Building Web Database Applications with Visual Studio 6

Building Web Database Applications with Visual Studio 6

DAN **RAHMEL**

Osborne/**McGraw-Hill**
Berkeley New York St. Louis San Francisco
Auckland Bogotá Hamburg London Madrid
Mexico City Milan Montreal New Delhi Panama City
Paris São Paulo Singapore Sydney
Tokyo Toronto

Osborne/**McGraw-Hill**
2600 Tenth Street
Berkeley, California 94710
U.S.A.

For information on translations or book distributors outside the U.S.A., or to arrange bulk purchase discounts for sales promotions, premiums, or fund-raisers, please contact Osborne/**McGraw-Hill** at the above address.

Building Web Database Applications with Visual Studio 6

1234567890 AGM AGM 019876543210

ISBN 0-07-212094-0

Publisher
Brandon A. Nordin
Associate Publisher and Editor-in-Chief
Scott Rogers
Executive Acquisitions Editor
Wendy Rinaldi
Project Editor
Betsy Manini
Acquisitions Coordinator
Monika Faltiss
Technical Editor
Steve Yolleck
Copy Editors
Andy Carroll
Bob Campbell
Proofreaders
Rhonda Holmes
Stefany Otis
Indexer
Valerie Robbins
Computer Designers
Gary Corrigan
Dick Schwartz
Jani Beckwith
Elizabeth Jang
Illustrators
Robert Hansen
Brian Wells
Beth Young
Series Design
Peter F. Hancik

This book was composed with Corel VENTURA™ Publisher.

This book is dedicated to my uncle Bill
(William Muckelberg, 1945–1999)
who left us this year.
He personified freedom, courage, loyalty, and self-reliance.
To me, he stood for America.
We will all miss him.

About the Author . . .

Dan Rahmel is a Visual Basic programmer with over 13 years of experience designing and implementing information systems and deploying mid-sized client/server systems using Visual Basic and Visual FoxPro. He has authored several books including *Visual Basic 6 Programmer's Reference,* first and second editions, *Teach Yourself Database Programming with Visual Basic in 24 Hours, Developing Client-Server Applications with Visual Basic,* and *Server Scripts with Visual JavaScript.* He is a regular contributor to *DBMS, Internet Advisor,* and *American Programmer* magazines.

AT A GLANCE

Part I The Telephony Environment

CONTENTS

ACKNOWLEDGMENTS

Acknowledgments are always hard to write because so many people are part of the process of placing a book like this in your hands. Individual contributions are also hard to single out because the length of time needed to finish a book brings almost every area of your life into play—so I'll try to thank everyone who helped me get here from there.

Thank you Ron and Marie Rahmel, David Rahmel, Darlene Rahmel, Uncle Bill, Don Murphy, Greg Mickey, John Taylor, Weld O'Connor, Bernard Arroyo, Juan Leonffu, Ted Ehr, Wendy Rinaldi, Andy Carroll, Steve Yolleck, Betsy Manini, Monika Faltiss, Megg Bonar, Ann Lush, Joel Harris, all of the Osborne staff, Ed Gildred, Thomas Rommel, Pacific Furlough Facility, Katz-Okitzu and Associates, SAIC, SANBAG, City of Poway, George Sullivan, Police Management Advisors, Reef Brazil, Microsoft, Sharp, Hitachi, Chrysler Plymouth, Ben Franklin, Guns 'N Roses, Roxy Music, and Kinko's.

Most of all, I'd like to thank you, the reader. By buying this book, you make it possible for all of us in the publishing industry to labor to produce good work. When we pull the long hours to complete a book, it is the knowledge that every little improvement will help you, our audience, that really makes the difference. Thanks.

Dan Rahmel

INTRODUCTION

Almost overnight, Web servers have become a key part of the information systems infrastructure in most organizations. The ease of creating Web pages makes Web publishing the key to communicating information instantaneously. Before the Web existed, there were few ways of presenting network-accessible information to a variety of platforms with both formatting and graphics.

Now that the Web is beginning to mature, Web solutions have begun to incorporate features beyond simple page presentation. Some Web applications present an interface with all the capabilities of a traditional client application in a client/server solution. Other applications provide robust access to object technology and comprehensive data-source capabilities. The single most important new feature is the ability to dynamically create Web pages from information stored in a database. This book will show you how to do just that.

In this book you will learn how to use the Visual Studio suite of tools to create Web database applications. These applications will incorporate the robust power of the Microsoft data access and Visual Studio tools.

You'll create a variety of solutions, from an interactive drill-down report to a Web-based forum. As you build each application, you will use tools as diverse as Visual InterDev and Visual Modeler. Most of the core Web application work will be done with Visual InterDev. Visual Basic will be used to create components that will be used with the Microsoft Web server and later deployed to Microsoft's object server (Microsoft Transaction Server). You will use the Java development environment, Visual J++, to create a simple bar-chart applet solution. By using this applet with data generated by an ASP page, you can see how client-side Java can effectively augment a server-side solution.

This book was written for hands-on use. As you progress through the chapters, you will be provided with simple examples that will demonstrate how each technology is actually used. These examples are meant to break up what might seem a large and difficult task into easily manageable chunks. That way, when you reach a complete application (such as the Web survey), you will understand how all of the parts fit together.

All of the solutions, large and small, have their complete source code listed in the text. I know how frustrating it can be when a book references source code on a CD when you're reading the book on a plane or other place without easy access to a computer. Additionally, the code is thoroughly commented so you can follow what is happening at each stage of execution.

WARNING: For all of the chapters, sample source code is provided for the particular Visual Studio development environment cited in the text. Because of the width limitations of a book page, code lines that extend beyond a single line are continued on the next line using the VB continuation character: the underscore (_). VBScript, however, does NOT support the continuation character. Therefore, for any code in VBScript that shows the underscore, simply enter all of this code on a single line without the underscore character to make it execute properly.

The book begins by laying the foundation of key concepts and information. In Chapters 1 through 5, you will learn about the basic technology used in building Web database applications. Visual Studio, the Web server, and the scripting languages must all be brought together in most applications. Therefore, it is important to know each technology to understand how each piece fulfills its role.

In Chapters 6 and 7, you will begin implementing solutions with the Web-server technology. The drill-down report uses the Northwind database included with VB, Access, and SQL Server to display how an interactive report can be created with Web data access. Chapter 7 then introduces the importance of Web sessions and how they can be used to permit user resources to be optimized for the length of the user visit.

Chapters 9 through 11 will take you through using Visual InterDev and the Visual Studio shared tool known as Database Designer to create a custom database, use the database to store survey information, and have IIS generate and send e-mail.

Chapters 12, 13, and 20 will introduce you to aspects of security that are very important to a Web database solution. Placing data on the Web offers great flexibility in accessing information, both for authorized and unauthorized users. By planning your security clearly, you can avoid the lion's share of Web security problems. Chapter 20 introduces some of the new security features present in Windows 2000 and offers an overview of the Active Directory system that will be at the heart of all future NT security.

Chapters 14 through 18 will take you through all aspects of component development and distributed systems deployment, which you will need to understand to create the next generation of Web solutions. The ability to place program logic on machines throughout the network is provided through the Microsoft DCOM and Microsoft Transaction Server technologies.

In Chapters 19 and 21, intranet development is addressed. The control available when deploying your solution on an intranet allows you to use such features as Dynamic HTML and file uploading. Chapter 21 guides you through the construction of an application that generates a formatted report that can be loaded into Excel or another spreadsheet software. The application then allows Web users to upload modified report files back to the Web server, all without leaving their browser.

In Chapter 22, you will examine some of the more advanced uses of ADO, including stored procedures and placing large amounts of data in a single data field.

Java is demonstrated in Chapter 23 for the non-Java programmer. The Java language is introduced from a perspective that the Visual Basic programmer will be able to understand. The Visual J++ development system is then used to create and deploy a Java applet to be executed within the client browser. The data displayed by the applet is retrieved from the Web server application, demonstrating how client-side and server-side execution can be used together.

Finally, in Chapter 24, you'll learn about the primary challenges of implementing a computing system that is distributed across a network. Because many database solutions use components to provide access to the background data source, special problems must be addressed when creating a distributed application.

In writing this book, I have endeavored to make the examples clear, the notes and tips helpful, and the applications useful to provide a solid foundation for your implementation needs. I hope you will find that all of the information presented here is useful in solving your problems. I tried my best to avoid mistakes or omissions, but if you discover any problems or would like to make suggestions for the next edition of the book, please e-mail me at danr@hobbyplanet.com.

Dan Rahmel

CHAPTER 1

Overview of Web Database Technology

With all of the technology and applications included in Visual Studio, embarking on a Web database project can be fairly overwhelming. The broad range of understanding required to create a scalable application requires either many years of experience or an effective map to aid a developer in reaching the goals set for the project.

This book will help you through the design, configuration, construction, maintenance, and upgrade of your Web database application. By explaining how all of the critical technologies (such as IIS, ADO, ASP, MTS, etc.) fit together and by directly demonstrating how they are used in a final solution, I'll help you through the jungle of confusion that surrounds advanced database application construction.

I have endeavored at every point in the book to show real-world examples, provide valuable tips, and useful diagrams. The diagrams will provide an overview of the relations between each piece of the project and the steps taken to reach each milestone.

Few people study technology for sheer enjoyment. Most people have real problems that need to be solved, often with very limited time and resources. A project leader wants to know how a task can be completed and understand the considerations that must be made before embarking on a particular course. The examples and source code in this book will show how this can be done.

WELCOME TO THE WORLD WIDE WEB

The growth of the World Wide Web took many people in the business community by surprise. Only now are organizations beginning to use the Web to its full potential for almost all forms of contact with customers and suppliers. One of the areas most critical to the success of a business on the Web is the dynamic connection of information systems (such as data sources) to Web content.

Web database connections are important in several key areas:

- Tracking visitor/customer interests
- Providing up-to-date information
- Real-time searching of database information
- Entry of user data directly into critical customer databases
- Personalization of served content

To aid you in creating Web database solutions, Microsoft has created and augmented powerful tools within the Visual Studio product family to facilitate the development of some of the most robust and solid Web applications. In this book, you'll learn how to use these tools together to create real-world Web database applications.

The Web itself has created an alternative to developing complete client applications (in a language such as Visual Basic or Delphi) to access server information by allowing the entire application to reside on the server. Web database applications have advantages over traditional client/server applications.

- Lowers cost of ownership
- Offers ease of upgrade
- Promotes centralization of data
- Provides the ability to run on various platforms
- Allows a return to back-end "server-centric" processing model
- Offers instantaneous publishing and access
- Permits separation of business logic from the user interface

With all of these advantages available to Web database applications, it is pretty clear why organizations have so quickly embraced this new technology. In terms of return on investment, corporate Intranets have repeatedly proven their value.

If there were only advantages to creating Web database applications, almost all client-server applications would be moving in that direction. Instead, the development community is seeing a split between the two types of applications as a clear picture develops of what solutions are most suited to Web deployment. Some of the disadvantages of a Web solution include:

- **Dependence on a server** When the server goes down, a Web application cannot be accessed. In contrast, many traditional client applications can be used for some functionality "off-line" including remote or replicated databases. Client application can also be programmed to initiate only specific functions to require server access.
- **Single window** A Web application can only effectively manage a single window. Although interface capabilities such as frames and cascading style sheets make the possibilities of a Web application more compelling, the simultaneous display of windows such as context help, toolbars, palettes, and floating summaries is not really available. Additionally, quirks in the implementation of the Web standards make controlling exactly how the application will appear on the user's screen a challenge.
- **Increased bandwidth requirements** On a traditional client application, most of the interaction over a network is simply an exchange of data. A Web application loads each piece of the application (usually as a Web page) with each access. This increases the strain on bandwidth as well as on the servers themselves.
- **More primitive user experience** Without complete control of the screen, a Web solution will rarely provide as pleasant experience as a custom application. Imagine trying to implement a program such as Excel with its drag and drop capabilities, cell expansion, right mouse button menus, and a variety

of other features in a Web application. Although this example is extreme (you probably wouldn't want to implement Excel on the Web), it makes the chasm between a custom program and a Web application immediately apparent. Fortunately, most database programming does not require this level of sophistication in the user interface.

- ▲ **Poor access to local resources** For security and deployment reasons, access to resources on a client machine such as the hard drive, printer, or CD-ROM is limited. While a traditional client-application can easily read and write to the local hard drive or print to a local printer, a Web app has to be implemented in a particular way to make this possible.

Although each limitation is important to consider, restrictions can be used as guideposts to determine whether the application you intend to create should be used as a Web database solution or as a more traditional client-server implementation.

Both the limitations and the advantages of Web solutions create a very different design environment than a traditional application. While the front-end prototype of a normal client would evolve into the final application, a Web database application requires far more planning. The trade-offs for various interface choices (DHTML, ActiveX DLLs, etc.) weigh very heavily on the appearance of the final application.

To understand a Web application, it is useful to have a general conceptual framework in order to approach it. Typically, a Web database program can be understood as it is broken down into the following functional parts:

Data source The data store (such as Microsoft Access, Oracle, or Microsoft SQL Server) that will record and retrieve your information

ASP programs Web programs that execute on the Web server to return a dynamic page to the Web user

Object components Components or controls that are written as ActiveX DLLs to hold specific business or program logic

Object models The framework through which the object components are used together to facilitate a process

For a Microsoft-based solution, understanding the technologies for a Web solution and how they work together is as important in knowing when a Web solution can most effectively be deployed. As you progress through this book, you will gain experience in how each piece can be deployed and when it most appropriately resolves a solution problem.

Overview of General Web Database Technology

Traditional database applications of the last several years have relied on a client/server model in which a client application handles a great deal of the processing before sending or receiving data from the server. In the new world of Web connectivity, most of the application logic and database control occurs on the server—much like the old mainframe-based database systems.

However, unlike the old mainframe systems from which all data would be accessed through a standard terminal (such as a VT-100 terminal) and stored in a common database, developers on the new frontier have to be prepared to handle a variety of browser-types, connection methods, and multi-database storage requirements.

You can see in Figure 1-1, that all of the Web database technologies can be brought together in a single system. This type of implementation is rare at the lower end of the Web solution world, but increasingly common at the database solution end.

For any Web solution that you construct using Visual Studio, there will be a minimum of two common elements: the Web server (IIS) and the Web execution engine (ASP).

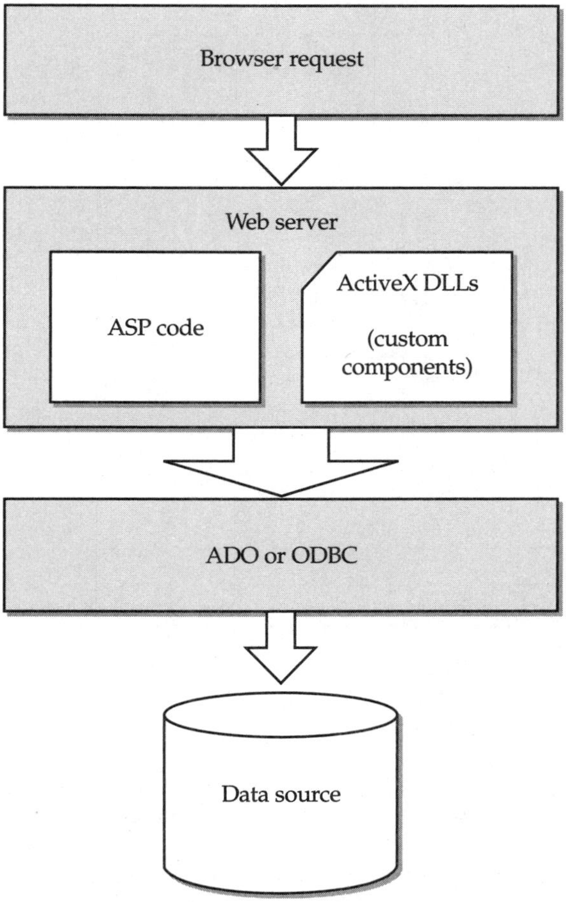

Figure 1-1. Master diagram of a possible Web database system

By examining how the rest of the technology relates to the dynamic Web system, you can accurately judge what the parameters of any Web system will be.

Web Server

The Web server provides the primary interface between the back-end server logic and data sources and the client's browser. The Web server communicates commands through the HTTP protocol over the TCP/IP protocol to deliver content to the browser.

Numerous types of server-side implementation models may be used to generate the content for display or execution on the browser (see Figure 1-2). Client-side scripting and

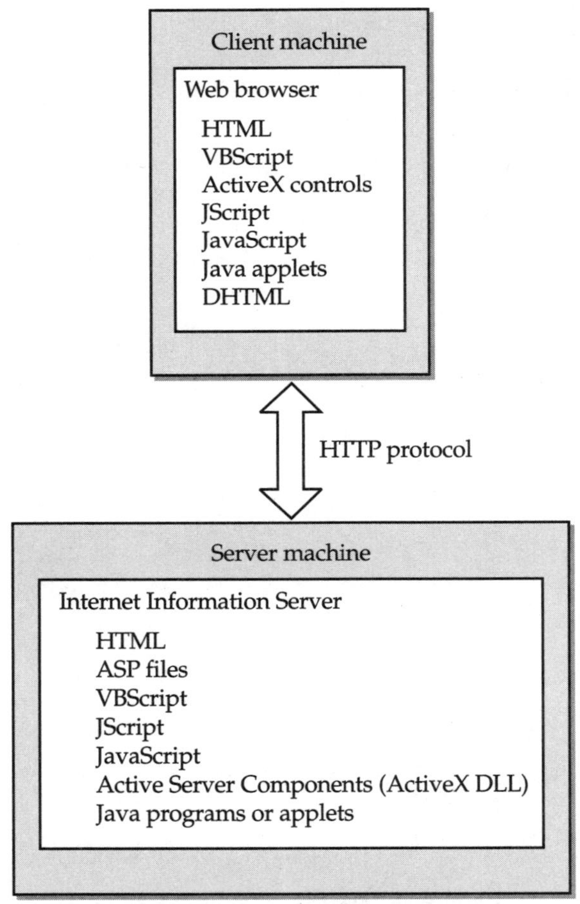

Figure 1-2. The Web browser communicates with IIS through HTTP

plug-ins (including Java applets and ActiveX controls) allow the browser to actually execute a process on the client-side, although security factors impede some types of access.

With the release of Windows NT 4 Server, Microsoft began shipping its free Web server to install with each copy of the operating system. Internet Information Server, or IIS as it's most commonly referred to, has become the foundation for the Web platform on NT.

When IIS reached Release 4, substantial technology was included in it, such as the ability to execute server-side code (through Active Server Pages), execute a process with or without its own protected memory segment, and manage Web access for everything from secure user login to protected directories. In the standard Web server installation, the Active Server Pages execution engine allows the Web server to execute code without reliance on primitive CGI connectors.

Active Server Pages and VBScript

From the standpoint of creating dynamic Web applications, the most important feature of IIS lies in the Active Server Pages (ASP) engine. ASP can process a Web page with server-side scripts, execute the code found in the scripting, and return a dynamically constructed HTML format file to the client browser.

When a file with an ASP file extension is requested from IIS, the ASP engine processes the scripted file (see Figure 1-3). The ASP file can contain code for any language that is supported through the Active Scripting plug-in architecture.

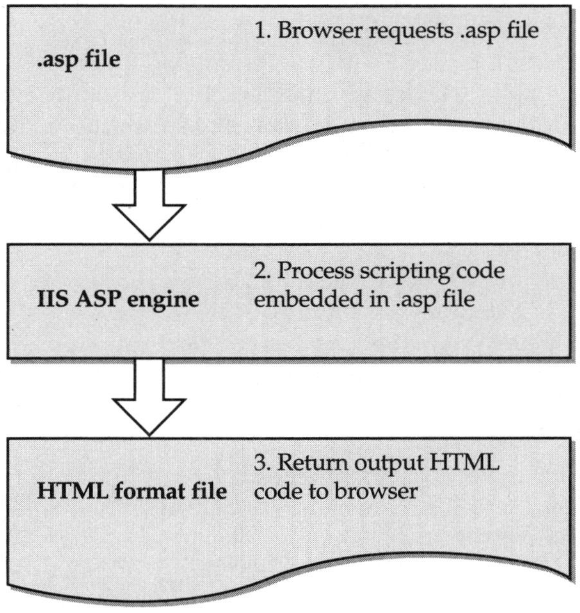

Figure 1-3. When a browser requests an .asp page, the ASP engine processes the script code and returns an HTML-format document

Most commonly, the scripting code is written in VBScript, a subset of the Visual Basic language. Since the scripting actually executes through the ASP engine, more than one scripting language can be supported. By default, both VBScript and JScript (a language compatible with the international standard for JavaScript) are available. The plug-in architecture of ASP allows languages such as Perl script to be used if the appropriate scripting engine is used. Several third-party vendors make engines to support the more popular languages such as Perl.

While the scripting language provides the basic dialect for executing statements, more complex execution occurs through objects contained in the Web server. Using ASP code and objects, the server can return HTML to a user, detect the browser being used, rotate a banner ad, etc. In ASP, even a session can be simulated for Web interactions.

Sessions

With traditional client/server software, a user login would start what is known as a session. A session is essentially a continuous trusted relationship between the client and the server. Until the user logs out of the session, it remains active between the two participants. Because of the structure of the HTTP protocol, there are no sessions in an HTTP connection. Each request and response between a browser and a Web server is considered unique by the protocol.

This introduces many problems to database applications that seek to provide specific and secure information to particular users. To help construct these common applications, Microsoft has created a simulated session that allows an application to execute as if a session has been created (see Figure 1-4).

For the initial access of an ASP page, IIS creates a session object that keeps a server-side session (and all variables associated with it) alive until a timeout period from the last access by that identified browser. Using the IP address of the client machine in conjunction with a uniquely identifying piece of information (called a cookie) written into the browser, a programmer of ASP code can address a single user as if a real session was taking place.

The ability to execute scripted code in ASP makes database solution construction possible. The session capabilities make a Web database application far more practical. In order to actually address a data source through ASP, a database access method must be used that will be available to all of the scripting engine through ASP execution. Microsoft provides a number of alternatives that make this possible.

Database Access Methods

Since it includes several distinct development systems,Visual Studio only needs a single common method of facilitating a connection to a data source. This facility would have to include more operations than simply creating a basic connection. It would also have to

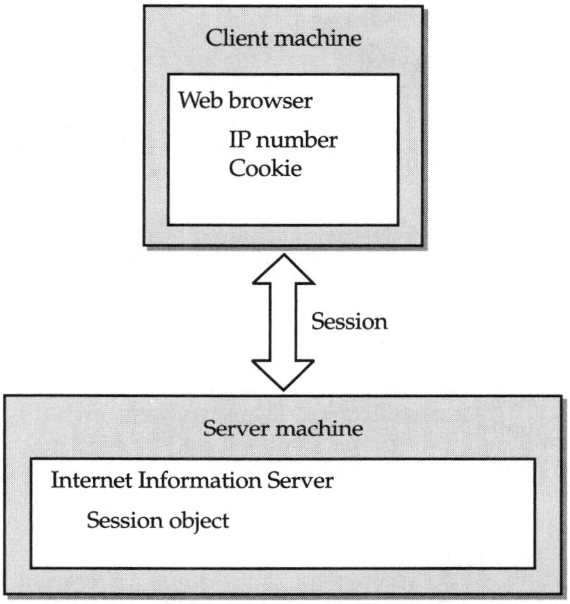

Figure 1-4. IIS uses an IP address number and a browser cookie to simulate a session

allow such advanced features as the use of recordsets, cursors, and other dataset operators that make database control effective.

To make universal database access possible, Microsoft implemented ActiveX Data Objects (ADO) and OLE DB. OLE DB is actually the common core technology that is used by low-level languages such as C++. ADO provides the interface to OLE DB for application-oriented languages such as Visual Basic and VBScript.

Although ADO is the new common standard, Visual Studio, in its myriad of development environments, actually includes many database access standards. These include:

- **Open Database Connectivity (ODBC)** The industry standard software solution that allows connection, through the SQL language, to query a data source. ODBC is still the fastest method of accessing heterogeneous data sources, but it lacks some of the advanced features supplied by OLE DB.
- **OLE DB** The new Microsoft technology that supercedes ODBC and allows access to numerous data types, including ODBC and other data sources. OLE

DB can access any type of information including media data (video, audio, documents), object data, and spatial data.

- **ActiveX Data Objects (ADO)** The high-level interface to OLE DB accessed through VBScript, J Script, and Visual Basic.
- **Remote Data Objects (RDO)** A thin layer atop the ODBC interface that provides high-level object access to an ODBC data source. Superseded by ADO.
- **Data Access Objects (DAO)** A database interface that allows access to local data sources (Microsoft Access, dBase, FoxPro, etc.) from Visual Basic. Superseded by ADO.

Although ODBC and ADO are the only two technologies you will need to know well to effectively use Visual Studio for database access, most of the technologies that preceded ADO (such as DAO) are still included in products such as Visual Basic. In fact, Microsoft Access 97 still makes DAO its standard database access method. In this book, ADO and ODBC will be the central focus as these are the methods you will use through VBScript and ASP.

ActiveX Data Objects (ADO)

Because ADO is the primary database access method for VBScript and ASP, it will also be the centerpiece in a Web database solution. ADO isn't just for addressing standard sequential data—it can also be used for hierarchical data, object data, and any other type of data source that has an available data source driver.

ADO provides a simplified interface to the OLE DB technology (see Figure 1-5) although it contains all of the features present in this lower-level interface. From ADO, a program can execute a SQL query, create a recordset, modify data, execute a stored procedure, perform a batch operation, or form a hierarchical view of data. All of the memory management and class handling necessitated by the lower-level of OLE DB is automatically managed for ADO solutions.

ADO evolved from the earlier DAO object model included in Visual Basic, but it has a completely new object structure. Although this structure may make it challenging to adapt older code, it will make current and future development more straightforward.

ODBC

Although there are ADO/OLE DB drivers available for the primary Microsoft data sources, many organizations will need to access a data source for which there is no custom driver. Alternately, you might want to use a driver that has been custom tuned to maximize efficiency with your particular data source.

The ODBC driver standard is almost universal in the database world. Drivers are available for nearly any type of database from the simpler systems such as dBase to the most complex Oracle or Informix server. The variety of ODBC drivers is broad, and since

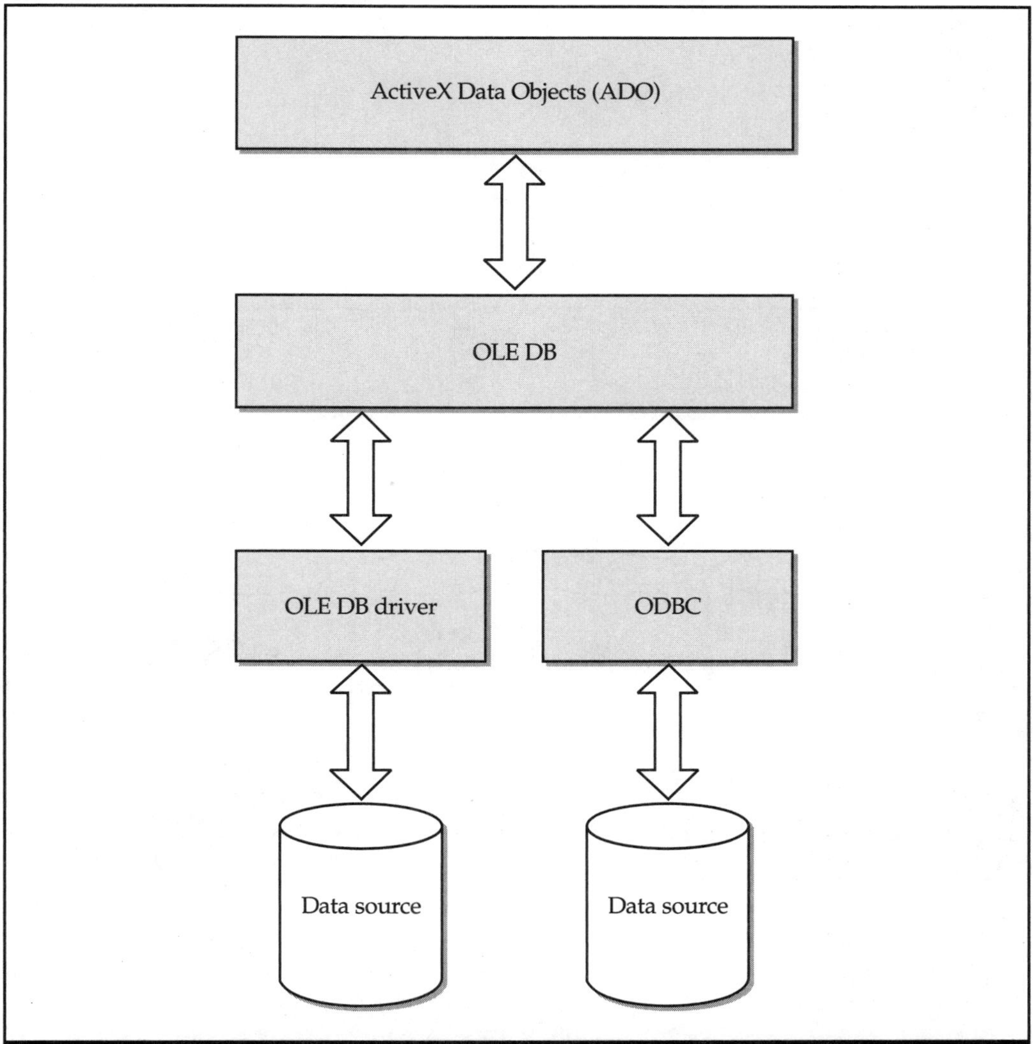

Figure 1-5. ActiveX Data Objects communicate with the lower-level OLE DB technology

they are all addressed through the common language of SQL (see Figure 1-6), programmers can write data source-independent code.

The ODBC interface is accessed transparently through ADO. The ASP program can access an ODBC data source in the same way that a Microsoft SQL Server database is addressed. Although ADO is robust enough to handle nearly any data source type, an

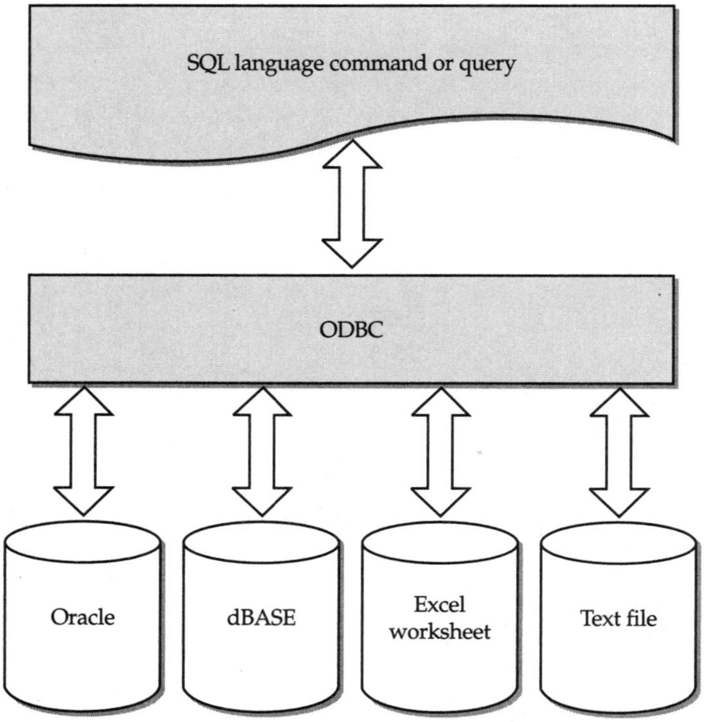

Figure 1-6. ODBC communicates with a variety of data-source types through standard SQL commands

ODBC driver may be more limited or the data source may not support certain capabilities. To ensure that you can exploit all of the features of an ODBC driver, ADO contains the ability to query the capabilities of a data source in order to properly address it.

Active Server Pages Components

Components provide self-contained objects that can be installed on a server and reused. Active Server Pages can access these components from any installed scripting language (most commonly VBScript). It is through components that the scripting language can execute almost any desired function.

When IIS is installed, ASP comes with a number of native components that provide core functionality such as access to server and browser resources. These components are activated in IIS by default, so they can be used on any IIS 4 Web server without additional installation. For custom functions, additional components can be installed and registered on the server as ActiveX DLLs that can then be controlled by the scripting language.

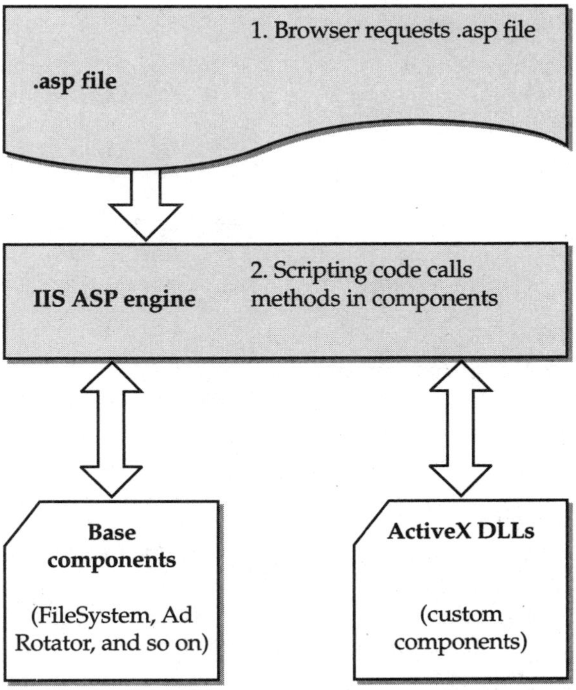

Figure 1-7. Structure of components as they are used by an ASP file

For any components that exist on the Web system, simply instantiating the proper objects (see Figure 1-7) will provide scripting access. Since the components are accessed in the scripting code, the object created from them can be instantiated at the time of Web page execution. In ASP, they can also be stored in the variables for session or in the application itself so they can remain alive past the execution of a single page.

BASE COMPONENTS There are a number of useful components already built into IIS, some of which are used for even the most basic ASP applications. The most commonly used objects include:

- **Scripting Runtime (Session, Request, Response, and Application objects)** Provides the interface for accessing the IIS environment such as variables submitted by the user through a form or included in a query string.
- **Ad Rotator** Used to display graphical or text banner ads according to a frequency specified in a rotator file.

- **FileSystem component** Pathway for accessing the server resources—including all directories and files.
- **TextStream component** The component to be used in conjunction with the FileSystem component to input and output files to the storage (hard disk, SCSI drive, etc.) of the server.
- **SMTP Connector** For sending e-mail from the Web server

Some of the components, such as the Ad Rotator component, will only be used in specific instances. Even a single use of the component, however, may prevent a good deal of repeated development of custom code. Other objects, such as the Response object, need to be used in nearly every ASP script.

ACTIVEX DLL COMPONENTS To add your own components, you can use C++, J++, or Visual Basic to construct them. Visual Basic 6.0 provides the entire framework to create object classes that can be compiled into an ActiveX DLL for use by ASP scripting code. This is probably the simplest and most straightforward method of generating an ActiveX DLL.

In addition to their uses for incorporating new logic into a component, ActiveX DLLs are also commonly used as "wrappers" for older technology. Older technology such as legacy data formats or even mainframe access may still be important to critical aspects of an organization; they may prove even more valuable if they can be accessed through a Web solution. By creating a component that interfaces with it, the old technology could be incorporated into an ASP project quickly and easily.

TIP: Breaking functionality up into several components usually requires tough management choices. Always consider security in regards to re-usability when deciding on the functions to include in a single component. If a component has many general capabilities, but also contains a sensitive function to which you want to limit access (a simple example would be a "Delete All" operation), consider placing sensitive functions in their own component. This will allow you to reuse the lion's share of the functionality you have created without jeopardizing the integrity of the system.

Transactions Through ADO

Within a database solution, one of the most critical functions of a new system should be to protect the data from possible corruption. To automate this protection, database vendors long ago came up with the implementation of a transaction. If you are unfamiliar with transaction technology, it is really very simple to use for a database programmer. Transactions were invented to prevent data corruption when multiple steps had to be completed for a single operation. If any of these steps fails, the whole operation should be aborted.

NEW TERM: **Transaction** A transaction encapsulates one or more operations and allows the operations that it contains to be treated as a single operation for abort purposes. This means that if any operation within the transaction fails, all operations can be rolled back.

The most common example of a transaction is that of a bank money transfer. If a sum of $500 needs to be transferred from John Smith's account into Fred Johnson's account, there are actually two operations that take place. As you can see in Figure 1-8, first the $500 is removed from the Smith account, and then $500 is added to the Johnson account.

If a failure were to occur, such as a power failure or hard disk crash, after the first operation succeeded and before the second one was completed, the fundamental accuracy of the database would be corrupted. Not only would Smith's account be $500 short and Johnson's account not be credited, but the bank would have an unaccounted for overage of $500.

To prevent these types of errors, a transaction encapsulates multiple operations into an all-or-nothing operation. A program initiates a transaction, and all operations are recorded, but not stored in their final form in the database. If all operations are completed properly, a *commit transaction* message is sent, and all transactions are actually written into the database. When an error occurs or the programmer detects a discrepancy, a *roll back* operation is performed and all the operations attempted within the transaction are revoked.

Building transaction technology into ADO and Web applications is critical. Because connections can so easily be lost and errors can occur in transmission over a WAN, transactions can be used to provide an extra level of safety to help prevent data corruption.

TIP: Transactions can also be used effectively for batch database operations. Because the operations are not actually committed until the end of the transaction, placing many small operations within a transaction can greatly speed operations.

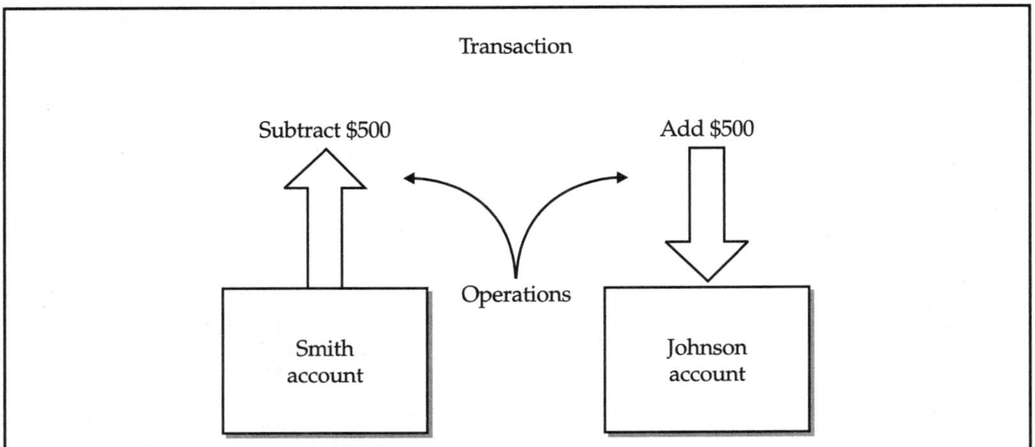

Figure 1-8. Two operations take place for an account transfer

Microsoft Transaction Server

When transactions are executing through ADO, the OLE DB technology handles all of the transaction operations automatically. If you want to create some ActiveX DLL components that encapsulate some of the interaction with a database, however, how do you still support transactions?

Microsoft Transaction Server (MTS) provides an environment where ActiveX DLLs designed to support transactions can be executed remotely. MTS is now added to NT Server automatically with every installation of IIS version 4. For earlier versions, MTS is available as a separate install.

The true advantage of MTS is its ability to manage several transactions that occur across objects (see Figure 1-9). This multi-object capability allows a single transaction to modify as many data sources (including different databases) as the task requires, and it has the ability to rollback the transaction because of an encountered problem.

In Visual Basic, a class simply needs to add some simple code to implement transaction capabilities. Since MTS can conduct a transaction across multiple objects, this opens up the transaction framework to allow undo features for almost any type of operation.

Unlike other types of servers such as NT Server or SQL Server, MTS does not do any actual processing. Instead it provides a centralized connectivity point so the objects stored within MTS can be activated and execute on the server to perform a requested operation. It also provides security and garbage collection for the objects on the server.

To communicate with the objects across the network, Microsoft's distributed object technology allows remote objects to interact. The objects that are held within MTS communicate through the Distributed Component Object Model (DCOM) standard (see Figure 1-10). DCOM allows a machine to access a remote object transparently. DCOM is a protocol, a standard, and an object interface. The actual code that executes to access the object operates no differently than if the object was installed on the executing machine.

An MTS distributed object solution is perhaps the most complicated and powerful form of a Web database application. Because independent business logic is stored within objects that may be called from ASP code, the entire system (and several servers) is involved with process execution. Although one of the substantial advantages of such a system is the ability to easily upgrade individual parts, proper project design becomes even more important than in a traditional solution.

Web Database Design Issues

The technology that you use for an application only determines some aspects of your Web solution. Equally important are the basic decisions that will determine how the application will be presented to the user, how it will be designed, how objects will fit into the deployment picture, and which database connectivity will offer ideal performance.

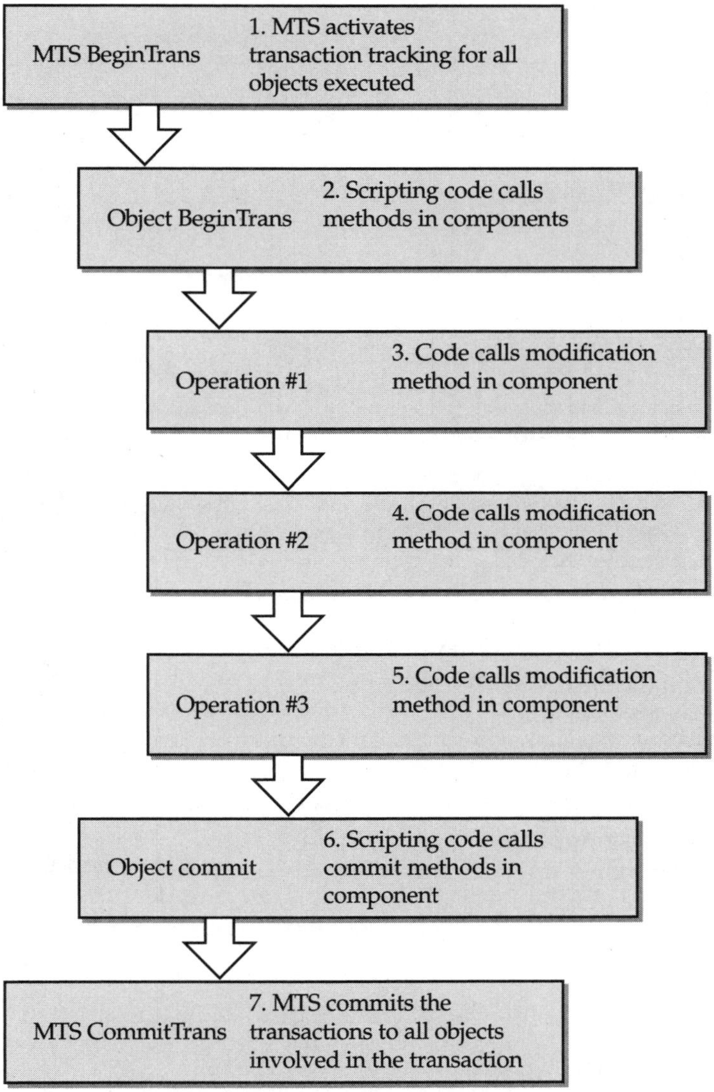

Figure 1-9. Transactions can occur through MTS objects

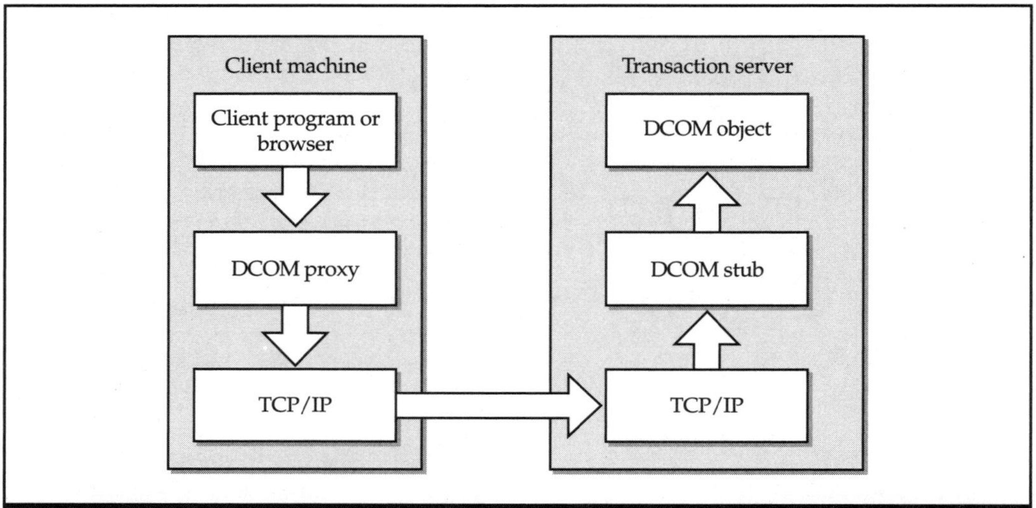

Figure 1-10. The client program communicates with the object stored in MTS through a TCP/IP connection

Static or Dynamic Web Database Applications

Before development on any application begins, it is important to do some amount of clear planning. For a Web application, one of the questions that needs to be asked near the beginning of the project is whether the information returned by the database needs to be dynamic (created on-the-fly) so that reports are up-to-the-minute accurate. If dynamic content is not required, there are a number of advantages to creating the pages as static HTML.

Static page creation does not indicate that each page is created individually with FrontPage or a similar layout package. Instead, it refers to the process of having script code generate a page or pages of HTML code once, rather than executing each time the page request is made.

STATIC (PREPARED) PAGES Administrators might consider the creation of an application to generate "prepared" pages that require frequent access but change very little. A special administrative page may be developed that actually generates the HTML page of a particular report, or a service might execute on the server at particular times or time intervals. The prepared or static pages are then placed in a directory under predefined filenames so that existing links can reference them.

Prepared pages are most frequently used for common reports such as monthly sales. Such a report will be accessed by numerous people at various times, and dynamic execution against the database each time will produce prohibitive processing requirements.

Since ASP provides the capability of writing text files to the server directories, prepared page creation can be fully automated and requires only slightly more code than a traditional dynamic page. Instead of writing to the browser, a prepared report execution page can be accessed by the administrator to create the required HTML file in a specified directory.

The advantages to using prepared pages include:

- **They can be indexed by search engines** Since the content of Web pages generated from database information will be dependent on the actual query, most dynamic content will be transparent to a search engine. If the page is dynamic and stored as a static Web page, however, the search engines will register the content as any other Web page.
- **They have lower processing requirements on the server** Instead of each request requiring complete report compilation, which uses a large amount of server resources, prepared pages of common reports will be served by the Web server like any other static Web page.
- **Their backing data does not have to remain online** With data accumulating at substantial rates in almost every business, archival of old and rarely used data is becoming increasingly important for the effective and fast execution of prevalent business queries. By creating a prepared page, the most critical aspects of dated information can be kept available without retaining the data in the active data source.

TIP: Because most Web database content is generated dynamically, some users may assume your report or query was created at the instant of access. To prevent confusion, you will want to be sure to place the time and date of the last update on the page itself, in an easy to see location. This will prevent any misunderstanding as to the relevance of the reported information.

In this book, you will learn how to create a solution that generates static pages automatically. Choosing when such a solution is advantageous is often a difficult proposition. Since the most commonly accessed queries are often the ones that can best be created as static pages, monitoring a dynamic implementation will often indicate which reports are best to prepare.

DYNAMIC PAGES The majority of database applications, however, do require pages to be dynamically generated from custom queried content returned from a data source. When a dynamic solution is chosen, the number of decisions that will be required is great, and tracking of the actual use must be watched closely.

The Web log file (traditionally stored in a Log files directory in the NT system directory) can provide important clues as to the most commonly made requests. For dynamic query applications, choosing to have the log information written directly to a data source (such as SQL Server) can be one of the most effective means of easily compiling usage information.

Since most of this book will delve into the aspects of dynamic Web page generation, the design factors and the choices that need to be made for these solutions will be detailed.

Levels of Web Database Development

A database Web application is seldom an all or nothing implementation. Although planning will minimize the number of changes required to the foundation structure of the application, there are general phases of an application that can be followed to allow it to scale properly.

Although any application may leap directly to a Level IV implementation, the progressive steps will allow you to judge which system you need to begin. It will also help you to plan for details of scaling as the system becomes increasingly mission-critical for a larger number of users.

- **Level I: Basic client application** Coded directly in ASP with a simple HTML front-end
- **Level II: Advanced client application** Client-side ActiveX control or Java applet provides custom user interface and server interaction
- **Level III: Object back-end** Critical business logic placed in ActiveX DLLs that are called directly by ASP code
- **Level IV: Distributed object deployment** ActiveX DLL objects are placed in a distributed system on Microsoft Transaction Server (MTS) and load-balanced with Microsoft Message Queuing Server (MSMQ)

How Do Objects Fit into the Structure of a Web Database Application?

Objects allow logic to be separated from a specific client or server, and modification of a single object can affect the entire system. Separating the logic from the main program has three distinct advantages:

- **Reuse** The functionality can be reused in different parts of the program or even among several programs.
- **Ease of upgrade** When changes are required, they can be made to a single object, rather than several times within a program.
- **Security** Once the logic is compiled into an object, the code cannot be examined or modified by any Web page developer. This is particularly effective when a project is shared among many members of a team and the possibility of accidental modification of critical code endangers the usefulness of the application.

A simple illustration of the usefulness of distributing business logic with an object is the credit-check problem. For example, in an attempt to capture drug money the government requires that all deposits of cash over the amount of $10,000 be reported. With a 2-tier system, the $10,000 limit would be coded directly into either the client or the server software. If the government were to decide that the limit will be raised to $15,000, either the central application would have to be modified (a complex procedure) or each individual client application would have to be updated (an expensive and time-consuming procedure).

If, instead, the checking logic were deployed in an object sitting between the client and the server, only the object itself would have to be modified. The change would be transparent to the clients and the main server. The object used to set up the necessary processing for the government notification could also be isolated on a secure object server to ensure that the dollar amount is not tampered with.

Objects are one of the key components of the implementation of an n-tier architecture system. Because of the flexibility they provide for isolating processes, companies can deploy a system that can be more effectively load-balanced, and for which updates and revisions to individual objects can be made.

DEFINITION: **n-Tier** A distributed architecture that breaks down a system among a client and one or more servers. Often this architecture consists of a client machine, multiple object or load balancing servers, and data sources on one or more database servers.

Initially, the standard multitier architecture was a three-tier architecture, as you can see in Figure 1-11. The three tiers consisted of a client machine, usually running a custom appli-

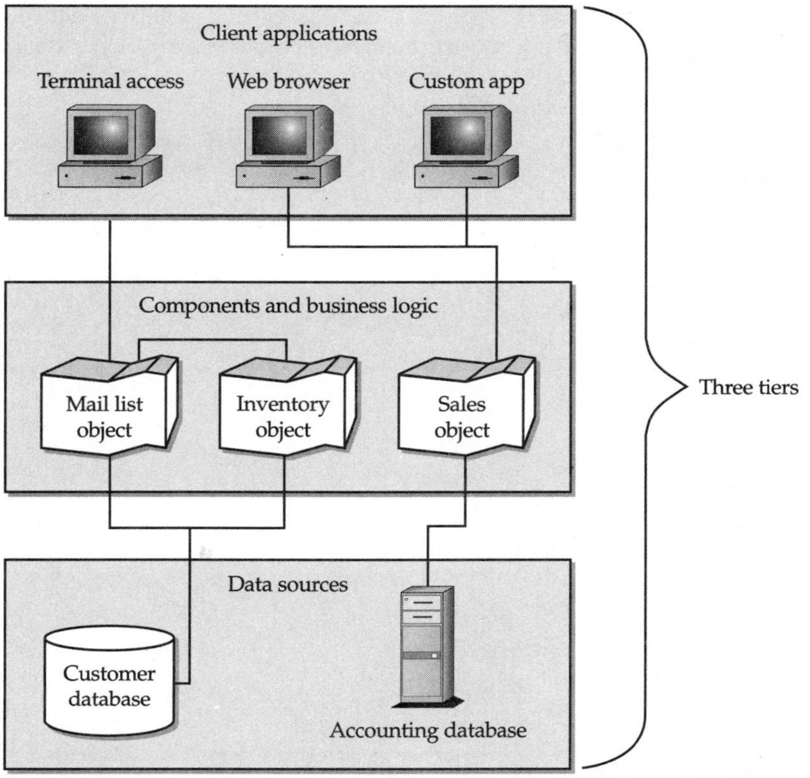

Figure 1-11. A three-tier architecture system typically has an object tier between the client and the data sources

cation (often written in Visual Basic), a specialized server (such as a credit processing or business rule server), and a centralized database (most popularly Oracle or IBM's DB2).

With the explosive growth of low-end servers and the rise of Windows NT, multiple tiers will likely become commonplace. Through MTS, and with the aid of Visual Modeler, a multitier solution finally becomes practical without having to invest tens of thousands of dollars in modeling software.

FrontPage is the ideal program for display and graphical editing and layout. Microsoft has constructed it to work well in conjunction with ASP code and to accurately load and save Visual InterDev documents without damaging the necessary coding and information.

Which Database and Connection Should I Use?

One of the questions that is often asked is which levels to choose for software. Although the prices shown in Table 1-1 may change, these prices and user levels (current as this book was being written) should give you at least a relative understanding of how cost will relate to the number of users you wish to support.

Note that the number of connected users given is the number of simultaneous users. This figure is a general number for typical database use, such as simple data entry or single table queries. If your Web database application allows complex queries or batch modifications by each user, you may put far more pressure on your resources and therefore decrease the number of effective simultaneous users.

If you are going to be using a LAN or a dedicated WAN for connectivity to your Web-based application, the bandwidth estimates provided will not be relevant, as the network will have a good deal of variability contingent on the amount of non-Web traffic on the network, the routing, and the number of users.

Name	Cost	Maximum recommended simultaneous users
Microsoft Access	$295	10
SQL Server	$1,500 + $2,995 internet connectivity	150
ISDN	$200 per month	25
T1	$1,500 per month	250
T3	$8,000 per month	2,000

Table 1-1. Costs and Access for Web Technology

Categories of Web Site

Understanding the type of Web database application you want to create is contingent on the access type, including not only how people will access it, but who and why. If customers will access it, how will you respond to data such as feedback and questions?

- **Internet** Will be accessed by the broadest range of users and browser types. Varying bandwidth and transmission rates must be taken into account (even 14.4K modems). World-wide exposure also makes security concerns very important.
- **Intranet** Only available within an organization. This does not necessarily limit geography, as security systems and remote dial-in accounts may still give remote access to the intranet. However, LAN access is usually assumed, providing large bandwidth for fast connections. Large file downloads and extensive graphics are permitted.
- **Extranet** Secure access to intranet-type applications available to distributors or other interested parties. Unless a dedicated connection is ensured, bandwidth is assumed to be of Internet variability (except when the minimum connection type can be specified). Security becomes a primary concern because secure internal information is available over a wide area network. Therefore, identification and effective monitoring are crucial.

TIP: The more general access that is required, the more limitations are required for the application to work properly. Therefore, if a majority of the access will be through an intranet, but parts of the application still need remote Internet access, consider breaking the application into two separate applications. By making this functional division, the strength of each application can cater to the medium that it will be deployed in, without having to reduce the whole application to the lowest common denominator.

Visual Studio Overview

To address most of the obstacles facing the modern developer, Microsoft has packaged all of the key development tools that it makes into a single package: Visual Studio. Visual Studio solves many integration problems for Web developers, because almost any project of reasonable size will often need to embrace several of these tools. These tools are not only packaged together, but share common tools (Visual Modeler, Database Designer), interface conventions (command keys, common menu options), and even a development environment (Visual J++, Visual C++, Visual InterDev).

The primary tool within Visual Studio for Web development, of course, is Visual InterDev—VI a pioneering tool created by Microsoft to facilitate easy incorporation of code (both client-side and server-side) into the HTML of a Web page.

Visual InterDev

The cornerstone of any Web database development effort will be the Visual InterDev application. Since all interaction with users will occur through ASP code, Visual InterDev provides the primary means of communicating with all of the back-end resources such as the Web server, data sources, and server components.

Using Visual InterDev,you can build HTML and Active Server Page code to serve the information from a database to the application users. Syntax checking, design-time components, and the data environment greatly increase the productivity of a developer creating a Web solution.

Visual Basic

Visual Basic (VB) is a powerful development system that can fill many roles in your Web database development tasks. Not only can it be used to create ActiveX DLL components for use with ASP code, it can also create IIS Applications, ActiveX documents, and DHTML applications.

The IIS Application is a component-based solution for deployment on the Web. All of the compiled Visual Basic code is encapsulated within one or more components. VB then auto-generates the necessary ASP code to place on a Web server to activate the components.

An ActiveX document is a form of a traditional VB application that is accessed through a Web server and appears in the browser window. Rather than simulating an application through Java or other means, it actually does a dynamic install and downloads and activates the application on the user machine. This provides for all of the advantages of dynamic updates and server-based content while not sacrificing any of the features available to a full client application.

The disadvantages, of course, include the client application being installed on each machine. This requires Internet Explorer browser use, acceptable Windows compatibility with the destination client, and disk access and space for the application.

A DHTML document, in contrast, can execute on any machine that supports this public standard. This type of application can be created in VB to include screen positioning and other elements of advanced browser application deployment. DHTML is traditionally used in conjunction with a client-side scripting engine such as JavaScript or VBScript.

CAUTION: Be sure to test compatibility of a simple DHTML application on the destination browser, as many browsers only partially implement the full standard. This is true in particular of Netscape Navigator, which implements a Netscape-specific flavor of this technology.

Visual J++

Currently the most popular development environment for Java code on any platform, Visual J++ is included in Visual Studio. Visual J++ builds on the years of experience that Microsoft acquired creating and refining the full-featured Visual C++ environment.

Visual J++ not only supports the traditional Java environment classes and features, but also provides Windows-specific classes and ActiveX access for creating applications tuned to the Windows operating system.

With Visual J++, a Web developer can build complete Java applets, as well as more robust server-side Java applications. IIS can call a Java application the way more traditional scripts call CGI applications. Although not the most effective use of server resources (a native solution will perform much better), it does allow a common server-based application to be deployed on the Windows NT platform, as well as on other Java-supported OS environments (such as Unix or OS/2).

Visual InterDev and Visual J++: A Common IDE

With Visual Studio 6, a movement has begun toward an integrated development environment (IDE) shared by all of the language tools within the Visual Studio family. With the Version 6 release, Visual J++ and Visual InterDev use the same IDE. Microsoft has declared its intention to place more of the Visual Studio products within this common environment.

The IDE shares many of the robust features of the Microsoft Office user interface, such as customizable menus and toolbars, docking windows, and linking windows. The Toolbox window can even contain code. Dragging code to the window will store the code as an icon for later drag-and-drop into other files in the application. It works like an organized clipboard. All of these features should make it easier to grow accustomed to the IDE, even if it is unfamiliar.

Within the common IDE, a "development solution" may be created. A single solution can incorporate projects in any language supported in the IDE. This means that as Microsoft continues to fold its various development environments into the single IDE, all projects can be managed in a single solution.

DEFINITION: **Solution** Although a solution is typically referenced in a general information-systems context as an information project, it has a specific meaning in Visual Studio. It refers to a project that can coordinate more than one language or file type. In Visual Studio 6, a development solution can contain both Visual InterDev and Visual J++ projects.

In addition to the other features that make the shared environment attractive, it also includes a task list with the solutions for various aspects of a project. This can aid management, as well as the programmers who have to track what remains to be created.

Visual Studio Analyzer

Visual Studio Analyzer (VSA) is a profiling tool that is used to examine and tune the performance of distributed applications created with the tools in Visual Studio. It also facilitates debugging the applications and tracking individual components of a distributed solution within the general framework.

VSA works by recording event information that is provided by COM, the COM Transaction Integrator (COMTI), and data source technologies including ODBC, OLE DB, and ADO. COMTI will even allow you to track transactions that occur on a mainframe computer included in the Visual Studio solution.

DEFINITION: **COM Transaction Integrator (COMTI)** Technology that lets MTS effectively manage transactions on mini and mainframe computers through the CICS or IMS implementations. COMTI requires SNA Server to function.

All of the key technologies that you will be using in a Web database solution including IIS, ASP, ADO, and COM generate traceable events for VSA. Even the ODBC framework and the VBScript language are VSA-savvy. Therefore, debugging and performance tuning a Web application is greatly simplified by monitoring how the pieces interact to form a whole.

NOTE: The Visual Studio Analyzer is only available with the Enterprise Edition of Visual Studio. Although it cannot be purchased separately, it really only makes sense to use it within the framework of the multidevelopment environment. If you are not constructing a project that requires more than one of the Visual Studio components, using VSA is not very effective.

VSA does not replace traditional debugging and profiling tools, such as the ones included with Visual Basic and Visual C++. Instead it provides an overview of the entire distributed application that allows a developer to track down bottlenecks and problems to a specific component. The VSA application can even create a general block diagram that can flowchart the progress of a particular process. Within the flowchart, the process can be examined for key factors that can reveal problems or bottlenecks.

VSA can also receive data from the Performance Monitor (PerfMon) application to structure analysis for precision measuring of desired factors. Correlations can then be drawn between the activity of the distributed application and the background execution that is actually taking place.

NOTE: To analyze an application, the target system must have the "VSA-friendly" components in place that provide the interface for monitoring. For Windows NT 4.0, these are present in Service Pack 4 and above. For Windows 95/98, the patches are shipped on the Visual Studio CD-ROM in the folder for the DCOM Version 1.2 patch.

What is Transaction Server?

Many developers are familiar with primary servers that Microsoft includes in the BackOffice package, such as Windows NT Server, SQL Server, and Exchange Server. Transaction Server, however, has not been as heavily promoted, because unlike the other servers that are cast in a specific and easily understood role, MTS is an object server that facilitates other programs.

MTS stores objects created in Visual Basic, Visual C++, or other COM-compatible environment for access by remote clients. MTS was created to allow objects to be used across a network to create a *distributed computing* infrastructure.

DEFINITION: **Distributed Computing** Distributed computing refers to a system structure that distributes processing functions among multiple machines in a network (usually a LAN).

CAUTION: If you are going to use an ODBC driver to access a data source through Transaction Server, you must be sure that the driver is thread-safe. This means that the driver can properly use the Windows NT threading capabilities for multiple connections. If a memory-access violation occurs in the driver after 60 seconds of inactivity, the driver may not be thread-safe. Check with the manufacturer of the ODBC driver to determine whether it is MTS-compatible. All of the standard ODBC 3.0 and higher drivers that ship with Microsoft products can be used with MTS.

You may have seen the Microsoft Distributed Transaction Controller (MS DTC) in your Control Panels folder. This service executes at the system level and allows transactions to span resources and processes.

Visual Modeler

You may be thinking that all of these components, data sources, and applications can make a project difficult to design, manage, or visualize. Fortunately, Microsoft has worked in conjunction with Rational Rose Software to create a tool called Visual Modeler that is included in Visual Studio.

Visual Modeler allows a multiple tier application to be designed, diagrammed, implemented, and managed. Once a project has been loaded into Visual Modeler, all of its forms, classes, and data sources appear in an easy-to-read diagram (see Figure 1-12).

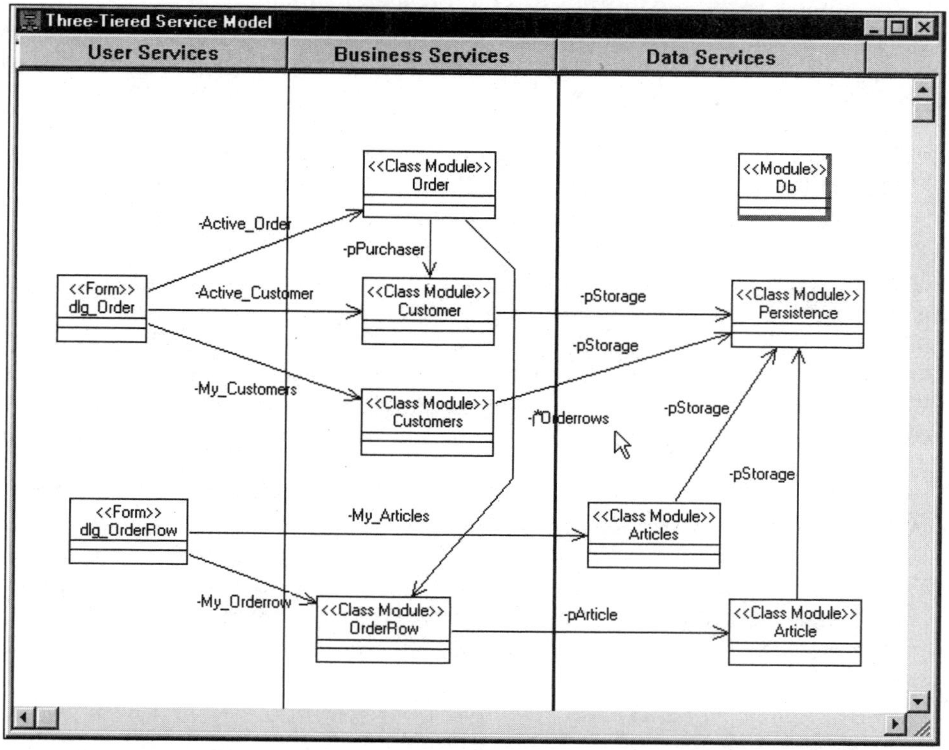

Figure 1-12. The Visual Modeler allows you to diagram the creation of a multitier system

Using an industry-standard modeling language (UML) at its core, Visual Modeler allows you to incorporate all aspects of the final solution into a visible project framework.

Visual Modeler works for more than simple setup and design. It has the ability to modify an ongoing system, so it can be used in every stage of implementation—what Microsoft calls "round-trip" engineering. It can also allow you to evaluate the project from three different perspectives: the logical, component, and deployment views. These perspectives will further help you refine how the project should be created.

For a complete multitier system created in Visual Studio, you will use Visual Modeler extensively. As you progress through this book and implement objects in MTS, you will rely more heavily on Visual Modeler to understand and maintain the project you create.

Q&A

Q: Is there a single best way to connect a Web page to a database?

A: No, the solutions that is needed varies dramatically with the size of the application you want to build, the deployment environment, and the number of users that will be accessing the page. This is one of the central objectives of this book: to provide examples from the simple to the complex for Web database solutions. Implementation generalizations are limited to the type of final application designed, but even then many variations occur.

Q: When should I demo my application to management?

A: The birth of GUI development tools such as Visual Basic have made developers aware that demonstrating an application too early can create an unrealistic expectation of when the application will be complete. With the user interface functional, many non-technically oriented people do not understand how much back-end work remains to be done.

This problem is even more apparent with Web applications, since a demo does not even require installation. One mistake my company made on an early Web database project should prove educational. We thought that since the application we were building was on the local intranet, management could watch its progress and make suggestions as the project evolved.

Instead, we were frequently confronted by management on our "visible" lack of progress since the back-end work did not generate many outwardly visible changes. We now structure our project to make an early presentation intentionally rough (no flashy graphics or UI bells and whistles) as a way to limit expectations. Then we focus on the back-end work and make sure this is well in order before another demonstration occurs.

Q: How can I make an accurate estimate to know how much database capability and bandwidth will be required?

A: The best method would be to take a look at existing applications that operate in a similar manner. For example, although the dynamics of the application are different, a client/server solution implemented for approximately the same number of users will provide a bottom-line estimate of the load on both the database back-end and the LAN requirements.

For the Web server itself, the best estimates can be made by understanding the amount of information that will be transmitted, rather than adjusting for user numbers directly. Given the size in kilobytes of all the graphics and text on a standard page, multiply this by the number of pages to be used in a typical session. Examining your bandwidth will then show how many users you can comfortably accommodate simultaneously.

SUMMARY

You should now have a fundamental grasp of how some of the technologies provided by Visual Studio, Internet Information Server, and Transaction Server can be used together to create a Web database application. This chapter covered the following:

- **Visual Studio programs** In this book, you will be using Visual InterDev, Visual Basic, Visual J++, and Visual Modeler to construct a series of Web database applications. By using these development programs and languages together, you can create robust client and server-side Web solutions.
- **Active Server Pages (ASP)** The ASP system executes scripting code (usually VBScript) to build dynamic Web pages to send to the client. ASP also has built-in objects, such as the Session object, that make database applications effective.
- **ActiveX Data Objects (ADO)** The data object model that is the successor to DAO. It can be used by all of the Visual Studio packages. In ASP code, ADO is the technology that provides advanced data access.
- **Multitier (or n-tier) systems** Unlike simple two-tier systems (client and server), multitier systems seek to break down a system into logic and reusable parts. The most common example is a three-tier system, where the client application (first tier) communicates with a number of objects (second tier) that actually address the data source (third tier).
- **Microsoft Transaction Server (MTS)** MTS serves remote objects through DCOM for execution and allows transactions to occur over multiple objects. Its transaction capabilities make it an important part of many advanced Web solutions and multitier systems.
- **Four levels of Web database systems** Understanding the level of complexity that will be required by the Web database system will allow you to more accurately estimate the needs of subsequently scaling it for heavier or more widespread use.

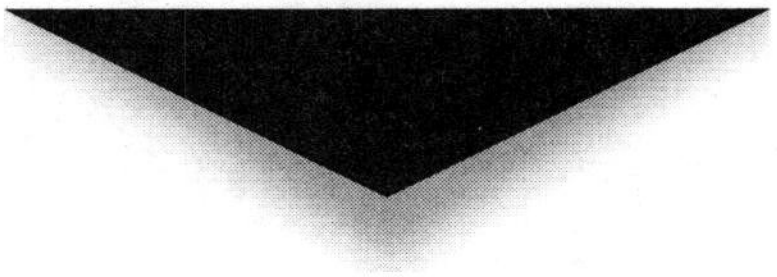

CHAPTER 2

Overview of Internet Information Server (IIS)

This chapter provides a detailed look at how Internet Information Server (IIS) and Active Server Pages (ASP) are used together to create dynamic Web pages. If you are already familiar with both of these technologies, I suggest that you skim this chapter to see if there is any information that you don't fully understand. If you're new to the ASP world, this chapter will give you everything you need to understand the basics of how ASP works in a solution.

After closely examining how IIS functions, you will be equipped to make critical choices about how to implement your Web database application. The two primary tools for doing so, Visual Basic and Visual InterDev, lend themselves to different types of solutions. If your task requires it, you may even need to use Visual C++ for low-level server interaction. Reviewing IIS and how it is used in conjunction with Visual Studio products will clarify these options.

BASIC INFORMATION ABOUT IIS

Internet Information Server (IIS) is Microsoft's free Web server that ships with every copy of Windows NT Server. In the simplest setup, the function of a Web server is to provide replies to HTTP command requests. Even at this simplest level, IIS is consistently rated as one of the most capable Web servers. For more advanced functions, such as server-side execution, IIS is truly in a league of its own.

The Active Server Pages (ASP) technology that is included with IIS is the cornerstone of the interface between scripting and the IIS engine. ASP is not the actual scripting engine, but merely a script preprocessor that sends the code to the script interpreter. Grasping this distinction is important in fully understanding the structure of IIS.

The overlap of the technologies present in Visual Studio can add to the confusion. The diagram in Figure 2-1 provides an overall picture of how these components work together. This diagram does not imply that all applications must be put together in this manner; in fact, few applications will be. Instead it demonstrates the files that are created and used together in a final application.

Visual Basic 6 (VB 6) can be used to construct both ActiveX DLL components (for use by an ASP file) or a complete IIS application. (If you are unfamiliar with IIS applications, they're explained in the "IIS Applications" section, toward the end of this chapter.) Both the ActiveX DLL components and the IIS applications must be processed through the ASP scripting engine.

When an ASP file is constructed, it is typically created using Visual InterDev. InterDev can be used to construct an ASP file from scratch, but it also includes the ability to easily insert an ActiveX DLL that you create in VB 6 into an ASP file. It can also accept ActiveX controls for client-side execution.

You might also notice that there is another type of DLL that can be used with IIS at the same level as ASP: the ISAPI DLL. The ASP engine is actually an ISAPI DLL that is shipped by Microsoft and automatically installed with IIS. All ISAPI DLLs address the

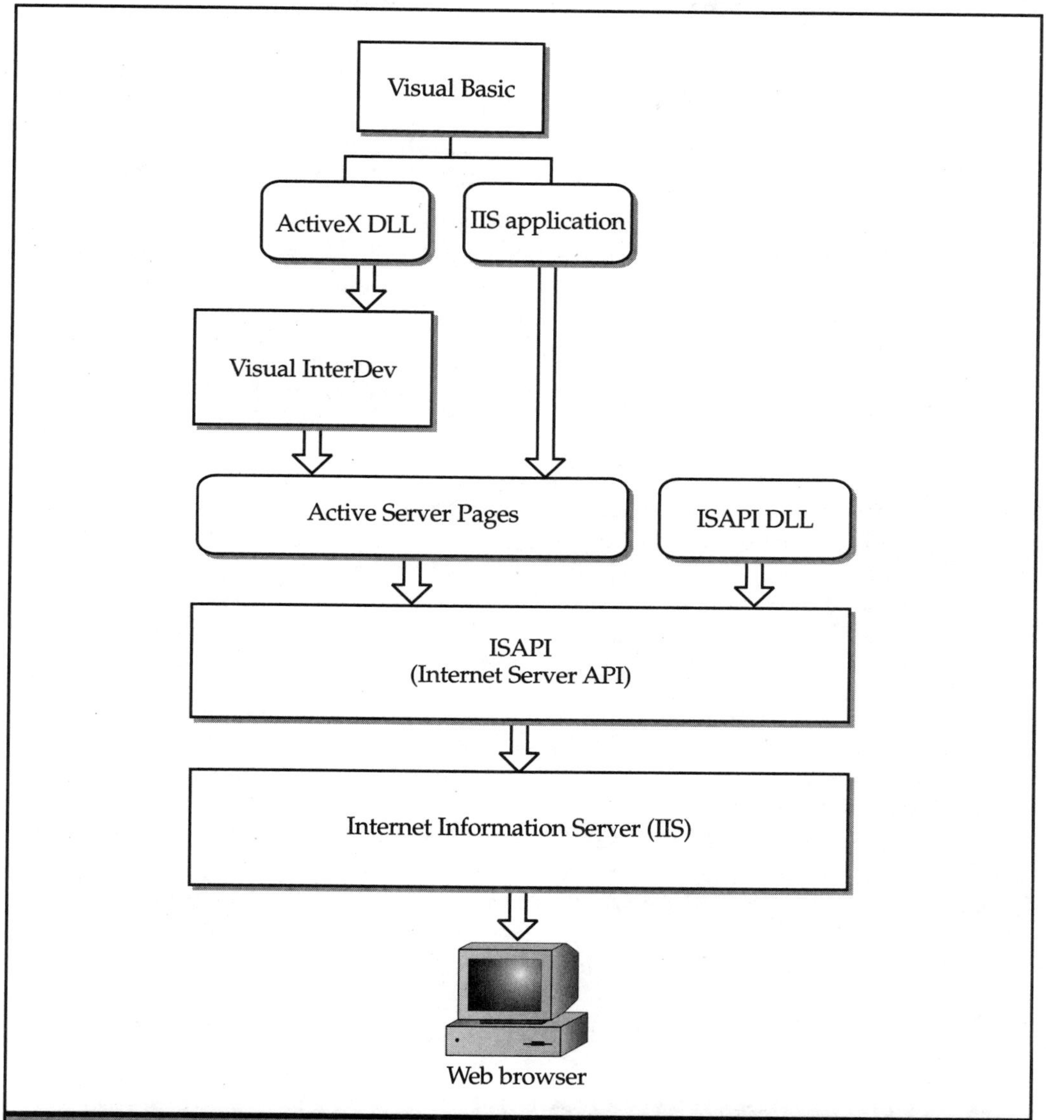

Figure 2-1. The entire IIS structure with Visual Studio products

foundation of IIS, which actually communicates with the user's browser. This means that commands and requests sent by the Web browser can be pre-processed by an ISAPI DLL to dynamically generate a return content.

The essential technologies used in creating a Web database solution include:

- **HTML** Markup language used for Web page coding and scripting code insertion
- **VBScript/JavaScript** The two primary scripting choices for code in Active Server Pages. The JavaScript implementation included with IIS is called JScript.
- **Visual Basic** Programming language used to create ActiveX DLL components, IIS applications, and client-side ActiveX controls (OCXs)
- **Visual InterDev** Web-page creation tool that helps you combine Web pages with client or server-side (ASP) scripting
- **FrontPage** Web-site creation tool that makes it easy to combine HTML, ASP, and template files (for IIS applications) using a What-You-See-Is-What-You-Get (WYSIWYG) interface

The preceding list is basically a top-down review, identifying the products that are used to construct the pieces of a solution. Each of these pieces is used in creating the application, but doesn't directly indicate how the solution will actually execute once it's created. Now we must review the IIS system with a bottom-up approach, looking at the technologies and operations that allow implementation. At the core of any Microsoft-based Web solution is IIS; it serves the actual Web pages requested. Beyond simply serving HTML pages, all of the more complicated functions available for IIS occur through the ISAPI interface layer.

ISAPI INTERFACE

The ISAPI interface is the key expansion interface that makes IIS more than a simple Web server. With a low-level ISAPI interface to a Web server, any HTTP requests can be preprocessed by a custom-designed piece of software. Through ISAPI, you could even create a custom server-side script processor, such as your own version of Active Server Pages.

There are three default ISAPI drivers included with IIS:

- Active Server Pages (ASP)
- Server-Side Includes (SSI)
- Internet Database Connector (IDC)

You will be using the ASP engine extensively in this book. Server-Side Includes will also be used in the solutions to minimize the amount of recoding. SSI essentially allows an HTML page to include another file in its processing stream as if the code in that file were actually included in the text of the primary file. The use of SSI is essential for banners, color coding, and other global attributes that allow a site to retain a particular look and feel across many individual pages.

The Internet Database Connector is actually a primitive precursor to the ASP database capabilities provided through the ADO model. The IDC is still in use by some organizations because of its short learning curve and instant implementation possibilities. However, once you learn to effectively build an ASP/ADO application, you will find that applications built with the IDC take an equal or greater amount of time to create—and they're not expandable.

NOTE: The Internet Database Connector is a very simple method of connecting database fields for display in a browser. Since the IDC is useful for only the most simplistic applications, it will be covered only briefly in this book. For complete information, see the IIS manual.

In addition to the three filters included, you can also create your own using a development language, such as C++. You may be wondering what you can do by programming ISAPI directly that you cannot do with a higher-level ASP page. Essentially, an ISAPI filter can be used to process a file, data, or HTTP request before any other processing, and before any modification has been made to it.

A simple example of something possible with the ISAPI interface that you may already be familiar with are the commercial page counters that are common on the Web. These free dynamic counters (such as those available from www.beseen.com) create an image that displays the count of accesses to a site. The counter is added to any HTML Web page by placing a standard remote image reference, like this non-working example:

```
<IMG SRC="http://www.mycounter.com/mycount.gif?id=2932">
```

When a browser loads this Web page, this code accesses the remote server (at www.mycounter.com) and grabs the GIF file of the current number. The GIF must be automatically generated and sent to the browser as a standard GIF file.

How could you offer this service through ASP? If all the pages were running on your Web server and each page was an ASP file, you could increment a counter in a database. Then an image creation component could be used to create the GIF file for display. A component such as Active Server Paint (www.cvisual.com) would be needed to create the actual image.

However, if it needs to be retrieved from a remote HTML file, the file would need to be sent before any other HTML content. From within ASP, writing binary directly to the request stream is much more difficult than from within an ISAPI DLL.

Since an ISAPI driver executes at a lower level, when the HTTP request is actually received, it can return the MIME type of a GIF to the browser and then send the necessary binary data. Remember that while the ASP filter was designed to process scripts code files and return HTML pages, a general ISAPI filter can return anything that the browser can recognize.

DEFINITION: **MIME Type** The type of file to be received by the browser. The MIME Type works much like a file extension (for example, .bmp) for the Web. Specific MIME Types let the browser know how the incoming file should be handled.

Possible uses that are ideal for ISAPI implementation include:

- **Scripting engines** ASP proves the effectiveness of this solution. Although it would rarely be necessary to design such an engine from scratch, it would be possible for specialized languages such as TCL, by using the ISAPI interface.
- **Automatic image or variable content** Image files for counters are not the only possible dynamic content that might be needed. VRML word files or custom multimedia data are two examples that come to mind.
- **Authentication** Security authentication must be provided in a low-level protocol. ISAPI makes it possible to implement a custom authentication process with each HTTP handshake.
- **Encryption** Like authentication, customized encryption is possible with an ISAPI driver.
- **Low-level API access** If a driver needs expedient access to system resources or driver API capabilities, an ISAPI filter may be the best method of implementation.

ISAPI functions can act as filters for receiving and sending any files. An ISAPI filter can even alter the way an incoming URL is mapped (for example, it can redirect a URL to a de-referenced directory). However, this power comes at the price of application complexity. Because the ISAPI bridge to the IIS functions is accessed directly from the IIS core, such interaction is not as sophisticated as that available through ASP.

In and Out of Process

When Microsoft first implemented ISAPI, it was the successor to the older CGI application model that had been migrated from Unix platform machines. ISAPI filters, like CGIs, were mostly coded in C++, which allowed many of the older CGIs to be converted.

The first version of IIS actually implemented a method for using CGI applications on Windows NT. As the ISAPI interface became more robust, however, CGI was phased out in favor of quicker and more effective methods—ISAPI filters—as well as easier and more powerful technologies—such as ASP pages.

CGI Applications and the Web

CGI (Common Gateway Interface) applications had their genesis in the Unix world where the entire operating system is optimized for multi-user/multi-application execution. A CGI acts much like an EXE in that it creates its own memory area and separate process in the operating system when it executes (known as an out-of-process application).

Each time a browser accessed a URL that contained a CGI reference, a file was created that contained the parameters to be passed to the application. An instance of the CGI executable was then run to process the request. The CGI would create a returned file that would fill in the HTML template information to send a page back to the browser.

CGI applications have numerous disadvantages, such as security issues with file creation, resource use for separate process execution, testing difficulty, and a complete recompile requirement for any small changes to the process.

The current wave of scripting engines from Netscape and Microsoft as well as the Java interfaces to Web and database servers has made CGI technology fairly obsolete. CGIs are still present in many organizations simply because the expense of transition to a newer style requires rewriting older applications that still function well.

A CGI application executed as an out-of-process instance for each individual access. Unlike Unix machines that target multiuser environments, Windows NT was not designed to effectively handle hundreds or thousands of independent processes.

DEFINITION: **Out-of-Process** A process that executes in its own protected memory space such as a program EXE. Out-of-process tasks prevent instability within the core of the Web server but use a great amount of memory and slow down processing execution.

Out-of-process tasks are also relatively slow whenever information needs to be exchanged between two or more tasks. For Web applications, because the Web server has to communicate with the process running outside itself, all communication occurs through the operating system's message channels.

Out-of-process applications use a tremendous amount of resources on a Web server. Each time a new instance of the task is needed (such as a new user entering the Web site), the operating system must create and manage a new application partition. In Figure 2-2, you can see the resource overhead that must be allocated with each additional process.

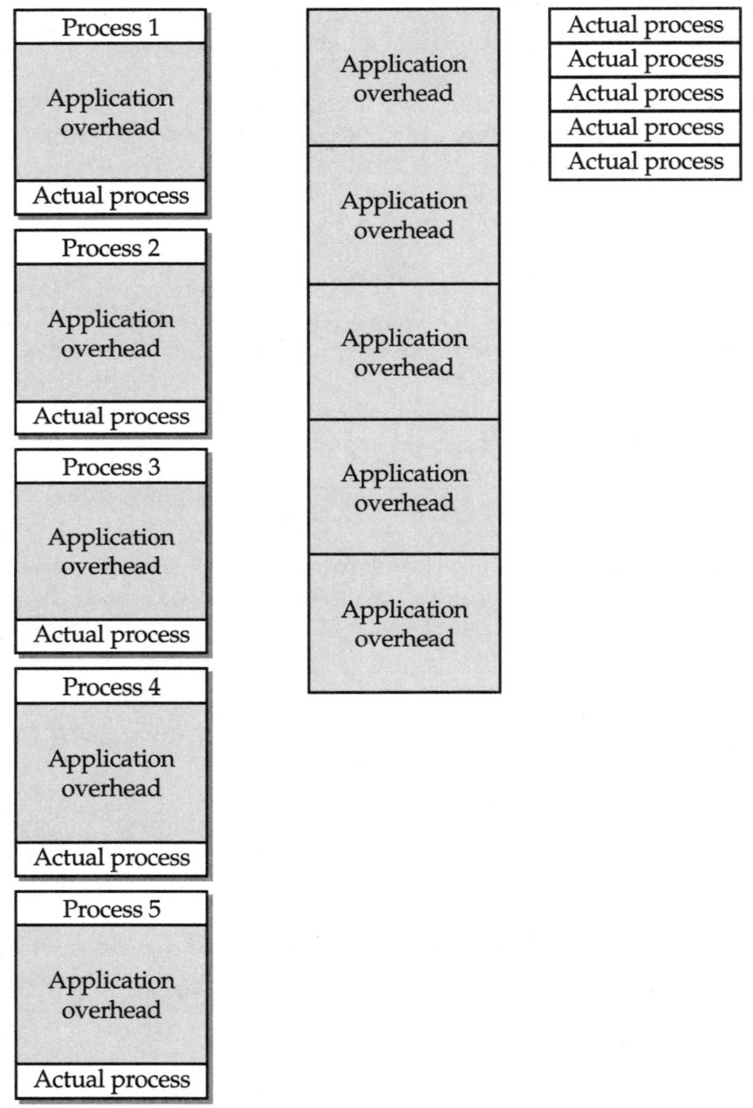

Figure 2-2. Out-of-process applications can take up substantial amounts of memory

The two stacked columns at the right of the diagram in Figure 2-2 demonstrate that a greater amount of resources are allocated to the overhead than to the processes themselves.

In-process operations, in contrast, execute the new tasks within the same protected memory space as the initiating task. Typically, the process is provided with its own processing "thread" that allows the operating system and processor to allocate it individual processing time based on its priority.

DEFINITION: **In-Process** A process that executes within the same memory space as the central application. In the case of a Web solution, the process executes within the protected memory of the Web server.

ISAPI filters are designed to be run within the same memory space as the Web server. This optimizes the execution of Web processes on the server. As in-process tasks, they also use dramatically less memory and processing resources than out-of-process tasks.

The Windows NT operating system is optimized to allow multiple threads within a single process. This design not only maximizes your Web server resources, but also minimizes communication delays between multiple operations occurring in individual threads.

The only real disadvantage to in-process structures is stability. If an out-of-process task crashes, it will only affect itself. In contrast, an operation fault on an in-process execution may take down the Web server. For this reason, extra attention must be paid when creating and debugging an ISAPI filter.

NOTE: Out-of-process applications are easier to debug, since they are isolated from all other processes. A memory leak can easily be detected, because the memory space of the independent process will steadily grow with each execution. Therefore, when debugging an application that runs on the Web server, including those that use ActiveX components, you might consider making them out-of-process for the duration of the debugging process. See the "Web Application Configuration" section in this chapter.

You might be wondering, since most documentation refers to the creation of ISAPI filters with C++, whether an ISAPI filter can be written in Visual Basic. With the new callback capabilities available in VB 6, it is possible to create an ISAPI filter. However, because of the low-level nature of the driver and the need for it to be optimized for speed, it is recommended that if an ISAPI filter is needed, it should be created with a language such as C++. Even with the power of the ASP scripting engine and the ability to create components in Visual Basic, most project requirements can be achieved without writing any ISAPI code.

An ISAPI filter responds to HTTP commands. There are three basic HTTP commands that are commonly used in Web communication. When you are considering implementing an ISAPI filter, knowing the function of each command is essential and it will assist you when you're creating ASP applications.

HTTP Commands

When a Web browser contacts a Web server, it is actually sending HTTP commands to the server that initiate a response. If a Get command is sent, the Web server looks for the file or information to fill that request. It will then either respond with the requested data or return an error code indicating why the request could not be granted.

There are three general HTTP commands a browser will send to a Web server:

- GET Requests for data or files from the server
- POST Sends data to the server
- HEAD Retrieves the header of a document

The GET command is sent to a Web server with a request for a particular directory or file. There is also a modified GET request that can include a "get if modified since a particular date" header. This method of GET is used extensively when the browser features a disk cache of Web content.

The POST command reflects the actions of a posting from a submit button. This command indicates that data that was entered into form fields will follow. The HTTP protocol accepts the data sent from the form and IIS makes it available either to the ISAPI driver or through the Request object in ASP. The POST command includes the information to be passed in an explicit data structure rather than through the URL as GET queries can be handled.

The HEAD command works almost identically to the GET command, except it only retrieves the header of an HTML document (the part surrounded by the <HEAD> tags). Browsers rarely use the HEAD command because the whole page is usually required. For automated solutions such as link checking, however, this command minimizes the amount of material that must be retrieved.

Understanding how the general functions of the HTTP protocol work is important if you want to develop more than basic applications for the Web. Many of the security holes that have been uncovered in Web servers have their basis in fooling various aspects of the protocol. These commands make up the contents of the Web log file, so if you need to examine it for individual interactions, you will know the function of each command. Additionally, Visual Basic includes the Internet Transfer Control that allows you to indirectly access the HTTP commands that the protocol uses.

ASP PROCESS STRUCTURE

Active Server Pages is really just another ISAPI filter. When pages with the .asp file extension are requested by a browser, IIS sends the file to the ASP ISAPI filter, which then returns the appropriate HTML response. The ASP ISAPI filter detects script code, and the code executes in whatever scripting engine is appropriate as specified in the default setting or within the <SCRIPT> tag.

Because ASP pages are primarily made up of standard HTML with the script code appearing between script tags, a traditional HTML editor can be used to create Web graphics. Microsoft FrontPage is an excellent graphics application that can be used to create the template files used in an IIS application, in normal HTML files, and in ASP files that can be edited in Visual InterDev (see Figure 2-3).

The ASP engine interprets files that have the .asp or .asa extensions by executing the pages through the currently selected scripting engine. The scripting engine is plugged into Active Scripting Engine (see Figure 2-4).

For server-side execution, the default language is set to VB Script. You can select a different default language in the IIS settings within the Microsoft Management Console (MMC), as described under "The Application Configuration Dialog Box," later in this chapter.

ASP Code

Active Server Pages code is stored on the Web server in the form of either .asp or .asa files. These files are like HTML files and act much like a template. When the ASP file is requested by the browser, it is executed by the ASP engine. Any text that appears outside server directives (the <SCRIPT> tags or <% %> brackets) or is output by the execution of the Write method to the Response object within the code is sent to the browser as HTML text.

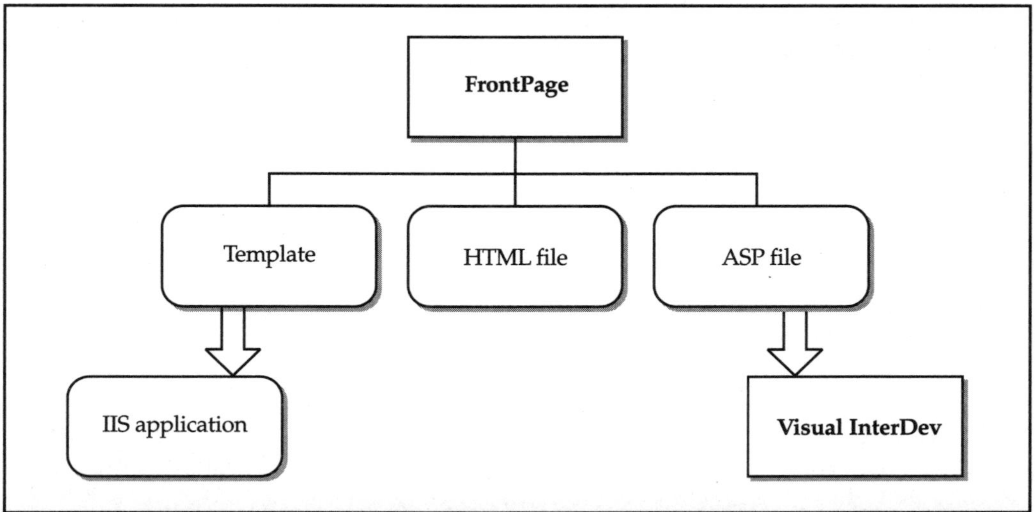

Figure 2-3. FrontPage can be used effectively to edit ASP files as well as standard HTML and template files

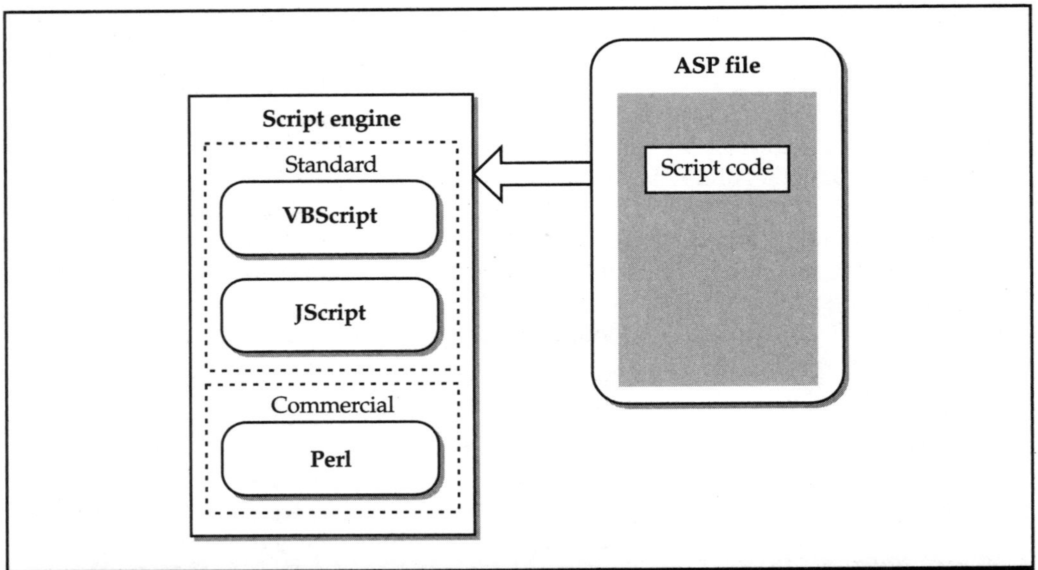

Figure 2-4. ASP allows any compatible scripting engine to be selected

The following code listing is from Sample HelloWorld.ASP, which uses a variable to display text. It provides the most rudimentary execution of an ASP page that contains VB Script code.

```
<HTML>
<BODY>
<%
   Language = VBScript
   a = "Hello World<P>"
   Response.Write(a)
%>
</BODY>
</HTML>
```

The preceding code shows a basic Hello World example. You've probably seen an example that displays this greeting in other languages such as Visual Basic. It defines a single variable to hold the greeting text and then uses the Write method to send it to the browser. All of the text that is not within the server execution directives (<% %>) is sent to the client browser as standard HTML code.

NOTE: When the Write method is used, the output is HTML. Therefore, be sure to include HTML tags for formatting and other needs, as the sample code demonstrates.

The language may also be selected in the code itself, using the Language statement:

```
<%@ Language="JScript" %>
```

This directive will set the scripting language, either for the duration of this ASP page execution or until it encounters another language directive. A single ASP page can hold script code in multiple languages. If a language isn't specified, the default setting is used.

Like the Language statement and tag, you may also notice that there are often several ways to accomplish special implementation features within an ASP file. For example, instead of using the Write method within a code block, there is a simpler way to print the value of a variable in the HTML that will be sent to the client browser. Like an HTML tag, you can use a command such as this:

```
<%=myVariable%>
```

The value contained in the variable *myVariable* will be inserted at the current cursor position in the HTML page that will be returned. This type of variable output is ideal for including a number of values within a table. The table can be designed and modified easily within a program such as FrontPage where the individual value directives will appear as script tags.

Global.ASA File

IIS provides the Global.ASA file to create global variables, methods, and event code that can be used by any of the Web pages within the project. The Global.ASA file can hold global functions and variables, as well as code that executes automatically when particular events occur. By default, a new Visual InterDev includes the Global.ASA file in the project window to help you manage it effectively.

NOTE: Every ASP Web application must have a root directory from which it executes. The Global.ASA file for the project must be located in this root directory to be used by ASP.

The code stored in the Global.ASA file can include script that executes in response to events such as Application_OnStart and Session_OnStart. Routines placed in these events can automatically initialize variables or routines when a Web user first visits the site. These events are often used by Web database applications to log a user, check cookies for personalization, or determine session settings. Events for closing a session or application also allow you to clean up any references or other settings that were initialized for the user session.

For Web database applications, you'll find that you will use the Global.ASA file extensively for connections and query text. Changing this file a single time will affect all of the pages within the particular Web application, so storing global connections and parameters within this file is necessary for most projects.

ACTIVEX COMPONENTS

While scripts provide the core coding of many Web database solutions, there are many solutions that cannot be approached or implemented effectively with scripting. ActiveX components are the perfect technology to use in conjunction with scripting to complete your Web database application.

Several of the key ActiveX features have been encapsulated within components and are included in IIS itself. The basic objects, known as Intrinsic objects, serve to allow a program to send text to the browser, access the form or request data, examine the browser features, and more. In addition to the Intrinsic objects, IIS also includes a number of Intrinsic components. These components contain functions for accessing the file system, automating banner ad rotation, and even sending mail from the Web server.

ASP Intrinsic Objects

The Intrinsic objects are part of the default IIS install and they can be accessed like any other available object. Because the object models for these components exist as part of IIS itself, there is no need to create an instance of these objects using the CreateObject method (as would be necessary if the objects were to be used within Visual Basic or VBA).

Instances of the Intrinsic objects are created automatically when the necessary conditions exist. One of the objects, known as the Sessions object, for example, is created when a new user addresses the Web server. All of the Intrinsic objects are collectively considered part of the HTTP Objects component.

HTTP Objects Component

All of the standard methods of communicating with the client browser are included within the HTTP Objects component. There are six objects that are available for use:

- **Application object** Represents the variables and properties that remain instantiated through access to the series of ASP pages located in the virtual directory that defines the application. Variables and resources may be retrieved from or stored in this object for use by all the ASP pages in the application.
- **Session object** Represents a simulated session for the current user. This object can be used to store variables and track user activities and authentication.
- **Request object** Retrieves information from the user in five forms: QueryString (parameters passed in the URL after the ? character), Form, Cookies, ClientCertificate, and ServerVariables.
- **Response object** Governs HTTP responses to the client, including HTML output and cookie modification.
- **Server object** Performs global functions, such as HTMLEncode (encodes text into a URL-compatible string), MapPath, and CreateObject.

▲ **Object Context object** Works with the Microsoft Transaction Server (MTS) to commit or abort a transaction.

All of these objects are critical for user interaction. The two most commonly used objects in ASP code, Request and Response, will provide all manner of exchanges with the Web client. Keep in mind that if the primary user of your application does not have a browser with the cookie feature (or has turned off the cookie feature), the Session object becomes essentially useless. Placing information in the Response, Request, or Applications variables is essential for simulating a single application across multiple ASP pages.

Using the Object Browser

Most development environments in Visual Studio (and in the VBA environment included in Office products, such as Excel, Word, Access, and PowerPoint) feature the Object Browser. The Object Browser allows you to examine all of the methods, properties, and constants associated with any object within an available object model.

You can use this object browser to examine the objects available for IIS. In the following illustration, you can see the HTTP Response object being examined from the Object Browser contained in Excel. You only have to select the object models you want to access in the References dialog box of the development environment.

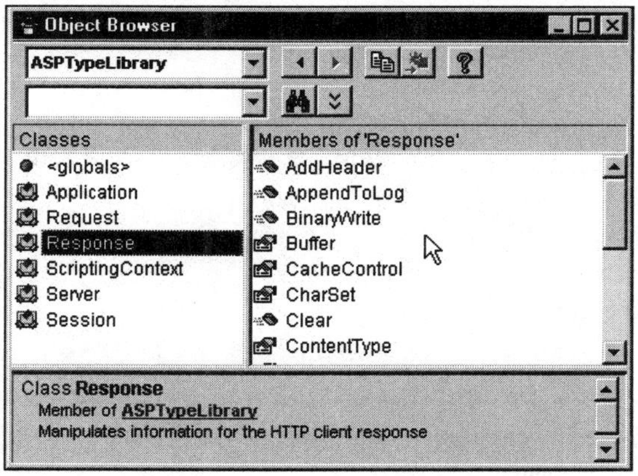

The primary object can be accessed by the Microsoft Active Server Pages Object Library selection in the References dialog box. The Object Browser provides a convenient method of quickly checking the information about an object without having to look in the IIS manual. In the Office applications, the VBA environment is activated by selecting the Visual Basic Editor option available from the Macro submenu under the Tools menu or by pressing ALT-F11.

Each of these objects will be used extensively as your Web database solutions become more complex. Keep in mind that these objects allow variables to be stored within them. Effectively judging the scope of the variables you wish to use can help minimize confusion about which variable is being accessed, and it can also simplify the number of parameters that must be passed between individual ASP files.

NOTE: When you need to create instances of objects, such as ActiveX DLLs, use the Server object's CreateObject method rather than the standard CreateObject method available through VBScript. The Server method can more effectively track objects and manage their disposal.

FileSystem Component

To read, create, or modify files contained on the Web server, you will need to use the FileSystem component. It provides complete filing capabilities, including the ability to access either ASCII or Unicode files, append to a current file, or create entirely new binary or text files. The FileSystem component is actually the *only* method of obtaining direct file access through VBScript, because the traditional VB file commands have been removed. With the release of VB 6, Microsoft is encouraging the standard use of FileSystem objects in all languages for general disk-related access rather than the use of traditional disk access language commands.

NOTE: From the Object Browser, the FileSystem component is listed as Microsoft Scripting Runtime in the References dialog.

The FileSystem object contains a TextStream object for file access once the file has been opened or created. Streams are treated in the same manner as numbered file paths, which are standard in environments such as Visual Basic.

Because the FileSystem object allows writing to the server machine, it is potentially more dangerous than the other standard components. Besides the ability to corrupt or delete current files, the dynamic creation of large files could strain your disk resources. Be careful to consider the possible ramifications of the use of this object in your solution.

NOTE: In the past, almost all text files have been written in the standard ASCII file format in which each character uses a single byte to represent a text value. With a single byte, that meant that there were only 256 possible values, making ASCII unable to record a number of languages that don't use the Roman alphabet, such as Chinese.

The newer International Unicode standard uses two bytes for every character to greatly increase the number of available possibilities; it encompasses most human languages. Almost all Visual Studio products now support Unicode in all file operations. However, many external tools, including a number of commercial text editors, do not yet support Unicode. Therefore, committing to using Unicode files in your project requires advance planning.

Ad Rotator Component

The Ad Rotator component allows you to place a banner ad on an ASP page, and it will automatically rotate the banner that is shown chosen from a list of banners. This component will allow you to display a number of banners with a preset frequency of appearance.

The component itself must have a text file known as the Rotator Schedule file (see Figure 2-5) that contains instructions concerning which adds to display with what frequency. The file is actually constructed in two parts: the header and the body. The header describes the entries found in the body, and the body contains each banner that is scheduled for rotation.

A redirect URL is also included in the header of the file to indicate a redirect when the user clicks on a banner. An ASP file records which banner was clicked before redirecting the user's browser to the final site. In this way, the page can track what banners users actually click on by recording a log entry of the banner type every time the redirect page is accessed.

TIP: Although primarily useful for banner ads, you can also use this component to add variety to your Web site. With this component, you can rotate the header graphics or even the headline content on various parts of your Web site. Users always enjoy seeing something new. For example, the Ad Rotator could be used to display one of four different company header graphics, providing users with a new look each time they enter your site.

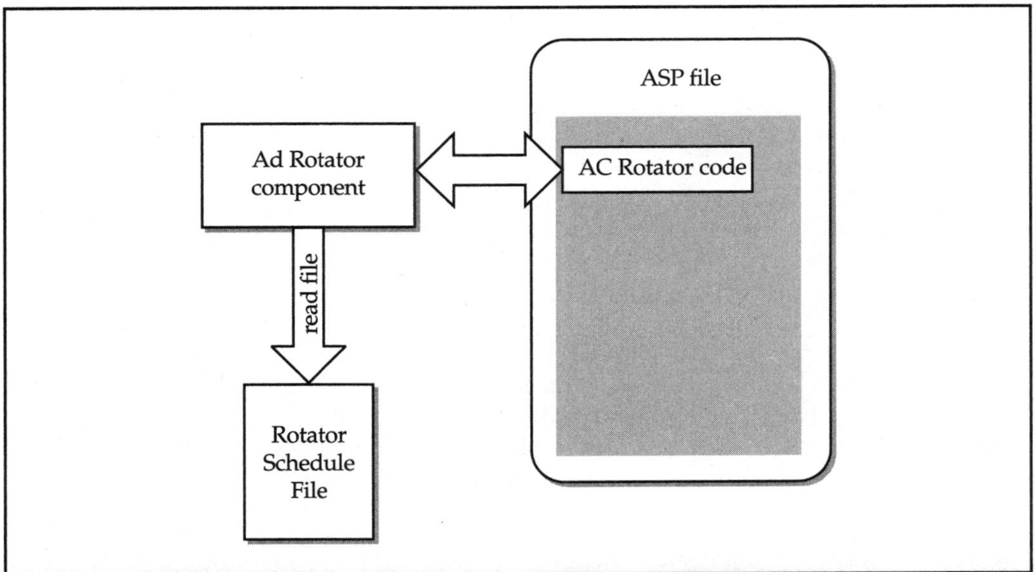

Figure 2-5. The Rotator Schedule file is accessed by the Ad Rotator component when it's called from ASP code

The file for the ad rotation is actually stored as a standard text file with a specific format. The first few lines specify a redirect URL (which can be used for traffic monitoring), and the Width, Height, and Border properties that will apply to all ads in the file. These are simply passed on as part of the IMG tag in the generated HTML. Each of the adds that follow must contain an HTTP address for the image, the destination link address, and the percentage of time that the ad should be displayed. The percentage numbers are really a ratio, so they may add up to more than 100, but it is usually easiest to keep them as true percentages.

NOTE: For the Object Browser, the Ad Rotator component is listed as MSWC Advertisement Rotator Object Library in the References dialog.

In the following listing, you can see an example of an add rotator file with three entries. Note that the third entry doesn't have a destination address. This entry demonstrates that the component can be used to rotate static graphics that have no link to click on.

```
redirect adRedirect.asp
width 460
height 60
border 1
*
ad_1.gif
http://www.coherentdata.com
Coherent Data
20

ad_2.gif
http://www.coherentdata.com/cscentral
Client/Server Central
20

ad_3.gif

Osborne
30
```

To use this file, a simple ASP page could be created like the one shown next. When this file is executed in the same directory in which the Rotator Schedule file is located, a banner will be shown on the page. Note that you will probably want to alter or eliminate the first line of the preceding Rotator Schedule file, which specifies a redirect URL.

```
<HTML>
<HEAD><TITLE>The Advertisement Rotator component</TITLE></HEAD>
<BODY>
<H3>The Advertisement Rotator component</H3>
```

```
<%  Set Ad = Server.CreateObject("MSWC.Adrotator") %>
<%= Ad.GetAdvertisement("adSchedule.txt") %>

<P>Click on the banner ad shown above.
</BODY>
</HTML>
```

SMTP Connector Component

One of the more powerful components now included with IIS is the Simple Message Transaction Protocol (SMTP) Connector component, which allows you to send e-mail from an ASP file. By configuring the SMTP Connector to point at a desired mail server, VBScript code can dynamically create and send an e-mail message to any desired address.

NOTE: For the Object Browser, the SMTP Connector Component is listed as Microsoft CDO for NTS Library in the References dialog.

In Chapter 11 you'll learn how to build a complete application using this technology to send a confirmation e-mail to a user who enters survey information into an application.

ActiveX DLL Components

Visual Basic can be used to create ActiveX DLL components for use on an ASP page. ActiveX DLLs are actually just Visual Basic class files that are compiled into stand-alone DLLs. With the proper methods and properties exposed through Public scope settings, they can be used in the same manner as the Intrinsic controls (instantiated through the CreateObject method of the Server object).

IIS Applications

In Visual Basic 6, Microsoft added the amazing new capability of creating what they have labeled an *IIS application*. Using all of the power and maturity of the Visual Basic environment, you can build an HTML-based server-side application that executes on IIS.

DEFINITION: **IIS Application** A type of application created with VB 6 that is essentially a collection of ActiveX DLLs that execute server-side on IIS. The ASP code that calls the IIS application is automatically generated by VB. A complete server-side HTML project can be created using only Visual Basic.

You might wonder why this possibility is so compelling when Visual InterDev is available. Granted, a project created with Visual InterDev can do many of the same things that an IIS application makes possible. However, a VB application offers several advantages that, as shown in the following list.

- Develop the solution within the world-class Visual Basic development environment.
- Use a single development environment for all projects, including Web-based projects.
- Use the complete power of the VB language, including class construction.
- Compile the final application for faster execution, security, and code privacy.
- More precisely address the transaction, connection pooling, and multi-threading capabilities of the server system

Visual InterDev will remain the primary environment for Web-application development and will become even more so as Microsoft enhances its features. However, the IIS application provides an excellent alternative for those who need any of the above advantages. In Chapter 15, I will demonstrate the creation of an IIS application using VB. Its creation is very similar to the process used to develop an ActiveX DLL, and, in point of fact, an IIS application is actually a series of ActiveX DLLs managed by the VB environment, including the automatic generation of the requisite ASP files to call them.

JAVA APPLICATIONS ON THE WEB SERVER

In contrast to a traditional Java applet, a Java application has complete access to all of the Java classes, including those that write to the disk drive. An ASP application can instantiate a Java application, pass it parameters, and execute methods through it.

Note that Java executes in much the same way as a CGI application, so it may be slower and more resource intensive than an equivalent ASP/VBScript solution.

> ***TIP:*** If you are going to use IIS to execute Java classes, I suggest you download and install the Activator from the Sun Web site. Although it is slower than the Java Virtual Machine (JVM) that Microsoft provides, it provides the reference implementation of the Java platform from Sun. Usually the reason for executing Java applications on IIS will be to allow the same application to be used across multiple platforms, so running the same JVM on each server will minimize the amount of debugging and the variation of execution between platforms.

PERSONAL WEB SERVER

With the integration of the Web browser into Windows 98, more companies have the impetus to create intranet applications. Because Web database applications can be expensive to create, critical solutions are often left undone or are partially implemented by lower-level personnel using Microsoft Access.

Personal Web Server (PWS), which is installed as part of Windows 98 (and is a free download for Windows 95), can provide the ideal small environment for simple applications. The ASP engine is integrated into Personal Web Server, so ASP code can be easily reused for smaller applications that do not need to be implemented at a higher organizational level.

Any Windows 98 machine with Microsoft Access can, therefore, be an ASP Web database deployment machine. Although Microsoft doesn't recommend PWS for anything but the smallest Web project, keep this technology in mind for department-specific or lower-priority implementation projects. PWS is available free in the Windows NT Option pack (even though it is a Windows 95/98 service). It also ships with every copy of Microsoft FrontPage.

TIP: If you use lower-power machines (especially portables) for general Web development, you can still use them to develop ASP applications. Since Personal Web Server runs under Windows 95 or Windows 98 and executes ASP code, simply install it on the lower-end machines. The final code will be compatible for execution on IIS 4.

CONFIGURATION ISSUES

Proper configuration of ASP is interwoven with IIS configuration. When your Web server is set up properly for application execution, ASP will function correctly. Configuration from the management console can be specified to affect the entire Web server, a particular directory, or a virtual (application) directory.

There are three primary questions that must be answered for each new ASP application that is installed on IIS:

- Does this application require its own memory space?
- What are the process and security considerations involved with this application?
- What debugging options should be present?

Determining whether independent memory space is needed will depend on speed versus stability concerns. If the application does not use any external components that might have memory problems, usually an in-process application is best. If there are concerns about a particular control, running it out-of-process may be the best choice.

Configuring Internet Information Server

The configuration of Internet Information Server, beginning with IIS 4, takes place through the Microsoft Management Console (MMC). The MMC is the same application that you will use later to configure the Transaction Server. Like the common IDE that Microsoft has been progressively moving toward for the Visual Studio products, BackOffice seems to be converging on the MMC as the common configuration environment.

The MMC for IIS allows you to configure the Default Web site as well as the Administration Web site. Clicking the right-mouse button and selecting Properties allows you to access the configuration settings.

Web Application Configuration

You can access the general properties of a Web server or virtual directory on the Home Directory tab of the Default Web Site Properties dialog box (see Figure 2-6). These are the properties that relate to each Web application. The Application Settings frame of the dialog box allows you to set specific parameters for various aspects of application execution.

Among the possible application settings is the option to Run in Separate Memory Space (Isolated Process), which was described earlier in the chapter as out-of-process execution. In the figure, you can see that this option is checked in order to ease debugging of an ActiveX DLL. For an independent memory space, the memory size may be tracked for memory leaks and any severe faults will only bring down the process, not the entire Web server.

The Permissions options describe the application's ability to execute processes in the virtual directory. By setting the permission to Script, ASP files can be executed out of this directory. The Execute setting provides for actual application execution, such as that re-

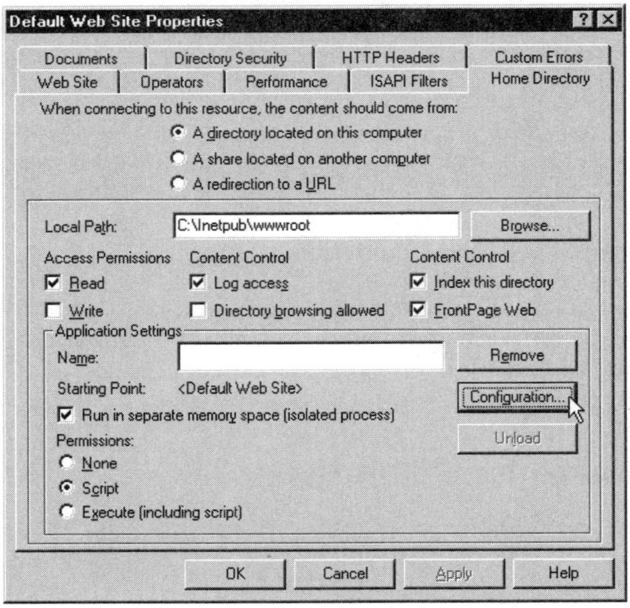

Figure 2-6. Configuring the Web application settings in the Home Directory Properties window

quired by CGI applications. There will be few IIS configurations for which the Execute setting will be appropriate.

These settings are very general when relating to Web applications. Clicking the Configuration button leads you to the Application Configuration dialog box, where settings much more specific to ISAPI filters (and thus to ASP) are applied.

The App Mappings Tab of the Application Configuration Dialog Box

The App Mappings tab of the Application Configuration dialog box is shown in Figure 2-7. The App Mappings tab contains the primary settings related to ISAPI filter execution.

As you can see from the figure, all of the currently available ISAPI filters are listed individually in the displayed list box. In addition to the file extension settings that determine which ISAPI filter is used, you can see that there are excluded functions displayed in the third column.

These functions are actually HTTP commands. If you double-click one of the list box entries, the dialog box related to that entry will appear (see Figure 2-8). From this dialog box, you can modify the filter used for an extension, add additional excluded HTTP com-

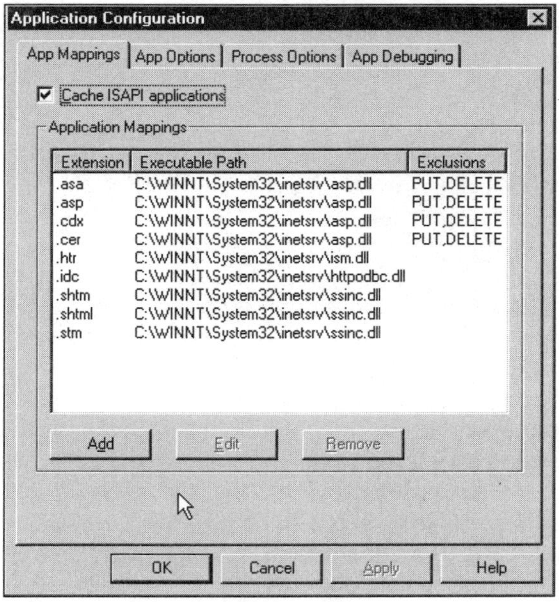

Figure 2-7. The App Mappings tab in the Application Configuration dialog box

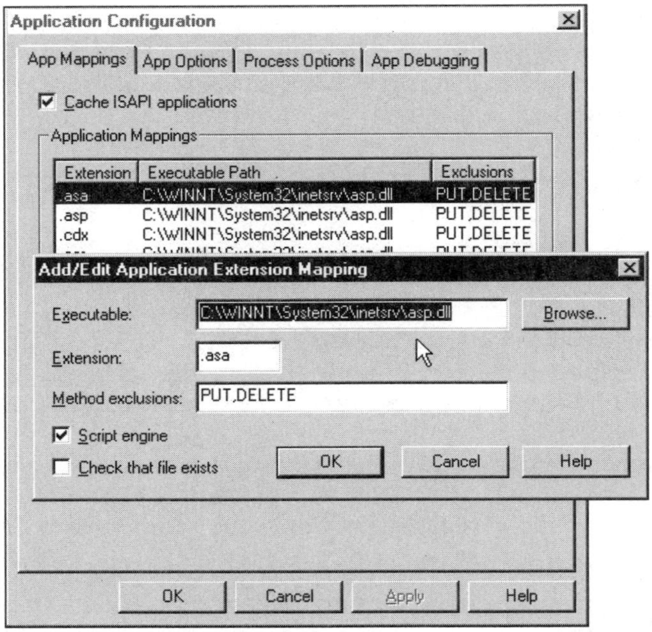

Figure 2-8. The Application Extension Mapping dialog box determines the ISAPI filter executed for a given file extension

mands, and set file checking. If you check the Script Engine check box this filter will not require Execute permissions to be available (it will only need Script permission).

The App Options Tab

The App Options tab of the Application Configuration dialog box provides general settings for configuring the application execution, as shown in Figure 2-9. Note that several of these settings, including the timeout values, can be modified with ASP code.

The decision to enable sessions is usually a policy decision within an organization. To simulate a session requires the storage of a cookie on the client browser. When catering to customers who find cookie creation on their machine an invasion of privacy, the *Enable session state* global setting allows you to disable it for a virtual directory or Web server.

To buffer output, check the Enable Buffering check box. By default, this box is left blank so that text written into the Response object is sent immediately to the client browser. Allowing buffering ensures that a user gets the entire contents of the page (although they must wait until it is complete), it also allows the HTTP headers to be modified anywhere in the ASP script, since they won't be sent until the conclusion of the page.

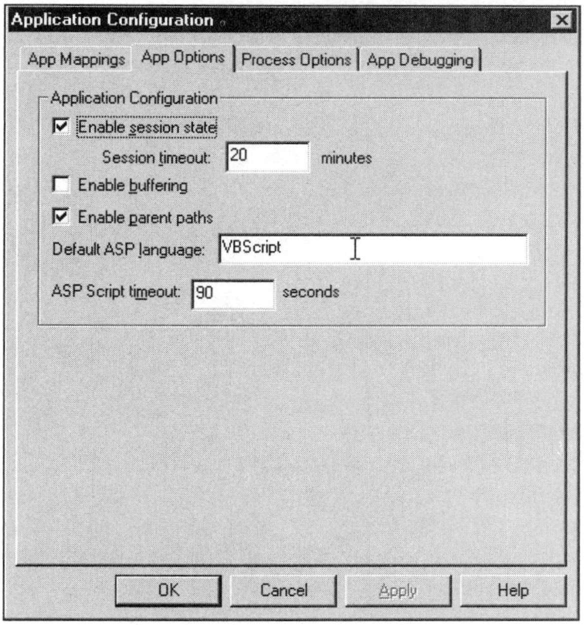

Figure 2-9. The App Options tab contains settings including Session capabilities

The Default ASP Language setting determines which language interpreter is used if none is specified. By default, the VBScript setting is used. When a general install of IIS is made, there are only two options available: VBScript and JScript.

Finally, the ASP Script Timeout option allows you to specify the length of time to wait before aborting a script. This value can range from 1 to 2,147,483,647 seconds.

TIP: Although the default is set to 90 seconds, I recommend setting it to a much shorter time, such as 35–45 seconds. Unless the query or process is extremely involved, it is unlikely that processing time will take over a minute. Creating a lower setting prevents the user from endlessly waiting, especially when the processing problem may have been due to a faulty input parameter.

The Process Options Tab

The Process Options tab of the Application Configuration dialog box, shown in Figure 2-10, has a few basic parameter settings for process execution. If the setting for the Web application specifies in-process execution, the settings chosen here will affect all applications that execute within the Web server process. On the other hand, for an out-of-process or isolated-process task, the settings in this window affect only that process.

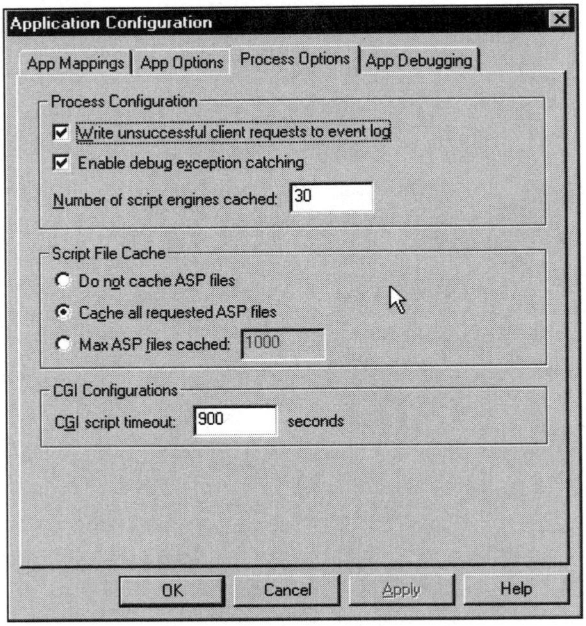

Figure 2-10. The Process Options tab contains options for either an isolated process or all processes

You can see that the default settings will comply with a majority of Web servers. Notice that the default CGI Script Timeout value is substantially longer than the equivalent scripting timeout. Because of the variability of CGIs, as well as the possibility that virtual memory requirements will slow down execution, this value is set high.

The App Debugging Tab

The App Debugging tab of the Application Configuration dialog box, shown in Figure 2-11, allows you to activate ASP debugging. The first check box allows you to enable server-side debugging. The client-side check box serves no function in IIS version 4 and is reserved for possible future implementation.

The response from a server error can be specified in the Script Error Messages frame. For debugging, you will most certainly want the detailed error messages activated. However, for deployment servers, you should consider selecting the generic Send Text Error Message to Client setting. Error messages can divulge private information when they occur, such as the name of a system ODBC data source. It is usually a good idea for an organization to decide on a standard setting for this option and stick to the policy.

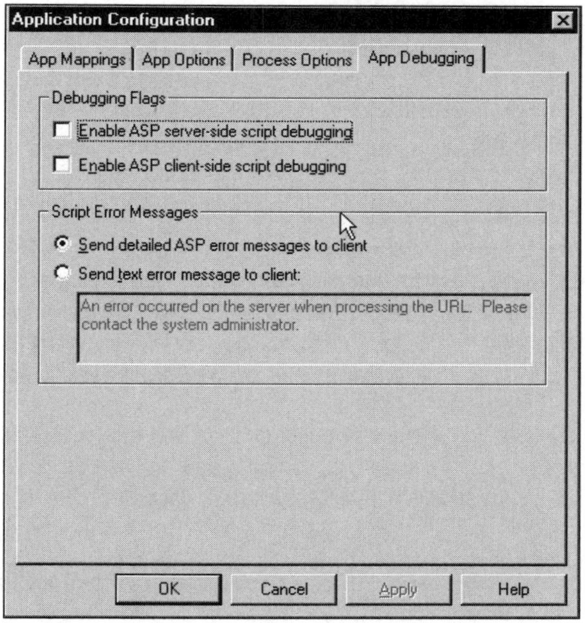

Figure 2-11. The App Debugging tab activates debugging

Providing FTP Access

A Web administrator will often want to provide upload access to the Web server. Although it is beyond the scope of this book to describe all of the ways this might be done, you should recognize that the abilities provided in Visual InterDev and Microsoft FrontPage can make this the most effective means of allowing Web updates.

The FTP server can even do automatic routing to individual directories. If you create a folder at the root FTP directory named *anonymous,* and inside it you place a folder that matches the username entered into the NT security framework, logging in without entering a default folder will automatically place the user inside the directory that matches their login name.

NOTE: When providing FTP access, remember that to use FTP Access, users must have the Log on Locally privilege set in the User Rights Policy dialog box of the User Manager application. The users may also belong to a group that has this privilege. If the setting is not configured, FTP access, even with the proper password and user ID, will be rejected.

EXAMINING THE EVENT LOG

Every HTTP command that is sent from the browser to the server is recorded in the event log, along with the return code if an error was generated. Examining the event log provides a clear picture of what actually occurred on the Web server.

Beyond that, the Web log can also serve as one of the best continuing methods for debugging your applications. The log will contain any queries or page accesses that generated errors, and help you track down and eliminate broken links or query errors.

NOTE: If you don't need a custom analysis solution, there are a number of products that report on Web server activity. One of the most popular packages is WebTrends (www.Webtrends.com). It will summarize the most popular pages, provide a breakdown of interaction by date and time, and produce many other statistics. All this is generated as a report in Web page format so that it can be placed on the intranet server for repeated evaluation.

WebTrends provides an excellent example of a solution that generates Prepared Pages. Processing a Web log, particularly a large one, can be a slow and resource-intensive operation. Therefore, executing WebTrends once generates a set of static pages that can become a permanent part of the site.

IIS provides extremely powerful options that allow you to place log data directly into a database for querying, summarizing, and processing. The logging settings can be adjusted under the Web Site tab of the Web Site Properties dialog box.

Options include how often a new log file should be created, what default log file directory should be used, as well as what information should be recorded in the log. Extended logging options include recording the following entries with each HTTP command occurrence: date, time, client IP, username, service name, server name, server IP, server port, method, URL site, URL query, HTTP status, Win32 status, bytes sent and received, time taken, protocol version, user agent, cookie, and referrer.

TIP: Although any ODBC data source can be used to store log information, including Microsoft Access, I recommend you use a complete database server (such as SQL Server) with its own database construct to hold the data. For a popular Web site, log files can run at least 150 megabytes per month. Storing and querying this amount of information effectively in a personal database, such as Access, will slow down the performance of the Web server.

Once the information has been stored in the database, a standard query can be used for the summary. At a minimum it is best to provide indexes for the date/time field, the request IP field, and the method.

SUMMARY

The entire structure of IIS can be simplified into two parts: the Web server and the ISAPI filters that provide dynamic capabilities. The ASP ISAPI driver allows pages with scripting code to be executed on the Web server to return dynamic content. With the recent addition of IIS Application creation to Visual Basic, the breadth of Web applications that can be developed using IIS is phenomenal. In this chapter, you've covered:

- **ISAPI** The interface that allows low-level access to Web server requests. Most ISAPI drivers are complex and written in C++, so they are not commonly constructed by application developers.
- **Active Server Pages** The technology within the IIS Web server used to execute scripts to return HTML to the client browser. The ASP engine includes the VB Script and JavaScript (JScript) languages in the default installation. ASP is actually an ISAPI filter DLL.
- **ActiveX DLL** An ActiveX DLL can be created using a number of Visual Studio products including Visual Basic, Visual C++, Visual FoxPro, and Visual J++. Once a class is compiled into an ActiveX DLL, it can be easily instantiated and used from within any ASP file on the server.
- **IIS application** Visual Basic now allows a complete server-side Web application to be constructed that compiles into a number of ActiveX DLLs. The DLLs are activate by ASP files automatically generated by the VB system. This allows an entire IIS project to be created using the reliability and maturity of the Visual Basic environment.
- **Event Log** The log containing every HTTP access command. Examining the event log can show which pages were accessed, the errors that occurred, and even the most commonly posted form requests.

CHAPTER 3

Overview of VBScript

The VBScript language is the default language used by Active Server Pages. Because it is a subset of the Basic language and is deployed across a wide variety of platforms, there is not a large amount of information that relates to VBScript specifically (as opposed to general Visual Basic information). Most documentation relates to general differences between the available versions of Basic or specific information for the VBScript environment used for deployment (such as Outlook, ASP, Windows Scripting Host, etc.).

This chapter provides a quick general summary of the VBScript language itself, no matter what platform it will be used upon. Microsoft seems to be broadening the deployment of VBScript with the addition of Windows Scripting Host to all its new operating systems. With the release of the Script Debugger which can be used to debug the scripting code, VBScript is becoming an increasingly robust solution for Web applications.

VBSCRIPT LANGUAGE

The VBScript language is a derivative of the Visual Basic/VBA languages. However, although it is a subset of these parent languages, it differs only in the broad number of environments in which it can be deployed. VBScript is now used for everything from operating system macro scripting to server-side Web execution. Although most designers are generally aware of the VBA environment that is present in Microsoft's Office applications, the VBScript subset is not as familiar.

VBScript is actually found in several Windows technology offerings. It can execute on both the client and the server: on the client, the script is typically retrieved from a remote resource, such as a Web server or Microsoft Exchange server; on the server, scripts are usually located on the server itself (see Figure 3-1).

In the diagram, you'll notice that Exchange Server is not included among the platforms that execute code on the server. Instead, forms may contain VBScript code that can be retrieved by client machines and executed within Outlook, via the Exchange client. Typically, the only execution of VBScript on the server takes place within IIS through an ASP page.

The features of VBScript are primarily limited by the role of the language. Scripting languages are never meant to be used for complete application development. Rather, scripts are traditionally used as "glue" code to coordinate several components of advanced technology. In fact, scripting languages are much too slow for execution when compared with compiled languages such as Visual Basic, which makes them less scalable for high-traffic volume solutions.

You might notice that VBScript is generally used in solutions that either have no direct user interface or that are vastly different from the traditional forms-based windowing interface common to client programs. Since VBA already fills the role when a complete environment is needed, VBScript is generally used when general language execution is required.

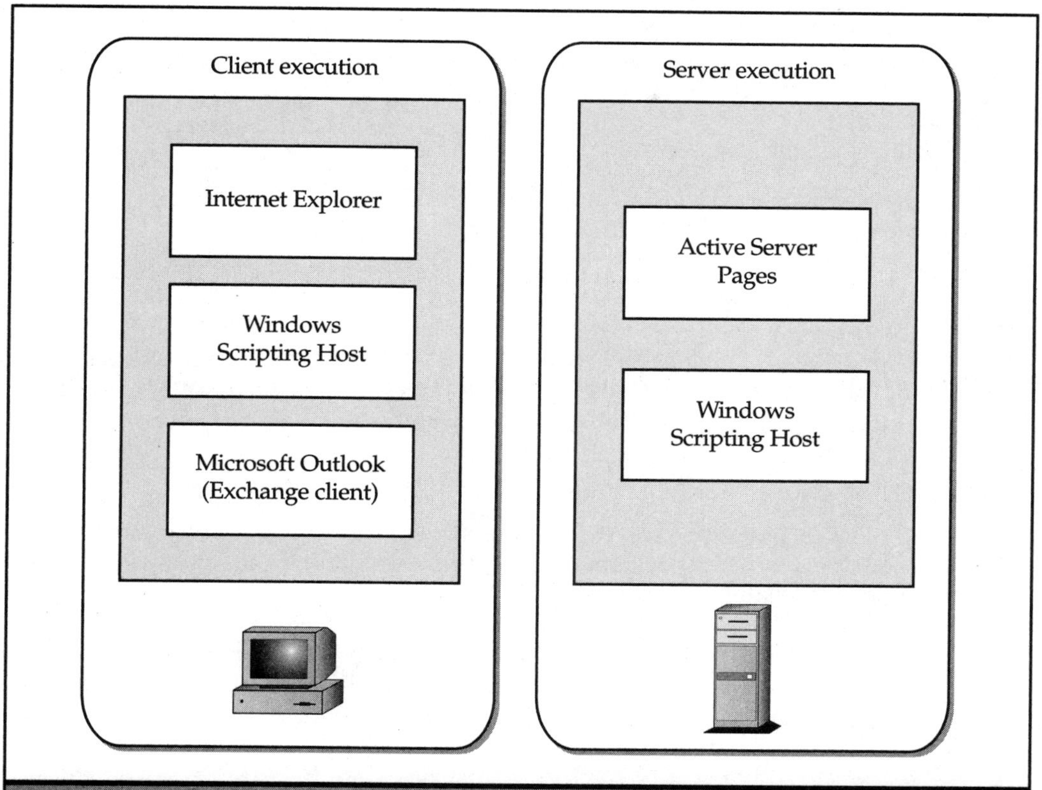

Figure 3-1. VBScript is used on both the client and the server

Data Types

Variables and the commands used to manipulate them are the most noticeable difference between VBScript and the parent languages. Unlike Visual Basic, VBScript does not have strong data-typing capabilities. In fact, the only true data type in VBScript is the Variant data type. A Variant variable can store any of the other traditional data types.

You are undoubtedly already familiar with the Variant data type. It is important to note, however, that while VBScript does not allow specific typing, it will generate errors when you attempt to combine inappropriate types (such as a number with a date).

When working with VBScript, you will regularly have to make explicit conversions. Simply use the supplied conversion functions:

- `CBool` Converts passed value to Boolean type
- `CByte` Converts passed value to Byte type

- `CCur` Converts passed value to a Currency numeric type
- `CDate` Converts passed value to a Date type
- `CDbl` Converts passed value to a Double numeric type
- `CInt` Converts passed value to an Integer numeric type
- `CLng` Converts passed value to a Long numeric type
- `CSng` Converts passed value to a Single numeric type
- `CStr` Converts passed value to a string

As a general rule of thumb, it is better to make these explicit conversions than not. If you do not, an incorrect value read from a database could cause your executing page to fault. As with VB, using the ampersand (&) operator will do an implicit conversion of any data type to a string when concatenating with a string.

Constants

A constant functions like a variable, except that once a constant's value is set, it cannot be changed. There are only a few constant values intrinsic in VBScript. The `True` and `False` constants are still available.

One of the largest differences you will notice as you begin to use VBScript extensively is the lack of object constants. In an object model, there are often many constant values to represent modes or other settings. For example, in Visual Basic or VBA, setting the scaling mode of a form can be done using an object constant:

```
Form1.ScaleMode = vbPixels
```

The value of the constant `vbPixels` is 8. If you used this statement in VBScript, the `ScaleMode` would be set to Null or 0, since the `vbPixels` constant does not exist. You could use code like this:

```
Form1.ScaleMode = 8   ' vbPixels
```

The value of the constant is placed in the code. The name of the constant has been included after the property setting both to clarify the function of the command and to allow for conversion to another language such as VB if necessary.

The reason for these missing constants is the portable nature of the scripting language. VBScript is used not only for server-based implementations, but also for applications where the code is sent over a network (such as in client-side scripts on a Web page or Exchange form). This means that an explicit reference will have to be made to the particular type library needed.

Since VBScript does not support explicit referencing, the constants are not available. Therefore, to use these constants in VBScript, you will either have to explicitly declare them at the beginning of a program or use their numeric value instead.

NOTE: The Immediate window, available in the Visual Basic and VBA environments, is a perfect companion to VBScript. When you need to learn the numeric value of a constant, simply add a reference in the References dialog box to the desired object model, and use the `Print` (`?`) command in the Immediate window to display the constant value.

Conditional Statements

Conditional statements affect the flow of the program. Like VBA, the two primary conditional statements are supported in VBScript:

```
If...Then...Else...ElseIf...End If
Select Case...End Select
```

These conditionals operate in VBScript almost the same way they do in the parent languages. Note that the `Select Case` statement in VBScript, although familiar from VB, is not as flexible as the version available in the parent language. Within the individual `Case` statements, VBScript does not include the ability to use `Is` or `To` (although type checks are possible using the TypeName function). Therefore, ranges and types cannot be handled within the `Case` branch of this statement. If such multiple-evaluation flexibility is required, `ElseIf`, although bulkier, can be used to accomplish the task.

Loops

VBScript features most of the standard looping commands. Just like in VB, the conditional check may appear at either the beginning or the end of the constructor. So, for example, to check at the beginning of the loop before an iteration has begun, you can use code like the following:

```
Do While i < 10
   ' Do operations
Loop
```

To make the evaluation process after an iteration is complete and before a new one has begun, use this code:

```
Do
   ' Do operations
Loop While i < 10
```

Often, programmers forget that these two possible execution models are available and write additional code to provide this functionality. In VBScript, where loop execution is much slower than in a compiled language such as Visual Basic, making sure loops are optimized for best execution is crucial to an effective application.

Objects

Referencing objects from VBScript in ASP can be done either directly for the intrinsic objects, such as Response, Session, and others, or by using the CreateObject method. Although the general CreateObject method may be used in an ASP document, it is recommended that you use the version included in the Server object.

Any ActiveX DLL that the Web server has permission to use may be accessed, unless it contains a flag denoting it as an application. For example, the Excel object model cannot be used from within an ASP file unless the IIS server has been specifically configured to allow this.

NOTE: To allow execution of an ActiveX EXE or non-ASP certified DLL, you must make an alteration to the Windows registry. See the IIS documentation for more information.

Keep in mind that VBScript does not include the `With...End With` statement for referencing objects. Therefore, all references must be made either explicitly or using a custom `CreateObject` reference. Also, using the Application object to store commonly used object references, especially database connections and recordsets, can speed program execution.

ERROR TRAPPING

One of the most overlooked but important features that should be included in a Web application is error trapping and handling. This topic is often given lip service by IS professionals, but is seldom well implemented. Error Trapping is *more* important in a Web application than in a typical application because of the number of layers between the user and the application.

When an error in a standard client application occurs, it can often be worked around. The most obvious problems are usually caught in basic testing. Since tasks such as data entry for a Web application usually take place over several pages, an unrecoverable error can actually cost far more time and frustration, since all entered information is typically lost (see Figure 3-2). Additionally, the multipage error that halts progress usually provides no way to complete the desired operation, whether it is a product registration or sales order entry.

With so much at stake, gracefully handling errors is the mark of a friendly application. Unfortunately, the work of the developer is more complicated in VBScript since it includes less basic error-handling machinery than is supplied with Visual Basic. In a Web solution, this prevents error recovery from being as elegant as is typical in a client application. Therefore, more planning is often required for effective error response.

Error-Catching

The only error-catching function included in VBScript is the `On Error Resume Next` statement. If this statement is not included, any error that occurs will halt application

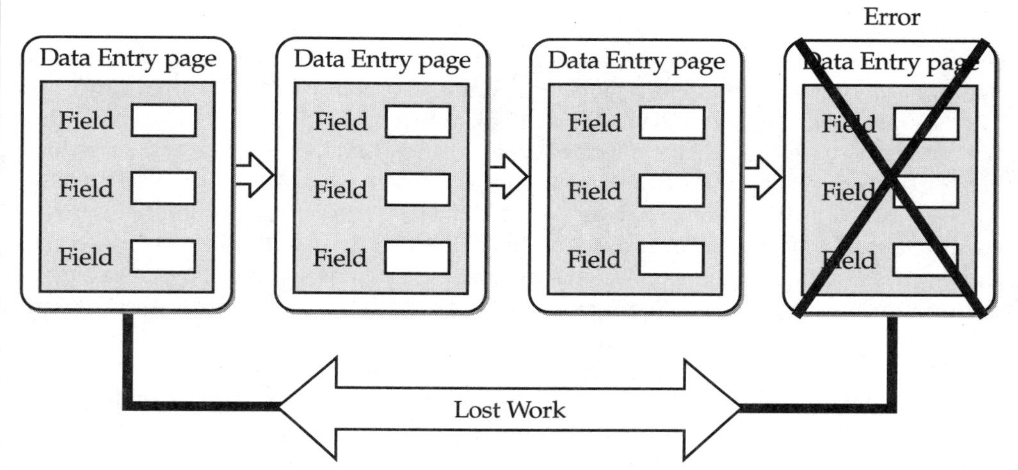

Figure 3-2. An error in a late page in a sequence can cause a great deal of work to be lost

execution. A VBScript routine that includes this code will ignore the error that occurred and continue to the next statement. You can then handle the error with an `If...Then` statement.

For example, the following code will generate an error of type 6, using the Err object. It will then check whether this type of error is present in the object. If so, the proper message will be displayed.

```
On Error Resume Next
Err.Raise 6
If Err.Number = 6 Then
   MsgBox "Error #6, Overflow occurred"
End If
```

While this example may seem simplistic, often errors are of common types and happen at predictable locations. If an ASP script is attempting to open a file for output, the possibility of a error caused by a lock on the file position or directory should be tested. Once you have finished the initial coding of a page, consider the most effective points in which to place error trapping routines to catch potential problems.

Error Reporting

In addition to focusing your efforts on error-catching in VBScript (which is limited by VBScript's capabilities), pay attention to the feedback systems that make Web applications more powerful than traditional clients. Users of a client often get errors and either do not report them at all or don't report them clearly enough for you to correct them. Since a Web solution talks directly to the server, both automated logging and providing a place for users to record their problems are possible.

Server-based applications, such as Web database applications, automatically record errors in several places. By examining exactly what occurred with these errors, you can ensure that they don't happen again. This feedback error strategy can allow developers to focus on the errors that are occurring and even to prioritize resources around the errors that occur most often or that have the most catastrophic results.

Page-access errors, the most common type of Web error, are listed in the IIS log file, indicating what error occurred and the URL where access was attempted. Writing a small program with one of the Visual Studio tools, such as Visual Basic, that can isolate and summarize these errors would not be a waste of time, by any means.

A more proactive strategy is to use the IIS error-page setting to send error-resulting pages to an error-handling page. The configuration dialog of IIS (see Figure 3-3), found under the Custom Errors tab, allows you to specify which page will be sent to the browser when an error occurs. By changing the Properties of an error, you can route it to a custom ASP page.

From the error page, you can execute code to do any of the following:

- Write specific errors to the IIS log
- Use the e-mail component to notify the IS department
- Write errors to a custom database log
- Allow the user to enter comments about the situation
- Record Response object data
- Record Form object data

As you progress through this book, you will see some of these solutions implemented. For now, just keep in mind that error checking and resolution in Web applications does not end at the capabilities of the scripting language; it begins there.

Err Object

Errors are trapped or generated through the Err object. The Err object is global in scope, so any errors that occur within the application are directed through this object. Since the object is global, you can even include a general err checking function in the Global.asa file.

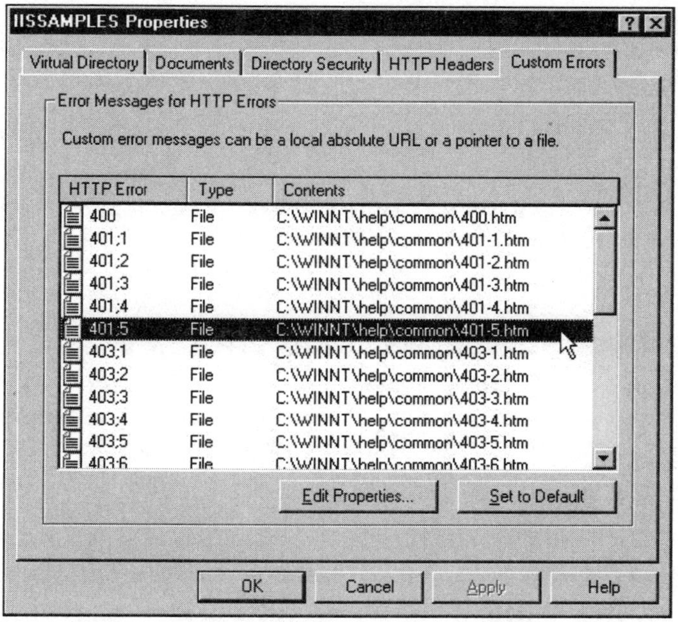

Figure 3-3. You can adjust IIS to send the error to a custom page

Microsoft has progressively made the Err object more powerful and designed it to be the central point for diagnosing errors. When an error occurs, all the information related to the error is stored in the properties of this object. These properties include:

- **`Number`** Contains the error number of the problem
- **`Description`** Contains a description in plain language (if available) of the error for possible display
- **`HelpContext and HelpFile`** Set the .hlp reference for the error; these properties are rarely used in a Web database application
- **Source** Contains the name of the object or application that generated the error; for objects, this property commonly holds the class name of the object causing the error

The Err object only has two methods:

- **Raise** Generates an error in the execution environment specified by a number passed to it
- **Clear** Clears the error and all of the properties associated with it

Using the Err object in conjunction with reporting can be the most effective means of keeping the user informed about problems that have occurred. The properties in the Err object can also be added to the log for more accurate later diagnosis of the cause of the problem.

Differences Between Visual Basic and VBScript

Although VBScript is a subset of the general Visual Basic language, the two languages become closer together with each revision as Microsoft adds missing commands. Following is a general overview of the commands that aren't present in VBScript:

- **Option commands** `Option Explicit`, `Option Base`, `Option Compare`, and the other Option commands
- **Collection commands** `Add`, `Count`, `Item`, `Remove`, `!`
- **Conditional compilation** Commands that disallow compilation of sets of code, such as `#If`, `#Const`, and so on
- **Non-structural control flow** Commands that jump to another part of the code, such as `GoSub`, `Goto`, `On Error Goto`, line numbers, and line labels.
- **Object mode** `With...End With`
- **Date and time commands** `Date`, `Time`, and `Timer`
- **User-defined types** `Type...End Type`
- **Declaration** `Static`, `Dim...As`, `Declare`, `New`, `ParamArray`, `Property Let`, `Property Set`, and `Property Get`
- **File commands** All file commands
- **Financial functions** All financial functions
- **String commands** Fixed-length strings, `LSet`, `RSet`, `Mid`, `StrConv`
- **Select statements** Evaluations using `Is` or `To` keywords

Since Microsoft is changing VBScript all of the time (at the time of this writing, version 5 is in early beta), check the Microsoft site at www.microsoft.com/scripting to get documentation on the newest version.

NOTE: Simply because the command is not directly available in VBScript does not necessarily mean that the functionality is not available to a VBScript programmer. For example, although VBScript does not have file access commands (such as `Open #`, `Input #`, and so on), from ASP you can use VBScript to access the FileSystem objects that essentially provide the same capability.

If VBScript is missing a function that you need, first check the available object models to make sure that the command is not available through one of them. As a last resort, you can always encapsulate the needed function in an ActiveX DLL that you can build in Visual Basic. Then you need only instantiate the object to have that function available.

With the release of Visual Basic 6, the Visual Basic language advanced beyond the version included in Office 97. Office 2000 remedies that gap and brings the VBA language up to date. However, until Office 2000 gains widespread acceptance, VBScript shares some features that are included in VB 6, but are missing from VBA.

You may also notice that there are some special implementation features that are provided for VBScript use within an ASP file. For example, to simply print the value of a variable into the HTML that will be sent to the client browser, you can use a command such as this:

```
<%=myVariable%>
```

The value contained in the variable `myVariable` will be instantly inserted at the current cursor position in the HTML page that will be returned. This method of using a variable is only available in the version of VBScript included in ASP.

Note that the standard method of denoting a script on the client side is using the `<SCRIPT>` tag. On the server, you will mostly see script code encapsulated within the `<% %>` brackets. However, you can use the `<SCRIPT>` tag for server-side code by using the `RUNAT` setting. For example:

```
<SCRIPT LANGUAGE=vbscript RUNAT=Server>
   ' Do operations
</SCRIPT>
```

Although you will probably not need to use this method, it is useful if you will be writing code that will be tested within a browser and then executed on ASP, because there is only a single setting that needs to be modified. It may also be handy if you need to create code that can be ported to a non-ASP machine that uses this standard.

The scope of variables in VBScript is also different from other VB implementations. Variables that are created within an ASP page retain their values until execution of the pages is complete. Therefore, unlike VB, where the scope of the variable can be determined within the code, variables must be added to the external environment to survive a single execution. For ASP, this includes placing values in objects such as Session and Application. These objects are unavailable to a typical VB solution.

VBScript also includes the following commands not available in versions of VB:

- `ScriptEngine` Returns a string indicating the script language currently in use (such as "vbscript" or "jscript")
- `ScriptEngineBuildVersion` Returns the version information of the actual scripting DLL
- `ScriptEngineMajorVersion` Returns the major revision version number
- `ScriptEngineMinorVersion` Returns the minor revision version number

Aside from these commands, the differences between Visual Basic/VBA and VBScript are not very substantial. The key difference is that the development environments do not tend to be as robust with VBScript. However, the new capabilities of the Microsoft Script Debugger provide an environment that is much closer to the one to which VB users are accustomed.

ASP DEBUGGING

With ASP, like a solution generated in Visual Basic, the code that you write will not execute as a traditional stand-alone application. Instead, the application will execute on the Web server to be sent to a Web browser. This two stage presentation can make debugging complicated. To partially solve this problem, Microsoft has created the Script Debugger. It is available for free download from the Scripting Web site (www.microsoft.com/scripting); installation requires Internet Explorer 4.01 or later.

The debugger is actually accessed through the browser. Under the View menu, a Script Debugger submenu is added. It allows the debugger to be opened or to automatically break on the next VBScript statement and open the page in the debugger. You can also use the `Stop` command in your VBScript code, which will cause the debugger to be activated and allow you to resume after that point in the code.

Server-Side VBScript Debugging

Debugging server-based software is one of the more difficult aspects of server-solution development. The complex systems that are created for Web information display may contain a jumbled combination of HTML, ASP, and component execution, making finding a problem difficult. Fortunately, debuggers are provided for client-side and server-side VBScript.

To activate debugging, you will have to use the Application Configuration dialog box for the Web application. Check the Enable ASP Server-Side Debugging check box. Once this is done, IIS can send instructions to the Web debugger when an ASP file has been accessed.

The Script Debugger can be activated from any ASP file that is being opened with the `Stop` command or when an error occurs. In Figure 3-4, an ODBC error was generated on execution of the ASP file, and the debugger was automatically activated at the line where the problem occurred.

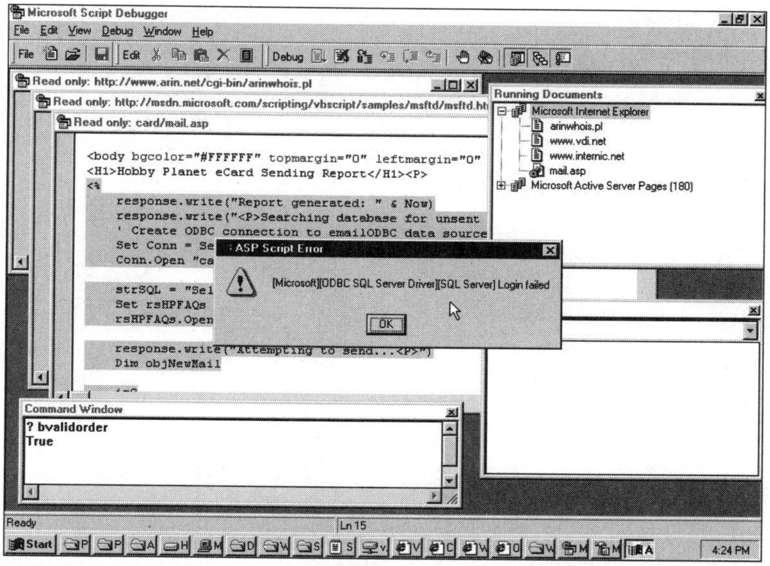

Figure 3-4. An ODBC error in the ASP file activates the Script Debugger

You can see that the debugger's Command Window provides a VBScript equivalent of the VB Immediate window. You can check the value of variables as well as execute simple commands from it.

All of the debugging occurs in the document windows, which have proper syntax coloring. The Running Documents window provides a hierarchical expansive view of all of the documents that are available for debugging.

Since the Global.ASA file cannot be opened from the Script Debugger, its execution must be halted for debugging within the code. To debug routines in the ASA file, you will need to use the `Stop` or the `Debugger` commands.

TIP: When an error occurs in an ASP page, the line number of the fault is displayed in the returned HTML. When you're not doing full ASP development in Visual InterDev, a fantastic and robust text editor called Ultra Edit (www.ultraedit.com) is excellent for quick modifications to ASP code. The Goto Line feature lets you jump immediately to the line at which the error occurred.

Client-Side VBScript Debugging

Client-side debugging of VBScript code is extremely simple because of the integrated VBScript debugger. Usually it is easiest to stop execution at the next statement (see Figure 3-5) that will transfer you from Internet Explorer to the Script Debugger.

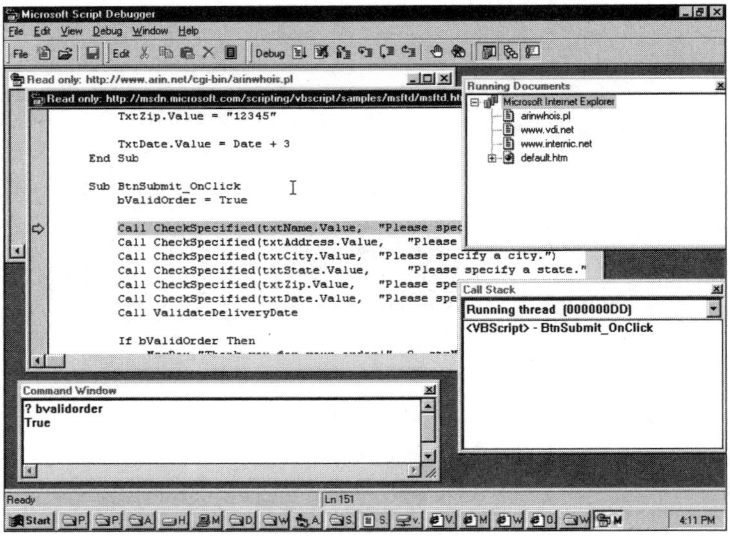

Figure 3-5. Debugging a client-side VBScript

From the debugger, it is also possible to load a file and set breakpoints. If your VBScript code is general (math routines, for example) the extra flexibility provided by client-side script debugging may provide a good reason to paste the code into a browser page for refinement.

Q&A

Q: Is the VBScript included with Microsoft Outlook the same thing that is used in ASP?

A: Yes. In fact, a new addition to the operating system included with Windows 98 and Windows 2000 is a technology called Windows Scripting Host (WSH). This technology actually embeds the scripting engine into the operating system itself. This allows programs to control the operating system in a way similar to older batch (.bat) files, as well as providing every program access to the same scripting engine.

VBScript's incorporation into the operating system means that through the ActiveX Scripting Engine, the exact same language will be available in Internet Explorer, Microsoft Outlook, ASP, and WSH.

Q: How can VBScript support all the features of ASP as well as those available in a browser?
A: Through the availability or exclusion of a particular object model. In ASP, VBScript has a great number of objects that are available for access, including the File System component. Inside a browser, these objects are excluded for security reasons. However, other browser-specific objects are available that provide access to the HTML Page model for manipulation of the currently loaded HTML document.

Q: Will VBScript eventually be discarded in favor of VBA?
A: Probably not. VBScript is a plug-in to the ActiveX Scripting Engine, while VBA usually encapsulates an entire development environment, such as the ones seen in the Office products. By having a plug-in architecture for scripting engines, Microsoft can easily embrace a variety of standards, including ECMAScript, that would be impossible through a closed-end solution such as VBA.

With other scripting languages, such as TCL, gaining acceptance in niche markets, Microsoft will most likely increase the development on the VBScript environment. This will help to ensure that Windows is the predominant platform for scripting languages as well as specialized environments.

SUMMARY

VBScript, a subset of the Visual Basic language, retains most of the core functionality. Because of the breadth of environments that use VBScript, its flexibility makes it more universal than VBA. VBScript is the core language that will be used in most ASP Web database applications. In this chapter, you learned about:

- **VBScript** The technology within the IIS Web server used to execute scripts to return HTML to the client browser. It is also available in the Internet Explorer browser, the Outlook client, and Windows Scripting Host.
- **Data types** The Variant data type is the only actual type supported by VBScript, but often you will need to do explicit conversions (such as with the `CStr` command) to avoid page errors.
- **Server-side debugging** For server application execution, you must configure the application settings in IIS to allow it to interface with the Script Debugger. Once properly set up, ASP files can be debugged with variable watches, single-code stepping, and breakpoints.
- **Client-side debugging** The most flexible VBScript debugging, client-side, will allow you to load pages, set breakpoints, and perform any operation for which the Script Debugger is capable. The VBScript debugger is available for download, and when installed, it becomes incorporated within Internet Explorer.

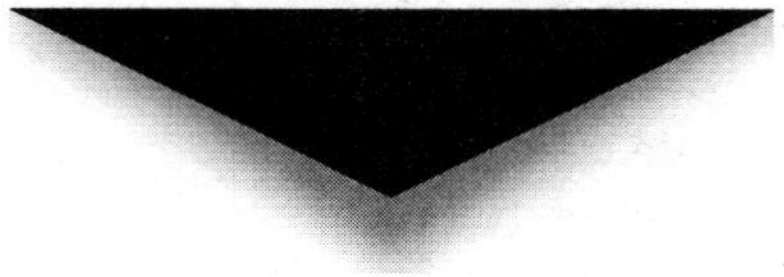

CHAPTER 4

ActiveX Data Objects

Web database applications require powerful data access capabilities to retrieve and modify data. When the ASP engine is used to execute code on the server, it can leverage the object technology that is part of the Windows platform. The high-level ActiveX Data Objects (ADO) is an object model that allows an executing program to address almost any data source. Through ASP, you can use ADO to connect your Web application to a database.

By unifying its products with the core ADO technology, Microsoft has created a central object model around which all of the Visual Studio projects can communicate with data sources. ADO provides a common driver interface that is significantly more advanced than the ODBC middleware that has in the past provided heterogeneous data access. ADO is actually a thin interface layer over the new low-level Microsoft OLE DB database middleware.

The highlights of ADO capabilities include:

- Creation of connections and recordsets as independent objects
- Support of offline data modification
- Event notification and code activation for programmed data environments
- Handling of distributed transactions
- A common framework across all Microsoft Visual Studio tools

These features are part of the reason that ADO is central to a polished middleware data solution. As the centralized database-access framework, ADO has a prominent place in Microsoft's Universal Data Access (UDA) initiative that seeks to make every type of data available through a common interface.

ADO OBJECT MODEL

If you have programmed Visual Basic before, you are no doubt accustomed to using the Data Access Objects (DAO) to provide connectivity to Microsoft Access, ODBC, and other data source types. DAO, although available for other programming languages, was used predominantly in Visual Basic programs. ADO is an evolution of DAO in both supported features, as well as supported development systems within the Visual Studio family.

When Microsoft created the database objects of ADO from the DAO foundation, the objects became more refined and powerful. While the capabilities of the objects have increased in ADO, they are easier to use than their DAO counterparts. The entire ADO object model is made up of only three primary objects: the Connection object, the Command object, and the Recordset object. There are also four minor objects (Error, Parameter, Field, and Property) that occur within the primary objects to contain settings for the objects and fill the role of multifaceted properties.

The three primary objects are used in conjunction with each other, but exist separately. One of the advances of the ADO model is the ability to create each primary database object independently. Unlike the previous incarnations of the database objects, which were strictly hierarchical, the ADO model allows all objects to be created separately and then attached together by a reference placed in the appropriate linking property (see Figure 4-1).

For an ASP solution, any of these objects is created using the `CreateObject` method that is part of the Server object. Once an instance of an object has been instantiated, it can be easily controlled through VBScript or JavaScript code.

Universal Data Access

Microsoft has announced its intention to create a framework so that any type of data can be accessed through a single interface. The combination of ADO and OLE DB provides the cornerstone technology of this strategic initiative. Because ADO/OLE DB can access not only general query data types but also object data, spatial data, and nearly any data type, UDA is set to be the standard method of data access on the Windows platform.

UDA (through OLE DB) already provides heterogeneous data access to data sources such as VSAM, AS/400, HP/UX, IBM AIX, and OpenVMS. Current Microsoft OLE DB

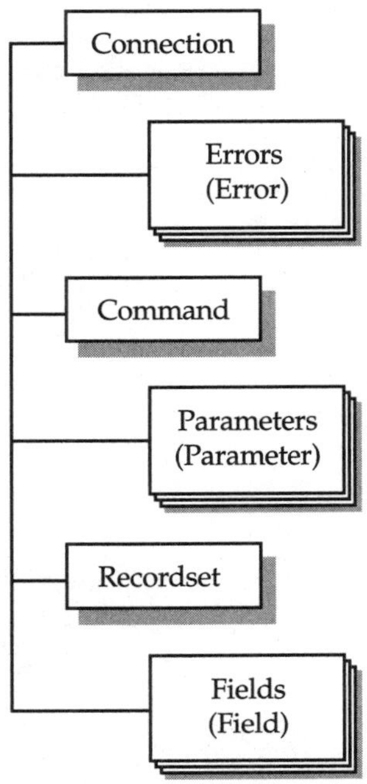

Figure 4-1. The ADO object model is not directly hierarchical, like the previous DAO model

data providers include ODBC, SQL Server, Oracle, and Microsoft Jet. Microsoft is working on ADO interfaces for such diverse resources as Microsoft Exchange and Active Directory. Third-party OLE DB drivers are available from vendors such as Simba for OLAP, which allows access to the OLAP API for Teracube.

Microsoft has begun describing all of the interface technology used to address a data source in terms of *data consumers* and *data providers*. A provider supplies the information that is consumed by objects, such as controls or recordsets. Using UDA is a matter of matching the right provider with useful consumers.

DEFINITIONS: **Data Providers** The data source that supplies information, such as an OLE DB driver, is known as a data provider.

Data Consumers Objects, such as controls (text boxes, grids, and the like), that use the data supplied by a provider are known as data consumers.

Developing your Web database applications with ADO will make them compatible with the entire thrust of the Microsoft database-technology path. As Microsoft expands the UDA initiative in the future, ADO/OLE DB will be the primary data-source interface for all of the products in the Visual Studio family.

Primary ADO Objects

To implement an ADO solution, ASP code uses the primary ADO objects. Each object facilitates a piece of the process of interacting with a data source:

- Connection objects provide the actual connected session with the data source.
- Command objects execute a command against the data source object.
- Recordset objects allow the retrieval and modification of records on the data source.

All three of these objects can be created and modified independently. The Connection object must be used by both the Recordset and Command objects, because it provides the session that enables communication.

Connection Object

To create a link to the desired data source, the Connection object is used either explicitly or implicitly. A single Connection object may be used by multiple objects to access the same source.

The Connection object has three primary parameters used to make the connection: `UserID`, `Password`, and `ConnectionString`. While the `UserID` and `Password` parameters are fairly self explanatory, the `ConnectionString` contains a number of attributes that must be set properly for the connection to work correctly.

The `ConnectionString` must contain the following settings:

- **Driver type** Determines the ADO driver that will be used to connect to the data source
- **Server name** Specifies the server on which the database is located
- **Database name** The name of the database to access on the default connection
- **Data source name** Specifies the name of the data source that will be used; most often the data source name refers to the name of the ODBC source that is configured on the executing machine
- **Connection type** Determines the type of connection

To access a Microsoft Access data source, the `ConnectionString` would look like this:

```
driver={Microsoft Access Driver  (*.mdb)};
dbq=c:\test\northwind.mdb;uid=Admin;pwd=etphone
```

To access an ODBC data source, the `ConnectionString` would look like this:

```
driver={SQL Server};
server=myServer;database=pubs;dsn=myODBC,,connection=adConnectAsync
```

The `ConnectionString` is the property that is used by the `Open` method if it is called without any arguments. Other properties and methods of the Connection object refine how the connection is made and maintained.

NOTE: There are two ways to specify the username and password when connecting to a data source. These parameters can be passed as arguments to the `Open` method or set within the connection string. In the `ConnectionString`, the settings are named `uid` and `pwd`. A connection string with the login would look like this: `driver={Microsoft Access Driver (*.mdb)};dbq=c:\test\northwind.mdb;uid=Admin;pwd=etphone`.

OPEN AND CLOSE METHODS To open a connection, the `Open` method requires several parameters for proper configuration. Many of these parameters can be set in the properties of the object rather than explicitly passing them to the `Open` method. In the previous section, you saw how the `ConnectionString` property might be defined. It may also be passed explicitly during the `Open` method call:

```
myConn.Open connectStr
```

Other properties, such as the `UserID` and `Password`, may be passed to the `Open` method as arguments:

```
myConn.Open connectStr, "joe", "snurgle"
```

The Options argument sets the connection that is being opened to the synchronous mode:

```
myConn.Open connectStr, "joe", "snurgle", adConnectUnspecified
```

By default, the Options argument is passed as a `-1` indicating `adConnectUnspecified`. This opens the connection in synchronous mode. To open the connection in asynchronous mode, the `adAsyncConnect` argument may be passed.

Once the `Open` method has been successful, the Connection object maintains a session with the data source. To end a session, the `Close` method can be used.

> ***NOTE:*** Using the `Close` method does not eliminate the Connection object nor does it clear any of the set parameters. Therefore, a connection can later be re-established with a lone call to the `Open` method.

MODE PROPERTY The `Mode` property specifies the type of connection that will be attempted when the `Open` method is executed. Afterwards, it contains the mode that the Connection object was able to establish. Possible values for the Mode property include: read only (`1`), write only (`2`), read/write (`3`), prevent others from opening with read permissions (`4`), prevent others from opening with write permissions (`8`), exclusive read/write (`12`), and completely exclusive (`16`).

ATTRIBUTES PROPERTY To control the functioning of the Connection object, the `Attributes` property allows the specification of many preferences. For example, setting the `Attributes` property to `adXactCommitRetaining` will make the Connection object begin a new transaction as soon as the initial transaction is committed. `Attributes` settings for the Connection object include:

aAdXactCommitRetaining	(131072)	Begins a new transaction automatically when one is committed
adXactAbortRetaining	(262144)	Begins a new transaction automatically when one is rolled back
adXactAsyncPhaseOne	(524288)	Sets the first phase of an asynchronous process
adXactSyncPhaseOne	(1048576)	Sets the first phase of a synchronous process

The `Attributes` property, which is also available in Parameter, Field, and Property objects, can accept multiple parameters. To make multiple settings, just add the constants together.

EXECUTE METHOD On the Connection object, the `Execute` method will call a stored procedure, send a SQL statement to the provider, or execute a query. If it is only a command to be executed and you do not need to receive the results, you can use code like this:

```
myConn.Execute cmdString
```

To receive the recordset returned by the execution, use code like this:

```
Set myRS = myConn.Execute(mySQL)
```

COMMANDTIMEOUT PROPERTY A SQL command that is executed against a connection may generate some type of unreported error or may take substantially longer to process a request than expected. Either case may make the server fail to return any response to the calling application for a prohibitively long period of time. Like an automatic Cancel button that is activated by a time-event rather than a user click, the `CommandTimeout` property can be used to abort an operation that exceeds the maximum time allowed to complete the operation.

The default setting for this time-out property is thirty seconds. The value in this property will determine the general timeout for all operations on this connection. However, a Command object linked to the Connection object can override this setting. If a specific command will take longer than the general Connection `CommandTimeout` setting, it can be set to a specific value.

> ***TIP:*** In a Web database solution, the `CommandTimeout` property can be the cause of difficulty when debugging. Remember that when you configure IIS, there is a setting to control the amount of time for an application to respond before it aborts. If the setting on the Web server is shorter than the one assigned to this property, the Web server will abort before the connection time-out is reached. Therefore, it is a good rule of thumb to always set the `CommandTimeout` value to about five seconds less than the timeout for the server.

OPENSCHEMA METHOD This method retrieves the database schema (or structure) from the data provider. The information about the schema is returned in a recordset. The schema information includes the structure of the tables, database, and other attributes of the database object. This recordset is read-only and the structure of the database cannot be modified by updating the records contained in the dataset.

The `OpenSchema` method allows you to specify exactly the type of information to be returned about the data source such as including which fields (columns) should be provided in the recordset. In Chapter 5, you will build a sample program that displays the structure of a database using the `OpenSchema` method to retrieve the details.

OTHER PROPERTIES In addition to the properties that have already been individually described, there are a number of additional properties that are useful and that are often provided by the ADO driver as access occurs. Some of these other properties of the Connection object include:

- **`Provider` property** Specifies the provider to be used for the connection. If none is specified, the default MSDASQL is used.
- **`State` property** Indicates whether the connection is opened or closed. Settings can be `adStateClosed (0)`, which is the default, or `adStateOpen (1)`,

which show that the connection is open. For asynchronous connections, there are also the properties: `adStateConnecting` (2), `adStateExecuting` (4), and `adStateFetching` (8).

- **`DefaultDatabase` property** Specifies the default database to open when the connection is made. The data source can specify a default database to be used for connections and can override this setting.
- **`ConnectionTimeout` property** The time to wait when establishing a connection. The default setting is 15 seconds.
- **`Version` property** Returns the version number of the current driver.
- **`CursorLocation` property** Holds the constant that indicates whether the cursor is client-side (adUseClient - 3) or server-side (adUseServer - 2).

TRANSACTIONS You initially learned about transactions and the ability to encapsulate multiple database operations within a single all-or-nothing commit in Chapter 1. In that chapter, the transactions were described in relation to an entire solution and Microsoft Transaction Server (MTS). The ADO framework itself provides the transaction functionality that can be used by MTS.

Transactions primarily occur at the database level, and the transaction commands available to the Connection object are the ones automatically activated by MTS when a database transaction occurs. ADO supports the ability to have a single transaction encompass operations that occur across multiple databases. Transactions can also be nested so a transaction can be started within another transaction. The number of nesting levels is determined by the ADO/OLE DB driver.

There are three methods included in the Connection object for managing a transaction:

- **`BeginTrans`** This command begins the encapsulation of all recording operations for the final commit.
- **`CommitTrans`** The `CommitTrans` method commits all of the operations contained in the transactions and writes them to the data source.
- **`RollbackTrans`** This command aborts the current transaction and revokes all operations that have occurred up to this point. A rollback is implicit if the database server or client fails and the transaction is abandoned.

Once a transaction has begun, all of the operations that execute against this Connection object are contained within it. If you need to alter the `IsolationLevel` property that sets the isolation of the transactions, it must be set before a new transaction has begun to take effect. Setting the property after a transaction has been activated will generate an error.

The default setting for the `IsolationLevel` property is `adXactChaos (16)` which specifies that pending changes are not overwritten for more highly isolated transactions. This property may be set to the values: `adXactUnspecified (-1)`, `adXactChaos (16)`, `adXactBrowse (256)`, `adXactReadUncommitted (256)`, `adXactCursorStability`

(4096), `adXactReadCommitted` (65536), and `adXactIsolated` or `adXact-Serializable` (1048576).

Command Object

The Command object is used to execute an operation against a data source. It works in much the same way that an Execute method may be used on a Connection object. The Command object has advantages over simply executing a method since it can be created through a variety of means (including the Data Environment in Visual Interdev) and stored until activation is necessary. Some of the operations that can be called using the Command object include:

- Executing a SQL statement
- Activating stored procedures
- Creating a Recordset object
- Executing a bulk operation
- Creating a new database structure, such as a table
- Modifying an existing database structure

The Command object is most often used to execute stored procedures on a database server. Because each data source will have different libraries or methods of calling stored procedures, the Command object is the object in the ADO model that is most likely to be programmed with vendor-specific statements.

DEFINITION: **Stored Procedure** Stored procedures are routines that exist on the database server itself—for optimized performance. Rather than sending a SQL `execute` statement containing numerous commands, a stored procedure can be created within the database and activated by a single command from the client. The procedure is precompiled for speed and encapsulation. Using stored procedures also allows business logic to be stored on the server rather than in the client programs.

COMMANDTEXT AND COMMANDTYPE PROPERTIES For the Command object, there are two primary properties: `CommandText` and `CommandType`. These properties are used to specify the way the object executes. The `CommandType` property defines the way the object will use the string found in the `CommandText` property.

Types that may be specified for `CommandType` include:

- **`adCmdText (1)`** Indicates that general SQL code is held in the CommandText property for execution by the data provider.
- **`adCmdTable (2)`** Uses the Command object as a table where all of the fields of the table are returned in the recordset. Provides essentially the same functionality of a SQL Select statement that requests all of the fields of all of the records in a table.

- **`adCmdStoredProc` (4)** Executes a stored procedure.
- **`adCmdUnknown` (8)** Indicates that the type of command found in the CommandText property is unknown; this is the default setting. The data provider must interpret the text which, if the provider is a database server, is generally assumed to hold a SQL statement.

The `CommandText` property specifies the command that will actually be executed by the Command object. This property usually contains a SQL command. These properties are used by the `Execute` method to perform a command operation against the data source.

EXECUTE METHOD The `Execute` method causes the Command object to execute the command specified in the `CommandText` and `CommandType` properties. The `Execute` method can be used as a procedure when either there is no information returned by the execution or the calling application chooses to ignore any information that the command generates. The `Execute` method can be used as a procedure like this:

```
myCmd.Execute
```

Like the `Execute` method on a Connection object, it may also be used to accept a returned recordset:

```
Set myRS = myCmd.Execute
```

Once the execution has completed, `Execute` will return a recordset of the information retrieved by the operation. If no records are to be returned by the operation, as is the case for many stored procedures, the returned recordset will be empty.

ACTIVECONNECTION PROPERTY `ActiveConnection` must specify a connection against which the Command object is executed. Unlike the Recordset object, which can dynamically create a connection, if the `ActiveConnection` property is not valid when the `Execute` method is called, an error will be generated.

> ***NOTE:*** To switch the connection of an active Command object, you must first set the `ActiveConnection` property to `Nothing` (that is, `Set myCmd = Nothing`). This operation will properly clear the Command object. Afterward, set the `ActiveConnection` property to the new connection.

PREPARED PROPERTY Because ADO is an advanced middleware solution, it allows you to make use of a data source that can compile a command for faster execution. This Boolean property notifies the data source that the `CommandText` property holds a valid command that can be compiled.

Recordset Object

The Recordset object is perhaps the most important object when creating a Web database solution. The Recordset object provides access to the actual data that will be retrieved and displayed or modified. Proper configuration of the object is critical to the effective functioning of your final solution.

There are three ways a Recordset object can be created or initialized:

- **Independently** The definition (or dimensioning) of a Recordset object, including all fields and settings, may be accomplished manually through ASP code, rather than reading the structure from a data source. This can be used for off-line recordsets, pre-connection configuration, or client-side data sets.
- **By executing a Command or Connection object** When a Command object is executed, it can return a Recordset object with the results from that execution. The same procedure occurs when the `Execute` method is used with a Connection object.
- **By opening a SQL query** The Recordset object can be created as an object variable (through the Dim, Private, or Public statements) and initialized using a SQL query that retrieves data from a data source.

Once the instance of the recordset has been created in memory, an additional memory structure called a *cursor* is created as part of the recordset. The cursor retrieves and holds the data that is accessed through the Recordset object. Think of the cursor as a pointer to a single record among all of the records held in the recordset.

DEFINITION: **Cursor** A structure in memory that points to and holds the information for the current record.

The cursor will define how the data set can be used. If you are accustomed to using Microsoft Access or SQL Server, you may have found that you need to manipulate the cursor to achieve certain results (such as sending the cursor to the last record in the set to obtain the number of total records).

Some older databases feature a cursor that can only move forward through a data set. Most modern databases, however, support the full cursor functionality. In present Web database solutions, recordset configuration requires the serious attention that was devoted to cursor feature verification in the past.

If the Recordset object is configured poorly, it can become the bottleneck that makes your application lack scalability. Choices such as the number of records to be buffered, the type of retrieval method to be used, and the cursor settings all affect performance.

The type of cursors available through ADO include the following:

- **Keyset cursor** A cursor that allows access to and modification of records in a recordset but does not update the recordset to reflect records added or created by other users since the initialization of the cursor.
- **Dynamic cursor** A general cursor that contains all of the features supported by the recordset, including record insertion, deletion, modification, and set updating.
- **Static cursor** A read-only cursor that cannot be dynamically updated as more records that match its query parameters are added to the data source. For example, if a Smith entry was added to the central data source by another user, and the query of the static cursor included all of the Smith entries, this cursor could not be updated to include this new entry. The static cursor is designed for faster access.
- **Forward-only cursor** A cursor that can only move forward (`MoveNext`) through a recordset. Although limiting, almost any type of ODBC data source (including older versions of Oracle) support this type of cursor at a minimum. It also provides better performance than other cursors.

Each of these cursor types should be considered when deciding how to code a Recordset object in a Web database solution. Often, the simplest type (such as a read-only or forward-only cursor) that will complete the intended task is the best.

NOTE: If a Recordset object is opened without an open or connected Connection object, a session is automatically created.

The `Open` method for a Recordset object attempts to make a connection to a data source and execute the specified query. The method will return an error code to notify the calling program whether the recordset creation was a success.

RECORDSET UPDATES All of the fields for a cursor in a Recordset object are contained in the `Fields` collection of the object (see Figure 4-2). The fields of the cursor are accessed through properties of objects in the collection. These properties allow you to access the name, the type, and the value of the field for the current record.

To display the name of a field from ASP, you could write ASP code to return it to the user's browser with a command such as:

```
Response.Write(myRS.Fields("Field1").Name)
```

The values of the fields can be accessed with a command such as:

```
Response.Write(myRS.Fields("Field1").Value)
```

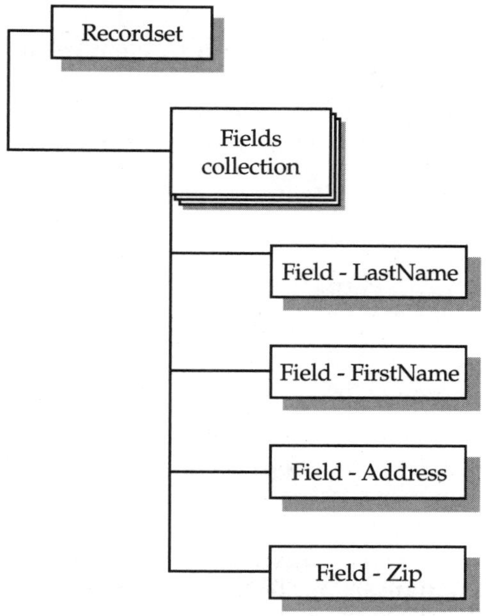

Figure 4-2. All the fields of the accessed table or view are held in the cursor

CAUTION: For convenience and faster coding, Visual Basic includes the `!` operator to access items in a collection. For example, instead of using the command `myRS.Fields("Field1").Value = "Hello"`, the shortcut command of `myRS!Field1 = "Hello"` might be used. Be aware that the `!` operator is not included in VBScript. Therefore, any ADO code that uses this operator will have to be modified to function correctly in ASP.

Once you've made changes to a record in the current recordset, the `Update` method is used to write the changes into the data source. By default, the update mode for the recordset will be set to `Immediate`. You can change the update mode so any changes are held in the recordset buffer. Then all the changes can be made at once in a batch, saving processing time and communication over the network.

In batch mode, calling an `Update` method does not actually write the changes into the database but retains the changes in the client-side recordset or record buffer. A call to the `UpdateBatch` method actually writes the change into the database.

To begin a batch operation, the LockType property must be configured before the recordset is opened. Setting the property to adLockBatchOptimistic (4) will set the recordset so that updates to the data source do not occur until the UpdateBatch method is executed.

In the following example code, the connection is assumed to be set to batch mode and changes are made to two different records before the update occurs for the batch.

```
myRS.Fields("ModDate") = #3/18/99#
myRS.Update
myRS.MoveNext
myRS.Fields("ModDate") = #3/18/99#
myRS.Update
' Update both records
myRS.UpdateBatch
```

Once an UpdateBatch method is called and all of the updates occur, a new batch is automatically opened. The CancelBatch method can be used to abort and revoke any changes made to the current recordset.

When you begin a transaction, a great deal of resources are reserved until the transaction is actually committed. It is possible within a single recordset to use the batch update capabilities to streamline a transaction. To do this, encapsulate the final UpdateBatch command in a transaction. This will ensure that all of the operations within the batch occur correctly. Updating the batch within a transaction can be accomplished with code like this:

```
myRS.BeginTrans
myRS.UpdateBatch
myRS.CommitTrans
```

The Delete method is also encapsulated within the batch process. Therefore, any record deletions within a batch do not take place until the code calls the UpdateBatch method.

ADDNEW METHOD The AddNew method adds a record to the current recordset. If the current recordset does not allow updates, an error will occur. The new record that is added may be blank, using the simple method call:

```
myRS.AddNew
```

You can also pass values in the FieldList and Values arguments. Both of these arguments can be passed as matching arrays (where the field name in element 1 in the first array matches the value in second array) or as a single value. For example:

```
myRS.AddNew "LastName", "Smith"
```

FIND METHOD The `Find` method is used to search within a current recordset. It allows specification of four parameters that constitute the search: `Criteria`, `SkipRecords`, `SearchDirection`, and `Start`. The `Criteria` parameter is the only one that is required, and executing the method with this parameter might look like this:

```
myRS.Find "LastName Like 'Smith'"
```

The `Criteria` parameter will only accept a search on a single parameter. No Boolean settings, such as AND or OR, may be used in this parameter. If you need Boolean parameters, you can use the `Filter` property for simple searches.

The `SkipRecords` parameter allows you to pass a numeric value of the number of records to skip before beginning the search. To skip 5 records, for example, the following command might be used:

```
myRS.Find "LastName Like 'Smith'", 5
```

The `SearchDirection` parameter can make the search proceed forward or backward through the data set. It can be set using either of two parameters: `adSearchForward` (`0`) or `adSearchBackward` (`1`). In VBScript, you must use the constants directly, so a backward search would look like this:

```
myRS.Find "LastName Like 'Smith'", 0, 1
```

Finally, the `Start` parameter can be used to specify where the search begins. Unlike the `SkipRecords` parameter, which specifies a number, the `Start` parameter is a Variant data type that can either accept a constant value or an object reference to an existing bookmark in the recordset. The constant values that may be passed include `adBookmarkCurrent` (`0`), `adBookmarkFirst` (`1`), or `adBookmarkLast` (`2`). For example, to search backward from the last record, a command like this could be used:

```
myRS.Find "LastName Like 'Smith'", , 1, 2
```

The `Find` method allows the direction of the search to be set. Using the `SearchDirection` argument, a search may be conducted forward or backward from the current record. Be sure to use the client-side index capability of ADO to speed up your searches.

NOTE: The `NoMatch` method that was commonly used with DAO does not exist in ADO recordsets. Use the `EOF` property, instead, to determine when no records are returned.

FILTER PROPERTY The `Filter` property allows you to set a criteria through which recordset data can be filtered. Setting this property automatically screens the existing data set and moves the cursor to the first record that matches the criteria. The filter can also be used to contain a number of records passed by an array of bookmarks.

A simple filter to find all of the people with the last name of Smith in a recordset could look like this:

```
myRS.Filter = "LastName = 'Smith'"
```

Wildcard characters can also be used to specify a general target. In the following example, all of the last names that begin with the letter *T* are filtered:

```
myRS.Filter = "LastName like 'T*'"
```

NEXTRECORDSET METHOD `NextRecordset` works on compound recordsets. You can specify more than one recordset by setting the `CommandText` property to multiple SQL operations separated by a semicolon (;).

```
"Select * from MyTable1; Select * from MyTable2"
```

The `NextRecordset` method only moves forward through compound command sets. If there are no available recordset query definitions, an empty recordset is returned.

CACHESIZE PROPERTY The `CacheSize` property determines the number of records that will be kept in the memory buffer at one time. The default buffer is set to hold ten records for a cursor unless it is a forward-only cursor, in which case only a single record is buffered. Modifying the size of the cache has various advantages and disadvantages.

With a large cache size, fewer requests must be made to the server as subsequent data is required. While this increases network performance, more memory on the client is used and a large data set can become out of date. When a system has a large number of frequent modifications, an increased buffer size may hold records that have been altered on the data source. The display would not reflect the current status of these records.

On the other hand, placing the buffer size too low requires frequent requests to the data source, increasing network traffic and possibly hurting performance. As you create a solution, use common sense based on the frequency of database changes and the speed of your database server to determine the optimal cache size.

EDITMODE PROPERTY The `EditMode` property indicates the update mode of the current record. This property is very useful in determining whether any changes have been made to the cursor record. The property can contain the following values:

- **`adEditNone (0)`** No editing of the record has occurred
- **`adEditInProgress (1)`** The record has been modified but not saved
- **`adEditAdd (2)`** A new record has been created with AddNew, but it has not been saved
- **`adEditDelete (4)`** The current record has been deleted

Note that this property is read-only so it cannot be set to determine the state of the current record. For example, a record cannot be undeleted by changing the property from `adEditDelete`. Instead, use the methods to edit, abort an update, and so on, to change the state of the record.

QUERIES The central property of a Recordset object is the `Source` property. It contains the actual SQL query of the desired data set. When querying tables, standard SQL syntax is used. For example, to retrieve all the records (with all of their fields) from a table named *sales*, a statement such as the following could be used:

```
Select * from sales
```

Of course, a view could be addressed by the same method. The `Source` can hold the desired SQL execution statement or the SQL can be passed directly during execution of the `Open` method.

DEFINITION: **View** A logical construct that makes one or more tables and the fields they contain appear as a single, physical table. Views are particularly effective when a query must be done against a combination of two or more related tables. It creates a type of 'virtual' table from one or more actual tables.

A view must be created in the database itself rather than through a query statement. From ADO, you can use a Command object to create a view in the required data source.

TIP: A view within a database is often read-only. Keep this in mind when designing your system, because attempting to write to a read-only cursor will generate an error.

BOOKMARK PROPERTY The `Bookmark` property may be used to get or set a reference to a particular record. That record can be quickly jumped to from anywhere in the data set. The `Bookmark` is a temporary setting and is lost when the recordset is closed.

CAUTION: Not all OLE DB drivers support bookmarks. If you're accessing a data source with an ODBC driver or OLE DB driver that did not ship with Visual Studio, check to make certain this feature is supported for your intended connection by using the recordset's `Supports` method.

MOVE COMMANDS While the `Find` method allows a simple search to be used on the recordset, the `Move` commands are made to move through all of the records returned by the query. The `MoveFirst`, `MoveLast`, `MoveNext`, and `MovePrevious` methods require no parameters to be passed to them and they go to the places in the records their names describe. A program can check whether the cursor has reached the beginning or the end of the data set by evaluating the `BOF` and `EOF` properties, respectively.

The `Move` method will move past a certain number of records. It requires a `NumRecords` argument to specify how many records to advance. The `NumRecords` parameter may be negative, to indicate the movement should be backwards. To move forward five records, you can use the command:

```
myRS.Move 5
```

The optional argument, `Start`, allows you to specify a bookmark (such as a record number) from which to begin the advance. If the `Start` argument is omitted from the method call, the `Move` begins from the current record position. To move backward three records from record number 17, you could use code like this:

```
myRS.Move -3,17
```

If the `Move` method causes the cursor to advance past the final record or before the beginning record, an error will occur. Make certain that your ASP code can handle that error if it occurs.

RECORDSET PAGES A recordset often has to manage a large amount of buffered data. To make this task more efficient, a structure called a *page* was created (see Figure 4-3). A page is a memory structure that contains one or more records. Pages reflect the actual structure of such data sources as Microsoft Access and older versions of SQL Server.

The `PageCount` property indicates the number of pages of records in the current Recordset object. The `PageSize` property defines the number of records held on each page. The `AbsolutePage` property indicates the page on which the current record is located.

NOTE: All of the page properties are affected by the `Filter` property. When a filter is set, it alters the references, such as `AbsolutePage`, to reflect the new locations of the records available.

CLONE METHOD To make a duplicate of the current recordset without executing the query again, the `Clone` method can be used.

```
Set newRS = myRS.Clone
```

Note that once a recordset is cloned, the bookmarks for the cloned recordset are usable on the original and vice versa. Bookmarks are normally not interchangeable among recordsets.

REQUERY AND RESYNC METHODS Executing the `Requery` method will make the recordset re-execute the query that was used to populate it. This makes all changes or additions to qualifying records appear in the recordset. You might consider providing a timed event to requery the data set if a client application will be left displayed for the duration of the work day. Updating the display every half an hour will ensure that current data will be used.

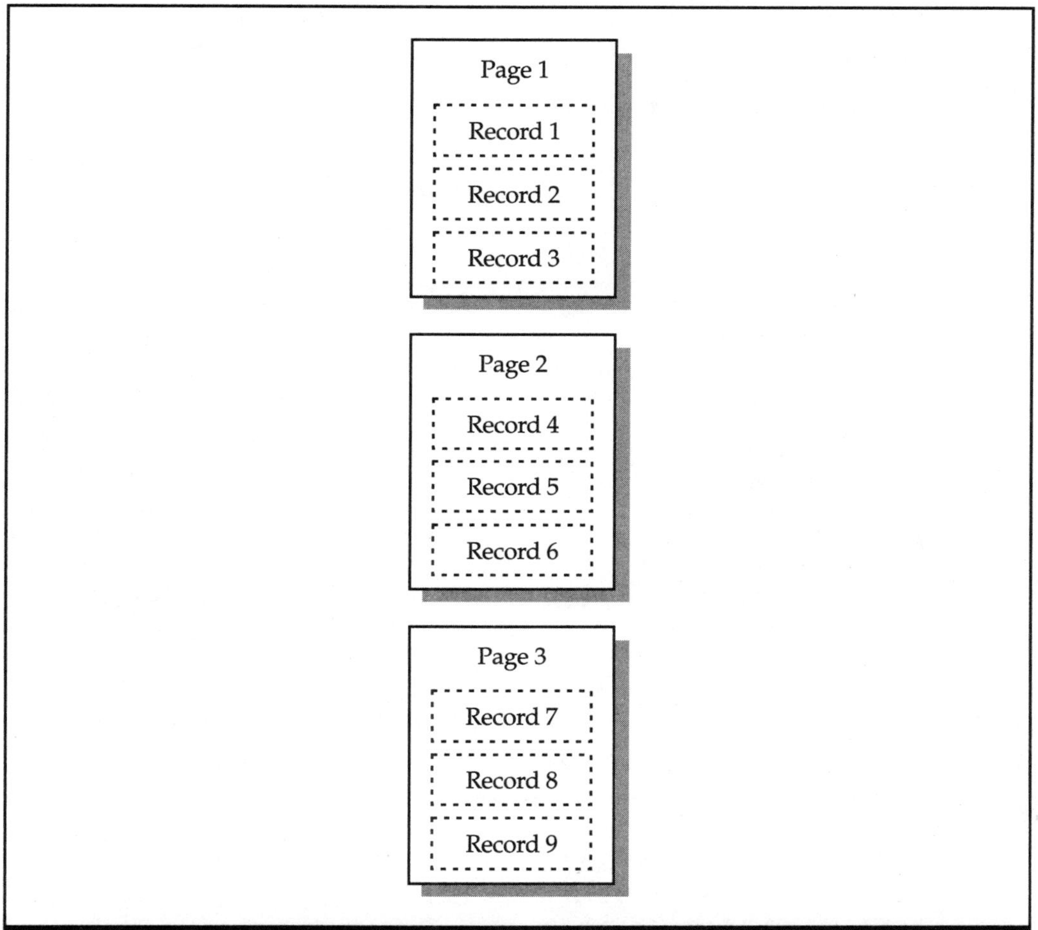

Figure 4-3. A page may contain multiple records

In contrast to the Requery method, which re-executes the entire query, the `Resync` method merely checks the underlying data in the records of the current recordset to make sure they are up-to-date. It will not add new records, but it will update existing records.

SUPPORTS METHOD The `Supports` method allows a recordset to query the data source to determine whether a particular type of cursor access is supported. This method, with parameter specifying the desired query, is executed against the recordset and a Boolean value is returned. For example, to determine whether the recordset supports the ability to add new records (`adAddNew` which has the value `16778240`), the code might look like this:

```
flag = myRS.Supports(16778240)
```

Other cursor options include `adApproxPosition` (16384), `adBookmark` (8192), `adDelete` (16779264), `adHoldRecords` (256), `adMovePrevious` (512), `adResync` (131072), `adUpdate` (16809984), `adUpdateBatch` (65536), `adNotify` (262144), and `adFind` (524288).

STATE PROPERTY In a Recordset object, the `State` property indicates not only whether the object is open or closed, but also the progress of a Recordset query. The possible settings include `adStateOpen` (1), `adStateClosed` (`0`), `adStateConnecting` (2), `adStateExecuting` (4), and `adStateFetching` (8).

STATUS PROPERTY The `Status` property is used to indicate a record status in relation to a batch operation. The settings of the `Status` property show whether the current record is new (adRecNew - 1), modified (adRecModified - 2), invalid (adRecInvalid - 16), deleted (adRecDeleted - 4), or pending changes (adRecPendingChanges - 128).

RECORDCOUNT PROPERTY The `RecordCount` property returns the number of records contained in the current data set. It is also related to the `AbsolutePosition` property, which has the index or ordinal number of the cursor of the recordset. Some ADO data providers do not support this property. Others require the cursor to be moved to the last record before the property becomes valid. Be sure to do a test on your target deployment data source before relying on this property in an application.

NOTE: The `RecordCount` property is only as current as the last query that was made. If other users have added records to the data source since the recordset was created, it may not show an accurate count of the number of records that match the criteria. Executing the `Requery` method before checking this property will ensure an accurate count.

LOCKTYPE PROPERTY The `LockType` property contains the locking mode of the current recordset. Note that this property can only be altered when the recordset is closed. Possible settings for the `LockType` property include: read only mode (adLockReadOnly - `1`), pessimistic locking (adLockPessimistic - `2`), optimistic locking (adLockOptimistic - `3`), and batch update optimistic locking (adLockBatchOptimistic - `4`).

SOURCE PROPERTY The `Source` property can contain the name of a table, a query, a Command object, or a stored procedure. If the `Source` property shows that the source of the recordset is a Command object, the `ActiveConnection` will contain an object reference to the same Connection object that the Command object references. This property most likely will hold a SQL statement defining the current query.

Events

ADO has evolved from the earlier DAO and RDO data models. Perhaps one of the most significant additions is the ability to set code to be executed automatically when certain events occur. These events include the completion of a query, the beginning or end of a transaction, and the interactive progress of record retrieval.

All of the events that are called before an operation is enacted (such as the `WillMove` event) allow that operation to be aborted. Therefore, checks can be performed to ensure that the attempted operation is valid.

Recordset Events

Events for the Recordset object will probably be the most commonly used for coding a Web database solution. Many of the change events can be used to effectively trap or reformat information that is in an unacceptable format.

- **`EndOfRecordset`** Activated when an attempt is made to move the cursor beyond the end of the recordset. Placing code in this event allows you to avoid creating error-trapping routines for this event.
- **`FetchComplete`** Executes after the retrieval of records in an asynchronous operation is complete.
- **`FetchProgress`** Executes periodically during an asynchronous operation and returns the progress toward completion.
- **`FieldChangeComplete` and `WillChangeField`** `FieldChangeComplete` executes after a change to the value of a field is complete. The counterpart event, `WillChangeField`, activates before the change has taken place.
- **`MoveComplete` and `WillMove`** `MoveComplete` executes after the cursor changes position. The counterpart event, `WillMove`, activates before the change has taken place.
- **`RecordChangeComplete` and `WillChangeRecord`** `RecordChange-Complete` executes after a change to one or more fields is complete. The counterpart event, `WillChangeRecord`, activates before the change has taken place.
- **`RecordsetChangeComplete` and `WillChangeRecordset`** `Recordset-ChangeComplete` executes after a change to recordset is complete (this event executes primarily upon execution of the Open or Requery events). The

counterpart event, `WillChangeRecord`, activates before the change has taken place.

Connection Events

For a Connection object, events are available for transactions, monitoring changes to the connection, and handling disconnections. Connection events are activated primarily when the `Open` method is executed.

- **`BeginTransComplete`, `CommitTransComplete`, and `RollbackTransComplete`** These events are called after the particular transaction operation is complete.
- **`ConnectComplete` and `WillConnect`** `ConnectComplete` executes after the connection is complete. The counterpart event, `WillConnect`, activates before the connection has taken place.
- **`Disconnect`** Executes after the connection ends.
- **`ExecuteComplete` and `WillExecute`** Executions against the connection by connected objects—such as Connection and Command `Execute` methods or the Recordset `Open` or `NextRecordset` methods—cause `ExecuteComplete` to activate. The counterpart event, `WillExecute`, activates before the command to be executed has taken place.
- **`InfoMessage`** This event is activated when a warning is issued during the opening of a connection.

These events are programmed most easily through the Data Environment in Visual Basic or Visual Interdev. However, you can create this event code simply by properly naming the event subroutines in the same way you create client-side script events such as Click().

TIP: Since the creation of connections in a Web database solution often exist in the Global.ASA for application-wide use, it is a good idea to place error-checking code at this point. This way you can re-use the definitions across many applications.

Other ADO objects

In addition to the primary objects of ADO, there are three other objects (Error, Parameter, and Field) in the ADO library that provide support and that give specifics for aspects of database access.

Field Object

The Field object is located in the Fields collection within the Recordset object. The Field object stores all of the information related to an open cursor, including the name, current value, data type, underlying field value of the current record, and original value. A Field object can be created dynamically and added to the current field collection in order to modify the database or to create an entirely new persistent recordset. By adding to the Fields collection, you can create a client-side recordset that has no connection to a data source.

For each Field object, the value stored in the Attributes property specify the definition of how the data contained in the field is handled. The possible values for the `Attributes` property currently include:

- **`AdFldMayDefer (2)`** Values contained in the field can be loaded when this field is addressed explicitly—instead of implicitly—with all of the other field values when the record is first loaded.
- **`AdFldUpdatable (4)`** Values of the field are updatable.
- **`AdFldUnknownUpdatable (8)`** Provider cannot determine whether updates are permitted to the field.
- **`adFldFixed (16)`** Fixed-length data is contained in the field.
- **`adFldIsNullable (32)`** Null values may exist in the field.
- **`adFldMayBeNull (64)`** Reading null values from the field is possible.
- **`adFldLong (128)`** A long binary field of general type, so chunks or BLOBs can exist or be added.
- **`adFldRowID (256)`** A unique identifier field that is read-only.
- **`adFldRowVersion (512)`** The field has a time/date stamp of some kind for replication.
- **`adFldCacheDeferred (4096)`** Field values are cached by data providers and values are read from the cache.

The Type property specifies the type of data that is held in a field. The possible values are as follows:

Constant Name	Value	Constant Name	Value
adEmpty	0	adGUID	72
adTinyInt	16	adDate	7
adSmallInt	2	adDBDate	133
adInteger	3	adDBTime	134
adBigInt	20	adDBTimeStamp	135
adUnsignedTinyInt	17	adBSTR	8
adUnsignedSmallInt	18	adChar	129
adUnsignedInt	19	adVarChar	200
adUnsignedBigInt	21	adLongVarChar	201
adSingle	4	adWChar	130
adDouble	5	adVarWChar	202
adCurrency	6	adLongVarWChar	203
adDecimal	14	adBinary	128
adNumeric	131	adVarBinary	204
adBoolean	11	adLongVarBinary	205
adError	10	adChapter	136
adUserDefined	132	adFileTime	64
adVariant	12	adDBFileTime	137
adIDispatch	9	adPropVariant	138
adIUnknown	13	adVarNumeric	139

Error Object

The Error object contains all of the error information when a Connection object encounters a problem. Note that the error may actually occur in a Command or Recordset object, but it is reported in the Connection object's Error object.

Within an Error object, the `Description` property contains an English description of the error that occurred. The number of the error is recorded in the `Number` property. The property setting that generated the error is held in the `Source` property.

The `NativeError` property contains error information returned by the OLE DB or ODBC driver. The `SQLState` property indicates the condition of SQL execution at the time the error occurred.

Parameter Object

The Parameter object is used for arguments that are passed for a Command query. Parameter objects are stored in the `Parameters` collection in the Command object. The ability to handle a parameterized query will depend on the capabilities of the data provider (Microsoft Access and SQL Server can both accept such queries).

> ***NOTE:*** The Parameter object provides the same basic function as the Parameter object on Oracle systems using PL/SQL. However, the ADO Parameter object is not as refined. When accessing an Oracle data source, only those properties supported by ADO will be available.

Calling the `Refresh` method on the `Parameters` collection retrieves the parameter information from a data source. If you already know the parameters that will be needed for a particular query, it is often much faster to add them by hand through the `CreateParameter` method.

ADDING A PARAMETER To add a parameter to the current Parameters object collection, you can use the `CreateParameter` method on the Command object. The data type, direction, and length of each parameter can be specified when it is created, as here:

```
Set myParm = myCmd.CreateParameter("name", _
   adVarChar, adParamInput, len(myStr), myStr)
' Add new parameter to collection
myCmd.Parameters.Append myParm
```

The `CreateParameter` method has five arguments: `Name`, `Type`, `Direction`, `Size`, and `Value`. Only the `Name` setting, the first of the properties, is required to be passed. If the `Type` setting is passed, then a `Size` argument must be passed as well, or the `Size` property must be set before the parameter is appended to the collection.

PARAMETER PROPERTIES In addition to `Name` and `Value`, there are six properties that set the characteristics of a Parameter object: `Attributes`, `Direction`, `Precision`, `NumericScale`, `Size`, and `Type`. All of these parameters must be set to coincide with each other (for example, a string parameter cannot have numeric precision set) or an error will be generated.

APPENDCHUNK METHOD Adding binary data to a field or passing it to a parameter cannot be accomplished simply within SQL code. Instead, the `AppendChunk` method can be used with either a Parameter or a Field object to add binary data. This method should only be used with Fields set to the type of `adFieldsLong`. These fields are traditionally used to store BLOB information.

DEFINITION: **BLOB** A Binary Large Object (BLOB) is a general description of untyped binary data, such as audio recordings (WAV, AU), graphic files (BMP, GIF, JPEG), and other data.

Property Object

The Property object is used to store information in any of the three primary ADO objects (Connection, Command, or Recordset), and Fields. You are already accustomed to built-in properties that are accessed simply with a dot (.) reference after the object. Property objects stored in the `Properties` collection are dynamic properties that are available to reflect values from the data-provider driver.

USE OF ADO

Using ADO from ASP is not really any more complicated than addressing any of the other intrinsic controls included with ASP. Since a connection is automatically created for a Recordset object if none is specified, retrieving records from a query is as easy as opening a recordset:

```
Set tempRecordset = Server.CreateObject("ADODB.Recordset")
tempRecordset.Open "SELECT * FROM customers", _
   "DATABASE=sales;UID=sa;PWD=;DSN=CustomerODBC"
```

Using Command objects is also extremely easy. Simply create an object of that type, and execute it against the desired data source.

In Chapter 5, we'll cover the use of ADO in a Web database solution in great depth.

ADO Constants

Since VBScript does not directly allow constants as part of the available object model, Microsoft has created ASP *include* files that can be used to define and initialize constants for the ADO objects. These constants are contained in a file called ADOvbs.inc. Simply including this file in your ASP solution will allow all of the ADO constants to be used in your ASP code.

To add the constants to an ASP execution file, you can add a line such as the following:

```
<!--#include file=" Adovbs.inc "-->
```

Loading this constants file with each ASP page will slow down the execution of each page. If the memory can be afforded on the server, you can add this include to the Global.asa file to make it available to the entire Web application.

NOTE: If you're using JavaScript instead of VBScript for ASP coding, the constants for ADO are stored in the ADOjavas.inc file.

Remote Data Services

For intranet applications, Microsoft has added features to ADO that support effective client/server communication. With Remote Data Services (RDS), ADO can provide client-side and server-side coordination. RDS is made to retrieve a queried data set for a server, load it to the client, and disconnect from the server. RDS comes in the form of an ActiveX control, so it can only be used on an ActiveX-capable browser.

The client-side RDS control can be dynamically installed in the browser when the page is accessed. However, RDS also requires objects to be executing on the Web server. RDS 1.5 is automatically installed with IIS 4 and higher. If your development machine is not executing IIS, you must have the RDS components installed to do RDS development.

To install RDS, download the Microsoft Data Access Components (MDAC) available free on the Microsoft site (use the search function to locate MDAC since it seems to frequently move around the site). The installation of MDAC will make the objects available to the development environments, such as Visual InterDev.

The components allow the instantiation of two objects types: the Advanced Data Space object and the Advanced Data Control. The Advanced Data Space allows the creation of client-side recordsets that have no visible user interface. The Advanced Data Control acts like a client-side data control and provides the standard recordset movement user interface. The Data Space can be used by client-side scripting code while the ADC, when linked with the Data Space, can provide the necessary user interface.

RDS is only useful in an environment where information systems can control the browser that will be installed by the user base. Since RDS relies on client-side ActiveX controls, the Netscape browser cannot be effectively used for this form of access.

ADO Recordset Library

If you attempt to examine the ADO object model using the Object Browser, you might notice a library named ActiveX Data Objects Recordset Library. This library is a subset of the entire ADO library. Instead of the entire ADO library, it contains only the following objects: Recordset, Property, and Field.

This ADO Recordset subset is used for client-side applications that only need to navigate a recordset, such as data supplied in an XML Web page. Because it only needs to address a simple data set, there are no Command or Connection objects included.

NOTE: The ADO Recordset library is not accessed from ASP. ASP code instantiates the entire ADO library.

Moving from DAO to ADO

Many developers who are now creating ASP solutions initially began development with Visual Basic. Since VB, up until version 6, exclusively used DAO and RDO for database connectivity, it is important to review the differences between the older and newer implementations.

ADO features all of the common features of DAO, such as Recordset, Field, Transaction, and Connection objects. Some of the features of DAO, however, have been discarded. These include:

- **Workspace objects** The workspace and the security objects that were used by the workspace (User, Group, and so on).
- **Database objects** These were used to create the connection and hold the appropriate foundation for recordsets; the functionality of the Database object has been split between the Command and the Connection objects.
- **Tabledefs** The Tabledefs could be used to create and modify the structure of a table or view. By making ADO allow the creation of a Recordset object independent of a Connection or Command object, this functionality is possible in ADO.
- **QueryDefs** The QueryDefs that formerly allowed parameterized queries and that called stored procedures have been subsumed by the Command object.

While these features have been modified from DAO, ADO added a number of new capabilities. The new ADO functions that have been added include the following:

- **Simpler object model** The object model is much flatter and hence more simplified than the DAO model.
- **Event notification** Activation of event code allows projects that use ADO to automatically perform actions when particular events take place, particularly the ability to handle asynchronous operations, such as queries.
- **Command objects** The Command object provides a much more elegant method of activating stored procedures on the data source, as well as making direct execution very simple.
- **Persistent recordsets** ADO allows a recordset to be decoupled from the data source that initialized it and also permits a recordset to be created from scratch in code. Especially in Web database applications, this permits effective connection management, as well as remote client modification if the connection is intermittent.

Missing from ADO are the `FindFirst`, `FindLast`, `FindPrevious`, and `Seek` methods. The `Find` method that was explained earlier in the chapter essentially contains all of the functionality that these methods previously supplied. ADO's powerful new implementation of the `Find` method allows you to eliminate much of the tedium normally associated with using these DAO methods.

Note that ADO has no direct equivalent of the `Seek` method because the `Seek` method was only available on Table objects. Since ADO supports tables through the Recordset object, the `Find` command is used for those actions that were previously implemented with `Seek`.

For additional information check the Visual Basic 6 manual included in Visual Studio. It provides a guide for converting DAO and RDO applications to ADO. The documentation also describes the features of the various versions of ADO and their relation to the equivalent versions of DAO/RDO.

ADO for Windows CE

You may have noticed that Microsoft has extended ADO to the handheld Windows CE device. Although Microsoft does include a version of Pocket Internet Explorer with each Windows CE device, key technologies such as XML and client-side recordsets have not been implemented as part of Pocket IE. Therefore, the ADO included in Windows CE is not relevant to Web database developers.

As Microsoft expands Windows CE into set-top boxes and thin terminals, a sophisticated, inexpensive client/server solution may be possible using an enhanced CE. Check the developer Windows CE site on Microsoft's Web site (www.microsoft.com/windowsce/developer) for more information.

Q&A

Q: Will ADO replace ODBC?

A: ADO is far more powerful than the solution presented by ODBC. However, ODBC has become a multivendor, cross-platform, database middleware solution. With the direct link to the COM object model required by the use of ADO, it looks unlikely that ADO will gain such broad industry support. ADO is also currently slower for many operations than the equivalent ODBC driver because of its added functionality. Therefore, it appears unlikely that ADO will supplant ODBC, at least in the near term.

Q: Is ADO a hierarchical object model like DAO?

A: The basic structure of ADO is hierarchical, but unlike DAO, objects can be created independently of their position in the tree. For example, a Recordset object can be created without a direct attachment to a Connection object. However, an object can be attached hierarchically in ADO so it can be used in a way familiar to DAO programmers.

Q: How is SQL used through ADO?

A: ADO has the capability to either use a general version of SQL or to allow the SQL code to be passed through it directly to the target data source. All three objects can use SQL for addressing a data source. The Recordset object uses it for data set selection. The Execute methods on the Connection and Command objects can execute using a SQL statement.

Although ADO primarily uses SQL, its object structure doesn't require SQL for non-SQL data sources. The ADO/OLE DB Provider for AS/400 and VSAM is such an example. It provides non-SQL record-level access when dealing with an AS/400. This provides a contrast to ODBC which requires SQL statements for all queries and data source interaction.

SUMMARY

A review of the ADO technology reveals that it is powerful enough to handle almost any data-management task. With the Microsoft UDA initiative, ADO will expand to provide access to new types of data and data sources. In this chapter, you learned about the following:

- **ADO** The ActiveX Data Objects technology that grew out of DAO and RDO. It is a flatter object model with the ability to activate event code, provide offline data sets, and perform batch operations and distributed transactions.
- **Universal Data Access (UDA)** UDA is the Microsoft initiative that seeks to unify all types of data (including traditional data types, object data, and multimedia data) under a single querying interface. The primary thrust of UDA is the ability to program ADO/OLE DB and access heterogeneous data sources.
- **Connection object** The foundation of interaction with a data source, a Connection object can be created to begin a session with a data source. The connection can be used by several objects, such as Recordset or Command objects.
- **Command object** Used to execute a SQL query or stored procedure or to access driver-specific functionality, the Command object can run against a data source and return a recordset.
- **Recordsets** The Recordset object holds all of the record data retrieved by a query or Command object. New to ADO is the ability to have hierarchical recordsets that hold related subquery data.

CHAPTER 5

Learning to Use ADO for Application Design

The ActiveX Data Objects (ADO) model provides simple access to almost any type of data source. Despite having only three primary objects, ADO's features support a broad range of possible solutions. Because the Web database solutions that you are going to develop will use ADO almost exclusively to access and modify data, it will be helpful for you to understand how ADO is used in a simple implementation. Building the more complete solutions that combine ADO with the features of the Web server will augment what you learn here.

In this chapter, you will also begin using Visual InterDev to create Web database applications—in this case, a basic application to examine the structure of a database. Make sure, before you begin, that Visual InterDev and the Internet Information Server (IIS) Web server are properly installed on your development machine. Additionally, you need the sample Northwind database (NWind.mbd) that is included with both Visual Studio (in the Visual Basic directory) and Microsoft Access (in the Office suite). If you don't know where Northwind is located, use the Find Files function on your system to locate it.

The ADO objects are very similar to the Data Access Objects (DAO) objects in Visual Basic. The two object models, however, have basic structural differences. Unfortunately for Web developers, much of the example code in DAO and ADO on the Microsoft Web site is constructed in Visual Basic. Since VBScript execution in an ASP file requires special considerations, it is important to have some key examples of the use of major objects within the ASP environment.

This section will enable you to create one-page examples that perform simple functions, such as creating a connection, using a Command object to return a recordset, or executing a query in a Recordset object. Each of these samples can be constructed with a simple text editor (such as Notepad) or through Visual InterDev. Later in the chapter, you will see how to use some of the more advanced capabilities of InterDev to make Web database construction much easier.

Chapter 4 briefly touched upon creating and using ADO objects. In this chapter, you will be given a more sophisticated and thorough example of how each object is instantiated as part of an ASP file that is executed. This will enable you to understand how the objects are connected together to return database information to the client browser.

CREATING A CONNECTION OBJECT

The Connection object is the cornerstone of any ADO database application. This object actually opens and maintains the connection to the requested data source. You can easily create the Connection object by using the Server object's `CreateObject` method, but you can't open the connection until you properly configure it. Proper configuration only requires setting a few parameters.

The following example performs only a single task: it makes a connection to the Northwind database. Depending on the results of the attempt, the status and some parameters are returned to the browser for display. To create the example using the Connection object, open your text editor and enter the code shown in the following listing:

```
<HTML>
<HEAD>
```

```
<TITLE>Connection Test (ADO)</TITLE>
</HEAD>
<BODY>
<H3>Connection Test (ADO)</H3>

<%
   ' Create a variable reference for the connection
   Dim myConn
   ' Create the connection object
   Set myConn = Server.CreateObject("ADODB.Connection")
   ' Attempt to open connection
   myConn.Open "driver={Microsoft Access Driver (*.mdb)};" & _

      "dbq=c:\Program Files\Microsoft Visual Studio\VB98\nwind.mdb"
   ' Check if the opening was successful and write the
   ' result to the client browser
   ' Possible values: adStateOpen(1), adStateClosed (0)
   If myConn.State = 1 Then
      Response.Write("Connection opened successfully<P>")
      ' Insert extra code
   Else
      Response.Write("Error. Connection could not be opened.<P>")
   End If
   ' Close the connection
   myConn.Close
   ' Eliminate the connection
   Set myConn = Nothing
%>
</BODY>
</HTML>
```

After you enter the Connection object source code, create a new folder named **WebDB05** in your Web publications directory (usually the \wwwroot folder). This is the folder that will be used to store all the other basic examples in this chapter. Save the file in the folder as **Connection1.asp**.

Enter the Microsoft Management Console (MMC) to set up the application. Create a new application called **WebDB05** and provide script execution privileges. You need to click the Create button which will initialize the application and change the Create button to a Remove button used to destroy the application (see Figure 5-1).

After you correctly configure the application, you can run it through a browser. Execute your Web browser and type the URL of the application. Once you access this page on the Web server, the returned page will display the success or failure of the connection attempt (see Figure 5-2).

You can also conduct a simple query from the Connection object. Add the following code after the comment (which has been included in the following listing for clarity) that states Insert extra code.

```
' Insert extra code
' Execute a SQL statement against the Connection
Set myRS = myConn.Execute("Select * from Customers")
' Add all of the records to the browser display
Do Until myRS.EOF
   ' Add all of the fields for the current record
   ' into a single line
   temp = ""
   For i = 1 to myRS.Fields.Count - 1
      temp = temp & myRS.Fields(i).Value & ","
   Next
   ' Write record to the browser
   Response.Write(temp & "<P>")
   myRS.MoveNext
Loop
```

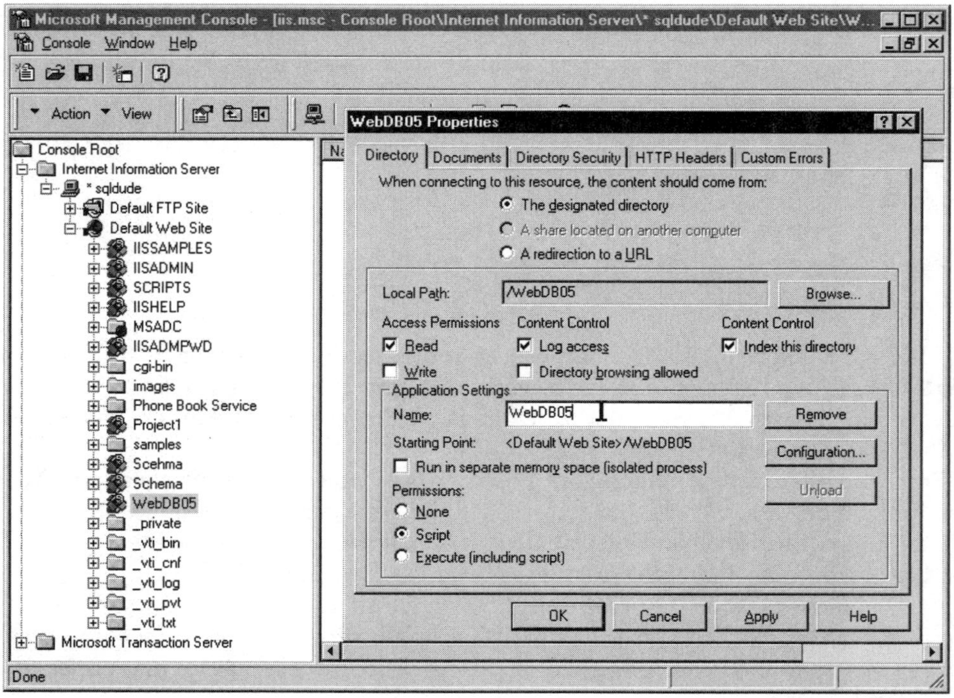

Figure 5-1. The folder must be set to allow script execution

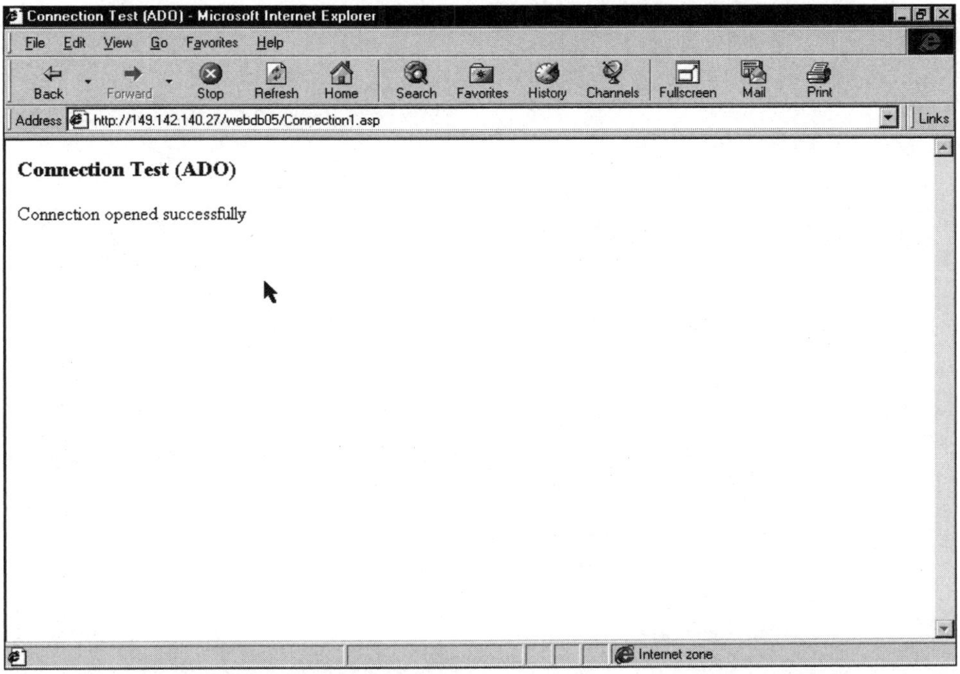

Figure 5-2. Display of execution from a Connection object

This sample code uses the `Execute` method on the Connection object. The `Execute` method may be used to execute a SQL command against the data source, much like a Command object. The recordset that is returned by the `Execute` method is always read-only, with a forward-only cursor. If you need other feature settings, you first need to create, configure, and open a Recordset object to execute the command.

CREATING A COMMAND OBJECT

The Command object provides great flexibility in the data object model because it can either execute a SQL command (such as a stored procedure) or generate a recordset. A recordset is always returned by a Command object execution, but you may choose to ignore it if the information is unneeded. The Recordset object may be empty if no records are retrieved by the execution or if a stored procedure does not return any data.

In this example, the Command object executes a query and returns a recordset. Enter the following code and save it in the WebDB05 folder under the name **Command1.asp**.

```
<HTML>
<HEAD>
<TITLE>Command Test (ADO)</TITLE>
</HEAD>
<BODY>
<H3>Command Test (ADO)</H3>

<%
   ' Create a variable reference for the connection
   Dim myConn
   ' Create the connection object
      Set myConn = Server.CreateObject("ADODB.Connection")
   ' Attempt to open connection
   myConn.Open "driver={Microsoft Access Driver (*.mdb)};" & _

      dbq=c:\Program Files\Microsoft Visual Studio\VB98\nwind.mdb"
   ' Check if the opening was successful and write the
   ' result to the client browser
   ' Possible values: adStateOpen(1), adStateClosed (0)
   If myConn.State = 1 Then
      Response.Write("Connection opened successfully<P>")
      ' Insert extra code
      Set myCmd = Server.CreateObject("ADODB.Command")
      ' Attach Command object to connection
      Set myCmd.ActiveConnection = myConn
      ' Set up command parameters
      myCmd.CommandText = "select * from Customers"
      myCmd.CommandType = 1'adCmdText
      ' Execute the SQL command
      Set myRS = myCmd.Execute ()
      If myRS.State = 1 Then
         Response.Write("Number of Fields: " & myRS.Fields.Count)
      Else
         Response.Write("An Error occurred. " & _

            Command couldn't create recordset.<P>")
      End If
   Else
      Response.Write("Error. Connection could not be opened.<P>")
   End If
   ' Close the connection
   myConn.Close
   ' Eliminate the connection
   Set myConn = Nothing
```

```
%>
</BODY>
</HTML>
```

The primary use of the Command object, however, isn't to execute a query since a Recordset object is generally used to accomplish this function. Most often, a Command object executes SQL commands or activates stored procedures on data sources more sophisticated than Access 97 or the Jet Engine (although Access 2000 with MSDE can use stored procedures). Therefore, an example can be created that calls a stored procedure to demonstrate how the Command object will be used for execution.

The following example executes a stored procedure on SQL Server. The example expects an ODBC data source called Pubs to exist on the server machine. This data source points to your SQL Server database server and has permission to access the basic stored procedures. The example accesses the data source through the system administrator (sa) account on the server.

CAUTION: Since the default sa account does not have a password when SQL Server is first installed, none has been included in the connection string. Be sure to set this to the password required on your system.

Save this code in the WebDB05 folder as **Command2.asp**.

```
' Create a variable reference for the connection
Dim myConn
' Create the connection object
Set myConn = Server.CreateObject("ADODB.Connection")
' Attempt to open connection
myConn.Open "driver={SQL Server};SERVER=sqlDude;" & _
   Database=pubs;UID=sa;pwd="
' Check if the opening was successful and write the
' result to the client browser
' Possible values: adStateOpen(1), adStateClosed (0)
If myConn.State = 1 Then
   Response.Write("Connection opened successfully<P>")
   ' Insert extra code
   Set myCmd = Server.CreateObject("ADODB.Command")
   ' Attach Command object to connection
   Set myCmd.ActiveConnection = myConn
   ' Set up command parameters
   myCmd.CommandText = "getauthorinfo"
   myCmd.CommandType = 4   'adCmdStoredProc
   ' Execute the stored procedure command
   Set myRS = myCmd.Execute
   If myRS.State = 1 Then
```

```
            Response.Write("Number of Fields: " & myRS.Fields.Count)
        Else
            Response.Write("Error. " & _
                Command could not get author info.<P>")
        End If
    Else
        Response.Write("Error. Connection could not be opened.<P>")
    End If
    ' Close the connection
    myConn.Close
    ' Eliminate the connection
    Set myConn = Nothing
```

You can determine whether the data source was effected by the execution. The `recordsAffected` property will notify you of how many records were changed by the executed statement.

CREATING A RECORDSET OBJECT

By far the most common object that you will use in your Web database solutions is the Recordset object. Since it provides the ability to receive data as well as add, modify, or delete records, learning to use it effectively is critical to application deployment. A Recordset object can be configured in many different ways. For a simple, read-only recordset, the code required is incredibly simple. The sample code shown in the following listing (save it as **RS1.asp**) uses the simplest operations to create a Recordset object and open it to access the data source. The count of the number of fields in the recordset is then sent to the browser.

```
<HTML>
<HEAD>
<TITLE>Recordset Test (ADO)</TITLE>
</HEAD>
<BODY>
<H3>Recordset Test (ADO)</H3>

<%
    ' Create a variable reference for the connection
    Dim myConn
    ' Create the connection object
        Set myConn = Server.CreateObject("ADODB.Connection")
    ' Attempt to open connection
    myConn.Open "driver={Microsoft Access Driver (*.mdb)};" & _

        dbq=c:\Program Files\Microsoft Visual Studio\VB98\nwind.mdb"
```

```
    ' Check if the opening was successful and write the
    ' result to the client browser
    ' Possible values: adStateOpen(1), adStateClosed (0)
    If myConn.State = 1 Then
       Response.Write("Connection opened successfully<P>")
       ' Insert extra code
       Set myRS = Server.CreateObject("ADODB.Recordset")
       ' Attach Recordset object to connection
       Set myRS.ActiveConnection = myConn
       myRS.CursorType = 2 ' adOpenDynamic
       myRS.CursorLocation = 2 ' adUseServer
       myRS.LockType = 3 ' adLockOptimistic
       myRS.Source = "select * from customers"
       ' Open the recordset
       myRS.Open
       If myRS.State = 1 Then
          Response.Write("Number of Fields: " & myRS.Fields.Count)
       Else
          Response.Write("Error. could not create recordset.<P>")
       End If
    Else
       Response.Write("Error. Connection could not be opened.<P>")
    End If
    ' Close the connection
    myConn.Close
    ' Eliminate the connection
    Set myConn = Nothing
%>
</BODY>
</HTML>
```

In a real case, the query generated by this routine would be output to the browser window as a list of items. This primitive example demonstrates how the source may be opened. Once the recordset has been generated, you will need to retrieve data, often data specified or selected by the Web user. Typically, even a simple query accepts parameters that modify what the query actually displays. Often, this information from the query comes in the Request string that is part of the URL (following the question mark symbol (?)) for the page.

To demonstrate this type of functionality, the example shown in Figure 5-3 accepts parameters in the query string. It uses the Request parameters to modify the SQL string used to create the data set. If you enter the page without any parameters, the ASP page uses the same query that was used in the previous example listing. The link at the top of the page includes a parameter to set the query.

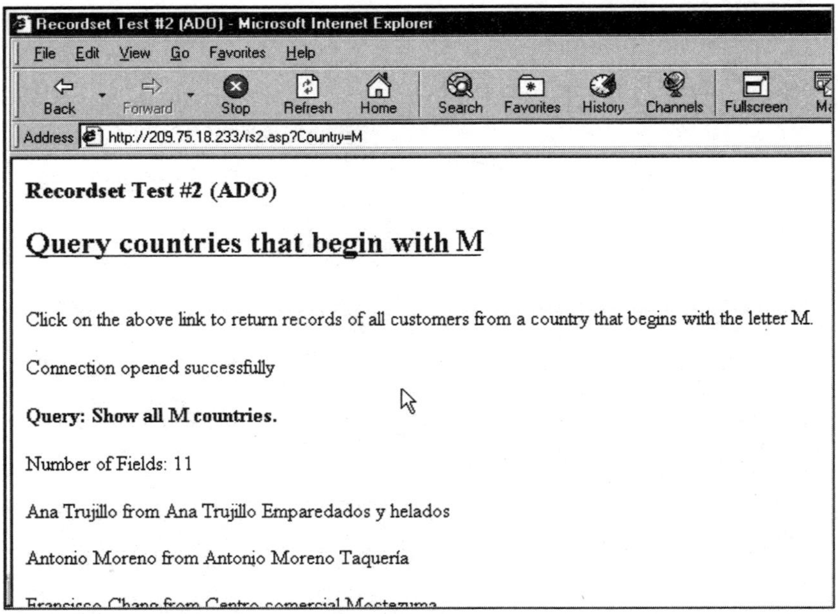

Figure 5-3. After accepting the query parameter, the Recordset only displays countries that begin with the letter M

This next sample code also demonstrates connecting the Recordset object to a Connection object. Multiple recordsets can be attached to a single Connection object.

```
<HTML>
<HEAD>
<TITLE>Recordset Test #2 (ADO)</TITLE>
</HEAD>
<BODY>
<H3>Recordset Test #2 (ADO)</H3>

<H2>
<A HREF="rs2.asp?Country=M">Query countries that begin with M
</A></H2><BR>
Click the above link to return records of all customers from a country that begins
with the letter M.<P><P>
<%
   ' Create a variable reference for the connection
```

```
   Dim myConn
   ' Create the connection object
       Set myConn = Server.CreateObject("ADODB.Connection")
   ' Attempt to open connection
   myConn.Open "driver={Microsoft Access Driver (*.mdb)};" & _
      dbq=c:\Program Files\Microsoft Visual Studio\VB98\nwind.mdb"
   ' Check if the opening was successful and write the
   ' result to the client browser
   ' Possible values: adStateOpen(1), adStateClosed (0)
   If myConn.State = 1 Then
      Response.Write("Connection opened successfully<P>")
      Set myRS = Server.CreateObject("ADODB.Recordset")
      ' Attach Command object to connection
      Set myRS.ActiveConnection = myConn
      myRS.CursorType = 2 ' adOpenDynamic
      myRS.CursorLocation = 2 ' adUseServer
      myRS.LockType = 3 ' adLockOptimistic
      If Len(Request.QueryString("Country"))=0 then
         Response.Write("<B>Query: Show all countries.</B><P>")
         myParam = ""
      Else
         Response.Write("<B>Query: Show all " & Request.QueryString("Country") & "
countries.</B><P>")
         myParam = Request.QueryString("Country")
      End If
      ' Open the recordset
      myRS.Open "select * from customers where Country like '" & myParam & "%'"
      If myRS.State = 1 Then
         Response.Write("Number of Fields: " & myRS.Fields.Count & "<P>")
         Do Until myRS.EOF
            Response.Write(myRS.Fields("ContactName") _
               & " from " & myRS.Fields("CompanyName") _
& ", " & myRS.Fields("Country") "<P>")
            myRS.MoveNext
         Loop
      Else
         Response.Write("Error. Could not create recordset.<P>")
      End If
   Else
      Response.Write("Error. Connection could not be opened.<P>")
   End If
   ' Close the connection
   myConn.Close
   ' Eliminate the connection
   Set myConn = Nothing
%>
</BODY>
</HTML>
```

Save this example as **RS2.asp** and try executing it with your browser. Click the link to execute the query with parameters. You can modify the URL so that it queries the records for the states that you specify.

All of the examples you've set up so far have created read-only recordsets. By default, when a new recordset is created, it is set to read-only access. This default read-only mode simplifies access because only recordsets that need write access must monitor record and database locking. However, almost every application that you create will have some aspect that requires an information entry that writes into the database. Most of the time, you will want to use the features of Visual InterDev that support such effective tools as bound data controls.

In the following example, the AddNew method is used to create a new item that is added to the Northwind data set. For the code to execute correctly, make sure that write capabilities of the NWind.MDB file are not disabled (in the Windows Explorer).

In contrast to the read-only recordsets you've used earlier, you might note that when opening the Connection, the Mode parameter is set to adModeReadWrite. This opens the connection to allow the creation of Recordset or Command objects that can modify the data source.

```
<HTML>
<HEAD>
<TITLE>Recordset Test #3 (ADO)</TITLE>
</HEAD>
<BODY>
<H3>Recordset Test #3 (ADO)</H3>

<%
   ' Create a variable reference for the connection
   Dim myConn
   ' Create the connection object
   Set myConn = Server.CreateObject("ADODB.Connection")
   ' Open with adModeReadWrite (3)
   myConn.Mode = 3
   ' Attempt to open connection
   myConn.Open "driver={Microsoft Access Driver (*.mdb)};" & _
      dbq=c:\Program Files\Microsoft Visual Studio\VB98\nwind.mdb"
   ' Check if the opening was successful and write the
   ' result to the client browser
   ' Possible values: adStateOpen(1), adStateClosed (0)
   If myConn.State = 1 Then
      Response.Write("Connection opened successfully<P>")
      ' Insert extra code
      Set myRS = Server.CreateObject("ADODB.Recordset")
      ' Attach Command object to connection
      Set myRS.ActiveConnection = myConn
      myRS.CursorType = 2 ' adOpenDynamic
      myRS.CursorLocation = 2 ' adUseServer
      myRS.LockType = 3 ' adLockOptimistic
```

```
      myRS.Source = "select * from customers"
      ' Open the recordset
      myRS.Open
      If myRS.State = 1 Then
         Response.Write("Number of Fields: " & myRS.Fields.Count & "<P>")



      myRS.AddNews
      myRS.Fields("CustomerID") = CInt(Rnd* 1000)
      myRS.Fields("CompanyName") = "Acme Products"
      myRS.Fields("ContactName") = "Jake McAdoo"
      myRS.Fields("ContactTitle") = "President"
      myRS.Fields("Phone") = "619-555-1212"
      myRS.Update
      myRS.MoveFirst
      Do Until myRS.EOF
         Response.Write(myRS.Fields("ContactName") _
            & " from " & myRS.Fields("CompanyName") & "<P>")
         myRS.MoveNext
      Loop
      Else
         Response.Write("Error. Could not create recordset.<P>")
      End If
   Else
      Response.Write("Error. Connection could not be opened.<P>")
   End If
   ' Close the connection
   myConn.Close
   ' Eliminate the connection
   Set myConn = Nothing
%>
</BODY>
</HTML>
```

The ADO example in this chapter has provided the simplest case scenario so far for implementing with ADO. For that reason, it is a good idea to keep them in a folder on your hard drive. Make the folders easy to find, as you'll likely reference them often when you need a quick-and-dirty implementation to test a data source or data access method.

ADO IMPLEMENTATION ISSUES

Knowing how the ADO objects work is the first step toward realizing a Web database application. However, before you create a complete application that can be deployed for realtime use, you must first consider many small implementation issues. Seemingly small details, such as handling strings properly, can be key elements in producing a polished application.

This section addresses some of the more important of these issues. Connection pooling, for example, functions in a way that is not ordinarily intuitive. However, proper configuration of pooling is one of the important methods of effective Web database scaling. By learning the fine points of some of the ADO technology, you can begin practicing correct implementation with your initial projects, which will help you well into the future.

Connection Pooling

In a Web solution, connections to a database are constantly being created and destroyed as new users enter the site. Likewise, individual recordsets are frequently used and discarded. ADO provides the capability of *connection pooling,* whereby multiple connections to a data source remain open and are simply assigned to the operation as they are needed.

DEFINITION: **Connection pooling** Denotes a process where a set of database connections are kept open and assigned upon individual requests rather than having to be created from scratch. By eliminating the constant creation and destruction of connections, performance is greatly increased.

Connection pooling is handled by the ODBC drivers that are version 3 and greater. Pooling, when activated, actually takes place within the current Windows NT Server process. Therefore, the application's execution setting (in-process or out-of-process) in the application configuration is very important. If the application is set to execute in its own memory space (out-of-process), then all connections within that application only will be pooled. This eliminates most of the potential efficiency gained through connection pooling.

However, if you set the application for in-process execution, the entire ASP process will pool connections. For in-process applications, pooled connections will include not only the connections of your application, but also all the ODBC connections used by applications executing in the ASP process. Before you activate pooling for a single application, either set the application to execute out of process or consider carefully how setting it to execute in-process may affect other applications executing within the Web server's memory process.

Pooling also only occurs for a single user login, which is exactly the method that is used by the Web server for database access. In IIS 4, altered from previous IIS versions, connection pooling is active by default. Thus, to have your connections pooled, you simply need to make sure that each login is done with the same username and password.

Connections contained in the pool are not kept open forever. By default, the timeout for a single connection is 60 seconds, so pooling primarily helps in the case of a heavily accessed application. Through the ODBC connection source, you can change the pooling timeout. Remember that the connection resources are kept allocated for all of the pool connections until the timeout. Make sure you don't set the timeout too long or the server will be starved for computing resources.

Handling Strings

In a Web database solution, you often have to retrieve information for display from a remote data source. Handling string data is one of the most time-consuming challenges that you need to address. For example, if the LastName field of a record contains a null, and you attempt to combine that field with another string, an error can result. Difficulties like this, in addition to VBScript's marginal string-handling abilities, can produce quite a challenge.

DEFINITION: **Null** A field that has not been set to anything. Unlike a field value such as an empty string ("") that still uses the field space in the database, a null takes up no space. It merely marks that the field is empty.

The Null problem actually has a fairly simple solution. The ampersand (&) can be used to combine a string data type with any other data type to return a string data type. For example, the LastName field in a database might contain a Null value. By combining the field value with an empty string, as follows, you will avoid a potential error:

```
a = myRS.Fields("LastName") & ""
```

Trimming string is the other problem that frequently appears when drawing to an HTML page. Many strings have trailing spaces that interrupt the flow of text, and which make an application appear unprofessional. For example, you may have received a form letter addressed like this:

You, Mr. Smith   , have already won one of many prizes...

Simply trimming these extra spaces ensures that your application has a much more polished look. VBScript includes the `Trim` function to remove leading or trailing spaces from a string. Using this function will ensure that white space is removed before you place it in the returning HTML text.

Making certain a string contains critical information before accepting page input is a function that often results in poor performance. If you need your ASP program to determine whether a string is empty, don't compare it to an empty string like this:

```
If myStr = "" Then
```

This method is slow because of the string-creation and character-checking routines required for execution to return the result. Instead, check the length of the string to make sure that it's 0:

```
If Len(myStr)=0 Then
```

Finally, if you have a value that you need converted to a string, favor the `Format`*`xxx`*`()` functions over the `CStr()` method. `CStr()` provides little control over spaces, commas, rounding, or other string factors, whereas the `Format`*`xxx`*`()` functions can help you with all of these. Here are some of the most common formatting function settings:

```
' Display in currency format using the regional settings
Response.Write(FormatCurrency(10.5) & "<P>")
```

```
' Display with two decimal places
Response.Write(FormatNumber(1110.5,2) & "<P>")
' Display as percentage
Response.Write(FormatPercent(.55) & "<P>")
' Display in long date format
Response.Write(FormatDateTime(#12/25/99#,1) & "<P>")
```

Multipage Handling

One aspect of a Web database application that is seldom addressed is the amount of information that should be available on a single page. A visitor can become quite fatigued if all of the information is contained on a single page that takes minutes to scroll through. One of the benefits of using a database with ASP execution is that problems such as this can be addressed in script code. Rather than having to institute a real-world procedure that will take extra time and effort, an automated solution can provide the functionality.

For breaking information into more accessible pieces, it is a good idea to design a multi-page handler into the foundation of your application. Thereafter, the routine can be used easily in one or more places. You can use multiple pages to accomplish the following:

- **Break up content** There may be simply too much information to send as a single page without forcing the user to wait excessively long. Breaking the data into more than one page makes downloading simpler.
- **Facilitate easier reading** Scrolling through a large amount of content or relocating a piece of information can be difficult in a single, long file. Additionally, returning to a piece of information that was being examined in the past is far more difficult.
- **Make data stealing difficult** For reasons of security or to deter possible sale of the contiguous data, companies break down data into multiple pages, which makes handling the data tedious for would-be pirates.
- **Tease with entries** A multi-page solution can provide the first page or "teaser" information (such as "Top 50" items) for free access. To be allowed further access, the user must become registered or pay a fee. Online magazines often implement this technique.

Here is the typical code listing to use a Request parameter to determine what page is currently being displayed. Enter this code and store it as **Multipage.asp** in the WebDB05 directory. The Northwind database has 91 records in the Customers table. Since the `numPerPage` value is set to 10, the data will be displayed in a series of ten pages.

```
<HTML>
<HEAD>
<TITLE>Multi-page Recordset (ADO)</TITLE>
</HEAD>
```

```
<BODY>
<H1>Multi-page Recordset (ADO)</H1>
<%
   ' Create a variable reference for the connection
   Dim myConn
   ' Create the connection object
      Set myConn = Server.CreateObject("ADODB.Connection")
   ' Attempt to open connection
   myConn.Open "driver={Microsoft Access Driver (*.mdb)};" & _
     "dbq=c:\Program Files\Microsoft Visual Studio\VB98\nwind.mdb"
   ' Check if the opening was successful and write the
   ' result to the client browser
   ' Possible values: adStateOpen(1), adStateClosed (0)
   If myConn.State = 1 Then
      Response.Write("Connection opened successfully<P>")
      Set myRS = Server.CreateObject("ADODB.Recordset")
      ' Attach Command object to connection
      Set myRS.ActiveConnection = myConn
      myRS.CursorType = 2 ' adOpenDynamic
      myRS.CursorLocation = 2 ' adUseServer
      If Len(Request.QueryString("page"))=0 then
         Response.Write("<B>Query: Show all pages.</B><P>")
         pageNum = CInt(1)
      Else
         Response.Write("<B>Query: Show page #" & _
            Request.QueryString("page") & "</B><P>")
         pageNum = CInt(Request.QueryString("page"))
      End If
      ' Open the recordset
      myRS.Open "select * from customers"
      If myRS.State = 1 Then
         pageSize = 10
         startNum = (pageSize * (pageNum-1)) + 1
         endNum = (pageSize * pageNum)
         recNum = 1
         Response.Write("Number of records per page: " & pageSize & "<P>")
         Do Until myRS.EOF
            If recNum >= startNum and recNum <= endNum then
             Response.Write("#" & recNum & ": " & _
                   myRS.Fields("ContactName") & " from " & _
                   myRS.Fields("CompanyName") & ", " & _
                   myRS.Fields("Country") & "<P>")
```

```
            End If
            If recNum > endNum then
            Exit Do
            End If
            myRS.MoveNext
            recNum = recNum + 1
         Loop
         If pageNum > 1 Then
            Response.Write("<A HREF=multipage.asp?page=" & _
               pageNum - 1 & "><< Previous Page </A>")
         End If
         Response.Write(" --- ")
         If Not myRS.EOF Then
            Response.Write("<A HREF=multipage.asp?page=" & _
               pageNum + 1 & ">Next Page >></A>")
         End If
      Else
         Response.Write("Error. Could not create recordset.<P>")
      End If
   Else
      Response.Write("Error. Connection could not be opened.<P>")
   End If
   ' Close the connection
   myConn.Close
   ' Eliminate the connection
   Set myConn = Nothing
%>
</BODY>
</HTML>
```

Using a Session for Database Objects

Any use of ADO on a Web server has associated performance issues that must be considered. One common mistake made by many beginning Web database developers is re-creating their database objects (such as Connection or Recordset objects) on each ASP page for small solutions. Not only does this require a lot of additional processing, it also slows the execution of the application from the perspective of the user.

Adding the Connection objects and some of the Recordset objects to the Session or Application objects can prevent much of this overhead. After the initial object creation, and for the duration of the session, the objects will remain intact for use by all subsequent ASP files. For infrequently used multipage applications, the increase in performance is significant.

CAUTION: Some people recommend against placing a variable in the Session object because it hampers scalability and connection pooling. Adding a Connection object to the Session object is not ideal in all Web applications. Since the Session object typically is kept alive for 20 minutes after the last use (unless explicitly eliminated), many connections and resources remain in limbo. If the application you develop will be consistently accessed by numerous users, avoid the Session-variable implementation method.

Remember that the default timeout for connection pooling is set to 60 seconds. If users access your Web database application less frequently than this, performance dictates that you use Session variables, because all connections are flushed from the pool at timeout. If access occurs more frequently, favor constant creation/destruction of connections because the pooling will eliminate much of the performance lag.

Batch Processing Issues

Batch processing of record updates, which is rather straightforward in a traditional client application, is a difficult design issue in a Web application. The discontinuous interface of the user moving from page to page makes it difficult to regiment a single path through data entry. Often, an innocent user action, such as clicking the Back arrow, can cause your entire application to fault.

For this reason, it is a good idea to make a design decision between two solutions, save all updates until the final page, or use a transaction to prevent data corruption. By placing information in Session variable, you can essentially cache entries across several pages. This allows all of the changes to be written at once on the final page.

Another method is to use the transaction capabilities of ADO to encapsulate multiple-page operations within a single commitment operation. In the event of a problem between one page and another, the data source will not be corrupted with an incomplete entry. If the transaction is not completed and the session times out, the operations will be revoked. Although this could lead to a loss of some data, it is often a better alternative than corrupting your source.

Validating Data

In more traditional client/server applications, data validity is tested on the client. For most Web applications, it must be checked by the server. Because client-side checking may be impossible (if scripting is turned off or not supported in the browser), you must rely on server verification to take place.

CAUTION: Even if client-side data checking is available through browser scripting execution, you can't be certain that the data has been checked. Although testing may confirm that a browser is capable of script handling, the scripting code might never execute. For example, a proxy server may strip the scripts contained in the page sent to the server for security reasons. Consequently, the server-side application will have no way to determine whether the client-side checking actually occurred.

One of the most effective methods of handling data verification is to create a series of global checking routines that can be used by any page in the application. You can use the ones already included in the VBScript language, but they may not cover all the possibilities. For example, to verify the entry of a date, you can use code such as this one.

```
If IsDate(myInput) Then
   ' Store information to database field
Else
   ' Set variable to alert user of problem
End If
```

However, what if you need a phone number in a certain format? Or what if you need to make sure that the date entered is a date that occurs after the current date? By creating singular functions to handle these situations, you can place them all in a single file (using ASP's Include or Global.asa capabilities) that can be used by all the pages that need such checking.

If you can determine at the beginning of the project the types of checking that will need to be accomplished, you will save a great deal of time by making all of those functions available for construction of the project. This is especially effective on projects requiring team development, preventing each team member from wasting time "reinventing the wheel." The code can also be generalized, so that it can be used with client-side execution.

DESCRIBING THE DATABASE SCHEMA

Chapter 4 briefly described the Connection object's `OpenSchema` method, which returns a recordset of the features of a database structure, such as a table. The `OpenSchema` method is the perfect device to demonstrate the use of an ADO recordset, as well as its own functionality. Since this function returns a recordset containing all of the requested schema information, the data in the recordset can be easily examined.

Before you begin, locate the Northwind database on your hard drive. You need to set a connection reference to match the location of the database on your system. To interpret the schema, you must perform the following steps:

1. Create a connection to the database.
2. Set up the variables to include the types of data to be returned.
3. Execute the `OpenSchema` method.
4. Use a loop to progress through the definitions stored as records.
5. Parse the record values.
6. Write the database records as HTML code to the user's browser.

This application will execute within IIS, so you also need to create a directory and an application setting to allow execution. Since it will be created in Visual InterDev, most of the primary database setup will be accomplished automatically.

ADO from Visual InterDev

Visual InterDev provides an essential GUI to simplify programming the ADO objects for a database solution. Primary among the features that simplify Web database development is the Data Environment of a project. The Data Environment allows references to be added for database connections, Command objects, and the other ADO structures. The Data Environment will aid you in selecting the database (as well as the objects in the database) to access from the ASP page.

With Data Environments added to your project, you can use Command objects or address the environment directly from within the project. The Connection object can also be used with server-side components, to minimize the time that you have to spend coding on the project. It can be used to provide an easy-to-use visual component to aid in development of data-driven projects, too.

After you create a project, adding a Data Environment is relatively easy. Under the Project menu, selections are available to add Connection and Command objects. You can use the Data View window to browse all the objects that are available in the project.

In Visual InterDev, you can use the server-side components listed on the tool palette to help you create your solution. These components act essentially like a Word macro, wizard, or Visual Basic add-in. They generate ASP code based on the selections that you make in a series of dialog boxes. They are design-time components that can provide such capabilities as bound controls, page navigation, and HTML presentation formating.

CAUTION: If you make modifications to the code that is generated by the server-side components, this code will be erased if you re-execute the component. The components do not read alterations made, so the new settings will simply write over the current definitions.

Creating the Schema Examination Application

The schema examination application will be a single ASP file that executes under the application name *Schema*. The application will request the database schema and display the schema as an HTML page. In the following steps, use the New Project Wizard to create the foundation of the project:

1. Open Visual InterDev, which presents you with the New Projects dialog box.
2. Select the New Web Project option.
3. Set the Name of the project to **Schema** and click the Open button. After you name the project, the New Project Wizard automatically executes, and guides you through the primary settings for creating an application. The first wizard dialog box shown allows you to enter the name of the Web server on which to locate the application.
4. Enter the name of the Web server, select Master Mode, and click the Next button to advance to the next step of the wizard. Master Mode gives you the maximum amount of flexibility and assumes that you have control of the staging server on which you'll be doing your basic development.

   When you click Next, Visual InterDev contacts the Web server to get the information it needs. Once this is accomplished, the wizard allows you to either create a new Web application or connect to an existing one.

Creating a Server Connection

For the most effective use of Visual InterDev, you need to create a connection to your Web server. Using a controlling connection to the Web server is known as *Master Mode*, in which Visual InterDev can manage the project on the Web server and update it automatically to reflect the new deployment changes. To use Master Mode, you must have the FrontPage Server Extensions installed on the Web server.

Local Mode, in contrast, enables you to work offline, but requires that you make updates to the Web server manually. When you save the project in Local Mode, the FrontPage extensions will not be used to automatically update the designated server.

If you don't know the name of the local Web server, you can load the Internet Service Manager and look at the default name of the machine that executes the Web server. You can then enter this name into the Web server box for a new project entry.

5. Leave the default selection of New Web Application and click Next. You are given the opportunity to pick a layout for the application. Because this example application is a simple, single-page application, you don't need a layout.
6. For the style of the project, leave the default selection of <none> and click Next. You don't need a theme for this project, so you can leave this default setting to <none> as well. However, since it's only an aesthetic change and doesn't interfere with the functioning of your Web database application, feel free to choose one.

You have now entered all the options for a simple project. The New Project Wizard has only four stages to select for creation. Click the Finish button. Visual InterDev begins building the project and all of its associated files. After the build is complete, you have the foundation of the project, as shown in Figure 5-4.

After the basic project generation, you can now add the code and the proper connections to the database. You can save the project now and it will automatically be created as an application on the Web server. To begin the actual project construction, you will need to add a data source to access the Northwind database.

1. Select Project | Add Data Connection, which displays the Select Data Source dialog box, for selecting a connection (see the following illustration).

   Creating a new connection requires you to select the NWind.mdb file. Once the connection is created, it can be used within the Data Environment for the entire project.

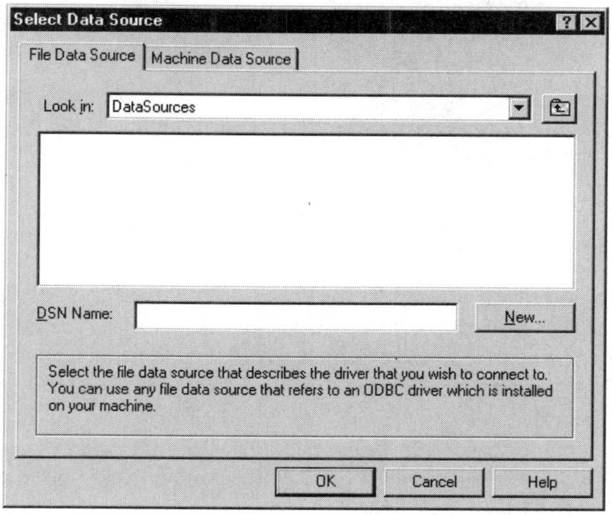

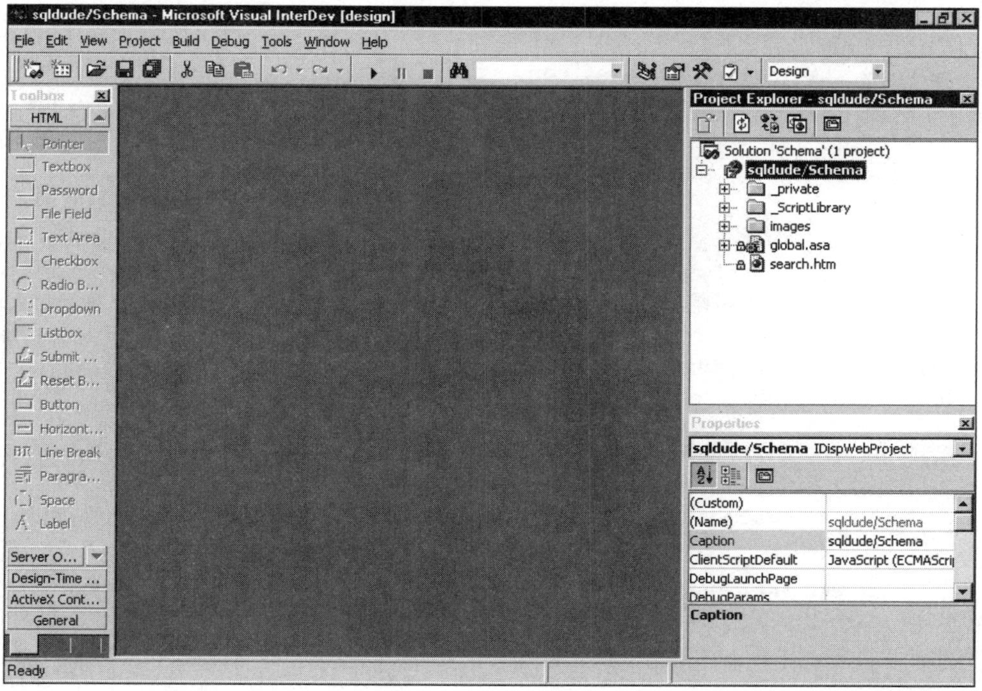

Figure 5-4. The new project automatically creates several files

2. Click New, which displays the dialog box that enables you to select the driver to use. In this case, the program needs to use the MS Access driver, so make that selection and then click Next.
3. For the filename, enter **schemaODBC** and then click Next. You have completed the basic configuration for the creation of the data source.
4. Click the Finish button.
5. Click the Select button and select the NWind.mdb source.

You must make one more change to the data source from the Advanced Options dialog box. For this simple schema example, you really don't need to change the default of 3 for the possible number of threads available through the connection. Nonetheless, you're going to alter it, which will help you remember to change this parameter when you create your own connections. Because an ASP session doesn't time out for 20 minutes and many developers place the connection reference in the Session, it doesn't take much to make all connections unavailable. To solve this problem, simply increase the maximum number of threads available for the driver, as follows:

1. Click the Advanced button and select the Threads parameter.
2. Set this parameter to 10 and click OK.
3. Click OK to create the ODBC connection. After you create the connection, you are returned to the data source selection window, in which you must set the source that you just created to be used in the Data Environment.

NOTE: For a File Data Source, the actual connection string for the data source is stored in a binary file called DataEnvironment.asa that is added to your project. Since it is part of your project, it is transported with the project if you move it to another machine. Visual InterDev simply reads the information from this file rather than resort to the file data source. This is referred to as a *DSN-less connection.*

A Machine Data Source, in contrast, uses the actual ODBC data source and must therefore exist on all machines that use the application. When deploying the application, you must make sure that the connections you use are replicated on the deployment server.

4. Select the schemaODBC source and click OK. The Connection Properties dialog box is displayed (see the following illustration). Notice that the Project Explorer window now contains entries for the Data Environment, with the connection in the Global.asa file.

This Connection Properties window provides a GUI for most of the settings that you normally make through the properties of the Connection object. You need to name the connection so that it can be used from the ASP code you will write. A good idea is to give the connection name a prefix of *dec,* for *data environment connection,* so that the object being referred to within the code is immediately apparent.

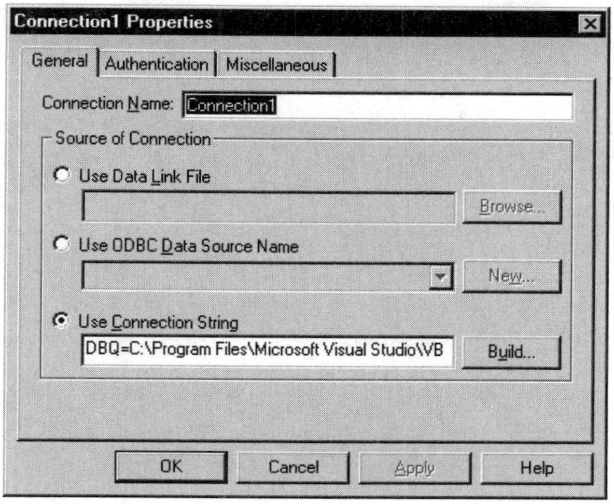

5. Set the connection name to **decSchema**.
6. Select the Miscellaneous tab, which contains the setting for the location of the cursor to be used with the connection. The default setting is to use client-side cursors. However, because you want your solution to be available for any Web browser—not just Internet Explorer, with its DHTML capabilities—you need to make the cursor execute on the server.
7. Set the Cursor Location to **2**. Use server-side cursors.
8. Click OK. You now have a complete data setup for this project.

After you add the main ASP page to display the schema of the structures, the application will be complete.

Examining the Data Source

After the data source is configured, Visual InterDev provides you with a method of examining both the structure of the source and its contents. The Data View window holds references to all the data sources that are being used within the current project (see Figure 5-5).

Expand the Northwind database in Data View and examine some of the tables and views it contains. Simply double-clicking a table or view item opens a browsing grid that is populated by data stored in the structure. In Figure 5-5, both the Orders and Order Details tables are open to show their current contents. Through Data View, you can see the fields that the application will detail.

Setting Up a Default Page

The data source is properly configured, but you haven't added the central ASP file that is needed to display the schema. Visual InterDev includes the Site Diagram feature, which

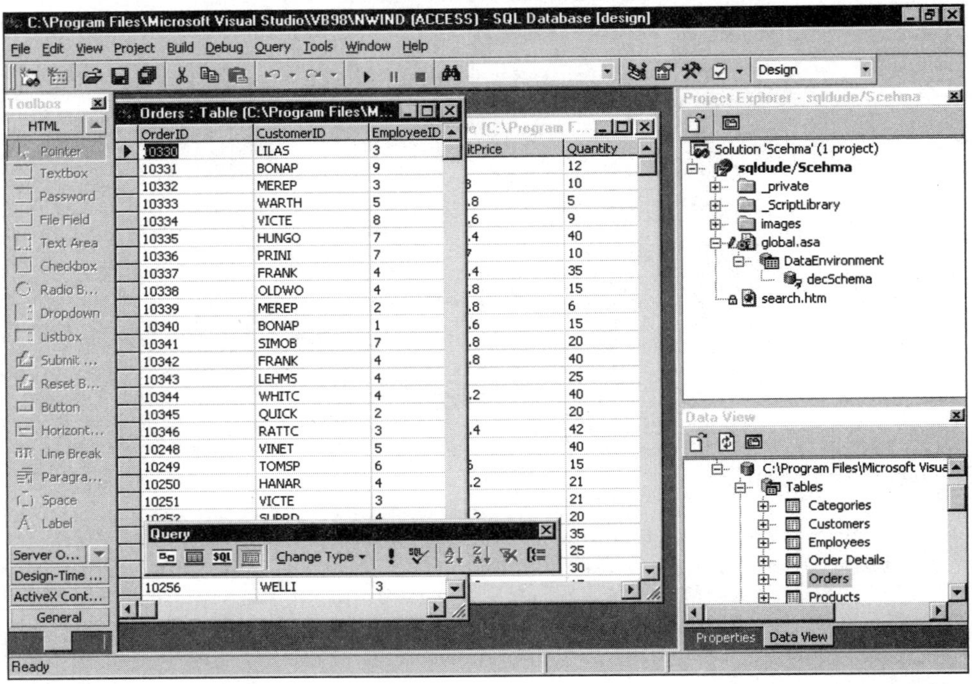

Figure 5-5. Visual InterDev provides the Data View window for you to examine the structure and contents of data sources

offers an attractive and functional way to maintain your application. A site diagram is a graphical display of each page in the project and its relation to the other files.

In the following steps you will create the default page for the application using a site diagram. With IIS properly configured, the Default.asp page you add to the project will, by default, be executed when the application is accessed.

1. Highlight the (Web server)/Schema entry in the upper-right portion of the Project Explorer pane.
2. Create a new diagram by selecting the Site Diagram option under Project | Add Web Item.
3. Click the Open button to create the site diagram. The Site Diagram tool provides the GUI to arrange the project. In this case, the project consists of only a single page, titled Home, which you can see in the Diagram window.
4. Replace the word Home with **Schema**.

5. Right-click the Schema object and select the Property Pages option.
6. Make sure the URL is set to **Default.asp** and click OK.
7. Double-click the Schema item in the site diagram; click Yes to save the changes. This opens the HTML page for editing. Since this is an ASP file, it opens with the bottom tabs set to Source mode, by default, to show the ASP code. You need to add some basic layout text to present the page, which is easiest to do from Design mode.
8. Select the Design tab and enter some introductory text. The introductory text should generally explain what the application shows (see Figure 5-6). You should at least enter a minimal description, even on your test pages, because HTML makes adding text so easy. This way, the functionality of quick ASP test applications that you generate can be identified months after you create them.

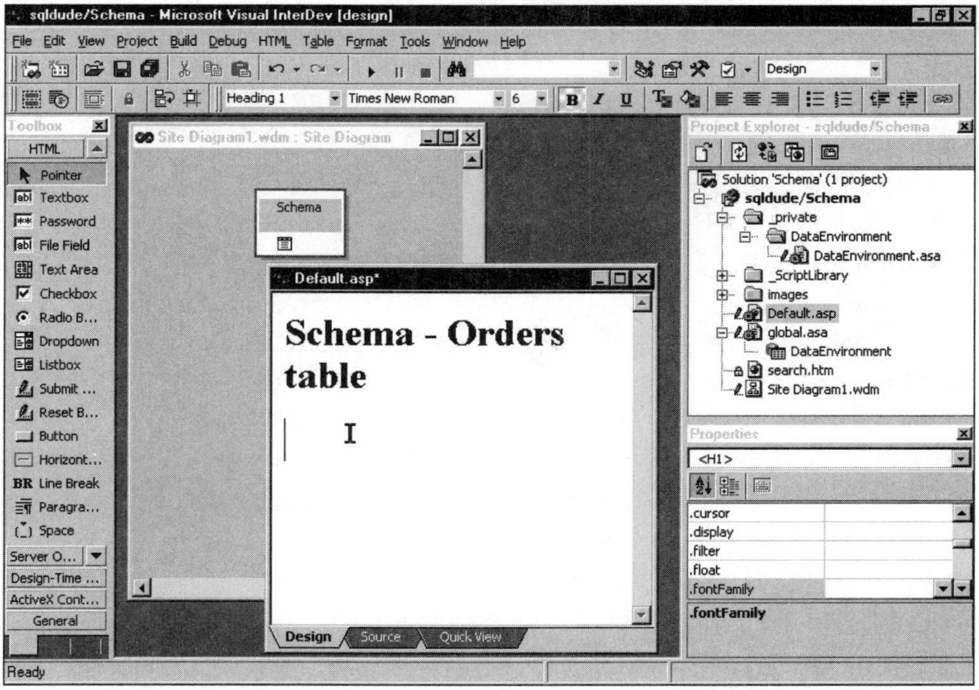

Figure 5-6. The Site Diagram tool allows you to open the file to enter some default text

You will be displaying the schema of the Orders table in an HTML table. From Design view, you can create an attractive table. In this case, since you will be using the special `OpenSchema` method, the table is coded by hand.

NOTE: Because you are using the `OpenSchema` method here to generate a custom data set based on unique parameters, it is more convenient to populate the table with custom code. However, in Visual InterDev, you generally would use the server-side component Grid, which correctly fills in the data from a Data Environment connection, without any coding.

Adding the Schema Addressing Code

The schema to be returned by the `OpenSchema` method can be as robust or as limited as you want to specify it to be. In this example, only the following items will be returned:

- Field name
- Field size
- Field type

To capture these values, you only need to pass the argument `adSchemaColumns`(4) to the `OpenSchema()` method. This will return the following 28 fields:

CHARACTER_MAXIMUM_LENGTH	CHARACTER_OCTET_LENGTH
CHARACTER_SET_CATALOG	CHARACTER_SET_NAME
CHARACTER_SET_SCHEMA	COLLATION_CATALOG
COLLATION_NAME	COLLATION_SCHEMA
COLUMN_DEFAULT	COLUMN_FLAGS
COLUMN_GUID	COLUMN_HASDEFAULT
COLUMN_NAME	COLUMN_PROPID
DATA_TYPE	DATETIME_PRECISION
DESCRIPTION	DOMAIN_CATALOG
DOMAIN_NAME	DOMAIN_SCHEMA
IS_NULLABLE	NUMERIC_PRECISION
NUMERIC_SCALE	ORDINAL
ORDINAL_POSITION	TABLE_NAME
TABLE_SCHEMA	TYPE_GUID

The fields may contain all the information for all the tables in the connection. Since this application needs to display only part of the field data, only the following three columns are used: COLUMN_NAME, DATA_TYPE, and CHARACTER_MAXIMUM_LENGTH.

When the `OpenSchema` command returns the recordset, it will contain all the fields for all the tables. For this example, because you want to display only the data for the Orders table, you need to use a filter on the recordset.

You only need to insert the code that isn't supplied by the Visual InterDev creation (see Figure 5-7). The application will be able to open the schema of the database, filter the Orders table's values, and display the various fields and types within an HTML table.

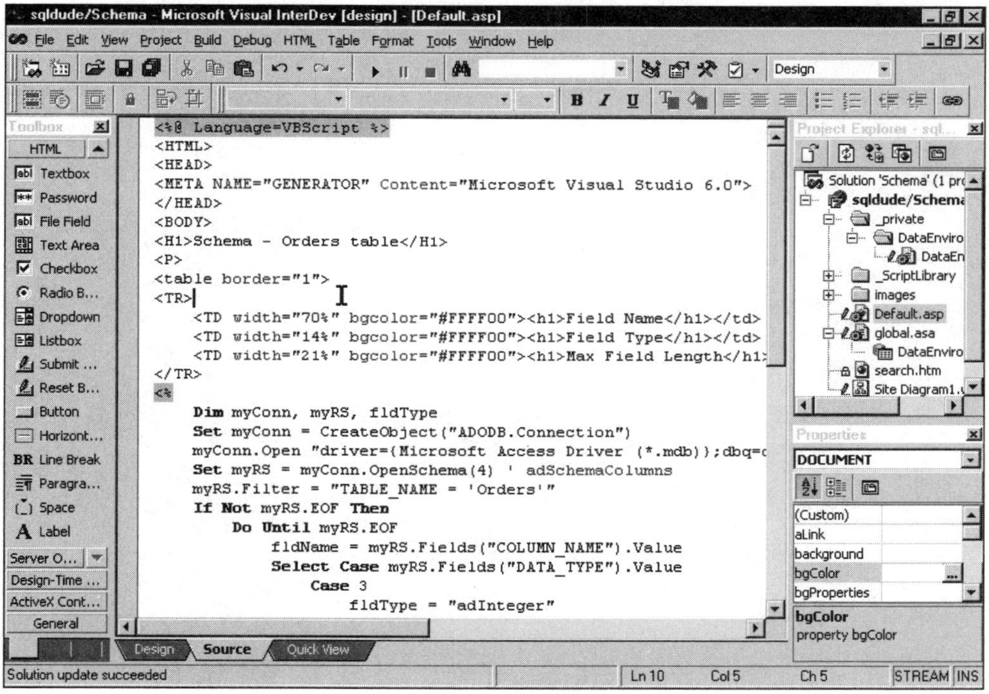

Figure 5-7. The code is placed in the Default.asp file

Click the Source tab and enter the following code, which adds a new record and writes information into the database:

```
<%@ Language=VBScript %>
<HTML>
<HEAD>
<META NAME="GENERATOR" Content="Microsoft Visual Studio 6.0">
</HEAD>
<BODY>
<H1>Schema - Orders table</H1>
<P>
<table border="1">
<TR>
   <TD width="70%" bgcolor="#FFFF00"><h1>Field Name</H1></TD>
   <TD width="14%" bgcolor="#FFFF00"><h1>Field Type</H1></TD>
   <TD width="21%" bgcolor="#FFFF00"><h1>Max Field Length</H1></TD>
</TR>
<%
    ' Create object variables
    Dim myConn, myRS
    ' Create and open a connection
    Set myConn = Server.CreateObject ("ADODB.Connection")
    myConn.Open "driver={Microsoft Access Driver (*.mdb)};" & _
        dbq=c:\Program Files\Microsoft Visual Studio\VB98\nwind.mdb"
    ' Open the schema to only return information about the columns (fields)
    Set myRS = myConn.OpenSchema(4) ' adSchemaColumns
    ' Filter the information so only the Orders table is shown
    myRS.Filter = "TABLE_NAME = 'Orders'"
    ' Make sure there are records in the recordset
    If Not myRS.EOF Then
        Do Until myRS.EOF
            ' Get the name of the current field
            fldName = myRS.Fields("COLUMN_NAME").Value
            ' Convert the data type number into a text description
            Select Case myRS.Fields("DATA_TYPE").Value
                Case 3
                    fldType = "adInteger"
                Case 10
                    fldType = "adError"
                Case 129
                    fldType = "adChar"
                Case 131
                    fldType = "adNumeric"
                Case 135
                    fldType = "adDBTimeStamp"
                Case Else
                    fldType = "Unknown"
            End Select
            ' Convert the field size to a string
            fldSize = CStr("" & myRS.Fields("CHARACTER_MAXIMUM_LENGTH").Value)
```

```
            ' If the string is empty, add a descriptor
            if Len(fldSize)=0 Then fldSize="N/A"

            ' Output values as rows in the HTML table
            Response.Write("<TR><TD>" & fldName & "</TD>")
            Response.Write("<TD>" & fldType & "</TD>")
            Response.Write("<TD>" & fldSize & "</TD></TR>")
            ' Advance to the next record
            myRS.MoveNext
        Loop
    End If
    ' Close and eliminate the objects
    myRS.Close
    myConn.Close
    Set myRS = Nothing
    Set myConn = Nothing
%>
</table>
</BODY>
</HTML>
```

Using a Staging Server

The server on which the application is finally placed for use by an organization is called the *deployment server*. For development, it is important to have a *staging server* that has the same software configuration as the deployment server.

DEFINITION: **Staging server** A server used for development that has the same setup as the final deployment server.

The following list contains problems that you might encounter when using the deployment server for development purposes.

- **Connection usage** If you are working with a database, your experimentation can use up a limited number of ODBC connections to the data source. Developers tend to bring up and drop sessions often. Unless all of the pooling connection guidelines are strictly followed, such as creating and destroying ADO objects after each page access, the application can fault by reserving all of the connections, making none available for your regular users.
- **Resources usage** Most development is strenuous on the system resources, because tests are being made to determine the outside parameters of system capability. The extra strain can seriously impede the speed of response, negatively affecting the experience of your users.
- **Data corruption** Early testing against a real data source is a very bad idea if any type of data modification can occur. A solution being built rarely has all the pieces in place to prevent a partially successful operation from committing these changes to authentic data.

- **Web server crash** It is very possible to crash the Web server itself due to a bug, especially if you are developing ActiveX DLLs for use with your application.

Most developers instinctively use a staging server, particularly because it can be installed on a local machine rather than a remote machine that may be maintained by someone else. Using a staging server, however, does create some of its own problems when the application needs to be moved to the deployment server. If an organization outsources the Web-serving operations to a third party, then proper consideration for mimicking the setup of the deployment server on the staging server can save a great amount of time.

The following short list includes some of the items that you must make sure transfer properly for your application to execute. If you transfer the application and it doesn't work, take a moment to consider each of these items and verify that you have completed it.

- **Database permissions** Most commonly, the database server has not had the permissions properly set, and the connections in the data environment attempt either an invalid account login or incorrect password. Check that the permissions, users, and groups on the deployment server match those on the staging server.
- **Application setup** Within IIS, the directory must be created and configured to hold the application. Make sure that execution privileges are set properly on the directory. Most often, only script execution privileges must be granted. Do not activation the full execution option unless a Java application or CGI must be run from that directory.
- **FrontPage Server Extensions** Visual InterDev cannot copy the application to the Web server unless the right version of the FrontPage Server Extensions is installed. If you installed the Windows NT Option Pack 4, you should already have the FP Extensions available on your Web server. If not, make sure you install them prior to executing Visual Interdev. Without these extensions, Visual Interdev is seriously handicapped and you will have to copy or FTP the files manually.
- **ODBC source** The ODBC connection that you use in your database application must be present on the deployment server. If it is a file Data Source Name (DSN), the file must exist on the designation system, whereas a machine or system DSN requires that you manually configure the source.
- **Directory permissions** If you are using the FileSystemObjects, make sure that the directory that you are trying to access has the correct permissions set to it. If your code will seek to write to that directory, be sure that write permissions are enabled for a Web user.

With all of the programming complete, you now need to place the application on the Web server. Visual InterDev actually does most of the work for you. As long as the project was created in Master Mode, each time that you save it, the new version is automatically updated on the Web server.

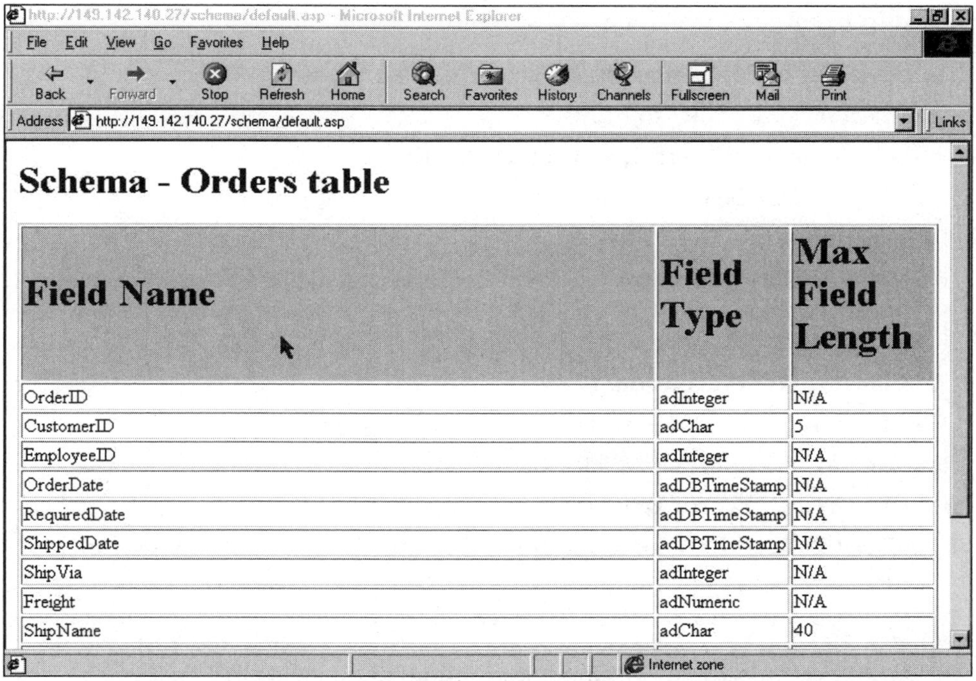

Figure 5-8. The Schema application will execute to display the structure of the Orders table in the Web browser

Execute the application in your Web browser. It should appear similar to the page shown in Figure 5-8. All the fields, field types, and sizes will be displayed in the table.

Adding the Application to Visual SourceSafe

The application can be added to Visual SourceSafe (VSS) very easily, because if you have VSS installed, it is automatically integrated into Visual InterDev. To provide you with an overview of the current projects that are under source code control, it is usually best to have Visual SourceSafe Explorer executing. To execute SourceSafe Explorer, choose Project | Source Control | SourceSafe.

NOTE: When Visual SourceSafe is executed, the default username is set to Administrator. However, the default Administrator account is actually labeled *admin*. If this is the first time that you've executed VSS, enter **admin** in the username text box and leave the password box empty. This should allow you entry, because it is the configuration default.

After you log in to VSS Explorer, return to Visual InterDev. All of the project files can be added from within Visual InterDev, as follows:

1. Select the folder icon in the All Projects frame of the window.
2. Select File | Create Project.
3. Set the name to **WebSchema** and click OK.
4. Click the WebSchema folder.
5. Return to Visual InterDev.
6. Right-click the first entry in Project Explorer that is titled Solution 'Schema' (1 project). It asks whether you want to add just the selection or the whole current solution.
7. Click the Solution button.
8. Click OK to accept the password.
9. Enter **WebSchema** and click OK.
10. Click Yes to create a new project.
11. Click OK to add to source control. The Enable Source Control window is displayed.
12. Click OK to add the project to Source Code Control.
    The process may take a few minutes as all the project files are added to the SourceSafe library. If prompted for individual file inclusion, click OK to accept their addition, but make certain the check box labeled Keep checked out is checked, so that you can continue to easily modify the project.
13. Reactivate the SourceSafe application.
14. Collapse and re-expand the main folder.
    You should now see your project added to the list of projects. Since this is the complete version 1 of the project, you should label it as such. A label enables you to examine all the files under a single, labeled version and even rebuild a set of files from a particular labeled version.
15. Right-click the WebSchema project item and select Label from the context menu.
16. For the label, set it to Version 1.0. Add any comments that you feel are appropriate. You might include a brief statement about the objectives of the project, for easy reference later.
17. Click the OK button.

This will label the version. To examine the versions that you have stored, simply select Tools | Show History. Checking the box labeled Labels only displays all the projects that you have supplied with a label.

> ***TIP:*** Source code control is almost essential for a team project, but even if you're working alone, you'll find that VSS is worth its weight in gold if used systematically. By regularly checking your files into the library, you'll have a record of all the changes made to a file.
>
> It has been my experience that clients often decide they don't want a particular feature, and just as you finish removing it, they decide they really want it after all. With Visual SourceSafe, you can retrieve the excised code in a matter of minutes.

You can add project files by hand either through the SourceSafe Administrator application or by right-clicking the file you intend to add. You can even add files outside the project, such as the documentation or supplemental graphics and imagining files. Although these files cannot be used effectively for difference comparison, they will be kept archived with the rest of the project.

The default folder for projects is in the Profiles directory on a Windows NT machine. On my machine, the pathway of the project is as follows:

```
C:\WinNT\Profiles\Administrator\Personal\Visual Studio Projects\Schema
```

With the application logged in to Visual SourceSafe, be sure to perform a check-in and check-out regularly, to update the archived version.

Q&A

Q: Is it better to create a Connection object for a recordset or to allow the implicit creation to take place?

A: The explicit creation of a recordset is justified in cases where several recordsets or commands must address the same data source. That way, the re-creation of the session isn't necessary. If only a single recordset is used on the page or each recordset accesses a different source, then let the implicit connection be used.

Q: What functionality is lost if I develop an ASP application without automatic updates (Local Mode) to the Web server?

A: The only difference is that you have to select the Deploy option manually to update the central Web site.

Q: Can connection pooling be done through ADO?

A: Connection pooling occurs through the ODBC drivers, so a direct interface to a data source does not provide connection pooling. However, one of the advantages of using Microsoft Transaction Server (MTS) is the ability to pool connections on the server. Later on, when you begin constructing the ActiveX DLL components and deploying them to MTS, you will see how these features can be used.

SUMMARY

Using the ADO objects in a Web database solution is not difficult, but a Web application has different requirements than a normal client/server application. You saw how simple implementations of each of the primary ADO objects can be accomplished. By using Visual InterDev, creating full-featured Web database solutions is dramatically simplified with the availability of the Data Environment and server-side components. In this chapter, you covered:

- **Connection pooling** ODBC has the capability to allocate to a data source a certain number of connections that can be assigned to objects as they request connections. This eliminates much of the overhead related to creating and destroying the connections.
- **Visual InterDev development** Using the Data Environment, you created a connection for use in a Web database project.
- **Site diagram** Within Visual InterDev, a site diagram can be created that graphically displays the structure of a Web application. Through the site diagram, you can add new pages or restructure and InterDev will manage items such as the connecting links.
- **Schema** The schema denotes the actual structure of database objects, such as tables and views. The `OpenSchema` method on the Connection object allows the structure to be queried and returned in a recordset.
- **Multipage applications** Since most Web applications exist across multiple ASP pages, appropriate design is extremely important. Taking the opening steps of drawing a rough diagram of the solution before you begin construction can literally save you hours of revision later.
- **Staging vs. Deployment Servers** A staging server is the server that should be used for development. It should mirror the general capabilities of the server on which the final solution will finally be deployed. The deployment server is the actual application will be made available for the users. The application should not be moved from the staging server to the deployment server until it is well tested.

CHAPTER 6

Drill-Down Interactive Report Application

One of the most powerful features of the Web, aside from instant publishing, is the ability to provide interaction. Although the return on investment is high for any report that is generated as a Web page (instead of distributed on paper), paperless reports only begin to tap the advantages of a Web solution. By having an interactive report, the viewer can take advantage of the following options:

- **Filtering for effective summaries** Only information that needs to be seen can be reviewed, so extraneous data doesn't cloud understanding
- **Requery possibilities** Report parameters can be instantly altered to examine the information from different angles
- **Large data quantities** Information that might require a thousand-page printed report can be presented in a navigable online form
- **Accessibility** Information that was previously hard to locate (in archives) can remain and be accessed online
- **Searchability** Advanced interactive reports can provide searching capabilities for locating specific data

The most common implementation of interactive reports is the drill-down report. These reports provide top-level summaries that the user can progressively work down through, until specific details are reached. Usually this method of reporting requires dynamic pages that alter the data query to show the selected information.

DEFINITION: **Drill-down** The idea of drilling down into data means that you select one part of a summary and progress to the finer details. Each selection will bring you closer to the actual figures summarized at the higher steps.

In this chapter, you'll again use the Northwind database as the foundation on which to build an application. The report that the application generates will be displayed in a table format (see Figure 6-1). Selections can be made by clicking on the links within the table or by selecting an item from the Option menu to further refine the choices of what will be displayed in the report.

The application will query the Northwind database to retrieve orders by month or by employee and will allow the user to drill down to see the exact items of each order. The solution presented in this chapter is complicated by the fact that it actually reuses ASP display pages to maximize the scripting code and minimize the number of ASP pages that must be maintained. Therefore, a single ASP page file will display several different resultant pages.

This example application demonstrates very effective use of an interactive report that could be easily accessed from anywhere on an intranet or even from the Internet. However, it also highlights some of the shortcomings of drill-down reports:

- **Possible inaccurate understanding** Since the ideal of the drill-down report is a refined examination, the user runs the risk of focusing on unimportant data or missing a higher-level understanding that might be possible if the data were viewed all at once.

- **Difficulty for output** With the information altered by the user selection, overviews are difficult to print. A single session may examine a dozen or more aspects of a given dataset, making printing each query difficult. A single report could make it easier to generate hard-copy reports.
- **Additional server processing required** Since the alterations to a page query will be sent back to the server for reevaluation, the server must do more processing than it would for a static report or a one-time generated dynamic report.

The technology available through ASP, ADO, and Visual Studio make a drill-down application reasonably cost-effective to create. The connection to the data source is easily facilitated through the Data Environment tool available in Visual InterDev. The Data Environment will help create the proper ADO objects to retrieve the desired data.

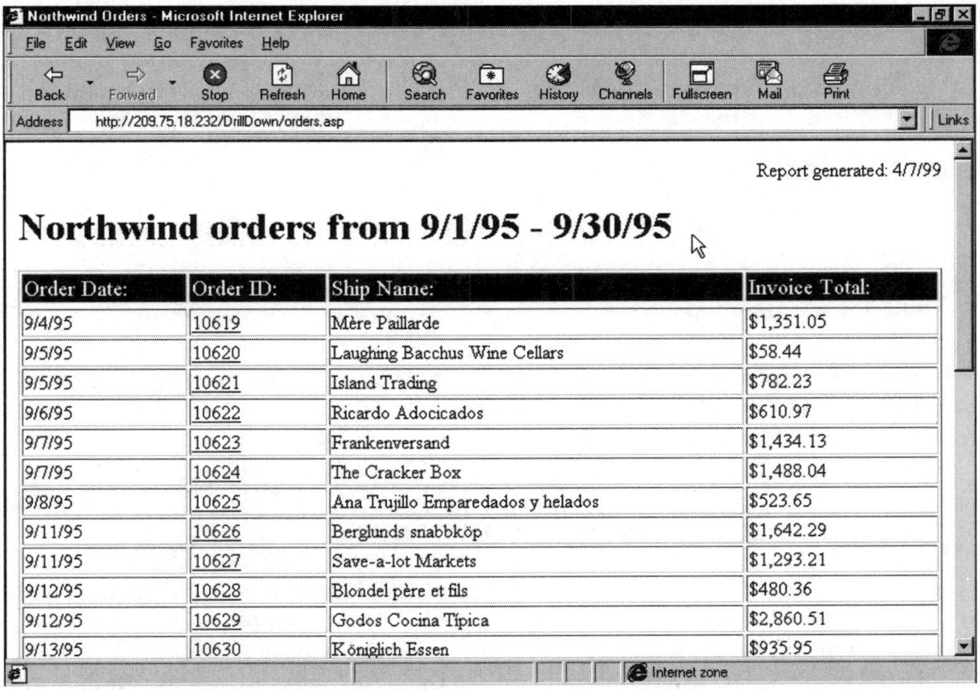

Figure 6-1. The final interactive report will be displayed in a table

As the user selects options and submits them to alter the report, ASP code examines the request and requeries the data. Most of the pages are then constructed using the `Write` method of the Response object.

THE NORTHWIND REPORT

The drill-down application will do much more than simply allow users to examine the order information. The Northwind Interactive Report will retrieve data from the Northwind database and display it in the following series of four page types:

- **Order by Month Summary** All of the orders that occurred during the selected month will be displayed. Each order will have a link that permits further drilling down.
- **Order by Employee Summary** Each employee name is displayed with the corresponding number of orders that they have made. Drilling down allows the orders for a particular employee to be viewed.
- **Actual Orders with Totals** When a series of orders is examined, whether they are orders for a particular employee or month, the summary information for each order is displayed. The order is summarized to provide a total dollar amount for the order, as well as a link allowing the viewer to drill down further to the items contained in the order.
- **Order Details** The details of the order are all displayed on the details page, with information such as customer name, shipping address, order items, and so on. This is the final level of drilling down available in this implementation of the application.

The first three selections, by month, by employee, and by invoice number, sit at the top level of the application. These reports will allow viewers to drill down to the actual orders that are behind the summaries. Since the Order Details page accepts different query options from the higher pages in order to display the correct order, that page is common to all of the selections.

APPLICATION STRUCTURE OVERVIEW

To properly implement any Web solution, you should begin by sketching a rough diagram of your design. Since a project will usually extend over multiple ASP pages, a simple diagram will help you immeasurably in conceiving the basic design.

In Figure 6-2, you can see the basic layout of the Northwind Interactive Report application, based on the pages that need to be created. The arrows in the diagram indicate whether the flow occurs through information entered into HTML forms or whether the

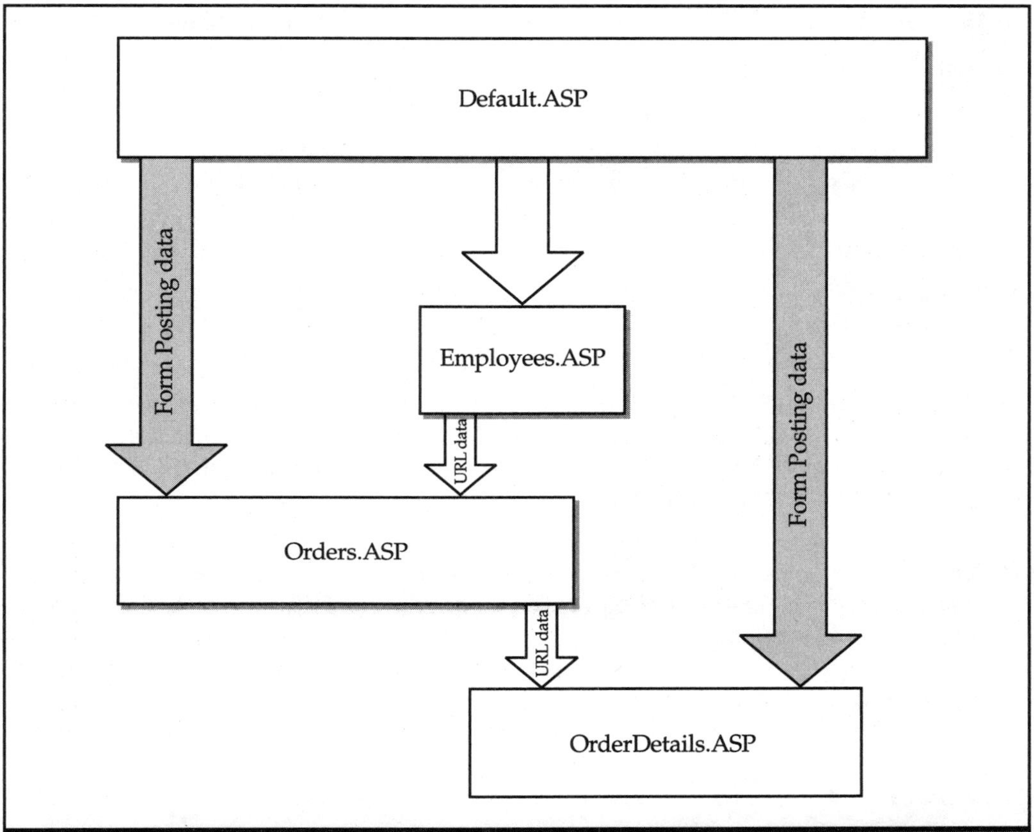

Figure 6-2. The application sketch of your drill-down application should show all the basic pages you will need

query specifications are held in the URL (as `QueryString` properties). Note that form data cannot be held in a bookmark, nor can it be easily included in a hyperlink. Arrows are used to demonstrate how the pages will be interconnected.

After the diagram is complete, it is usually a good idea to list the pages that you will be creating and determine the data sources that will need to be accessed. When when you actually begin the implementation, you will already know the fundamental elements that will be required from your SQL statements.

The following pages are used in the solution for this example:

- **Default.ASP** This is the main page that will display the three possible options for the report. This page accepts input for the Monthly report (month and year), the Employees report, and the Invoice/Order report (the order number) and passes them to subsequent ASP pages.

- **Employees.ASP** This page presents a list of all of the employees and the number of orders attributed to each. Selecting a drill-down link from any of the employees displays a summary of the orders that the employee participated in making.
- **Orders.ASP** This page displays a list of orders and their total amounts for either a specified month or employee ID. It receives information from either the URL (through the `QueryString`) passed by the employees.asp page or from the form (on the Default.asp page).
- **OrderDetails.ASP** The details of an order include both the top-level summary information (the customer, shipping address, and so on) as well as an itemized list of all the items sold in that order.

These four pages work together to provide the interactive solution that you'll build in this chapter. The creation of each page is facilitated by accessing ADO through pages constructed using Visual InterDev. Now that you have an understanding of the overall structure, you can begin creating the solution.

> ***TIP:*** Writing out a list of data structures to be accessed by the pages will also clarify which tables could be optimized with indexes. Even a cursory examination of this implementation allows you to see that the data retrieved on the Orders.ASP page will be accessed the most, since many users will have no need to drill-down to the details level. This overview will help you in the initial stages of optimization before a true user load can be examined.

CREATING THE DRILL-DOWN APPLICATION

The drill-down report will use the sales data contained in the Northwind database. A drill-down report will allow a user of the application to progressively refine examination of the data. Two tables in the database define each order: the Order and Order Details tables. You have already reviewed the intended structure of the final application. Now it is important to examine the data source you will be addressing.

Northwind Database

When you used the Northwind database in the previous chapter, it was used simply as a generic data source to demonstrate some basic principles, such as the schema of an ADO data source. The data contained within the database was not actually retrieved for any useful purpose. This application will present the data in a meaningful way.

To actually implement the drill-down report that needs to be created, a closer examination of the structure of the database and the actual data is required. You will need to know how each table relates to the application. The following tables exist within the NWind.MBD file:

- **Orders** Contains summary information for each order, including who sold it, who bought it, when the sale occurred, where the order was shipped, and so on. This table is used extensively by the three reporting pages.

- **Order Details** Lists the items that were sold with each order. The relationship between this table and the Order table makes it possible to determine which products were sold with which order.
- **Products** Contains information about all of the stocked products. This table is used by the interactive report to generate the itemized order list.
- **Employees** Contains all of the information about who sold a particular order.
- **Customers** Contains customer information, including name, address, phone number, title, and so on.
- **Shippers** Identifies the shipping companies used to distribute the orders.
- **Suppliers** Links to the Products table to determine where the goods were purchased for Northwind. This table is not used by this application.
- **Categories** Describes several general categories used to specify the products. This table is not used by the drill-down application.

All of these tables are related and work together to manage the sales and inventory of Northwind Traders. In Figure 6-3, you can see the relationships between the various tables in the database. These relationships are critical to establishing an effective interactive report, because they allow the users to move down from a general level to specific data.

The most obvious interactive report that could be created from this dataset would display a list of all of the orders in the database. A click would then generate an HTML page of all the details for that particular order. Clicking the browser's Back button or selecting a Back link would return to the Default page, allowing the viewer to examine another order.

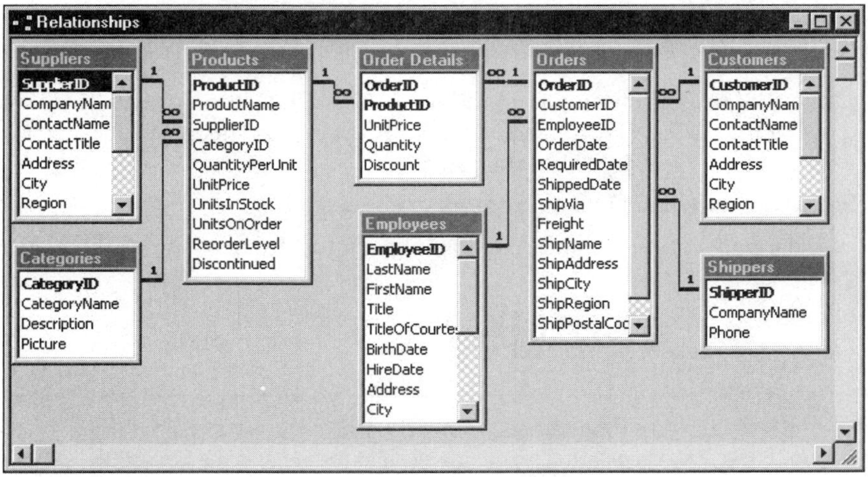

Figure 6-3. The relationships between the tables of the Northwind database are very clear

It is easy to see the usefulness of creating such an application, especially with a Web interface. From anywhere on the LAN, an authorized user could immediately examine not only a particular order, but all of the orders that took place within the same time frame. The simplicity and abilities of ADO, ASP, and Visual InterDev can allow you to create far more ambitious applications.

Starting a Visual InterDev Project

To begin creating the application, you will follow many of the same steps that you completed in Chapter 5. Essentially you will use Visual InterDev to create a connection to the Northwind database and then construct and add pages that use this connection to generate the HTML output that will be sent to the user.

As the first step for this project, start Visual InterDev and begin a new project by selecting the New Project option under the File menu. In the new project dialog box, select the standard Web project type and set the name to DrillDown. Once the project has been created, you will need a starting ASP page that will distribute the users to one of three directions. Before you start adding pages, it is always a good idea to begin a project by defining the necessary data sources that the application will use.

Adding the Database Connection

For this solution you will need a connection to the Northwind database. The data source is the same one you created in the last chapter. If you skipped the last chapter, return to the "Creating the Schema Examination Application" section and construct the schemaODBC source. You can recreate the data source with a more appropriate name or simply use it as it is. If you use a different name, make sure you alter the name when creating your connection for the report application.

Once the data source has been created, select the main Project item in the Project Explorer. Then follow these steps:

1. Under the Project menu, select the Add Data Connection option. This item will display the dialog box that allows you to select a connection. Use the one that was created in the previous chapter.
2. Select the schemaODBC data source, and click OK.
3. In the Connection Properties dialog box, set the name of the connection to decNWind.
4. On the Miscellaneous tab, set the cursor location to option number 2 (server-side cursors) and click OK.

TIP: The Project menu is dynamic and changes depending upon which item in the Project Explorer is selected. If the solution is selected, rather than one of the items in the project, the Connection and Command addition items do not appear in the Project menu. Therefore, if a menu item has gone missing from a menu, check which item is selected.

By default, the setting for the data source uses client-side cursors. Client-side cursors require the browser to be ActiveX-enabled and they support the DHTML specification compatible with Microsoft Internet Explorer. Therefore, in any solution that is not using the Remote Data Services (RDS) to allow for client-side data set interaction, you will need to change this property to server-side cursors.

Creating the Default Page

With the connection created, you need to create a home page for the application. Defining a general Web page project in Visual InterDev, as in Chapter 5, will not create a default Web page. Instead, you will begin generating your pages on the site diagram. Follow these steps:

1. Select Project | Add Web Item | Site Diagram.
2. Click the Open button to generate the diagram. Leave the primary page title as Home.
3. Right-click the Home item and select the Property Pages icon.
4. Set the URL of the page to Default.ASP.
5. Save the Site Diagram.

Your page should now look like the one shown in Figure 6-4.

The default Home page is just the first page to be added to the solution. You will need three other pages to display all of the necessary reports. Before you create the other pages, it will be best to add the text and hyperlinks that will be displayed on the home page.

Double-click the Home page to begin, and click the Design tab. Although the page will be dramatically changed as you implement the solution, we'll create temporary links that will allow you to properly test the names of the other pages and the soundness of the project. Enter some text (see Figure 6.5 for suggested text) and the following items:

- Northwind Sales by Month
- Northwind Sales by Employee
- Northwind Invoice/Orders Examination

Highlight each line in turn, and use the Link icon on the far right of the InterDev toolbar to set the hyperlink of each report. In the URL field of each report, replace the "http://" as follows:

- Set the URL for Sales by Month to Orders.ASP
- Set the URL for Sales by Employee to Employees.ASP
- Set the URL for Invoice/Order Examination to OrderDetails.ASP

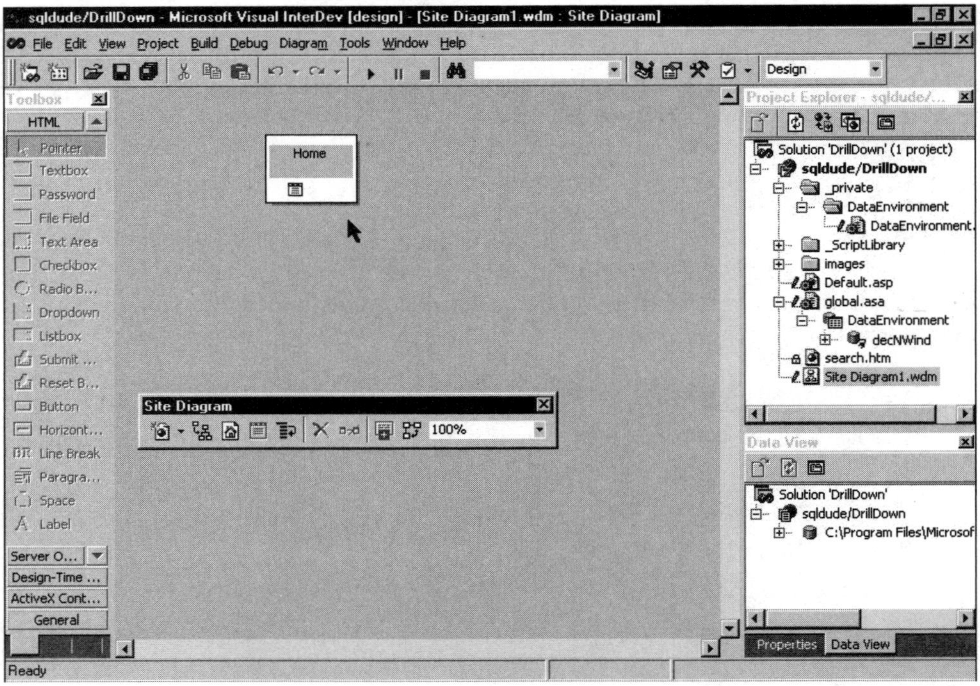

Figure 6-4. With the basic project set up, you are ready to begin constructing the report project

Your form should now look like the one shown in Figure 6-5. This page has the basic links to the three report pages.

Creating the Other Pages

When the Default page is complete in a basic form, the other pages need to be created. Follow these steps:

1. Return to the Site Diagram by selecting it from the Window menu.
2. Right-click on a blank area to show the Site Diagram context menu, and select the New ASP Page option.
3. Click on the text in the page box and set the title of the new page to Orders.
4. Right-click the page and select the Property Pages option.
5. Make sure the URL is set to Orders.ASP.

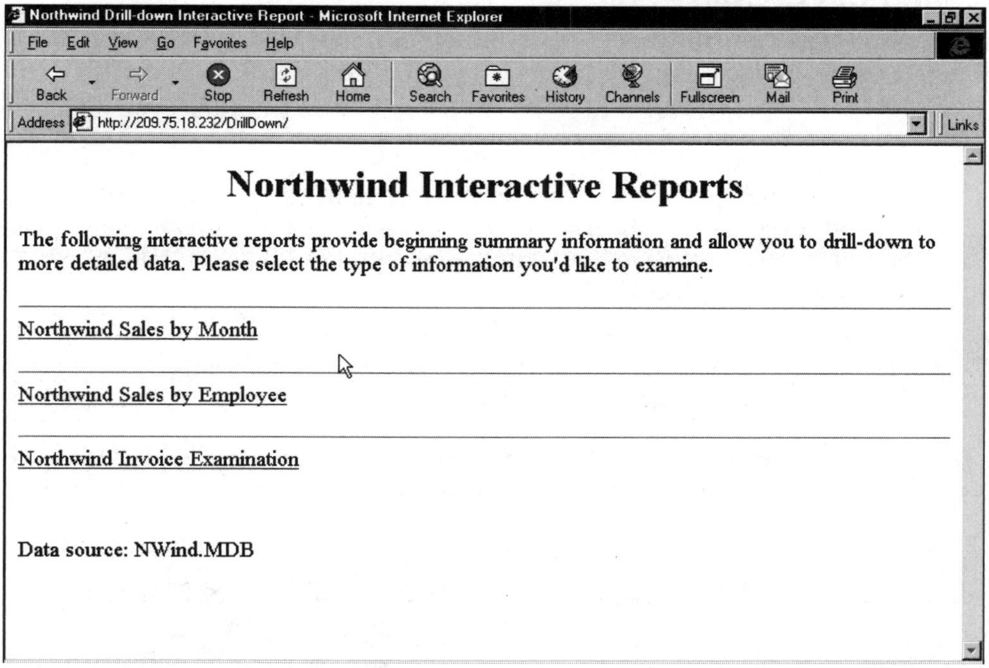

Figure 6-5. The complete design of the introductory page

When the Orders page is created, follow the same process to create and name the following pages:

- Employee Orders, named Employees.ASP
- Order Details, named OrderDetails.ASP

When you've completed creating all of the pages, your Site Diagram should show all four pages in the diagram window. To demonstrate one of the useful features of Visual InterDev, you can have the program check for broken links. Select View | Broken Links Report to determine whether you've set the project up correctly. If any broken links are displayed, you will need to alter either the filename of one of the pages you created or the link on the home page.

You will be editing these pages primarily in source mode to add the design elements. The Visual InterDev general page-design tools are not very effective, so for basic page design you might want to load the pages into the FrontPage Editor to create the look that you want for them.

Completing the Default Page

The Home page will actually provide the basic access for the other drill-down reports. In the form as you have it currently, it simply links to the three pages. The modifications described next will make it possible to enter a month and year on the Default page to be passed to the Orders page, or an invoice number to be passed to the Order Details page (as shown in Figure 6-6).

Because the existing plain links do work, you can choose to skip the modifications in this section and continue with the next section where the first report is actually created. Then, when all of the report pages are complete, you can come back and modify the Default page to access them properly.

NOTE: To debug your application, you must set a start page. Do this by right-clicking the Default page (Default.ASP) in the Project Explorer window and selecting the Set as Start Page option.

The following listing contains the final code for the home page. This code simply creates two forms: one for the Monthly report and one for the Invoice/Order report.

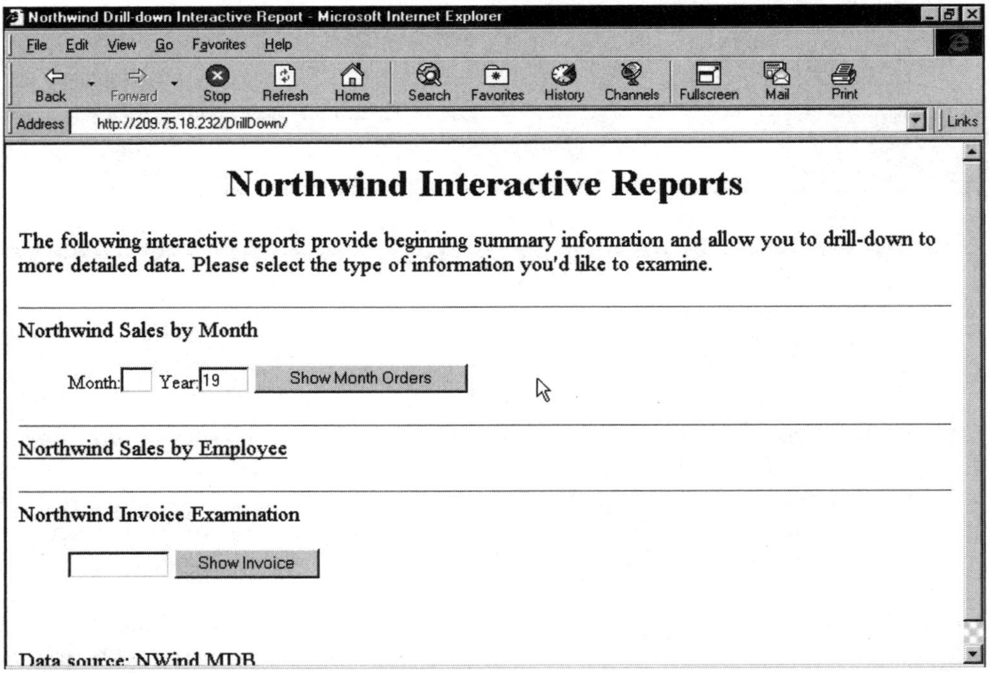

Figure 6-6. The Default page allows proper access to all three reports

These forms pass the necessary data directly to the Orders.ASP and OrderDetails.ASP files, respectively.

In the code, you can see that neither client nor server-side error checking is implemented in this solution. Because this is the first full Web database solution you've created, the code will be much more direct and clear without the error-checking routines. In a real solution, you would use a combination of the `On Error Resume Next` command and checking the Err object during questionable operations to provide error catching.

```
<%@ Language=VBScript %>
<HTML>
<TITLE>Northwind Drill-Down Interactive Report</TITLE>
<HEAD>
<META NAME="GENERATOR" Content="Microsoft Visual Studio 6.0">
</HEAD>
<BODY>
<H1 align=center>Northwind Interactive Reports</H1>

<P><FONT face="" size=4>The following interactive reports
provide beginning summary information and allow you to drill-down to
more detailed data. Please select the type of information you'd like
to examine.</FONT></P><P><HR>

    <FONT face="" size=4>Northwind Sales by Month</FONT>
    <Form method="POST" action="Orders.asp">
       <blockquote>
       Month: <Input type="Text" name="Month" size="2" value="09">
       Year: <Input type="Text" name="Year" size="4" value="1995">
       <Input type="submit" name="SubmitMonth" value="Show Month Orders">
       </blockquote>
    </FORM>
    <P><HR>
    <FONT face="" size=4><A href="Employees.asp">
    Northwind Sales by Employee</A></FONT>
    <P><HR>
    <FONT face="" size=4>
    Northwind Invoice Examination</FONT>
    <Form method="POST" action="OrderDetails.asp">
       <blockquote>
       <Input type="Text" name="OrderID" size="10">
       <Input type="submit" name="SubmitInvoice" value="Show Invoice">
       </blockquote>
    </FORM>

<P><FONT face="" size=4>Data source: NWind.MDB</FONT></P>
</BODY>
</HTML>
```

Completing the Orders Details Page

All of the reports ultimately need to drill-down to the detail level and address the order items, so constructing this page first makes the most sense. The Order Details page takes an Order ID, either from form input or through a query string. Once the ID is obtained, the program opens the connection provided by the Data Environment using the DERuntime object (described below).

Visual Interdev provides a way to access all of the objects for the Data Environment (DE) from code. These objects are available through the Data Environment Runtime or DERuntime object. Using the DERuntime, an Interdev program can use the connections, recordsets, commands, and other Data Environment structures to access the data sources. Using this object allows you to effectively combine the easy user interface provided by the DE while retaining the power of direct coding.

CAUTION: In some cases, Visual Interdev does not automatically activate the Data Environment runtime for the final application. This can cause the application to not execute properly. To turn on the DERuntime manually, there are 2 lines that are commented out in the Global.asa file that initialize the runtime. Uncomment them manually and the runtime will be activated when the solution executes.

When the connection is open, recordsets can be created to access the data source designated in the Data Environment. First, simple queries are made to determine the name of the employee that sold the order, the shipper of the order, and the name of the customer, obtained from those individual tables. An HTML table is then generated to display all of the general ordering data.

After the ordering data table is complete, another table is created to display the individual order items. This itemized HTML table will show all of the records linked to the given order.

As each item is displayed in the table, the total price is calculated. The amount of each item is added to the subtotal, which is then added to the freight costs to generate the total amount of the order. The final result is shown in Figure 6-7.

TIP: You might notice that the final sum for the order information is not found in the actual table. Since Northwind is merely a sample database, this doesn't matter, but in a real situation this would be a poor design choice. Keep in mind that whenever money or other critical information is involved, a final amount tendered should be stored in the database. Working up the total each time is a poor idea because prices and tax rates in your database may change—the source data itself is not a valid tracking method for determining final totals .

In Figure 6-7, you'll notice that the URL contains a query string that determines the order that is being shown. The actual application, however, can also accept the Order ID from information posted in a form. In Figure 6-8, you can see that the URL does not contain any query information. If you were to reload this page, unlike the query string access, you would be asked whether you wanted to repost the form data.

The next listing shows the code that makes the Order Details page work. Note that the opening lines of the ASP code check for the presence of query information and use a default Order ID if none is found. Due to the complexity of adding error checking to this ap-

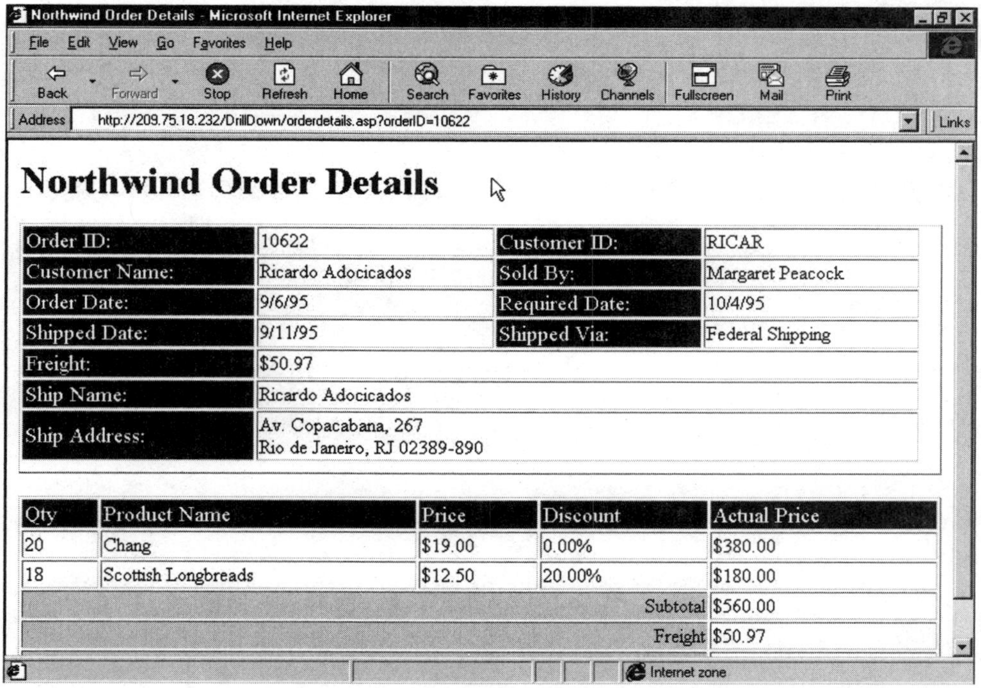

Figure 6-7. The Order Details page displays two tables that contain all of the information related to an order

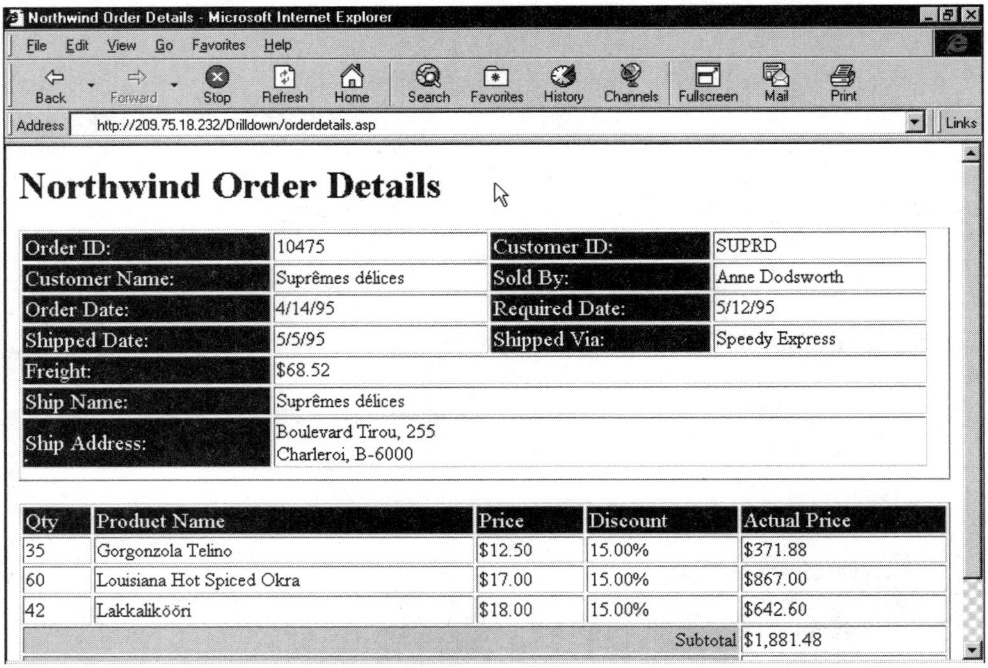

Figure 6-8. The Order Details page using the form information to display the order

plication, only this minimal device was included. The default Order ID also allows you to execute the page using the link you initially created from the Default page.

From Visual InterDev, enter source mode and add the following code to make your OrderDetails.ASP page match the following listing. When you are done, save the application in Visual InterDev and access it from the Web server.

```
<%@ Language=VBScript %>

<HTML>
<HEAD>
<TITLE>Northwind Order Details</TITLE>
</HEAD>
<BODY>
<H1>Northwind Order Details</H1>
<P>
```

```
<%
  ' Has either a query or form request been entered?
  If Len(Request.QueryString("OrderID"))=0 and _
     Len(Request.Form("OrderID"))=0 Then
     ' Use a known order if no info was supplied
     orderID = 10643
  Else
     ' If there is no query, use the form info
     If Len(Request.QueryString("OrderID"))=0 Then
        orderID = CLng(Request.Form("OrderID"))
     Else
        orderID = CLng(Request.QueryString("OrderID"))
     End If
  End If
  ' Create a variable reference for the connection
  Dim myConn
  ' Get the connection object from the Data Environment
  Set DE = Server.CreateObject("DERuntime.DERuntime")
  DE.Init(Application("DE"))
  Set myConn = DE.Connections(1)
  myConn.Open
  ' Check if the opening was successful and write the
  ' result to the client browser
  ' Possible values: adStateOpen(1), adStateClosed (0)
  If myConn.State = 1 Then
     Set orderRS = Server.CreateObject("ADODB.Recordset")
     Set orderRS.ActiveConnection = myConn

     ' Find the order that matches the specified OrderID
     orderRS.Source = "select * from Orders where OrderID=" & orderID
     ' Open the recordset
     orderRS.Open

     ' Set up a temporary recordset to use for quick queries
     Set tempRS = Server.CreateObject("ADODB.Recordset")
     Set tempRS.ActiveConnection = myConn

     ' Find out the name of the employee that sold the order
     employeeID = orderRS.Fields("EmployeeID").Value
     tempRS.Source = "select FirstName,LastName from Employees " & _
        "where EmployeeID=" & employeeID
     ' Open the recordset
     tempRS.Open
```

```
        soldBy = tempRS.Fields("FirstName").Value & _
           " " & tempRS.Fields("LastName").Value
        tempRS.Close

        ' Find the name of the shipping company
        shipID = orderRS.Fields("ShipVia").Value
        tempRS.Source = "select CompanyName from Shippers" & _
          " where shipperID=" & shipAD
        tempRS.Open
        shipVia = tempRS.Fields("CompanyName").Value
        tempRS.Close

        ' Find the name of the customer
        customerID = orderRS.Fields("CustomerID").Value
        tempRS.Source = "select CompanyName,ContactName " & _
         "from Customers where CustomerID='" & customerID & "'"
        tempRS.Open
        ' If there is no company name, use the contact
        If Len(tempRS.Fields("CompanyName").Value) = 0 Then
           customerName = tempRS.Fields("ContactName").Value
        Else
           customerName = tempRS.Fields("CompanyName").Value
        End If
        tempRS.Close

        shipName = orderRS.Fields("shipName").Value
        shipAddress = orderRS.Fields("shipAddress").Value & "<br>" & _
           orderRS.Fields("ShipCity").Value & ", " & _
           orderRS.Fields("ShipRegion").Value & "   " & _
           orderRS.Fields("ShipPostalCode").Value
        freight = orderRS.Fields("Freight").Value
        requiredDate = orderRS.Fields("RequiredDate").Value
        shippedDate = orderRS.Fields("ShippedDate").Value
        orderDate = orderRS.Fields("OrderDate").Value
        connectFlag = 1
     Else
        Response.Write("Error. Connection could not be opened.<P>")
        connectFlag = 0
     End If

%>
<TABLE border=1 height=48 width="100%">

    <TR>
```

```
        <td bgcolor="#0000FF"><font color="#FFFFFF">
<big>Order ID:
</big></font></td>
        <TD><%=orderID %></TD>
        <td bgcolor="#0000FF"><font color="#FFFFFF">
<big>Customer
ID:</big></font></td>
        <TD><%=customerID %></TD>
    <TR>
        <td bgcolor="#0000FF"><font color="#FFFFFF">
        <big>Customer Name:</big></font></td>
        <TD><%=customerName %></TD>
        <td bgcolor="#0000FF"><font color="#FFFFFF">
        <big>Sold By:</big></font></td>
        <TD><%=soldBy %></TD>
    <TR>
        <td bgcolor="#0000FF"><font color="#FFFFFF">
        <big>Order Date:</big></font></td>
        <TD><%=orderDate %></TD>
        <td bgcolor="#0000FF"><font color="#FFFFFF">
        <big>Required Date:</big></font></td>
        <TD><%=requiredDate %></TD>
    <TR>
        <td bgcolor="#0000FF"><font color="#FFFFFF">
        <big>Shipped Date:</big></font></td>
        <TD><%=shippedDate %></TD>
        <td bgcolor="#0000FF"><font color="#FFFFFF">
        <big>Shipped Via:</big></font></td>
        <TD><%=shipVia %></TD>
    <TR>
        <td bgcolor="#0000FF"><font color="#FFFFFF">
        <big>Freight:</big></font></td>
        <TD colspan="3"><%=FormatCurrency(freight) %></TD>
    <TR>
        <td bgcolor="#0000FF"><font color="#FFFFFF">
        <big>Ship Name:</big></font></td>
        <TD colspan="3"><%=shipName %></TD>
    <TR>
        <td bgcolor="#0000FF"><font color="#FFFFFF">
        <big>Ship Address:</big></font></td>
        <TD colspan="3"><%=shipAddress %></TD>
    </TR>
        </TABLE>
<P>
```

```
<TABLE border=1 height=48 width="100%">
    <%
       if connectFlag then
          ' Begin the first row for the details
      Response.Write("<TR>")
      ' Setup start and end formatting for the headings
      sTD = "<TD bgcolor=#0000FF><font color=#FFFFFF><big>"
      eTD = </big></font>"</TD>"
      Response.Write(sTD & "Qty" & eTD & sTD & _
         "Product Name" & eTD & sTD & "Price" & _
         eTD & sTD & "Discount" & eTD & sTD & _
         "Actual Price" & eTD & "</TR>")
      ' Begin a row for the data
      Response.Write("<TR>")
      Set myRS = Server.CreateObject("ADODB.Recordset")
      Set myRS.ActiveConnection = myConn
      myRS.Source = "select * from [Order Details] " & _
         " where Order=" & orderID

      myRS.Open
      If myRS.State = 1 Then
         Do Until myRS.EOF
            qty = myRS.Fields("Quantity").Value
            Response.Write("<TD>" & qty & "</TD>")
            Set myRS2 = Server.CreateObject("ADODB.Recordset")
            Set myRS2.ActiveConnection = myConn
            myRS2.Source = "select * from Products " & _
               " where ProductID=" & _
               myRS.Fields("ProductID").Value
            ' Open the recordset
            myRS2.Open
            If Not myRS2.EOF then
               Response.Write("<TD>" & _
                  myRS2.Fields("ProductName").Value _
                  & "</TD>")
               unitPrice = myRS.Fields("UnitPrice").Value
               Response.Write("<TD>" & _
                  FormatCurrency(unitPrice) & "</TD>")
            End If
            myRS2.Close

            discount = myRS.Fields("Discount")
            ' Calculate the total for the item
```

```
            itemTotal = qty * ((1-discount)* unitPrice)
            ' Add it to the invoice total
            total = total + itemTotal
            Response.Write("<TD>" & FormatPercent(discount) & "</TD>")
            Response.Write("<TD>" & _
                FormatCurrency(itemTotal) & "</TD>")
            Response.Write("</TR>")
            myRS.MoveNext
         Loop
      Else
         Response.Write("Error. " & _
                Command could not create recordset.<P>")
      End If
      Response.Write("<TR><TD align=right colspan=4" & _
        " bgcolor=#FFFF00>Subtotal</TD>")

      ' Format the total for currency and output
      Response.Write("<TD>" & FormatCurrency(total) & "</TD></TR>")

      Response.Write("<TR><TD align=right colspan=4" & _
        " bgcolor=#FFFF00>Freight</TD>")
      Response.Write("<TD>" & FormatCurrency(freight) & "</TD></TR>")
      Response.Write("<TR><TD align=right colspan=4" & _
        " bgcolor=#FFFF00>Total</TD>")
      Response.Write("<TD>" & _ &
         FormatCurrency(total + freight) & "</TD></TR>")
      myRS.Close
      ' Close the connection
      myConn.Close
   End If

   ' Eliminate the object references
   Set myConn = Nothing
   Set myRS = Nothing
   Set myRS2 = Nothing
   Set tempRS = Nothing
%>
</TABLE>
</BODY>
</HTML>
```

The Order Details page, although it provides error processing in the form of the default Order ID, was not meant to be accessed directly. Instead, it should receive an order request from the Orders.ASP page.

Completing the Orders Page

The Orders page is actually created to handle two types of queries: by month and by employee. If the Request object holds form information that specifies a month and a year, all of the orders for that month are shown in the output table. If an Employee ID is passed to the page through a QueryString object, all of the Orders sold by that employee are displayed.

This provides a very simple framework for changing the query to return almost any set of orders. Once the order type is determined, a string named `mySQL` is set to specify the query. The query contained in the string is used to populate the Orders HTML table. In Figure 6.9, you can see that the string was set to display all of the orders sold by one of the employees.

The table, itself, is interesting because within it, in the Order ID column, a link is created for each order. The link is custom set to access the OrderDetails.ASP page and pass

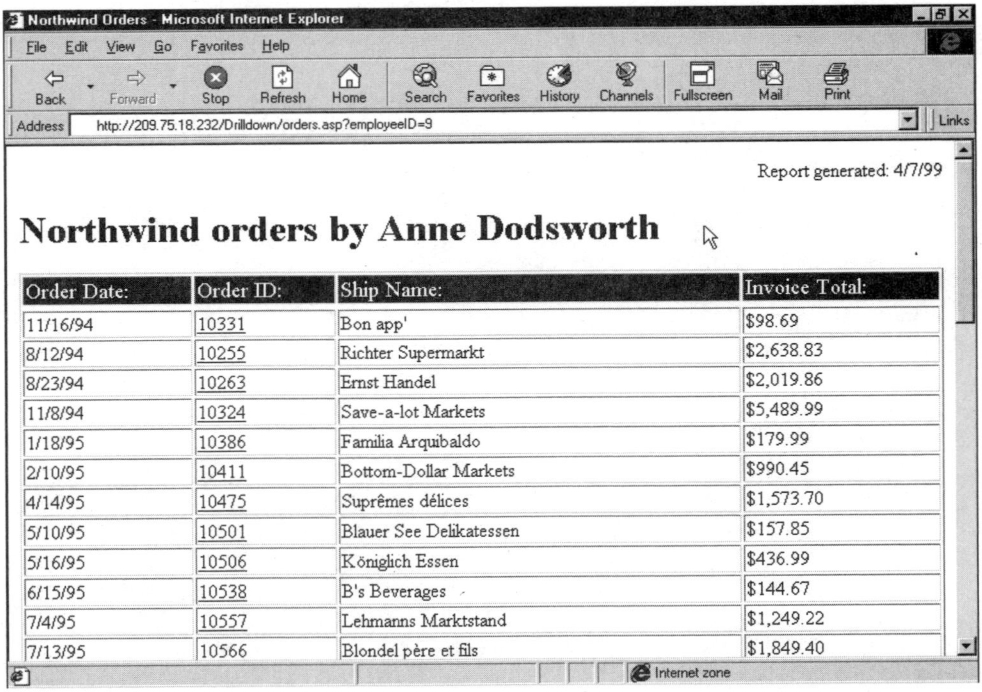

Figure 6-9. The Orders page generates a table containing all of the orders sold by an employee

the Order ID to be displayed. Using dynamically constructed links is one of the most effective ways of providing a solution with drill-down capabilities.

The code for the Orders.ASP page, shown in the following listing, displays all of the orders either for a particular month or employee. It is much simpler than the Order Details code you entered earlier—most of the complexity in this page occurs when the program needs to determine the date range for the month specified. This is most easily accomplished by using the `DateAdd( )` method, adding a month to the specified one, and then subtracting one day.

Enter the code in the listing and then test the page. Clicking on any of the links will take the browser directly to the details of that order.

```
<HTML>
<HEAD>
<TITLE>Northwind Orders</TITLE>
</HEAD>
<BODY>

<%
   ' If no parameters were passed, substitute
   ' samples that will work
   If Len(Request.Form("Month"))=0 and _
      Len(Request.QueryString("EmployeeID"))=0 Then
      sDate = "9/1/95"
      eDate = "9/25/95"
      dateFlag = 1
   Else
      ' Determine whether an employee or date query
      ' is requested
      If Len(Request.Form("Month"))=0 Then
         employeeID = CLng(Request.QueryString("EmployeeID"))
         dateFlag = 0
      Else
         ' Retrieve month and year values
         orderMonth = CLng(Request.Form("Month"))
         orderYear = CLng(Request.Form("Year"))
         sDate = orderMonth & "/1/" & orderYear
         eDate = DateAdd( "m", 1, sDate )
         eDate = DateAdd( "d", -1, eDate )
         dateFlag = 1
      End If
   End If

   Response.Write("<p align=right>Report generated: " & _
       Date & "</p>")
```

```
' Create a variable reference for the connection
Dim myConn
' Get the connection object from the Data Environment
Set DE = Server.CreateObject("DERuntime.DERuntime")
DE.Init(Application("DE"))
Set myConn = DE.Connections(1)
myConn.Open
' Check if the opening was successful and write the
' result to the client browser
' Possible values: adStateOpen(1), adStateClosed (0)
If myConn.State = 1 Then
   ' Place the correct header and SQL string depending on
   ' type of page generated.
   if dateFlag then
      Response.Write("<H1>Northwind orders from " & _
         FormatDateTime(sDate,0) & _
         " - " & FormatDateTime(eDate,0) & "</H1><P><P>")
      mySQL = "select * from Orders" & _
         " where orderDate > #" & sDate & _
         "# and orderDate < #" & eDate & "#"
   Else
      ' Get name of employee from Employees table
      Set tempRS = Server.CreateObject("ADODB.Recordset")
      Set tempRS.ActiveConnection = myConn
      tempRS.Source = "select FirstName,LastName from " & _
      "Employees where employeeID=" & employeeID
      ' Open the recordset
      tempRS.Open
      FullName = tempRS.Fields("FirstName").Value & _
         " " & tempRS.Fields("LastName").Value
      tempRS.Close

      Response.Write("<H1>Northwind orders by " & _
         fullName & "</H1><P><P>")
      mySQL = "select * from Orders" & _
         " where EmployeeID=" & EmployeeID
   End If


   Set orderRS = Server.CreateObject("ADODB.Recordset")
   Set orderRS.ActiveConnection = myConn
   orderRS.Source = mySQL
   ' Open the recordset
   orderRS.Open
```

```
    Else
       Response.Write("Error. Connection could not be opened.<P>")
    End If

%>
<TABLE border=1 height=48 width="100%">

    <TR>
        <TD bgcolor=#0000FF><font color=#FFFFFF>
         <big>Order Date: </big></font></TD>
        <TD bgcolor=#0000FF><font color=#FFFFFF>
         <big>Order ID: </big></font></TD>
        <TD bgcolor=#0000FF><font color=#FFFFFF>
         <big>Ship Name: </big></font></TD>
        <TD bgcolor=#0000FF><font color=#FFFFFF>
         <big>Invoice Total: </big></font></TD>
    </TR>
<%
    Do Until orderRS.EOF
       ' Get values of fields
       shipName = orderRS.Fields("shipName").Value
       freight = orderRS.Fields("Freight").Value
       orderDate = orderRS.Fields("OrderDate").Value
       orderID = orderRS.Fields("OrderID").Value

       Set totalRS = Server.CreateObject("ADODB.Recordset")
       Set totalRS.ActiveConnection = myConn
       totalRS.Source = "select " & _
           "sum((UnitPrice*Quantity)*(1-Discount)) as subTotal " & _
          "from [Order Details] where OrderID=" & orderID
       ' Open the recordset
       totalRS.Open
       subTotal = totalRS.Fields("subTotal").Value + freight
       totalRS.Close

       Response.Write("<TR><TD>" & orderDate & "</TD>")
       Response.Write("<TD><A HREF=OrderDetails.asp?orderID=" & _
          orderID & ">" & orderID & "</A></TD>")
       Response.Write("<TD>" & shipName & "</TD>")
       Response.Write("<TD>" & FormatCurrency(subTotal) & "</TD></TR>")

       orderRS.MoveNext
    Loop
    orderRS.Close
```

```
    ' Eliminate the object references
    Set myConn = Nothing
    Set totalRS = Nothing
    Set orderRS = Nothing
    Set tempRS = Nothing
%>
         </TABLE>
</BODY>
</HTML>
```

Completing the Employees Page

The Employees.ASP page creates the data set for all of the employees. The Employees table must be used in conjunction with the Orders table to determine how many orders are attributed to each employee (see Figure 6-10).

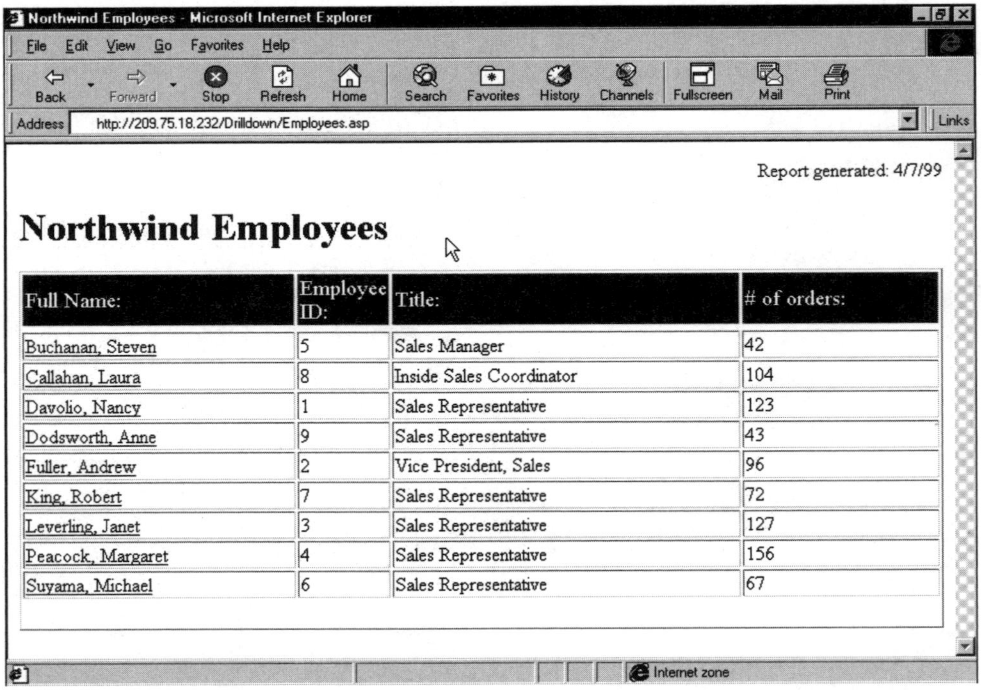

Report generated: 4/7/99

Northwind Employees

Full Name:	Employee ID:	Title:	# of orders:
Buchanan, Steven	5	Sales Manager	42
Callahan, Laura	8	Inside Sales Coordinator	104
Davolio, Nancy	1	Sales Representative	123
Dodsworth, Anne	9	Sales Representative	43
Fuller, Andrew	2	Vice President, Sales	96
King, Robert	7	Sales Representative	72
Leverling, Janet	3	Sales Representative	127
Peacock, Margaret	4	Sales Representative	156
Suyama, Michael	6	Sales Representative	67

Figure 6-10. The Employees table shows each employee and the number of orders for which they are responsible

The aggregate function `Count ( )` is used in the SQL query each time a new employee record is accessed. In the following listing of the Employees.ASP page, you can see that the links are also dynamically created to allow drilling down to the Orders.ASP page for a specific employee. Enter the following code in the Employees.ASP page.

```
<HTML>
<HEAD>
<TITLE>Northwind Employees</TITLE>
</HEAD>
<BODY>

<%
   Response.Write("<p align=right>Report generated: " & Date & "</p>")
   Response.Write("<H1>Northwind Employees</H1><P><P>")
   ' Create a variable reference for the connection
   Dim myConn
   ' Get the connection object from the Data Environment
   Set DE = Server.CreateObject("DERuntime.DERuntime")
   DE.Init(Application("DE"))
   Set myConn = DE.Connections(1)
   myConn.Open
   ' Check if the opening was successful and write the
   ' result to the client browser
   ' Possible values: adStateOpen(1), adStateClosed (0)
   If myConn.State = 1 Then
      Set empRS = Server.CreateObject("ADODB.Recordset")
      Set empRS.ActiveConnection = myConn
      empRS.Source = "select * from Employees Order " & _
         " By LastName,FirstName"
      ' Open the recordset
      empRS.Open
   Else
      Response.Write("Error. Connection could not be opened.<P>")
   End If

%>
<TABLE border=1 height=48 width="100%">

    <TR>
        <TD bgcolor=#0000FF><font color=#FFFFFF>

         <big>Full Name: </big></font></TD>
        <TD bgcolor=#0000FF><font color=#FFFFFF>

         <big>Employee ID: </big></font></TD>
```

```
        <TD bgcolor=#0000FF><font color=#FFFFFF>

         <big>Title: </big></font></TD>
        <TD bgcolor=#0000FF><font color=#FFFFFF>

         <big># of orders: </big></font></TD>
    </TR>
<%
   Do Until empRS.EOF
      lastName = empRS.Fields("LastName").Value
      firstName = empRS.Fields("FirstName").Value
      fullName = lastName & ", " & firstName
      title = empRS.Fields("Title").Value
      employeeID = empRS.Fields("EmployeeID").Value

      Set totalRS = Server.CreateObject("ADODB.Recordset")
      Set totalRS.ActiveConnection = myConn
      totalRS.Source = "select count(orderID) as numOrders " & _

         from Orders where EmployeeID=" & employeeID
      ' Open the recordset
      totalRS.Open
      subTotal = totalRS.Fields("numOrders").Value
      totalRS.Close

      Response.Write("<TR><TD><A HREF=orders.asp?employeeID=" _

         & employeeID & ">" & fullName & "</A></TD>")
      Response.Write("<TD width=10% >" & employeeID & "</TD>")
      Response.Write("<TD>" & title & "</TD>")
      Response.Write("<TD>" & subTotal & "</TD></TR>")

      empRS.MoveNext
   Loop
   empRS.Close
   ' Eliminate the object references
   Set myConn = Nothing
   Set totalRS = Nothing
   Set empRS = Nothing
%>

</TABLE>
</BODY>
</HTML>
```

Like the other pages, the Employees table makes certain that each object reference (recordsets, connections, and so on) are cleared when the page is finished displaying. This prevents unnecessary memory use on the server.

USING PAGE REFRESHES FOR UPDATED DATA

Queries that are made to the server take a snapshot of the current data on the server. After it is downloaded to the client browser, this information remains on the client for the duration of time that the browser is running. In the application presented in this chapter, most of the data that will be examined is historical and therefore will not change within the short period of time the user is browsing it.

However, in an online analytical processing (OLAP) system, such as a point-of-sale tracking system, updates may be frequent, and data that remains on a client-browser for even a few minutes may be out of date. To prevent inaccurate data from remaining in the browser, a refresh time can be added to a Web page. When the refresh time reaches its expiration date, the client will automatically request that the server send updated data. This is identical to the user clicking the browser's Refresh button.

To have the page refresh itself, simply place the following HTML code in the header of the document:

```
<HEAD>
<META HTTP-EQUIV="REFRESH" CONTENT=60>
```

In this example code, the refresh has been set to occur every sixty seconds. You can also make the document refresh to a different page. Simply change the value in the `CONTENT` parameter:

```
<HEAD>
<META HTTP-EQUIV="REFRESH" CONTENT="60;URL=http://www.cvisual.com">
```

Coding the refresh in your database solution, preferably for a longer duration, such as an hour, can ensure that the displayed information is valid.

Q&A

Q: Can a drill-down report be bookmarked?

A: If the query string in the URL contains the drill-down information, then the answer is yes. Bookmarks in a Web browser store only the URL information and the title of the link. Data posted through a form submission, however, is not stored. The example in this chapter showed methods of using both the URL/QueryString approach as well as the form-based information approach. To allow bookmarks, the application would be required to create parameters as part of the criteria string available through the QueryString collection.

Q: Can drill-down functionality occur on the client side?

A: Yes. This can be done most effectively using a combination of DHTML and XML executing on the browser. In Chapter 19, you will learn how to create a DHTML client application. Client-side execution requires much more stringent definition of the target browser (usually specifying the vendor and version number), while server-side drill-down functionality can be used by any intended browser.

Q: Can drill-down reports use hierarchical recordsets?

A: Yes, but be careful of the number of levels you add to the hierarchy. Since drilling down only displays a single tree branch of the query at a time, the query may incur unnecessary overhead by creating the hierarchy before drilling down. On the other hand, once the structure is created, object navigation is much easier for the application. You will need to examine each application individually to determine whether this provides an appropriate solution.

SUMMARY

Drill-down reports provide an effective interactive presentation of a large amount of data. The user-criteria selection aspect of the report allows the report to be customized to show exactly the information that's requested. Creating a drill-down report for Northwind helped you to examine how a real-world application could be constructed around an existing data set. In this chapter, you covered:

- **Drill-down report** This type of report allows the data displayed to be refined based on user selections. A drill-down report is one of the most effective methods of making large quantities of related information available.
- **Application structure overview** Creating a series of basic diagrams to illustrate the intended construction of the ASP application can greatly aid in anticipating problems and considerations for the final construction.
- **Multiple paths of drill-down** An effective drill-down report uses single pages from several different starting points. This promotes code reuse and simplifies maintenance of the application.
- **Option selection** Most drill-down reports rely on the use of the HTML option list selector to let viewers choose from a list of alternatives. Once a choice is made, the information is submitted as part of the form data.

CHAPTER 7

Using a Web Session

During most Web site visits, many pages are often accessed by the user. Together, all of these requested pages make up a Web session. Each individual user interacting with your Web server will be automatically allocated a session by IIS. The session instance created on your Web server can be used to store information for that user or access the current session parameters. Managing session information properly can greatly ease your Web development. Variables stored in the Session object can exist across all the pages that a user accesses. A Session can even be programmed to react to events such as the user's first page accesses and the termination of the session.

Some of the more obvious ways to use Session variables include:

- **Variable persistence** Normally, variables are lost after a user leaves a Web page. Variables created in a session remain until either the session is abandoned or the timeout is reached.
- **Storing user preferences** Simple user preferences, such as whether to display graphics or the choice of a Web theme, may be stored in a session and retrieved on each page, thus presenting each user with a customized display.
- **Avoiding information duplication** Factors that are dependent on continuing page access, such as the time the session was started or the banner ads that have been displayed, can help to maximize a user's experience.
- **Preserving the login ID** If you have a low-security login (one that does not require Secure Sockets Layer), the login can be tracked throughout the user session.
- **Avoiding object reinitialization** Some objects take a lot of time to initialize. You can prevent the re-creation of such objects by placing them higher in the variable scope, which preserves them.

Although using the Session object appears to be one of the simpler aspects of creating a Web database solution, proper utilization of it requires considering how resources and variables are deployed. Microsoft has created the Session object to provide extra capability that was not included in the HTTP protocol.

USING THE SESSION OBJECT

As mentioned in Chapter 2, HTTP is inherently *stateless*, which means that no continuous connection is made between the client and the server. Each request from the Web server is treated essentially as a new user. To overcome this limitation, ASP uses cookies stored in the client browser to simulate a connection state. When a request is made, the Web server queries the browser for a cookie that was placed there at the first page access (see Figure 7-1).

The cookie may appear like this:

```
Set-Cookie: ASPSESSIONID=TDHFYXYHDGEJSWEB;
```

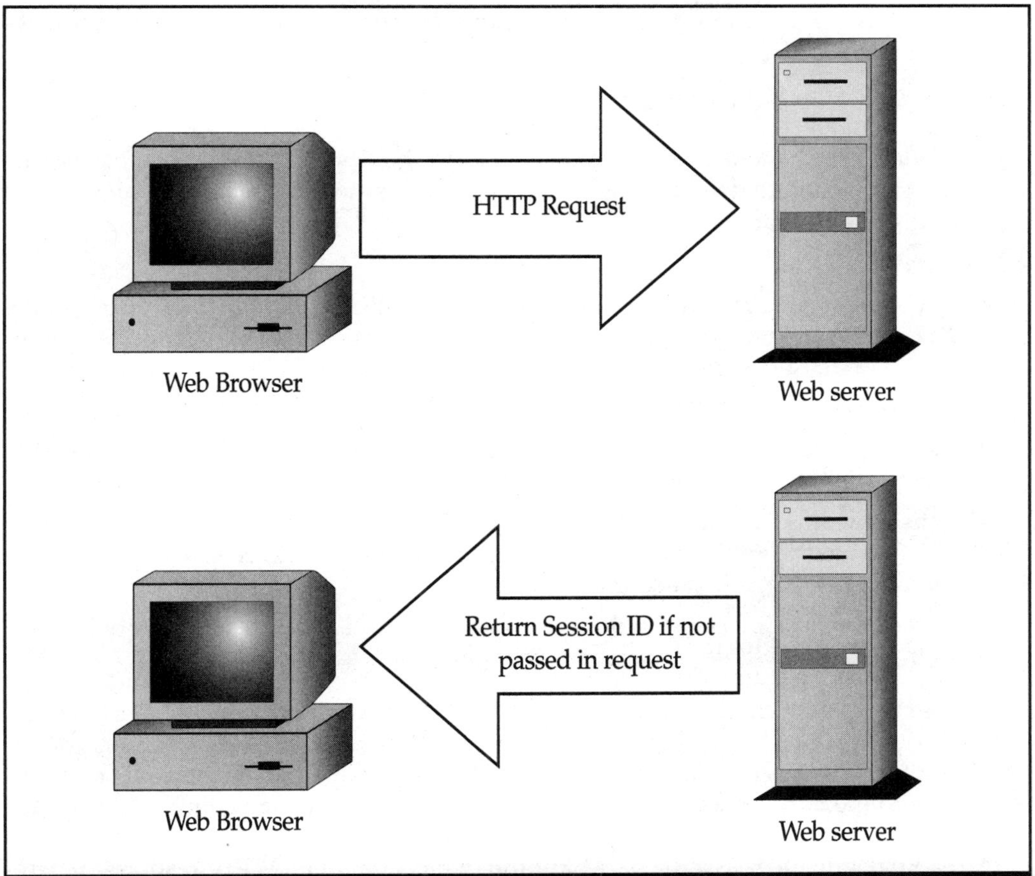

Figure 7-1. With each page access, the Web server requests the ID number of the user which was stored in a cookie

The cookie remains on the Web browser and is tracked by the Web server until the session either times out or is explicitly abandoned. The default timeout for a session is 20 minutes, after which the cookie information is destroyed on the server. If the user accesses the site again, the server won't have a cookie to match the one in the browser, and thus the session will reinitialize. Also, on the browser, the cookie is set to be eliminated when the browser shuts down.

Storing a value in the Session object is very simple. Values are implicitly created in the Session object by setting a variable name, like this:

```
Session("myValue") = 20
```

To retrieve this value, simply access it in the same way data is read from the Request object items:

```
myVar = Session("myValue")
```

Variables, objects, and arrays may be stored in the Session object. You can use the `IsEmpty()` function to determine whether any value is stored in a Session variable.

Starting a Session

A Session is not created for every user that accesses a Web server. In fact, access to simple HTML files does not instantiate the Session object. Although each ASP page access generates a `SessionID`, a session is not actually created until an event occurs that causes a need for a session. The following are the three ways to initialize a Session object:

- **Set a Session variable** Placing a value in a Session variable creates a session if one hasn't already been created.
- **Insert event code in the Global.asa file** If code for the `Session_OnStart` event is in the application's global file, a session is initialized when any ASP application file is first accessed.
- **Use a server-side component** When an ActiveX DLL or server-side object is initialized, the server automatically begins a new session.

A `SessionID` is generated each time that an ASP file is accessed until a session is declared through one of the preceding means, because the default mode of transmission for Internet Information Server (IIS) is unbuffered HTML transmission. This means that content is sent to the browser as it is generated, instead of waiting for a completed page before beginning transmission.

The cookie information must be sent within the header of an HTTP response. Therefore, if a session is initialized within the body of the Web page, it already is too late for IIS to send over a `SessionID`. Therefore, a new ID is sent with each ASP page access and is simply discarded if a session is not used. If a session is used, this `SessionID` remains the same for the duration of the user session.

`SessionID` is a number of the Long data type that is created by the server through a random process. The actual ID may be accessed through the `SessionID` property of the Session object. To display the `SessionID`, simply add the following code to an ASP file:

```
<% Response.Write(Session.SessionID) %>
```

NOTE: Checking this property to determine whether the browser supports Sessions (via cookies) does not work. If the browser is unable to store cookies and therefore unable to handle a Session, the SessionID is simply a new, random ID each time a new page is accessed.

Storing a Connection in a Session

For small applications, you can store a Connection object in the Session so that the user does not have to initialize a new connection for subsequent pages, which takes time and resources. If you do not have enough users regularly hitting your Web site to justify connection pooling (whereby connections are destroyed after 60 seconds of inactivity), setting up a connection in the Session object can dramatically increase your application's performance.

If you enter the code shown in the following listing and execute it, the first time the page is accessed a new connection will be created. Clicking the Refresh button will then use the Connection object that was created with the initial page access when the first Session variable was set.

```
<HTML>
<HEAD>
<TITLE>Session Connection Test</TITLE>
</HEAD>
<BODY>

<H1>Session Connection Test</H1>
<P>
<%
   If Not IsObject(Session("myConn")) Then
      Set myConn = Server.CreateObject("ADODB.Connection")
      ' Attempt to open connection
      myConn.Open "driver={Microsoft Access Driver (*.mdb)};" & _
         "dbq=c:\Program Files\Microsoft Visual Studio\VB98\nwind.mdb"
      Set Session("myConn") = myConn
      ' Display the creation of a connection
      Response.Write("New connection.<P>")
   Else
      On Error Resume Next

      Set myConn = Session("myConn")
      ' Let the user know an existing connection is being used
      Response.Write("Using existing connection.<P>")
   End If

   ' Create a simple query
   mySQL = "SELECT * FROM Customers"
   ' Execute the query against the connection
   Set myRS = myConn.Execute(mySQL)
   Response.Write("Contact: " & myRS.Fields("ContactName") & "<P>")
   Response.Write("Company: " & myRS.Fields("CompanyName"))
```

```
    myRS.Close
    ' Eliminate the recordset object
    Set myRS = Nothing
%>
</BODY>
</HTML>
```

Objects can be stored in the Session object by using either the `Set` command or the `<OBJECT>` tag within the Session `OnStart` event. For example, to create the Ad Rotator component, you could use code like the following in your Global.asa file:

```
<OBJECT RUNAT=Server SCOPE=Session ID=MyAd PROGID="MSWC.Adrotator">
</OBJECT>
```

One of the advantages to using this method for object creation is that the object isn't actually created on the server until the first access to it (in the code) is made. Therefore, if the object is never used, it will not use any resources on the Web server.

NOTE: You can't store any of the ASP built-in objects in a Session. For example, the code `Set Session("myRequest") = Request` will generate an error. The objects that can't be added to the session include: Application, Request, Response, Server, and Session.

Storing Arrays in a Session

Variables and objects are used in a session in the same manner as local variables. All the session variables are stored in an object collection in the Session object. This prevents arrays from being initialized within the Session object. However, a workaround is available that allows arrays to be stored at the Session level.

The Session object holds all variables in the Variant data type. Although this prevents storing an array data type in the object, it allows a reference to an array to be placed there to retain the array information. To create an array and store some values, you can use code like this:

```
<%
    Dim myArray()
    Redim myArray(10)
    For i = 1 to 10
       myArray(i) = i * 2
    Next
    Session("sessionArray") = myArray
%>
```

Unfortunately, it is not recommended that you directly access the array elements because they are stored in the Session object. To manipulate the information, the array must be recopied into a local array variable, as follows:

```
localArray = Session("sessionArray")
```

Since you are copying the array to a local variable, changes to the array value will not be placed in the array stored in the session. To accomplish the update, you must set the Session object variable again:

```
Session("sessionArray") = localArray
```

If changes or updates to the array are not re-stored in the Session object, the changes will be lost.

Scalability of Sessions

Keep in mind that each variable, array, or object that you define within a Session remains in server memory throughout the user session and 20 minutes past the final interaction. This means that large objects placed in every session can actually starve a server for resources if too many users access a site within a limited amount of time.

Remember also that if you create a Recordset object in the Session variable, connection pooling is effectively eliminated as a useful technology. This rule applies most critically if your server is managing a few hundred simultaneous sessions.

These warnings are not to discourage the use of the powerful tool that the Session objects represent. Rather, you are encouraged to consider carefully the type of environment that you will deploy in the final application. If the application will need to be rapidly scaled with a large number of simultaneous users, try to avoid placing any large objects or arrays in the Session object.

Checking for Cookie Abilities

The Session object requires the use of cookies to track users. Unfortunately, not all browsers support cookies, and some users disable the cookie feature. Chapter 6 describes how to use automatic refresh to reload the page. You also can use this feature to facilitate detecting a cookie.

The code necessary to detect a cookie relies on the refresh feature to load a different page after a certain duration. Try creating some code such as the following:

```
<HTML>
<HEAD>
<META HTTP-EQUIV="REFRESH" CONTENT="5;URL=testcomplete.asp">
</HEAD>
<BODY>
<%
On Error Resume Next
Session("myValue") = 13
%>
```

```
</BODY>
</HTML>
```

If the capability to use cookies isn't available, setting the Session variable will cause an error. The `On Error` routine will prevent any error from being shown. In five seconds (the duration specified in the `CONTENT` parameter), the page will refresh to the page testComplete.asp. Although you can reduce the timing from five seconds, make sure that the update doesn't occur before the script has the opportunity to execute on the server—otherwise, the results will state that cookies are not available, even though that may not be true.

On test completion, the query can simply read the variable to determine whether it was successful. To determine whether the Session variable wrote correctly, you can use straightforward code, such as this:

```
<%
   On Error Resume Next
   If IsEmpty(Session("myValue")) then
      ' Doesn't accept cookies
   Else
      ' Accepts cookies
   End If
%>
```

You can then modify the display of the page or use the `Redirect` method of the Response object to send the browser to the appropriate Web page. If sessions are not available, you can notify the user to use either a different browser or one of the techniques to simulate a session, as described later in this chapter.

Using Session Variables in a Frame-Based Application

A Web application that uses frames is slightly more complicated in its use of Session variables. If no Session is established before the frameset is accessed, all the loaded pages will be treated as independent sessions. Each page that is loaded within the frameset will create a new Session object. Therefore, the session `OnStart` and `OnEnd` events will also be executed for each file.

To prevent this behavior, change the frameset foundation page from an HTML file to an ASP page. In the ASP page, initialize a Session variable after the `</FRAMESET>` tag. This forces the creation of the Session before the documents in the frames are actually initialized. For example:

```
<HTML>
<BODY>
<FRAMESET FRAMEBORDER=0 SCROLLING=YES ROWS="15%, *">
   <FRAME NAME="Top" SCROLLING="NO" SRC="Top.asp">
   <FRAME NAME="Body" SRC="Body.asp">
```

```
</FRAMESET>
<% Session("myValue") = 13 %>
</BODY>
</HTML>
```

If the frameset foundation page must be an HTML page, you can either turn off the Session capabilities for this application (to streamline execution) or make sure that an ASP page that initializes the session is accessed before the frameset.

Communication with the Application Object

The Application object is one level higher for the scope of variables. All of the sessions access the single Application object and may store variables there that are held in common. A simple application of this capability would be to track users that access a Session, such as with the code shown here:

```
Sub Session_OnStart()
   Application.Lock
   Application("visitorNum") = Application("visitorNum") + 1
   Application.Unlock
End Sub
```

Unlike the Session object, for which only one page at a time is likely to access a variable, the Application object can be addressed by all currently running instances. Therefore, the `Lock` and `Unlock` methods are used to prevent user conflicts.

> ***TIP:*** Don't use this method for any counter in which you need to keep solid information. The variables contained in the Application object exist only as long as the application is active. Therefore, if the application times out, these variables will be lost. Additionally, if the Web server is shut down for any reason, all of the variable information will be cleared.

Turning Off Session Capabilities

If none of the applications on your Web server need session capabilities, you can turn off the session features. Disabling session capabilities is possible for individual applications or for the entire Web server. You can also eliminate the availability of Session from ASP code by using this statement:

```
<%@ EnableSessionState=False %>
```

You will need this line on every ASP page that will try to disable the session.

Shutting off the session service for the entire Web server is fairly drastic and isn't recommended unless most of the browsers accessing your site do not allow cookies. Because writing a session cookie is attempted with each page access if no current Session variable exists, a multi-frame application accessed by a browser without cookie capabilities could experience a performance decrease.

To turn off the session features, set the Session state in the Application Configuration dialog box for the entire server (see Figure 7-2). This dialog is available from the MMC through the Properties menu option on the right-click menu. On the App Options tab, simply uncheck the *Enable session state* check box to deactivate the session capabilities. You can also use this Configuration window for individual applications.

SESSION OBJECT MODEL

The Session object can be accessed directly from any ASP page, because it is one of the built-in ASP objects. The object is uncomplicated and consists of the Contents collection (see Figure 7-3) and a few methods and properties.

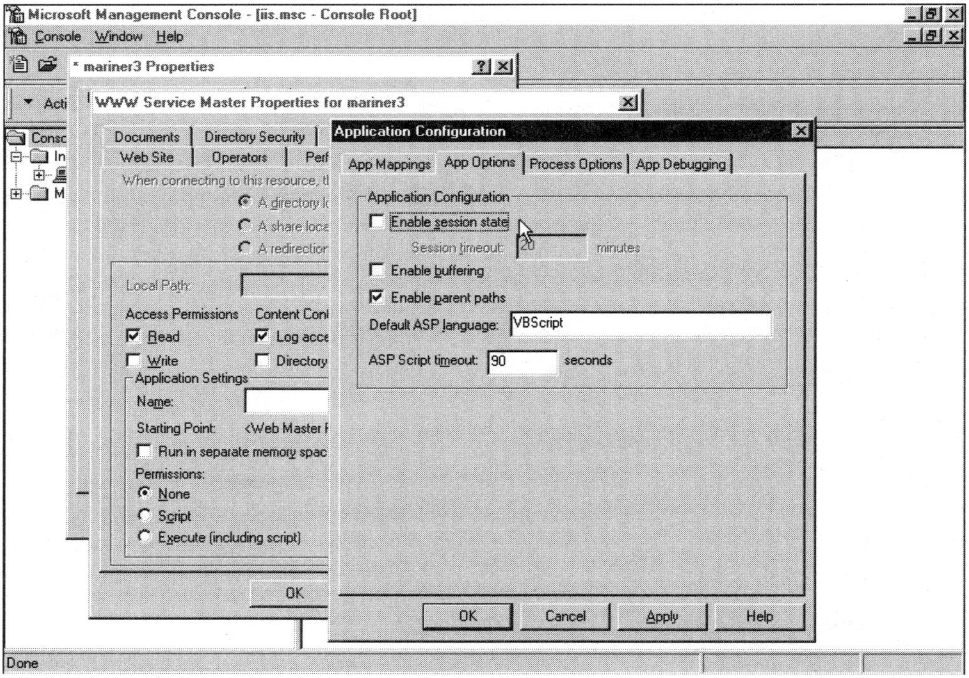

Figure 7-2. The Microsoft Management Console can be used to turn off Session capabilities for the entire server or for individual applications

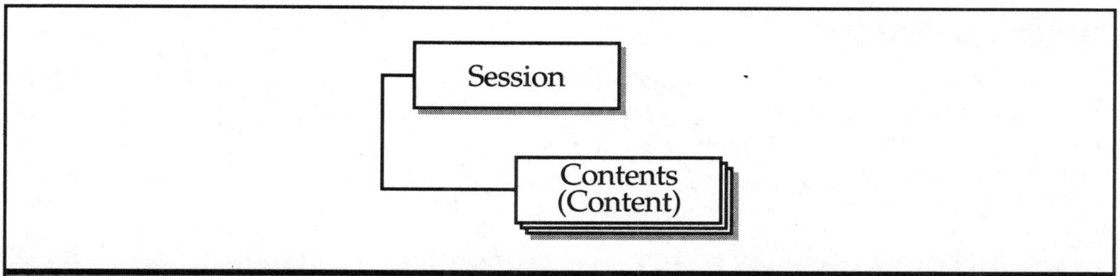

Figure 7-3. The Session object contains the Contents collection

Session timeouts may be set by using the `Timeout` property of the Session object. The default, stored in minutes, is 20. The following code will set the timeout for only 10 minutes:

```
Session.Timeout = 10
```

You may choose to include the necessary setting in the `OnStart` event for the session or application in the Global.asa file. This would allow the timeout value to be changed for the particular session or application without having to set it on a specific page.

NOTE: Make sure you don't set the timeout too low. If your page contains a lot of information, the session may expire while a user is reading the page. This is why the default is set to the 20-minute duration.

Session Abandon Method

`Abandon` is a method that may be called from ASP code to flush a Session from the server's memory. All variables and objects created within the Session are eliminated, and the `Session_OnEnd` event is activated.

When the `Abandon` method is called, the objects and variables are not actually destroyed. They are queued to be destroyed when the page completes execution of all the page code. Therefore, you can continue to access variables after calling the `Abandon` method, until the page finishes execution.

NOTE: To eliminate an object or variable immediately from a Session, you can use the `Delete` method on the specific item in the Contents collection. You can use the Delete method on a variable named myValue like this:

```
Session("myValue").Delete
```

Contents Collection

All information entered into the Session object is actually held in the Contents collection of the object. Since it is a collection, you can access named elements (as you have done so far) or use an index value to specify an ordinal reference.

To examine the elements in the Contents collection, you could use simple code like this:

```
<%
Session("myValue") = "Hello World!"
Response.Write("Number of items in the Contents collection: " & _
   Session.Contents.Count)
Response.Write("Value of the first item: " & Session.Contents(1)
%>
```

To enumerate all the individual elements in the collection, either use the index values, as shown in the example, or the `For Each...Next` structure. You can use methods such as `IsObject()` and `IsArray()` to determine whether the object in the collection is simply printable as a single value.

Session Events

Session events are activated when a Session has been created or is being destroyed. These events provide the opportunity to setup or destroy parameters and variables for the session. The code that will execute for these events is stored in the Global.asa file.

Session_OnStart

The `OnStart` event executes any time that a user accesses an ASP page and no session has been previously established. This code initializes the first value in a session when placed in the Global.asa file:

```
Sub Session_OnStart
   Session("myValue") = 10
End Sub
```

The event code will execute before the page is executed to allow the proper SessionID cookie to be sent to the browser. The Response object should not be used in this event routine since the page has yet to be initialized.

TIP: Make sure that you don't have an empty `Session_OnStart` procedure in the Global.asa file. Even if no code is present in the routine, the Session will be initialized when a page of the application is accessed. Therefore, each user accessing the application will take up session memory whether it is needed or not. By default, Visual InterDev places the stubs of the subroutine for the `OnStart` event in the Global.asa file, but it is remarked out so that it isn't recognized by the ASP engine.

Session_OnEnd

The `OnEnd` event executes either when the session times out or when the `Abandon` method is called. You can use code in this event to clean up or close out any files or objects that need a graceful exit. As a general rule of thumb, make sure you explicitly destroy any objects (by setting them to `Nothing`) that you've created in the `OnStart` event.

SIMULATING A SESSION

If the cookie capabilities of a user browser are turned off or simply not available, a session can be simulated. This method is actually used by many sites, such as Amazon.com, that balance a great amount of traffic and don't want to risk losing track of a customer's journey through the site. Many Web farms use this technique to implement load balancing while retaining session abilities.

DEFINITION: **Web farm** A Web farm consists of a group of Web servers that contain the same content. A load-balancing machine receives the HTTP requests and distributes the request to the machine that is most available.

When a user first accesses the Web site, an ID is randomly generated. All subsequent page access includes this ID in the request string. For example:

```
http://www.myserver.com/order.asp?id=200123
```

The server uses this number to store related information about the session in a component, a database, or the Application object. Each page access by the user is recorded and associated with this ID number. This also requires that any hyperlinks that exist in the ASP pages must be dynamically generated in order to include the ID in the request string.

Note that a problem occurs if you use a Web load-balancing server that distributes Web access among several Web servers. You can create explicit links rather than relative links to make the page addresses access a specific server after the initial connection is made. This allows the server to maintain the Session connection.

When used in conjunction with a database that contains the user preferences, this method can be used to create a flexible equivalent of the Session object. Using this custom session method does require some added complexity. In addition to managing the hyperlink references, recognize that you must code to handle the invalid IDs. If a user places a bookmark on one of the pages, when the page is accessed again, the temporary ID will not be located and a fresh one will be generated.

Q&A

Q: Can Session object resource usage be monitored explicitly?

A: No. Because the Session is managed as part of the memory model of the Web server, the memory allocation does not appear as part of an application, even if the application is set to execute out-of-process.

Q: Can Sessions exchange information between them?

A: Not directly. However, the Application object is held one level above the Session objects, so variables that are set at the Application level of scope can be accessed by all the sessions. For example, using the Application object to count the number of users was demonstrated earlier in the chapter. This is possible because all the variables in the Application object are available to all the sessions.

SUMMARY

The Session object of ASP can provide you with a powerful method of tracking users and maximizing resources across multiple pages. Judicious use of the Session object can help you to track information on the server, extend the lifetime of difficult-to-initialize objects, and hold information important to users for their continuing site access. In this chapter, you examined the following:

- **Session object** The Session object can hold variables, objects, and arrays for the duration of a Web session. A session can be ended either from disuse for the specified timeout period or by activating the `Abandon method`.
- **Arrays in Sessions** Arrays cannot be accessed within the Contents collection. An array can be stored there and copied to a local array, as needed. Any updates that occur to the local array must be recopied to the Session object; otherwise, they are lost when the page execution ends.
- **Session security** A session is no more secure than any other Web page access. Therefore, if security is required, consider getting a Web server key that will enable an SSL session between the client and the server.
- **Cookies** Since the HTTP protocol doesn't support sessions, a cookie is used by ASP to provide the session. If a browser doesn't support cookies, the ASP Session object can't be used.
- **Simulating a session** For Web farms or browsers that don't support the ASP session, you can use a user ID as part of the QueryString to simulate many aspects of the ASP session.

CHAPTER 8

Recognizing and Recording Browser Data

On the Web, numerous customizable sites provide a "home" page. You can tailor the display of information that you want to see when you visit it. Sites such as Netscape's Netcenter, MSN, and most of the search engines all provide some type of customizable visit. Increasingly, sites are also modifying their presentation based on knowledge about users' browsers. WebTV is known to have a resolution of 640 × 480, so many Web sites now present a page that accommodates this resolution.

To create such a site, your application needs to be able to determine information about the browser that is addressing the system. ASP includes a component that enables the server-side application to determine the functions available to a particular browser type.

The Browser Capabilities component can provide the following information about the functions of the browser:

- Browser name
- Major version number
- Minor version number
- Whether it supports frames
- Whether it supports JavaScript
- Whether it supports VBScript
- Background-sounds capability
- Whether it supports tables

Each of these parameters is available from the Browser Capabilities component, which can be easily accessed from your server-side code to modify the user experience to fit the capabilities of their browser. These properties can also be used by your application to determine what technology (such as Java or JavaScript) may be transmitted to the user for page presentation.

CREATING BROWSER-SPECIFIC PAGES

Depending on the browser features available to the user, you can either dynamically create different versions of the same page or direct the user to pages that are customized for their use. You may also disallow visitors to your page whose set up does not qualify with the features you require for adequate presentation.

Currently, browsers can be categorized into four groups:

- **Primitive browsers** Support basic HTML, usually up to the HTML 2.0 standard. Formatting is limited to basic styles and tables are typically not supported.
- **No-frames and primitive scripting** Frames support did not come for the primary browsers until after Navigator 2.0 and Internet Explorer 1.5. Scripting was supported, but was primarily incompatible with later versions.

- **Netscape Navigator 4 and above** Some support for Cascading Style Sheets (CSS) and new layering document object model supported.
- **Microsoft Internet Explorer 4 and above** ActiveX controls, DLLs, VBScript, and complete DHTML support including CSS and DOM are supported.

Undoubtedly, a mix of all of these types will be accessing your site, so you need a strategy for effectively addressing each one. To cope with the various browsers, you can adopt the following strategies:

- **Use a lowest-common denominator** Essentially, by placing all the execution pieces on the Web server and eliminating the use of frames and scripting, nearly anyone can access your site.
- **Specify minimum browser** Do not let people enter your Web site if they don't have a minimum-capability browser.
- **Dynamically create the page** Use ASP scripting code to output a page in a custom way depending on the browser.
- **Automatically redirect the browser to a different page** Check out the features available on the browser and redirect to a page appropriate for that level of functionality.
- **Allow manual direction to a new page** Simply provide links on the home page that allow the user to choose the most effective presentation of the page for their purposes.

Before you learn how to handle these various strategies, you need to understand how the server-side application can detect the features of the browser that is accessing the Web server.

Server Variables

Whenever an HTTP request for a page is issued to the Web server, a number of properties are sent with the request. All of these values and general server properties are held in the ServerVariables collection of the Request object. The variables held in the collection can be accessed by their names, like traditional elements.

For example, to find out the actual `QueryString` that was passed by the browser (rather than the preparsed collection), you would use code such as this:

```
Response.Write("QueryString = " & Request.ServerVariables("QUERY_STRING")
```

Using these variables provides you with a method of obtaining the raw elements that are used in HTTP communication. The IP address of the browser machine, for example, can be obtained through the `REMOTE_ADDR` variable. The browser information from the user variable can be obtained via `HTTP_USER_AGENT`. Most of the variables included in this collection are written into the log files, so they don't necessarily need to be written into a custom database for user tracking.

NOTE: If you need more exact feature notification of the capabilities of the browser than can be obtained from these variables or the server log, a commercial product known as BrowserHawk from Cyscape (www.cyscape.com) can be used. It will return notification of whether features are supported, including cascading styles sheets, file uploads, SSL encryption, and more. BrowserHawk can even detect whether cookies are supported.

Table 8-1 lists and briefly describes the names of the core server variables.

Because Microsoft upgrades the available variables, you may want to explicitly examine which variables are available on the Web server. Retrieving the variables is simply a matter of addressing the collection in the Request object. The following code will display all the available server variables; add an ASP page to a Visual InterDev project and then enter this code:

```
<%@ Language=VBScript %>
<HTML>
<HEAD>
<META NAME="GENERATOR" Content="Microsoft Visual Studio 6.0">
<TITLE>Browser Capabilities - Server Variables</TITLE>
</HEAD>
<BODY>
<H1>Browser Capabilities - Server Variables</H1>
<P>
<%
   ' Open the HTML table
   Response.Write("<TABLE border=1>")
   Dim tempVar
   For Each tempVar In Request.ServerVariables
      Response.Write("<TR>")
      ' Display string of variable name
      Response.Write("<TD>" & tempVar & "</TD>")
      ' Display variable value
      Response.Write("<TD>" & Request.ServerVariables(tempVar) &
"</TD>")
      Response.Write("</TR>")
   Next
   ' Close the table
   Response.Write("</TABLE>")
%>
</BODY>
</HTML>
```

When you execute this code in your browser window, you should see all the server variables and their values displayed in the table (see Figure 8-1). This program is a handy display that enables you to examine the values the server is actually using on a lower level of the protocol.

Variable Name	Description
ALL_HTTP	All the HTTP information sent by the browser, including cookies, IP number, SessionID, etc.
ALL_RAW	Same as ALL_HTTP, but no preprocessing occurs. HTTP headers are exactly as they come from the client
AUTH_PASSWORD	Available if BASIC authentication was used for entry of the user password
AUTH_TYPE	Authentication type, such as BASIC, used to validate user's access to protected script
CONTENT_LENGTH	Length of the content information sent by the browser
CONTENT_TYPE	The data type of the content sent with attached information of POST and PUT queries
GATEWAY_INTERFACE	The version of CGI interface supported
HTTP_<HeaderName>	The values of direct HTTP parameters that are passed
LOGON_USER	The Windows account of the user
PATH_INFO	Extra path information that was sent by the browser
PATH_TRANSLATED	Translated PATH_INFO into physical path
QUERY_STRING	The entire query string passed in the URL
REMOTE_ADDR	The IP address of the user machine
REMOTE_HOST	The name of the user machine
REQUEST_METHOD	The GET, HEAD, POST, or other method that made the request
SCRIPT_NAME	Path of the script being executed
SERVER_NAME	The server's name as used in self-referencing URLs
SERVER_PORT	The port that the request was sent to
SERVER_PORT_SECURE	If the request was secure, a string containing a 1; if not, a string containing a 0
SERVER_PROTOCOL	The information protocol name and revision returned by a request command
SERVER_SOFTWARE	The Web server name and revision
URL	Holds the base URL

Table 8-1. Numerous Variables Available Through the ServerVariables Collection

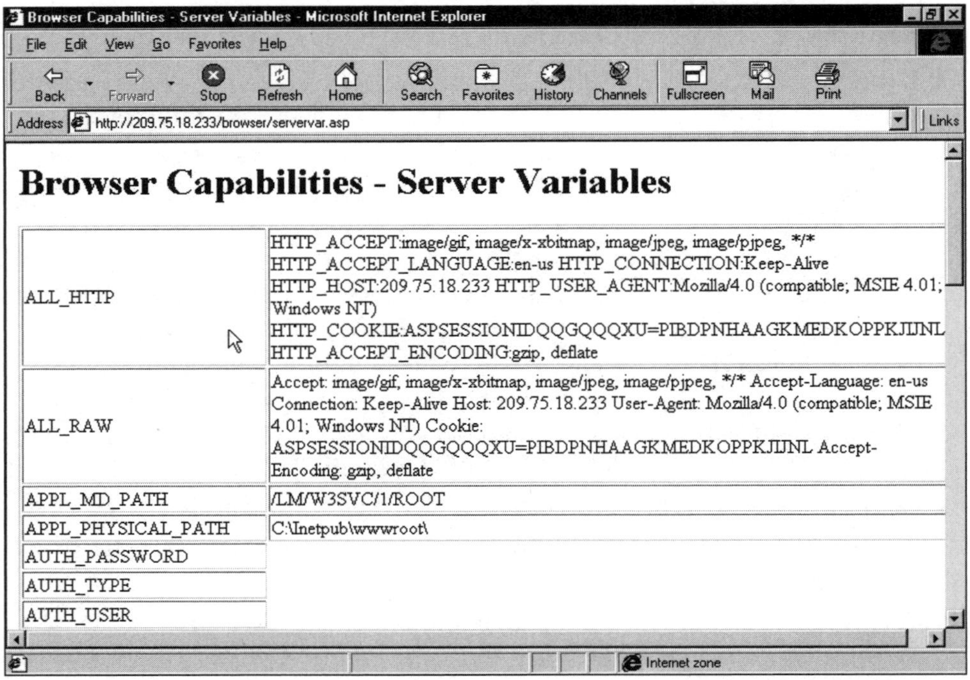

Figure 8-1. The servervar.asp page displays all the variables and their current values available on the server machine

HTTP Header

When a connection is made to the Web server, an HTTP header is broadcast from the client. The information about the browser is held in the HTTP `USER-AGENT` value. From this information, the Web server can understand which browser is being used, the general capabilities of the browser, and the user's version. The key information is held in the Browser Type field, which is an ASCII string that identifies the browser. The browser type field appears as follows to the Web server:

```
Mozilla/4.0 (compatible; MSIE 4.01; Windows NT)
```

NOTE: In the Browser Type field, the term "Mozilla" refers to the unofficial mascot of the Netscape Web browser. When Netscape initially created its browser, a character not unlike a popular fire-breathing movie monster was invented by the Netscape crew. Mozilla has since become the name of the Open Source version of the Netscape browser, available through the Mozilla Web site (www.mozilla.org). If you are interested in obtaining the C++ source code for almost the entire Netscape Web browser (SSL security code and Java interpreter are not included), it is available for download on the Mozilla Web site.

Other than this browser data, very little information about a client browser is actually available from the HTTP protocol. For example, the HTTP information doesn't identify whether the browser is capable of executing JavaScript. How, then, does the Browser Capabilities component provide this information? Microsoft has created a file that can provide the individual capabilities based on the browser type.

Browser Capabilities File

With so little information about the browser provided by the HTTP protocol, Microsoft has created a reference file to simplify the task for Web developers. Stored on the Web server is a file that contains individual listings for each browser type available at the time the Web server was released. The description file can—based on the browser type and version—report the functions supported within that browser.

All of this information is held in the *browscap.ini* file, in the system's InetSvr directory. On a Windows NT machine, this file typically is located at C:\WinNT\System32\InetSvr. Stored as an ASCII text file, the format of browscap.ini is actually the same as a traditional INI file, with the sequential stream of data divided into sections and items. The section title provides the name of the browser and the items describe the individual characteristics.

The following listing shows a sample entry of the browser descriptions held in the browscap.ini file. Notice that the variety of parameters supplied by this file match the properties available from the component.

```
;;;;;;;;;;;;;;;;;;;;;;;;;;
;;; Microsoft Browsers ;;;
;;;;;;;;;;;;;;;;;;;;;;;;;;

;;;;;;;;;;;;;;;;;;;;;;;;;;;;;;;;;;;;;;;;;; IE 1.x
[IE 1.5]
browser=IE
version=1.5
majorver=1
minorver=5
frames=FALSE
tables=TRUE
cookies=TRUE
```

```
backgroundsounds=FALSE
vbscript=FALSE
javascript=FALSE
javaapplets=FALSE
beta=False
Win16=False

[Mozilla/1.22 (compatible; MSIE 1.5; Windows NT)]
parent=IE 1.5
platform=WinNT

[Mozilla/1.22 (compatible; MSIE 1.5; Windows 95)]
parent=IE 1.5
platform=Win95
```

When the HTTP request is made, the INI file is searched to locate the browser that is currently being used. If a match is made between the browser type text and an entry in the file, that information is used to provide the settings for the Browser Capability component. If not, the component searches for the closest match by using wildcard characters. It uses the closest browser type and completes the property list.

When no match can be found, the default settings included in the INI file, under the heading *Default Browser Capability Settings*, are supplied by the component. If default settings are not specified in the INI file, all the properties of the component are set to the string "UNKNOWN". The following listing shows the default browser settings returned in the Browser Capability component when the browser type cannot be found in the INI file.

```
;;;;;;;;;;;;;;;;;;;;;;;;;;
;;; Default Browser    ;;;
;;;;;;;;;;;;;;;;;;;;;;;;;;
[Default Browser Capability Settings]
browser=Default
Version=0.0
majorver=#0
minorver=#0
frames=False
tables=True
cookies=False
backgroundsounds=False
vbscript=False
javascript=False
javaapplets=False
activexcontrols=False
AK=False
SK=False
```

```
AOL=False
beta=False
Win16=False
Crawler=False
CDF=False
AuthenticodeUpdate=
```

If your INI file does not contain a default group of settings, you can add the values shown in the previous listing.

NOTE: To be used, the browscap.ini file must be located in the same directory as the Browscap.DLL ActiveX DLL control. If the file is not located in this directory, all properties will be set to the string "UNKNOWN", regardless of the browser type.

It is not important that you study the format of this file. Essentially, you need only a basic understanding of how the features of a particular browser are discovered. You should, however, make a point of routinely upgrading this file with the newest version (available at www.cyscape.com/browscap), even if you don't upgrade the IIS Web server itself.

The continuing proliferation of Web browsing devices (such as set-top boxes, handheld devices, PDAs, and so forth) will make updates to the INI necessary if you want to allow your Web server to properly address the wide variety of users of your system.

Internet Information Server 5 Custom Properties

IIS 5 has added a new method of determining the capabilities of the browser that is accessing the Web server. In addition to the defined properties that are included with the Browser Capabilities component, the browser itself can specify custom settings that are added to the property collection of the object.

Instead of just using the INI file, IIS 5 can retrieve a cookie supplied by the browser. This new method has been created to make it possible for new browser types to notify the Web server of features that are available, even if they are too new to be recognized in the INI file.

The items are stored in a cookie with code such as this:

```
Document.cookie = "BrowsCap=&userLanguage=Spanish"
```

For the Web server, this cookie will be recognized as a browser type property. From the Web server, these values can be retrieved as a custom property:

```
Set myBrowsCap = Server.CreateObject("MSWC.BrowserType")
userLanguage = myBrowsCap.userLanguage
```

Most of these capabilities will have been specified by the user in a user preferences list. This example provided a server-side implementation; client-side DHTML can also be used to retrieve the browser settings. This allows the content itself to manage the presentation based on the browser settings.

For server-side solutions on IIS 5, your ASP page code can automatically attempt to retrieve custom properties from the user browser. The status code will call back to the client when a request does not return the browser capabilities cookie. Simply include the following code at the beginning of your ASP code on the server side:

```
<!-- METADATA TYPE = "Cookie" NAME="BrowsCap" SRC="sendcook.htm" -->
```

IIS 5 automatically executes the sendcook.htm file to create a cookie describing the browser capabilities.

NOTE: Microsoft has a robust example online to help you evaluate whether to use client- or server-side browser detection. The Client Capabilities workshop (http://msdn.microsoft.com/msdn-online/workshop/author/clientcaps/overview.asp) provides sample code and evaluation tables to determine the browser information.

Browser Capabilities Component

Now that you have a good idea of how the information is retrieved from the Web browser and parsed for use by ASP, you can begin using the Browser Capabilities component. The component itself is an ActiveX DLL named browscap.dll, located in the InetSvr subdirectory of the System32 directory.

NOTE: The BrowsCap.DLL object model, because of the way it is structured, can't be loaded into the Object Browser. This prohibits easy reference of the properties and methods for the component. For these component details, consult the IIS operating manual.

To demonstrate the capabilities of the component, the following listing includes some basic code to return the elements of the browser features. Note that instead of creating the object by using the `CreateObject` method of the Server object, the `<OBJECT>` tag is used. This tag allows the server to more effectively manage the objects that are created on it.

```
<%@ Language=VBScript %>
<HTML>
<HEAD>
<META NAME="GENERATOR" Content="Microsoft Visual Studio 6.0">
<TITLE>Browser Capabilities - Component</TITLE>
</HEAD>
<BODY>
<H1>Browser Capabilities - Server Variables</H1>
<P>
<OBJECT RUNAT=Server ID=myBrowser
   PROGID="MSWC.BrowserType">
```

```
</OBJECT>
<H2>Browser properties:</H2>
Browser Type: <B><%= myBrowser.Browser %></B><BR>
Version: <B><%= myBrowser.Version %></B><BR>
Major Version: <B><%= myBrowser.Majorver %></B><BR>
Minor Version: <B><%= myBrowser.Minorver %></B><BR>
Frames: <B><%= CStr(CBool(myBrowser.Frames)) %></B><BR>
Tables: <B><%= CStr(CBool(myBrowser.Tables)) %></B><BR>
Cookies: <B><%= CStr(CBool(myBrowser.cookies)) %></B><BR>
Background Sounds: <B><%=
   CStr(CBool(myBrowser.BackgroundSounds)) %></B><BR>
VBScript: <B><%= CStr(CBool(myBrowser.VBScript)) %></B><BR>
JavaScript: <B><%= CStr(CBool(myBrowser.JavaScript)) %></B><BR>
<P>
</BODY>
</HTML>
```

Most of the programming that you've done with Visual InterDev so far uses the Data Environment and the Site Diagram tools. The primary reason to use the `<OBJECT>` tag is its availability as an insertable object from the Visual InterDev toolbox. Simply select the Server Objects tab to see a component listed as Browser Capabilities. Drag and drop this item onto your page to generate a reference like the one in the preceding application.

By default, the object is named object1. Change the name of the object to **myBrowser**, so that you can clearly reference it from the script code. You need only change the ID parameter to the name that you want to use in your code.

NOTE: Because *<OBJECT>* is an HTML tag, it can't appear within the scripting code area (in other words, between <% %> brackets).

You can see that all the characteristics of the browser are stored as properties rather than as items of a collection (like the ServerVariables collection). When this page is accessed by a Web server, the proper browser values are displayed. Figure 8-2 shows that when the page is addressed from Netscape 3, the features of the browser are properly listed.

Frame Redirect

The most common way to deal with these browsers is to redirect the browser to a different page, depending on the properties of the browser. Keeping a separate page prevents voluminous alternate presentation code to be present in the page and also generally allows a user to select the appropriate page, sometimes over-riding the features available to the browser.

You may have noticed that the browscap.dll file recognizes whether or not the browser supports frames. Because frames-based sites are becoming more popular for cer-

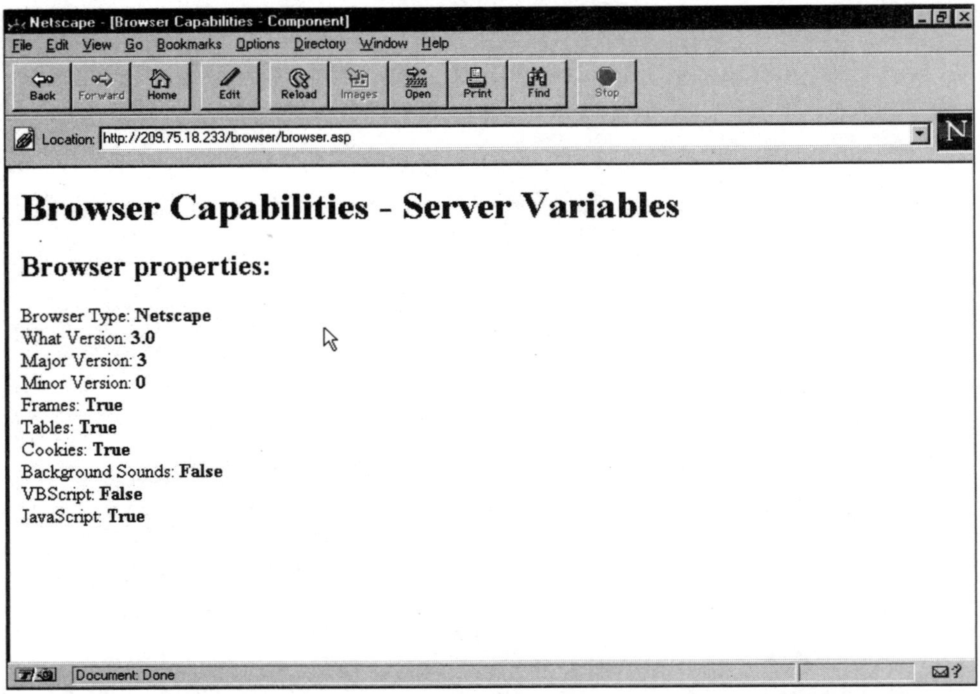

Figure 8-2. The application displays the characteristics of the client browser

tain applications, automatically redirecting the user's browser to either a frames or nonframes version may be a feature you want to include in your Web database solution.

The next listing shows a sample page that detects whether or not the browser supports frames. If frames are not available, the user is sent to the noframes.asp page. Otherwise, the frames.asp page is used.

```
<%@ Language=VBScript %>
<%
On Error Resume Next
Set myBrowser = Server.CreateObject("MSWC.BrowserType")
' Check if the browser supports frames
```

```
If myBrowser.Frames="False" then
   ' The browser doesn't support frames.
   Response.Redirect("noframes.asp")
Else
   ' The browser supports frames.
   Response.Redirect("frames.asp")
End If
%>

<HTML>
<HEAD>
<META NAME="GENERATOR" Content="Microsoft Visual Studio 6.0">
<TITLE>Browser Capabilities - Frames Redirect</TITLE>
</HEAD>
<BODY>
<H1>Browser Capabilities - Frames Redirect</H1>
<P>
</BODY>
</HTML>
```

Any script code that activates a redirect must be placed before the `<HTML>` tag occurs. The <HTML> tag begins the server-side Web page send. Redirects must occur before any page information is broadcast to the browser. If you place the code after the HTML tag or attempt to use the Response object to write to the output stream, the Web server will generate an error.

NOTE: Although you can provide *automatic detection* of frame support in the browser, you might allow the user to choose anyway. Often, users prefer one presentation style or the other regardless of their browser features. Allowing your visitors to select will make your site more user-friendly.

Additionally, if the browser supports frames, the browser may be accessing a page through a proxy server that doesn't support passing frame information. The popular Web surfing service called the Anonymizer (www.anonymizer.com) shields a server's ability to directly access the browser that you're using. If you attempt to go to a page on a Web server through such a server, features normally available from a browser may be disabled (see Figure 8-3).

Therefore, even if you believe that visitors to your site are sophisticated enough to use the latest version of a browser, an Internet or extranet application should provide a nonframes version to enable users to address your Web site.

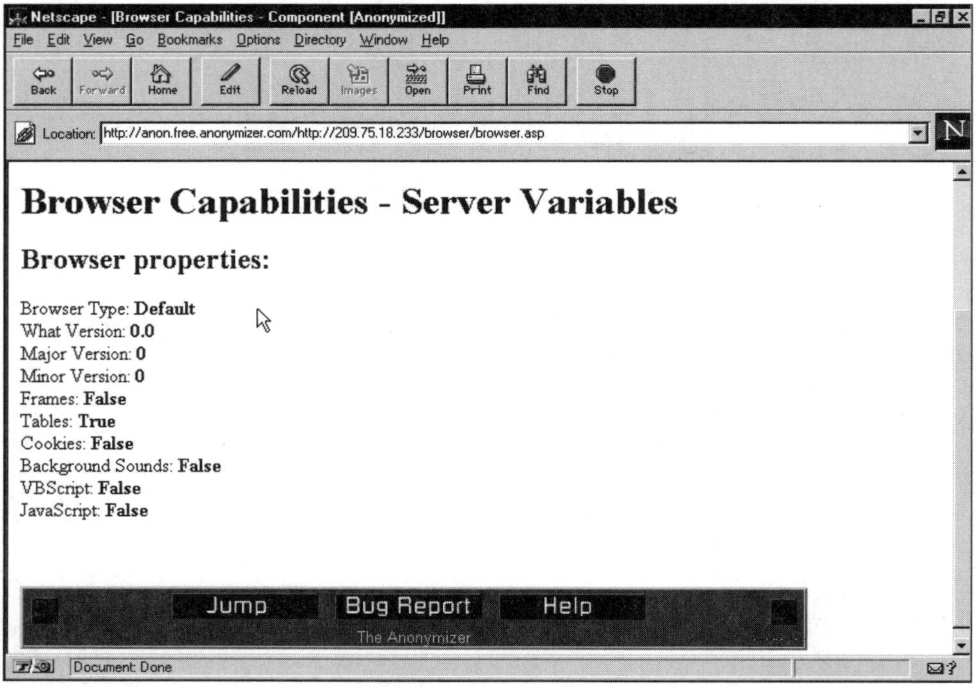

Figure 8-3. Passing through a proxy server may limit the browser features

Creating a Browser-Customizing Application

Rather than provide some form of redirection, you might want to support custom page creation. For features such as client-side scripting, tables, and cookies, actually generating a different page on the fly may be the most advisable path.

The most obvious advantage to using custom page creation is that you avoid having multiple pages of the same content. In fact, this is the method that I use with many of my clients, because it provides a single, unified group of pages, even if the coding is more tedious at the beginning. In the long run, it prevents many linking and content errors.

One of the features that many sites take for granted is the ability to display tables. Many older browsers are unable to provide table display and need an alternative coding. In the following example, script code is used to generate the table. Subroutines are created to handle the opening and closing of tables, rows, and so forth. If the browser has no support for table functionality, the preformatted table is used (see Figure 8-4).

However, if table functionality is available, the same information will be shown in HTML table format (see Figure 8-5). Although this technique may be cumbersome, it provides great flexibility for later formatting and even for possible output as XML data for advanced information uses.

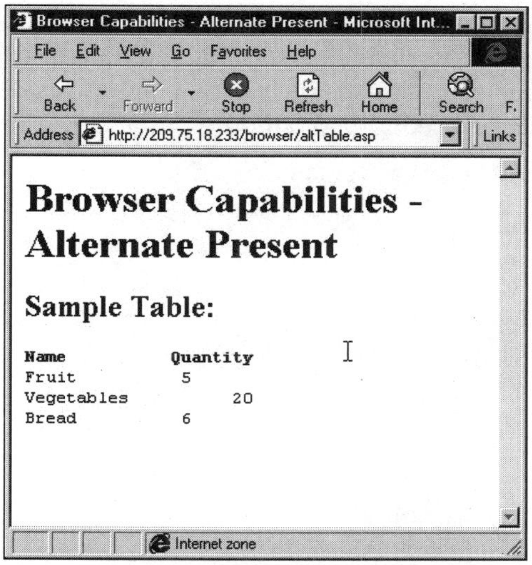

Figure 8-4. Preformatted table for a browser that doesn't support tables

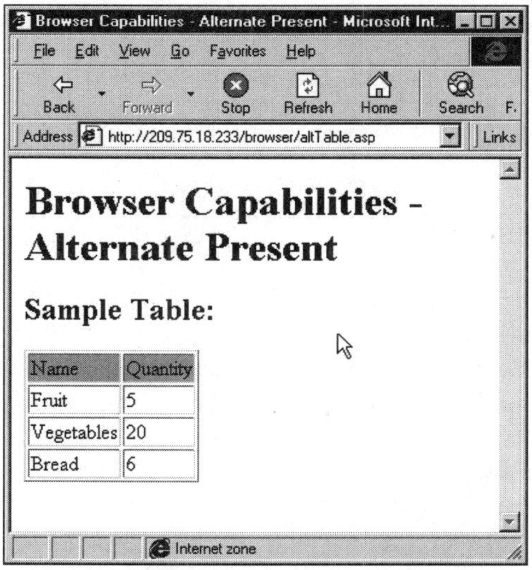

Figure 8-5. The same table information displayed in an HTML table

The code shown in the next listing creates the display through the table subroutines (`openTable` and `closeTable`), row subroutines (`openTitleRow`, `openRow`, and `closeRow`), and column routine (`outputCol`). All the HTML commands are handled by these routines. This example simply outputs three rows of two-column information, but the generalized routines can actually be used for any amount of data.

```
<%@ Language=VBScript %>
<HTML>
<HEAD>
<META NAME="GENERATOR" Content="Microsoft Visual Studio 6.0">
<TITLE>Browser Capabilities - Alternate Present</TITLE>
<OBJECT RUNAT=Server ID=myBrowser PROGID="MSWC.BrowserType">
</OBJECT>
<%
Dim myItem

If myBrowser.Tables="True" Then
   tableFlag=1
Else
   tableFlag=0
End If

Sub outputCol(ByVal myItem)
   If tableFlag Then
      Response.Write("<TD>")
      Response.Write(myItem)
      Response.Write("</TD>")
   Else
      Response.Write(myItem & space(10))
   End If

End Sub

Sub openTitleRow()
   If tableFlag Then
      Response.Write("<TR bgcolor=#00FFFF>")
   Else
      Response.Write("<B>")
   End If
End Sub

Sub openRow()
   If tableFlag Then
      Response.Write("<TR>")
```

```
    End If
End Sub

Sub closeRow()
    If tableFlag Then
        Response.Write("</TR>")
    Else
        Response.Write("</B><BR>")
    End If
End Sub

Sub openTable()
    If tableFlag Then
        Response.Write("<TABLE Border=1>")
    Else
        Response.Write("<P><PRE>")
    End If
End Sub

Sub closeTable()
    If tableFlag Then
        Response.Write("</TABLE>")
    Else
        Response.Write("<P></PRE>")
    End If
End Sub

%>
</HEAD>
<BODY>
<H1>Browser Capabilities - Alternate Present</H1>
<P>



<H2>Sample Table:</H2>
<%
openTable
openTitleRow
outputCol("Name")
outputCol("Quantity")
closeRow
openRow
outputCol("Fruit")
```

```
outputCol(5)
closeRow
openRow
outputCol("Vegetables")
outputCol(20)
closeRow
openRow
outputCol("Bread")
outputCol(6)
closeRow
closeTable
%>
<P>
</BODY>
</HTML>
```

Each value that is sent to the `outputCol` subroutine is sent to the browser as a column in the table. In this example, the script code displaying the information may seem slightly tedious since each column is uniquely coded. However, when a loop is used for displaying database information, the code appears much more elegant.

Q&A

Q: Will future browsers significantly differ from current browser features?

A: Most of the features that have been added in the last few years, including Cascading Style Sheets (CSS), Java applets, Dynamic HTML, XML, and others, have yet to gain wide acceptance or development in actual deployed Web sites. Although the many browsers can handle these additions, Web authors have not found that the investment of time and energy spent implementing them is justified in terms of the number of targeted users. However, because the installed base is now so large for version 4 browsers, it will probably be a long time before solutions can rely on the use of those features that are not already available in these browsers.

Therefore, if you limit your application to the features available in these browsers, your application should function well for the foreseeable future. Making your application compatible for both version 4 browsers is ideal if it will be accessed over the Internet; you can make it browser-specific if it will be accessed over an intranet only.

Q: Can I allow customization if the user has cookies turned off?

A: Most users don't completely turn off the cookie capabilities of their browsers, but instead request notification when the accessed site attempts to read or write a cookie. If your site provides obvious benefits to the use of a cookie (such as presentation preferences or automatic sign-on), most users will accept the cookie information from the site.

Most often, the elimination of cookies means that site personalization/customization is not available. To provide this service to users without cookie capabilities, you could offer a login capability so the users don't need to lose the advantages of a custom presentation.

SUMMARY

Determining the type of browser that is accessing your page is an effective way to provide automatic customization of the site, and offers an improved user experience. Browser type, scripting capabilities, frame support, audio features, and more can be tested by using the Browser Capabilities component. This chapter covered the following:

- **Browser Capabilities component** This server-side component executes under ASP and uses information returned by the browser to detail the features that it supports. It uses an INI file, browscap.ini, to read the browser type and extrapolate that information into the individual properties that are returned.
- **IIS 5 cookies** With version 5, the IIS capability to retrieve browser features has been modified so that those features can be returned in a cookie. This functionality enables newer browsers to state their capabilities, so that the browscap.ini does not have to be updated constantly to include such new devices as WebTV and set-top boxes.
- **Auto configuration** A Web page can automatically customize its appearance and functionality based on the capabilities of the user's browser. This can include dynamically building a custom page based on the browser's capabilities.
- **Frame or frameless configuration** Using frames is one of the most difficult user issues, because some still popular browsers are incapable of displaying frames. By checking whether the user's browser supports frames, the page can automatically redirect frames-incapable browsers to frameless presentation.

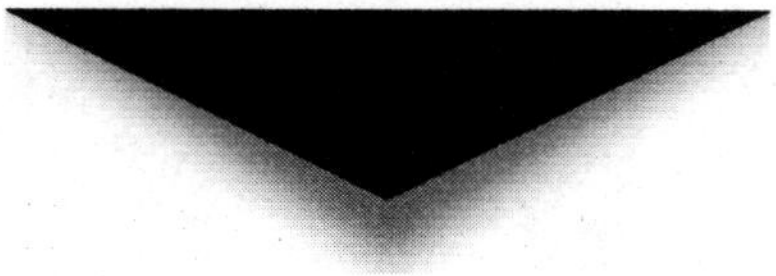

CHAPTER 9

Using Database Designer

Up to this point in the book, all the applications that you have created have used existing data sources. This was an effective way of introducing you to some of the ASP and database tools without requiring bottom-to-top application construction. However, most of the Web applications that are built in the real world will require you to create, or at least modify, the data source.

In this chapter, you'll learn how to use Database Designer in Visual InterDev to construct a database from scratch in Microsoft SQL Server. In the Visual Studio package, Database Designer enables you to construct a database schema with both the basic diagramming techniques, such as those shown in Microsoft Access, and the documentation capabilities.

NOTE: If you don't have SQL Server installed, Visual Studio includes the SQL Server Developer Edition of the database server. Also, Access 2000 comes with the Microsoft Development Environment (MSDE) that is actually a feature-complete version of SQL Server 7. MSDE only lacks the scalability of the full server. SQL Server, SQL Server: Developer Edition, or MSDE can be used for the examples in this chapter.

Database Designer is one of four visual database tools included with Visual Studio. These tools can be used in Visual InterDev, Visual Basic, Visual J++, and Visual C++. Therefore, the techniques that you learn in this chapter will help you to use nearly all the Visual Studio applications.

The sample solution in this chapter will do the following:

- Demonstrate browser viewer customization/personalization
- Store browser cookies for user identification
- Link the cookie to a database profile
- Use Database Designer to create and document a database
- Install and configure SQL Server

When the application is complete, your Web solution will be an effective prototype for general login applications. A Web page can appear much more professional when it provides either automatic or selectable customized features. With a combination of a database tracking system and a client-side cookie or user login, a user-friendly experience can be created.

CONSTRUCTING A DATABASE FOR A WEB APPLICATION

The cornerstone of the Web application will be a database that is used to store user selections for personalization of the browsing experience. When users first enter the site, they may select options that reflect how they want their version of the site to appear. Once selections are complete, this information is stored in a database for later retrieval. Subsequent visits will automatically capture a cookie that contains the user identification number, retrieve the corresponding configuration record, and then use that information to display the site.

Before you actually begin building the application, you must design the fundamental aspects of the database that will contain the user preferences. After you complete this design, you can construct a user interface (UI) that presents or records the proper data.

Database Structure Design

Proper design at the beginning of database creation is far more critical than proper design of a program. Poor decisions made when beginning a program can usually be remedied, or a workaround can be found. If a database structure is poorly designed or a piece of vital information is left out, it can affect everyone's work on the entire project. A poor design affects so many areas, because the design does the following:

- **Dictates how data will be entered** In designing a UI, decisions regarding the order in which data is entered and the minimum types of data required to be entered depend on which fields are critical to the information flow of the database. When the dynamics change regarding critical information, the entire process flow of data entry may be upset, thus requiring changes to the structure of the UI.
- **Governs the user interface** How the interaction occurs, including the process (such as wizards), the type of UI needed (frames or nonframes), and deployment options (Dynamic HTML, XML, ActiveX, or primitive HTML), depends on how you want the user to interact with the information.
- **Controls use of screen acreage** The fields and tables that make up the data source usually determine the layout of the display that is required to show the necessary information. HTML table design, option menus, and other user interface features are dependent on the data that must be presented.
- **Determines how queries and indexes are implemented** Multitable queries are complicated and must be well designed. Late design changes to the location of a single field can affect all the queries and index optimization that has occurred up to that point.
- **Affects field coding and data type checking** All code for field entry or data checking (on the client or the server) must be designed to evaluate the field information to be entered and the field names. A simple change of a field from a number to a character field (such as changing a ZIP code field to a ZIP+4 field) can break every page of code that accesses it.

For these reasons, the database must be well planned *before* substantial construction begins. The database that you construct in this chapter will be flat in structure and will not include related tables. In the next chapter, you'll expand the design principles you learn here to include relational design issues.

The Need for Documentation

Documentation has long been overlooked as a way to minimize the cost of additions or upgrades to a database system. Unlike coding, for which programmers can often puzzle out the reasons and functionality behind the origins of a piece of code, the structure of a database indicates almost nothing about the design decisions made when the structure was initially created.

As a very basic example, imagine a database constructed to accept only five digits for a ZIP code. Upon later examination, a decision is made to update the field for ZIP+4 coding. When this upgrade is made, all of the accounting reports from another system begin failing. Only then is it discovered that the commercial accounting program downloads the data every month from the central database and can only handle the five-digit format.

Another example, unrelated directly to the computer implementation, is a mailing list that allows 10 letters for the first name of a recipient. Years after initial deployment, a decision is made that 10 letters is insufficient space for the first name and should be expanded to 15 letters. Only after hundreds of misprinted sheets occur does someone realize that the form used to output the data only has space for 10 letters.

These are just two obvious and simple examples of problems that could have been averted if the design rationale was actually documented with the system. Prior to Database Designer, this form of documentation nearly always required the purchase and installation of additional programs and/or substantial extra time and effort for manual documentation.

Database Designer's features enable you to do the following:

- Create a table or modify an existing one
- Diagram existing relationships
- Add text annotations to a diagram
- Format display in viewable or printable layouts

Database Designer can even view the tables and relations in various ways. You can view a table with either all of its field information, only the fields, only the key fields, or only the table titles.

Installing and Using SQL Server 6.5 Developer Edition

In the previous chapters, you have always used the Northwind Microsoft Access sample database file. For many of the remaining solutions presented in this book, you need to use Microsoft SQL Server. You may have never used SQL Server before, but explaining the entire functioning of the SQL Server database server is beyond the scope of this book (see *SQL Server: The Complete Reference* by Gayle Coffman).

Whereas use of a complete database server used to be relegated to high-end information system developers, application developers are increasingly called upon to maintain or augment a SQL Server solution. Therefore, this chapter presents a basic step-by-step guide to using SQL Server to implement a Web solution.

Microsoft includes the Developer Edition of SQL Server on the Visual Studio CD-ROMs, so installation is easy and convenient. The Developer Edition is a trimmed-down version of the entire server, so it can't handle numerous real-time users (nor are you licensed to use it that way), but it contains all the features of the complete server. SQL Server Developer Edition is rated to support up to five simultaneous users, but the license agreement for this edition does not allow you to deploy a real application with it. You can use MSDE, however, which has similar limitations, for legal deployment. By creating a database on SQL Server, you will gain at least a rudimentary understanding of how the server works.

TIP: If you don't want to use SQL Server for your Web database prototyping, either Microsoft Access or Visual Basic's Visual Data Manager can be used to create a compatible database. Since the basic field types, sizes, and structure of the databases are provided, you should be able to create, with only simple modifications, all the solutions that don't require stored procedures.

The primary difference in field types between a SQL Server database and the equivalent Access database (.MDB file) is the Identity field. In Access, this field type is known as an Auto Number or Auto Increment field. This field type is generally used to provide a unique ID field for each record.

Installing the Server

If you haven't already installed SQL Server Developer Edition, included with Visual Studio, you need to do that now. The easiest way to accomplish this installation is to find the SQL folder (usually on Visual Studio CD-ROM 2) and execute the installer in the folder. You can also add SQL Server to your machine by re-executing the main Visual Studio installer and selecting the BackOffice installation application.

After the installer begins execution, follow most of the default settings. When you come to the Select Network Protocols window, however, be sure to allow connections to SQL Server through TCP/IP (see Figure 9-1). By default, the protocol used is Named Pipes. To allow access to SQL Server from almost anywhere (including through the Internet), check the TCP/IP setting to enable that protocol.

After installation is complete, you will probably need to start SQL Server manually. Unless you selected autoboot during the installation process, you need to start SQL Server services through SQL Service Manager (see Figure 9-2). Double-clicking the green light begins SQL Server execution. Note the listed name of the database server, because you have to enter it manually when you first register the connection in SQL Enterprise Manager.

TIP: On a development machine, it is usually advisable to allow manual starting of SQL Server service. Otherwise, the database server is automatically opened at startup, using processor resources and memory, and increasing system boot time.

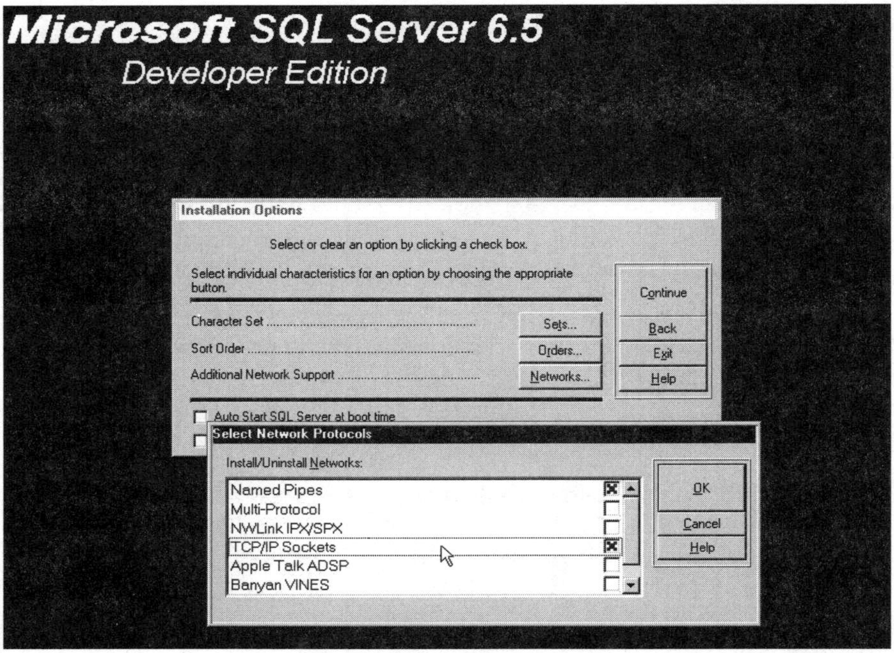

Figure 9-1. Make sure that SQL Server accepts connections through the TCP/IP protocol

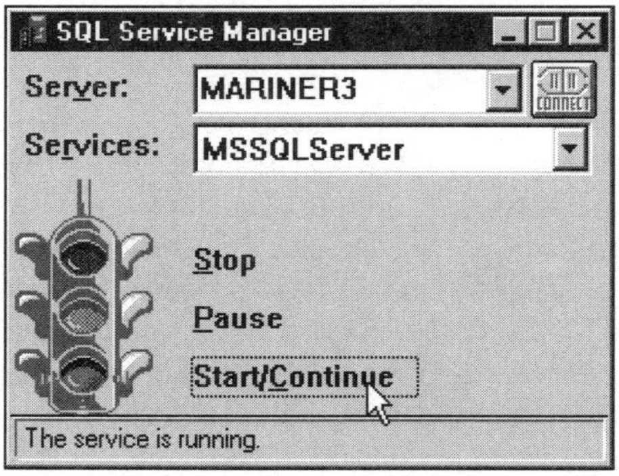

Figure 9-2. Start SQL Server through SQL Service Manager

After SQL Server service starts, you can exit SQL Service Manager. You now need to execute SQL Enterprise Manager, to complete configuration of the databases. The first time that you execute your SQL Server, you must register it with Enterprise Manager, so that you can administer it from Enterprise Manager.

A dialog window will automatically be displayed on the first execution to allow you to register the default database server. If you dismiss this window, you can display it again by selecting the Register Server option under the Server menu.

In the registration window, enter the name of the server (which you got from Service Manager), the username (Login ID field), and the password of the administrator account (see Figure 9-3). By default, the username is set to *sa*, for *system administrator*, and the password is left blank. Clicking the Register button registers SQL Server, and it then appears in the Server Manager window, located behind the Register Server window.

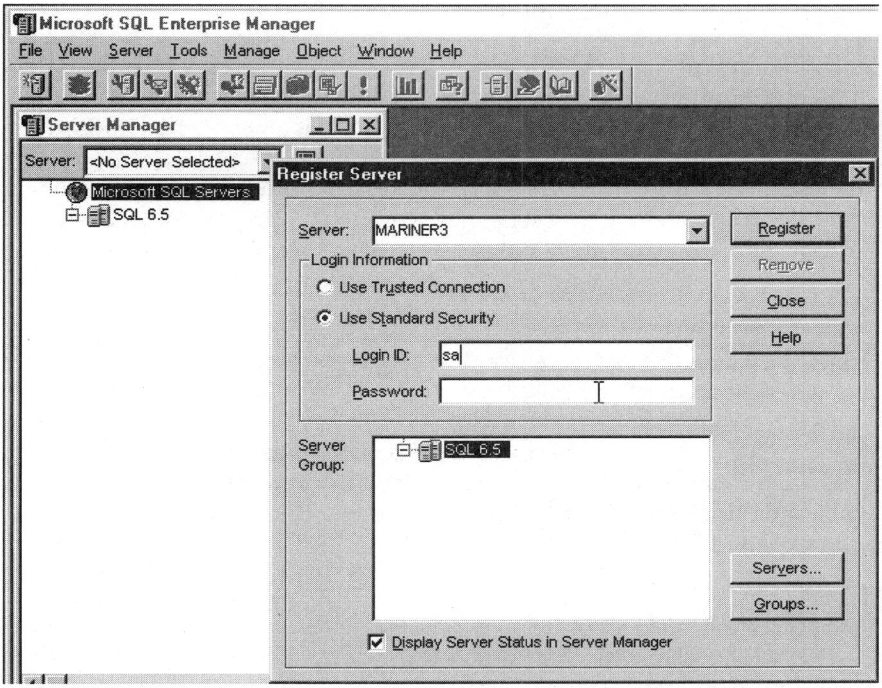

Figure 9-3. Register SQL Server in SQL Enterprise Manager

To expand all the hierarchies of SQL Server that you just installed, click Close to exit the Register Server window. At the top level, the folders include:

- **SQL Mail** Mail connector to send e-mail messages from SQL Server through stored procedures
- **SQL Executive** Allows scheduling of time- and date-based SQL tasks including backups, log truncation, etc.
- **Distributed Transaction Coordinator** Management of SQL Server transactions
- **Database Devices** The device files are a disk-based construct that actually hold the databases
- **Backup Devices** Device to store backups of SQL Server databases
- **Databases** Database objects—including the database itself—login permissions, tables, views, stored procedures, rules, defaults, and user-defined data types
- **Logins** Security settings for the database

The most unfamiliar piece of SQL Server to the new user is probably the database device. SQL Server handles all the file read/write of the database operations itself rather than letting Windows NT provide data space allocation management. For this reason, the logical construct of a database device was created.

A database device appears to the operating system (OS) as one very large file. When you allocate a database device, you set aside a certain amount of hard disk space. Within this allocated space, you can create databases, tables, indexes, and log files. SQL Server handles all the space management.

DEFINITION: **Database device** An allocated amount of hard disk space that is used to store databases, tables, indexes, and log files.

After you create a database device, multiple databases can be stored in it. Also, a database and its log file can be split, to exist on different devices. After you create and configure a database device properly, you don't have to pay much more attention to it unless you need to expand its size.

NOTE: The structure of database devices is the reason SQL Server features its own backup functionality outside the general NT Server backup. While SQL Server is running, all the database device files are kept open as far as Windows NT is concerned. When a traditional NT backup is attempted (using the Backup utility), these files can't be backed up because they remain open.

To make a backup of your SQL Server databases, you need to either shut down SQL Server or use SQL Server's backup capabilities. Third-party utilities that allow complete backup of an NT system and SQL Server files at the same time are available from companies such as ARCserve (www.cheyenne.com) and Seagate Backup Exec (www.seagatesoftware.com).

Constructing a Database

You now are going to create a SQL Server database and a device to hold it. Once the device has been defined, there are a variety of ways of creating the database itself, including through direct SQL code. You'll be using Database Designer to define the tables that are held in the database. Database Designer, however, cannot create the database devices and other low-level constructs required to define a new database from scratch.

Creating a Database Device

You need a database device to hold the databases that you create in this and upcoming chapters. Since most of these databases will be examples that do not require large amounts of storage, you can make the device fairly small (approximately 30MB). Follow these steps to create a database device:

1. Right-click the Database Devices folder and select the New Device option.
2. Set the Name to WebDB (see the following illustration) and click Create Now, which causes the device to appear in the device list. This device will be used to store most of the databases that are created in the remainder of this book. If the device is too small, it can be expanded later.

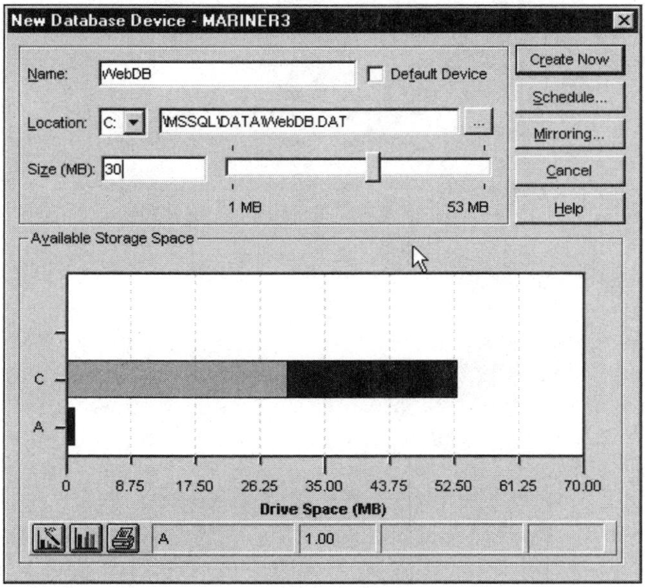

3. Right-click the Databases folder and select the New Database option. The database for this chapter is used to record personalized information, and therefore doesn't require much space on the device.
4. Set the Name to **Customer**.

5. Set both the Data Device and the Log Device to WebDB. The log device will store a log of all of the transactions that are attempted against the database and will be used to recover the integrity of the database if a system failure occurs.
6. Make the Data Device allocate 5MB of storage.
7. Make the Log Device allocate 1MB of storage. The log file for SQL Server must be either backed up or cleared regularly to function properly.
8. Click the Create Now button (see the following illustration).

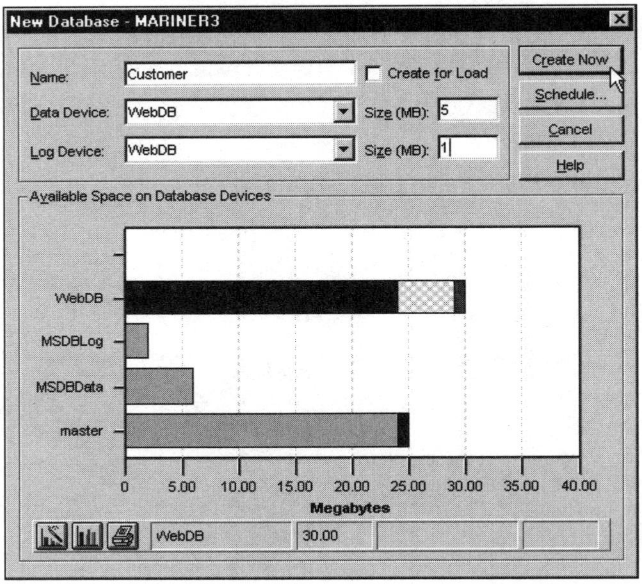

After you create the database, it will appear in the Databases folder. Although you can use it immediately, you should first set an option to automatically truncate the database log by following the steps presented next. By doing so, the system will not be overwhelmed by a tremendous log size. It will also prevent an operation such as loading a large amount of data into the database upsizing from Microsoft Access, for example, from aborting because of log overload. It will prune the log at the appropriate times.

1. Right-click the Customer Database and select Edit.
2. Select the Options tab.
3. Set the Truncate Log on Checkpoint option (see the following illustration) and click OK.

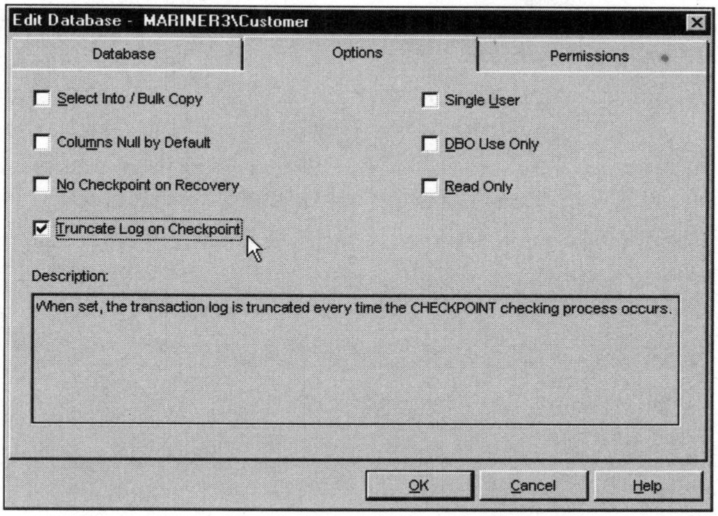

You're done. All other modifications that you need to do are most easily performed in the Database Designer window. You can exit SQL Enterprise Manager (you'll use it briefly at the end of the chapter to examine the logins that have been created).

TIP: The system administrator (sa) account currently has the default password of empty string (""), so the examples here use the sa account to provide the login. However, security usually is one of the first things that you configure, so that it doesn't get overlooked later. Consider skipping to Chapter 12 and checking out the section "Configuring Security to Your SQL Server." That way, you can establish the basic security before you begin constructing the database.

Creating an ODBC Link to the Table

To allow the Database Designer to create the necessary tables, you need an ODBC link to the WebDB database in SQL Server. This can be created when the connection is added to the project. However, the connection-adding dialog box does not allow an existing connection to be edited. Therefore, this time you can use the ODBC settings program which is contained in the Windows Control Panel and provides complete ODBC facilities:

1. Select Start | Settings | Control Panel.
2. Double-click the ODBC applet.
3. Under the File DSN tab, click the Add button to add a new data source.
4. For the driver option, select SQL Server and then click the Next button.

5. For the Name of the data source, type **customerODBC**, and then click the Next button.
6. Click the Finish button. The SQL Server ODBC setup window will appear.

   This setup dialog box differs significantly from the Access setup dialog box that you are accustomed to using. SQL Server is far more powerful and thus provides several options that govern how the source can be addressed.
7. Select (local) as the Server in the drop-down list box (as shown in the following illustration), or enter the IP address if your SQL Server is not on the development machine, and then click the Next button.

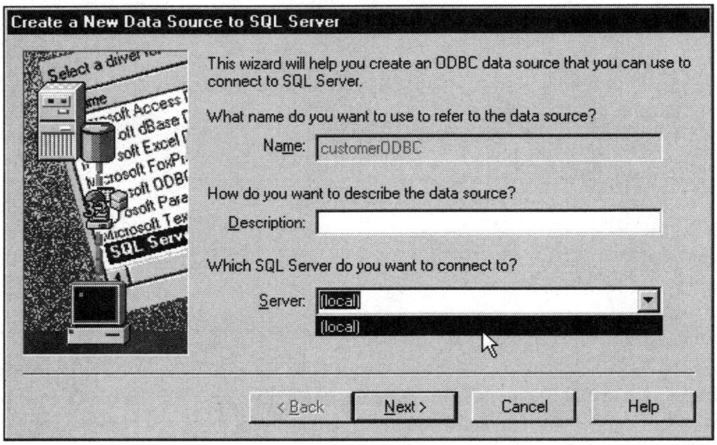

   The next page of the wizard contains the SQL Server security options. Leave these security settings to the default. For both intranet and Internet applications, the TCP/IP protocol should be used for communication between the Web objects and the data source. Therefore, you use the Client Configuration utility included in the ODBC driver to specify the protocol that will be used.
8. Click the Client Configuration button.
9. Under the Net Library tab of the SQL Server Client Configuration Utility, set the protocol to be used by selecting the TCP/IP Sockets option for the Default Network (as shown in the next illustration) and then click the Done button.

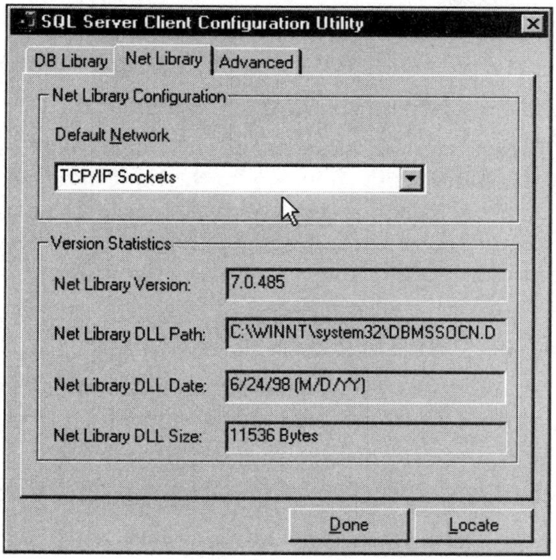

10. Click the Next button. The Create a New Data Source to SQL Server window appears.

    The traditional setting for accessing SQL Server is to map the user into the Master database. In this solution, you want to set the default database for this data source to be the Customer database.

11. Check the box labeled Change The Default Database To.
12. Use the drop-down list box to select the Customer database (as shown in the next illustration).

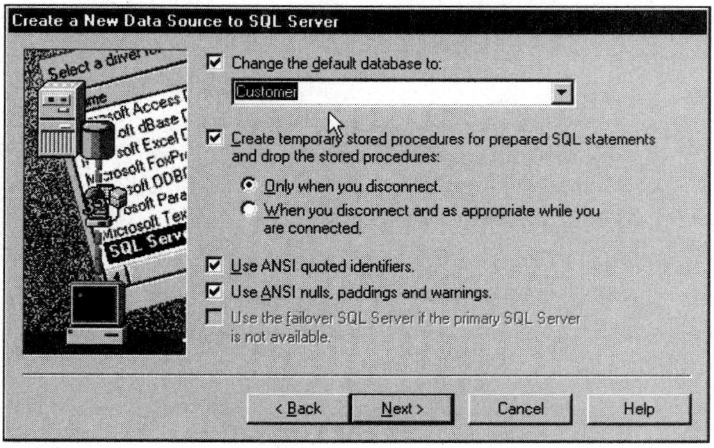

13. Click the Next button to advance to the next page.
14. Click the Next button to accept the default character set translation options.
15. Click the Finish button to create the data source.

    You are now presented with a final window that displays all the options that you've selected. Additionally, a button at the bottom of the window enables you to make an access test through the driver that you've just configured. This can help you confirm that the ODBC configuration is working properly, so that if you have difficulty connecting, you'll know the cause probably isn't the ODBC driver.
16. Click the Test Data Source button.

    The test will be attempted and should succeed. If some problem occurs, go back through the configuration steps and make sure that you have made all the proper settings.
17. Click the OK button to accept the data source.

The list of data sources is shown again, and the customer ODBC source should now be available for use.

Creating the Personal Project

Now that you have created the database, you need to make the pages that will access it. Figure 9-4 shows a diagram of the general Web design. You can see that the eight pages do not all interlink. The creation of a new, personalized presentation is available only if no cookie is found for the existing user.

You need to create the following eight ASP pages in this exercise:

- **Default.asp** is the home page for this application. It checks whether the user ID is present in the Cookies collection. If so, the user information is read from the database, and the Web page display is altered appropriately.
- **addPersonal.asp** provides the form to enter personal and configuration information, including the user's name, e-mail address, and password; scripting capabilities; choice of whether to receive e-mail updates for the site; and the user's color preference for the background display of the page. Form information is submitted to writePersonal.asp.
- **writePersonal.asp** receives the user-entered information and writes it to the database. It also stores the cookie of the added user ID to the client browser.
- **loginPersonal.asp** accepts the user e-mail address and password in an HTML form to submit to enterPersonal.asp for verification and login.

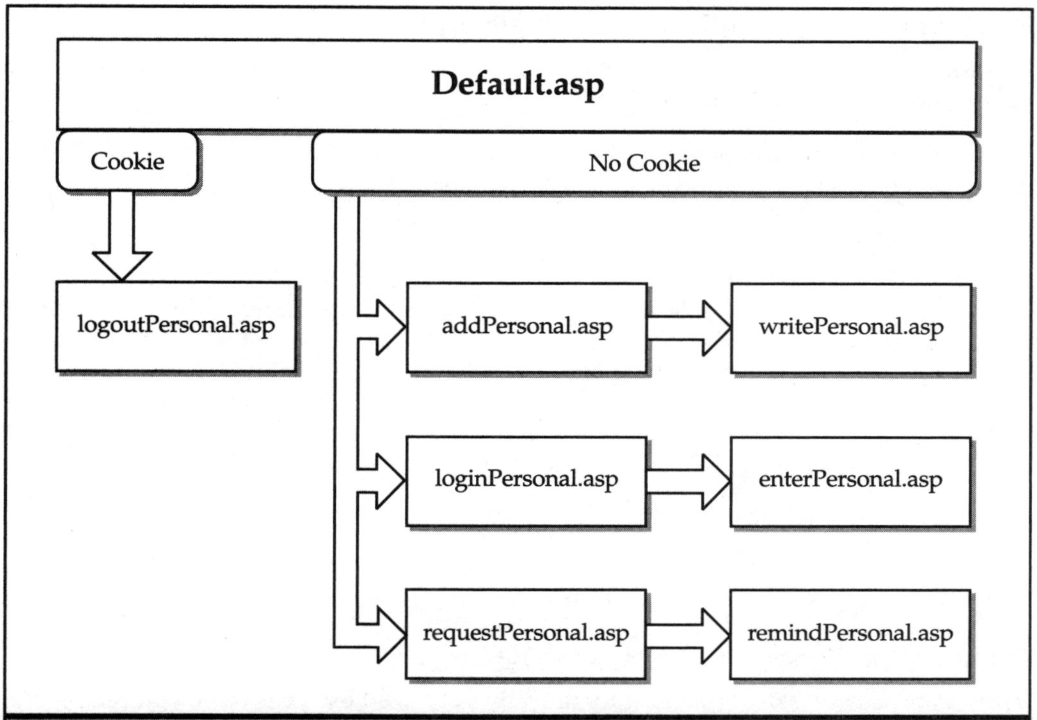

Figure 9-4. The design of the Personal Web database application

- **enterPersonal.asp** receives the e-mail address and password information, locates the requested user in the database, and loads the user ID into a client browser cookie.
- **logoutPersonal.asp** simply clears the user cookie so that login is possible with a different user ID.
- **requestPersonal.asp** requests an e-mail reminder of a user password. The request is submitted to the remindPersonal.asp page.
- ▲ **remindPersonal.asp** reads the password from the database, and in this simplified version, displays it in the Web page.

Each of these pages are constructed within the Visual InterDev project titled Personal.

Starting the Database Project in Visual InterDev

You can use the Database Project type in Visual InterDev to provide the foundation for the creation of this eight-page project.

1. Select a new Database Project and name it **Personal**.
2. Select the customerODBC source when asked for a data source.

The server controls that are featured in Visual InterDev enable you to select these controls from the palette. You can drag and drop any of the controls in the palette to anywhere within a page that is open in the development environment. Using the palette items does not create server-side code. Rather, the pallet items use the <OBJECT> tag to provide the instance for use on the page.

With the <OBJECT> tag, the object will not actually be instantiated until the first code reference to it occurs. If you drag an object onto the VI document, the tag is added into the header portion of the page (outside of a script). It will create an object reference like this:

```
<OBJECT RUNAT=Server ID=myBrowser PROGID="MSWC.BrowserType">
</OBJECT>
```

This object can then be used by any of the code on the page.

Creating the Table with Database Designer

In the Data View window that is automatically initialized by the project, you can see the Customer database. Expand the Customer folder in the Data View window for SQL Server objects by clicking the plus sign to the left of the item. One of the items contained within the Customer folder is Database Diagrams (see the following illustration). Because no diagrams currently exist for the Customer table, attempting to expand Database Diagrams doesn't work.

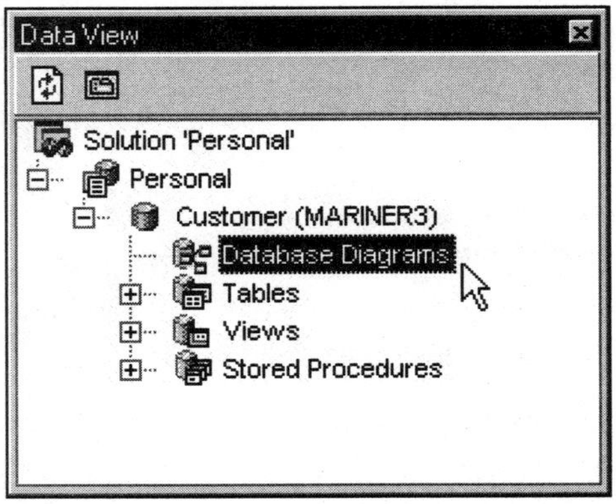

1. Right-click the Database Diagrams item and select the New Diagram option. The Database Designer will appear. When the diagram is first created, it is a blank slate. Onto this blank area, you can create tables or link to existing tables.

2. Click the New Table icon on the Database Diagram toolbar. You are asked for the name of this new table.
3. Name the table **Personal**, because all the personal preferences of the user will be kept in the table.
4. Click the OK button and the table creation window appears (see Figure 9-5), in which you can add fields (columns), set the field type, length, precision, and scale, and adjust other parameters.

   To construct the table, you need to enter the fields that it will contain.
5. Enter the items listed in Table 9-1. This table lists all the fields and the entry values that they should have. The Personal table will be constructed to store the information provided by the user.

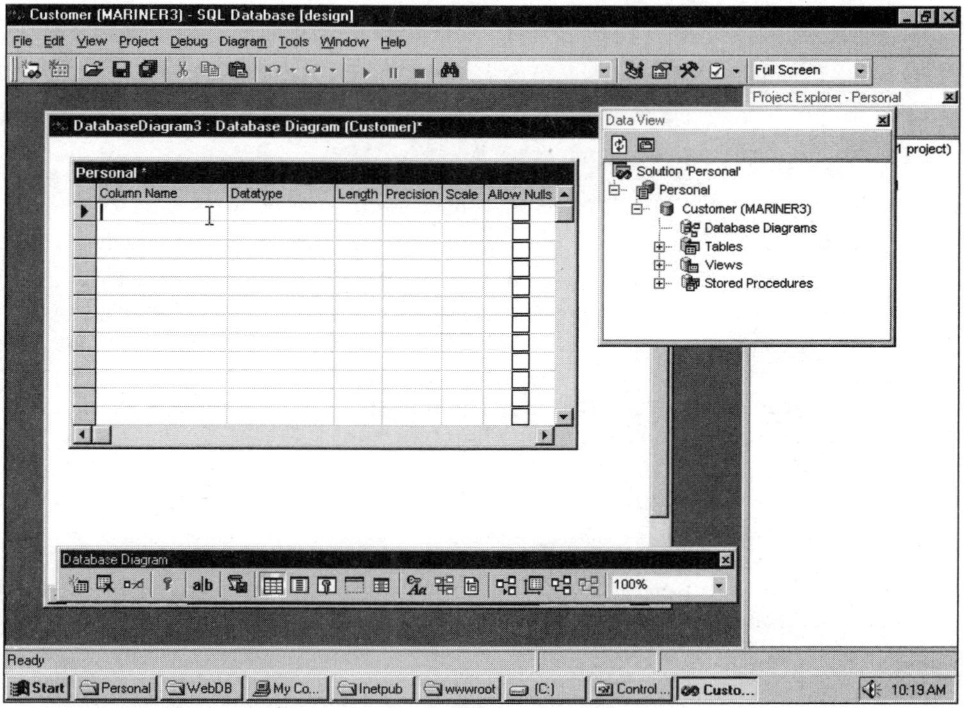

Figure 9-5. The table creation window for the Personal table enables you to set all the fields and field parameters

Name	Data Type	Length	Precision	Scale	Nulls?	Default Value	Identity?
userID	int	4	10	0	No		Yes
FirstName	varchar	20	0	0	Yes		No
LastName	varchar	30	0	0	Yes		No
Password	varchar	20	0	0	Yes		No
ClientJS	bit	1	0	0	No	0	No
updateEmail	bit	1	0	0	No	0	No
bground	varchar	8	0	0	Yes		No
browserType	varchar	50	0	0	Yes		No
email	varchar	30	0	0	Yes		No

Table 9-1. The Personal Table Field Definitions

For the fields that are fixed length, such as ClientJS and userID, Database Designer automatically fills the entries for precision, scale, length, and so forth.

NOTE: When you're constructing a table, the bit fields (ClientJS and updateEmail) are unique in two ways: bits fields definitions can't be altered after the table is created, and they must have a value before the record can be written. Bit fields are combined by SQL Server in the background into a single, multibit field for increased execution speeds. Therefore, they can't be altered once they are created. For this same reason, they require a set value when a new record is created or an error occurs. This is why the default value of 0 is included when constructing the table.

If these limitations are a problem, use the smallint field to hold Boolean values. Fields defined as the smallint type can also be bound to data-aware controls such as the check box, but can be modified like any other general field type.

After all the columns for the table are set, you will need to make several special modifications.

6. Reselect the row that contains the userID field. Every table should have a key field that can be used to identify a record uniquely. In the Database Diagram toolbox, you should see a small key icon.
7. Click the key icon to set the userID field as the primary key field for the table. Your table should now look like the one shown in the next illustration. To the

left of the userID arrow, you should now see a small key icon, indicating that userID is the key field of the table.

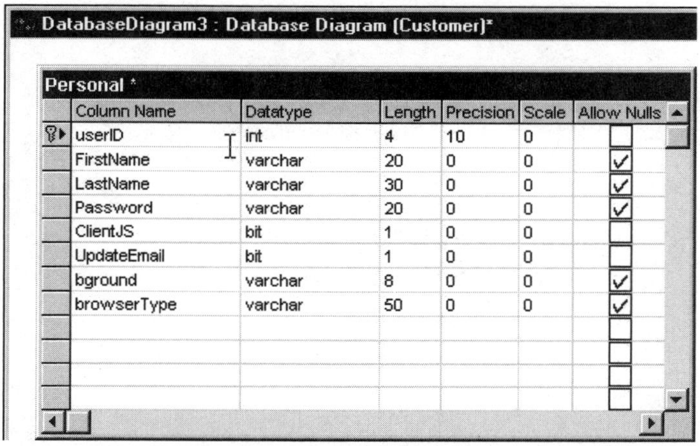

DatabaseDiagram3 : Database Diagram (Customer)*

Personal *

Column Name	Datatype	Length	Precision	Scale	Allow Nulls
userID	int	4	10	0	
FirstName	varchar	20	0	0	✓
LastName	varchar	30	0	0	✓
Password	varchar	20	0	0	✓
ClientJS	bit	1	0	0	
UpdateEmail	bit	1	0	0	
bground	varchar	8	0	0	✓
browserType	varchar	50	0	0	✓

8. With the table constructed, you should place a simple description of the table within the diagram so that its purpose is clear for other users. The Database Diagram toolbar includes several viewing options for each table. By default, Show Column Properties is set (this icon looks most like a table). To document the table more easily, you can collapse some of the characteristics so that they remain hidden.
9. Click the Show Column Names icon on the Database Diagram toolbar. The diagram automatically adjusts to show only the field names and the table title. The two other views of the table are available (Show Key Columns and Show Table Names) in addition to a custom view that can be created. With the extra room that hiding the specifics of the table provides, you can place text annotations on the diagram.
10. Click the New Text Annotation icon on the Database Diagram toolbar to see a box that allows text to be entered.
11. Enter a basic description of the table and its intended use. A description might be something like this:

```
Personal Table
Stores the information supplied by the user in the web
database solution called Personal created in Visual
Interdev. The userID field is used to match a cookie
stored in the client browser.
```

12. Resize the box and move it close to the actual table so that it can be easily read. You can change the font by right-clicking within the text box and selecting the

Set Text Annotation Font option. After you enter the necessary text, your final diagram should look similar to the following illustration.

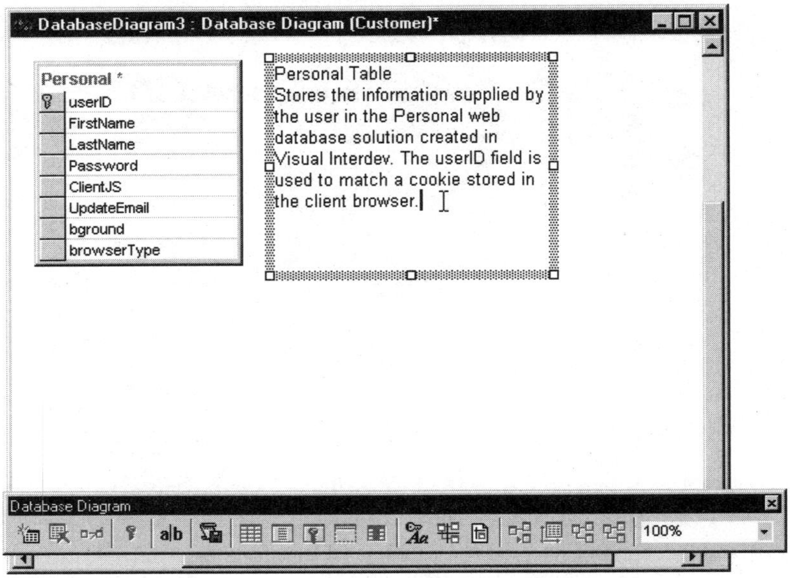

The diagram is now complete. Saving it is slightly more complicated than saving a standard Web page. The designer actually needs to create SQL code that is executed against SQL Server to modify the Customer database. Database Designer will automatically track future changes to the structure.

13. Select the Save Change Script icon on the Database Diagram toolbar. Since the diagram is stored on SQL Server for community access, you are asked to give the diagram a name. (A copy will also be stored on your local machine as a diagram file.)
14. Name the diagram **diaPersonal**, and then close the diagram window. After you close it, you can use Data View to open the table.
15. Right-click the Personal table item in the diaPersonal folder and select Open (shown next). The Open command displays the Query Designer editing window, which you can use to create new records or modify existing data. Then the recordset will open, and you can enter a sample record if you want.

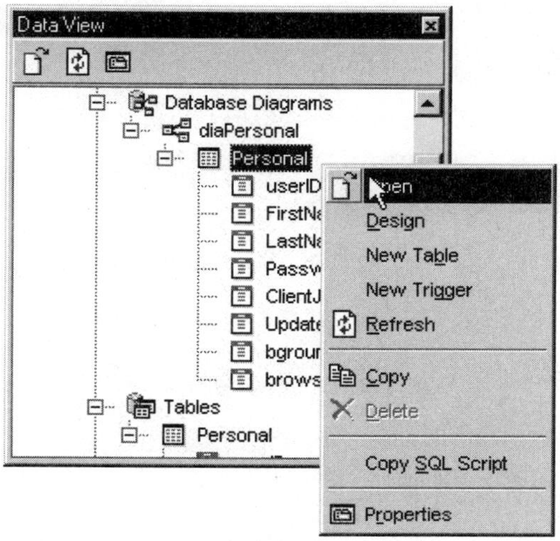

The Home Page (Default.asp)

The home page is accessed when the user first browses to the application. This home page will modify the way that it initially greets the user depending on the cookie configuration in the browser. The Default.asp page has four tasks:

- Check whether a cookie is available to indicate a user ID.
- If the user ID exists, look up information from the database and display the page in personalized mode.
- If no user ID exists, present options to look up the user ID or create a new one.
- Allow the entry of an e-mail address to obtain a password reminder.

Completing these tasks actually takes very little ASP code. Since the cookies are read from the collection in the Request object, the user ID, if available, is very easy to recover. If the cookie is valid, then the database must be accessed to determine if the ID is valid.

All the information from the database record is read directly into a series of Session variables. This allows any subsequent pages to retrieve preferences without having to access them in the database. When the page is initially displayed (see Figure 9-6), all the possible login options are displayed, because no cookies or Session variables exist yet.

1. Add a Web page to your Visual InterDev project (through the site diagram or new page wizard).

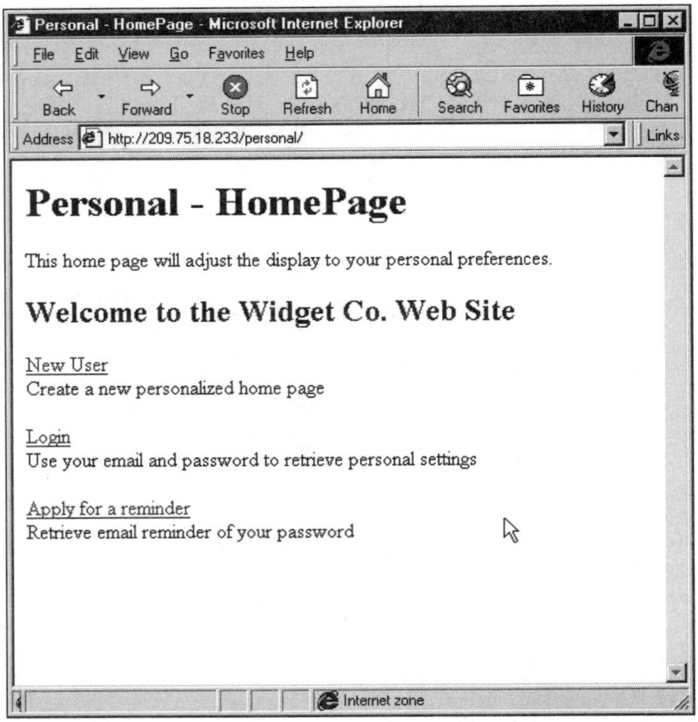

Figure 9-6. The initial view of the Personal application home page

2. Enter the following code:

```
<HTML>
<HEAD>
<%
   ' Check for the userID cookie
   If IsNumeric(Request.Cookies("userID")) Then
      Session("userID") = Request.Cookies("userID")
   Else
      Session("userID") = -1
   End If

   ' Set default background to white
   Session("bground") = "#FFFFFF"
```

```
    If Session("userID") <> -1 then
       Dim myConn

           Set myConn = Server.CreateObject("ADODB.Connection")
       connString = "PROVIDER=MSDASQL;DRIVER={SQL Server};" & _
          " UID=sa;PWD=;SERVER=MARINER3;DATABASE=Customer"
        myConn.Open connString

       If myConn.State = 1 Then
          Set myRS = Server.CreateObject("ADODB.Recordset")
          Set myRS.ActiveConnection = myConn
          ' Find the record that matched the userID
          myRS.Source = "select * from personal where userID =" _
             & session("userID")
          ' Open the recordset
          myRS.Open
          If myRS.State = 1 and Not myRS.EOF Then
             ' Place values in Session variables
             Session("FirstName") = myRS.Fields("FirstName")
             Session("LastName") = myRS.Fields("LastName")
             Session("Email") = myRS.Fields("Email")
             Session("Password") = myRS.Fields("Password")
             Session("clientJS") = myRS.Fields("clientJS")
             Session("updateEmail") = myRS.Fields("updateEmail")
             Session("bground") = myRS.Fields("bground")
          Else
             Response.Write("Error. Recordset could not " & _
                "created or no records found.<P>")
          End If

       set myRS = nothing
       End If
       myConn.Close
    End If
    Set myConn = Nothing
%>

<TITLE>Personal - HomePage</TITLE>
</HEAD>
<BODY bgcolor=<%=Session("bground") %> >
<H1>Personal - HomePage</H1>
This home page will adjust the display to your personal
preferences.<P>
```

```
<%
   ' Personalize introduction
   introStr = "<H2>Welcome to the Widget Co. Web Site"
   If Session("userID") <> -1 Then
      ' Greet user by name and allow logout
      Response.Write(introStr & ", " & Session("FirstName") &
"</H2>")
      Response.Write("<A HREF=logoutPersonal.asp>Logout</A><P>")
   Else
      ' Allow user to create personal record, login, or request a
      ' forgotten password
      Response.Write(introStr & "</H2>")
      Response.Write("<A HREF=addPersonal.asp>New User</A><BR>")
      Response.Write("Create a new personalized home page<P>")
      Response.Write("<A HREF=loginPersonal.asp>Login</A><BR>")
      Response.Write("Use your email and password to retrieve ")
      Response.Write("personal settings<P>")
      Response.Write("<A HREF=requestPersonal.asp>" & _
         "Apply for a reminder</A><br>")
      Response.Write("Retrieve email reminder of your
password<P>")
   End If
%>
</BODY>
</HTML>
```

3. Save the file to Default.asp in the project:

This page will be the cornerstone of the application.

addPersonal.asp

With the personalization page, a form is presented that allows entry of all the key user data. This page collects the following items:

- First and last name of the user
- Password
- E-mail address
- Client-side JavaScript execution preference

- Permission to send e-mail updates of the site
- Preferred background color

The input information is entered into the form and then submitted to writePersonal.asp. The ASP code in this page is primarily used to retrieve the scripting capabilities of the client browser. If JavaScript functionality is available, the Client JavaScript check box is automatically set (see Figure 9-7). If the browser lacks scripting ability, the check box is left clear.

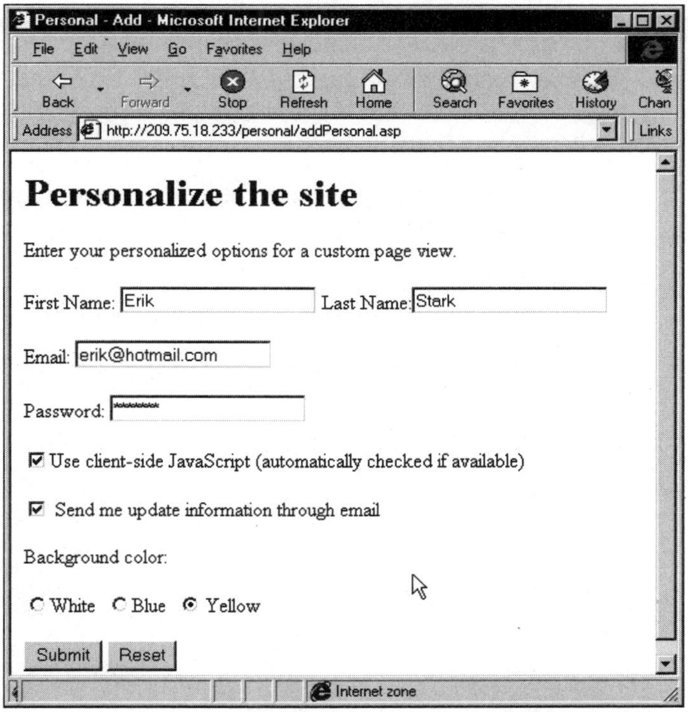

Figure 9-7. The browser scripting check box is automatically set if the browser is capable of JavaScript

TIP: Logins to Web sites are proliferating at an enormous rate. Most people have difficulty keeping track of all of their logins. Most of the more advanced sites now allow entry of your e-mail address in addition to a password. As opposed to a user ID, people always know their e-mail address. Consider using this means of identification.

Chapter 11 explains how to use the Web server to e-mail a message. This functionality can be easily used to send users a reminder of their password if they request it.

Chapter 8 describes how to simulate a session using a QueryString to track the user through the site. Another method of tracking is made possible through the Request object. As you probably known, every machine on the Internet must be assigned an Internet Protocol (IP) address to send and receive data. The IP address acts essentially like the computer's phone number.

A computer's IP address may be either static, identifying the machine on the network, or dynamic, assigned by a service provider (such as an ISP or AOL) each time a dial-in connection is made to the network.

Either way, for the time that the user is accessing Web sites for that session, the IP address remains the same. Your ASP code can read the IP address used by the computer and use it to uniquely identify and track the user, at least for that session.

Add a Web page to your Visual InterDev project, enter the following code, and save the file to addPersonal.asp in the project.

```
<html>
<head>
<title>Personal - Add</title>
<meta name="GENERATOR" content="Microsoft FrontPage 3.0">
</head>
<OBJECT RUNAT=Server ID=myBrowser PROGID="MSWC.BrowserType">
</OBJECT>
<body>
<h1>Personalize the site</h1>

<p>Enter your personalized options for a custom page view.</p>

<form method="POST" action="writePersonal.asp">
  <p>First Name: <input type="text" name="FirstName" size="20">
  Last Name:<input type="text" name="LastName" size="20"></p>
  <p>Email: <input type="text" name="Email" size="20"></p>
  <p>Password: <input type="password" name="Password" size="20"></p>
  <p><input type="checkbox" name="clientJS" value="ON"
   <%
   ' Read browser JavaScript capability
   If CBool(myBrowser.Javascript) Then
```

```
      Response.Write(" checked")
Else
      Response.Write(" disabled")
   End If
   %>
  >Use client-side JavaScript (automatically
  checked if available)</p>
  <p><input type="checkbox" name="updateEmail" value="ON" checked>
  Send me update information through email</p>
  <p>Background color:</p>
  <p>
  <input type="radio" name="R1" value="V1" checked >
   White 
  <input type="radio" name="R1" value="V2">Blue 
  <input type="radio" name="R1" value="V3">Yellow</p>
  <p><input type="submit" value="Submit" name="B1">
  <input type="reset" value="Reset" name="B2"></p>
</form>
</body>
</html>
```

writePersonal.asp

After the information from the form is returned, it needs to be written into the Personal database. The database table also returns the current value of the userID column, which is sent to a cookie in the browser.

This page has several unique features, the most apparent of which is the ASP execution code that appears before the `<HTML>` tag is sent. Cookies must be written to the browser before any HTML is sent, because (like the `Redirect` command) the information is sent to the browser in the initial HTTP response. Therefore, before any HTML is transmitted, the information must be added to the table, the user ID must be retrieved, and the cookie must be set (see Figure 9-8).

Because the settings come before the HTML page text, local variables are not kept intact when the page begins executing. Therefore, setting a variable such as `myVar = 3` in the initial code does not allow retrieval of the value in the main page body. This is why Session variables are used to effectively provide the information-passing capacity that is required.

Certain variables sent from the form require special handling. HTML check boxes provide the text "ON" or "OFF" instead of sending an actual Boolean value. For this reason, an `If...Then` structure is required to set the database field properly. Also, the value of radio buttons is returned as a string setting. In this example, a `Select Case` statement is used to process the correctly selected background color.

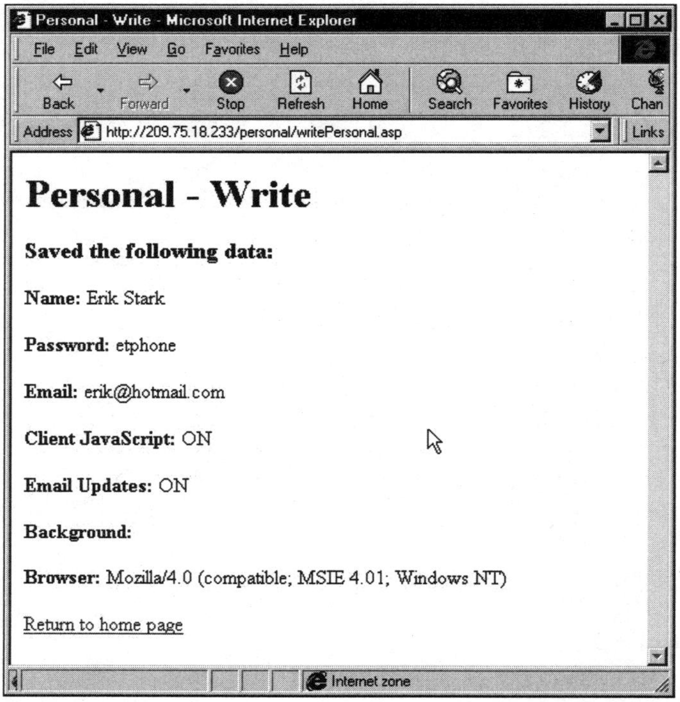

Figure 9-8. The data is written to the database and displayed on the Web page

Add a Web page to your Visual InterDev project, enter the following code, and save the file to writePersonal.asp in the project:

```
<%
   Dim myConn
       Set myConn = Server.CreateObject("ADODB.Connection")
   connString = "PROVIDER=MSDASQL;DRIVER={SQL Server};" & _
      " UID=sa;PWD=;SERVER=Mariner3;DATABASE=Customer"
    myConn.Open connString
   If myConn.State = 1 Then
      Set myRS = Server.CreateObject("ADODB.Recordset")
      Set myRS.ActiveConnection = myConn
      myRS.CursorType = 2 ' adOpenDynamic
      myRS.CursorLocation = 2 ' adUseServer
      myRS.LockType = 3 ' adLockOptimistic
```

```
myRS.Source = "select * from personal"
myRS.Open
If myRS.State = 1 Then
   ' Add a new record
   myRS.AddNew
   ' Record user information
   myRS.Fields("FirstName") = Request.Form("FirstName")
   myRS.Fields("LastName") = Request.Form("LastName")
   myRS.Fields("Password") = Request.Form("Password")
   myRS.Fields("Email") = Request.Form("Email")
   ' Read browser information from ServerVariables
   myRS.Fields("browserType") = _
      Request.ServerVariables("HTTP_USER_AGENT")

   ' Evaluate HTML checkbox variables
   If Request.Form("clientJS") = "ON" Then
      myRS.Fields("clientJS") = 1
   End If
   If Request.Form("updateEmail") = "ON" Then
      myRS.Fields("updateEmail") = 1
   End If

   ' Determine which radio control was selected
   Select Case Request.Form("R1")
      ' White
      Case "V1"
         bground = "#FFFFFF"
         txtColor = "White"
      ' Blue
      Case "V2"
         bground = "#000020"
         txtColor = "Blue"
      ' Yellow
      Case "V3"
         bground = "#FFFFA0"
         txtColor = "Yellow"
   End Select
   myRS.Fields("bground") = bground
   Session("txtColor") = txtColor
   myRS.Update

   ' Write the new identity value
   Response.Cookies("userID") = myRS.Fields("userID")
   ' Indicate there was no error
```

```
            Session("Error") = ""
        Else
            Session("Error") = _
                ("Error. Recordset could not be <P>")
        End If
    Else
        Session("Error") = _
            "Error. Connection could not be opened.<P>"
    End If
    myConn.Close
    Set myConn = Nothing
%>
<HTML>
<HEAD>
<TITLE>Personal - Write</TITLE>
</HEAD>
<BODY>
<H1>Personal - Write</H1>

<%
    If Len(Session("Error")) > 0 Then
        Response.Write("<B>An error occurred:</B><P>")
        Response.Write(Session("Error"))
        Session("Error") = ""
    Else
        Response.Write("<H3>Saved the following data:</H3><P>")
        Response.Write("<B>Name:</B> " & Request.Form("FirstName") & " ")
        Response.Write(Request.Form("LastName") & "<P>")
        Response.Write("<B>Password:</B> " & _
            Request.Form("Password") & "<P>")
        Response.Write("<B>Email:</B> " & Request.Form("Email") & "<P>")

        Response.Write("<B>Email Updates:</B> " & _
            Request.Form("updateEmail") & "<P>")
        Response.Write("<B>Background:</B> " & _
            Session( "txtColor" ) & "<P>")
        Response.Write("<B>Browser:</B> " &
Request.ServerVariables("HTTP_USER_AGENT") & "<P>")
    End If
%>
<A HREF=default.asp>Return to home page</A><P>
</BODY>
</HTML>
```

Notice that the browser information is stored with each user profile. Since you have the INI browser definition file (browscap.ini) on the server's hard drive, you can correlate the database information with this INI database to render a report on your registered users. This might be a particularly effective method of watching your intranet to see which browsers are actually being used to access your Web solution.

loginPersonal.asp

You need a page that enables users to reestablish their records on the browser. Too many sites forget to provide this option, and thus require complete reentry of all the user information. Not only is this irritating to the user, but it also can clutter the database with duplicate information.

The loginPersonal.asp page presents a simple form that allows the user to enter their e-mail address and password (see Figure 9-9). The data entered is submitted to enterPersonal.asp.

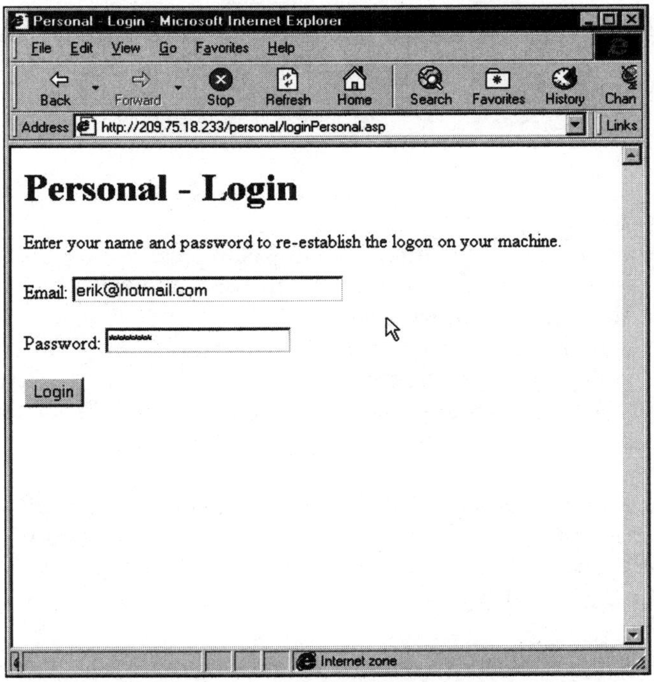

Figure 9-9. The e-mail address and password can be entered to create the browser cookie

Add a Web page to your Visual InterDev project, enter the following code, and save the file to loginPersonal.asp in the project:

```
<html>
<head>
<title>Personal - Login</title>
<meta name="GENERATOR" content="Microsoft FrontPage 3.0">
</head>
<body>
<h1>Personal - Login</h1>

<p>Enter your E-mail address and password to re-establish the
logon on your machine.</p>

<form method="POST" action="enterPersonal.asp">
   <p>Email: <input type="text" name="reqEmail" size="30"></p>
   <p>Password: <input type="password" name="reqPassword"
size="20"></p>
   <p><input type="submit" value="Login" name="B1"></p>
</form>
</body>
</html>
```

enterPersonal.asp

Once the information has been requested from the login page, it must be retrieved from the database. Like the writePersonal.asp page, this page must modify a cookie if the user login is correct. Therefore, the ASP code must occur before any HTML is sent to the browser.

The supplied e-mail address is queried in the Personal table. The `Like` keyword is used in the SQL query to ignore case sensitivity, which might otherwise prevent the e-mail address from being located. If the e-mail login is authentic, the password for that user preference account is checked. The `equal (=)` operator is used in this case to ensure an exact match.

After the user is confirmed by their e-mail address and password, the `userID` parameter of the Response object's Cookies collection is set to the located user ID. The client browser is now set to have the user information retrieved when the user accesses the Default.asp page (see Figure 9-10).

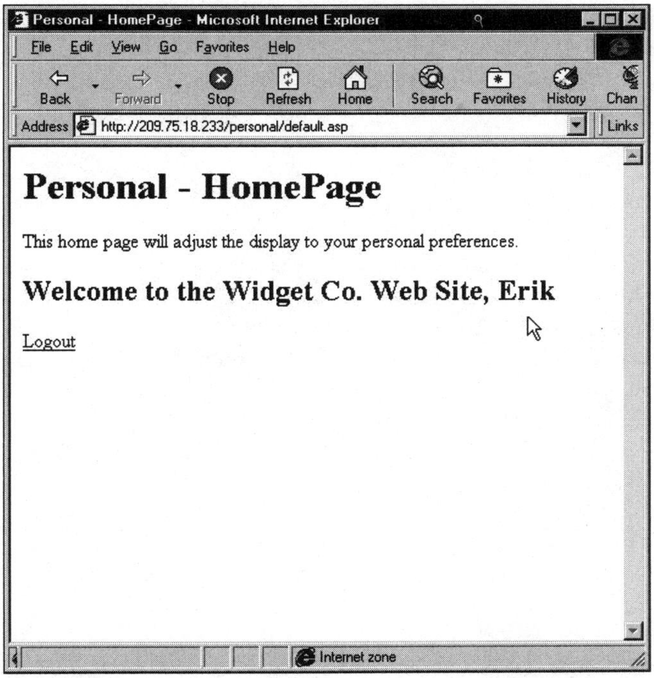

Figure 9-10. The Default.asp, when accessed, now displays a custom presentation

Add a Web page to your Visual InterDev project, enter the following code, and save the file to enterPersonal.asp in the project:

```
<%
Dim myConn
       Set myConn = Server.CreateObject("ADODB.Connection")
   connString = "PROVIDER=MSDASQL;DRIVER={SQL Server};" & _
      " UID=sa;PWD=;SERVER=Mariner3;DATABASE=Customer"
    myConn.Open connString
```

```
    If myConn.State = 1 Then
       Set myRS = Server.CreateObject("ADODB.Recordset")
       Set myRS.ActiveConnection = myConn
       myRS.CursorLocation = 2 ' adUseServer
       Session("login") = 0
       Session("Error") = "The Email address and/or password is invalid"
       myRS.Source = "select * from personal where email like '" _
          & Request.Form("reqEmail") & "'"
       myRS.Open
       If myRS.State = 1 and Not myRS.EOF Then
          ' Check for a valid password
          If myRS.Fields("Password") = Request.Form("reqPassword") Then
             Response.Cookies("userID") = myRS.Fields("userID")
             Session("login") = 13
             Session("Error") = ""
          End If
       End If
Set myRS = Nothing
    Else
       Session("Error") = "Error. Connection could not be opened.<P>"
    End If
    myConn.Close
    Set myConn = Nothing
%>
<HTML>
<HEAD>
<TITLE>Personal - Login Entry</TITLE>
</HEAD>
<BODY>
<H1>Personal - Login Entry</H1>

<%
    If Session("login") = 13 Then
       Response.Write("<H3>Login successful</H3><P>")
    Else
       Response.Write("<H3>Login failed</H3><P>")
       Response.Write("<B>An error occurred: </B>")
       Response.Write(Session("Error") & "<P>")
       Session("Error") = ""
    End If
    Session("login") = 0
%>
<A HREF=default.asp>Return to home page</A><P>
```

```
</BODY>
</HTML>
```

logoutPersonal.asp

For a variety of reasons, including multiple users on a single browser or multiple server accounts, the user may want to destroy the cookie that ushers them personally into the site. When a cookie is destroyed, the logoutPersonal page simply sets the userID cookie to an empty string.

Add a Web page to your Visual InterDev project, enter the following code, and save the file to logoutPersonal.asp in the project:

```
<%
   ' Clear the userID cookie
   Response.Cookies("userID") = ""
%>
<HTML>
<HEAD>

<TITLE>Personal - Clear</TITLE>
</HEAD>
<BODY>
<H1>Personal - Clear</H1>

This page clears the login connection for the current browser.<P>
<H2>Login cleared</H2>
<A HREF=default.asp>Return to homepage</A><P>
</BODY>
</HTML>
```

requestPersonal.asp

Once the requestPersonal page receives the information from the Default.asp page, the e-mail address is looked up in the Personal database. In this solution, the page displays the password directly, which isn't a good idea in a real application. (Chapter 11 explains how to add e-mail capabilities to your Web server.) When a reminder is requested, the Web page can send an e-mail message to that address to remind the user.

Add a Web page to your Visual InterDev project, enter the following code, and save the file to requestPersonal.asp in the project:

```
<html>
<head>
<title>Personal - Request</title>
<meta name="GENERATOR" content="Microsoft FrontPage 3.0">
</head>
<body>
```

```
<h1>Personal - Request</h1>

<p>Send me a reminder of my password.</p>

<form method="POST" action="remindPersonal.asp">
   <p>Email: <input type="text" name="reqEmail" size="20"></p>
   <p><input type="submit" value="Submit" name="B1">
</form>
</body>
</html>
```

remindPersonal.asp

The final piece of the Web solution involves reading the forgotten password of a user from the Personal table. In a real solution, the password would be sent to the user at the specified e-mail address. Here, you create a dummy page that simply displays the password (not too useful) until you use the Web server e-mail capabilities to mail back the information to the user.

If you want to use this system for a real application, be sure to delete this page before deployment. Without the e-mail connector, security is nonexistent. However, other than the general settings, this solution includes no methods for editing the existing record information. Therefore, capturing a user's password won't jeopardize the information available in the table.

Add a Web page to your Visual InterDev project, enter the following code, and save the file to remindPersonal.asp in the project:

```
<%
Dim myConn
      Set myConn = Server.CreateObject("ADODB.Connection")
   myConn.Open connString
   If myConn.State = 1 Then
      Set myRS = Server.CreateObject("ADODB.Recordset")
      Set myRS.ActiveConnection = myConn
      myRS.CursorLocation = 2 ' adUseServer
      ' Search for the record with a matching email
      myRS.Source = "select * from personal where email like '" _
         & Request.Form("reqEmail") & "'"
      ' Attempt to open the recordset containing the information
      myRS.Open
      If myRS.State = 1 and Not myRS.EOF Then
         ' If password is located, add it to a session
         ' variable that won't be lost once the page begins
         Session("myPassword") = myRS.Fields("Password")
      End If
```

```
   Else
      Response.Write("Error. Connection could not be opened.<P>")
   End If
   myConn.Close
   ' Eliminate the connection
Set myConn = nothing
%>
<HTML>
<HEAD>
<TITLE>Personal - Reminder</TITLE>
</HEAD>
<BODY>
<H1>Personal - Reminder</H1>
Here is the reminder of your password from the
 email address you supplied.
<%
   Response.Write("<H3>Your password is:</H3><P>")
   Response.Write(Session("myPassword") & "<P>")
%>
<A HREF=default.asp>Return to home page</A><P>
</BODY>
</HTML>
```

Your solution is now complete, at least for the moment. This temporary example enables you to read the passwords of users until you add the e-mail capabilities in Chapter 11.

Examining the Logins

Since the cookie writes to the local browser, you should use several different browsers (perhaps from different machines) to test to make sure the cookie writes properly and that the solution is working. After you test the application, you can check all the data that is contained in the table. In SQL Enterprise Manager, a simple query tool is included that enables you to execute SQL statements against the server, and then displays the results. When you have to use SQL Server in your everyday work, this window becomes almost indispensable.

Using the query tool, you can examine the entered data by following these steps:

1. Execute SQL Enterprise Manager.
2. Open the database folder and expand the Customer database. You'll see two folders: Groups/Users and Objects. In the Objects folder, you'll find the Tables folder, which contains the table you created in Database Designer. Although you can make changes to the structure of the database here, to keep the structural modification and documentation limited to a single place, you should make all changes from within Database Designer.

3. Select the personal table.
4. Select Tools | SQL Query Tool. This tool is equivalent to the iSQL tool in the Start menu's SQL Server folder. From the iSQL window, you can easily select any of the databases in the current SQL Server. Because you executed the window from the Enterprise Manager objects, the drop-down list box should already be set to the Customer database.
5. To display all the user records in the query window enter:

```
select * from personal
```

6. Click the Execute Query button on the toolbar.

On the Results tab, you will see all of the fields and data represented by the table. The query tool can actually hold many different queries and SQL statements; they simply become additions to the combo box listing in the top of the window. Individual queries can also be saved as .sql files for later retrieval.

For additional testing, you can leave the query window open. Changes to the database can be seen simply by clicking on the Execute Query button again to update the Results tab.

Q&A

Q: Can I use Database Designer with existing databases?
A: Yes. In fact, Database Designer will create a SQL `ALTER` statement to modify the existing table. Try adding another field to the database diagram of the Personal table, and the modification code will be displayed.

Q: After the user enters information, can I have ASP code modify a cookie?
A: No, writing to a cookie, like a redirect command, can only be done before HTML is sent to the browser. One modification method is to write a cookie in conjunction with a redirect command. Have the user click to a linked page that writes the cookie and then immediately redirects the browser to the intended destination page.

SUMMARY

You've created your first complete bottom-to-top Web database application. The application uses a cookie stored in the client browser to link to a preferences profile that is stored in the database table named Personal. Options are provided to recall the password, log in, and log out to clear the user cookie to log in with a different browser. In this chapter, you covered:

- **Database Designer** In Visual InterDev, Database Designer allows you to diagram a database for creation on SQL Server. It also allows you to add text annotation to the diagram for more robust documentation.
- **SQL Server Developer Edition** Visual Studio includes the Developer Edition of Microsoft's database server, which makes development possible even on smaller machines. The Developer Edition is completely feature-compatible with the full version of SQL Server.
- **Identity field** Similar to the Microsoft Access Autonumber field type, an Identity field in SQL Server automatically increments the number stored in the field when a new record is created.
- **userID cookie** The user ID is stored in a client-side cookie so that each access to the site can simply read the cookie and look up the related record held in the server-side database. A cookie can be written to the Response object only before any HTML is sent to the browser. Cookies can be read from the Request object at any time.
- **Database device** Within SQL Server, all databases exist within contiguous files that appear to the NT operating system as a single file.

CHAPTER 10

Creating a Customer Survey Database Application

In Chapter 9, you created your first database in SQL Server to use for Web application data entry. The table that was used for input was actually very simple. From this foundation, you can now build on that application to create a more robust set of related tables to allow for a customer survey.

THE POWER OF WEB-BASED SURVEYS

Survey questionnaires are perhaps the simplest, yet most useful and direct method of getting opinions about a variety of topics for an organization. You can create applications such as the following:

- **Management review** The number of forms that management requires, from performance evaluations to project assessments, can be staggering. The time taken processing these forms is further increased because these forms require respondents to fill them out by hand. This makes data correlation difficult, in addition to putting a strain on the data-entry infrastructure when the data must be entered. An intranet-based form allows the user to easily type responses online. The final data can be quickly and easily tabulated.
- **Customer satisfaction** On Internet or extranet sites, a survey can be the perfect tool for judging outside perceptions of your organization. Even a suggestion box can be established as a Web page.
- **New product features** The desire for new product features are often difficult to quantify. By categorizing the requests for specific features, a single query can quickly provide information to give you a competitive edge.
- **Demographic information** Many organizations spend large amounts of money to acquire demographic information. These costs can be dramatically lowered with the use of a Web database application. Initial registration forms can be used to retrieve customer information that would be expensive to acquire by other means.

These applications are only a few of the possibilities that organizations have found for Web-based forms. In the past, data collected from survey forms has been difficult to convert into useful information. The large number of steps involved from collecting the data (i.e. paper forms, telephone surveys, etc.) to placing the data into a database for correlation and summarization was troublesome. Early attempts at computerizing forms have been cumbersome and expensive.

Even deploying a survey form electronically was difficult. In a client/server system, a new application must be sent to users for each new form. Another method has been to send a word processing document for manual entries into provided spaces. Neither of these methods has proved very effective or satisfactory.

The Web has broken open this field by making truly inexpensive and accessible methods available. A Web-based survey offers the following advantages:

- Data is entered directly into a database.
- The form is accessible from any Web browser anywhere on the network.
- Entry error–checking provides instant feedback and prevents invalid information from being entered.
- Data is available as soon as it is entered for query and tabulation.

You may have noticed that many cutting-edge Internet sites even feed the survey data directly back to the users. For example, www.msnbc.com allows users to rate how useful (on a scale of 1 to 10) the story they just read was to them. One of the most popular pages on MSNBC is the Viewer Top 10 which takes that simple survey information and displays the stories readers have rated as being the most useful.

RELATIONAL DATABASE CONCEPTS

In Chapter 9, you created a simple flat database that contained only a single table; thus there were no relationships between tables. Creating effective relationships, as you've seen in the Northwind database, is critical to effective categorization of data. Relations between tables can avoid duplication of data, improve the flexibility of queries on the data, and promotes better information organization. Before you actually create the new table and link it to the existing table, it will be useful to review the core database concepts that are used when establishing the relationships.

Joins

When two or more tables are linked together, that is said to be a *join*. A join between tables is made possible by each table containing a field that relates to a field held in the other table. For example, in a financial database, the taxpayer ID field could exist in the address book table as well as a transactions table. The value stored in the taxpayer ID field of each transaction record would relate to a taxpayer ID found in the address book table. In the Northwind database that you've been using, there are numerous joins that relate information between tables such as the orders and order details.

DEFINITION: **Join** A conceptual linking of multiple tables through the use of corresponding field values. A join requires a field (known as key fields) in each of the involved tables that can hold a value that indicates a record in the other table.

The fields that are used to create the join are known as key fields. Most often, the data type of key field for the relationship is an AutoIncremented or Identity field (see Figure 10-1). The key field used to connect tables does not have to be a number, but using a numeric data type allows for the fastest join execution.

In the tables of the Northwind database, the CustomerID field is actually a character string. A key for a single database can also span across multiple fields. For example, you could make both the first name and last name fields the key fields for a database. Since only the first name or only the last name fields alone would probably not be unique, using both fields can allow safety for individual record tracking.

There are actually two types of key fields: a *primary key* and a *foreign key*. The primary key exists in a table to uniquely identify each record. Although a primary key can span multiple fields, the fields are used together to act as a single unique identifier. Foreign key fields store the referencing value of the primary key field for a particular record to provide the relation.

DEFINITIONS: **Primary key** A unique identifier for each record that is typically used to provide a reference in another table to allow relationships. For example, a CustomerID field in a Customer table. A primary key may consist of one or more fields.

Foreign key The field in a table that references a primary key field value in another table. For example, a CustomerID field in an Invoice table that indicates a specific customer record in the Customer table.

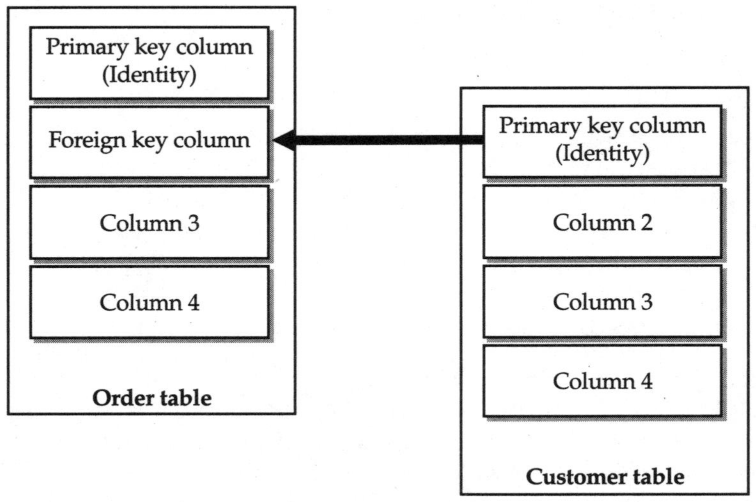

Figure 10-1. Two or more tables are joined through unique key fields

The relationships of the Northwind database are shown in Figure 10-2. The primary key of the Customers table is CustomerID. This field uniquely identifies each record. One of the foreign keys in the Orders table is the CustomerID field, which holds values that connect it to the records in the Customers table.

In Chapter 9, when you created the Personal table, you set the userID field to be the key field. The userID field becomes the primary key that can be related to another table. This primary key will be used in this chapter to link it to a related foreign-key field stored in the Survey table you'll create.

Unlike table structures, field types, and other items that are actually stored within the database, a *join* is an explicit relationship that is sent with each query. For example, this code shows a simple join:

```
select * from customers, invoices where customers.userid = invoices.userid
```

You can see in this code that the equal operator (=) actually generates the relationship between the records in the two tables. Constructing these joins can be extremely complicated. The Query Builder, included in Visual InterDev, simplifies the process of making joins.

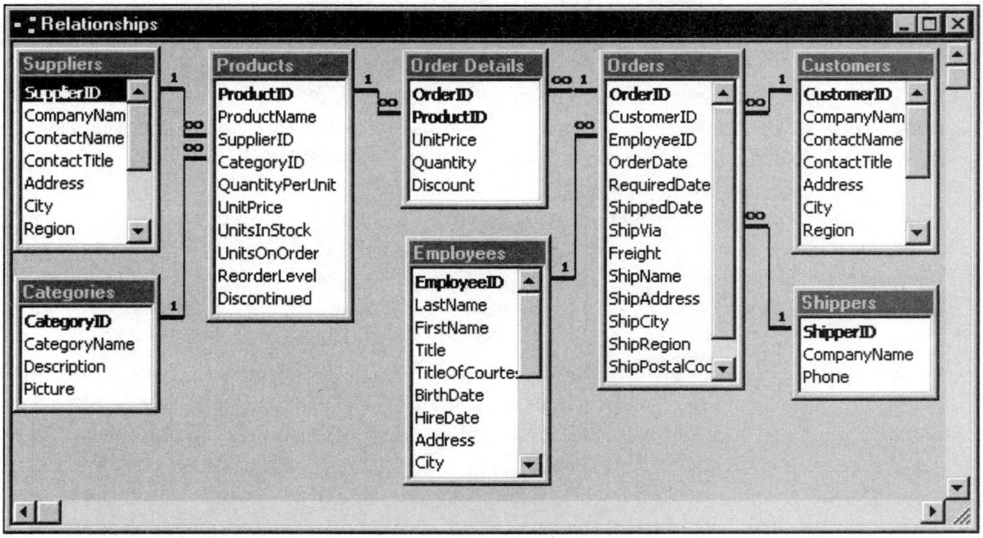

Figure 10-2. The Northwind database contains numerous primary and foreign-key relationships

DEFINITIONS: **Inner join** The default method of join, which combines the returned values of the records for two tables only when the values of the joined fields are equal.
Left outer join A left outer join takes all of the records from the table on the left side of the join in the result set and combines them with those on the right side of the join only when the values of the joined fields are equal. For each record in the left table that has no matching entry in the right table, the right table fields are returned filled with Nulls.
Right outer join Exactly like the left outer join except that the right side table is made primary.

TIP: When you are just beginning to understand queries, you should try to test your knowledge. For example, you already know the Northwind database very well. Make a copy of the file and name it TestWind.mdb. Load it into Microsoft Access and examine the relationships by selecting the Relationships option under the Tools menu.

Now delete the current relationships. For practice, recreate the relationships between the tables. Checking your relationships with those of the original file will help you understand how the joins are used.

For a join there are three primary types of relationships: one-to-many, many-to-one, and one-to-one. The most common, one-to-many, allows many records of one table to be linked to a single entry in another. One-to-one relationships are the least common, but you will use one in the survey application because each user will only be able to enter information for the survey once.

DEFINITIONS: **One-to-many** When a single record in one table relates to many records in another table. For example, a single customer record may be related to many order records.
Many-to-many When records in both tables can hold multiple relationships between the two tables. A database that contains inventory information may have one table for the manufacturing locations and one table for the products. The products may be made in several different locations and each location may make several different products.
One-to-one A single record in one table relates to one and only one record in another table. This would be the case if a table of Social Security information were linked to a driver's license table via the SSN. Each individual would only have one record of Social Security information and one driver's license.

New records can be added to a multi-table join. When this occurs in a one-to-many relationship, the "one" record will perform an auto-lookup. If the key exists, a record will only be added to the "many" table. For example, if a query joined an Orders table to an Invoice table, adding a record to the result set would indicate whether an invoice already existed with that invoice number. If so, the order item entry would be created, and it would assume the link to the primary table.

NOTE: To allow updates of a query that has a join, the INNER JOIN and OUTER JOIN keywords must be stated explicitly. A query that uses the Where clause only for the join will not be updateable.

As mentioned earlier, a join is not an actual structure that is stored in the database itself, but rather a clause held within a query. Although the join isn't part of the database, there are two types of representation of a join that can be placed within a table: a relationship and referential integrity.

The relationships are the connections that you see in the Relationships window in Microsoft Access. When using the query building wizards in Microsoft Access, these relationships help the wizard to generate the proper join within the query. The relationships can also form the basis of database rules known as referential integrity.

Referential integrity refers to a set of rules that ensure that relations between tables remain valid for all the records they contain. For example, if there is an orders table and an orders detail table, what happens if an order record is deleted? In a normal database, the table that contained the order details would have a number of orphaned records that no longer point to a valid order record. To prevent this from occurring, referential integrity can be created for a database to ensure that any changes to a record that hold a primary key, affect the related records as well.

Services such as cascading updates and deletes enforce this integrity and simplify the amount of manual maintenance that must be performed. Cascading updates will update the foreign keys in a related table when changes are made to the primary key. Cascading deletes will delete all of the related records when a primary record is deleted. These two services enforce the rules set up for referential integrity.

DEFINITIONS: **Cascading update** Changing the primary key automatically changes the foreign key values of the related tables.
Cascading delete Deleting a record in the primary table deletes all of the related records in the foreign key table.

Adding referential integrity to a set of tables enforces a number of additional rules to make certain all of the relations are valid. These rules include:

- A foreign key value cannot be entered unless a record with that primary key exists in the related table. A foreign key may, however, contain a Null to specify that it is not related to any record in the primary table.
- A record in the primary table cannot be deleted if connected records exist in the attached table.
- The primary key cannot be changed if there are related records.

Referential integrity on a SQL Server database can be configured in the Database Designer that is part of the Visual InterDev, Visual Basic, and Visual J++ development environments. When you construct a Database Diagram in the designer and you draw a connection between two fields, the Create Relationship window will appear, offering the option to "Enable relationship for INSERT and UPDATE." Selecting this option will create the integrity for that relationship.

Normalization

When you create a relational database system where several tables are interconnected, your design requirements are more stringent than when a single table is used. If the relationships between tables are well constructed, SQL queries work well, reports are simple to generate, and database interaction executes quickly.

The process of deciding how the information will be stored among several tables is known as *normalization*. Normalization seeks to minimize duplication of information within the database.

DEFINITION: **Normalization** The process of grouping information around key fields and minimizing the duplication of information within a table. Preventing duplication is most often done by breaking the fields out into other related tables.

The first step to designing a database is listing the columns (or fields) that you know you will need. Once most of the fields are known, you can begin deciding which fields should be placed in which table. All of the columns could be placed in a single table, but that would be incredibly inefficient.

To decide which columns belong together in the same table, you must consider their *functional dependencies*. Functional dependency indicates a direct relationship between a particular field and the table's primary key. For example, in an address book table where the primary key field is a social security number (SSN), the lastName and firstName fields are functionally dependent on the SSN for identification. It would make little sense to place the lastName and firstName columns in another table since they require the SSN for their unique identity.

A person's work address, in contrast, may be held by many different people and is not functionally dependent on the individual's primary key. The primary key is a very good indicator of the exact function of the table, since it defines how the record will be uniquely accessed.

You should also take into account the rules for normalization when determining which columns belong in a given table. There are three basic levels of data normalization:

- **First Normal Form** There are no repeating groups of fields and all values are atomic
- **Second Normal Form** Every field in the table is fully dependent on the primary key
- **Third Normal Form** Non-key fields are fully dependent on the primary key and not on another key field in the table

These forms are hierarchical in that by the time the database is compliant with the third normal form, the rules of the first two are already assumed to have been fulfilled. The forms are described in more detail in the following sections.

First Normal Form

To achieve the first normal form, also known as structural or syntactic normalization, you need to eliminate repeating fields. For example, a customer record may have fields named contact1, contact2, and contact3. Complying with the first normal form, these references would be placed into a related one-to-many table where the customer record would be linked to a number of contact records.

The requirement that values be atomic means that each field represents one and only one thing. Therefore, you wouldn't have a column that stored the address, city, state, and zip code. This practice assures that querying and sorting can be done on atomic values, such as locating all the records with a particular zip code. Combined fields make searching for data far more difficult.

Second Normal Form

The second normal form specifies that all fields must be dependent on the primary key. This form requires you to ask of each field: Is the field directly related to the primary key? In a Customer table, an address field would be directly related to the unique primary key. However, if the table contained order items, fields for the order items would not comply. There would have to be a customer record for each order item, making the orders not strictly dependent on the customer record, but on the order that contained them. You usually don't have to worry about the second normal form, because if the primary key of a table is a single field and the table is in the first normal form, it is automatically compliant with the second normal form.

Third Normal Form

The third normal form requires that each non-key column be dependent on the primary key and only the primary key. For example, if you add a field to the Customer table that contains a companyID that relates to the employer of the customer, you would have a link to the Company table. It would be a violation of the third normal form to store the name of the company in the Customer record. Storing the companyName field in the Customer table would mean the company name value was dependent on the companyID field, not the primary key.

Learning Limits of Normalization

The process of properly normalizing a database takes practice. When normalization is optimal, data entry and data reporting are significantly easier because the organization of the data is almost self-explanatory. As you begin creating tables on your own and use the normal forms to guide your decisions, keep in mind these general guidelines:

- **Don't normalize excessively** Many beginners end up creating far more tables than are necessary. Not only does this complicate the solution, but it also creates a significant penalty in performance. Not every piece of data that has the *potential* of requiring multiple values needs to be broken into a separate table.

- **Use the normal forms as guidelines** The normal forms were created to maximize the capabilities of your database. If a solution requires bending one of the form rules (usually the nonrepeating field maxim in the first normal form), it may be appropriate to ignore the rule in that particular case.
- **Examine the potential queries you will need** Sometimes, single-table queries on a complex inner relationship can be cumbersome. Understanding the queries that will be needed for the solution can aid in deciding what amount of normalization should take place.

AUGMENTING THE PERSONAL APPLICATION

The example survey application you will create in the chapter will have a single point of data entry (the survey page). Like the drill-down report you created in Chapter 6, there will be many ways to examine the information entered by the survey visitors.

The application will also take advantage of the table and application structure that you created in Chapter 9 to use the primary information already entered by a user. To take part in the survey, the user will be required to register with the system.

This modification will also provide the chance to learn some of the concepts that make relational databases so powerful. The new Survey table will be linked to the existing user tables in the database. Enforcing the relational database structures within the database will prevent orphaned survey data if the user is removed from the system.

Design-Time Controls

This book has introduced the basic Visual InterDev methods of using object controls and hand-coding to facilitate most solutions. The controls have been simple visual representations of objects that exist on the ASP server. Visual InterDev also includes the more powerful option of using *design-time controls* (see Figure 10-3).

Design-time controls execute within Visual InterDev to provide a user interface for configuring the features of the control. The user interface available to the designer is hidden at run-time when the controls merely execute their configured functions.

> ***DEFINITION:*** **Design-time control** A design-time control allows properties to be set and wizards to be invoked in the development environment. When the application is compiled to a final ASP page, the control outputs standard ASP code that will execute on the Web server. Therefore, from the standpoint of the Web server, no control is executing—only ASP code.

Visual InterDev comes with numerous controls of this type, and they can be found on the Design-Time tab of the toolbox palette. Some of these design-time controls include:

- **Recordset** Like the Data Control in Visual Basic, the Recordset design-time control allows controls to be bound to it to provide display, insertion, and

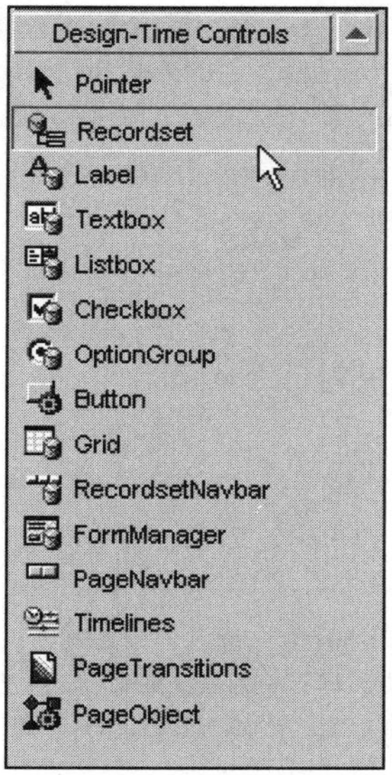

Figure 10-3. The design-time controls are located in the Toolbox palette

editing of table records. The recordset can be configured to provide records from a particular data source and table.

- **Bound controls** The bound controls include all of the standard HTML controls such as Label, Textbox, Listbox, Checkbox, OptionGroup (radio controls), and Grid. These controls are attached to a design-time Recordset.
- **Button** Button objects can be displayed as either an image or an HTML button, and scripting for the control is available through either the Server Objects and Events (for server-side controls) or Client Objects and Events properties.
- **FormManager** The FormManager manages the display of controls, records, and navigation for form-based projects. This powerful control allows you to create a single page that can be used for adding, editing, and browsing records in a database.
- **PageNavbar** The PageNavbar provides forward and back paging through a recordset. When used in conjunction with the Recordset and FormManager controls, an interface very similar to a Visual Basic Data Control form can be created.

- **Timelines** For DHTML-capable browsers, Timelines provide a time-based event structure to be created on the client that allows pieces of code to be activated based on time events, user events, or code loops. This is similar to the functionality provided by the Timer in Visual Basic.
- **PageTransitions** This control specifies an animated transition for moving off the current ASP page. The results of this control are only displayed when the user is accessing the page with an Internet Explorer browser.
- **PageObject** The PageObject treats the page as an object so that properties of the page itself can be retrieved and set.

Although design-time controls will add some overhead to the execution time of your ASP solutions, they generally dramatically decrease the development time and maintenance of many common database applications.

NOTE: To have the PageObject work on your ASP page, you must enable the page to execute the scripting model. This is done by right-clicking the page itself (rather than the PageObject) and setting the Enable Scripting Object Model setting on the General tab of the Properties dialog box.

Use of a control should be determined by evaluating whether the control fulfills all of the needs of your application. Each control is self-contained, so even slight modification is difficult. Some developers will find their capabilities restrictive.

Creating Global Procedures

In this example, you will begin using the Global.asa file, which holds routines and variables that are available to all of the pages of an application. You will construct few Web database applications that don't use the global file for something. When Visual InterDev initially creates an application, it automatically generates a dummy Global.asa file. With a single connection added, the Global.asa file appears like the one shown in the following listing:

```
<SCRIPT LANGUAGE='VBScript' RUNAT='Server'>

' You can add special event handlers in this file that will be
' run automatically when special ASP events occur.
' To create these handlers, just create a subroutine with a name
' from the list below that corresponds to the event you want to
' use. For example, to create an event handler for Session_OnStart,
' you would put the following code into this file
' (without the comments):

'Sub Session_OnStart
'**Put your code here **
'End Sub
```

```
'Session_OnStart
' Description: Runs the first time a user runs any page in
'              your application
'Session_OnEnd
' Description: Runs when a user's session times out or quits
'              your application
'Application_OnStart
' Description: Runs once when the first page of your application
'              is run for the first time by any user
'Application_OnEnd
' Description: Runs once when the Web server shuts down

</SCRIPT>
<SCRIPT LANGUAGE=VBScript RUNAT=Server>
Sub Application_OnStart
   '==Visual InterDev Generated - startspan==
   '--Project Data Connection
      Application("decCustomer_ConnectionString") = & _
         "DRIVER=SQL Server;SERVER=(local);UID=sa;" & _
         "APP=Microsoft(R) Windows NT(TM) Operating System;" & _
         "WSID=MARINER3;DATABASE=Customer;User Id=sa;PASSWORD=;"
      Application("decCustomer_ConnectionTimeout") = 15
      Application("decCustomer_CommandTimeout") = 30
      Application("decCustomer_CursorLocation") = 2
      Application("decCustomer_RuntimeUserName") = "sa"
      Application("decCustomer_RuntimePassword") = ""
   '-- Project Data Environment
      'Set DE = Server.CreateObject("DERuntime.DERuntime")
      'Application("DE") = DE.Load(Server.MapPath("Global.ASA"),
"_private/DataEnvironment/DataEnvironment.asa")
   '==Visual InterDev Generated - endspan==
End Sub
</SCRIPT>
```

The Global.asa file, in addition to containing application-wide variables, holds the events that are executed for a new session or new application. Near the top of the file you can see the comments that list the available events (`Session_OnStart`, `Application_OnStart`, and so on). By adding the `Sub...End Sub` constructor, these routines can be added for execution when the event occurs.

Although you will not be directly modifying the Global.asa, the Design-time controls use it to store important private information such as the connection name and passwords. Each time you make a modification to the Connection contained within the project, alterations are being made to the Global.asa.

Database Structure

For the database, you'll actually create a new table (Survey) and link it to another table through the key field. The Survey table will be constructed within the Customer database that you created in Chapter 9. Placing the new table within this database will provide easy access to the logon information in the Personal table for relationships with the new table.

Survey Table

The Survey table will hold the primary information from the survey. Since all of this information must be displayed on an HTML page, it will be a simple affair to construct the information within a single table.

Use Table 10-1 in conjunction with the Database Designer to add the table Survey in the Customer database. Be sure to set the surveyID column as the primary key of the table.

The foreign-key field, userID, will be related to the userID field in the Personal table to link to the information stored there.

Name	Data Type	Length	Precision	Scale	Nulls?	Default Value	Identity?
surveyID	int	4	10	0	No		Yes
userID	int	4	10	0	No		No
buyRegular	bit	1	0	0	No	0	No
buyFuture	bit	1	0	0	No	0	No
hear	int	4	0	0	Yes		No
hearOther	varChar	20	0	0	Yes		No
ageGroup	int	4	0	0	Yes		No
serviceLevel	int	4	0	0	Yes		No
qualityLevel	int	4	0	0	Yes		No
comments	varChar	20	0	0	Yes		No

Table 10-1. The Survey Table Field Definitions

Linking the Survey Table to the Personal Table

Once the Survey table has been created, you will need to create a relationship to the Personal table. Relational links can easily be added to the Database Diagram in a visible way. Making connections only requires you to drag the intended foreign key to the primary key of the source table.

Simply drag from the userID column in the Survey table to the same field in the Personal table. The Database Designer will prompt you with the relationship dialog box (shown in the following illustration). The default referential integrity rules are already enabled in the dialog box. Click the OK button to accept these settings and create the relationship.

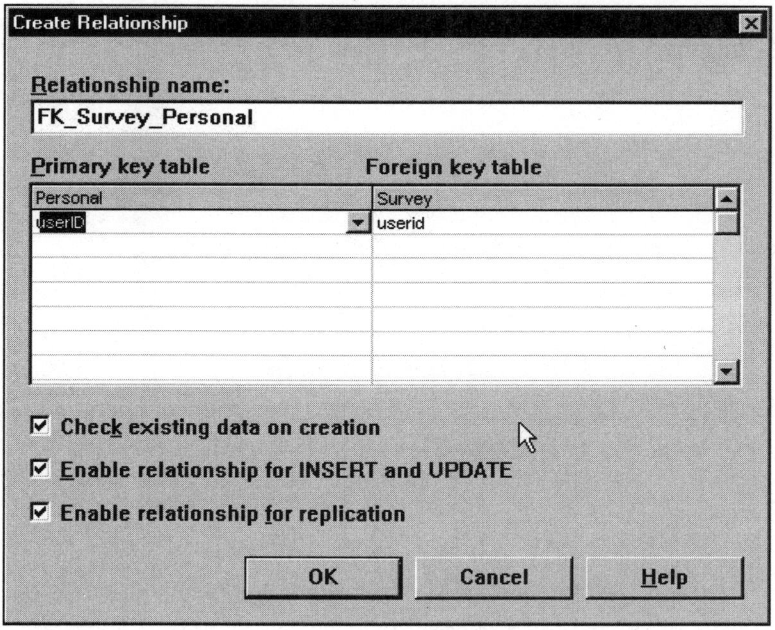

After the connection is made, you will be able to see the link in the database diagram (see Figure 10-4). More than one link can be made between tables as you have seen in the Northwind database. Since our needs are simple, there is only a single foreign-key field contained in the Survey table.

Now the two tables have an enforceable link between the related fields. This relationship will be enforced whenever insert or update events occur to either table.

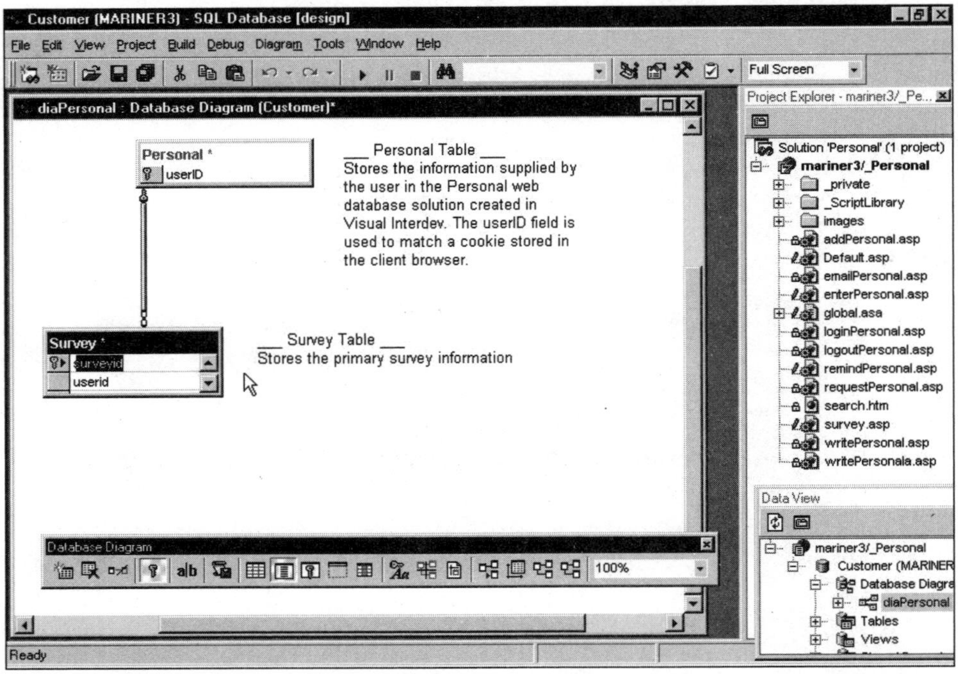

Figure 10-4. The connection between the two tables will appear as a thick line in the diagram

APPLICATION STRUCTURE

The application will consist of three Web pages. These pages will actually be divided into three sets: survey, reporting, and administration. The survey pages will accept the information that the user is entering, and the reporting page will summarize the collected data.

You will need to add the following pages to the Visual InterDev project:

- **Survey.asp** The main page that accepts the entry of survey information.
- **doneSurvey.asp** The page that confirms that the survey information was received and written to the database.
- **Report.asp** The page that generates the report from the survey information.

These three pages will augment the features currently available in the Personal application. The cookie that was created in that application will be checked before survey access is granted to confirm that the user login has occurred. Once verified, the user will be presented with the survey form.

Visual InterDev actually allows the use of a data control that isn't dramatically different from the Visual Basic data control. You can create a page, place text boxes, option lists, and other controls on it, and bind them to a data source. Thereafter, attaching specific controls to fields in the data source will automatically display the current field values and write user changes into the database.

Augmenting the Personal Table

The Personal table needs an additional column in order to specify who has access to the management report. By linking this table to the userID cookie as you did in Chapter 9, you've greatly simplified adding future options to a user profile. If each preference had been kept in individual cookies on the client machine, a great deal of information could be easily lost or compromised.

Add a column entitled `surveyReport` and make the type a bit field. Don't forget to set the default value to zero (0) to prevent any errors when creating a new record.

Constructing the Survey Form

The survey form will ask a number of generalized questions. The questions themselves are not important, since each survey will be different. These questions do, however, represent each of the possible data types and HTML controls that can be used on a survey to allow user input into the database. The items that the user will enter for this survey form are:

- Where did you hear about us?
- Age Group (optional)
- General Comments
- Please rate the following:
  - Quality of the product
  - Service
- Have you ever bought a product from us before?
- Would you buy this product again?

The answers to these questions provide common information that would be useful to nearly any organization.

NOTE: Only one radio button in a group can be selected at a time. In HTML, each group has a group name. All radio buttons in a group share the same group name, and the value changes depending on which item is currently selected. Multiple groups can exist in the same form—they just need separate group names. Therefore, if you have a number of radio buttons that you copy and paste into the form, be sure to change the name of the second group of buttons.

Add the Survey to the Default.asp File

In the original Personal application, the only option available to an established user was the ability to log out. Now, once you've added the Survey application, two links will be available to the confirmed user (shown next). The survey form will actually confirm that the user is logged into the system or it will redirect the user to the login page.

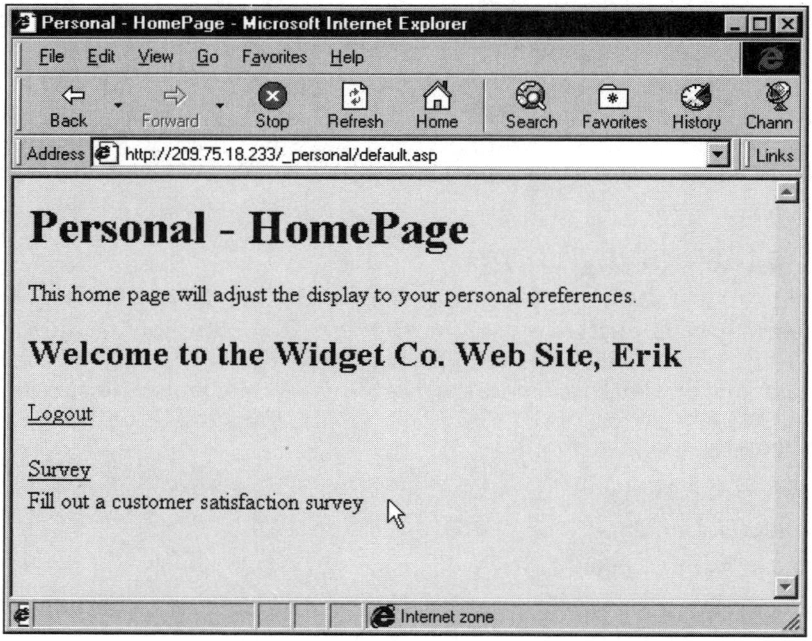

The modification required for the existing default page includes adding a new link to the confirmed options. Enter the code shown in the following listing to the Default.asp file. This scripting code is inserted where the detected cookie options are presented.

```
' Greet user by name and allow survey or logout
Response.Write(introStr & ", " & Session("FirstName") & "</H2>")
Response.Write("<A HREF=logoutPersonal.asp>Logout</A><P>")
Response.Write("<A HREF=survey.asp>Survey</A><BR>")
Response.Write("Fill out a customer satisfaction survey<P>")
```

This additional code will provide the gateway to the survey application page.

Construction of the Survey.asp Form

In the past solutions, you used ADO directly in your script code to access a data source through the Recordset object. In the survey application, rather than using the general server-side object for the recordset, you will need to place a design-time control for recordsets on the Web page. Since design-time controls feature a graphical interface on the page, you will be able to see the connection and selections before you compile them to the final page.

You will need to begin by creating a page that can hold the recordset and all of the form controls to accept the survey information. This page will actually present the form required for data input. Instead of standard HTML form input, however, you will use a design-time recordset control to bind controls to the current record.

To create the application, follow these steps:

1. Create a new ASP page called Survey.asp. This page will be addressed through the link on the initial Default.ASP page.
2. Select the Design-Time tab in the controls toolbox.
3. Drag a Recordset control onto the page. You will be asked if you want to add the Scripting Object model to the project. The Scripting Object model contains all of the server-side objects that Visual InterDev needs to provide the design-time object execution at run time. It is necessary to add this scripting model when using these controls. The model only has to be added once to a project using the controls.
4. Click OK to add the object model.

When the recordset object is placed on the page, you should see the item as shown in Figure 10-5. You can see that it provides a complete user interface, unlike the traditional server controls available from the toolbox palette.

In the last chapter, you created an ODBC data source called customerODBC that connects to the Customer database. This connection will be used by both of the pages that you create. The design-time controls can use any connections that exist within a project's data environment.

First you will need to select and display the connection, and then you will need to make some adjustments to the default properties of the control so that it will function properly. Follow these steps:

1. Add a connection to the project by selecting the Project | Add Data Connection menu option. The Connection wizard will appear to take you through the steps of setting up the connection.
2. When prompted for a data source, select the customerODBC data source.
3. Set the connection name on the General tab to decCustomer.
4. On the Authentication tab, be sure to set the proper username and password for both Design-time and Run-time modes. If you haven't made changes to the

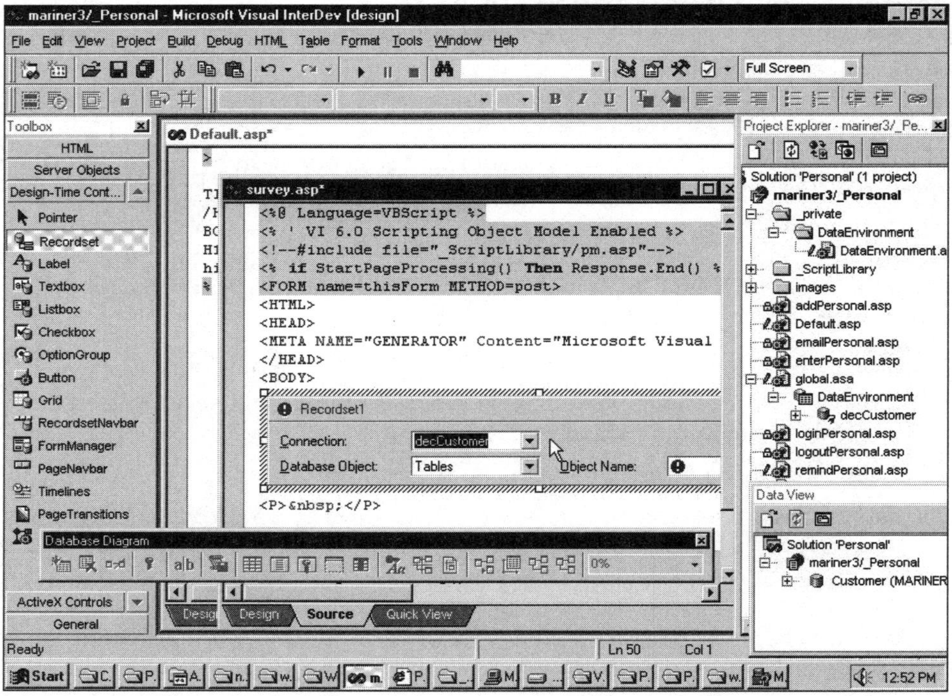

Figure 10-5. The design-time Recordset control inserted into the Web page

default account or created a special Web SQL Server client account, the username will be *sa* and the password will be left blank.

5. On the Miscellaneous tab set the cursor location to option *2 - Use Server-Side Cursors*.
6. Click the OK button to accept these changes. The connection will now be created so that the project can access the tables in the database. Now the design-time control that you placed on the page needs to be configured.
7. Select the Survey.asp page window.
8. Right-click the Recordset control and select the Properties option.
9. Click the Connection combo box and select the decCustomer connection.
10. In the Database object combo box, make sure that the Tables option is selected. This option allows you to set one of the tables as the data source.
11. From the Object name combo box, select the Survey table.

Your page should look like the one shown in Figure 10-6.

With the Recordset object configured, the individual controls for the survey (checkboxes, text entry fields, etc.) can be added and set up. These controls are also design-time controls, and as such they can be bound to the recordset through the individual properties of the controls. You'll begin by adding a checkbox to the page.

It is easiest to see if you place the controls underneath the recordset control in the viewing window, but the position won't affect the operation of the page. The recordset is actually instantiated before the HTML page has been sent to the browser.

To begin constructing the survey form, follow these steps:

1. Type a title for the page (such as `Survey Form`) in the Body of the HTML document.
2. Enter the text `Do You:` after the title to introduce the next options.
3. Drag the design-time control labeled Checkbox onto the page.

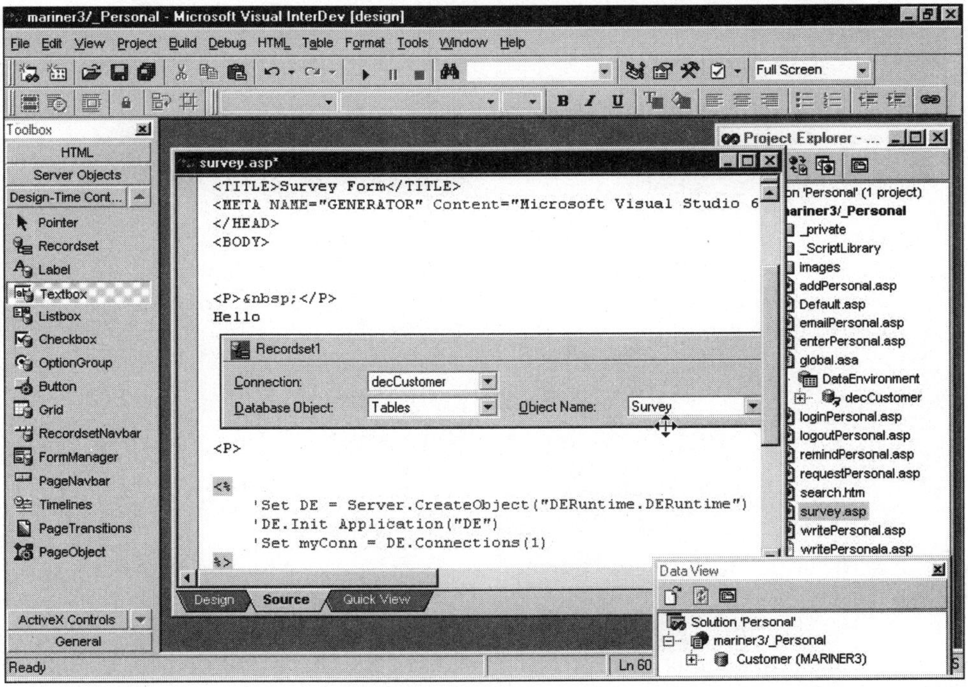

Figure 10-6. Once the recordset has been added, you can select the connection

4. Right-click the control and select the Properties option.
5. Set the Name property to `chkRegular` and the Caption property to `Regularly buy our products` and click the OK button. This checkbox will be used by the visitor to indicate that they are a regular customer.
6. Add the text `<P>` after the checkbox to make the next control appear on the next line when the user accesses the page.
7. Drag the design-time control labeled Checkbox onto the page.
8. Right-click the control and select the Properties option.
9. Set the Name property to `chkFuture` and the Caption property to `Want to buy from us in the future` and click the OK button. This checkbox will be used by the visitor to indicate that they intend to continue as a customer.
10. Add the text `<P>` after the checkbox.
11. Enter the text `Age Group:` on the new line to introduce a combo box that allows the user to select the age group. In the design-time controls, the equivalent of both a list box and a combo box are contained within a single control called the *listbox*. This listbox is configured in the Properties dialog box as either one of the traditional Visual Basic controls. By default, the Visual InterDev listbox is set to display a combo box on the Web page (listed as the Dropdown style in the control's properties).
12. Drag the design-time control labeled Listbox onto the page. Once the combo box is placed on the page, it will need to be edited for the proper values.
13. Right-click the control and select the Properties option.
14. Set the Name property to `cmbAgeGroup`.
15. Select the Lookup tab and enter the desired values. The values to be displayed within the listbox can come from the recordset or from a static list. Since this listbox only has a few unchanging values for the survey, they can be entered by hand into the static list. Only the first three entries are shown in the next illustration, but feel free to continue the list if you like.

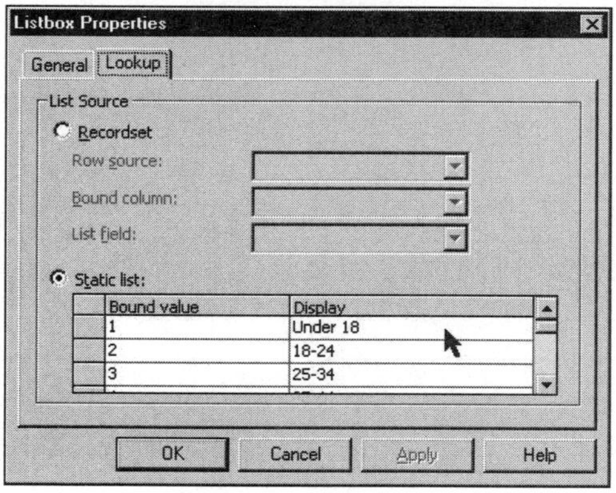

16. Click the OK button to accept the lookup entries.
17. Follow the same procedure as shown in Steps 10–16, except this time add the introductory text as Where did you here about us? Then set the Name of the combo box to cmbHear and the lookup values to the following: Banner Ad, Magazine, Word of Mouth, Newsgroup (Usenet), and Other.

Once the listbox is configured, you will need to add a text box for the other places that people might have heard about the company.

1. Enter the text <P>If other, please enter where: after the combo box to allow the visitor to indicate other places they might have heard of the organization.
2. Drag the design-time control labeled Textbox onto the page.
3. Right-click the control and select the Properties option.
4. Set the Name property to txtHearOther and the Display Width to 20 characters.
5. Click the OK button to accept these settings.

At this point in the form, you will need an option group to allow the visitor to rate the quality and service received from the organization. The user may rate factors for service and quality from “Excellent” to “Poor.”

1. Enter the text <P>Please rate the following: <P> <B>Service: </B> after the text box.
2. Drag the OptionGroup design-time control onto the form and drop it after the text you just entered.
3. Right-click the control and select the Properties option.
4. Select the Lookup tab and enter the desired values. In the next illustration, you can see that the Lookup tab for the option group is very much like the one you previously configured for the listbox. Unlike the listbox, however, each additional value adds another option button to the display.

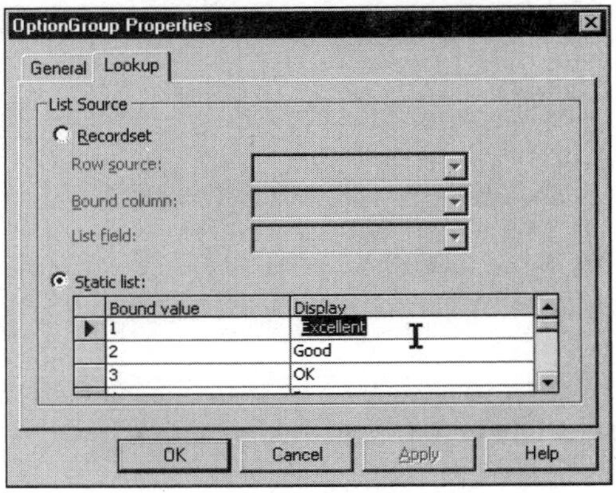

5. Click the OK button to accept the list.
6. Follow the same procedure in Steps 1–5 except make the introductory text read `Quality:` instead of `Service:`. Since the option list is the same, you could just copy the whole option group control and paste a duplicate after the new introductory text. To complete the form layout, you need to accept miscellaneous comments.
7. Enter the text `<P>Comments:` after the last option group.
8. Drag the TextBox design-time control onto the form and drop it after the text you just entered.
9. Set the Name property to `txtComments`
10. Set the Style property to `TextArea` and the Lines property to `3`.
11. Set the Display width property to `60`.
12. Click the OK button to accept the text box configuration.
13. Drag a Command button design-time control onto the form.
14. Set the Name property to `cmdSubmit` and the Caption property to Submit `Survey Entries`
15. Enter the text `<P>` after the command button.
16. Drag a Label design-time control onto the form. This label will be hidden when the user is filling out a survey and it will be displayed once the survey is complete to allow access to the survey report.
17. Right-click the control and select the Properties option.
18. Set the Name property to `lblShowReport`
19. In the Field/Expression property, enter `<A HREF="SurveyReport.asp">Show Survey Report</A>` to provide a link to the report. The Label Properties window should now appear like the illustration here.

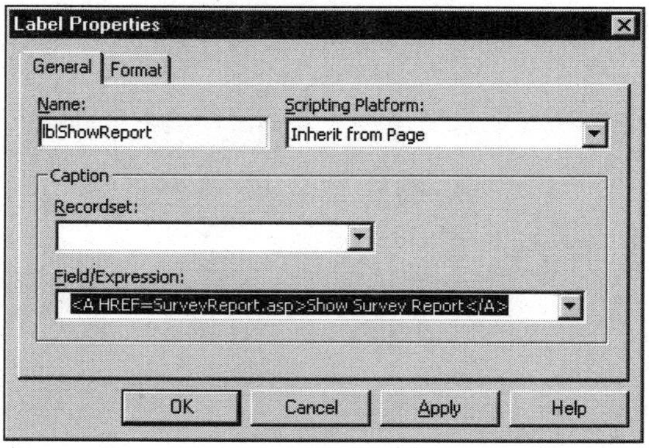

20. Select the Format tab and check the Data Contains HTML checkbox and uncheck the Visible checkbox. These selections will treat the code set in the

Field property like HTML code and hide the label control until the Form Manager makes it visible.

21. Enter the text <P> after the command button.

Now that all of the controls have been placed on the form, you will need to configure each control to bind it to the recordset. Follow these steps for each of the controls on the Web page:

1. Right-click the control and select the Properties option.
2. In the Data frame, set the Recordset property to Recordset1.
3. Set the Field property to the field appropriate to that control. In Table 10-1, you can see a list of all of the controls and the field names to which each corresponds.

Control name	Field name
chkRegular	buyRegular
chkFuture	buyFuture
cmbAgeGroup	ageGroup
cmbHear	hear
txtHearOther	hearOther
optionGroup1	serviceLevel
optionGroup2	qualityLevel
txtComments	comments

Configuring the Form Manager

You will need to add the form manager to accept the data entered by the user and write it into the database. The form manager can actually perform operations on the various bound controls to allow for editing, displaying, and adding records. Follow these steps:

1. Drag the Form Manager control onto the page. Your form should look like this:

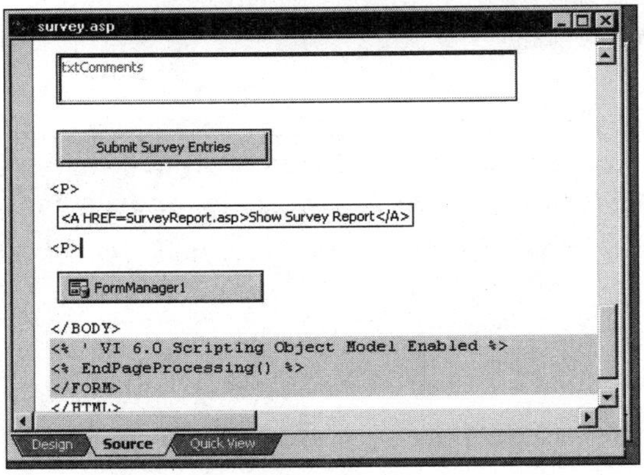

2. Right-click the control and select the Properties option.
3. In the New Mode box, type **Insert** and click the right arrow button to move it into the Form Mode listbox.
4. Select the Insert item in the Form Mode listbox.
5. Set the Default Mode property to Insert so that mode will be executed when the page is first loaded.
6. Under the Actions Performed For Mode grid, use the Object column to select the chkFuture control.
7. In the Member column, select the Show method from the combo box. The Value column will automatically fill with the option to send no arguments.
8. Repeat Steps 5 and 6 for each of the controls on the form except the label and the recordset objects. The FormManager Properties window should appear like this:

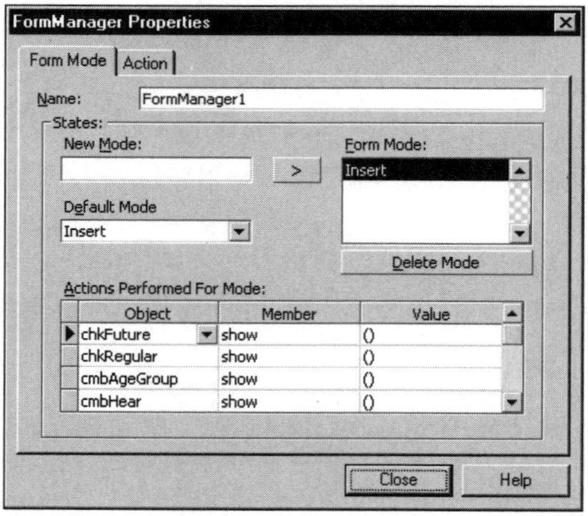

9. After you have completed setting the Show execution for the other controls, select the Recordset object in the Object column. You will need to add a new record to the table when the page is first viewed and the Insert mode is executed.
10. In the Member column, select the `addRecord` option from the combo box. Now you need to create the conditions to have the survey information submitted. That means creating a new mode for the submission process.
11. In the New Mode box, type **Submitted** and click the right arrow button to move it into the Form Mode listbox.
12. Select the Insert item in the Form Mode listbox.
13. Add all of the objects as in Steps 6 through 8, only this time select the `hide` method for the controls.

14. In the Object column, select the lblShowReport object and set the method in the Member column to `show`. That will provide the link once the user has entered the survey information.

Once the Insert and Submitted modes has been created, you will need to add the actions that will be performed when this mode is enacted. In this application, the data in the bound controls should be available for modification. You will need to set the proper actions for each control on the form.

1. Select the Action tab in the Form Manager properties.
2. Under the Current Mode, select the Insert option.
3. In the Object column, select the cmdSubmit button. This button will be used to change the mode to enter the information into the database and show the Show Report hyperlink.
4. For the Event column, select the onclick event.
5. Set the Next Mode to the Submitted option. Now the actual operations to be performed when the action of moving from the Insert mode to the Submitted mode must be configured. The action performed consists of only a single operation—saving the user-submitted survey information.
6. In the Object column of the Actions Performed Before Transition grid, select the Recordset option.
7. In the Member column, select the `updateRecord` method (shown here).

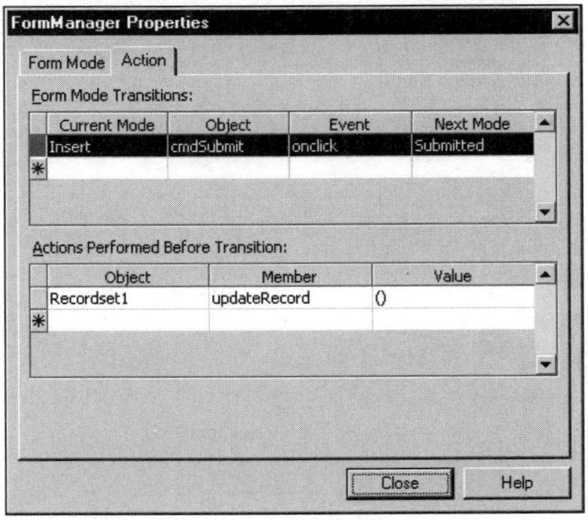

8. Click the Close button to accept all of the Form Manager settings you have made.

When the Submitted mode executes, it will hide all of the controls and expose the hyperlink to the report (as shown in the next illustration).

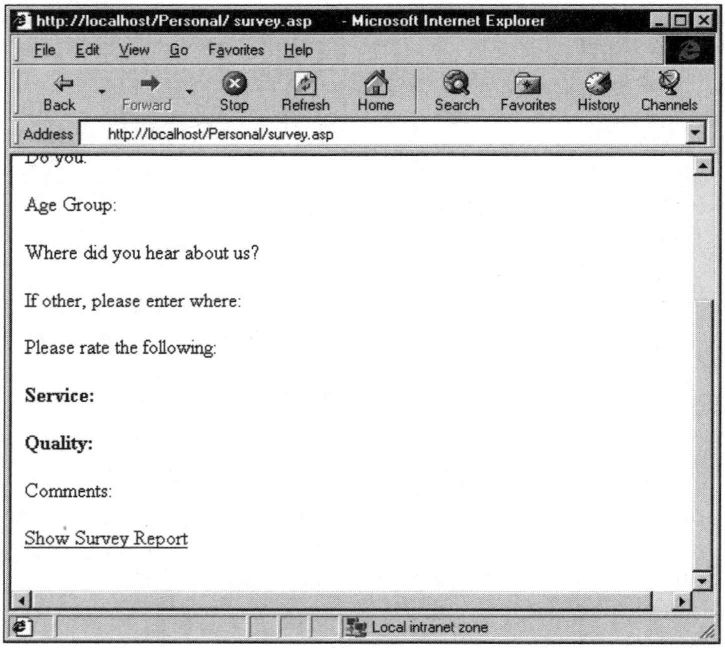

After you have created the initial controls on the page, try executing the report page from the link after the survey was filled out to make certain that it works properly. The following illustration shows the Survey form as it executes for the first time.

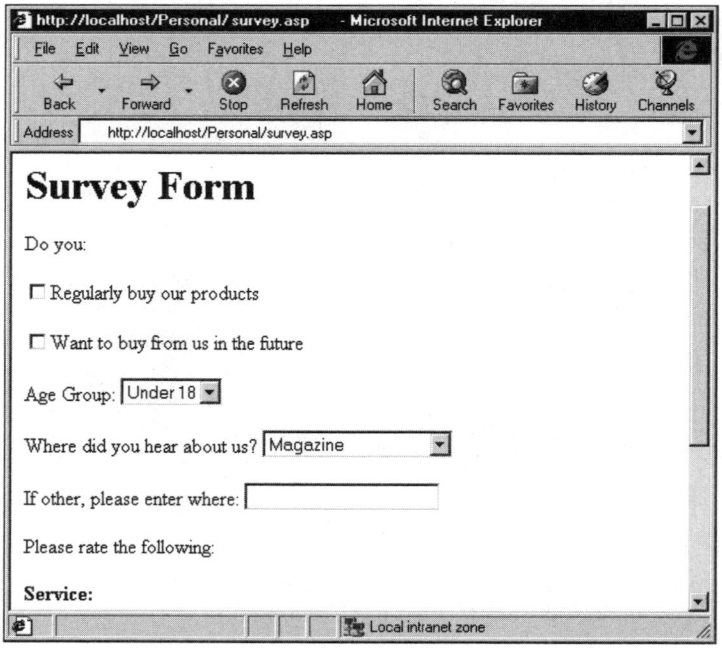

REPORTING DATA

One of the primary reasons that Web surveys are so powerful is that the data is written directly to the database. That means that retrieval can be instant and reports can be generated dynamically. The link on the Survey page will take you to the reporting part of the application. You will need to construct this report in Visual InterDev so that it can return the proper results.

1. Create a new page in the project called SurveyReport.asp.
2. Drag the Recordset object onto the page from the Design-Time controls palette. You will need to configure the control so that it can return the summary data needed for the report.
3. Right-click the Recordset control and select the Properties option.
4. Click the Connection combo box and select the `decCustomer` connection.
5. Select the SQL Statement radio button. You will see that the text box below it will activate. This text box is where SQL code can be entered.
6. Type in the following SQL code:

```
Select count(buyRegular), count(buyFuture), Avg(ageGroup), avg(hear),
   avg(serviceLevel),avg(qualityLevel) from survey
```

7. Click the OK button to accept the settings.
8. From the Design-Time controls palette, drag the Grid control onto the page. The page should now appear like this:

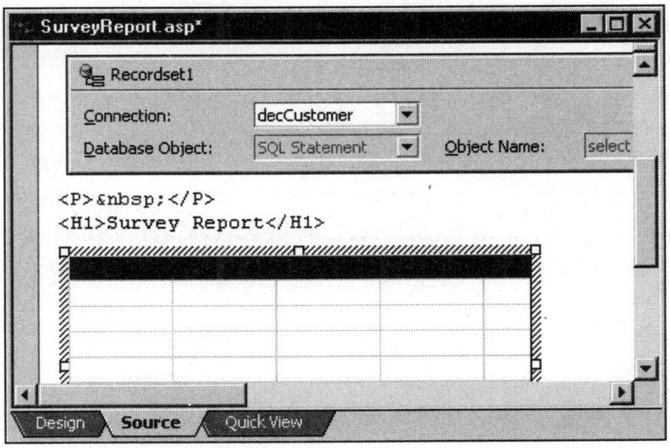

9. Right-click on the Grid object and select the Properties option.
10. Select the Data tab in the Properties window.
11. Select the Recordset1 in the Recordset combo box.
12. Check all of the fields displayed in the Available fields listbox. With each check, the field will be placed in the Grid columns list that determines the

order in which they'll be displayed in the grid. The up and down arrows to the right can be used to change the order of any of the columns.

13. Click the OK button to accept the property changes. The solution is now complete; it just needs to be executed.
14. Select the View in Browser option under the View menu to execute the solution.

After you enter the proper survey information and submit it, a link will appear that allows you to access the report page. Clicking on the link will display all of the summary information regarding the surveys that have been entered.

NOTE: There has been a great amount of debate in the database world on whether object databases make sense. Forms such as a survey are one of the applications for which an object database implementation makes a lot of sense.

Rather than defining a new table each time a new survey needs to be constructed, as well as a complete application interface, a Form object type could be created to store all of the information accepted in the fields of a form. A single database could hold all of the surveys for numerous different studies as different objects. Queries could be done across the survey objects for common fields. Implementing such a solution with a current database server would be difficult and resource prohibitive. Right now SQL Server does not incorporate object storage.

Possible Additions to the Report

As an addition, the activity report could identify how often the surveys were entered and provide a time-based breakdown of the results. This information is important because it is provided over time. Since most surveys are generally not open-ended and have start and end dates, you can evaluate the progress.

If you are advertising for a survey ("take the survey and win a prize"), the time-based reporting also aids you in determining the immediacy of your advertising. The majority of the respondents may not actually take the survey until two weeks after the ad drops. Analyzing this will aid you in future campaign planning.

Q&A

Q: Can the survey information be placed within a data warehouse?

A: A data warehouse is a database server dedicated to retaining summary information specifically for large-scale querying and reporting. If your organization is large enough to do an immense number of surveys, then data results from these surveys are exactly the type of information that is ideal for summary in a data warehouse.

Q: Is the FormManager control useful for general Web database applications?

A: The design-time FormManager control is perhaps the most powerful control that is included with the Visual InterDev system. Not only can it manage the Recordset and bound controls, but it may also be hooked into the record navigation design-time control. It can even modify the page that will be displayed, based on settings and the proper events. Using the survey form was a simple introduction to this control.

SUMMARY

A Web-based survey can be extremely effective in terms of cost for use and deployment. Essentially, the time taken to build a few simple pages and a relational database can provide a substantial amount of information. Developing a relational database involves creating and connecting multiple tables using key fields. Once the database is created, Visual InterDev greatly simplifies generation of the necessary survey pages. In this chapter, you covered:

- **Surveys** The usefulness of automating survey forms into a Web database application cannot be overstated. Not only do they allow users to easily enter the form information from anywhere on the network, but the information can be easily and cheaply summarized for management.
- **Joins** Query joins are used to connect two or more fields together to relate the tables. A join relies on a unique primary key in one table and an associated foreign key in the other table.
- **Normalization** The process of deciding how to divide data between multiple tables is called normalization. The three levels of normalization provide general guidelines as to how this separation can be done.
- **Design-time controls** In Visual InterDev, a number of design-time controls, including the Recordset object and various bound controls allow a complete user interface for the developer to configure them. Once their settings are adjusted, deploying the controls to the Web server will turn them into executable scripting code.

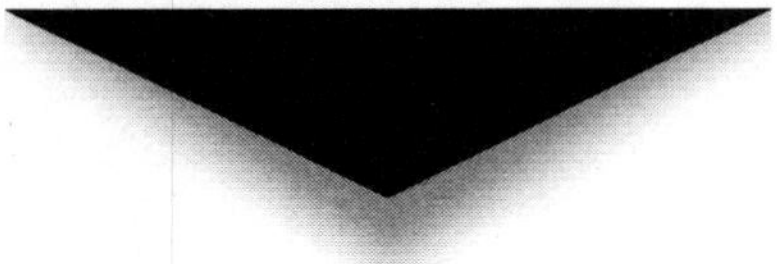

CHAPTER 11

Using CDO for Auto–E-Mail

One of the most powerful ways to enhance a Web application is to connect the database storage to an auto-e-mailer. This can provide you with the opportunity to distribute updates, respond with automated material, and issue "thank you" e-mails for a user signup or purchase. Increasingly popular on sites is the "E-mail this to a friend" option that will send an online article to a destination address.

The Survey application that you created in the last chapter included a page to thank the user for entering the survey information. The original application that you built in Chapter 10 also had a reminder page for a forgotten password. Both of these Web pages can be augmented to send an e-mail. The survey can deliver a thank you message to the user and the forgotten password page can be mailed out as a reminder. Adding such features can provide a substantial amount of professionalism and polish to your Web site.

Adding e-mail support to a Web application isn't difficult, thanks to a technology built into IIS 4 and later versions. IIS has an e-mail object model called Collaboration Data Objects (CDO) that can create and send e-mail using a few simple scripting commands.

NOTE: Most of the e-mail addresses in this chapter are fictional. If you see an address such as you@destination.com in the source code, replace this with a valid address in order for the code to properly function.

AN OVERVIEW OF COLLABORATION DATA OBJECTS

Collaboration Data Objects (CDO) is an object framework that allows access to an e-mail server. By accessing the CDO data model, messages can be created and sent either through the batch SMTP server included with IIS 4 or directly through your Microsoft Exchange Server. CDO makes it possible to build messaging and groupware applications from either a scripting environment (such as ASP) or through a complete development system (Visual Basic, Visual J++, and so on).

Before you get into the complexities of building a complete application that uses CDO, first look at how easy it is to send a message from ASP code. A version of CDO is installed automatically with IIS 4 on your NT server, and this version can be made to send an e-mail message with only two lines of code: one to instantiate the CDO object and another to send the e-mail.

This simple mail-transmission code would look like the following:

```
<HTML>
<BODY>
<%
Set objMail = Server.CreateObject("CDONTS.Newmail")
objMail.Send "phil@hotmail.com", "danr@coherentdata.com", "mySubject", "Great Dummies book"
Set objMail = Nothing
%>
Mail sent!<P>
</BODY>
</HTML>
```

Two Versions of CDO

There are actually two main versions of CDO that are currently in use: CDO 1.2 and CDO for NTS (Collaboration Data Objects for NT Server). CDO 1.2 is the version included with Exchange Server; CDO for NTS is installed with IIS 4. Although the object models and programming methods look the same, the implementations of mail capabilities are actually very different. In the solution that you'll create in this chapter, CDO for NTS will be used because it ships with IIS 4 and does not require administrative access to an Exchange Server.

CDO for NTS is designed for simple and flexible e-mail transmission from a bulk sending platform, such as a Web server. CDO 1.2 was created to allow complete groupware capabilities, and it provides a way to mail-enable an e-mail application. In Table 11-1, you can see a rough comparison of the overall features contained in each CDO implementation.

Perhaps the most important thing to understand about these two versions is that they use different protocols for e-mail communication. CDO 1.2 provides a complete interface to Microsoft's Messaging API (MAPI), which makes it an ideal choice for managing an Exchange Server that uses MAPI as its base protocol. CDO for NTS, on the other hand, uses the SMTP protocol that is common to Internet e-mail servers. This allows it to easily send messages using the standardized Internet protocol for HTML-based messages, known as MHTML.

E-Mail Feature	CDO 1.2	CDO for NTS
Protocol used:	MAPI	SMTP
Usable from ASP?	Yes	Yes
NewMail object available?	No	Yes
Requires authenticated user login?	Yes	No
Remote and multiple-server access possible?	Yes	No
Calendars, filters, and sorting available?	Yes	No
Writing to Message object available?	Yes	Yes
Reading from Message object available?	Yes	No
Render messages in HTML for browser display?	Yes	No
HTML/MHTML for transmission of rich text and graphics?	No	Yes

Table 11-1. E-Mail Features Available in CDO 1.2 and CDO for NTS

DEFINITION: **MHTML** MIME HTML is a subset of the complete HTML specification that allows HTML styles (such as bold and italic) and other formatting to be used within the body of an e-mail message.

CDO 1.2 can handle calendaring, scheduling, and advanced management re-engineering processes such as workflow. It can manipulate messages on a variety of servers including Exchange Server, GroupWise, and cc:Mail. Most Web database solutions don't need the level of power offered by the complete CDO implementation, so Microsoft created the object model CDO for NTS.

CDO for NTS

CDO for NTS is a subset of the complete CDO 1.2 implementation. While CDO 1.2 communicates with the e-mail server through the MAPI interface, CDO for NTS uses the SMTP protocol, usually to access the SMTP service included with IIS. When CDO for NTS is installed on an Exchange Server, the Exchange SMTP interface can be used instead.

Unlike CDO 1.2, CDO for NTS does not allow access from remote machines. Therefore, the SMTP or Exchange service must be on the same machine that is running IIS. By not allowing remote access to foreign users prevents them from accessing the SMTP service on the Web server that was specifically intended for use by CDO and not for complete e-mail services. Since no authenticated logon is required, remote access to the SMTP services would make every IIS 4 Web installation a magnet for spammers (those who send unauthorized e-mail advertising).

NOTE: The SMTP service included with IIS cannot be accessed from a remote machine. This was probably designed to prevent spammers from abusing the service and illegally transmitting messages from other people's servers. These spammers could then send out chain letters, pyramid schemes, etc. with your mail server as the source. Note that this is a danger with any mail server, because most SMTP servers must either be specifically configured to ignore mail from outside the line or must provide firewall protection against illegal access. Be on guard if you do set up any type of e-mail server—this type of transmission can and does occur.

The SMTP service installed with the IIS 4 Web server uses the same transmission process of a typical SMTP server. This process, with its basis in writing small files to folders, may seem unfamiliar to developers more accustomed to manipulating object models. CDO actually shields the developer from the behind-the-scenes details of the SMTP server. However, having a general understanding of the workings of the service will help you properly maintain it.

HOW SMTP WORKS IN CDO FOR NTS When IIS is installed, the SMTP service is installed by default. If it was not installed on your server (you will see the SMTP item in the MMC if it was installed), you can add it by using the Windows NT Option Pack setup application. Once installed, the service will automatically start each time the server is booted.

NOTE: The SMTP service is a Windows NT service. Therefore, it cannot be installed on a Windows 95/98 machine. If you are using the Personal Web Server for some of your development, it cannot be used to address the CDO for NTS object model.

During SMTP installation, a number of folders are created that will be used by the service. The directory that contains all of the SMTP folders is, by default, located in the InetPub directory. All of the SMTP folders are located in the main directory called Mailroot. The common path for the folder is C:\inetpub\mailroot.

Messages are stored as files in individual directories within the Mailroot directory. The SMTP service is completely directory-based in that all incoming and outgoing mail is actually placed in the proper directory for the service to handle. The service checks the directory periodically to determine whether new message were received or need to be sent.

Within the Mailroot folder, there are four folders that actually handle the mail. These folders are:

- **Pickup** Holds outgoing messages. Any file in the proper e-mail format can be placed in this folder for transmission.
- **Queue** If the mail found in the Pickup folder cannot be transmitted immediately, it is placed in the Queue folder to await transmission. The SMTP service will attempt to resend the messages in this folder at regular intervals. In the MMC, you can configure the number of attempts that are made before delivery is aborted.
- **BadMail** After the maximum number of failures in the Queue directory, the message will be marked Undeliverable and placed in this folder.
- **Drop** This folder will contain all of the incoming messages sent to the SMTP service. Since the SMTP service does not have any method of providing mailboxes to receive mail (if mail, such as a reply, was routed to this SMTP service), any messages sent to the service are simply stored in this folder and not processed.

The SMTP service was not designed to receive e-mail. However, to support the SMTP specification, if an e-mail message is sent to an address in the local domain, the message is placed in the Drop folder. Otherwise, the message is placed in the Queue directory for transmission. E-mail messages are queued so they can be delivered at once.

The SMTP service can be configured in the MMC. Simply open the IIS object and select the SMTP item. You can enter either an IP address or a domain name for the intended server. Most of the configuration for the service is done with individual messages when sent through the object model.

Using the CDO for NTS object library, you really don't have to worry about the folder structure, because most of your interaction will occur through the objects. By examining the folders, particularly the BadMail and Drop folders, you can determine whether any mail was undeliverable and what was received by the service.

CDO 1.2

CDO 1.2 is a far more robust implementation of mail objects than CDO for NTS, but it also requires more coding in order to broadcast e-mail messages and it requires login access to an Exchange Server. CDO 1.2 is installed when the Outlook Web Access component or the complete Exchange Server is selected on the Exchange Server 5.5 CD.

> ***NOTE:*** CDO 1.2 was initially called OLE Messaging. When Microsoft upgraded most of the OLE family of products to the ActiveX specification, OLE Messaging became known as Active Messaging. Subsequently, the next revision added the collaborative groupware functions available through Exchange Server, hence the name change to CDO.

Management of CDO 1.2 occurs through the MAPI interface. Using MAPI, CDO 1.2 can access any public folders on an Exchange Server, use the MAPI drivers to address almost any other supported e-mail server, and manipulate advanced functions, such as the calendaring functions of Exchange Server. Although CDO 1.2 has more features than CDO for NTS, it can also be less flexible, because sending any mail requires activating a session with a proper logon account on the server. CDO 1.2 requires a Session logon for all e-mail transactions because it lacks the NewMail object that is standard in CDO for NTS. The NewMail object was created explicitly for the types of e-mail tasks that would be required from a Web server.

CDO, because it requires a session, must have an authenticated logon before new messages may be added. This prevents programmatically setting a different return address for each e-mail since the return address from the user session is used. CDO for NTS allows you to specify any return address desired.

For groupware solutions, the entire message box framework can be accessed through CDO 1.2. It can be used to access public-folder applications on a Microsoft Exchange Server including retrieval or posting of messages to the public sections.

CDO consists of two object frameworks: CDO library and CDO rendering:

- **CDO library** Creates the e-mail messages
- **CDO rendering library** Renders Exchange data into HTML

The central CDO library requires the creation of a session with login user ID and password. Once the session is created, the MAPI hierarchy for folders can be navigated for message creation, posting, or retrieval. Since this library requires an Exchange Server, presenting an example is beyond the scope of this book. Check the MSDN CD for extensive MAPI programming examples.

The CDO rendering library is used to create messages that hold HTML formatting. MIME HTML (MHTML) is a new message type that allows the styles supported by HTML to be sent in a message. Rather than a message being sent as plain text, it is sent designated as MHTML. That allows advanced mail clients, such as Eudora, Outlook, and Netscape Messaging, to display formatting-rich e-mail messages. MHTML can also contain references to objects, such as embedded scripts, inline images, and Java applets.

NOTE: The object model for CDO 1.2 is contained in the file CDO.DLL. If you need to control the Exchange Server from a remote machine, the CDO 1.2 libraries can be moved simply by copying and registering the appropriate DLL. You can transfer it to a machine and place it in the Windows\System folder. Then the DLL can be registered using the regsvr32 cdo.dll command.

With Windows 2000, Microsoft intends to ship an update to CDO 1.2. The newer CDO 2.0 includes MIME, NNTP, and SMTP. CDO 2.0 does not directly support mailboxes, although it does support protocol events, allowing a program to process incoming messages. At the time of this writing, CDO 2.0 was not shipping with any products, so its adoption will be gradual.

CAUTION: CDO 2.0 is not code-compatible with CDO 1.2 (included with Exchange Server 5.5). The object models of each are similar, however, so CDO 1.2 code won't require substantial revision to allow it to work with version 2.0. Additionally, both object models can coexist on the same machine, saving a developer from having to rewrite existing code immediately.

USING CDO

Programming is very similar for either version of CDO. With the exception of the NewMail object available to CDO for NTS, the objects contained in the models function in the same manner. Since most of your Web database work will be done using the NewMail object, however, a thorough knowledge of it is more important than general CDO session work.

Figure 11-1 shows a simplified object model of CDO for NTS. The primary objects, NewMail and Session, are used to either send an e-mail message or open a session to the current e-mail server. The other objects exist once the Session object has been initially created.

Notice that the NewMail object is off by itself and not part of the object hierarchy. This is because the NewMail object is created independently from the rest of the objects and cannot be directly referenced by them. In fact, its write-only nature precludes it from actively interacting with the other objects in the model.

NewMail Object

The sample code given at the beginning of this chapter to send an e-mail message uses the NewMail object in conjunction with the `Send` method. The object needs to be created, and the `Send` method must be passed the required arguments, as follows:

```
Set objMail = Server.CreateObject("CDONTS.Newmail")
objMail.Send "me@source.com", "you@destination.com", _
    "My Subject", "MyBody"
```

The complete syntax of the `Send` method looks like this:

```
objEmail.Send [from] [,to] [,subject] [,body] [,importance]
```

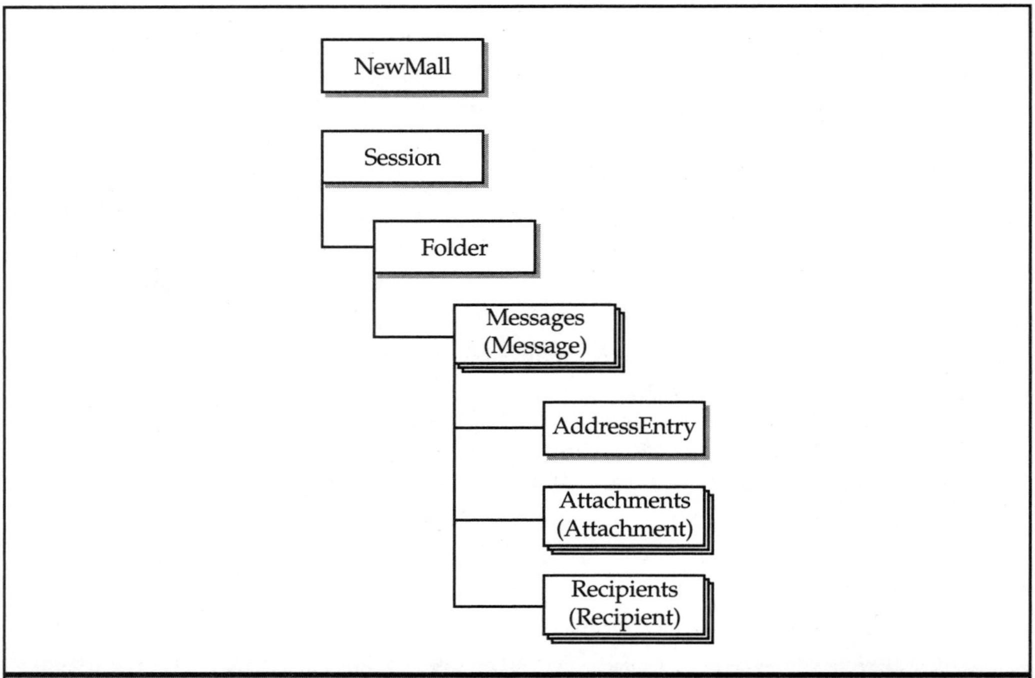

Figure 11-1. The CDO object model used by CDO for NTS

The arguments passed to the `Send` method are used in place of setting the properties for the NewMail object. Any argument that is omitted will be read from the equivalent property instead. The properties for the NewMail object include:

- **From** The source e-mail address, which must be in a format understandable to the SMTP service.
- **To** The destination e-mail address or addresses.
- **CC** The destination e-mail address for those who should receive a copy of the e-mail. This must be a list of e-mail addresses with each address separated by a semicolon.
- **BCC** The destination e-mail addresses for those who should receive a blind copy of the e-mail. The list of BCC addresses is not revealed to each recipient, unlike the CC recipients. Instead, the message appears addressed individually to each person. This can be done with a list of e-mail addresses.
- **Subject** The text that will be entered in the subject line of the e-mail message.

- **Body** The content of the message to be sent. The Body can contain plain text or HTML.
- **BodyFormat** The type of content stored in the Body property.
- **ContentBase** The base address for the URL contained in ContentLocation (for URL attachments).
- **ContentLocation** A URL that provides a root path for any URLs contained in the Body of the message.
- **MailFormat** The format in which the e-mail message will be sent. By default, this specification is plain text. Other options include MIME and uuencoding. Changing this property automatically alters the default coding type for attachments.
- **Importance** The importance of the message. Options include cdoLow (0), which is the default, cdoNormal(1), and cdoHigh(2).
- **Version** Returns the version number of the CDO framework.
- **Value** Settings for information that will be included in the header of the message.

NOTE: To send e-mail to multiple recipients in the To, CC, or BCC properties, separate the addresses with a semicolon (;).

All of these properties, except the Version property, are write-only. The NewMail object was created strictly for sending e-mail, not for interacting with the e-mail server. Any properties that are left blank are simply omitted from the transmission. Anonymous e-mail can be sent from the server if the From property is left blank. However, be aware that any mail will contain the source IP address, which in this case is the address of the SMTP service, so the e-mail will not be truly anonymous.

By default, the attachment coding is set to uuencoding. Base64 encoding is also available. The uuencoding protocol is more widely supported by e-mail carrier services, although either can be used with most modern servers.

NOTE: If you use an IP address for your e-mail server, the address must be enclosed in square brackets ([ ]). Therefore, if the IP address of your e-mail server is 209.75.18.100, the IP address you would specify is [209.75.18.100].

Send Method

The `Send` method accepts five arguments: `From`, `To`, `Subject`, `Body`, and `Importance`. All of these arguments can be specified through properties for the NewMail object instead of being passed directly via the `Send` method.

Once the `Send` method is invoked, the NewMail object is automatically eliminated. Therefore, you cannot send a message twice without recreating it. The following is an example of using the NewMail object to create and send a piece of e-mail that contains HTML formatting. You can see from the example that both the `MailFormat` and `BodyFormat` must be set properly in order for the receiving e-mail client to get the style enhancements in the message.

```
Set objEmail = Server.CreateObject("CDONTS.Newmail")
bodyStr = "<HTML><BODY>"
bodyStr = bodyStr + "<P>I <STRONG>love</STRONG>"
bodyStr = bodyStr + " Visual Studio!</P>"
bodyStr = bodyStr + "</BODY></HTML>"
objEmail.From = "danr@coherentdata.com"
objEmail.To = "joe@widgetco.com"
objEmail.MailFormat = 0 ' cdoMailFormatMime
objEmail.BodyFormat = 0 ' cdoBodyFormatHTML
objEmail.ContentBase = "http://www.coherentdata.com/"
objEmail.ContentLocation = "danr/"
objEmail.Body = bodyStr
objEmail.Send
Set objEmail = Nothing
```

Other Methods

The `Send` method is not the only method available for use with the NewMail object. Two of these methods are used to attach content to the message itself. These methods include the following:

- **`AttachFile`** Attaches a file, specified by path and filename, to the current message using the specification of the format for encoding it.
- **`AttachURL`** Adds an attachment and associates a URL with the attachment.
- **`SetLocaleIDs`** Includes the local ID to be used to examine the e-mail messages. If left empty, the local ID is retrieved from the registry of the sending machine.

Attaching a File

When you create a message containing HTML, you can also attach a file to be referenced within the HTML body code. Most often, this attachment will include an image. In this example code, a logo file is placed in the body for display at the top of the message:

```
objEmail.Body = "<HTML><BODY>Widget Co<IMG SRC=logo.gif><P>" _
   & "</BODY></HTML>"
objEmail.AttachFile "file://c:\logo.gif", "logo.gif"
objEmail.Send
```

Message Headers

A typical e-mail message, when viewed in an e-mail program such as Outlook, will only display the primary details of the message, such as those set by the NewMail object properties. There is, however, far more information contained in the message. This information is stored in the message header. In the following listing, you can see the amount of information contained in a simple header message:

```
From ???@??? Tue Sep 01 08:48:45 1998
X-Persona: <CDI>
Received: from xox.lifelike.com (209.60.124.1 [209.60.124.1]) by
hobbyplanetserv.hobbyplanet.com with SMTP (Microsoft Exchange Internet Mail
Service Version 5.5.2232.9)
   id SDXGNJ29; Wed, 2 Sep 1998 22:54:28 -0700
Received: by xox.lifelike.com (8.9.0.Beta5/8.9.0.Beta5) id UAA05650
   for ogo-nospamoutgoing; Wed, 2 Sep 1998 20:03:03 -0700 (PDT)
Received: from dfw-ix8.ix.netcom.com (dfw-ix8.ix.netcom.com [206.214.98.8])
   by xox.lifelike.com (8.9.0.Beta5/8.9.0.Beta5) with ESMTP id UAA05644
   for <myName@lifelike.com>; Wed, 2 Sep 1998 20:02:49 -0700 (PDT)
Received: (from smap@localhost)
          by dfw-ix8.ix.netcom.com (8.8.4/8.8.4)
     id WAA08463 for <myname@lifelike.com>; Wed, 2 Sep 1998
        22:01:56 -0500 (CDT)
Received: from sji-ca9-67.ix.netcom.com(209.109.236.67) by dfw-ix8.ix.netcom.com
via smap (V1.3)
   id rma008445; Wed Sep  2 22:01:52 1998
Message-ID: <32EE06D0.A2E8F74C@ix.netcom.com>
Date: Wed, 02 Sep 1998 20:02:40 -0700
From: My Name <MyName@ix.netcom.com>
Reply-To: myName@ix.netcom.com
Organization: MyName Co.
X-Mailer: Mozilla 4.05 [en] (Win95; I)
MIME-Version: 1.0
To: OmniGo list <ogo@lifelike.com>
Subject: database to PC
Content-Type: text/plain; charset=us-ascii
Content-Transfer-Encoding: 7bit
Sender: myMail@xox.lifelike.com
Precedence: bulk
Hi, just thought I would write.
```

As you can see, the header of the message contains information about content type, the sending e-mail program, and numerous other details used for identification and routing. Most of the information in the header is automatically generated. However, through CDO you can add your own header information. This is done by using the `Value` property of the object. Each Value property within the collection is specified by a name. In the following code, the `Reply-To` value is set.

```
Set objMail = CreateObject("CDONTS.Newmail")
objMail.Value("Reply-To") = "jdr@homeemail.com"
objMail.Send "rob@here.com", "jdr@there.com", "Bad news", "I owe you £50"
Set objMail = Nothing
```

Some of the standard header types you might use include: Reply-To (to set the address for an e-mail reply to a different address than the sender), Keywords, and References. To add these header items, you need to specify the property by name in the `Value` collection.

The `Value` property can be set any number of times, each time adding a new object. If you wanted to add some keywords and specify a different reply-to address, you could write code like this:

```
Set objMail = CreateObject("CDONTS.Newmail")
objMail("Reply-To") = "otherbox@widgetco.com"
objMail("Keywords") = "Alert,Hobby,Planet,World"
objMail.Send "me@source.com", "you@destination.com", "My Subject", "My Body"
Set objMail = Nothing
```

Header values, like attachments, cannot be removed from a NewMail object once they've been added. Therefore, if a mistake has been made, the whole message should be eliminated and reconstructed from scratch.

Session Object

While the NewMail object is the most rudimentary method of sending mail, the Session object provides much more complete mail interaction. The Session object opens a session with the mail server using a complete profile, including a user name, password, and the mail server to access. Unlike the NewMail object, which requires explicitly sending

Sending Mail Through the Exchange Server

Using Microsoft Exchange Server instead of the SMTP service included with IIS requires a few special considerations. The advantages of sending all mail traffic through a single centralized machine (the Exchange Server) is certainly attractive. The disadvantages include installing a compatible object model to allow ASP code to communicate with Exchange Server.

If you want to use CDO for NTS (CDONTS.DLL), IIS 4 must be installed on the Exchange Server. Alternatively, you can install CDO 1.2 on the IIS Web Server to access the remote Exchange Server machine. In Exchange Server, you must run the IMS Wizard, Web applications will use the SMTP service installed with IIS otherwise.

addresses, the Session object actually logs on to the e-mail server, allowing the use of an address book stored there.

The e-mail server to be used for login is specified in the e-mail profile on the machine that is sending the message. A profile is typically created through Outlook, but can be created in the Mail and Fax application of the Control Panels.

ADDING THE PASSWORD REMINDER

In Chapter 9, when you created the login application, the password reminder page simply displayed the requested password. A small modification to the remindPersonal.asp page will set it up to e-mail the requested information to the user.

1. Open the page remindPersonal.asp. In the body of the page, there are two Response.Write commands that tell the user the current password. You will need to replace these commands with the e-mail code.
2. Enter the following code in place of the two Response.Write calls:

```
<%
   Set objNewMail = Server.CreateObject("CDONTS.NewMail")

   fromStr = "postmaster@widgetco.com (Postmaster)"
   toStr = Request.Form("reqEmail")
   subjectStr = "Widget Co. requested reminder"
   bodyStr = "This is the reminder you requested from Widget Co"
   bodyStr = bodyStr + " about your forgotten password." + chr(13)
   bodyStr = bodyStr + chr(13)+ "Your password is: " _
      & Session("Password")
   bodyStr = bodyStr + chr(13)

   objNewMail.Send fromStr, toStr, subjectStr, bodyStr
   Response.Write("A reminder has been sent to your email account.<P>"
%>
```

Now when a request is made, a message containing the password reminder will be sent.

MODIFYING THE SURVEY APPLICATION

E-mail confirmation of received registration information is one of the fine touches that sets apart a well constructed Web solution. In the previous chapter, the doneSurvey.asp page contained a commented line that stated, "Insert e-mail code here." This is, of course, where the e-mail code can be entered.

1. Open the doneSurvey.asp page.
2. Add the following code to replace the insert comment:

```
Set objNewMail = Server.CreateObject("CDONTS.NewMail")
fromStr = "postmaster@widgetco.com (Postmaster)"
toStr = Session("curE-mail")
subjectStr = "Widget Co. Survey confirmation"
bodyStr = "Thank you for filling out the survey on " + CStr(Now)
bodyStr = bodyStr + chr(13)
bodyStr = bodyStr + chr(13) + "We appreciate your the time you've given to us."
bodyStr = bodyStr + chr(13)

objNewMail.Send fromStr, toStr, subjectStr, bodyStr
```

CREATING A SENDING APPLICATION

To provide an example of what a delayed e-mail processing system might look like, I've included the following code, which sends e-mail messages based on information found in a database. This code is a piece of an application that demonstrates how a link to an electronic greeting card can be sent, something like the cards provided by BlueMountainArts.com.

In a solution of this sort, you may want to review the e-mail destination addresses. When a card entry is added to the database, a flag field named Sent is created, which is initially unchecked. When the page is accessed with a Web browser, all of the unsent mail will be e-mailed. If the e-mail is successfully sent, the Sent flag is marked and the broadcast date is recorded. Once the loop sends all of the unsent mail, a report is generated to display the addresses to which the e-mail was broadcast as well as the total number of messages that were sent.

You could easily add an HTML form solution to allow you to individually evaluate and alter any of the e-mail settings before it is dispatched. This would allow remote administration of the system as well as remote sending activation.

The code shown next will automatically create and deliver batch e-mail via the NewMail object:

```
<html>
<META HTTP-EQUIV="REFRESH" CONTENT="90;URL=mail.asp">
<head>
<title>Card sending</title>
</head>


<body bgcolor="#FFFFFF" topmargin="0" leftmargin="0"
   LINK="#0080FF" VLINK="#0080FF">
<H1>Hobby Planet eCard Sending Report</H1><P>
<%
   response.write("Report generated: " & Now)
   response.write("<P>Searching database for unsent cards...<P>")
   ' Create ODBC connection to emailODBC data source
   Set Conn = Server.CreateObject("ADODB.Connection")
   Conn.Open "cardODBC"
```

```
strSQL = "Select * from cardInfo where sent = 0"
Set rsHPFAQs = Server.CreateObject("ADODB.Recordset")
rsHPFAQs.Open strSQL, conn, 3, 3, 1

response.write("Attempting to send...<P>")
Dim objNewMail

' Step through the recordset to send email where the sent Field
' is set to 0 (unsent)
i=0
Do Until  rsHPFAQs.EOF
   Set objNewMail = Server.CreateObject("CDONTS.NewMail")
   ' Get the values from the db and place them in local variables
   fromName = rsHPFAQs("fromName")
   fromEmail = rsHPFAQs("fromEmail")
   toName = rsHPFAQs("toName")
   toEmail = rsHPFAQs("toEmail")
   cardType = rsHPFAQs("cardType")
   fromStr = "postmaster@hobbyPlanet.com (" & fromName & ")"
   toStr = toEmail & "(" & toName & ")"
   ' Determine the type of card to be sent to the user
   if cardType = 1 then
      subjectStr = "Holiday Greetings - from "  & fromName
   else
      subjectStr = "Holiday Beanie Greetings - from "  & fromName
   end if
   ' Generate the body content of the message
   bodyStr = "Guess what!!! You have just received a greeting " & _
      "card from " & fromName & ". You can pick up your " & _
      "personal greeting by connecting to the following " & _
      WWW Address:"
   bodyStr = bodyStr + chr(13)
   bodyStr = bodyStr + chr(13)+ "http://www.hobbyPlanet.com/card/card.asp?friendshipID="
& friendshipID
   bodyStr = bodyStr + chr(13)
   bodyStr = bodyStr + chr(13)+ _
      "This service is FREE! Have a good day and have fun!"
   bodyStr = bodyStr + chr(13)
   bodyStr = bodyStr + chr(13)+ "___________________________________________________"
   bodyStr = bodyStr + chr(13)+ "You're welcome to send a " & +
      "free card to someone at this location: " & _
      "http://www.hobbyPlanet.com"
   response.write("From: " & fromStr & " To: " & toStr & _
      " at: " & now & "<BR>")
   if len(trim(fromStr)) > 1 and len(trim(toStr)) > 3 then
      objNewMail.Send fromStr, toStr, subjectStr, bodyStr
   else
      response.write("bad FROM or TO field")
      rsHPFAQs("comments") = "bad TO field"
   end if
   ' ---- Create and send the mail ----
   if rsHPFAQs("sendToMyEmail") then
```

```
            Set objNewMail = Server.CreateObject("CDONTS.NewMail")
            if len(trim(fromStr)) > 1 and len(trim(fromEmail)) > 3 then
               objNewMail.Send fromStr, fromEmail, subjectStr, bodyStr
            else
               rsHPFAQs("comments") = "cc: bad TO field"
               response.write("cc:bad TO field")
            end if
            response.write("CC From: " & fromStr & " To: " & _
            fromEmail & " t: " & now & "<BR>")
         end if
         rsHPFAQs("Sent") = 1
         rsHPFAQs("sendDate") = Now
         rsHPFAQs.update
         i = i + 1
         rsHPFAQs.MoveNext
      Loop
      Set objNewMail = Nothing
      rsHPFAQs.Close
      response.write("<P><b>Sent " & i & " message(s)</b><P>")

      ' Display the number of cards sent in this batch
      strSQL = "Select count(sent) AS NumSent from cardInfo"
      Set rsHPFAQs = Server.CreateObject("ADODB.Recordset")
      rsHPFAQs.Open strSQL, conn, 3, 3, 1
      response.write("Total cards sent: " & rsHPFAQs("NumSent") & "<P>")

      Conn.Close
      Set rsHPFAQs = Nothing
      Set Conn = Nothing
%>

</body>
</html>
```

The advantage of this system is the ability to manually check which confirmations will be broadcast before the e-mail is actually transmitted. It also allows the e-mail to be efficiently transmitted as a batch. The page will return a report of the number of messages actually found and transmitted.

At the top of the listed code, you'll notice the META tag used to refresh the page every 90 seconds. Leaving a browser running with the page active will keep the page activated and sending batches of messages regularly. Although this is not an elegant programming solution for most tasks, it provides an example of how a batch process might be activated remotely, and it can be stopped by simply displaying another Web page.

Sending Mail Through SQL Server

There is a stored procedure called xp_SendMail that is built into SQL Server that allows you to send e-mail. It can be activated through a Command object execution, within a stored procedure, or through a trigger. It can even be used to send the entire returned recordset of a query automatically. The simplest execution of the stored procedure can send a message with a brief amount of body text, such as the following:

```
xp_sendmail 'myName@widgetco.com', 'A new record was added'
```

A number of variables can be provided with this stored procedure so that you can be more specific in the message that is sent:

```
xp_sendmail @recipients = 'myName@widgetco.com,
yourName@widgetco.com',
   @message = 'A new record was added',
   @subject = 'New record alert'
```

You could easily create a new record trigger to accomplish almost the same process that is created here through the CDO. When a customer adds new card information, the process of adding a new record to SQL Server could activate an e-mail message.

Q&A

Q: Is there any way to use CDO 1.2 to send a message without logging on for a session?

A: No. Unlike CDO for NTS with the NewMail object, CDO 1.2 requires that a session be initiated before transmission can take place. Therefore, there must be a user account created on the Exchange Server through which the e-mail is sent. The ability to send e-mail without a session is why CDO for NTS is the ideal technology for sending quick batches of e-mail.

Q: Is there any way to confirm that an e-mail sent from the NewMail object was received?

A: With the NewMail object, any return address may be entered. Therefore, you can specify a known account to receive rejected messages, and you can even use the CDO Session object to check for the returned mail.

SUMMARY

The Collaboration Data Objects (CDO) allow you to send e-mail easily from an ASP script. The CDO for NTS that is included in the IIS 4 installation can provide an easy and effective way for a Web solution to send e-mail through scripted code. Using the NewMail object, an e-mail message can actually be created and sent in only two lines of code. In this chapter you covered:

- **Collaboration Data Objects (CDO)** CDO is the object framework that makes e-mailing possible through ASP scripting. New messages can be generated and sent by using the CDO object model.
- **CDO for NTS versus CDO 1.2** CDO for NTS, the version of CDO installed with IIS 4, is a subset of the more robust CDO 1.2. CDO for NTS uses the SMTP protocol to send messages. CDO 1.2 (available for Exchange Server install) contains the higher-level functions for addressing an Exchange Server services such as the calendar, address book, filtering, and workflow functions. CDO 1.2 uses MAPI services for e-mail server access.
- **NewMail object** This is the primary object that simplifies sending mail through the CDO. The NewMail object allows a message to be sent with a single method call. The object is write-only and perfect for bulk or automated e-mail transmission. This object is only available in the CDO for NTS object model.

CHAPTER 12

Security Overview

Security is often the last item implemented in a project, and when schedules get tight, it is often only marginally addressed. Ensuring good security is further impeded because many of the concepts are not intuitive and require different knowledge than traditional design and deployment considerations.

For Web database solutions in particular, where security extends over at least three separate servers (the Web server, database server, and network operating-system server) security is complicated. To minimize the potential security risks, planning a basic security foundation as you create new Web applications will aid you tremendously in preventing intentional or unintentional security breaches.

In this chapter you will learn about some of the technologies available for making your Web database solution secure, as well as some of the planning steps necessary for properly evaluating and deploying security plans. Security should not only prevent outside attacks, but also provide the ability to keep information from individuals in the organization who are not authorized to view it.

IMPORTANCE OF SECURITY

After the most basic security holes are plugged, such as changing the name and password on the administrator account and taking other simple steps, many developers simply ignore security considerations on a Web-based platform. After all, most data collected through the Web would be useless to all but the company's most direct competitors.

Additionally, security procedures are not always applied in the required division of labor. Typically a network administrator or database administrator is responsible for the vulnerability of the network, so it's not within the job description of the Web solution developer to handle security issues. However, many potential security holes are inherent within the construction of each solution, so everyone involved in the project should consider these aspects.

Here are a few security dangers that are important to consider, even at the level of an individual project:

- **Accidental damage to data** Users without proper training or who are not paying close attention to their actions can often delete or incorrectly change information unintentionally. These people often should not have data-changing access in the first place.
- **Unauthorized data access** The more routes available for accessing secure data, the more likely unauthorized access will be obtained. Given that many Web applications require access to the system itself (through a data source), this security window must be guarded.
- **Misinterpretation of information** If a user is not trained or instructed on how to view data, the data can be misleading and allow the spread of misinformation. A salesperson might examine current inventory and believe there is no stock, without being aware that refurbished entries may be contained in a separate table.

These potential dangers simply highlight the need to pay attention to the security structure you plan to deploy. Too often, developers consider security only in terms of a hacker trying to penetrate a system, but internal security lapses are far more common.

SECURITY PLANNING

In most development, planning should occur before the project starts. A re-examination of the security plan should usually occur again, at about halfway through the project, when the exact extent of deployment is known. Be sure to place a milestone in your overall plan to ensure that the security evaluation takes place at the proper time.

One of the best ways to begin a security plan is by asking yourself some questions that will outline the parameters of the desired security protection. The answers will help define the terms under which the security framework will be designed and put into place.

Web Security Questions

There is no question that security is expensive in terms of time and maintenance needs. To minimize the obstacles in creating a security framework, it is necessary to examine the problem from several different angles and determine exactly what security is necessary. After all, spending time and energy reinforcing the main barn door isn't very effective if you leave the side doors open.

Here is a list of questions that, when answered, should help you determine where you should focus the resources you intend to commit to security. Answering these basic questions can help, whether you are evaluating the security that you have in place or creating a new system. These questions will also aid you in determining how your solution will merge into the general security framework created by the network administrator.

These sample questions include:

- Is there one network or are multiple networks joined together? Does the connected network have high-level administrative privileges on your network? Does the point that joins the networks act as a firewall, so your solution only must contend with access on the LAN?
- How is it possible to monitor network traffic? Is someone in your team training to examine Web traffic? In Web systems, surges in traffic are often warnings of possible penetration.
- What happens when you access Web pages out of order in a Web application? Does the application crash or does it provide a loophole where custom (non-application) information can be fed from the outside through a query, form, or cookie?
- Is secure transmission between the browser and the server necessary? If someone intercepted the communications, would the problem be significant? Are cleartext passwords being sent over a WAN connection?

- Does the firewall protect against dangerous content, such as applets or client-side scripting code?
- Is it necessary to verify that applets or ActiveX controls have not been modified on the way to the browser?

These questions provide an overview of the potential holes in a Web application framework.

To really judge your security needs, you need to ask yourself five basic questions:

1. How important is the information being accessed?
2. What is it worth, in terms of dollars, to protect it?
3. If the data is stolen or intercepted, what is the possible danger?
4. If data is lost or changed, what would be the cost of the loss? Is there a recovery system in place?
5. Can seemingly unimportant information be leveraged to access important private data?

Answering these questions will help you determine realistic goals and limits when designing a workable security plan. One of the most effective means of performing this evaluation is using the data dictionary or data model as a template from which to ask these questions. If you can answer them for every data object (table, database, etc.) used by your solution including data sources external to your application, you can create a fairly good overview of your system's security parameters.

TIP: When examining the security that is implemented on your system, you might check out the L0pht (that's L-Zero-P-H-T), Heavy Industries Web site at www.l0pht.com. They often have updates on security issues for IIS and ASP, as well as warnings of potential danger areas in Windows NT Server.

Planning Security

Once you've examined the type of protection that you need and how security can affect the safety of your systems, it is important to properly plan how security will be implemented. Any security plan should address internal and external threats in these three categories:

- **Transmission interception** The transmission over a network could be intercepted for the information contained in it, to stop it from reaching its destination, or to be modified and retransmitted.
- **Password breach** Passwords are the most common low-tech breach, because people often use popular (guessable) passwords, such as birth dates, marriage dates, popular movies, and so on. Besides using easily predicted passwords, the user may use the same password on both a secure network and on an insecure one-visit Web site.

- **System compromise** If an unauthorized person obtains control of a server, information contained on that server, or available through that server's authorization, can be compromised. The system may be compromised not only through a network; physical security must be considered as well. Physical security includes restricting physical access to the servers, passwords, and so on.

As you can see, most of these areas don't apply directly to Web database services. With ASP execution, however, there is a great deal of overreach in potential effects. Since an ASP script has access to the server resources of the machine, it can be used to facilitate all three categories of threat. An ASP page can intercept outgoing or incoming data, provide a "Trojan horse" to fool a user into providing an important password to a fake page, or compromise the system by gaining control over available server resources.

Defining Groups and Users

For key server resources, most security planning comes down to properly defining and granting permission to the groups of users on the system. After the groups have been defined, the individual users are created and added to each group. Only for special exceptions should security be granted on a user-by-user basis. By creating groups and assigning users to the groups, many problems of improper access can be avoided.

For Web database developers, setting up security will most often occur within the database that is used such as Microsoft SQL Server. Defining groups on SQL Server is accomplished through the SQL Enterprise Manager. Objects within the database are defined to allow permission by users or groups (see Figure 12-1).

The SQL Server security controls allow you to define access down to the column level. Because of the difficulty of maintaining column-level security, most organizations seek to separate private data into related tables to prevent any accidental access or configuration mistakes.

NOTE: Setting security access on SQL Server is not only available through the graphical user interface. Stored procedures such as sp_addgroup, sp_adduser, and sp_addlogin let the system administrator manage security from the SQL execution command line (through iSQL, for example). All modification of security access through the command line applies only to Standard security and will not be extended to NT Server.

Network Traffic Analyzer

For management of networked Windows platform machines, Microsoft includes Systems Management Server (SMS) in the BackOffice suite. SMS is used to allow remote configuration, debugging, and installation of a network infrastructure. Included with SMS is an application called Network Traffic Analyzer. This application will allow you to examine all of the traffic that is progressing over your IP network. A version of the utility is available that can monitor the traffic from a single machine. All monitored traffic is actually viewed using the unique MAC address of each machine that is broadcasting and receiving.

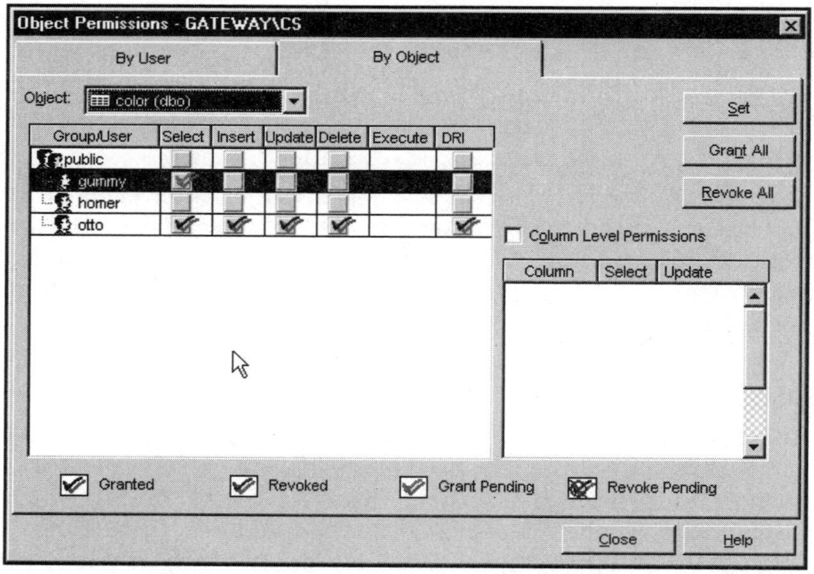

Figure 12-1. The Enterprise Manager is used for objects on SQL Server to configure the users or groups that have permissions

DEFINITION: **MAC address** Every network card has a unique identifier assigned to it when it is created at the factory. The identifier, or MAC address, remains unchanged for the life of the card and can be used to establish a unique identifier for the machine.

Filters can be applied to allow you to watch specific origination or destination addresses. This feature is helpful if a small percentage of the overall network traffic needs to be watched.

NOTE: The Network Traffic Analyzer is a low-level tool used primarily by network administrators. Although you may never use it, it is useful to know that traffic can be monitored at the IP traffic level in case any questionable access occurs.

Traffic analysis using the Network Traffic Analyzer is far more rudimentary than a monthly Web log report—this analysis allows viewing the user activities in real-time. If the MAC address of a particular system is known, traffic analysis patterns can be filtered specifically to watch the traffic from that machine.

CAUTION: Most of the products in Microsoft Office since the Office 95 version (including Word, Excel, and PowerPoint) write the MAC address of the machine into each and every document created by these programs. This means that all documents created by a user can be traced back to the originating machine. Microsoft offers a patch to registered users of Microsoft Office that removes this feature, but by default it is left on.

You should consider patching all of the copies of Microsoft Office active in your office. Because any knowledgeable user could modify this ID to make it appear that the origin (of a virus, for example) is another user, it is a false authentication danger. It also means that any Microsoft documents distributed outside your organization will publish the unique identifiers of each machine on your network at the same time. Privacy and security organizations are just beginning to recognize the magnitude of this security problem.

WEB APPLICATION SECURITY

In addition to the security placed on groups that will access a server, execution privileges on individual applications must also be closely examined. For example, if a directory that allows FTP access can also execute ASP scripts, the security of that entire server can be compromised. In Figure 12-2, you can see the various aspects of the Web application and how it relates to the security of other systems executing under NT server.

Execution dangers apply to any code that executes on the server at the prompting of a remote request. For a Web database application, the threat will most likely come through a dangerous ASP file. The potential danger of an ASP application lies in its broad reach. Once the application executes, it has access to the following:

- **The complete file system, through the FileSystem component** The FileSystem component can allow read and write privileges to every file on the server, potentially including the system registry, transaction log, and source-code directories.
- **Data sources and possibly data-source passwords** If the data-source passwords are stored in the Global.asa files of the application, they can be read directly from the files.
- **Component execution** Any components authored for access through a Web server process can be tapped for use. In a distributed computing system that uses technology such as DCOM to execute a component on a remote server, an ASP file could potentially breach far more than the single server machine to which access has been gained.

The potential for Web-application security violations is perhaps the most dangerous possible breach with which a Web developer must contend. Unauthorized execution

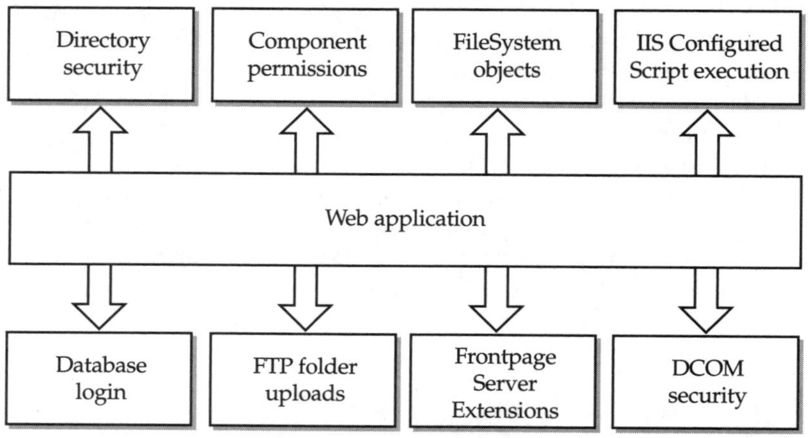

Figure 12-2. The Web application contacts almost every security aspect of a server system

control can be far more dangerous than unintended data access disclosure. If the proper Web application security is not in place, exposure through the Internet makes it possible for someone to obtain nearly untraceable access. This would permit a gateway to introduce or modify executing ASP code on a server.

As a simple example, imagine that an application is created to display photographs of corporate personnel. An application directory that contains the ASP code to display these images is given script execution permission. Within this directory is another folder called `\Images` that actually contains the photos in JPEG format. To simplify management, the personnel department is given FTP access to this directory to update the photos as necessary.

A gigantic security hole has now been created in your infrastructure. Since execution privileges are inherited, an ASP file can be placed in the `\Images` directory that can be called for execution through any Web browser. This ASP file can have access to any resource on the server and any other server resources that are permitted to the server via DCOM or Active Directory.

The entire problem would be avoided if there had been guidelines in place as to the creation of new directories within an execution structure. When the directory was configured for FTP access, it could have also been set so that it won't allow execution. It is important to consider these types of problems when defining application execution.

Safety-Lock Password

Any evaluation of the level of security should also take into account the level of training given to the system operators. Increasingly, intranet applications are being used for basic data entry, and the operator is only coached on the most rudimentary features. Some destructive functions, such as a Delete Record button, can be made much safer if a simple safety-lock password is put in place.

A safety-lock password is a general password known by all of the administrators. When a destructive button is pressed, the user is prompted for the password before the change can be made. Advanced users will have learned the password, but beginners will have to consult more senior personnel. At this point, the intended action can be checked and the user can be instructed as to the general policy regarding the feature.

This function can be easily implemented in client-side JavaScript code. A simple input dialog box accepts the password, the value entered is checked, and the action is allowed or disallowed. Although this is not a replacement for logon security, the safety-lock password can be useful in many areas of a Web application to prevent unintended operations.

Database Security

Properly configuring your database server for security is at least as important as setting up Web-application security. Most likely, your database system administrator will handle the security on the database server. However, if you are going to do it yourself, it would be worth getting a good book on SQL Server.

SQL Server actually has three different modes of security: Standard, Windows NT Login, and Mixed. For Web database solutions, Standard security is usually the best choice, because SQL Server–specific security can be easily managed. Even when the security is integrated with Windows NT, database resource settings for the login accounts must be independently configured. Therefore, standard security assures that all users in the system are meant to have SQL Server access.

When using Windows NT Login or Mixed security, the general NT security must be contended with. This can add complexity and potential security holes for maintenance of group definitions and unmonitored, unused, but unpurged accounts. However, with the addition of Active Directory in Windows 2000, maintenance of multiple accounts and passwords can be minimized. If you are using a Windows 2000-based network, NT Login security may be the best option.

Cleartext Transmission

One of the inherent security problems with the Web is that most transmissions take the form of plain ASCII text, or what is known as *cleartext*. Because any information broadcast over a network can be intercepted by a program called a packet sniffer, even user names and passwords entered into a standard Web page can be captured.

DEFINITION: **Packet sniffer** A program that reads packets that are being transmitted over a network. Rather than receiving only the packets that are intended for a specific computer, a sniffer allows the capture of any packets being broadcast on the network, regardless of the intended source or destination.

When a normal logon to a network such as Windows NT occurs, a challenge/response security model is used (see Figure 12-3). Once the session has begun, the broadcasts are unencrypted. The actual password and username, however, are encrypted at the client with a special time code and transmitted to the server. The server decodes them and checks for authentication. If they are valid, a session is opened between the client and the server.

NOTE: Windows NT challenge/response is available through the Internet Explorer Web browser. It is activated much the same way as traditional security is placed on shared folders. Netscape Navigator, however, does not support the Windows NT Login. Therefore, if you secure your site with challenge/response security, no Netscape users can log on to the system.

Even with a valid NT logon, all information passed between the client and server is sent in cleartext. Therefore, the challenge/response overcomes the problem of secure

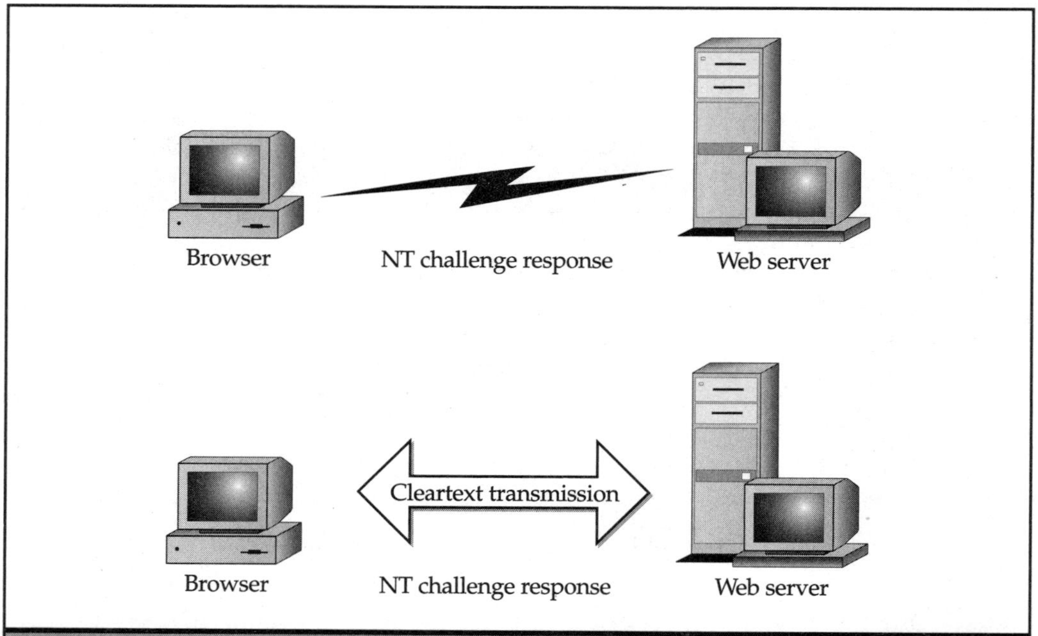

Figure 12-3. After the initial secure challenge/response exchange, all further communication occurs in cleartext

logon, but does not address the problem of data interception. To handle secure data exchange, IIS includes the ability to communicate with the browser through an encrypted session.

Encrypted Web Sessions

When the Web was first beginning, a number of Web industry companies and standards bodies united to create a sister protocol to HTTP that allowed encrypted, and hence secure, communication to take place over the Internet. This new protocol, called HTTP Secure, actually allowed HTTP communication between the Web browser and server to take place with all of the data encrypted.

The HTTP protocol simply added another layer, Secure Sockets Layer (SSL), to allow this communication. SSL provides the secure protocol layer for HTTP to transmit encrypted information to and from a Web browser.

DEFINITION: **SSL (Secure Sockets Layer)** The protocol layer available for encrypted HTTP communication between the Web browser and server.

When you access a site secured by SSL, instead of the traditional http prefix on the URL, the https prefix (for http secure) is used. A secure URL would look like this:

```
https://www.mySecureWeb.com
```

The user of the Web browser will also see either a lock icon close (Internet Explorer) or a broken key made solid (Netscape Navigator) at the bottom of the browser window to indicate that a secure session is in progress.

An SSL session actually uses a combination of public- and private-key (generally just called public-key) and symmetric-key systems. The public key is used to initiate the session and authenticate the user. Once the proper identities are established, the server sends the browser a time-based symmetric key. From that point forward, all communication between the client and server for the duration of the session is encrypted with that key.

The level of security of a public-key system is based on the length of the key used. A 40-bit key, which the United States allows for export, is fairly secure and takes a concerted effort to break. A single transmission can be broken over time with supercomputer-level power. The 128-bit key standard, also supported for US-based Web servers, is almost completely secure from attack at the present time. It takes so much computing power to break a single transmission that to break it is not very feasible even for the government to try to do. However, as computers get faster, the length of the key will also have to increase to prevent decoding.

Encryption and decryption can place a processing strain on a computer even with the proper keys. Public/private key security is particularly processor intense. For a 40-bit key, the encode and decode time for a piece of information can be substantial—public-key algorithms are approximately 1,000 times slower than symmetric-key encryption. For this reason, the public-key system is used to exchange a symmetric key password (see Figure 12-4).

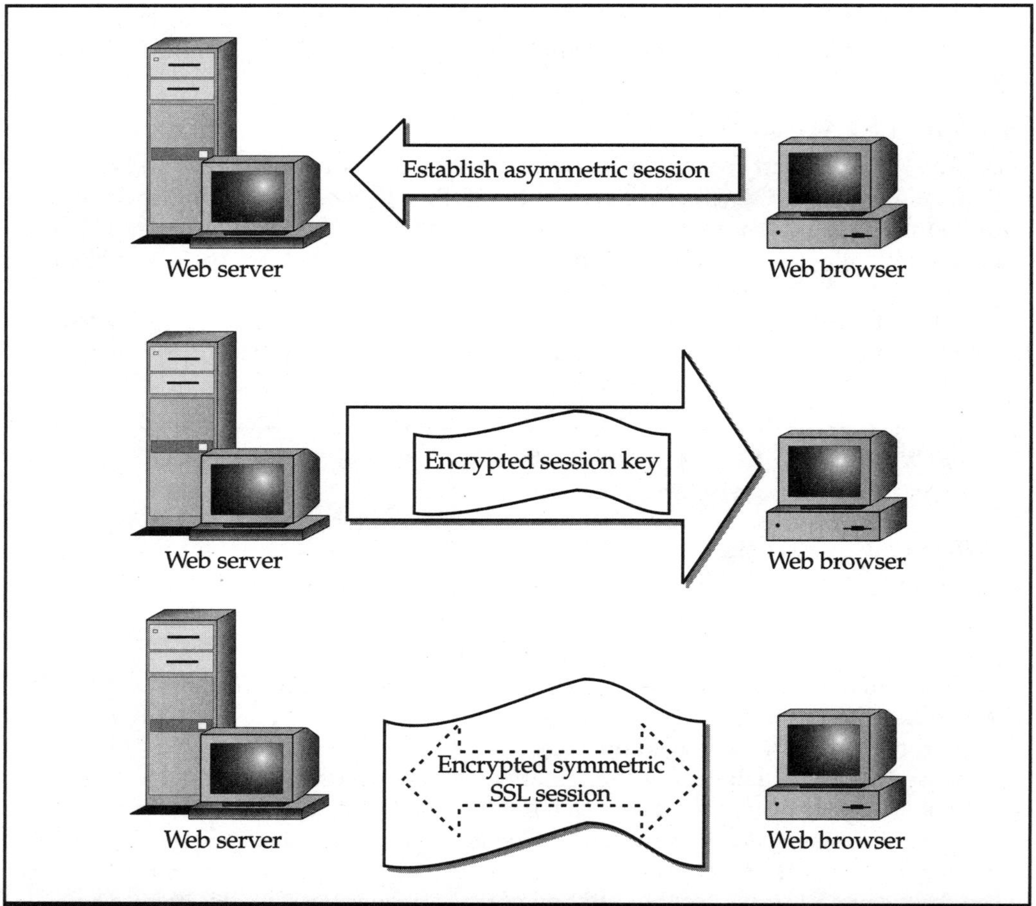

Figure 12-4. To begin an SSL session, an encrypted symmetric key is passed between browser and server

Some of the most popular symmetric algorithms include RC2, RC4, and the Data Encryption Standard (DES). Although for years 56-bit DES encryption has been considered extremely safe, recent advances in computing power and distributed architecture have made it possible (if still slightly expensive) to crack data encrypted with this method.

Any code can be cracked just using mathematical trial and error if enough time and processing power is supplied. Previously it was too expensive for any code breaking to be done by anyone but the best-funded organizations and governments. The increase in workstation computing power, however, has made previously secure techniques vulnerable. This is the primary reason why newer security models with longer keys are being adopted.

Once both sides of the session have the symmetric key, all communication between them is encoded with it. That means that all HTTP transmissions use the symmetric key to encrypt the send and receive information. Since this key changes with each session and is based on random factors and time, it is extremely difficult (nearly impossible) to decrypt during the data-exchange period.

NOTE: When an HTTPS session is active, all data transferred between the browser and the server is encrypted. This includes any graphics that are being sent by the server. On the pages that require security, try to minimize the amount of the data (text and graphics) that must be transferred. Large graphics files, for example, will slow down decoding and display, degrading the user experience.

Public-Key Encryption

Public-key encryption is a very important technology for security. Only within the last decade and during the rapid increase in internetworking of computers has this method of key security come to the forefront of encryption technology. It is a two-key encryption system that uses one key for encryption and the paired key for decryption. In Internet implementation it is being used to provide:

- Encrypted communication between a Web server and browser
- Encrypted transmission of data, such as documents or e-mail
- Absolute identification

This system of privacy has become increasingly popular over the last few years because of the flexibility it affords. A public-key system works with a matched pair of keys. A key looks like a bunch of random data. For example, a public key might look like this:


```
MIIBGTCBxAIBADBfMQswCQYDVQQGEwJVUzESMBAGA1UECBMJU2FuIERpZWdvMQsw
CQYDVQQHEwJDQTESMBAGA1UEChMJV2lkZ2V0IENvMQ4wDAYDVQQLEwVTYWxlczEL
MAkGA1UEAxMCV0MwXDANBgkqhkiG9w0BAQEFAANLADBIAkEA1OLA+v8WjiucfUd1
fGpwtAFmJYGd+vPAX9St1IigTl+34S6qNHeiLlMuZjK/jbd7JnA0DMSpXKBOlBtR
zSW4UwIDAQABoAAwDQYJKoZIhvcNAQEEBQADQQB0NnbtqLO8ycmXShdggsQOvWxi
5UFObjo06i1hrMAtfz14JPh0gf9Nx1l91QXTdiLF3/yCyCEgrX61djzWqaIH
```


The public key can be used to either encrypt or decrypt data (see Figure 12-5), as can the private key. If one key of the key pair is used to encode information, the other must be used to decode that same information. Data encrypted with the public key requires the private key for decryption. The same is true for the opposite route: if data is encrypted with the private key, the public key is required for decryption.

This two-key system is good for more than data security, it is also the method used to provide unique identification for users, systems, and resources. Since only the data encrypted with the private key can be decrypted with its matching opposite, authentication is ensured. Traditionally, a trusted third party keeps the public key on file to be accessible so the identity of the submitted encrypted data can be confirmed.

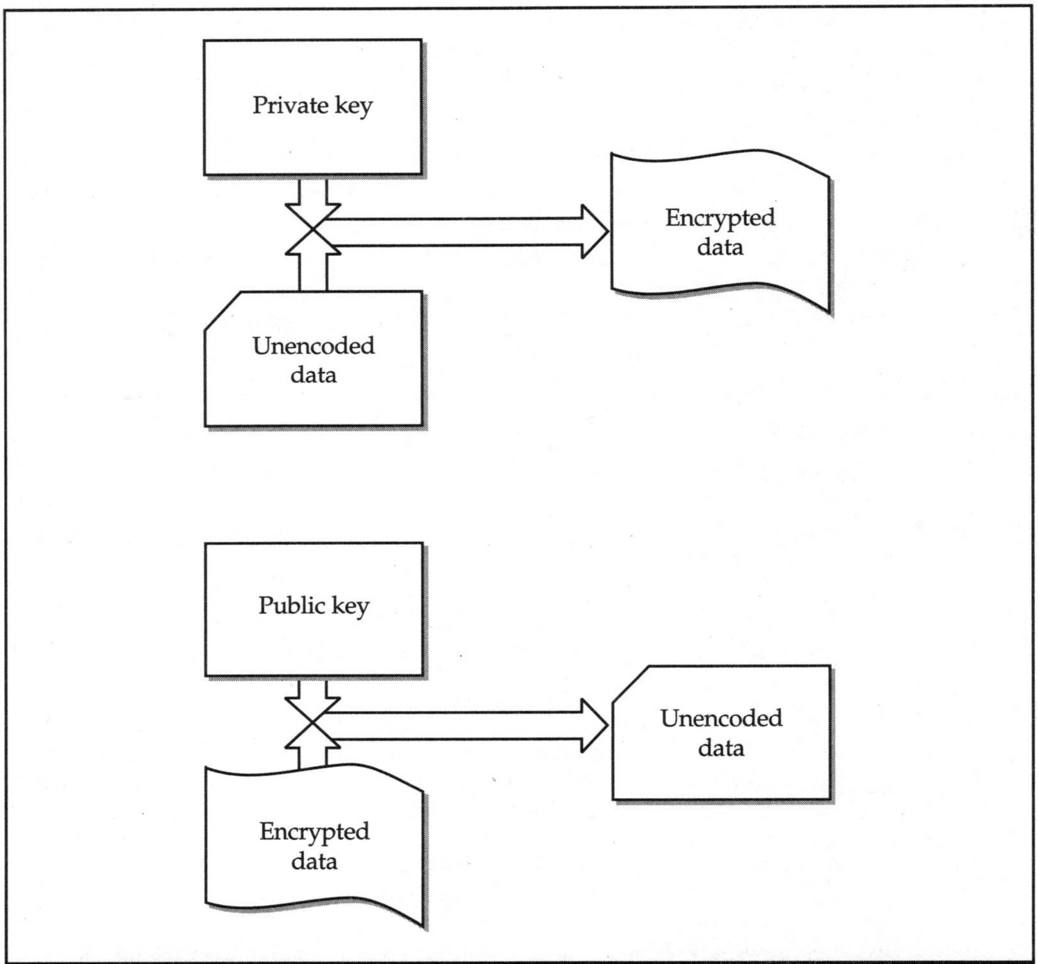

Figure 12-5. Once the public key is used to encrypt the data, only the matching private key can decrypt it

For example, the president of the United States might encrypt an e-mail message with his private key and send it to someone. A trusted source, perhaps the White House Web site, would contain the public key of the president. Any information that could be unencrypted with the recognized public key would establish that it had been initially encoded with the matching private key.

NOTE: Two-key encryption is sometimes known as asymmetric encryption. Single-key encryption, which you are probably more familiar with, is called symmetric encryption. This method uses a single password key for both encryption and decryption, like a Little Orphan Annie decoder ring.

Although public-key encryption has achieved widespread acceptance, it is very expensive for small- to medium-size companies to implement. RSA holds the patents on the technology and requires substantial fees for its inclusion in both commercial and noncommercial products. Therefore, many companies have opted to include compatibility with the Microsoft Crypto API so a user can acquire and "plug-in" any encryption engine that is needed. This allows a company to ship a product with a royalty-free symmetric engine while still allowing the use of an independently available asymmetric key system for customers that need the extra security.

Registering IIS with Secure Keys

To make your Web server capable of hosting a SSL secure session, you need to install a proper key. The IIS Microsoft Management Console (MMC) application will generate a key pair that can be submitted to a certificate authority. The certificate authority will process the pair and return a certificate that is installed into IIS and that will be accepted by Web browsers for trusted communication.

DEFINITION: Certificate An encrypted set of information that validates the identity of the source or requestor.

The process of setting up a trusted Web server is fairly straightforward. From the MMC, select the Key Manager icon on the toolbar. You will be presented with the Key Manager application (see Figure 12-6).

From the Key Manager, you can generate a key-pair certificate to allow activation of encrypted communication with your Web site. Under the Key menu, select the Create New Key option to generate a key pair. The wizard will ask you for information relating to your organization. You will need to submit this information to a certificate authority, such as Verisign. They will verify that you represent the company or organization that the key represents by accepting a fax or mailed-in report of documentation, such as articles of incorporation. Once you have satisfied their checklist to prove your identity, you will be e-mailed your certificate.

Once you receive the certificate file, it must be activated on the Web server. Simply start the Key Manager and install the confirmed key. If the key validates properly, any access to the domain using the https:// prefix will enter encryption mode.

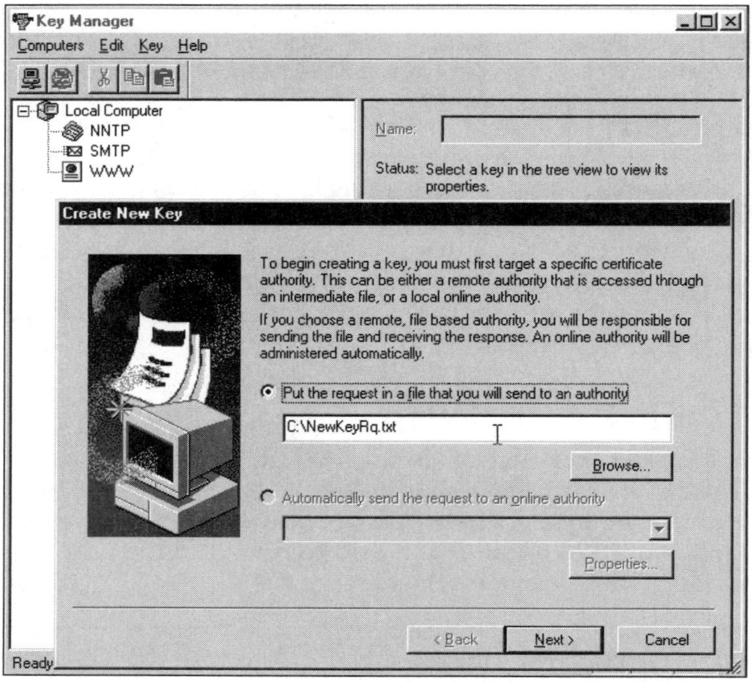

Figure 12-6. The Key Manager helps with the administration of keys for the Web server, NNTP, and e-mail

NOTE: For secure Web-server transmission, the key is specifically keyed to the machine on which the key was created (using the MAC address) and TO the domain name desired. Separate keys must be purchased for each domain and each machine that provides secure access.

A certificate authority (CA) is an organization that provides verification of keys. The most popular public CAs are Verisign (www.verisign.com), Thawte (www.thawte.com), and IBM Registry (www.software.ibm.com/commerce/registry). A key that will allow either Netscape Navigator or Internet Explorer to enter encrypted mode may be purchased from these CAs.

If you start up Internet Explorer and look in the Internet Options dialog box, you will see the settings for the certificate options and trusted CAs. Under the Content tab, click the Authorities button to open up the Certificate Authorities dialog box (see Figure 12-7). More authorities can be added through this dialog box (such as a Certificate Server run within your organization).

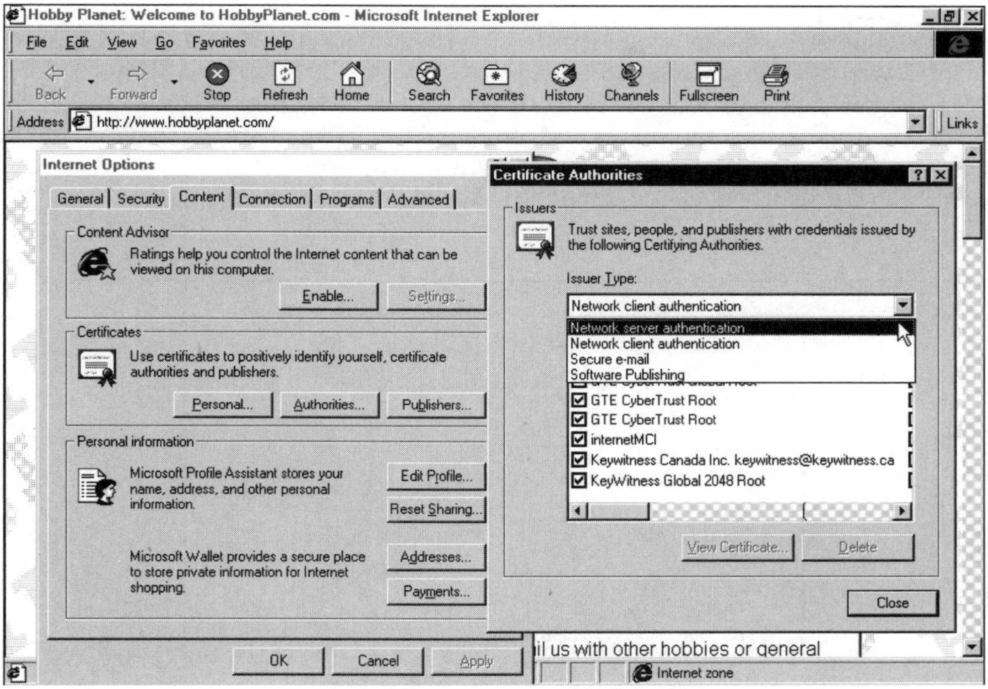

Figure 12-7. Which certificate authorities are to be trusted is set in the Web browser

The Publishers button in the Content tab of the Internet Options dialog box will display a list of companies that can install authenticated programs (such as ActiveX controls) to the current system without prompting for approval. From the Publishers dialog box you can manage control over which sources can be trusted by the Web browser.

Each key contains an expiration date when it is constructed. When the key has expired, encryption mode is still supported but the user is warned with a dialog box that states that the key is either unconfirmed or expired.

Code Signing

Code signing is the process of encapsulating a control or download with an encryption signature and checksum. Like digital signatures, code signing assures that a file that is sent across the Internet is the same one that is actually received. By maintaining a checksum of the file length and content, the client can determine whether any tampering occurred in the process of transmission.

Code signing is especially important with technologies such as ActiveX controls that can be downloaded, installed, and executed within the client browser. Tampering with such a control could endanger the client system. Microsoft has created the Cabinet (CAB) file format to allow for compression and code signing. CAB files are the standard method of encapsulating ActiveX controls for deployment where the originator, checksum, and actual control are all contained within the CAB (see Figure 12-8).

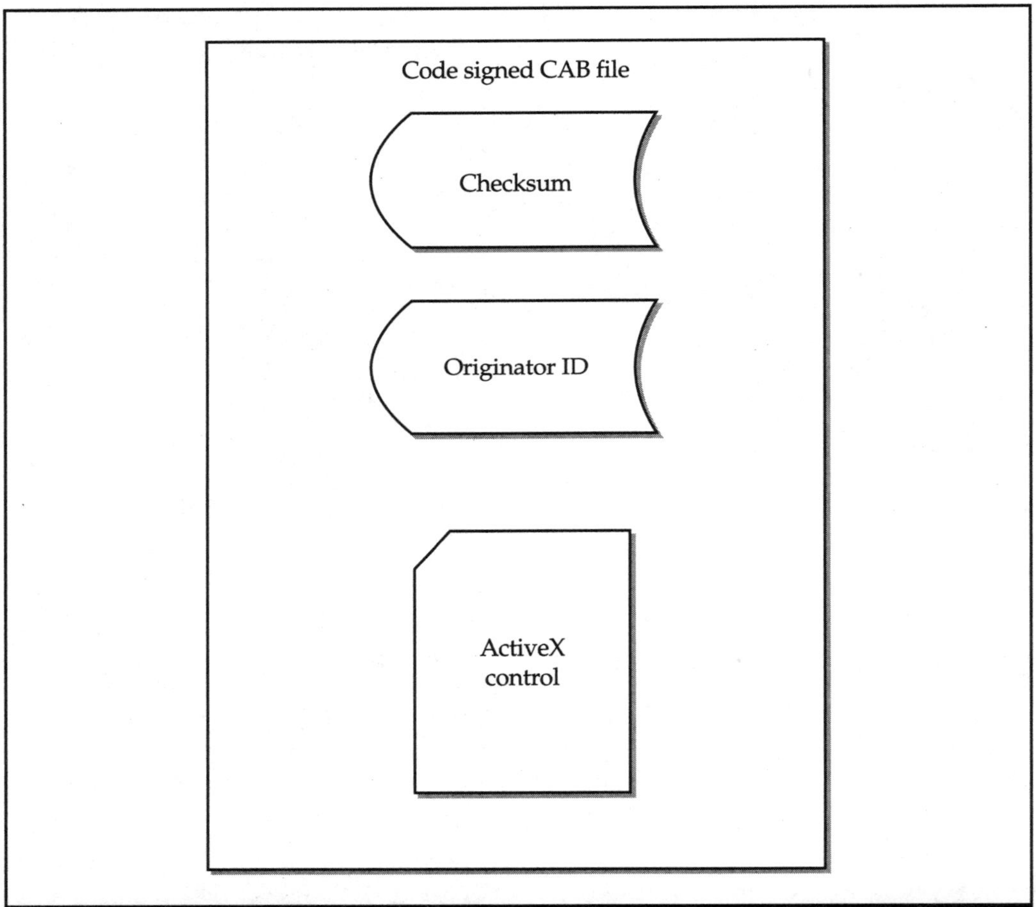

Figure 12-8. CAB files are secure because they encapsulate the control, checksum, and originator information in a single file

NOTE: The code-signing technology is mostly used for transmitting important data or executable files. Therefore, ActiveX controls (OCXs) have code-signing capabilities in CABs. ActiveX DLLs, however, since they are installed directly onto the server, do not usually need this type of protection unless they will be sent to a remote user through some type of eCommerce application.

Digital IDs

Establishing your identity in the world of the Internet is a challenge with many possible solutions. With eCommerce at an all-time high and growing fast, we can probably expect an escalation in credit card fraud, since this type of fraud simply involves entering a number. Additionally, people are being overwhelmed with passwords, PINs, and logon codes. One solution to this "identity crisis" is to use a digital signature. An automated form of DigitalID is actually the foundation technology of an SSL session.

Building on the technology of public-key encryption, a digital signature encodes information with a key given to you and no one else. The public key would be kept by a trusted third party using the same technology Web servers use for encrypted communication. Only information created using the private key of the specific user can be decoded with the key on the third-party server.

ACCESS CONTROL

The security that is included in any Win32 operating system (Windows 95/98 or Windows NT) provides access control to resources such as servers, files, directories, and printers. If the security is integrated with IIS or SQL Server, the Win32 security affects these server resources, as well. The resource permissions for Win32 are stored in the Access Control List (ACL) that contains all of the security preferences for the machine.

The ACL affect the accessibility of Web directories. Through the ACL, you can restrict a directory to be read-only, or even make it unbrowseable so that visitors (through Web or FTP access) cannot see the files that are contained in the directory.

NOTE: One of the largest advances present in Windows 2000 is the inclusion of Active Directory. The Active Directory logon allows global resource access with a single logon. In Chapter 20, more information on the new Active Directory technology is provided.

Q&A

Q: Does security on the Windows NT File Server translate to Web security?

A: Yes. If you set the security preferences on a folder, even a Web logon will require proper confirmation before access is allowed. Attempted access to the folder will be halted, and the user will be presented with a Windows NT Challenge/Response Login window if they are using Internet Explorer.

Q: How many different sets of security groups and users are required by a standard Web database application?

A: Each Web application will be different. The Windows NT security will be used to maintain the users and groups for folder permissions. The Web server (IIS) will require independent settings for application script execution privileges.

A database server, through a Web solution, may require either a Web user login (for general access) or individual user login. Because of the mixed security of SQL Server and NT Server, an application may have more or less complicated categories to maintain. With the growing use of components and distributed systems, the number of user security settings that need to be maintained may increase dramatically. In the next chapter, you will learn how to determine where your Web application requires protection and how testing should be done.

SUMMARY

Security is an important consideration when implementing your Web database solution. Because of the large number of facets of security that relate to such an application, a security strategy should be planned and put in place before the application is deployed. In this chapter you covered:

- **Varieties of security concerns** Security is more than simply preventing hackers from entering the system. It also includes protecting private data from those who are not authorized or trained to see it, as well as placing barriers to unintentional data corruption. Security is not only the responsibility of the network administrator, but also the Web solution developer.
- **Public/private key encryption** Two-key encryption (asymmetric encryption) provides the core technology that allows encrypted Web communication, unique identification, and general e-mail encryption. Using certificates are one form of a public/private key system.
- **Symmetric key encryption** Single-key encryption requires both the sending and receiving party to have the secret password. Symmetric-key encryption is up to 1000 times less processor-intensive than asymmetric encryption, but doesn't provide unique identification. An example of a primitive form of this type of encryption would be the decoder rings that many of us played with as children.
- **SSL** Secure Sockets Layer permits an encrypted session between a Web browser and a secure server. The URL for an SSL session must have the https:// prefix. SSL is widely used in eCommerce applications.

CHAPTER 13

Internet Security Issues

The growth of the Internet and the cost savings that can be achieved by using the Internet backbone as the primary corporate WAN have brought potential security risks directly into the heart of many organizations. This danger has been increased by the power of Web database applications that make information more accessible electronically. Firewall technologies were only used in the rarest circumstances 10 years ago, but now almost every organization with Internet connectivity uses some form of firewall technology to protect itself. As lower-cost, high-speed technology, such as DSL, opens the Internet to even the smallest businesses, simple security implementations will become essential.

In Chapter 12, general security considerations were examined. The Internet, however, poses special problems for identification and login. In this chapter, we'll look at some of the technology that has been specifically created to handle the problems of the Internet and what you can implement for your Web server, identification problems, and e-commerce security.

Some of the technology described here will overlap areas of responsibility that are typically associated with a system administrator, and will not be covered fully. The details of using Certificate Server, for example, are far more complex than can be handled in a short chapter. However, since the Certificate Server can be installed as part of the free Windows NT Option Pack, it is accessible to intermediate users. A general familiarity with the server, as presented in this chapter, will help you understand how Web security can be handled, even if you are not directly responsible for its administration.

TIP: Check out the security portion of the Microsoft site (www.microsoft.com/security) for bulletins, services, government issues, and products made to complement Windows NT security capabilities.

MICROSOFT CERTIFICATE SERVER

For some applications, it is critical to allow secure identification, validation, and tamper-proof transmission over the Internet. To promote secure communications, Microsoft has created a server that can create and verify digital certificates. In Chapter 12, you learned about public-key encryption, digital certificates, and digital signatures. Certificate Server can provide these certificates to provide unique identification and validation of users and data.

For electronic commerce with unknown users accessing a site, a certificate needs to be issued by a trusted third party, such as Ensign or VeriSign. For internal organizational communication, or even extranet usage, going to a third party is inconvenient, expensive, and limits the administrative level of control you have over authentication. Setting up an in-house certificate server allows you to control the certificates, their issuance, and the resource to which a certificate grants access.

Additionally, Microsoft Certificate Server (CS) can be programmed through its OLE Automation interface. This allows an organization to develop custom applications that can control the server for verification of certificates or for designing custom policy applications. There are a number of samples for various development environments included with Certificate Server. One shows how a policy module could be constructed in Visual Basic.

The server runs as a service under Windows NT, so it is always available while the server is running. It executes as shown in Figure 13-1.

The entry module accepts the request for a certificate. The policy module handles the request in the appropriate way. Through the OLE interface, a custom policy module can be created if you want to program how the requests are handled. The policy module also has access to the certificate repository to validate certificates and answer certificate requests. Depending on the results of the request, a response is issued from the server.

Certificates can be stored in the internal database or, through the Lightweight Directory Access Protocol (LDAP), in other locations. Microsoft Exchange Server, in particular, allows LDAP access to the user list to allow verification of identities through public certificate decoding.

NOTE: At the time of this writing, Microsoft Exchange Server includes its own Key Manager to allow automatic encryption and decryption of e-mail with certificates. Future releases of Exchange Server will eliminate the Key Manager and integrate directly with Certificate Server for comprehensive certificate management.

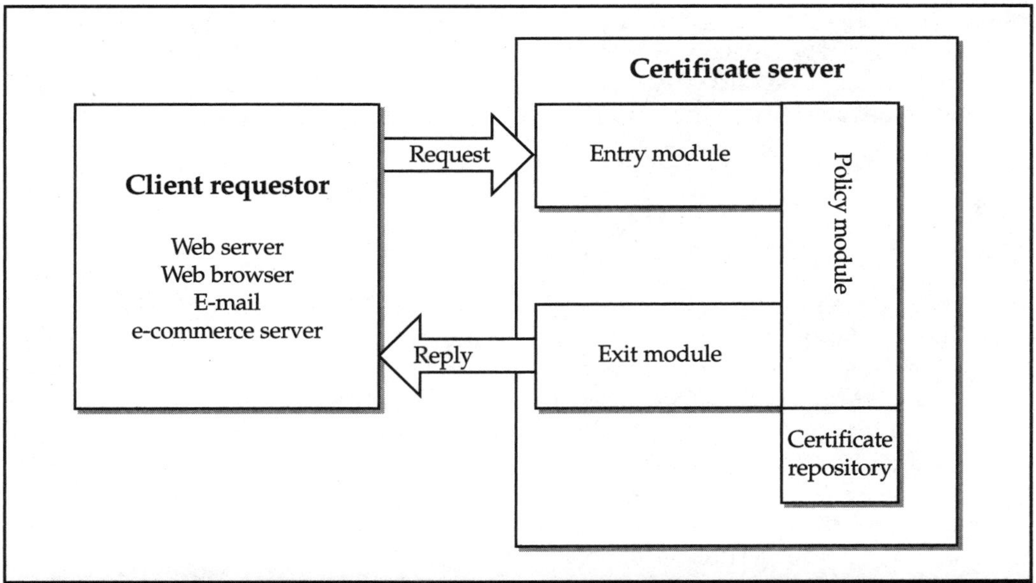

Figure 13-1. The process of a certificate request

Maintaining a list of revoked certificates is as important to the proper functioning of a certificate-based system as verifying existing certificates. Revoked certificates are tracked by a certificate revocation list (CRL). Every certificate issued by a certificate authority (CA) contains the path back to the originating CA. By checking the CRL for this CA, you can be assured that the certificate that is being used is still valid. Microsoft Certificate Server supports the publication of a CRL.

Certificate Server accepts certificates provided in the international certificate standard format (defined by the X.509 specification for versions 1 and 3). It also accepts standard requests of PKCS #10 certificates. The server can issue certificates in a variety of formats:

- **X.509 version 1 and 3 in PKCS #7 format** The international standard for certificates
- **SSL client and server certificates** Certificates that establish the identity of a particular server, as well as forming the basis for secure encrypted communication between a Web browser and a server
- **S/MIME certificates** Certificates for secure e-mail, allowing e-mail to be encoded and authenticated to ensure that it actually originated from the designated source
- **SET-compliant certificates** Certificates for electronic commerce applications and for the transmission of financial information

Certificate Server is now integrated with Windows 2000 Active Directory, so the two resources can be coordinated. Active Directory can be used to make the certificate server into an Enterprise CA. The Enterprise CA can publish certificates and CRLs to Active Directory.

Once the certificate server has been set up as a CA, there are a variety of methods of retrieving a certificate from the server. Certificate Server supports three methods:

- E-mailing the server
- Using the LDAP protocol
- Addressing the server through the object model

Certificates can be stored in an e-mail message, in an LDAP-compatible directory, or in an ODBC data source, such as SQL Server. They can also be placed in a certificate repository. The server keeps an event log for all certificate transactions. For live examination of the Certificate Server processes, you can use the Performance Monitor to view event quantities.

The Certificate Server also has the capability of being included in a CA hierarchy. A CA hierarchy allows multiple CAs to be used together for certificate authorization. The server can generate a CA certification request to another authority in the chain and also distribute the CA root certificate when requested.

Installing Certificate Server

For Web transactions and identity verification, setting up a Certificate Server within your organization can be very useful. The server is available as one of the custom installation options when you install the Windows NT Option Pack. If you haven't already installed Certificate Server, you'll need to follow these steps:

1. Execute the Windows NT Option Pack installer.
2. Select a custom installation (or Add/Remove Component if you've already installed the option pack).
3. Check the box for Certificate Server installation.
4. Click the OK or Finish button to begin the installation. The installer will eventually begin prompting you for the installation configuration for Certificate Server. The first screen of the wizard will prompt you for the storage folders.
5. You will need to set a shared folder to hold the certificate of the server itself, so enter a path that can be shared as a network drive (see the following illustration). In this example, a folder named certsrv was created in the root directory. The Database Location will hold all of the actual certificates stored on the CA. You can change the locations of the log files if the specified location is not appropriate.

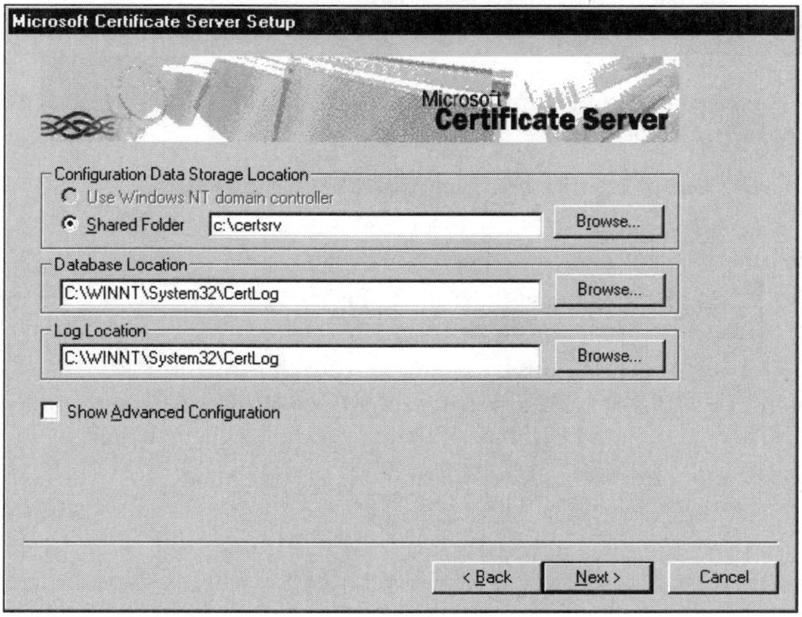

6. Enter the organization information for the CA. This information will be encoded in the central certificate to be distributed to requestors (shown here).

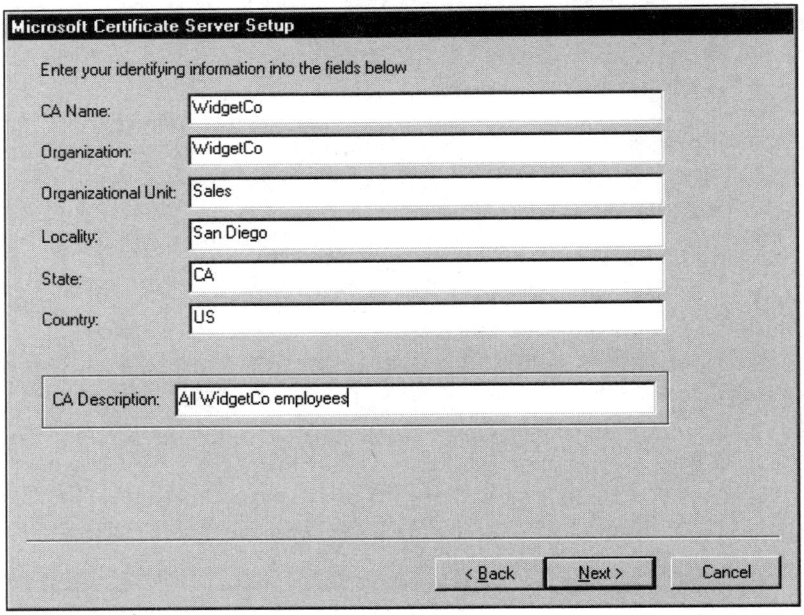

After all of the user-supplied information is entered, the Setup Wizard will automatically perform several operations:

- Generate a public/private key pair for the CA.
- Create a self-signed certificate to be stored in the shared folder for CA verification.
- Set up a certificate request file if the CA is a non-root CA, which can be submitted to the root CA for certificate requests.
- Select a cryptographic service provider (CSP) for the certificate services. The default provider of such services is the Microsoft Base Cryptographic Provider (MBCP). For the MBCP, the hashing algorithm MD5 will be used.
- Specify whether this certificate server will act as a root CA (if you configured it as a non-root CA, you need to specify the CA from which the certificates will be obtained).
- Add the Certificate Server service to the Windows NT system services.

From here, the installer should tell you that installation is complete. You should verify that the certificate server is operating properly by going to the Settings | Control Panel | Services application. If the certificate authority item has a status of Started, the certificate server can now be used to issue new certificates and provide verification of keys stored in the CA database.

However, if the CA has not started, you will probably have to make a few adjustments. At the time of this writing, the Certificate Server installer makes two mistakes, both of which prevent the Certificate Server from executing with a default install.

The first problem relates to the ODBC data source that points to the server store where the certificates are held. This data source must be created as a System DSN, but the installer creates it as a User DSN. Open the ODBC application in the Control Panel. If the data source CertSrv is located in the User DSN tab instead of the System DSN tab, you will need to move it.

NOTE: Available on the Microsoft site, along with the technote that describes this problem (Q217339), is code for an executing file that is supposed to move the data source from the User type of DSN to the System type. When I executed the file included in the tech note, it failed to resolve the problem. To get the system working I simply destroyed the old data source and recreated it in the appropriate place.

To move the DSN entry, delete the entry that exists in the User DSN category. It uses all of the default settings for an Access DSN, so you won't be losing any information. Under the System DSN tab, click the Add button to add a new Microsoft Access data source. Set the name of the source to CertSrv and set the location to be the path of the certsrv.mdb file. For a default installation on Windows NT, the path will be:

```
C:\WinNT\system32\CertLog\certsrv.mdb
```

Click the OK button to create this data source. It should now appear in the System DSN list. Certificate Server will run now, but the administrative reports may still be inaccessible.

The second problem is that the CertAdm folder is not set up as a Web application, so executing the administration interface will return an error. To correct this problem, you'll need to execute the Internet Services Manager for IIS in the MMC. When the IIS configuration tree is displayed in the MMC, expand the Default Web Sites folder. You should see an entry named CertAdm.

If this item has an icon indicating that it is an application, then it is installed properly. If not, right-click it and select the Properties option in the menu. Under the Application Settings frame in the Virtual Directory tab, click the Create button. The button name will be changed to read "Remove" once the application is created.

Certificate Server should now be ready to run. Go to Settings | Control Panel | Services, select the Certificate Authority item, and click the Start button. After a delay as the service begins, the service should be active and the Status column of the window will display "Started".

NOTE: From the console, the configuration information about Certificate Server can be examined with a command line utility called CertUtil.exe. If the utility was executed with the -dump switch, all of the information about the CA will be placed in a file named CertSrv.txt. Without the switch, the information will be displayed on the screen.

Managing Certificate Server

Certificate Server is managed via a Web-based interface (see Figure 13-2). Since most interaction with the server occurs behind the scenes, it wasn't necessary for Microsoft to create an entire MMC snap-in for administration.

Oddly, there isn't an item in the Start menu of the Certificate Server program group to activate this management page menu. To access it, load Internet Explorer and execute the CertSrv application on the local host. Typically, this application can be referenced with this path:

```
http://localhost/certsrv
```

When the page is returned, you will see the Certificate Server main page options. Click the Certificate Administration Log Utility option. If you receive a database error (E78), try to restart the publishing services as the page instructs. If you still have a problem,

Figure 13-2. The Certificate Server management page allows access to logs, queues, tools, and documentation

return to the earlier Installing Certificate Server section and make sure that you have followed the proper steps for correcting the two problems with the default installation.

If you don't receive the error message, the log will be displayed and it will be empty because no certificates have been accessed on the current server. Click the Back button on your browser to return to the main menu. From the menu, select the Certificate Enrollment Tools option. The enrollment tools are used to manage the certificates available from the server (see Figure 13-3). You can obtain the certificate of any CA in the CA chain, process a certificate request, or request the generation of a new certificate.

Select the Install Certificate Authority Certificates tool. This option will help you install the current certificate server as a CA on your browser (see Figure 13-4).

To make this CA the server for a Windows 2000 domain, you need to change the settings in the Group Policy area. The Group Policy snap-in in the MMC allows you to point a Windows 2000 domain at a specific CA. If you open the Group Policy for the current domain, you can follow this setting's path:

```
"Default Domain Policy" Policy\Computer Configuration\Windows
Settings\Security Settings\Public Key Policies\Trusted Certification
Authorities
```

In the Trusted Certification Authorities area, you can add CAs.

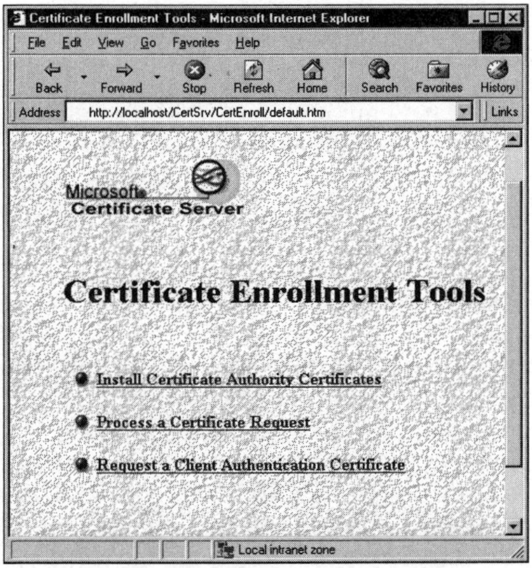

Figure 13-3. The enrollment tools will allow you to obtain the CA certificates, process a certificate request, or request a certificate

Figure 13-4. All of the certificate servers registered on this machine will be displayed in the certificate list

CRYPTO API

In the interest of supporting new methods and implementations of cryptography technology, Microsoft has created a plug-and-play architecture for encryption engines known as the Crypto API. The API architecture allows any compatible encryption technology, including both software and hardware security systems, to be used by a program that accesses the API. The Crypto API supports both symmetric and public- and private-key encryption types.

In addition to the breadth of support that is possible because of the single API plug-in architecture, export restrictions also promote this technology. Vendors, previously hampered by the difficult-to-adopt export restrictions on encryption technology, can now create an application that simply supports the Crypto API. The program can then use any compatible component available in the destination country.

The Crypto API also automatically uses encryption hardware if available on a system for any application that addresses the API. Encryption hardware might be used for either an additional level of security or to accelerate complex and slow routines.

Certificate Server uses the Crypto API to encode the certificates. If you need to alter the algorithms or encryption capabilities of Certificate Server, you can obtain another Crypto API–compatible engine and plug it into the system.

CAUTION: At the time of this writing, there are still strict controls on exporting cryptographic technology from the U.S. Before you ship an application with encryption capabilities, even as freeware, be sure to check the appropriate trade policies. You can find more information on U.S. cryptography export controls at the Bureau of Export Administration's Web site (www.bxa.doc.gov/Encryption).

OTHER INTERNET-SPECIFIC SECURITY TECHNOLOGIES

Certificate Server provides one of the most obvious pieces of the Internet security puzzle. The functionality provided by the Windows NT Challenge/Response login, Microsoft's implementation of the SET protocol, and the Microsoft Proxy Server can all help you to create a secure Web-based system.

Windows NT Challenge/Response

For disk access on a Web server, traditional security can be used if the browser is Internet Explorer. Traditional Windows NT security settings will affect access through the Web server. You can set folder security to allow access to certain group members in the Directory Permissions window (shown in the following illustration) available through the standard file and directory properties.

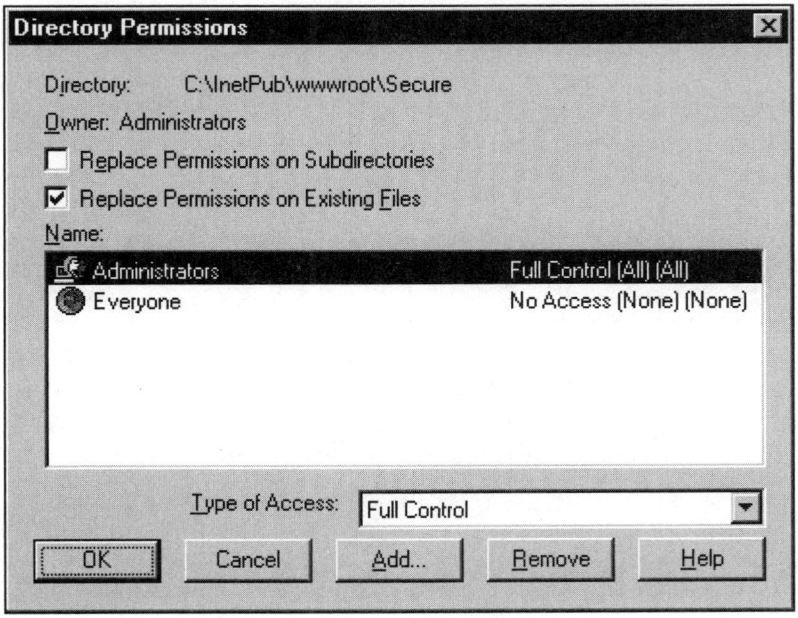

When a user attempts to access a directory which has group or user security placed on it, the standard Challenge/Response dialog box will be presented (shown next).

If a user enters a valid login, he or she will gain access to the folder. If the login fails, an HTTP 401 error will be generated, and the user will be notified that the proper clearances were not available (see Figure 13-5).

Netscape Navigator users may become confused when accessing this same page. Although Navigator does not support NT Challenge/Response, the login dialog box will still be presented. When a user enters the proper username and password, they are rejected

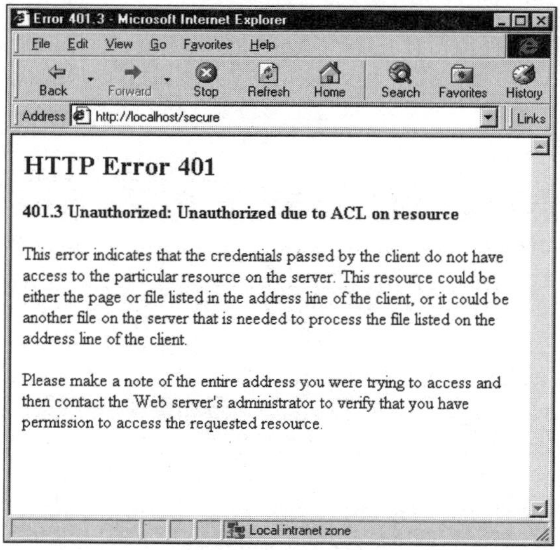

Figure 13-5. Login failure will generate an HTTP 401 error

as invalid. Navigator uses its own form of secure interaction, and the information sent from the login dialog by Navigator is not provided in a format that IIS can understand. Netscape created its own format to allow compatibility with Netscape servers across a variety of platforms (such as Unix, Macintosh, and Windows).

Since no indication or warning of the actual problem is provided to Netscape users within the login dialog box or the login rejection page, you might want to create a custom rejection page in the Properties dialog for the Web application. The custom error page can state that an Internet Explorer browser is required for secure login.

Microsoft Wallet and SET

Electronic commerce, also known as e-commerce, is one of the fastest growing sectors of the Web. In an attempt to encourage electronic commerce, Microsoft has created an application known as the Microsoft Wallet. The Wallet can securely hold private information, such as your credit card or ATM numbers, for transmission over the Web. Rather than requiring you to repeatedly retype and reverify this important information, the Wallet stores the information and can securely pass it to a compatible server.

A program designed to use the Wallet can request a financial charge. If you approve the Wallet's request to pass the information to the requestor, it will be authenticated and shipped in an encrypted format. The Wallet is available free through Microsoft's Wallet site (www.microsoft.com/wallet).

To allow the type of e-commerce made possible by the Wallet, Microsoft has adopted an industry standard protocol known as SET. The Secure Electronics Transactions (SET) protocol standardizes the performance of credit card transactions over the Internet. It is being developed by Visa, MasterCard, Netscape, Microsoft, IBM, VeriSign, and others. This protocol is embraced by banks as well as technology companies. It provides a secure method, not only of allowing vendors to interact with customers, but also of allowing charges between vendors and banks to occur securely.

TIP: There is an organization that has been formed explicitly to maintain and upgrade the SET standard. Check out the Web site (www.setco.org) for complete information on the specification.

SET uses digital certificates, just like SSL, to provide authentication and privacy with electronic transactions. While an SSL session provides a general secure session between two parties, a SET exchange can send specific financial information in a predefined format. Microsoft Wallet has the SET protocol built into it for this information exchange.

Web developers who wish to use SET for credit card interaction or Microsoft Wallet for customer purchases can find more information on the Webmasters portion of the Wallet site (www.microsoft.com/wallet/security/Webmasters.asp). There are also server-side extensions to IIS available that allow communication with Microsoft Wallet.

Microsoft Proxy Server

Firewalls have traditionally been hardware-based, often located within the router that transfers traffic from the Internet to the LAN. Microsoft has created a software router known as Proxy Server. Proxy Server is included in the BackOffice family of products. With the low cost of a stripped-down PC these days, using a software-based proxy server becomes an attractive option.

There are several advantages to using Proxy Server:

- **Easier management capabilities** The often cryptic command-line configuration in hardware-based proxy servers is replaced by the common GUI user interface for Proxy Server.
- **Caching capabilities** Frequently accessed pages can be cached on the local server to provide internal users with faster access speeds.
- **Dynamic packet filtering** Proxy Server can be configured to handle selected packets for tracing, routing, and distilling in real-time.
- **VPN support** Support for Virtual Private Networks (VPNs) that allows traffic to be filtered for a logic network grouping instead of a physical/geographic grouping allow remote users to access a network as if they were physically plugged into it.
- **Virus scanning** The server can scan incoming content for damaging viruses.

Most of these features are extremely expensive or completely unavailable on hardware firewalls. To a Web developer, proper configuration of a proxy server is critical if access must be enabled for remote users. You can find more information about Microsoft Proxy Server at the Proxy Server home page (www.microsoft.com/proxy).

Q&A

Q: Do I need to know about these security technologies as a Web developer?

A: Yes. A wide variety of Web technologies must be used for final application deployment. All the pieces of your application, including form data, logins, and even e-mail transmission, may incorporate data that would be damaging if corrupted or leaked to hostile outside sources.

By maintaining an understanding of the basic security systems, you will be better able to protect the information that your application will handle. Microsoft is beginning to place many of these technologies at the intermediate developer level so that, for example, certificates are available for authentication within every browser. Learning how to use Certificate Server, a central component of the Windows Option Pack installation, can help you learn about a system that will eventually become a basic part of the Web system.

Q: Can I add Windows Challenge/Response login to browsers other than Internet Explorer through a plug-in?

A: If such plug-ins were available, then you could. The specification for implementing this method of security is available to browser vendors. Unfortunately, no vendors have provided support for this login method. With the growth of the Mozilla browser community, you may see a Netscape-type browser capable of this login in the future.

SUMMARY

The widespread adoption of the Internet has prompted the development of a number of technologies to handle the increased security concerns of organizations going online. These systems have evolved to allow secure information transmission, identification and authentication, and e-commerce. In this chapter you learned about the following:

- **Certificate server** This server creates and distributes unique digital certificates. The server can be used to verify the identity of a certificate holder or to issue new certificates for later identification.
- **Root and non-root certificate authorities (CAs)** A root CA provides the top level of certificate storage in a CA tree. Other CAs will defer to the root CA for authorization. A non-root CA is any certificate server that references the root for certificates.
- **Crypto API** Microsoft's plug and play API for encryption engines that allows a program designed to use it to select a desired method of encoding.
- **Microsoft Wallet** A piece of software that safely stores and transmits private financial data (such as credit card or ATM accounts) without requiring the information to be entered repeatedly.
- **SET protocol** The core security protocol used to allow encrypted financial information to be exchanged securely.
- **Microsoft Proxy Server** Proxy Server combines a proxy server and a software-based router to allow secure control over a network.

CHAPTER 14

ActiveX DLL Overview

In Visual Basic, you can easily create components that can be used to augment the Web server and encapsulate secure and fast execution of code. An ActiveX component, in the form of an ActiveX DLL, is like an ActiveX control except it has no user interface. The ActiveX DLL is a compiled Visual Basic class file that can be accessed by any language once it is installed and registered.

ActiveX DLLs are currently used to encapsulate nearly every type of business process within an organization. These DLLs also make up the foundation of a distributed system that can be managed by Microsoft Transaction Server. ActiveX DLLs can be used for making compiled code available to the IIS Web server for ASP script execution.

When you used the CDO compenent to send e-mail in Chapter 11, you were using an ActiveX DLL component. In this chapter, you'll create a simple charting ActiveX DLL that can be accessed with the same techniques you used to control the CDO class. Once the component has been registered on the server system, you'll use the `CreateObject()` method to instantiate the DLL. The instance can then be addressed like the intrinsic controls available with IIS.

ACTIVEX HISTORY

The ActiveX technology that is used for ActiveX DLLs represents the evolution of object technology that has been available for years. Microsoft pioneered object technology in the Windows operating system with a system called OLE, which was short for object linking and embedding. OLE allowed a user to paste or link an object from one program into another. OLE provided the ability to take a spreadsheet from Microsoft Excel and paste it into Microsoft Word or any other OLE-capable application.

Before OLE, pasting from one application to another required the destination application to understand the format of the pasted information, much like importing a file. The advent of OLE allowed the pasted data to be received by the destination application as an object. The object could be treated as a black box by the receiving application, allowing the acceptance of data from any program that could output an OLE object.

The *linking* feature of OLE would create a reference to the object in the receiving application instead of placing the actual object in the document. This allowed the linked object to exist autonomously on the disk. Any changes to the disk-based object would be reflected in the document where the link had been inserted.

When the new version of OLE, known as OLE 2.0, was released, it included so much new technology that it went beyond the initial linking and embedding that made up its original acronym. OLE 2.0 expanded features included the following:

- **OLE automation** The ability to control an object through scripting, in much the same way as objects are controlled through Visual Basic and VBA. This made it possible to script Microsoft Excel and other applications from outside out-of-process applications.

- **OLE controls (OCXs)** A standardized control format that allowed a component built to the OCX specification to be used by any development environment. OCXs evolved from the VBX (Visual Basic custom controls) modules, which were components that were only practical when used within Visual Basic.
- **OLE storage** A hierarchical method of storing files (rather than the standard sequential file format) that is used by Microsoft Word, Excel, PowerPoint, and other applications. An OLE Structured Storage document is organized much like a hard disk, with data stored within internal folders.

When Microsoft embraced the Internet, it extended the OLE technology further and changed the name of all of the technologies to the *ActiveX* moniker. ActiveX more accurately described the new breadth of capability than the older OLE acronym. Microsoft also began promoting the underlying foundation technology that supported ActiveX, which is known as the Component Object Model (COM).

COM can be thought of as a protocol, like TCP/IP. ActiveX, in this metaphor, would be the HTTP layer that sits atop the foundation. COM is the technology that allows for standardized communication between objects, whether they are in process or out-of-process.

COM was further augmented in a version known as Distributed COM (DCOM). DCOM provides a transparent way for COM objects to communicate over a network. Traditionally, ActiveX controls have been installed on the machines used to execute them. Since ActiveX sits above COM, DCOM can be used instead to locate the executing component on a different machine. To the object that uses the ActiveX control, the access is transparent and is no different from calling a local instance of the object (see Figure 14-1).

Microsoft strengthened its position as a key technology provider for the Internet by embracing the Web with ActiveX object functionality. Since Microsoft incorporated the Web technology into the ActiveX infrastructure, even more technology has been added under the ActiveX umbrella:

- **ActiveX Scripting** The plug-and-play scripting engine that allows different languages to be used. ActiveX Scripting is the engine accessed by the ASP technology to execute scripting code.
- **ActiveX Documents** A new way to deploy VB applications by automatically downloading them from a Web page. When an ActiveX document is accessed by a browser, the application installs on the local computer and appears within the user interface of the browser. ActiveX Documents offer an easy installation process for existing VB applications.
- **ActiveX EXEs** A method of allowing multiuse, multithreaded applications to exist within the EXE framework.
- **ActiveX DLLs** In contrast to traditional DLLs, ActiveX DLLs have a complete COM interface for instantiation and access through COM automation support. An ActiveX DLL can therefore be easily addressed by VBA and VBScript, which were limited in DLL capabilities in the past.

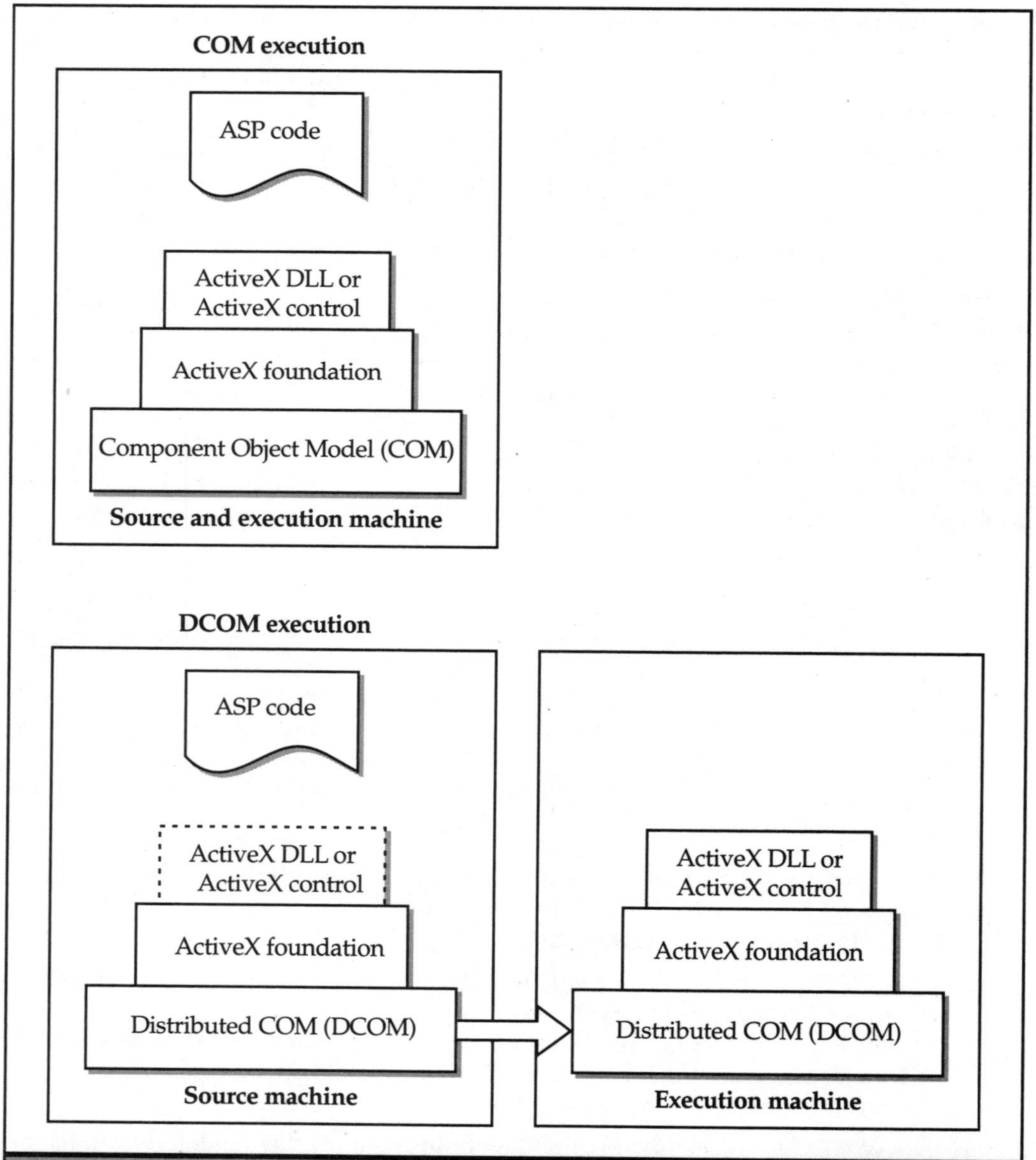

Figure 14-1. Remote ActiveX execution is possible simply by switching the foundation from COM to DCOM

You may not realize it, but you've used many of these new ActiveX additions . You're already using ActiveX Scripting to provide the language capabilities to ASP. The components you've accessed have all been available through ActiveX technology. In this chapter you'll learn how to construct an ActiveX DLL to use with the scripting code.

ACTIVEX GENERAL INFORMATION

For a Web database application, it is most appropriate to deploy an ActiveX component when it can be used in place of a large quantity of ASP code. Execution will be much faster and the code can be more effectively organized. Special considerations may be required, however, since a component is more powerful than direct ASP code and therefore must be more precisely configured. While the Web server handles most of the details of ASP execution for you, an ActiveX DLL will be dependent on the choices you make when developing the control.

Why an ActiveX DLL?

Since ActiveX DLLs require more consideration for configuration, more lengthy development time, and are more difficult to modify than ASP code, you may wonder why you would want to create an ActiveX DLL at all. Nearly all primary programming tasks can be accomplished with ASP scripting code, so the advantages of writing an ActiveX DLL may not be immediately apparent. These advantages include:

- **Compiled execution** Unlike script code that must be interpreted, an ActiveX DLL is compiled and its code optimized for execution on the machine. For processor-intensive operations, such as loops or recursive iterations, an ActiveX DLL can be orders of magnitude faster.
- **Reduced execution time** Each time ASP code is executed, the ASP engine must load the scripting code, parse it, and then proceed with execution. Even without the speed gain from the compilation, an ActiveX DLL would execute much faster because it doesn't have to be dynamically processed by the scripting engine.
- **Protected source code** Source code in an ActiveX DLL is not available for examination or modification. Scripting code contained in ASP pages can be accessed and modified with any text editor (assuming access to the server). The compiled ActiveX DLL protects the integrity of the code and guards against unwanted plagiarism or modification.

- **Ease of upgrades** All Web database projects that use the ActiveX DLL will automatically be upgraded simply by installing a new version of the DLL on the machine. This is in contrast to an ASP solution which often requires that a file be separately upgraded for each Web application.
- **Compatibility with other programming systems** Once the ActiveX DLL is created, its use is not limited to ASP. It can be addressed by any ActiveX-capable environment, including Visual Basic, Visual C++, Visual J++, and Delphi. This promotes code reuse.

These are the primary arguments for encapsulating code within ActiveX DLLs. There are also requirements (such as direct access to DLL calls and the Windows API, which are unavailable to VBScript) that make an ActiveX DLL the only solution for some Web projects.

Deciding Which Functions to Place in the DLL

It is rarely a good idea to place most of your ASP application in the DLL. Because each change requires that the component must be recompiled and reinstalled, it is more useful to put only functions that provide core capabilities that will not frequently change into the DLL. To decide if a function should be placed within an ActiveX DLL, ask yourself the following:

- *Is it processor intensive?* Loops, mathematical calculations, manual (non-SQL) data crunching or searching, and recursive algorithms are all good candidates for inclusion in a DLL.
- *Should the code be secure?* Often organizations have proprietary code or business rules that need to remain unseen or intact. However, a Web database application usually needs to be accessible for modification by a great number of people (graphic articles, scripters, HTML coders, and so on), so including this code in a DLL will keep it hidden and prevent modifications.
- *Does a function fit into a broader group?* It is usually too much work to make an ActiveX DLL that contains only a single function. A component that encapsulates several functions that address the same general area of work is usually more appropriate.

Once a function is decided to be appropriate for inclusion in a DLL, consider some of the problems with placing it in the DLL. Think twice before placing a function inside an ActiveX DLL if any of the following apply:

- **Specialty modifications are necessary** If there are many pages that have slightly different needs that cannot be easily placed in function arguments, it might be wise to leave the code as ASP code. Having many slightly different versions of an ActiveX DLL on a server creates extra management and upkeep work.

- **Changes are frequently made** If frequent changes must be made to the application, the time and energy required to recompile and reinstall the DLL may become prohibitive. The Web server must be stopped while upgrading if the control is used on active pages, making each upgrade unpleasant for your users.
- **Web server inaccessibility** If you don't have physical access to the Web server, or if it is a deployment Web server with too many concurrent users to be conveniently restarted, updating an ActiveX component will be difficult. Remote Web server administrators may even refuse to install any type of component on the server.
- **Other secure functions might be compromised** Placing a general development function within a DLL that contains secure operations (such as financial-transaction business rules) is usually a poor idea. The critical component then must be recompiled and installed when a generalized function is changed. This either requires general access to the source code or requires that the secure component team spend time making general upgrades. Either process may make secure code available and subject to unintentional modification.

Creating ActiveX DLLs for a Web solution is usually an evolutionary process. Basic functions are much more easily designed and refined as raw ASP code, and this code can then be converted to the final ActiveX DLL implementation. Since Visual Basic is almost entirely compatible with VBScript (some objects like the FileSystem object must be specially activated in VB), conversion takes little time. Therefore, even functions that will become a part of a component can be prototyped with ASP early in the development cycle.

Threading Model

When Web database applications originally appeared, Web servers used CGI technology to execute an instance of a separate application for each access. This process was extremely memory- and processor-intensive. IIS was one of the first Web servers that allowed an application to execute within the same memory space as the Web server, making it substantially faster; it also reduced the memory requirements for the server. At the same time as this advance was made, IIS also enabled the Web application to execute using processor threading. Threading allows a process, normally treated as a single unit, to be broken into smaller execution pieces to be handled by the operating system. Microsoft Word's background printing is a good example of the use of a thread model. Rather than the entire application execution being treated as a single unit, the main Word application becomes one thread and the printing another thread.

In Microsoft Word, this freed the main application to continue executing, thus allowing entry, editing, and all of the normal word-processing features to take place while the operating system executes the printing thread in the background. Without this threading capability, the user would have to wait for the printing to finish before they could use Word again.

The IIS Web server is automatically multithreaded to handle simultaneous users. When you write VBScript code in ASP, all of this threading is taken care of by IIS, so you do not even have to be aware of it. When building your own ActiveX DLLs, however, you must configure your control for the proper threading model.

Available Threading Models

For the most part, when you create an ActiveX DLL for use on a Web page, you will use the standard threading and class settings. However, there are several different types of threading, and gaining a general understanding of how these work in relation to an ActiveX control will be useful when you expand your projects and begin working with Microsoft Transaction Server. Visual Basic supports two of the common threading models for ActiveX DLLs:

- **Apartment threading** All objects created by the class exist within an "apartment" and are unaware of objects that exist in other apartments.
- **Single threaded** Threads are queued to execute on a single thread.

Apartment threading creates an isolated instance of all objects for each instance of the class that is created (see Figure 14-2). In contrast, the single-threaded model uses a single thread and queues the requests, making execution much slower.

Within the project, each class that is created can be set to a specific type of instantiation (creating an instance of an object in memory) that defines the scope of its threading use. An ActiveX component must be set to an instantiation type so the ActiveX system can understand which threading model to use for execution. Therefore, the type must be set at the project level for ActiveX DLLs since these only contain a single class. The available instantiation types are:

- **Private** The object will not be available outside the control.
- **PublicNotCreatable** These objects can be accessed after they have been created by your application, but they can not be created using the New keyword or CreateObject method.
- **Multiuse** This allows one instance of the object to create as many objects as required.
- **Global Multiuse** This is similar to Multiuse, but it allows methods and properties to be called as if they were global functions. If an instance of the class has not been created explicitly, Global Multiuse will automatically create one for you.
- **SingleUse and GlobalSingleUse** Because these are single use, they are not allowed in an ActiveX DLL.

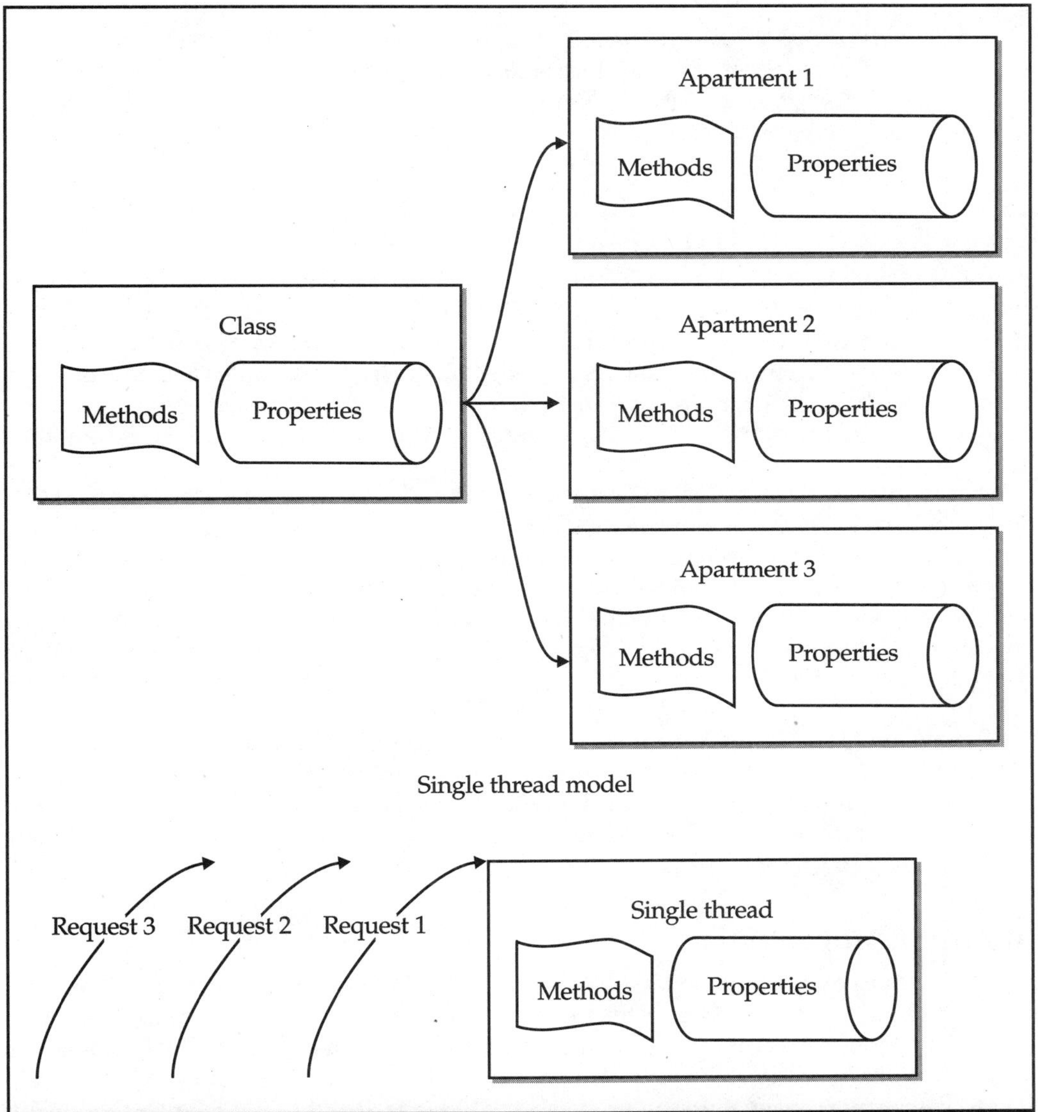

Figure 14-2. Apartment threading creates an apartment for each instance of the object, while single threading requires queuing

The Multiuse selection is the default when you create a new ActiveX DLL and it serves for most uses of a component in a Web solution. If you use another selection for the class, be sure to test your solution well, because threading problems are common when the access factors are not properly considered.

NOTE: Do not call the DoEvents procedure within an ActiveX DLL method. Because it pauses to allow the system to activate other events, an event in another apartment thread may be waiting to use the current class procedure. This will cause problems as the queued method will believe the currently executing method has completed.

CREATING A NEW ACTIVEX COMPONENT

You should now have a fair idea of how the ActiveX technology is placed within the execution framework of the system processes. Visual Basic can be used to very easily create an ActiveX control for use on a Web page. In fact, because of the simplified ActiveX DLL project type included in Visual Basic, it will only take you a few minutes to create one. An ActiveX DLL has no direct user interface, so it cannot be directly executed from the VB environment. It must instead be compiled and loaded into another program that instantiates an object of its object type.

In this chapter, the component that you'll create will construct a bar chart as an HTML table. There is no simple way to create a bar chart for display on the user's browser. You could use a server-side control, such as Active Server Paint by Coherent Visual (www.cvisual.com), to dynamically create a graphic image. Alternatively, a Java applet like the one you will construct in Chapter 23 could accomplish the task, but it requires Java client support in the browser. Finally, DHTML can provide this capability if linked with a drawing interface (such as Microsoft DirectAnimation), but it would also require a compatible client-side technology.

For this project, the component will set the background color of different cells in a table to display the values from 0 to 100 percent. Nearly every browser supports tables, so this solution requires neither special client nor server technology. The component itself will accept several values and return the proper HTML code in a string, which will then be sent to the browser for display.

Coding the Component

In this section you will create the basic component and test the generation code. You should be aware, however, that testing an ActiveX component might be complicated and frustrating. Since the component is compiled, debugging must take place laboriously in the general Visual Studio debugger. If you are using IIS, it can be even more exasperating. When IIS executes a page with the ActiveX DLL, it loads the DLL into memory and locks it. Replacing it with a different version requires flushing the control, if not shutting down the Web server.

There is an easier method of debugging a component prototype. An ActiveX DLL is really nothing more than a Visual Basic class with the addition of an ActiveX wrapper. Therefore, it is possible to test the code for your ActiveX control within Visual Basic and, once it is tested and debugged, simply transfer the solid code into the DLL.

The project will activate the component to generate the HTML table code. Rather than sending the returned HTML text to the browser, the application will write it off to a text file. The text file can then be loaded into the Web browser by hand. For this project, you'll first create and test the code as a class instantiated within an EXE. Once the code has been tested, the class will be moved into a complete ActiveX DLL.

1. Start Visual Basic and create a new project. You will need a standard EXE project, because the testing will be done from an executable form. Adding a class to the existing project will provide the framework into which the component code will be placed.
2. Under the Project menu, select the Add Class Module option. The class will hold all of the code that will eventually be compiled into the DLL. The class needs to be properly named so it can be addressed within the form code.
3. In the Project window, select the class item named Class1.
4. In the Properties window, set the Name property to WebDB.

The class is now ready for the method code to be entered. This component will only have a single method (`tableChart`) that will accept four values for graphing. It will return a string containing HTML code for the table chart.

Within the class file, enter the following code:

```
Public Function tableChart(wid As Integer, widPort As Integer, _
    widPro As Integer, widLite As Integer) As String
    Dim r As String
    Dim myArray(), colorArray(), origArray()
    ReDim myArray(4), colorArray(4), origArray(4)

    ' Load values in an array for easy handling
    origArray(1) = wid: origArray(2) = widPort
    origArray(3) = widPro: origArray(4) = widLite

    ' Set up colors for each of the 4 bars
    colorArray(1) = "#008000": colorArray(2) = "#FFFF00"
    colorArray(3) = "#FF0000": colorArray(4) = "#0000FF"

    For i = 1 To 4
        ' Round to the nearest 10%
        myArray(i) = CInt(origArray(i) / 10)

        ' Adjust for min and max values
        If myArray(i) < 0 Then myArray(i) = 0
```

```
        If myArray(i) > 10 Then myArray(i) = 10
    Next

    ' Add header
    r = "<table border=0 cellspacing=0 cellpadding=0 width=542>"
    r = r + "  <tr>"
    r = r + "<td width=53 align=right></td>"
    r = r + "<td width=24></td>"
    r = r + "<td width=90>" + _
      <p align=center><strong>Widget</strong></td>"
    r = r + "<td width=24></td>"
    r = r + "<td width=90><p align=center>" + _
      "<strong>Portable Widget</strong></td>"
    r = r + "<td width=29></td>"
    r = r + "<td width=84><p align=center>" + _
      "<strong>Widget Pro</strong></td>"
    r = r + "<td width=30></td>"
    r = r + "<td width=84><p align=center>" + _
      "<strong>Widget Lite</strong></td>"
    r = r + "<td width=34></td>"
    r = r + "</tr>"
    ' Display 100% to %10 + Value row
    For i = 1 To 11
        ' Begin new row
        r = r + "<tr>"
        r = r + "<td width=53 align=right>"

        ' Show percentage values for all but the
        ' actual value row
        If i < 11 Then r = r & (11 - i) * 10
        r = r + "</td>"
        ' Leave a blank column
        r = r + "<td width=24></td>"

        For j = 1 To 4
            ' If not value row, display color if
            ' appropriate
            If i <> 11 Then
                If myArray(j) >= (11 - i) Then
                    ' Color bar
                    r = r + "<td width=90 bgcolor=" _
                        + colorArray(j)
                    r = r + "></td>"
                Else
```

```
                ' No color
                r = r + "<td width=90></td>"
            End If
        Else
            ' Value row
            r = r + "<td width=90><p align=center>"
            r = r & origArray(j) & "</td>"
        End If
        r = r + "<td width=24></td>"
    Next
    r = r + "</tr>"
Next
r = r + "</table>"
' Return string for HTML bar chart
tableChart = r
End Function
```

You now have a class that can generate the proper HTML, but no method of calling it. However, when you started the new EXE project, a default form was automatically created. You're now going to use this form to instantiate the class and execute the method. Open the default form (Form1) in the project, and follow these steps:

1. Add a command button to the default form by selecting it from the palette and drawing the button frame.
2. Set the Name property of the button to cmdTableChart. The command button will need to create a new instance of the class. Since you will want to test the class in a realistic setting for its final destination (execution on a Web server), the button will be used to export a simple HTML file that contains the appropriate table.
3. Add the following code to the command button:

```
Private Sub cmdTableChart_Click()
    Dim myWebDB As New WebDB
    Dim tableChartStr As String

    tableChartStr = myWebDB.tableChart(42, 22, 7, 29)
    Open "c:\chart.htm" For Output As #1
    Print #1, "<HTML><BODY>"
    Print #1, "<H1>Widget Sales</H1>"
    Print #1, tableChartStr
    Print #1, "</BODY></HTML>"
    Close #1
End Sub
```

That's all. Now just execute the application, and click the button—a file named chart.htm will be created at the root directory of your C drive. You can change the path to write directly into the Web-server folder, if you'd like.

The file that is created can be directly accessed in a Web browser. Simply double-click the file from Windows Explorer, and you'll see the chart displayed, as in Figure 14-3.

This output establishes that the class is functioning properly. If you made any mistakes entering the source code, you may notice that a fault drops you directly into the VB debugger at the line of the problem. From there, any standard debugging practices can be employed. This method is much more convenient than using the Visual Studio debugger process.

NOTE: In Chapter 15, you will learn about Web classes that allow an ActiveX component to access elements on a Web page. A Web class allows a Visual Basic program to address intrinsic Web objects such as the Session object or the Application object. Using a class for testing as described above cannot be used to address Web objects because they are not available when executing in a Visual Basic environment.

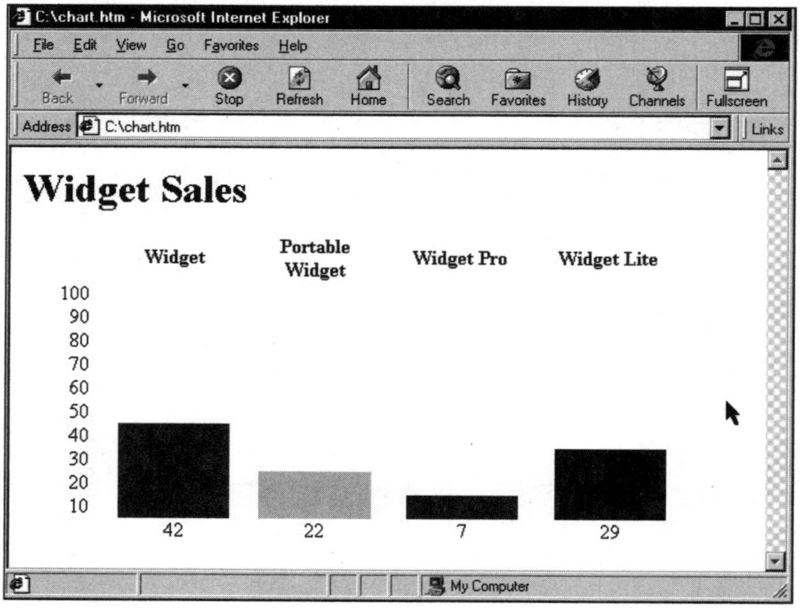

Figure 14-3. The bar chart displays the data in a table

Moving to a Complete Component

While the class you have created is usable within this Visual Basic project, it cannot be accessed from ASP, which is the goal. Therefore, you will have to convert the class into the proper ActiveX DLL. First, though, save the current project in case you want to make further additions or do some debugging.

The easiest method to convert the class to a DLL is to follow these steps:

1. Select the Procedure View icon in the lower-left corner of the code window to display all of the code within the class. (In this example, a single method is used, so doing so is not essential. With a more elaborate class, this icon will allow all code and variable definitions to be captured in a single clipboard stream.)
2. Select the code in the method and copy it to the clipboard. Once on the clipboard, it can be easily added to the final DLL project.
3. Start a new project as an ActiveX DLL (see the following illustration of a selection from the New Project dialog box).

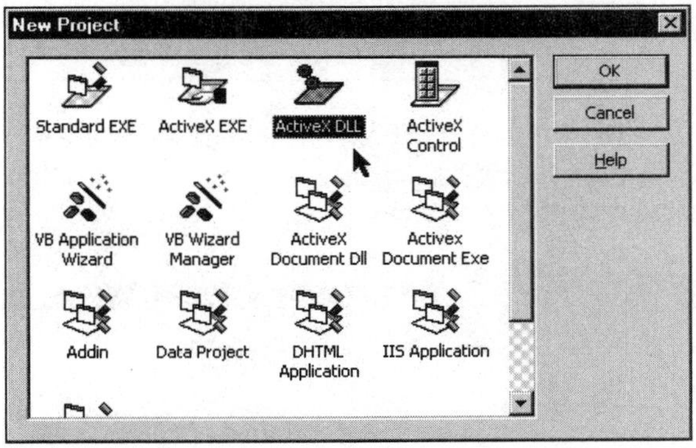

4. Under the Project menu, select the current Project Properties. In the Project Properties configuration dialog box, you will need to change the name and execution settings.
5. Set the Project Name to WebDBClass. The project name will be the prefix used to reference the class from the `CreateObject()` method, and for this class the `CreateObject("WebDBClass.WebDB")` reference will be used.
6. Select the check box for Unattended Execution. Unattended Execution suppresses any user interface calls, such as `MsgBox`, that would halt execution of the application. This option is typically used when the component that is being created will be executing on a server. In this case, you'll be installing the component to execute without interaction on the IIS Web server.

You can see in the following illustration of the General Tab that the Apartment Threaded model is used to allow multiple simultaneous use of the component.

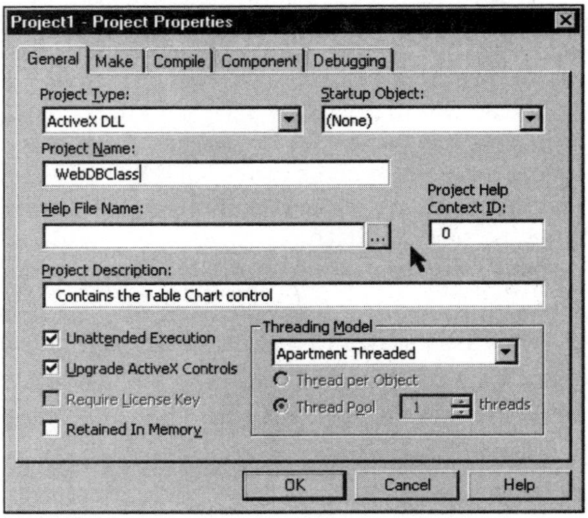

7. Click the Make tab of the dialog box, and check the AutoIncrement option. The following illustration shows the proper settings for enabling the Make tab to provide auto-incrementing of the version number.

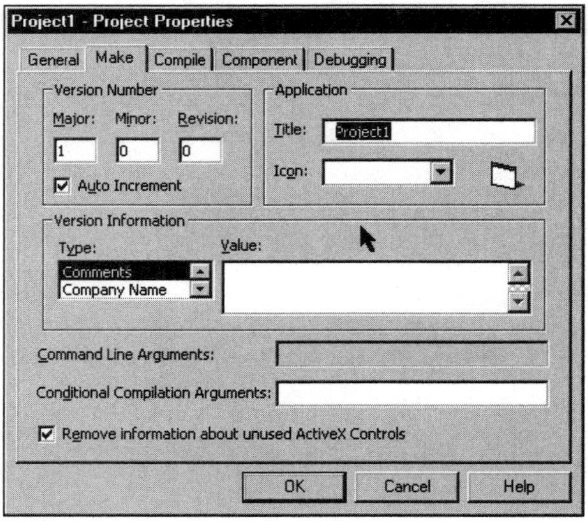

NOTE: Compatibility with an ActiveX DLL is critical, so setting the version number to automatically increment assures that you will know exactly what version of the DLL exists on a machine. This information can be viewed by looking at the file properties in Windows Explorer.

8. Click the Compile tab to display a number of options that will be set specifically to relate to the type of DLL you intend to deploy (see the following illustration). Set the DLL Base Address to &H11A00000.

   The Base Address defines where the DLL will be addressed by the instantiating platform. If this address is already taken, the DLL will be reassigned and the reassignment managed. However, you should attempt to set a unique address for each component in order to maximize execution and minimize memory overhead on the server.

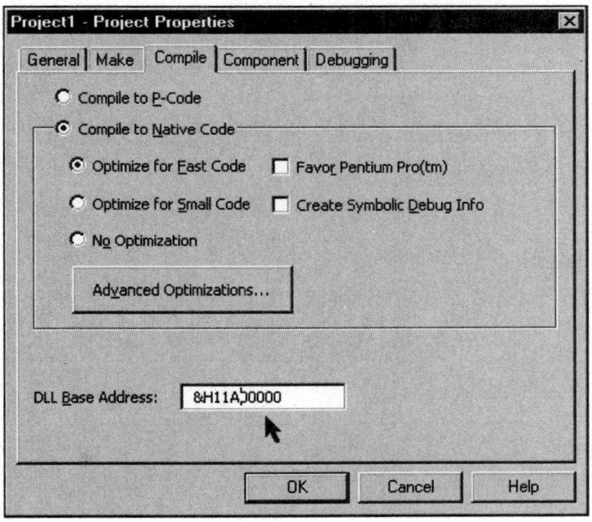

9. Check the Create Symbolic Debug Info option if you intend to use the Visual Studio debugger for the control.
10. Click the Component tab to make specific settings for an ActiveX component (see the following illustration). Since the execution will take place without DCOM, you don't need to select the Remote Server Files option.

    The Version Compatibility options allow your component, through subsequent compiles, to retain its general identity. With the Project Compatibility option checked, any projects that use the component will automatically be upgraded if a newer version is installed. Binary compatibility ensures that the component is identical in its basic interface to an older version of the control.

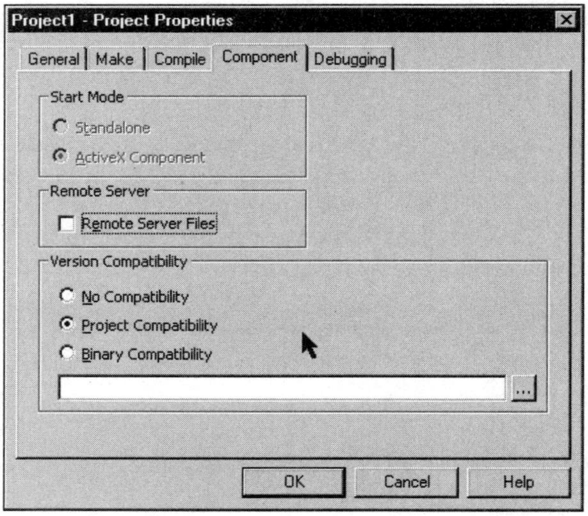

11. Click OK to accept the project properties.
12. Under the File menu, select Make WebDBClass.DLL to compile the ActiveX DLL.

Once your ActiveX DLL is compiled, Visual Basic will automatically install and register the component on the current system. If you need to place it on another server, simply use the Application Setup Wizard to create some install images to use for deployment. The following section, "Registering the Component on the System" explains what to do if you want to install and register the component yourself.

With the component complete, you will need an application to execute it. To create this Web application, you can return to using Visual InterDev.

1. Start the Visual InterDev application.
2. Create a new Web project, and name it TableChart.
3. Add an ASP Page through the Project | Add Web Item option.
4. Name the page Default.ASP. This page will now be executed with the TableChart application on the Web server. The project only needs the specific ASP code to instantiate and use the object.
5. Enter the following code into the Default.ASP file:

```
<%@ Language=VBScript %>
<HTML>
```

```
<TITLE>Example of Table Chart control</TITLE>
<HEAD>
<META NAME="GENERATOR" Content="Microsoft Visual Studio 6.0">
</HEAD>
<BODY>
<H1>Widget Co. Sales for Quarter 1</H1>

<%
    Dim myWebDB
    Dim tableChartStr

    ' Create an instance of your new class
    Set myWebDB = Server.CreateObject("WebDBClass.WebDB")
    ' Request a new table generated
    tableChartStr = myWebDB.tableChart(42, 22, 7, 29)
    Response.Write(tableChartStr)
%>

</BODY>
</HTML>
```

The preceding code simply uses the `CreateObject()` method to instantiate your component. Alternately you could have used the `<OBJECT>` tag for the same results. Once the component is created, the `tableChart()` method in the ActiveX DLL is executed to return the HTML definition of the table data that was passed. This HTML is then sent to the browser.

To see the result, select View in Browser under the View menu of Visual InterDev. You should now see the dynamically generated table.

Congratulations on making your first ActiveX DLL! You can now see how easily standard VB class-file code can be compiled into an ActiveX component and used by a Web server.

Registering the Component on the System

If you don't install a component on a remote machine with the installer created by the VB Package and Deployment Wizard, you can register it in the OLE registry manually. Before you register it, however, you should unregister the old version of the control (if it exists on the target machine).

To unregister the control, you will need to use the `-u` or `/u` (unregister) switch. At the command prompt, type the following command, replacing *`myControl.dll`* with the name of the control you wish to upgrade:

```
regsvr32 myControl.dll -u
```

Copy the new control to the server over the old version. You might want to right-click on the file and check the properties to make sure you have the version you want to install. Then, type the following command:

```
regsvr32 myControl.dll
```

The registration application will attempt to execute and place the DLL or OCX within the registry. You should be presented with a dialog box notifying you that the registration was successful. The component is now registered on the system in the directory where the OCX file is located.

CAUTION: When attempting to register a control, make sure that no copy of the control exists in the root directory of the boot drive. Even if you include the entire path of the control that you wish to register, regsvr32 will check the root directory first and register the version it finds there, rather than the one you specified.

Registering an ActiveX component is also handled automatically in Visual Basic when you compile and save the component. The control is registered at the working directory to which it is compiled. The preceding registration method can also be used to move the location of the registered control.

NOTE: If you want to upgrade an existing control, and the control is in use by the Web server, you will not be allowed to write over it. The best way to accomplish an upgrade is to open the Services control panel. Find the service labeled World Wide Web Publishing Service, and click the Stop button. This will stop the Web server and flush the memory of any ActiveX DLLs that were in use.

Once the service is stopped, you can replace the control and restart the service when you're finished. Stopping the service works better than using the Microsoft Management Console (MMC) to shut down the Web server. Using the MMC does not explicitly release the resources used by IIS, such as ActiveX DLLs.

Q&A

Q: Can I have two versions of the ActiveX DLL installed on the same machine?

A: Yes, but providing access to them is difficult. Each control has a global universal identifier (GUID) that uniquely identifies it on the machine. If you install more than one version on a machine, they must have unique GUIDs.

Also, the OLE Automation identifier (such as "Application.Excel") must be unique in order for your ASP scripts to access the component. Therefore, if you included the version in the identifying name (such as "Application.Excel10" and "Application.Excel11") this would be possible. However, all code would have to be modified when the version was upgraded.

Q: Can an ActiveX control or ActiveX EXE be used from within ASP code?

A: Yes, but it usually is not recommended. Most ActiveX controls have user-interface components or single-use instancing settings that prohibit effective use of the control from a server. An ActiveX EXE (such as Microsoft Excel) usually provides too large a memory footprint to be used effectively.

However, it is possible. To allow the Web server to access these types of OLE Automation applications, you will need to alter a value in the registry file on the server system. Consult the IIS documentation to determine the registry key that must be modified and the value to which it must be set.

SUMMARY

ActiveX DLLs can be easily constructed from existing VBScript code or new Visual Basic code. Once compiled, they provide fast-executing and effectively encapsulated components for use by ASP scripting code. In this chapter, you covered the following:

- **ActiveX** Evolved from the original OLE technology. The ActiveX family provides everything from components to scripting to automation.
- **ActiveX DLL** An ActiveX component is like an ActiveX control (OCX) without a visible user interface. ActiveX DLLs can be created in Visual Basic and instantiated and used from ASP.
- **Threading** The technique of breaking a single process into separate, autonomous execution units. When building an ActiveX DLL for use with ASP, you can use either the apartment- or the single-threading models.
- **Class testing** By using a VB class in a standard EXE, you can more easily define and debug the methods and properties you intend to use in the ActiveX component. This code can then be easily transferred and compiled within an ActiveX DLL.
- **regsvr32** The regsvr32 application is used to manually register and unregister ActiveX components in the OLE registry. The `-u` switch is used to specify that the component should be unregistered.

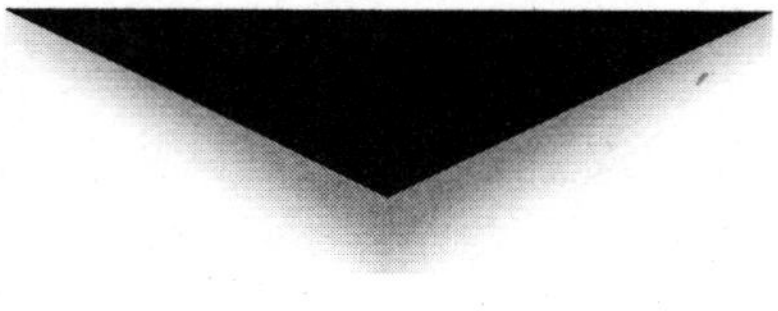

CHAPTER 15

Creating an IIS Application

In Chapter 14, you used Visual Basic to create a simple ActiveX DLL to return information that was subsequently linked to an ASP page. The ActiveX DLL was limited to working only with the information passed directly to it. To use the full abilities of VB in your Web database solutions, VB needs to be able to interact with the IIS Web server in order to access Web page elements.

To add this capability to Visual Basic, Microsoft added a new project type: the IIS Application. Many Visual Basic programmers are unaware of how easy it is to interact with a Web server through IIS applications. An IIS application combines the display capabilities of HTML with the compiled advantages of the VB language. Code is written in standard Visual Basic and compiled into an automated ActiveX DLL/ASP solution.

INTRODUCTION TO IIS APPLICATIONS

When you begin designing IIS applications, the process may appear confusing at first. Since all of the code is actually written in Visual Basic, it is sometimes hard to grasp how this will relate to an ASP solution. It is usually easiest to imagine an IIS application as a series of HTML templates in which certain fields can be filled dynamically with content (such as data or HTML instructions). Figure 15-1 shows a simplified diagram of an HTML template file that is part of an IIS application. As the application executes, the dynamic fields are processed and filled by the VB code that is executed. An HTML standard file is then sent to the browser.

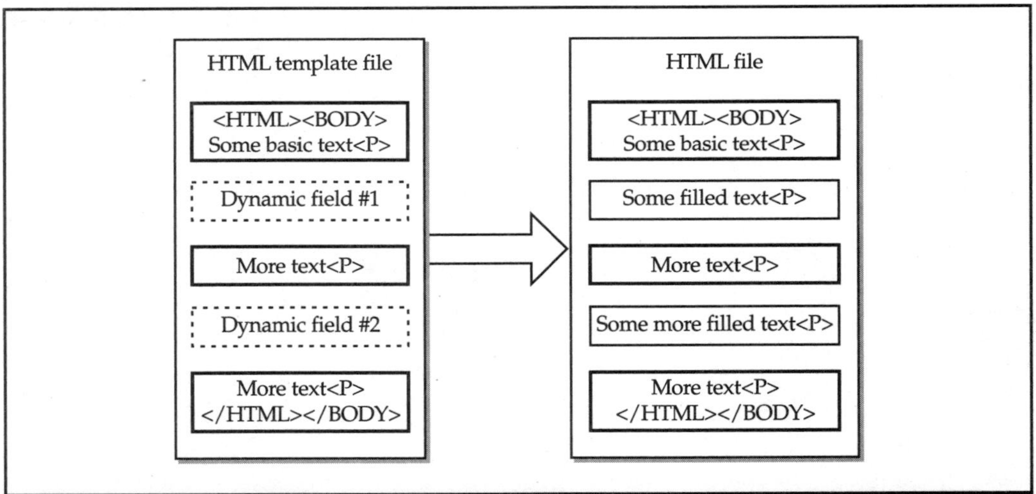

Figure 15-1. The HTML template is processed by the IIS application, and the browser is sent a standard HTML file

All of the processing of the template file occurs within an ActiveX DLL that contains all of the logic for the IIS application. The VB application can even choose which template to send to the browser, depending on the user selection. The only ASP code that is executed is the small amount of script needed to activate the ActiveX DLL on the Web server.

CAUTION: An IIS application is created with the apartment-threading model, in which an instance is placed in the Session object. If you keep a WebClass alive between requests, be careful that you don't leave large objects in the Application or Session objects that the WebClass uses. This will starve the Web server for system resources.

The HTML templates that are contained in an IIS application can be filled with any data available to the VB application. The templates contain a number of tags that can be set to the values provided by the data. These tag replacements can be broadly applied within an IIS application to allow:

- Query responses to a user request from a database
- Retrieval of HTML template pages, replacing portions with dynamic content
- Dynamic creation of HTML that generates events for the application to handle

All of these functions are possible within the framework provided by the IIS application. Using the replacement and event functionality allows an IIS application to appear to the user like a traditional multi-page ASP application.

Differences Between IIS Applications and ASP Applications

An IIS Application is developed almost exclusively in Visual Basic; only the template files used by the application are created elsewhere. A small amount of code executes in VBScript to activate the compiled ActiveX DLL generated by Visual Basic, but there is no execution logic beyond the component activation that is stored in these scripts. Therefore, the application logic itself is contained within the specific DLLs; it is not contained in ASP files.

In addition to the advantages of developing your application in an environment you already know well (Visual Basic), IIS applications also offer these benefits:

- **Event capabilities** There is really no equivalent in standard ASP applications for the event model available to IIS applications. These events use form and URL submissions to activate specific processes, much like the event code in traditional VB solutions. All of the event handling and resolution takes place on the server-side, which doesn't require a special browser like DHTML and other client-side event processing.
- **Automated ASP generation** All of the ASP code used by the application is automatically generated by VB for the IIS solution. Therefore, no time working on an IIS application is spent editing ASP code.

- **VB debugging features** Rather than using the more primitive VBScript debugger, all of the code for an IIS application is written in Visual Basic. Therefore, the superior testing capabilities included in VB can be used. The execution of an IIS application can be halted with breakpoints and standard debugging methods for robust examination of variables, tracing code, and so on.
- **Compiled code** Since all of the code is contained in the ActiveX DLL, it is all compiled. Unlike ASP code that must be executed from script in an ASP file, precompiled ActiveX DLLs make execution much faster.

The general structure of an IIS application (shown in Figure 15-2) uses an ASP page to activate the component on the server. When the application executes, the selected template is combined with the necessary code process to return an HTML page. This page also contains the necessary linking code to allow URL requests to be passed into the IIS Application as events.

All of the advantages listed above are embodied in an IIS application without requiring any script code maintenance normally associated with an ASP Web solution. In some ways, the VB foundation for this type of Web application is more flexible and cost-effective than an ASP-based Visual Interdev Web application.

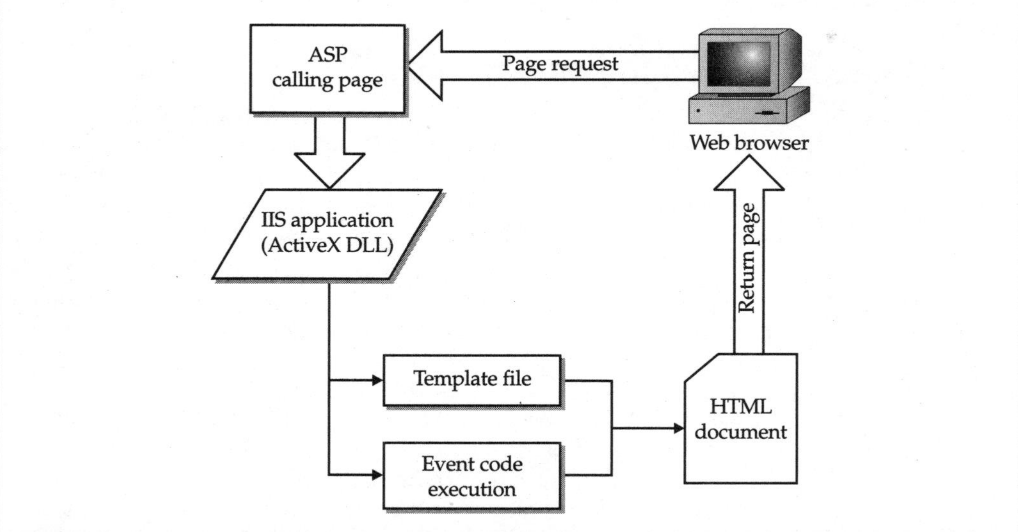

Figure 15-2. When the browser requests the IIS application, a number of processes are "set" in motion

The power of an IIS Application can supply:

- **Substantial interactivity** The event model used in conjunction with template files allows you to provide much more dynamic range in an HTML presentation than would be feasible with a standard ASP solution. Since most of the event maintenance is taken care of for you, flexibility is maximized while specific coding is minimized.
- **Seamless interaction between graphic artists and developers** An IIS application effectively separates content from logic, unlike most ASP solutions, which combine them on a single page. Since the HTML can be created and updated with any HTML editor, you only need to send the specific file in the project that has been updated.
- **Page reuse** A template and even a WebClass can easily be reused for many applications.
- **Access to the ASP object model from VB** An ActiveX DLL cannot easily address and manipulate objects contained in IIS. In an IIS application, all of the objects (including Application and Session) are available for the application to use.

All of these features do not come without some cost. This application type isolates the VB logic from traditional ASP script code logic, making integration with existing Web applications difficult.

Disadvantages of an IIS Application

IIS applications do have some disadvantages when compared with traditional ASP applications. The most pronounced issues involve the deployment and maintenance of an IIS Application when compared with a strictly ASP coded application.

Because IIS Applications are written in Visual Basic, each modification or addition requires a recompile. This means that entirely new DLL and execution files are generated with each change. It makes a Web application created in VB lack the simple change-and-update cycle that is available with Visual InterDev ASP development.

Once the application is complete, VB does not provide the final automatic deployment to the Web server that Visual InterDev offers. Whereas Visual InterDev can upload your applications, create the application directory, and perform basic configuration, VB merely provides a finished project. You will have to create an installer through the Package and Deployment wizard, install it on the Web server, and configure it for use manually.

The IIS application is also more complex because of the number of files that must work together for proper execution (templates, DLLs, ASP pages, and so on). Given these considerations, you must decide whether the project would be best constructed as an IIS application or not. The ease of creation, the polish of the Visual Basic environment, and the flexibility of the application all favor IIS applications in an Enterprise situation. If an ASP integration solution is required, however, an IIS application is not the proper choice.

Movement in a Browser-Based Application

Within a traditional VB application, the sequence of steps involved in the user-interface process can be controlled. In a browser-based application, the user might click the Forward or Back buttons, alter the URL, or use a bookmark to jump into a process. These occurrences cannot be controlled in the way a dimmed menu item can limit the activation of events in a traditional application. Therefore, there are special considerations when creating a Web application.

These considerations include:

- **Don't use cross-page transactions** The user may abandon the page or click the Back button at any time. Keeping a transaction open during these events would hold up a percentage of server resources. Depending on the size of the transaction and the objects involved, server performance could be affected. To allow all transaction operations to be executed on a single page, save all changes and information in a Session or Application variable and provide a single page that makes all of the changes.
- **Structure for random page access** Like random-access files, users can instantly jump to any page by supplying a URL. Take this into consideration by providing navigation buttons from each page. This can reduce the unintended access your system must be designed to handle.
- **Plan for multiple submits** Use a unique field, such as the user ID to record all submissions. If the database itself doesn't ignore or reject a repeated submission, then pruning the database of repetitive data will be much easier with a unique identifier.
- **Refill forms** When the user moves backwards or jumps to an out-of-sequence form, fill the form with values held in the Session variables.

DEFINING WEBCLASSES

An IIS application has, at its heart, an object class known as a *WebClass*. Like an ActiveX DLL class, the WebClass is registered for access on the serving system. A WebClass has a special management window that allows integration between class code, HTML template files, and the ASP objects available on the Web server. The IIS application provides its own general interface, in the form of a wizard, within the VB IDE. Figure 15-3 shows an example of the basic window.

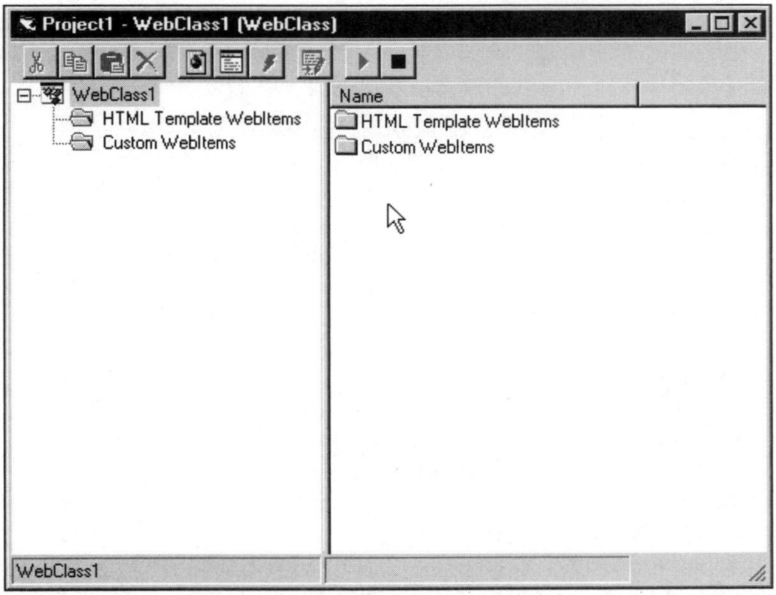

Figure 15-3. With the Visual Basic IDE, the WebClass has its own interface

DEFINITION: **WebClass** A special class within Visual Basic that forms the basis for an IIS application. The class can receive events from the user via browser hyperlinks and forms, as well as from interaction directly with the Web server.

The WebClass is used to contain all of the code that will be compiled for the IIS application. When you develop an application for Web deployment in Visual Basic, you will work within this class by creating code for methods and code that is activated by events fed to the class. To define a new WebClass, it must be uniquely named and execution events must be defined to begin showing the templates that will be used to display the application.

NOTE: Like any ActiveX DLL, a new instance of the WebClass object is generated for each client that accesses the application. This object is only used for that particular client. When the session timeout expires to indicate abandonment, the instance is destroyed.

Each WebClass has an ASP file that is used to activate it. The WebClass executes using an extension to a URL to provide the relevant information regarding an event. In a simplified example, a URL to activate a custom event named `ReturnTable` might look like this:

```
MyForm.ASP?WCI=MyTemplate&amp;WCE=ReturnTable&amp;WCU
```

The ASP code automatically generated by VB will process the URL and pass the information to the WebClass that you have defined. Once the event is activated, other HTML tags are used to identify the slots that are to be filled with dynamic content. *Tag substitution* is the term used for the core method of providing dynamic HTML pages. Tags that have a prespecified tag value are located and replaced in the HTML file by the proper ActiveX DLL methods before the document is sent to the user's browser.

A WebClass usually consists of a minimum of two items: an HTML template file and a custom WebItem. The HTML template provides the basic template for the page that will be sent to the client once the dynamic content is added. The custom WebItem is the class that holds all of the code that will execute when Web and user events occur. A WebClass can contain multiple templates and WebItems.

To allow you to address how parts of the IIS Application will execute on the Web server, you can use the State property to keep the WebClass active between requests. It can be set for each WebClass object using the Properties window.

Templates for use in the IIS application need to be created from an HTML construction program. FrontPage is probably your best bet for creating them, as it provides an effective graphic interface for page construction. Once the general look has been defined as an HTML page, the page can be converted into a template for use by the WebClass.

TIP: When creating a WebClass, use relative URLs for referencing pages. This allows the application to be placed in any directory for final deployment. A single reference omitting a path (for example, logo.gif) is used for current directory access. For a folder contained within the current folder, use the dot slash (./) reference command (for example, ./images/logo.gif). For a directory above the current one, use the double dot slash (../) reference (for example, ../pub/logo.gif).

IIS Application Events

In the development process, when a new HTML template is added to the project, the HTML is scanned for the tags that mark where dynamic replacement should take place. If you are familiar with HTML coding, then you will readily understand how the event model can be implemented through a template. The items in the template act in a manner similar to an `IMG SRC` tag. An `IMG SRC` tag makes the browser request the image file while the display is taking place. In the same manner, the tags make requests to the WebClass to handle the events of the user.

Each tag within a template file that needs to be addressed can contain the ID attribute so that it can be accessed directly by the WebClass. By giving this attribute a unique name, the IIS Application can process it and allow VB events to be coded to react to events related to it.

DEFINITION: **ID Attribute** An optional attribute in an HTML tag that can be parsed by the methods of a Template object. The attribute name is assigned in the WebClass properties, and each value is assigned in the template text.

Buttons are the primary methods of generating events for a traditional server-side solution. While hyperlinks are used most often to provide event notification to the server, buttons can also be used for events. Make sure the buttons on the template page all contain the attribute `Type=Submit` so they'll execute properly in application.

Any HTML file can be added as a template. If there are no identified tags within a template, the IIS Application will simply display it like a normal HTML file. A template file differs from a normal HTML file only in the tags that it contains to allow processing and the generation of events.

Tags for the WebClass have the prefix letters `WC@`. This default setting can be changed to a different prefix in the WebClass properties. The `TagPrefix` property defines the tags that will make the parsing routines activate. For an event, the name of the tag is listed after the prefix.

NOTE: When you add an HTML file to a project as a template, the images and other files referenced by the HTML will not automatically be copied. Make sure you copy them to the application directory to ensure that the IIS application functions and that all files associated with the application are centralized.

Once a template has been loaded into a VB project, only the most rudimentary changes can be made to it. By configuring Visual Basic to set the HTML editor that will be the external editor launched for the templates (through the Advanced tab in the Options dialog box), you can select a file for editing by right-clicking the item in the Project window. The Edit HTML Template option will open the file in the external editor. Once the file is updated, the VB project will automatically update for any changes made.

When you use an editor not executed by VB, or make any changes to the page while the IIS application is loaded into Visual Basic, the project will still contain the old file when you load it. Be sure to use the Refresh HTML Template option for the page when you open the application again in VB. Right-click the page and select the Refresh command, and VB will scan it for any changes and update the displayed tag list.

NOTE: When you are working on a Web application, the graphic artist will probably have a number of updates for the template file. If you need to alter a template file, it is recommended that you delete the current file from the project and add the new one, rather than altering the existing file. Doing so allows Visual Basic to reprocess all of the tags and items in the HTML file.

All WebItems can access the custom WebItem event. The `URLFor` method can be used instead of writing a handling procedure. Custom WebItems encapsulate frequently used code and are stored in the Custom WebItems folder.

NOTE: In an IIS application, you can use frames to display information. Content can be dynamically generated for each frame with processing defined in WebClass events.

A custom event, such as `ShowList`, could be created to generate a list of possible options available in a left-hand navigation frame.

An IIS application actually intercepts hyperlinks and takes action. Actions can include firing a standard or custom event that matches the request, firing the respond event, launching ASP pages, or firing the WebClass `Start` event.

Here is the order of processing for an event call:

1. Standard event
2. User event
3. `Respond` event
4. ASP application and WebClass `Start` event

The `Respond` event is the default event activated for templates and WebItems. A WebItem can be activated by the client or the server. Within the Visual Basic development environment, the `Respond` event doesn't appear in the designer's Detail panel like other events. Instead, it occurs in the Proc combo box. Client-side (user) events occur after a URL request is made. When a user clicks on an item, this will submit an event to the WebClass. In contrast, server-side events (such as the `Start` event) are activated on the WebClass when the `NextItem` property is changed to a different value by the server (such as when a server is initially accessed).

Standard Events

In an IIS Application, standard events are predefined events, such as `Respond` or `ProcessTag`, which are available in the combo box of the Code Editor. The `Start`, `Initialize`, and `Terminate` events parallel the Visual Basic Form events `Load`, `Initialize`, and `Terminate`, respectively.

The standard events (shown in Figure 15-4) include the following:

- **`Start`** Executes when the WebClass is first loaded. This event is only executed the first time an HTTP request is received by the application.
- **`Initialize`** Called when the WebClass begins execution.
- **`Terminate`** Executes when the WebClass is being terminated from the server memory.
- **`BeginRequest`** Executes at the beginning of the HTTP request when the user sends a request to a WebClass.
- **`EndRequest`** Executes when the processing is complete on the HTTP request and the HTML page has been returned to the browser.

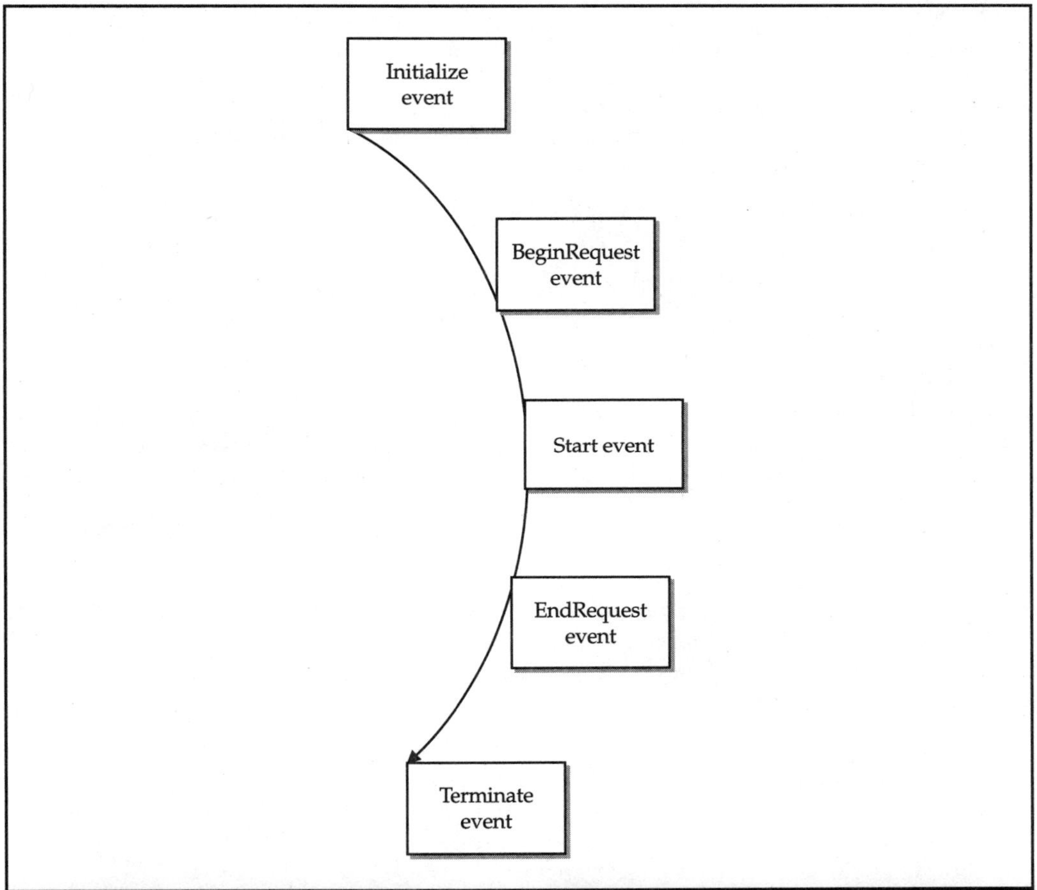

Figure 15-4. The process cycle of a WebClass executes each initiation or termination event in sequence

The `BeginRequest` and `EndRequest` events are usually used for various application-setup routines. You can use these events to gather requests for intense server-side resources with `BeginRequest` and release the resources with `EndRequest`. All of the standard events are automatically predefined for every template in a WebClass.

Template Events

Template events are generated in a WebClass by tags within the template file when it is processed by Visual Basic. A browser request connecting to the Web application activates the event by adding tag attributes that can be addressed by the WebClass when a page is requested. Most tags have a single event attribute, although the `IMG` tag has multiple attributes. Attributes that are available are displayed in the Detail panel of a selected template.

Each template has its own available code and events. The template events include the following:

- **Respond** Executed in response to a request from a Web item. The code in this event usually contains the `WriteTemplate` method call to return a Web page to the user.
- **ProcessTag** Activated when a WebClass tag (`WC:`) is encountered. Text can then be substituted for this tag, or other scripting logic can be executed.
- **UserEvent** Initiated when a `UserEvent` call is placed by one of the elements on the HTML page. User events must be specifically defined.

Custom Event

Custom events are events that are added by the developer that do not automatically relate to an object in the browser. These events are used by activating the `URLFor` method to relate a custom event to an element of the browser. This is done with code such as this:

```
Response.Write "<A HREF=""" & URLFor(CustomWebItem1,"CustomEventName") _
   & """>Link</A>
```

When a user selects the hyperlink, the custom event is activated. Custom events are the events that you will define to allow interaction with the Web user, and they will be triggered when the user clicks on a specific hyperlink to activate the event. Custom events use standard VB syntax:

```
ObjectName_EventName()
```

User events are events generated by user actions in the browser. A user event is actually located in the WebClass under the `UserEvent` item. `UserEvent` only returns a single parameter called `EventName` as a string.

Visual Basic Access

All of the events of an IIS Application execute Visual Basic code inside the DLL. From within the IIS application, you have complete access to the IIS objects, including the Server, Application, and Session objects. These objects can be manipulated in the same manner as in ASP.

Additionally, there is a method and a property to add for dealing with the interaction of a Web application. These are:

- **WriteTemplate method** Sends the template to the browser.
- **NextItem property** Sets the template that will be used next. Used to explicitly determine which template the user will access, based on user information. For example, once a response to a currently tagged file is generated, the Web item stored in this property will be sent to the browser.

Default Start Event Code

When you first create a WebClass, default code is automatically created in the `Start` event. This code will use the Response object to return a basic HTML page to the browser. In the following listing, note that the WebClass automatically creates a default Response object in the `Start` event. You can see the code that is used to return this page. Notice that this code parallels code normally executed within ASP to return information through the Response object.

```
Private Sub WebClass_Start()
    'Write a reply to the user
    With Response
        .Write "<html>"
        .Write "<body>"
        .Write "<h1><font face=""Arial"">WebClass1's Starting Page</font></h1>"
        .Write "<p>This response was created in the Start event of WebClass1.</p>"
        .Write "</body>"
        .Write "</html>"
    End With
End Sub
```

In an application, this code provides a starting point. You can alter the script as necessary. Most often, the `WriteTemplate` method is used in the `Start` event to send the first template to the user, or the `NextItem` property is set to the desired template for the same results.

NOTE: You might have noticed that using the `With` statement makes the Response code far more brief than it would be if you included the full object reference in each line. Remember that this code is complete Visual Basic code, and it will be compiled into an ActiveX DLL. The `With` statement is not available in VBScript, so it cannot be used on ASP pages.

Form and QueryString Objects

Every Web page uses the HTTP protocol to govern the interaction between the page and the server. When a QueryString is used at the end of a URL (for example, www.widgetco.com?id=123), the actual HTTP command executed is a `Get` command. The `Get` command is used for any request by the client browser for a Web page. Since the query is included in the URL, it is passed along with the request.

Form content, on the other hand, is sent to the Web server in a specialized HTTP command known as `Post`. The `Post` command sends data to a particular Web page for retrieval. This command will transfer the information in fields of the form. The data contained in these fields can be accessed from within Visual Basic using the Form object, just as you would access them using ASP code.

CAUTION: Be sure to use the Post command for all form submissions. If the `Get` command is used with a form, the WebClass will not be able to handle events properly.

CREATING IIS APPLICATIONS

You can begin experimenting with the IIS Application project type by creating a simple application and then augmenting it. The foundation project in this chapter will be a Hello World IIS application. You will also construct a more advanced MyForm application that demonstrates the use of events that are handled by the compiled application—completely on the server-side. It will allow a form entry to determine which of several pages will be displayed in response to an event interaction.

NOTE: You must first save the IIS application before you can add any template pages to it. Since the project copies the added template files into the destination project folder, it must have a location in which to place them.

The Hello World Application

To begin building WebClass solutions, you can start by creating a Hello World application. This example will not simply display a message greeting. To demonstrate the template and tag capabilities of an IIS application, this program will retrieve the "World" text of the greeting from a WebClass procedure.

In the steps below, you will create a new IIS Application project and name it HelloWorld.vbp. When you begin a new project in VB 6, the IIS Application item is the selection you'll use. You will then need to import the file to use it as a Web page template. When you install the template, you can select it from the HTML Template WebItems folder. The tags contained in the document will be displayed in the Content frame.

NOTE: When you import a template, your IIS Application project will automatically make a duplicate of the file and place it in the project folder. Therefore, to have additional edits to the template reflected in your solution, make sure you edit the version stored with the project.

Creating a New IIS Application Project

You'll need to begin by creating a new project much like any other VB project:

1. Start Visual Basic and select the New Project option from the File menu.
2. From the Project Types, select the IIS Application icon (see the following illustration) and click the Open button. This selection will create all of the core structures needed for the Web solution. Note that a default class file named WebClass1 has been added to the project. This is the WebClass that will be used to hold your execution and event code.

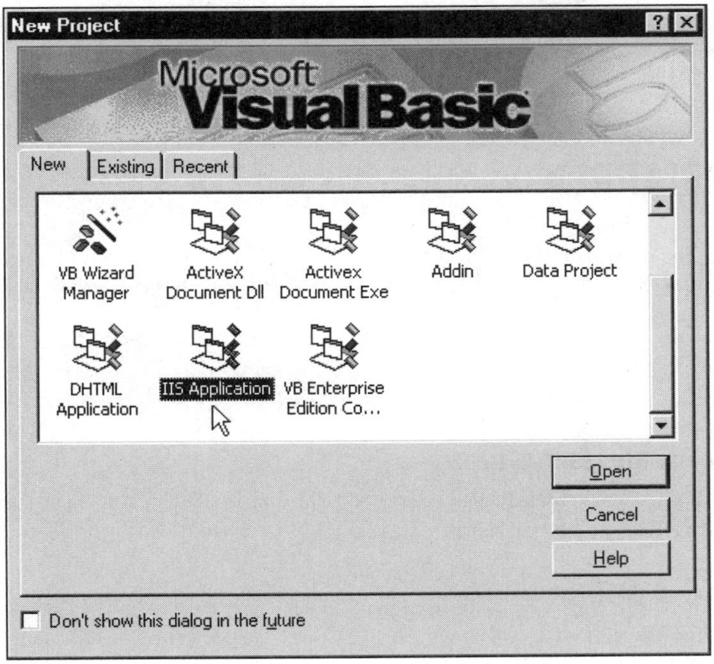

3. Double-click the WebClass1 item to open it in the Web designer (see the next illustration). Two folders contain all of the pieces of a WebClass: HTML Template WebItems and Custom WebItems. Since no templates or items have been entered, the project will appear empty.

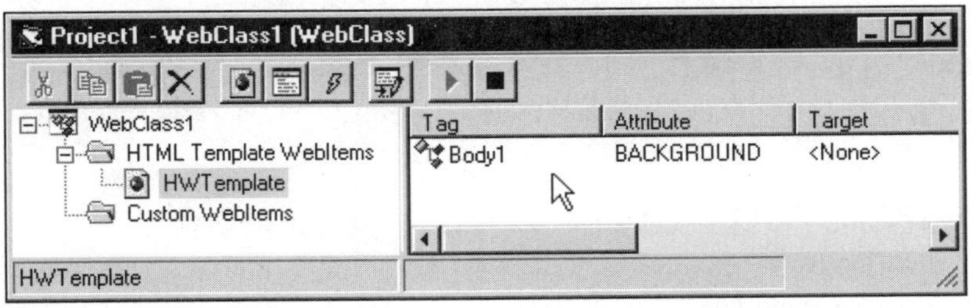

Before you add any code to the project, it is best to set the properties of the project itself to the naming parameters under which the project will be deployed (and accessed through a URL).

Setting Project Properties

The `Name` and `NameInURL` properties define the name that the component for the project will be constructed under and the name of the application that will be deployed on the Web server when you execute it, respectively.

1. Select the class in the Project window and from the right-button menu select the Properties option. You will see the Properties window.
2. Set the `Name` property to *wcHelloWorld.*
3. Set the `NameInURL` property to "HelloWorld". The `NameInURL` property will define the title of the ASP file that calls the Web application. If you set this value to Default, for example, the project would create the page as Default.asp.
4. Select the Save Project option from the File menu.
5. Save the designer files as HelloWorld.dsr and the project as HelloWorld.vbp.

Make sure that you save the project in a folder that can handle the template files as you add them. Since all of the images, class, and template files are used together in the application, it is usually a good idea to create a separate folder for each new IIS Application.

Creating the HTML Template

You will need a simple template to create your first file. Open the Notepad application or another simple text editor and enter the following code.

```
<HTML>
<TITLE>Hello World WebClass sample</TITLE>
<BODY>
<H1>Sample of an IIS Application template</H1>
<P>Hello...<WC@MYTAG>insert text</WC@MYTAG>
</BODY>
</HTML>
```

This file should then be saved under the name HelloWorld.htm.

Note that unlike an ASP file, this code does not contain any script. It contains traditional HTML with the exception of the `<WC@MYTAG>` opening and closing tags. These are needed for tag substitution by the IIS Application and they serve to define an item for event access.

Import the HTML File for Use as a Web Page Template

Once the HelloWorld.htm file has been saved, you will need to import it into the current WebClass. Visual Basic will process the file and display it in a special window to show the various accessible items that were found in the page.

1. In the Project Window, right-click the HTML Template WebItems folder, and select the Add HTML Template option.
2. Select the HelloWorld.htm file, and click the Open button.
3. Change the default name from "Template1" to "HWTemplate".

4. Click OK. The Web designer will import and parse the template file you created earlier. The tag (`<WC@MYTAG>`) that was included in the file will show up in the Details window, and if you expand the folder, you will see all of the tag items from the template.
5. Double-click the HWTemplate item. With the template added, you can add VB code to the project to replace the tag with the text that is generated by the code. Adding logic or event code is done in the same way that a normal VB application is edited.
6. Select the HWTemplate item from the object (left) combo box, and ProcessTag routine from the procedure (right) combo box to display the `ProcessTag` event.
7. Insert the following code into the `ProcessTag` event of the HWTemplate:

```
Private Sub HWTemplate_ProcessTag(ByVal TagName As String, _
TagContents As String, SendTags As Boolean)
    Select Case TagName
        Case "WC@MYTAG"
            TagContents = "World!"
    End Select
End Sub
```

8. Insert this code commenting out the default code:

```
Private Sub WebClass_Start()
    'Write a reply to the user
    'With Response
    '    .Write "<html>"
    '    .Write "<body>"
    '    .Write "<h1><font face=""Arial"">WebClass1's Starting Page</font></h1>"
    '    .Write "<p>This response was created in the Start event of WebClass1.</p>"
    '    .Write "</body>"
    '    .Write "</html>"
    'End With
    HWTemplate.WriteTemplate
End Sub
```

This code comments most of the default code out of the execution. You can eliminate it instead if you like, but since this is your first solution, retaining the code as a sample may help you when adding features to the project.

Executing the Application

The first time you execute an IIS application from Visual Basic, you will be prompted to set your browser to allow out-of-process component execution. Out-of-process execution is required in order for VB to allow debugging on the currently executing application. If you approve it, you will let the `AllowOutOfProcessDLL` registry property to be set to 1. This option will allow Visual Basic to access the component to allow for debugging.

TIP: Allowing out-of-process component execution can allow your browser (and potentially harmful script code) to access out-of-process components on your system, so you might consider changing the parameter back to its initial value when not doing IIS Application development. You'll find the attribute set to 1 in the registry. Returning the value to 0 will reset it.

Execute the application by clicking the Start icon on the toolbar or pressing the F5 key. The application will compile and install on the current Web server. The first time you execute the application, it will prompt you to install it to the current Web server. Name the virtual root directory HelloWorldProj, as the next illustration shows.

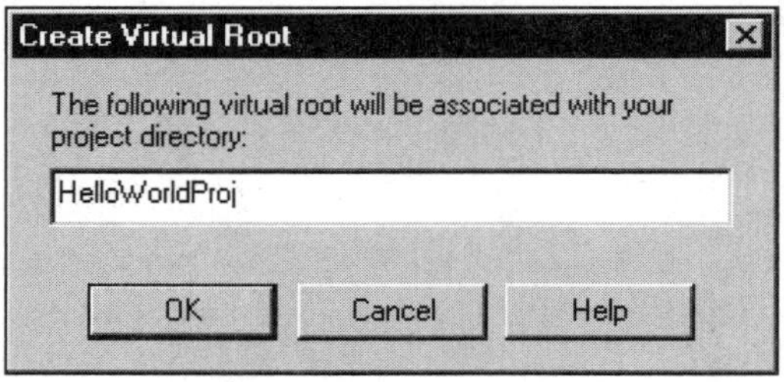

The project will be registered automatically as an executable application on the Web server that is available on the development machine. A browser will be opened that activates the Web page of the application (see Figure 15-5). Visual Basic will continue to execute, and all of its debug capabilities will be available. To stop execution, close the browser and click the Stop button on the VB toolbar.

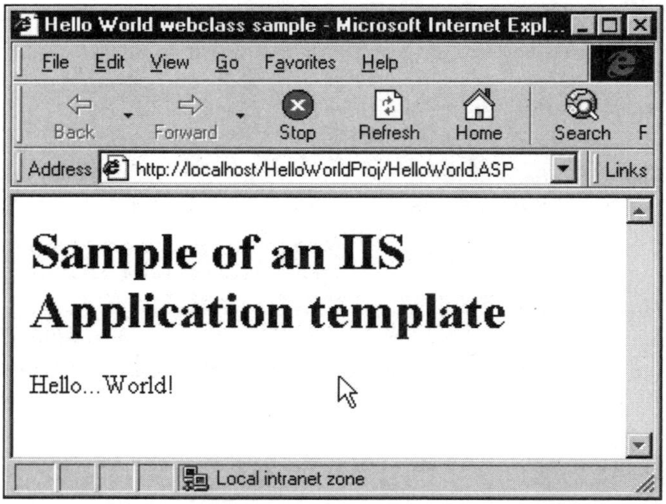

Figure 15-5. The browser will display the string in place of the specified tag

TIP: Every time you execute the application, a new instance of the browser will be created. The only way to avoid this process is to use the Make...DLL option in the File menu. You can then move to the Web browser and click the Refresh button to load the new instance. However, when you use this technique, the debugger will be unavailable. Therefore, it is usually best to simply close the browser and stop the application after each test.

Form/Event Application

With the construction of the Hello World application, you have created your first example of a WebClass. You learned how to parse a tag contained within the template to return a customized page. The real power of an IIS application comes from its event model. The application's ability to receive events and send custom output makes developing Web applications much more like traditional event-based VB solutions.

To demonstrate this functionality, you can construct an HTML form application that will receive events and display different templates depending on those events. The template file used in this project is a simple form file that accepts a name field (into the control named NameVal) and posts it to MyForm.asp. Shortly, you will learn how to augment the application to show specific pages, depending on the input.

Create the MyForm Application

To construct the IIS Application, follow these steps:

1. Start a new IIS Application project.
2. Open the WebClass1 designer.
3. Set the `Name` property of the class to "wcMyForm" and the `NameInURL` property to "MyForm".
4. Save the designer as "MyForm.dsr" and the project as "MyForm.vbp".
5. Use Notepad or another HTML editor to create the Default.htm template file shown in the following listing:

```
<html>
<head>
<title>WebClass Demo</title>
</head>
<body>
<h1>WebClass Event Demonstration Example</h1>
<form method="post" action="MyForm.ASP">
<p>Please enter your name below.
<p>Name: <input name="NameVal" ></p>
  <p><input type="submit" value="Send" name="B1"></p>
</form>
</body>
</html>
```

6. Right-click the HTML Template WebItems, and select the Add HTML Template option.
7. Select the Default.htm file in the dialog box. This will add the template file to the project.
8. Name the newly added Web item "tplMain". You should see two items in the Details pane on the right side of the window: Body1 and Form1.
9. Right-click the Form1 item and select the Connect to Custom Event option. You will now see the event under the tplMain template. This event will be used to display the information entered into the name field.
10. Name the event `ShowData` as shown in the following illustration.

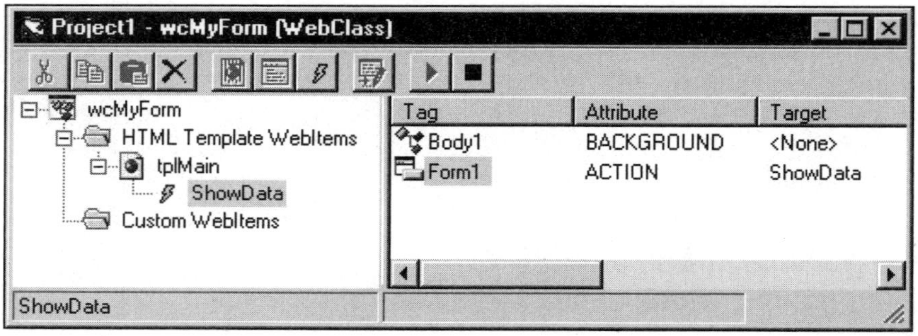

If you examine the code contained in the HTML template now, you'll see that the form action includes code like this:

```
<form method="post" action="MyForm.ASP?WCI=tplMain&amp;
  WCE=ShowData&amp;WCU">
```

Notice that the ASP file is requested along with three additional parameters: WCI, WCE, and WCU. The WCI argument is the WebClass item that is to be referenced. The WebClass event (WCE) names the event that will be activated when the `POST` command is activated by the button. Since all the data are passed in the form, the WebClass URLData (WCU) contains no information.

11. Double-click on the ShowData item to see the code window. The code window will be opened and the code stubs for the event will be displayed. When the `ShowData` event occurs, any code contained in this procedure will be activated in the WebClass application. In this case, your code will check to make sure that

the user entered a name in the supplied text box. An empty Name box will cause the event to send the user a Web page that requests that they use the Back button and enter a name. This page is displayed using the Response object in IIS.

When the Name field is valid, the user is showed the tplWelcome template. The template itself will display the value that was returned in the form which is set in the Session variable as `NameVal`.

12. Enter the following event code into the ShowData method:

```
Private Sub tplMain_ShowData()
    If Len(Request.Form("NameVal")) = 0 Then
        With Response
            .Write "<html>"
            .Write "<body>"
            .Write "<h1>Error in data</h1>"
            .Write "<p>There was no information entered in the name field."
            .Write "<p>Please press the back arrow on your browser and enter<br>"
            .Write "the requested information."
            .Write "</body>"
            .Write "</html>"
        End With
    Else
        Session("NameVal") = Request.Form("NameVal")
        tplWelcome.WriteTemplate
    End If
End Sub
```

Setup the Start Event

Before the application can be run, you need to set up the `Start` event to execute the template that will begin the process. In this case, the template called tplMain must be written to the browser. To set up the `Start` event, follow these steps:

1. Open the `WebClass_Start` event code.
2. Comment out or delete the existing default code, in order to start with an empty page.
3. Add the following code, which will send the template tplMain to the browser:

```
Private Sub WebClass_Start()
    tplMain.WriteTemplate
End Sub
```

4. Create the tplWelcome page in a text or HTML editor and save the file as Welcome.htm. The `ShowData` event executes this template. It needs to be an HTML page that contains a tag that can be supplied by the IIS application, such as the following:

```
<html>
<head>
<title>Welcome</title>
</head>
<body>
<p>Welcome to the IIS Application,
<WC@NAMEVAL></WC@NAMEVAL>!
</body>
</html>
```

   This tag will be filled with the value held in the `NameVal` session variable.

5. Add the Welcome.htm file to the project as a new template, and set its name to **tplWelcome** as shown next. When you add another template, it will appear, listed in alphabetical order in the template folder.

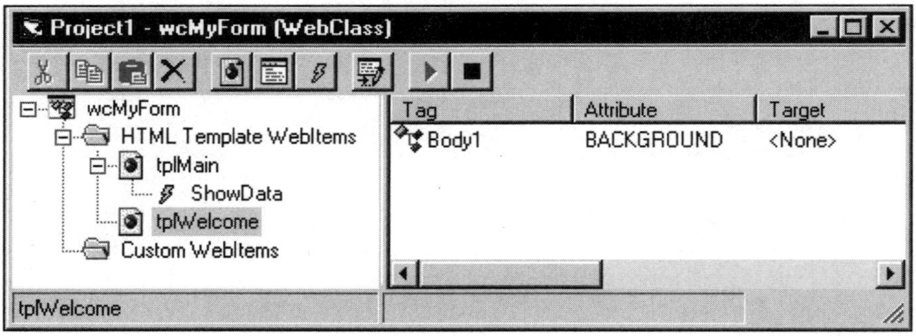

6. Double-click the tplWelcome item and place the following code in the `ProcessTag` event:

```
Private Sub tplWelcome_ProcessTag(ByVal TagName As String, _
TagContents As String, SendTags As Boolean)
    Select Case TagName
        Case "WC@NAMEVAL"
            TagContents = Session("NameVal")
    End Select
End Sub
```

The application is now complete and ready to execute. The first page that will be displayed is the central form page that requests that a user name be entered (see Figure 15-6).

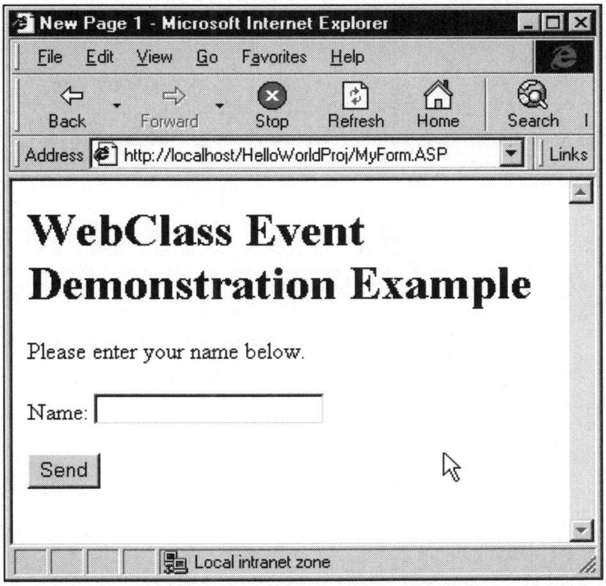

Figure 15-6. The main page of the MyForm application prompts for a name to be entered

If you enter your name into the Name text box, the Welcome template will be executed and the welcome message displayed with the value stored in the Session object variable. (See the following illustration.) The value for the name is placed into the HTML through the tag-event parsing routine.

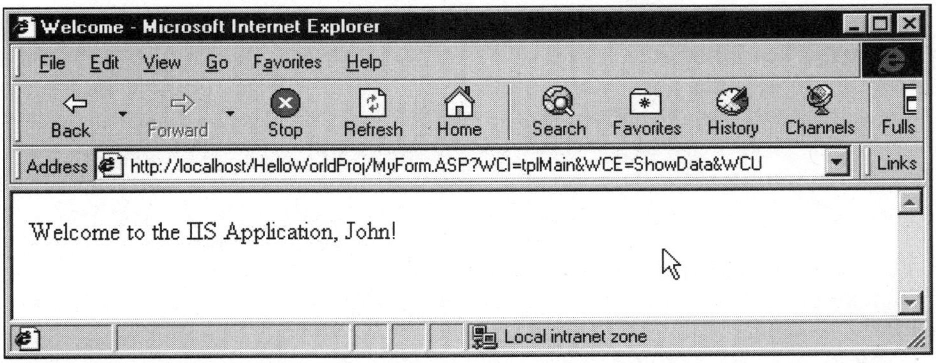

When the text box is left blank, the Empty Field page (which is generated by the Response object) will be shown (see Figure 15-7). This error page could have been generated as a template and the `URLFor` method could also be added to provide a link to the previous page.

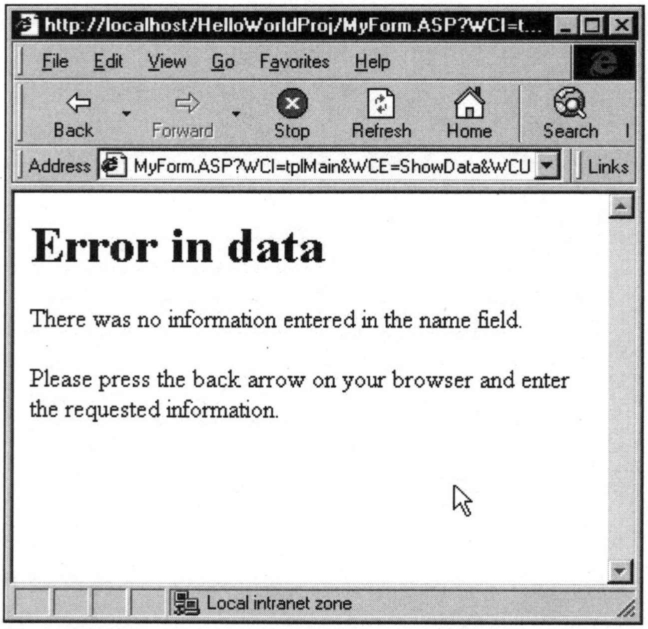

Figure 15-7. The dynamically created error page will be displayed if the Name text box is empty

Q&A

Q: Can an IIS application be used in conjunction with Visual InterDev development?
A: Yes, the application itself can be loaded into InterDev and deployed to a Web server, or you can use hyperlinks within ASP pages to jump to the IIS application. An ASP page cannot be added to the IIS application as a template. If an ASP page is added to a project, VB makes it the default page to be executed when the application loads. This disables the main ASP page that is automatically generated to activate the WebClass stored in the DLL, which means that the IIS Application will never be activated and hence won't execute.

Q: Can a template be used in multiple projects?
A: When a template file is inserted into a project, a duplicate is actually made, and this file is added—any subsequent editing occurs to the project copy. Therefore, you can keep a source file that could be added to multiple projects. However, the template cannot be used like an Include file, where the update to a single file will revise all the files that use it.

SUMMARY

An IIS application provides an ideal way to develop comprehensive Web applications from within Visual Basic. Because the entire object model of IIS is exposed to a WebClass, all development can be done within VB. The pages that activate the WebClass (that compile into ActiveX DLLs) are created by VB when the project is executed. In this chapter, you covered:

- **IIS application** A Visual Basic–based application that compiles into an ActiveX DLL and automatically generates ASP pages to activate it.
- **WebClass** The class of an IIS application that contains event code and interprets events sent from the user via hyperlink clicks or form submissions. The term *WebClass* is largely interchangeable with the general term *IIS application*.
- **WebItems** The individual items in an IIS application, such as the imported HTML templates and custom events, are known as WebItems within the solution.
- **Template file** An HTML file that can contain tags that are parsed by events within a WebClass.

CHAPTER 16

Distributed COM (DCOM)

So far, you have used ActiveX DLLs extensively and even created a few. All of these components have been installed on the machine on which they will run. For database access, encapsulating logic in a component can provide security. It also adds an extra level of abstraction that can allow you to centralize and standardize the method used to access a data source. The power of ActiveX DLLs is augmented dramatically if they can be placed on remote machines for execution over a network. Distributing components on a LAN or WAN offers numerous advantages, including load balancing for incoming execution requests, placing the location of components within an organization to the group that is responsible for maintaining them, distributed development possibilities, and more.

Microsoft makes it easy to take advantage of distributed computing by augmenting the object communication technology that you've already been using. The ASP scripting environment uses an underlying object technology, known as COM, for communication with components. COM, short for Component Object Model, provides the foundation for standardized object interaction on the Windows platform. COM was designed to provide a method of creating objects and communicating with them. Although the COM framework allows interaction across processes (such as between different EXEs), it does not natively allow connections between objects on different machines.

Microsoft created Distributed COM (DCOM) to allow components to be placed on remote machines and still communicate over a network. DCOM was originally designed for use with components developed in C++, but Microsoft has extended it for use by ActiveX components generated by development systems, including Visual Basic, Delphi, or Visual J++.

DEFINITION: **DCOM** Distributed COM is an object model that allows objects to be called and executed on remote machines transparently to the calling application. DCOM provides the network communication layer for COM objects.

There are many solutions that are ideal for locating process execution on a machine other than the one on which the calling script or application resides. One example of distributed processing is the computer rendering required to create many of the flashy special effects in today's big screen movies. While the graphic artist works at a single machine, the processor-intensive calculations that actually generate the final image execute on a separate, specialized, high-powered machine (see Figure 16-1).

Distributed computing offers benefits for many applications that don't require intensive calculation. Some reasons for creating a distributed system include:

- **Encapsulating business logic** Business logic in the form of a component can be placed on the appropriate server. Common applications, such as credit validation and inventory reorder checking can be placed in a distributed component. When changes need to be made to the logic, only the remote component used by all of the solutions needs to be modified.

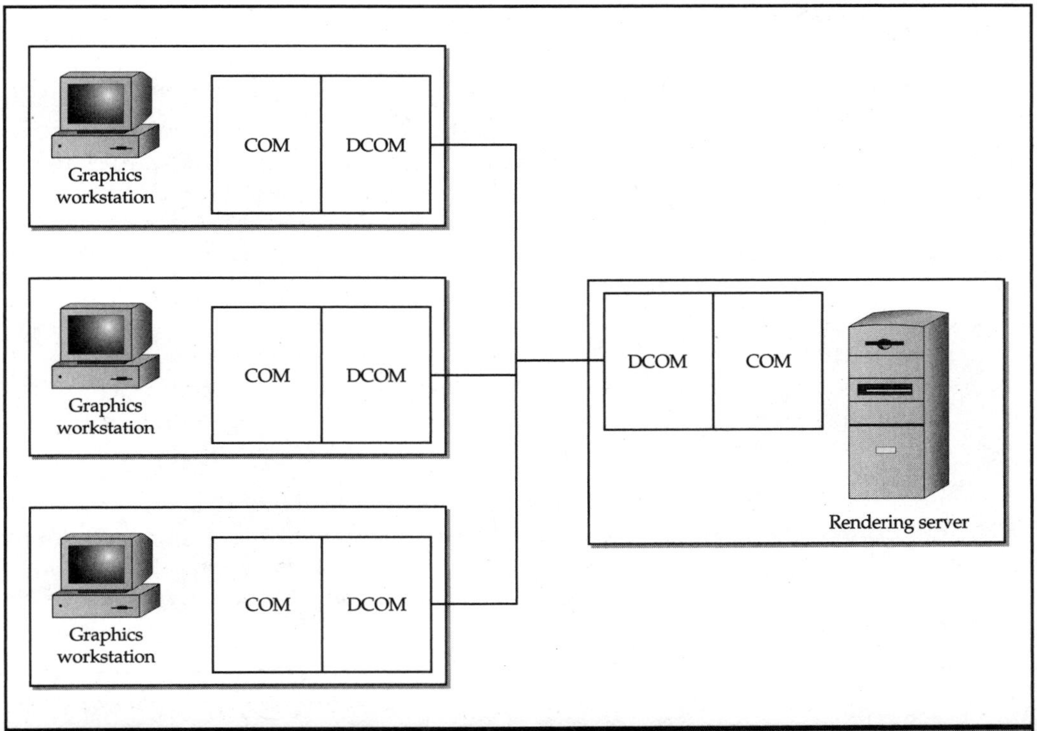

Figure 16-1. DCOM provides a transparent layer that allows COM objects to communicate over a network

- **Encapsulating departmental logic** By creating specialized objects, the responsibility for development and testing can be kept within one department. For example, the accounting department could maintain the objects that make alterations to the accounting data. Applications that need to retrieve or make alterations to this data would have to access them via a DCOM object. Accounting could then control the necessary checks and balances for the processes they understand.
- **Specialized servers** Components can be placed on servers that provide special hardware resources or separate processing locations required for special tasks. Computer graphics rendering is one example of specialized distributed processing.
- **Shielding data or resource access** In Chapter 11 you learned that, for security reasons, the SMTP mail service could only be used on the machine on which it was installed. A distributed object could be created to execute on that machine, and yet expose a method that allows remote invocation of the secure

capabilities. Access to the component would be limited to those who have authorization through DCOM security.

- **Sharing resources** Using distributed objects, you can share resources such as database connections, fax servers, and modem servers.
- **Custom processes** Proprietary processes, such as clearing a credit-card charge amount, can be encapsulated in a distributed object. The object can then be used remotely by any application that needs to charge the credit account. A custom process could also interface with a proprietary API, such as a communication protocol, to retrieve data.
- **Distributing processing power** Using DCOM, you can break up a complex process into smaller pieces. Each piece could then be used as a separate object executing on a different machine. Using this method, a complex, processor-intensive solution can be computed without using expensive supercomputer resources.

Common business uses of distributed objects include customer database access, tax calculation, order entry, credit verification, inventory management, and accounting functions. As the technology becomes better known and integrated into the Windows 2000 system, distributed applications will most likely become the standard deployment model for enterprise solutions.

NOTE: To understand the potential of widespread distributed computing, you might examine the SETI (Search for Extraterrestrial Intelligence) program's project for searching the sky. SETI has released a screensaver (www.setiathome.ssl.berkeley.edu) that, when active, downloads a piece of information from a huge dataset of radio frequencies acquired by the Arecibo telescope. Each machine running the screensaver processes the part of the dataset that it receives, and then returns the results to the central computer.

In the past, processing this quantity of information required a tremendous amount of expensive supercomputer hours to execute. By distributing the problem to be processed on thousands of individual machines, all of the processing power can be brought together to create a solution. Although the implementation of the SETI project uses specialized software, the processing could conceivably have been set up using DCOM components remotely executing the process on all of the individual machines.

With all of the advantages of distributed technology, using it in a Web-based solution has been Microsoft's primary objective. In fact, Microsoft Transaction Server (MTS), the distributed component server, has become an integral part of IIS. By default, MTS is automatically installed when IIS is installed. DCOM makes a complete distributed system possible in the Windows environment as well as in other platforms supporting COM.

Currently, the COM foundation (including the DCOM transport layer) is available for the Windows platform, as well as for the Tru64 UNIX, DEC Alpha, OpenVMS, and Solaris operating systems. Software AG also has a Linux version of DCOM available. This foundation allows components to be interconnected and activated on any of these platforms and used across a network.

In this chapter, you'll use DCOM to distribute a simple ActiveX component to a different machine. The component will then be used by an ASP page as if it were located on the Web server machine. Although it is possible to use DCOM without knowing how the distribution layer functions, to properly design a distributed solution, you will need to understand how connections are made and maintained, as well as the limitations presented by the technology.

HOW DCOM WORKS

The DCOM technology, which works transparently to the scripting environment, actually progresses through a number of stages to create a remote connection. Because of the number of pieces that must be properly configured, failure can occur at any step of the establishment of a session. By examining how these configurations are properly set, you can create a reliable solution each time.

Figure 16-2 shows the process of connecting and instantiating a remote COM component. Once the program places a call for execution on a remote machine (in this case, the Server machine), the object is activated over the protocol specified for use by DCOM (TCP/IP, in this example).

When the script code initially calls the component, the ActiveX system goes to the registry to locate the component. If the component is not located on the client machine, the DCOM system is activated. DCOM places a request over the network to the machine hosting the component. To provide a connection between the calling machine and the server that will instantiate the component, DCOM must first use a standard protocol to

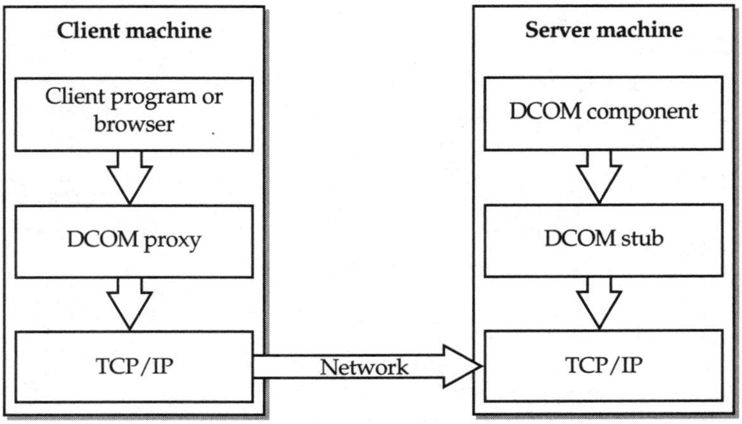

Figure 16-2. The DCOM session process connects to the remote DCOM component

negotiate the session. This negotiation process is similar to the connection process between two fax machines, where capabilities and protocol expectations are coordinated.

Once the negotiation is complete, an instance of the component will be created on the hosting machine and a reference to this object will be returned to the client. Calls to the component are processed through the client reference and submitted for execution on the hosting machine.

The structure on the client machine that describes the interface for the component is called a client *proxy*. The proxy is the interface (methods and properties) of the component without any of the component code. The proxy works through DCOM to broadcast messages to the remote component.

DEFINITION: **Proxy** A client-side interface that receives method calls and property-access requests for a component and broadcasts them over the DCOM communication session to the remote component. A proxy contains only the interface of the component and no actual component code.

The *stub* interface is located on the server side, where the component is actually located. The stub receives the DCOM messages and feeds them to the actual component, making the component believe that the request occurred on the local machine.

DEFINITION: **Stub** The server-side stub receives DCOM requests and interfaces with the component executing on the server to return the necessary information.

The complete COM system detects when a call is made and whether the process is local or needs to be activated as a remote call (see Figure 16-3).

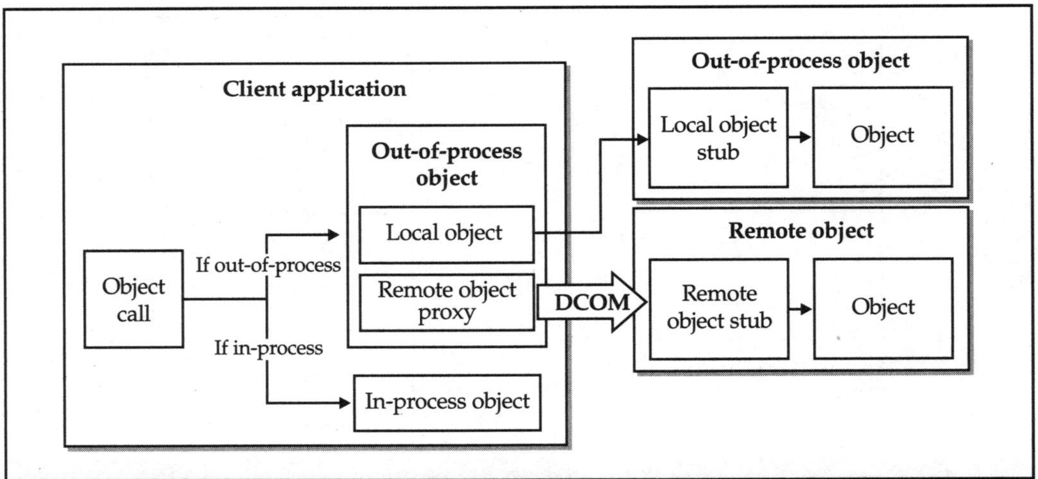

Figure 16-3. An overview of the COM system shows the similarity between an out-of-process object and a distributed one

DCOM provides communication between objects across a network using Remote Procedure Calls (RPC), a low-level calling mechanism, over the default TCP/IP protocol. DCOM adds a layer on top of simple RPC execution in much the same way that the HTTP protocol sits atop TCP/IP for Web communication.

Communication takes place between the DCOM client proxy and the DCOM server stub. The proxy and the stub connect to the COM interfaces on either side to allow for a transparent connection. You can even execute a remote component within the client browser as an ActiveX control that communicates directly with the server stub.

One of the advantages of DCOM's proxy and stub implementation over more primitive RPC remote invocation is the layer of error checking that can occur automatically within the connection code. If a disconnection occurs between the two objects, the stub and proxy can continue to function in order to report the error to the calling program. If direct RPC calls were being made to the remote object, the loss of connection might cause system instability.

CAUTION: The loopback mode, which allows a computer to call a network address that loops back to call itself, cannot be used for Windows NT 4.0. If you use standard addresses, such as localhost or 127.0.0.1, DCOM will not recognize them. This is an acknowledged bug in some editions of DCOM that may be fixed by the time you read this note. If you encounter problems using the loopback, check the Microsoft site (msdn.microsoft.com) for tech note information.

One of the most important executables in the DCOM install is the hosting utility for Windows NT, Dllhost.exe. The Dllhost.exe utility allows in-process classes to be executed out-of-process or across a network.

The DLLHost is critical to enabling remote execution. When the system receives a call from a remote procedure, the DLLHost application is executed as a shell program to hold the DLL. You will need to configure the remote component for execution under DLLHost as a surrogate process. Later in this chapter, you will see how this is used to enable an ActiveX DLL.

NOTE: A DCOM object must be registered on every machine that will use the component. The only way to avoid registration on each machine is through Visual C++, which can use the MIDL proxy/stub code that is compiled directly into the final application and thus does not require the registry for remote object access.

COM and DCOM are members of Microsoft's *component services*. Component services are used to enable and manage component technologies. In addition to COM and DCOM, IIS, MTS, and MSMQ are included in these services. If you see documentation on Microsoft component services, the documents will usually contain information about system-wide component implementation.

The COM object model is language neutral. The programming constructs such as data types that usually vary in different language implementations and across different microprocessors, are standardized in the object model. This allows a COM object to be used by C, C++, Visual Basic, Java, and other languages. This language neutrality is critical to the proper functioning of DCOM objects when a distributed application will most likely be created using several different development systems.

TIP: Because DCOM can be accessed at a lower level than C++ or Visual Basic, many of the documentation pages and online examples will contain code in this language. Although they are difficult for non-C++ programmers to understand, the general ideas of the following examples will provide useful information. Keep in mind that you can take advantage of most of the capabilities of DCOM from a high level.

DCOM Functional Overview

To allow a component to execute on a remote machine, you must use a properly configured DCOM layer that holds references to all objects on the system and their locations. The DCOM system uses the object registry to locate the information to make the connection between the calling application and the execution of the object on a remote machine.

Using this object location registry, COM determines where the object is located in a way that is transparent to the program instantiating the component. The program will be calling a remote object that it actually believes is located on the local machine.

When communication occurs between objects, the actual transmission of information occurs using a process called *marshalling*. Marshalling uses a programmed structure to map local memory locations for remote access. When marshalling is initiated, a stub and a proxy object are created. All exchanges of information actually occur between the stub and the proxy.

DCOM Execution Process

When a program places a call to an object that is actually just a DCOM proxy, a series of operations are set in motion. The operations begin on the client in the proxy and progress to the server. Each object instantiation follows these steps:

1. The proxy on the client tests to see if the registered control is a remote object.
2. The proxy determines the location (using either the domain name or the IP address) of the intended control.
3. The proxy attempts to make a connection with the remote DCOM server.
4. The proxy connects to the remote stub on the server.
5. The proxy requests an instance of the object to be generated.
6. The server returns a reference to the object instance.

In step 2, when a COM object is first requested by a program, the COM Service Control Manager will locate where the object resides. This control manager looks in the object registration database for the location of each component.

DCOM for Windows 95/98

There are many special considerations when running DCOM on Windows 95/98. The primary consideration is security. These operating systems have no security capabilities at their core for resources and logon. Instead, security features have been added on top of the general features so the actual security protection is primarily superficial. This makes DCOM security difficult, and, as a result, the Windows 95/98 security features are fairly limited. Although it is unlikely that you'll execute important components for a Web-based system on these platforms, it is useful to cover some of the special considerations for Windows 95/98 so that testing can be done on the platform.

For DCOM to be available, both printer and file sharing must be activated. These options are set in the Network control panel on the Client for Microsoft Networks option.

To run DCOM Config on Windows 95/98, the system must be configured to use user-level security. This means that you should also set the Logon validation capabilities to log on to a Windows NT domain (available in the Properties window of the Client settings). The DCOM utility cannot be executed if an NT domain is not specified.

For security reasons, DCOM cannot automatically launch a component on a remote Windows 95/98 machine. Instead, a DCOM server program must be manually activated before a calling machine can activate an instance. Although this requires an extra step, it ensures that remote calls (which may cause damage or may drain resources) cannot control an unsecured system.

For Windows 95/98 machines, you can also execute the program Rpcss.exe. Rpcss is a DCOM-enhanced System Control Manager that controls memory allocation and allows the configuration of memory (on Windows 95/98) for interprocess communication.

Finally, you should enable the system configuration on the server machine. This can be done through the OLE Viewer (Oleview.exe) that is included in the Visual Tools of Visual Studio. Execute the application, and select the System Configuration option under the File menu. There are two options: Enable Distributed COM (Windows 95 and 98) and Enable Remote Connections (Windows 95 only). Make sure both of these are checked. When you make changes to these settings, they won't be enabled until you reboot the system.

NOTE: The actual technology that generates the instance on a remote machine is called a Class Factory. If the Class Factory is of type 2 and it has licensing options set, a license must exist on the machine attempting to create the instance. If no license is located, an error is returned to the request. You can find more information on Class Factories and licensing in the COM SDK documentation on the MSDN CD.

Object Life Cycle

The object that is created on a remote machine has a more complicated life cycle than a local COM object. If the client doesn't actively set the object references to Nothing, the remote object can remain on the remote machine for some time, using valuable server resources.

DCOM keeps a count of how many different applications are referencing the same object. This count is incremented each time an additional user requests the creation of the object and decremented when a user is finished with that object. When the instance count reaches zero, the object is not immediately removed from memory so that an access can be made in a short time. Instead it is marked for removal, and the garbage-collection routines, based on time or resource shortage factors, will dump the marked objects.

To make certain that the client is still in contact with the server, a DCOM client actually uses a form of a network ping. A ping requests packets from a remote machine to verify that it is accessible.

NOTE: With DCOM, if the connection is lost between the object and the client that has requested it, the connection cannot be reestablished. The client must request the creation of a new object and start again.

USING DCOM

To use the DCOM technology, DCOM must be installed on all of the desired machines (Windows NT and Windows 98 have DCOM preinstalled). The default configuration of DCOM can be used effectively after you set the properties of the individual components by using the DCOM Config utility.

NOTE: Internet Explorer 5 installs DCOM to Windows 95 if it does not exist. This installation is needed to allow ActiveX components that use DCOM to communicate with DCOM objects across the Internet.

Using DCOM Config

As mentioned previously, in order to configure programs for use with DCOM, you will need to use the DCOM Config utility to set the class options, such as location, security, and protocol. For Windows NT, the program DCOMCnfg.exe is stored in the Windows\System32 directory. For Windows 95, you'll have to install the DCOM services to use this application. Afterwards, it is located in the System directory. It is included in the System directory of Windows 98 by default. Executing it will display a window like the one shown in Figure 16-4.

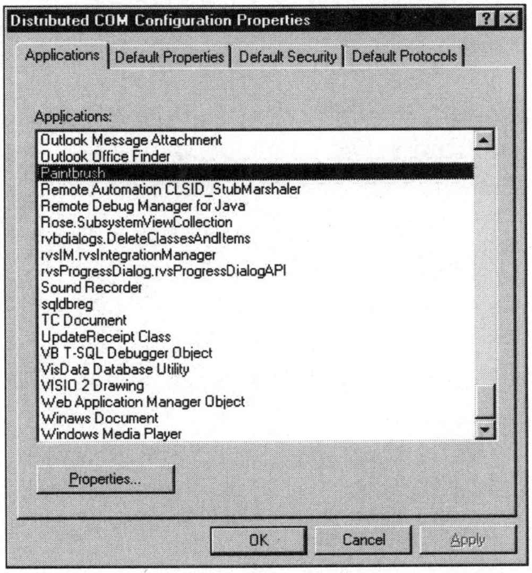

Figure 16-4. Choose the Paintbrush application in the Distributed COM Configuration properties dialog box

There is no shortcut to DCOM in the Start menu, so you will have to start it by double-clicking the application icon. When you do, it will open a window displaying all the components installed on the machine that are compliant with the DCOM component rules.

The main settings of the configuration utility are specified on the four tabs:

- **Applications** Provides a list box of all of the DCOM-compatible components available on the system and a Properties button for configuring individual components.
- **Default Properties** Sets properties that apply to the DCOM system, including whether the DCOM interface is enabled, and basic security settings.
- **Default Security** Allows you to specify users and groups with permission to various aspects of DCOM.
- **Default Protocols** Includes all of the protocols that are supported by DCOM on the local machine. Default protocols include UDP/IP (stateless communication), TCP/IP, IPX, NetBEUI, and NetBIOS tunneled over IPX. Note that changing the protocol is not possible on Windows 98; it enforces the default.

All of the DCOM components installed on the machine are listed in the list box on the default Applications tab. When you select a class from the Applications tab, the Properties button at the bottom of the tab can be clicked. If you click this button, you will see the extensive options that can be set for each object. If you pick an object such as the one listed as

Paintbrush and click the Properties button, you will see a new window displaying all of the properties related to that class.

The Properties window contains the following option tabs:

- **General** Supplies information on the component, including the application name, type, authentication level (only on Windows NT, not 95/98), and local path or remote execution machine (if applicable).
- **Location** Specifies where the application will execute, including setting the location of a remote computer.
- **Security** Sets access, launch, and configuration permissions (access permissions only in Windows 98).
- **Identity** Specifies the account to use when running the application (not available on Windows 98).
- **Endpoints** Sets the protocols and endpoints that can be used by DCOM (not available on Windows 98).

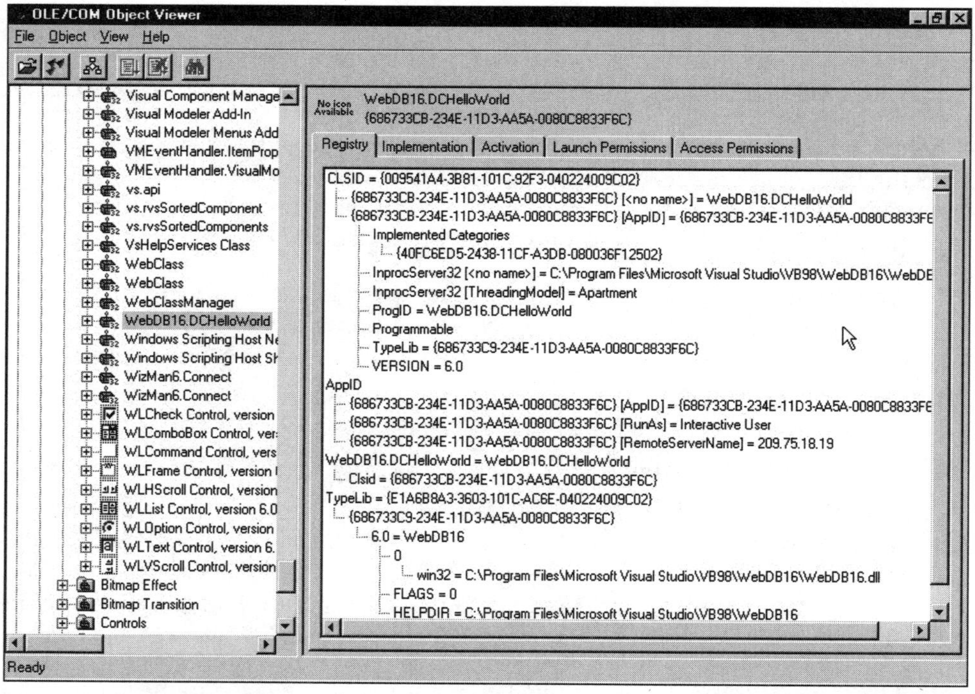

Figure 16-5. The OLE Viewer utility allows you to access all of the settings for a COM object

For most of the client configuration of DCOM, the DCOM Config application will handle the task. It provides a simplified user interface to the various COM settings available for each class. However, most developers will find that the information provided by this utility is too limited for specific settings. For this reason, the OLE Viewer utility is far more powerful for complete COM and DCOM management. The OLE Viewer utility is included in the Visual Tools library of Visual Studio (see Figure 16-5 on the facing page).

From the Implementation tab you can set the DLL to execute on the DLLHost application (see Figure 16-6) by checking the Use Surrogate Process option. The DLLHost will run a shell EXE to hold instances of a DLL that has been remotely instantiated.

In Chapter 17, you will begin using Microsoft Transaction Server, and won't have to rely on the relatively primitive execution capabilities included with DLLHost.

TIP: The OLE Viewer program has a handy feature which ensures that you won't always have to type the long ClassID for an ActiveX component. This comes in handy when you have to insert the ClassID directly into the object reference, such as when you're inserting an ActiveX control with an <OBJECT> tag in your browser script. When you select the component in the list box of the OLE Viewer, you'll see that the Object menu has a Copy CLSID to Clipboard option which makes the long string available for pasting.

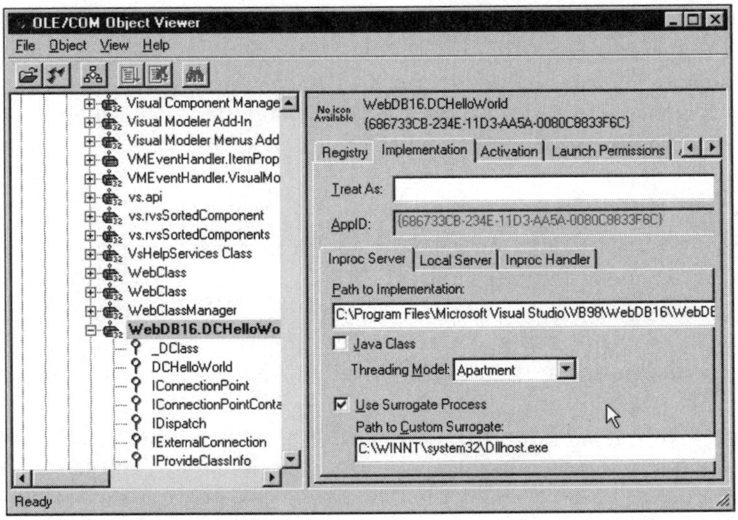

Figure 16-6. Checking the Use Surrogate Process check box allows a custom process to be specified

Configuring the Table Chart Component

In Chapter 14, you created a TableChart ActiveX DLL that returned a chart using HTML tables. Here you will use this component, placed on another machine, to create a basic distributed system. The component is excellent because it can be used to return HTML, and since no ADO configuration is necessary, it provides a simple example. For testing, you will need to have the component installed on both the Web server and a remote machine so that it can communicate with the calling application through the DCOM protocol layer.

The DCOM Config utility allows you to very easily set the component for remote access. By setting the DCOM properties on the client machine and the remote machine that will actually be executing the component, all of the instantiation and object management will be handled by the DCOM system. Chapter 18 demonstrates the use of the Visual Modeler application, which will greatly simplify distributing database-oriented Web applications.

NOTE: The IIS applications that you created in Chapter 15 were actually WebClasses, not strict ActiveX DLL components. Unfortunately, distributing a WebClass object is very difficult and not recommended. It essentially needs direct access to the capabilities of the Web server that will be executing the component. Therefore, for distributed development, it is best to stick to creating pure ActiveX DLL components.

The component will have to be installed and registered on the remote machine. If the remote machine does not have VB 6 installed on it (necessary in order for the single component file to be transferred and registered), use the Application Setup Wizard. The Setup Wizard will create install files with all of the necessary DLLs and runtimes, and it will also register the components with the desired system.

The component can be executed on a Windows 95/98 or Windows NT machine, although NT is recommended for its stability and security.

Setting Up the Remote Server

To activate the system, you must install the component on the remote machine for execution. The main Web server machine will place DCOM calls to this machine to create and access the component, and the DCOM system will run in the background of the Windows system and will respond to remote DCOM requests. When a request is made, the system will establish whether the component is registered on the machine, and if so, instantiate it.

The first task is to install and register the component on the remote machine. There are actually several methods of deploying the component on a remote machine. You can use the installer that's created using the Package and Distribution Wizard, which is included as a VB 6 Add-In, and is available through the Visual Studio Tools menu. This wizard can create a standard EXE installer or a CAB file. If you create a CAB file, the component can be installed over the Internet via a Web page.

A component can also be manually copied and registered on the client system. If the proper VB 6 runtime files and necessary support components are already installed, the OCX file of your DLL may be the only new file needed. You can also copy the component into the System32 directory and use the regsvr32 application to register it.

NOTE: There are several disadvantages to installing the component via a CAB file over the Web. The CAB file, with its automatic download and install feature, requires that the security setting on the browser be set to Low for installation. This means that each client copy of Internet Explorer must be changed for installation and subsequently changed back after the download takes places (to ensure a proper level of security).

The installation of the component actually takes place in the Downloaded Programs folder in the Windows directory. This causes the component to be treated specially (as a registered program) and it cannot even be deleted without a system reboot. Further, upgrades to the control by any method other than Web access becomes problematic. Therefore, before using the Web installation option, weigh the disadvantages against a traditional EXE installation method.

Once the component is installed, you need to configure it to execute when a request is made from a remote machine. For the purposes of this example, the security of DCOM will be turned off to make configuration and access easier. In a real deployment environment, you'll want to make certain the proper settings are in place.

To configure the component, execute the DCOM Config utility on the remote machine, as described previously (see Figure 16-7).

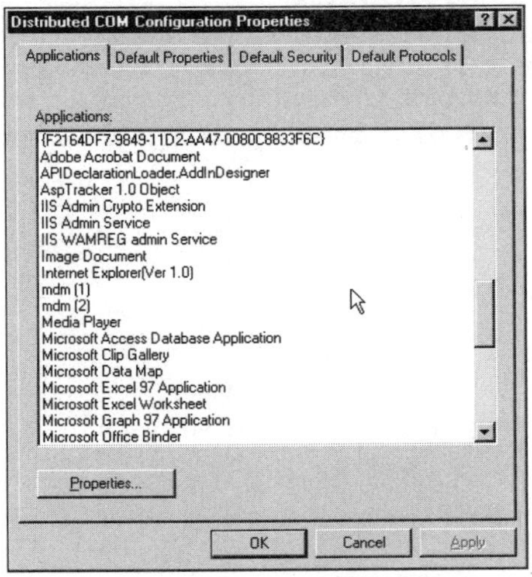

Figure 16-7. Execute the DCOM utility used to configure DCOM settings

Once the Distributed COM Configuration Properties window is opened, select the Default Properties tab. Within this tab are a number of options, including the default settings for DCOM security. In this example, you'll need to essentially disable security. This is the most flexible setting for development testing, but make sure that you never have security removed for your deployment servers. That would enable any remote user to activate any DCOM-capable registered components on your server.

If you are executing the DCOM configuration utility on Windows NT, you may notice the setting for COM Internet Services that are now available for DCOM. These services allow DCOM to communicate over the Internet despite the restrictions of a corporate firewall or stub server. By default, DCOM dynamically selects a communications port anywhere in the range of 1,024–65,535. Since most firewalls restrict the ports that allow access in and out of a network, COM Internet Services establishes a DCOM connection over the HTTP port address, allowing DCOM objects to communicate.

If you are running IIS 4 or above, and you need to construct a DCOM solution in a restricted environment, you can check the box to enable COM Internet Services. See the technical note on the MSDN site (msdn.microsoft.com) regarding other configuration settings of the clients and firewall for Internet deployment of DCOM.

If you will be executing the component on Windows 95/98, you can skip the following section as the security privileges are already set to these values. To deactivate security on an NT server machine that will be executing the component, change the following settings shown in Figure 16-8. Set the Default Authentication Level to None and set the Default Impersonation Level to Anonymous. These options will remove security from the DCOM system so the component can execute most easily.

Click the OK button to accept the security settings. DCOM doesn't require a reboot to activate these settings. With the security configuration completed, you will need to make changes to the component that will be available for remote activation.

NOTE: These settings place the NT Server in an equivalent security mode to Windows 95/98 when it is running DCOM.

The final configuration must be set in the DLLHost application, which will need to execute when the component is requested. To configure the component for execution, follow these steps:

1. Start the OLE Viewer application.
2. Select the component in the Automation list (under Object Classes/Grouped by Component Category/Automation Objects).
3. Under the Implementation tab, check the Use Surrogate Process option.
4. Use the browse button to select the Dllhost.exe application.

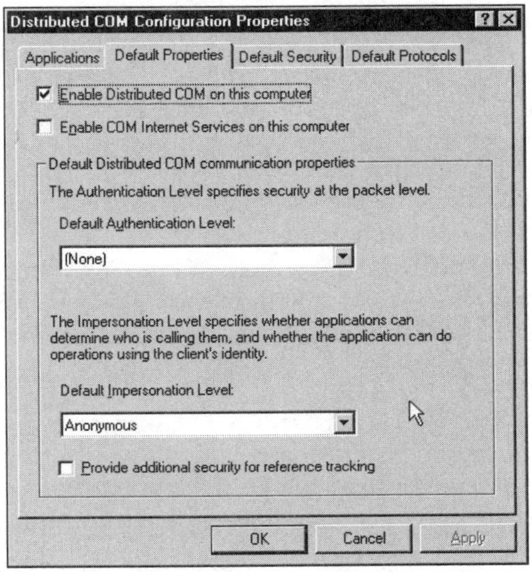

Figure 16-8. Set the security levels on your staging server to low

The DLLHost application is installed in your Windows\System32 directory. Once this item is selected, you can quit the OLE Viewer. Any changes made are automatically recorded.

Setting Up the Client Machine

For this example of using the Table Chart component, the client machine will actually be the ASP Web server that will address the component. It will use DCOM to instantiate and execute the component on the remote machine. Since DCOM is transparent, you don't need to make changes to the ASP code that executes the component.

1. Execute the DCOM Config utility again.
2. Select the component WebDBClass.WebDB from the list on the Applications tab.
3. Click the Properties button. A configuration window will be displayed to allow you to select the DCOM options for this component. You can leave the Authentication Level to Default for now. Since you removed the security from the entire DCOM system in the last section, setting it for the component is not important.

NOTE: Some of the components created in VB 6 that are properly named as classes and projects do not appear with their names in the DCOM Config utility. Instead, they are merely listed by their ClassID. If your component does not appear in the list, use the OLE Viewer (which will properly display the classes and projects by name) and note the ClassID. Then, when you enter the DCOM Config application, you will find your class or project listed numerically in the list box.

1. Select the Location tab. The location tab allows you to specify where the component will execute. You can actually specify more than one option for execution. By default, the Run Application on This Computer option is grayed out. Since the component is installed on the machine, DCOM will use this component to execute if the remote system is unavailable.
2. Check the Run Application on the Following Computer option.
3. Set the field to a WINS address, DNS name, or direct IP number of the server that will be executing the component. The Browse button (in Windows 95) for this field provides the standard NetBIOS browser, but since you will be using TCP/IP for this example, you can ignore the Browse button. DCOM defaults to communication over the TCP/IP protocol, so simply enter the IP address of the remote machine (see Figure 16-9).
4. Click OK to accept the property settings, and the component is now ready to execute.

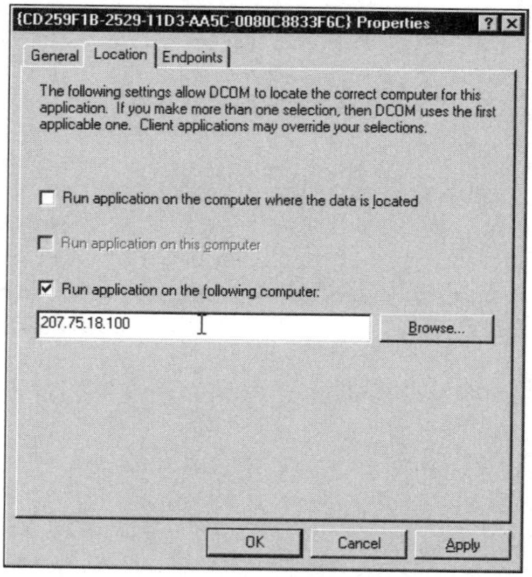

Figure 16-9. Set the IP address or DNS entry that holds the remote component

When an instance of the component is requested, it will automatically instantiate the component on the remote computer.

Executing the Distributed Application

Once all of the layers have been prepared, accessing the Default.asp Web page that you created in Chapter 14 will activate the DCOM connection. This connection will instantiate the component on the remote machine. Once the instance has been created, each method call will be sent to the component on the remote machine. There should be no apparent difference in the execution of this Web page, apart from an initial delay as the objects communicate over the network.

For testing, you can use the OLE Viewer to make sure that an instance can be created on each machine. In the Object menu of the viewer is an option to Create Instance for the selected component. The Create Instance On option allows you to specify a machine name on which to remotely instantiate the object.

Try suspending connections from the remote machine by unchecking the Create Instance On option. Now access the Default.ASP Web page again. See what happens? The component interface returns a component creation error, much as if you had a faulty component on the server machine.

OTHER DISTRIBUTED TECHNOLOGIES

DCOM does not work in isolation—it is part of a larger distributed object system. Additions made to the COM object model, as well as to other object technologies, such as CORBA, will determine the breadth of the applications that you deploy in the future. DCOM is a technology competitive with two other popular object technologies: Enterprise JavaBeans and CORBA.

The specification for Enterprise JavaBeans actually encompasses the functions of not only the basic object model and distributed behavior, but the serving mechanism as well. This makes the specification more like that of all the COM technologies (including DCOM), as well as Microsoft Transaction Server. Current deployment of JavaBeans is fragmented and Sun and IBM, the primary proponents of the standard, are redefining the implementation.

IBM has embraced Enterprise JavaBeans for all of its Java offerings. For non-Java solutions, IBM promotes an industry standard distributed object model known as CORBA.

Common Object Request Broker Architecture (CORBA) is a multi-company (IBM, Sun, and others) standard for distributed objects that is a competitor of DCOM. It provides a standard architecture for object interfaces over a network, as well as on a single machine. CORBA is dominant primarily in the Unix industry, where there had previously been no widely accepted standard available.

CORBA is a standard that is superior to DCOM in some ways and inferior in others. CORBA, unlike DCOM, is very effective at reestablishing a link between a server and a remote object. If the connection is severed, both sides retain a reference ID, and the client may request a reconnect to the process with that ID. If the object hasn't been flushed, a new link will be created, and the processing can continue. CORBA, however, suffers from serious performance and compatibility issues. CORBA implementations, though a multi-vendor standard, have problems interoperating among the various products.

CORBA has become well established on UNIX-based platforms at the same time DCOM became standard on Windows. Increasingly, companies have sought to bridge the two standards via server software to enable a CORBA request to marshal a DCOM object, and vice versa. In fact, Iona Software, one of the leading vendors of CORBA systems, has worked with Microsoft to make its server software interface fluidly with the two types of objects.

Since CORBA is better at some operations (such as inheritance, Java interfacing, reconnection, and so on) than DCOM, these new solutions that integrate both standards have been a blessing for many developers. Information about CORBA can be found at the Object Management Group's Web site (www.omg.org). The multi-company Object Management Group (OMG) manages the CORBA standard.

NOTE: In CORBA documentation, the terms stub and proxy are used in the opposite fashion of those in DCOM. In DCOM, a client proxy is used to connect to a server stub. In CORBA, however, a client stub connects to a server proxy/skeleton. Recognizing this difference in terminology will aid you when reading CORBA documentation.

Keep in mind, though, that DCOM offers organizations the added advantage that the same object technology (COM) built for local system use can be distributed across the enterprise. Most of the alternative object technologies, including CORBA, have execution speed and installation problems when placed on individual desktop machines. These problems are much less common in COM-based components because of the advanced tools already built into the Windows operating system.

Q&A

Q: Can DCOM be used to share objects over a Unix system?

A: Depending on the flavor of Unix that needs to be accessed, yes. If there is not a version of DCOM that can be used on the desired platform, or if the Unix implementation is too limited, you might consider deploying a CORBA server. Most of the CORBA servers, such as the one available from Iona Technologies (www.iona.com), now support bridging capabilities between DCOM and CORBA objects.

Q: Is there any way to restore a connection to an object that has been broken?

A: Currently there is no way to restore a failed connection. In an uncertain environment where the method of connection can be intermittent, it is recommended that you use MSMQ server to allow asynchronous object communication. If asynchronous communication is not appropriate for your solution, but you need to reconnect after a transport failure, consider using a CORBA-based solution. CORBA can reconnect to a remote object and restore an executing session.

SUMMARY

Distributed computing using DCOM is quickly becoming a standard technology in advanced enterprise applications. As the distributed environment becomes easier to deploy, more mid-level and lower-tier solutions will use it as well. For Web database applications, DCOM is useful for proper load balancing solutions. In this chapter we covered:

- **Distributed computing** A solution structure where the program logic is dispersed among one or more servers (usually object servers) across a network.
- **DCOM** Distributed COM is an object technology that allows transparent connection and use of objects across a network. DCOM can be used with appropriately programmed Visual C++ and Visual J++ ActiveX DLLs and all DLLs created in Visual Basic.
- **Life cycle** Each object, once created, remains alive on the server. As long as there is a connection between the client and the remote component, the instance will remain alive.
- **DCOM Config** The utility used to specify where a component is located. This configuration utility also allows the specification of security settings, the protocol to be used by DCOM, and other connection parameters.
- **COM+** The next generation of the Component Object Model (COM) features the integration of MTS, better security, in-memory databases, event publishing, and more.

CHAPTER 17

Deploying a Component to Microsoft Transaction Server

The DCOM technology gives you the power to create a distributed system. However, once you begin creating such a system, you will recognize that component management is a difficult and tedious task. To solve the problem of the difficulty and complexity of creating a distributed system, Microsoft Transaction Server (MTS) was created to manage all types of COM objects. Microsoft has integrated MTS with IIS and many Web database solutions have started using the technology. MTS, however, introduces its own challenges. Creating a distributed system is a new paradigm, so MTS must introduce a number of new concepts and terms that may be confusing to the beginner. Additionally, the Microsoft documentation for MTS is not very hand-holding and few of the examples lead you through the process of creating and deploying components on it.

This chapter will help you get started. It will guide you through the use of MTS for both COM and DCOM-based solutions. After describing the basic operational processes behind MTS, you will be led through creating a Web-based forum solution that can be deployed on the server. In this chapter, the basic API of the forum component will be created and installed as part of MTS. In Chapter 18 you will augment this application to build a distributed solution using the Visual Studio tool, Visual Modeler.

When you are creating components, you should design them to take advantage of the MTS object features, where appropriate. MTS offers scalability, security, transactions, configurable security through the MTS roles, connection pooling, thread support, component state management, process isolation for packages, and integration with mainframe transactions through CICS. Recognizing some of the available features for MTS can help you optimize your component for deployment on the server.

CAUTION: In Chapter 16, you turned off the security for DCOM to simplify testing. With security disabled, MTS will not execute—the error #800706BE will be returned. Return the Default Authentication Level to Connect and the Default Impersonation Level to Identity. Note that these changes won't take effect until the machine is rebooted.

MTS can be used to simply manage components on an NT-based machine. However, most of the real power of MTS is utilized when a distributed solution is created with DCOM. When DCOM is used to allow objects to communicate over a network, it rarely looks like the component that you used in Chapter 16. It is rare to just have two objects communicate, except in specialized applications, such as two-person chat software. More often, many clients will be addressing many instances of an object. In a Web-based solution, those clients will be accessing the Web server, which in turn will address one of the object instances.

WHAT IS MTS?

To develop an effective distributed system, you need a server that can hold many objects, can allocate resources, and can specify security on a component basis. Without the centralizing influence of MTS, objects would be haphazardly located on machines around the network—MTS provides a way to consolidate component and transaction management.

To give you an idea of the problems MTS solves, try to imagine the answers to these questions:

- What components are on each machine that can handle transactions?
- How can access for a specific group of users be limited to a set of components?
- What transactions are currently open and executing?
- How can I make a component that has transactions that link with transactions from another object technology?

MTS allows any COM objects that do not include a user interface (such as ActiveX DLLs) to be placed on a central distributed server for access and execution by client applications. Any component registered for use on the server machine that is running MTS can be managed by it.

Microsoft Transaction Server provides:

- **Resource pooling** Component resources including instances, transactions, database access, disk resources, and others can be managed from MTS.
- **Concurrency** Provides isolation for the simultaneous access of components by interweaving the execution of multiple operations. This allows components to be deployed without worrying about transaction collisions since MTS handles the process.
- **Security** MTS offers six levels of security that can be defined for user, group, and component access.
- **Context management** MTS supports process isolation to allow for the server to keep track of the identity and state of each user-addressable component.

MTS fully supports transactions generated through the ADO, DAO, RDO, and ODBC database access methods. Even the ADC object model for client processes can address MTS transactions, because ADC uses ADO for its actual database access.

For Web database access, you already know how powerful encapsulating primary operations within the controls can be. If there is ever a need to completely change the back-end format of the data source, or the data source itself, the exposed interface offered by your component can remain the same.

MTS can be used to manage in-process or out-of-process components, as well as local or remote components. Normal components used on MTS must be created as in-process DLLs. Out-of-process components are specially executed with an MTS *server process*. This process will appear in the Process tab of the Task Manager (which may be accessed from the Ctrl-Alt-Del menu window) as an executable named `mtx.exe`.

DEFINITION: **Server process** An execution space used specifically to run components. As with an application execution space, if a component faults, only the other components within that execution space are affected. MTS and the calling application remain intact.

A server process can be used to execute one or more components in this memory space and can provide instances of each component to potentially thousands of calling applications. Multiple server processes can execute on a single machine, and they will remain isolated from one another.

In order to execute on an MTS server, a component must comply with more specific implementation criteria than a common COM object. The component must be an ActiveX DLL (not an ActiveX EXE, such as Excel), and it must be built to certain specifications (such as class factory requirements, standard marshalling interfaces, and so on). Fortunately, all ActiveX DLLs compiled with Visual Basic conform to this standard, so any DLL created in the VB environment can be used with MTS.

To ease deployment for a number of components that work together in a solution, MTS has created a structure called a *package*. A package contains one or more components that can be treated as a unit by MTS. Defining a package allows you to set security and execution controls for all of the components within the package at once.

All of the components available to the MTS system for inclusion in a package are stored within the MTS *catalog*. To use a component, it must first be added to the catalog that tracks all of the MTS-specific properties of the component.

DEFINITION: **Catalog** A catalog is used to list all of the components available on an MTS server. The catalog listing describes to the server all of the MTS-specific properties.

MTS OVERVIEW

Configuring and using MTS is actually fairly simple in comparison to the setup process of other servers. Since most of the activity actually takes place in the execution of the COM/DCOM objects, the framework that the server places around these objects is minimal and primarily aids the system administrator in managing the objects.

You can use MTS to serve component requests that are issued from the MTS machine itself or that are called from remote machines through the DCOM architecture. In a Web solution, ASP script code can access the MTS components located on the Web server or located on a remote MTS machine. The location of the object will be transparent to the script code, as are DCOM components. Figure 17-1 shows a simplified diagram of a common Web server use of MTS where the MTS Executive is the server process that actually executes the components.

N-Tier Structure and Design

Multiple-tier applications are applications where the executing logic is spread across multiple servers. A simple two-tier application only has a client and a server (for example, a Web browser and a Web server). Most Web applications are at least three-tier solutions, with a Web browser, a Web server, and a database server (see Figure 17-2).

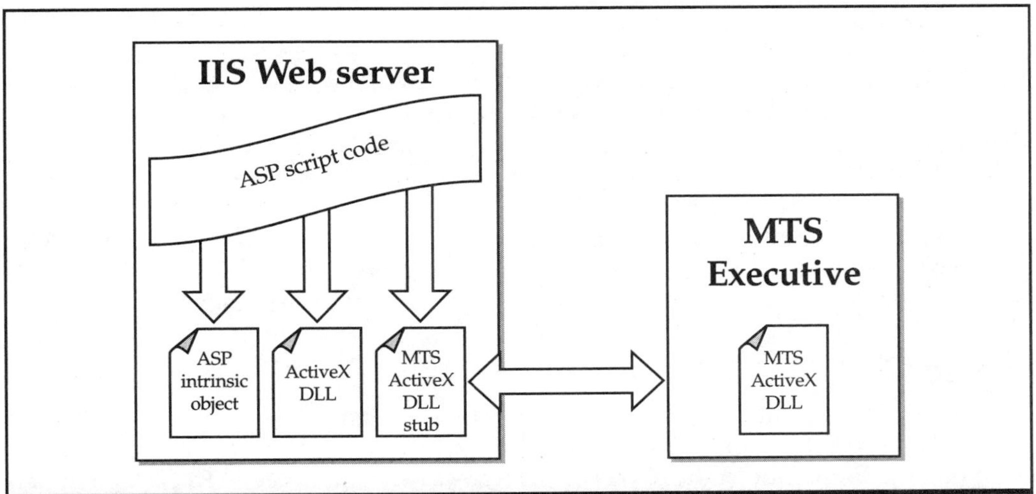

Figure 17-1. Structural overview of an MTS-based Web solution

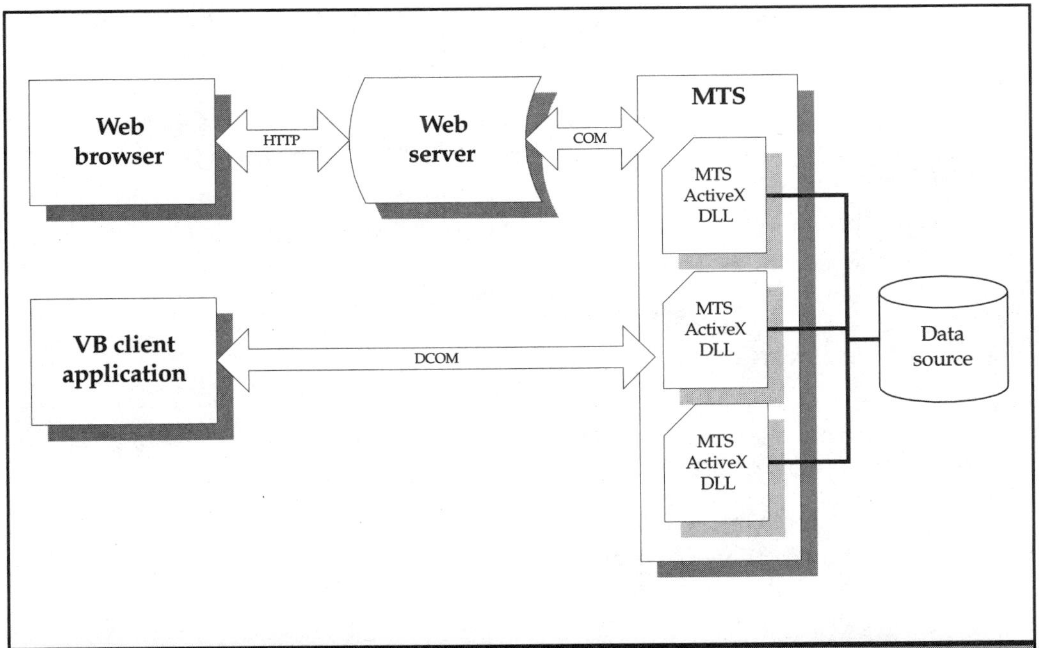

Figure 17-2. A typical Web application has three tiers: a Web browser, a Web server, and a database server

With MTS, applications can extend beyond three tiers. The terms *multiple tier* or *n-tier* are typically used to refer to an object-based system that uses objects that sit between the data sources and the client logic. Before Web solutions existed, two-tier deployment was standard for a client/server system, while three-tier implementations used the object layer to add an extra level of bridge logic. Web solutions, however, make a four-tier system a common implementation when a solution uses each of the four layers: Web server, components, database, and clients.

These multi-tier forms of distributed computing are made possible by the DCOM technology, which is used for interobject communication. When DCOM is used in conjunction with MTS, a completely managed distributed system is possible.

Setting Up MTS

MTS is installed through the NT Option pack, like IIS itself. To use MTS after it is installed, you should set up a custom user account that you can use to manage access to components. There should already be an MTS group account called MTS Trusted Impersonators. You merely need to add a custom user to this group for component use.

If you installed Windows NT 4 Option Pack, the default components of MTS were installed, but some of the key developer tools were not. You will need to rerun the installer to add these tools. To set up MTS for development, follow these steps:

1. Run the Option Pack Setup, which is a selection on the Start menu in the Option Pack folder. From the setup you will be able to make the developer headers, libraries, and samples available for your distributed project development.
2. When you reach the step in the install wizard to select the items for installation, open the Transaction Server item and check the Transaction Server Development option.
3. Click the OK button to accept the Transaction Server options.
4. While you have the Option Pack installer running, check the Microsoft Message Queue (MSMQ) option to install it. This will add the Message Queue server to your system in case you want to allow for asynchronous object execution on an application.

NOTE: You must have SQL Server installed on the system prior to installing MSMQ. MSMQ uses SQL Server for a primary information store.

After you have the MTS server installed, you need to change some of the security settings on the system to allow the prevention of unauthorized access to the server. When MTS is first installed, the System package is not set to have any administrators, so the administrator security is disabled. Without administrative security, any user is allowed to configure MTS. You need to set the identity of the System package before you install any new packages to make the system secure.

In MTS, security is based on *roles*, which define the types of operations a user will be allowed to perform. There are two default roles that can be granted for accessing MTS:

- **Administrator** Users with this role can read, modify, install, delete, or create any objects on MTS.
- **Reader** Users with this role can only view objects stored on MTS.

The administrator can create new roles that have other privileges. For example, the administrator might create a Developer role whose users can modify or execute packages, but not create or delete a complete package.

Obviously, the first task will be to limit the administrative privileges to a specific authorized group of users. This will require you to create a new user and group in NT Security.

1. Execute the User Manager for Domains application from your Administrative Tools menu in Windows NT.
2. Add a group called MTSAdministrators using the User | New Local Group menu option.
3. Add a user called MTSAdmin using the User | New User menu option.
4. In the Properties of the MTSAdmin user, set the Groups of this user to MTSAdministrators.
5. Set the identity of the System package to MTSAdmin.
6. Reboot the system.

The MTS system is now configured for use. Components that you create in Visual Basic, Visual C++, or Visual J++ are not automatically used by MTS. However, Web solutions registered as applications are added for management by MTS.

USING MTS

The Microsoft Management Console (MMC) is used to manage MTS for configuring users and security, creating new packages, and adding controls. All of the configuration of MTS occurs through MMC. You are already familiar with MMC, as you've used it to change the settings of IIS for Web applications.

Once the server properties have been set, new packages can be created to hold the various components that will make up the complete solution. Since the MMC supports both the IIS and MTS administration, you can conveniently configure most of a distributed application from within it.

In order to use a component on MTS, it must be placed within a package. Each package can contain one or more components that are grouped to provide security capabilities. The package should contain related components since you may, in the future, want to export the package for distribution

TIP: When you define a package, make sure that all of the objects within the package are functionally consistent. This process is much like the evaluation of which fields belong in which database tables. Since security is governed primarily by package access, placing sensitive components with general components is not a good idea. Attempt to define what components are used together based on their roles in the final application.

Creating a New Package

You can either create a package from scratch or, if you've built a package previously, you can simply add this package to MTS. Any package defined in MTS can be saved to a package (.pak) file that can be loaded into another MTS server. All components in a package will execute within the same server process.

You will have to set a package identity and a role for each package you create. The default package identity is Interactive User. An Interactive User is a person or process that is logged on to the server that is running the component. In this case, your IIS Web server would be an Interactive User, since it will be located on the same machine as the component.

Once the package is created, you can use the Component Wizard to add ActiveX DLLs to the new package.

Examining the Microsoft Distributed Transaction Coordinator

You may have noticed the Microsoft Distributed Transaction Coordinator (MS DTC) that has appeared in the Windows Control Panel since Windows NT was first released. MS DTC is a system service that manages a transaction across multiple resources. MS DTC uses a two-phase commit that provides a protocol to ensure a transaction either completely succeeds or isn't executed, even across multiple machines.

MTS can start and stop the MS DTC service from the MMC. Under the Action menu, the Start MS DTC and Stop MS DTC options allow you to change the state of the service.

If you double-click the MS DTC icon in the Control Panel folder, you will see a configuration dialog box like the one shown in Figure 17-3. This dialog box allows you to set the central server that will manage the distributed transactions. It also provides a means of configuring the protocol that will be used to communicate between the systems handling a transaction.

CAUTION: If the MS DTC protocol is set to use NetBEUI (Named Pipes), and more than 40 connections are attempted from a Windows 95/98 machine, the transaction controller will freeze. At the time of this writing, there is no fix for this problem, but changing the protocol to IPX or TCP/IP will work around it.

Creating a MS DTC Account

If you run a transaction across multiple computers using DCOM, make sure that the machines have the proper user accounts needed to communicate. All of the transactions occur through MS DTC, including those activated through MTS components.

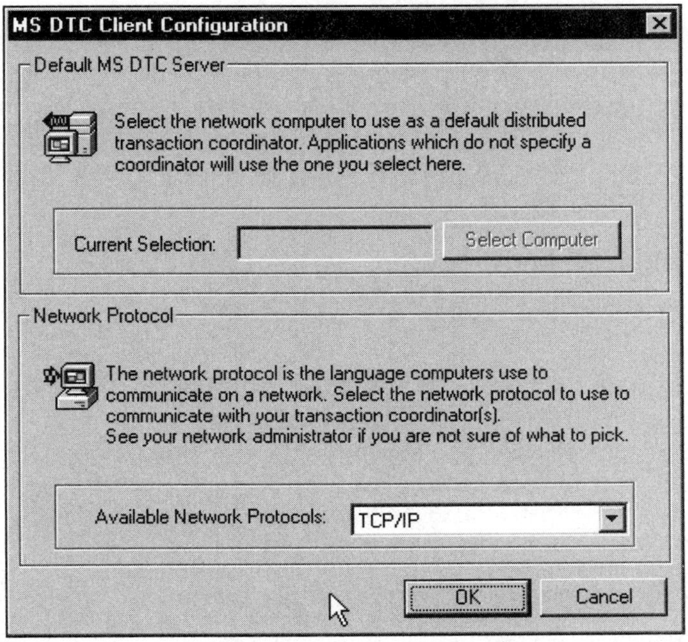

Figure 17-3. MS DTC allows you to set the server and protocol for distributed transactions

To allow communication between computers, the Guest account on each computer must be active, but for security reasons it is best to remove or disable the Guest account. To still allow transactions to occur when the Guest account is inactive, you will need to create a specific account on each machine that can be used for communication.

Execute the User Manager for Domains applications under the Administrative Tools menu of the Start menu to create the new user accounts. Once the accounts are created, you will need to alter MS DTC to make it use the newly created users. From the User Manager, the user must be added to the MTS Impersonators group on the client and the MTS Trusted Impersonators group on the server.

NOTE: When changes are made to a configuration that affect MTS components, it is best to reboot the system. However, you can flush all of the component information held in MTS from MMC by opening the MTS snap-in at the MMC, and right-click the My Computer icon. The Shut Down Server Processes option will reset the state of the components running on MTS.

Creating a Forum Prototype DLL

Making a component that provides all of the key functions of the eventual Forum object is probably the best place to begin for MTS incorporation. Once the component has been generated, you can register it in an MTS package. You will create a component that allows users to read and post messages to a Web-based forum. To create this solution, you will need to create a new database, an ActiveX DLL component in Visual Basic, and a few ASP pages to activate the component.

Connecting the Forum Component to the Data Source

You will need a new database device to store the message data for the forum. Execute the SQL Enterprise Manager in order to construct the device to hold the database information (database and log).

Allocate 8MB for the database and 2MB for the log file. Since this is a sample, it will be unlikely that you will use that much space for the posts.

With the data source created, you can begin coding the component that will be used to read and add information to the source. The new Forum component needs to access the data source to send the information to the browser. Therefore, create an ODBC data source called connForum that connects to the database you just allocated.

Creating the Forum Table

You'll first use the Database Designer to create a table which will be stored in a database named Forum. Open Database Designer through the connForum data source and create the primary table with the fields shown in Table 17-1.

Create this table in the Forum database. You might consider entering some sample topic categories that have a ParentID of 0. That way, when you first load the solution, you will see some existing topics.

Name	Data Type	Length	Precision	Scale	Nulls?	Default Value	Identity?
uniqueid	long	8	0	0	No		Yes
title	varChar	50	0	0	Yes		No
messagecreated	datetime	8	0	0	Yes		No
body	text	-	0	0	Yes		No
ParentID	long	8	0	0	Yes		No
messagefrom	varChar	40	0	0	Yes		No

Table 17-1. The ForumTable Table Field Definitions

Create the Control Project

With the data source ready for access, you will need to build the component that will be used for the forum. Follow these steps to create the component:

1. Start Visual Basic 6.
2. Create a new ActiveX DLL project in VB.
3. In the Project window, set the project name to ForumCtl.
4. Set the name of the class file to clsForum.
5. Under the `MTSTransactionMode` property, set the value to 3 - UsesTransaction (see Figure 17-4).
6. In the References dialog box, check the Microsoft ActiveX Data Objects Library.

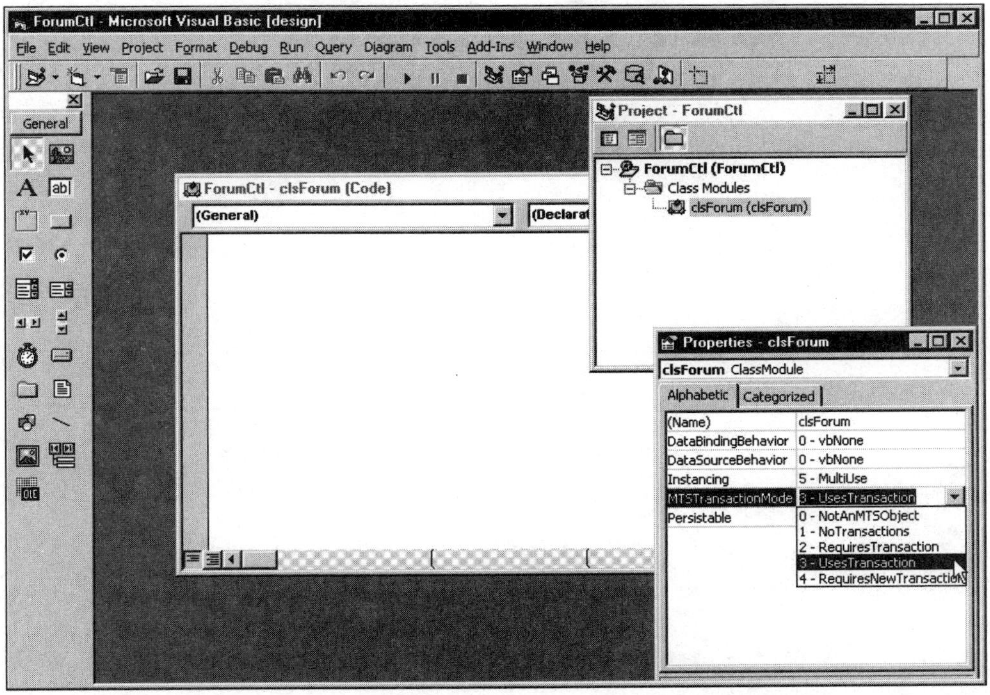

Figure 17-4. Set the MTSTransactionMode so some of the methods can activate transactions

7. Enter the code shown in the following listing. MTS expects certain functions to be present even if they are not used, so we must enter stubs for these.

```
Dim myConn As Connection
Dim myRS As Recordset, myRS2 As Recordset

Public Function PostMessage(parentID As Long, postName As String, _
      subject As String, body As String) As Long
    Dim r$

    Set myRS = CreateObject("ADODB.recordset")
    myRS.CursorType = 3
    myRS.CursorLocation = 2 ' Server-side
    myRS.LockType = 3 ' Optimistic locking
    Set myRS.ActiveConnection = myConn

    ' Select the general table for insertion
    strQuery = "Select * from forumTable"
    ' Open the recordset
    myRS.Open strQuery
    ' Add a new record
    myRS.AddNew
    ' Set the values to the arguments passed
    myRS.Fields("title").Value = subject
    myRS.Fields("body").Value = body
    myRS.Fields("messagefrom").Value = postName
    myRS.Fields("messagecreated").Value = Now
    myRS.Fields("parentid").Value = parentID
    ' Write the information into the database
    myRS.Update

End Function


Public Function DisplayThread(parentID As Long, _
      messageLink As String, replyLink As String) As String
    Dim r$

    Set myRS = CreateObject("ADODB.recordset")
    myRS.CursorType = 3
    myRS.CursorLocation = 3

    Set myRS.ActiveConnection = myConn
    strQuery = "Select * from forumTable where parentID = " & parentID
    myRS.Open strQuery
    ' Create header
    r$ = "<H2>Messages</H2>"
    r$ = r$ + "<HR>"
    r$ = r$ + "<CENTER><H2><A HREF=" & Chr(34) & replyLink & _
      parentID & Chr(34) & ">Post new message</A></H2></CENTER>"
    ' Cycle through top level of messages
```

```
    Do Until myRS.EOF
        currentRecord = myRS("uniqueid")
        r$ = r$ + "<HR>"
        mystr = "title=" & myRS("Title")
        titleStr = "<B><I><FONT Size=+2>" & myRS("Title")
        titleStr = titleStr & "</FONT></I></B><BR>"
        r$ = r$ + titleStr
        r$ = r$ + "Message from: <B>" & myRS("messagefrom") & "</B><BR>"
        r$ = r$ + "<FONT Size=-2>Date posted: " & _
            myRS("messagecreated") & "</FONT><P>"
        r$ = r$ + "<FONT Size=+1>" & myRS("body") & "</FONT><P>"
        Set myRS2 = Nothing
        Set myRS2 = CreateObject("ADODB.recordset")
        Set myRS2.ActiveConnection = myConn
        strQuery = "Select * from forumTable where parentID = " & _
            myRS("uniqueid")
        myRS2.Open strQuery
        ' Display all replies to current message
        Do Until myRS2.EOF
            r$ = r$ + "<blockquote>"
            r$ = r$ + "<B><I><FONT color=#0000FF>" & myRS2("Title") _
              & "</FONT></I></B><BR>"
            r$ = r$ + "Message from: <B>" & myRS2("messagefrom") & _
              "</B><BR>"
            r$ = r$ + "<FONT Size=-2>Date posted: " & _
              myRS2("messagecreated") & "</FONT><BR>"
            r$ = r$ + "<FONT Size=+1>" & myRS2("body") & "</FONT><P>"
            r$ = r$ + "</blockquote>"
            messagecount = messagecount + 1
            myRS2.MoveNext
        Loop
    r$ = r$ + "<FONT Size=+1><A HREF=" & _
       Chr(34) & replyLink & myRS("uniqueid") & _
       "&" & mystr & Chr(34) & _
       "> [Reply to message]</A></FONT><P>"
    messagecount = messagecount + 1
    myRS.MoveNext
Loop
    r$ = r$ + "<HR>"
    r$ = r$ + "<CENTER><H2><A HREF=" & Chr(34) & replyLink & _
        parentID & Chr(34) & ">Post new message</A></H2></CENTER>"
    r$ = r$ + "<HR>"
    r$ = r$ + "Total messages: " & messagecount
    DisplayThread = r$
End Function


Public Function AdminReport() As String
    Dim r$
```

```
    r$ = "<H1>Admin Report</H1>"
    r$ = r$ + "Figures will appear here"
    AdminReport = r$
End Function

Private Sub Class_Initialize()
    connectStr = "{SQL Server};server=myServer;database=forum;" & _
      "dsn=connForum"
    Set myConn = CreateObject("adodb.connection")
    myConn.Open connectStr
End Sub


Private Sub Class_Terminate()
    Set myRS = Nothing
    Set myConn = Nothing
End Sub

Public Function DisplayTopTitles(parentID As Long, _
   messageLink As String, replyLink As String) As String
    Dim r$

    Set myRS = CreateObject("ADODB.recordset")
    myRS.CursorType = 3
    myRS.CursorLocation = 3
    'myRS.LockType = 3
    Set myRS.ActiveConnection = myConn
    strQuery = "Select * from forumTable where parentID = " & _
         parentID
    myRS.Open strQuery

    r$ = "<H2>Topic categories</H2>"
    messagecount = 0
    Do Until myRS.EOF
        currentRecord = myRS("uniqueid")
        myHREF = "<A HREF=" & Chr(34) & messageLink & _
            myRS("uniqueid") & Chr(34) & ">"
        r$ = r$ & myHREF & myRS("Title") & "</A><P>"
        messagecount = messagecount + 1
        myRS.MoveNext
    Loop
    r$ = r$ & "<HR>"
    r$ = r$ & "<CENTER><H2><A HREF=" & Chr(34) & replyLink & _
         parentID & Chr(34) & ">Create new topic</A></H2></CENTER>"
    r$ = r$ & "<HR>"
    r$ = r$ & "Total topics: " & messagecount
    DisplayTopTitles = r$
    Set myRS = Nothing
End Function
```

With all of the proper functions enabled, you will need to change some of the default settings of the project so that it can be used effectively by MTS. The most important change is the Unattended Execution option that allows the component to be used not only on the object server, but over DCOM, as well.

Follow these steps to change the settings:

1. Open the Project Properties window.
2. On the General tab, check the Unattended Execution checkbox.
3. On the Compile tab, set the DLL Base Address to `&H11B00000`.
4. Click OK to accept these project settings.
5. Save the project.
6. Under the File menu, select Make ForumCtl.dll.

When the DLL is created, it will automatically be registered with the system. Note that although the automatic registration process is useful, MTS can also install and register components that are not currently registered by the current system. Therefore, if you place the component on another system, adding it to MTS can provide the system registration to use the component.

Installing a DLL in MTS

You will need to create a new package to hold your component. This package can be given security capabilities to govern how the component will be used. In this example, you can leave the security at the default settings.

NOTE: MTS Explorer used to be a separate application. Now it has been adapted to be a snap-in in the MMC. The snap-in contains all of the features initially available in the stand-alone executable version.

To add the forum control to the MTS system, follow these steps:

1. Launch MTS Explorer.
2. Expand the My Computer item, and select and right-click the Packages Installed item. This folder will show all of the packages currently available to MTS. You will need to add a new package to hold the forum control.
3. Select New | Package | Create an Empty Package from the context menu.
4. Set the name of the package to pkgForum, and click the Next button.
5. Set the user information to MTSComponent, and enter the proper password.
6. Click Finish and a new package will be added to the MTS server. Once the package has been created, you need to place the component into it.

7. Double-click the pkgForum item. You should see two items, Components and Roles. Since you have not added to the component nor set up security preferences yet, both of these items will be empty.
8. Right-click the Components folder and select the New | Component option. The wizard window will allow you to select preinstalled components or to install them from a file.
9. Click the Import Components That Are Already Registered button.

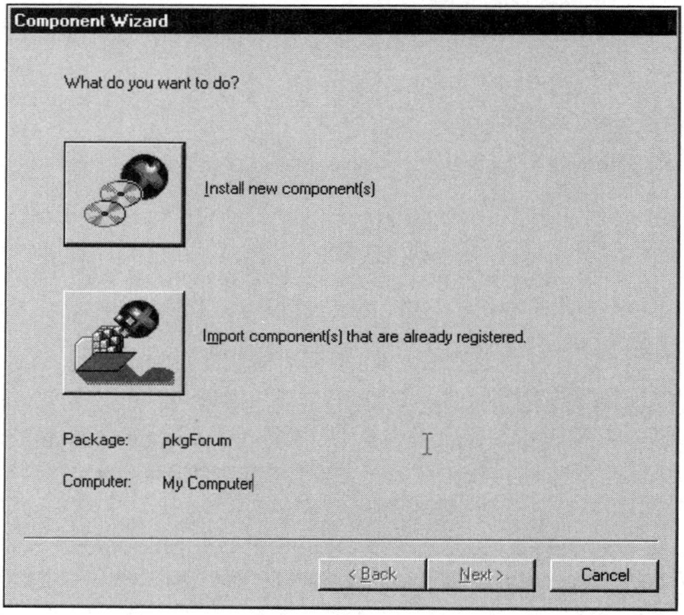

The MTS Explorer will build a list of in-process components that are currently registered on the machine. This list may take a few moments to generate, because the computer must determine whether the registered component can be used by MTS. Once the list is complete, select the Forum component from the list (see Figure 17-5) and click Finish.

The MTS wizard will retrieve the information on the ActiveX DLL and store it in the MTS directory. If you expand the Components folder of the pkgForum item, you will now see the Forum component listed (see Figure 17-6).

Running the Forum

Now that the component is ready for execution on MTS, you need to create some ASP files to instantiate the component and accessing the necessary methods. You will need to use an HTML editor such as Visual InterDev or Notepad to create three files: a message display page, a posting form page, and a page that stores the posted information. For these files, you will need to create a Forum folder application in IIS where the files will be placed.

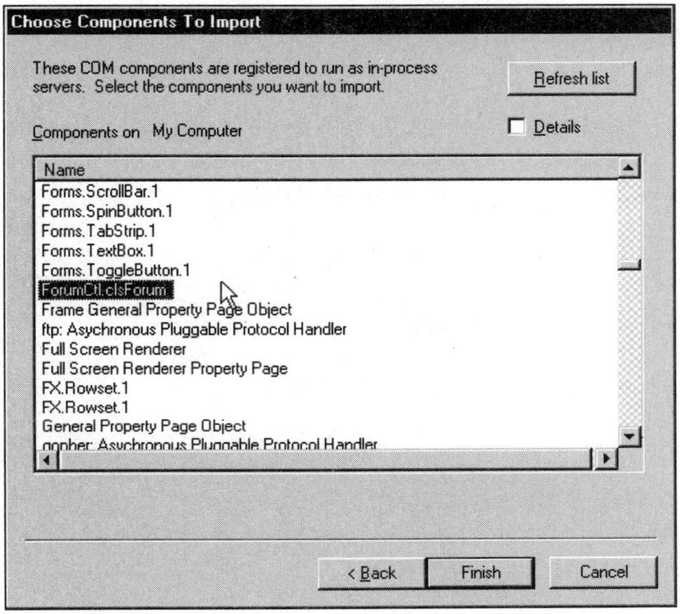

Figure 17-5. The ForumCtl component is displayed in the list of available components

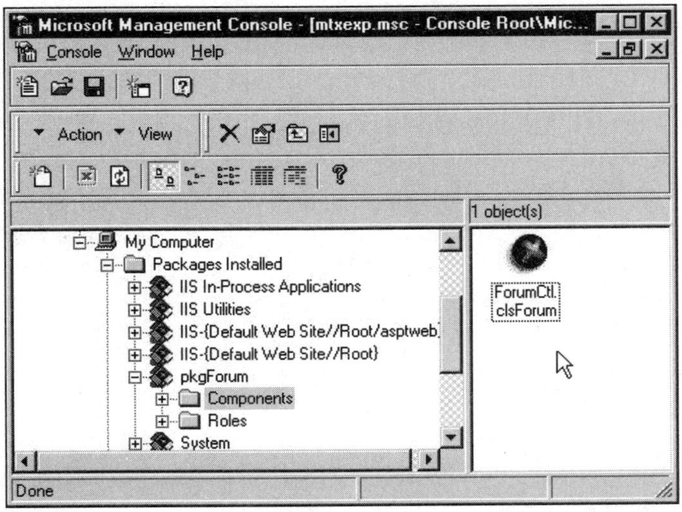

Figure 17-6. Your new component can be accessed in the pkgForum package

To begin, enter the following code and save it as the Default.asp file in the Forum application folder.

```
<HTML>
<HEAD>
<% @ LANGUAGE="VBSCRIPT" %>
<%
   Set myForum = Server.CreateObject("ForumCtl.clsForum")
   'Session("myForum") = myForum
   If request.QueryString("parentID") <> "" Then
      parentID = request.QueryString("parentID")
      Session("parentID") = parentID
   else
      Session("parentID") = 0
      parentID = 0
   End If
%>
</HEAD>
<BODY>
<blockquote>
<H1>Forum</H1><P>
<%
if parentID = 0 then
   response.write(myForum.DisplayTopTitles(0, _
        "default.asp?parentID=", "post.asp?replyID="))
else
   response.write(myForum.DisplayThread(CLng(parentID), _
        "default.asp?parentID=", "post.asp?replyID="))
end if
%>
</blockquote>
</BODY>
</HTML>
```

Enter the following code and save it as the file Post.asp in the Forum application folder. You might notice that there is only a small piece of ASP code in this page. Since the form will submit all of the information for saving to the page named Post2.asp, only the title and reply ID that are received for posting need to be processed.

```
<HTML>
<HEAD>
<% @ LANGUAGE="VBSCRIPT" %>
<%
   if request.QueryString("replyID") <> "" then
      Session("replyID") = request.QueryString("replyID")
```

```
      if request.QueryString("title") <> "" then
         Session("messageTitle") = "Re:" & request.QueryString("title")
      else
         Session("messageTitle") = ""
      end if
   else
      Session("messageTitle") = ""
   end if
%>
</HEAD>
<BODY>
<H1>Post to Forum</H1><P>
<form method="POST" action="post2.asp" name="frmContent">
  <p>Title: <input type="text" name="txtTitle" size="60" value="
<%=Session("messageTitle")%>"></p>
  <p>Date: <%=Now%></p>
  <p>Message from: <input type="text" name="txtFrom" size="20"></p>
  <p>Message:</p>
  <p><textarea rows="4" name="txtMessage" cols="60"></textarea></p>
  <p><input type="submit" value="Submit" name="cmdSubmit"><input
   type="reset" value="Reset"
  name="B2"></p>
</form>
</BODY>
</HTML>
```

Enter the following code and save it as the file Post2.asp in the Forum application folder. This page will call the component to write a new message into the data store.

```
<HTML>
<HEAD>
<% @ LANGUAGE="VBSCRIPT" %>
<%
   Set myForum = Server.CreateObject("ForumCtl.clsForum")
       myForum.PostMessage CLng(Session("replyID")), "" & _
       request.Form("txtFrom"),"" & request.Form("txtTitle"), "" & _
       request.Form("txtMessage")
%>
</HEAD>
<BODY>
<H1>Post to Forum</H1><P>
Your message was posted:<BR>
<%
   response.write request.Form("txtTitle")  & "<BR>"
   response.write Now & "<BR>"
```

```
   response.write request.Form("txtFrom")  & "<BR>"
   response.write request.Form("txtMessage") & "<BR>"
   valueStr = "('" & request.Form("txtTitle") & "','" & _
     request.Form("txtMessage") & "','" & request.Form("txtFrom") & _
      "',#" & Now & "#," & Session("replyID") & ")"
response.write("<HR>")
response.write("<A HREF=" & chr(34) & "default.asp" & chr(34) _
   & ">Return to forum</A><P>")
'response.write("Total messages: " & messagecount)
%>
</BODY>
</HTML>
```

Once you have all three of these pages complete, execute the application by typing the following path into your browser:

```
http://localhost/Forum
```

To start, there will be no topics or messages. Try posting a few to get the forum started. Now that the component is being used, you can examine how it is actually executing under MTS through the MTS portions of MMC.

Monitoring MTS

You can use MTS to watch the live activity of the components and packages that it manages. In MMC, where all MTS management takes place, select the Components folder in the left pane so that the Forum component is displayed in the right pane. The default view of the right pane is set at the Large Icon view by default. There are four other views. The Small Icon view and the List view mimic their equivalents in Windows Explorer. The other two views are Property view and Status view. These views are available from the View menu on the MMC toolbar.

> ***NOTE:*** There is an excellent program called MTS Spy that allows live monitoring of all MTS components on the server. See the "MTS Spy" section later in this chapter for information on compiling and using the program.

The Property view allows you to examine all of the static attributes of the components and packages, such as the unique ID of each component, the transaction setting, the location of the actual execution DLL, the threading model, and the security settings.

To use the Property view for the components, select that view option from the View menu in the toolbar. The right pane lists the available components, as well as their transaction support and the location of the actual DLL. This view provides a convenient way of quickly determining the capabilities and location of installed components.

The Status view displays the status of packages, components, and execution computers. It will also allow you to see whether the DTC has been started. The Status View can be used to quickly see what computers are active and which packages are executing on them.

From the View menu in the toolbar, select the Status view. The Status view displays a number of essential columns of information. The Objects column shows the number of object contexts that are created for the class, and the Activated column displays how many instances of the object are executing on MTS at the present time. The In Call column shows when the execution is currently in the process of a call. The Status View does not show the status of Utilities or System packages.

Now it's time to instantiate the forum component so you can examine it executing in the Status view. You will be able to monitor it from within MTS Explorer. You can create an instance of the component in the Immediate window of the VB programming environment. Follow these steps to create the object:

1. Load Visual Basic 6.
2. Display the Immediate window either by selecting it in the View menu or by pressing CTRL-G.
3. In the Immediate window, type the following code, and then look at the Status view of MTS (see Figure 17-7).

```
Set myObj = CreateObject("ForumCtl.clsForum")
Set myObj2 = CreateObject("ForumCtl.clsForum")
```

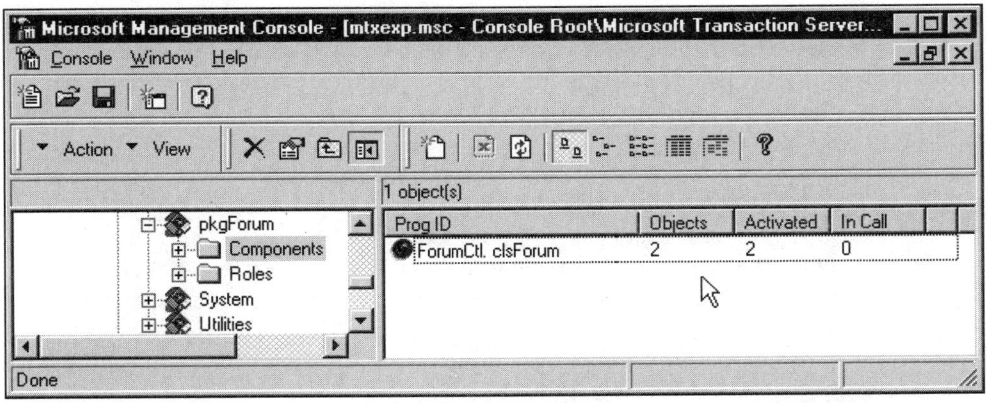

Figure 17-7. The Status view of the component shows that two instances are active

4. Now clear the second instance by entering the following code into the Immediate window. When you return to MTS Explorer, you will see that only a single object is active.

```
Set myObj2 = Nothing
```

The Sample Bank Application

In addition to installing your own components as packages in MTS, you can examine the predefined example that is included with MTS. It is a banking application, called Sample Bank, which demonstrates simulated banking functions, such as credits, debits, and transfers between accounts.

Because the component of the Sample Bank application is built using Visual C++, it also provides a demonstration of cross-language development. Remember that one of the advantages of COM objects is their language independence, which allows a component created in any language to be used by any other language. By installing it on your system, you can actually access the components that are included with the sample solutions or create some of your own test applications.

NOTE: The Sample Bank application is not installed by default. If you haven't installed the Transaction Server Developer yet, go back to the "Installing MTS" section earlier in this chapter for instructions.

MTS DETAILS

You now know the basics of creating a component and registering it with MTS. If the capabilities ended there, MTS would not be as useful as it is. MTS has a number of features that facilitate the creation of custom components specifically adapted for use on MTS. These include the ability to manage the login context for users and to configure resource dispensers.

Examining Context

Each object is contained within an MTS context. A *context* determines what type of user is accessing the object and whether the operation with the component is inside a transaction or not. There are four possible transaction settings for a context: requires a transaction, requires a new transaction, supports transactions, or does not support transactions. The setting of the context will determine how the component will be created in relation to a current transaction.

To examine the context from within one of your components, you need to instantiate the MTXAS object. For example, the following code will create the Context object:

```
Set myMTX = CreateObject("MTXAS.AppServer.1")
Set myContext = myMTX.GetObjectContext()
```

From the Context object, you can also execute a manual commit (SetComplete method) or rollback (SetAbort method) for the transaction from within the component. A Context state is inherited—an object called by a package will inherit the state of its caller. When the object is released, so is the object context.

The following properties and methods are available for every Context object.

- **`Count`** `property` Provides the number of Context items available
- **`CreateInstance`** `method` Instantiates another MTS object
- **`DisableCommit`** `method` Indicates that the transaction is an incomplete state and a commit should not be attempted
- **`EnableCommit`** `method` Indicates that the transaction is progressing properly
- **`IsCallerInRole`** `method` Indicates what MTS role is being used for the direct call to the component.
- **`IsInTransaction`** `method` Indicates that a transaction is in process
- **`IsSecurityEnabled`** `method` Returns a flag used to determine whether MTS security is turned on or off.
- **`Item`** `property` Provides a reference to the Context object
- **`Security`** `property` Provides a reference to the SecurityProperty object
- **`SetAbort`** `method` Indicates to MTS that an error occurred and the transaction must be aborted
- **`SetComplete`** `method` Indicates to MTS that the transaction completed successfully

Each object created on MTS has an associated Context object that holds the transaction, security, and activity information about the instance.

Resource Dispensers

A Resource Dispenser is the key to resource balancing on the server machine that holds MTS. The Resource Dispenser acts like a load balancer by managing the pool of available database connections and providing a bridge between the current transaction and the

Resource Manager. The Resource Dispensers will automatically be activated when they are needed. If you have the need to develop your own, documentation and sample source code is included in the MTS SDK available on the MTS COM Web site (msdn.microsoft.com/com/mts.htm).

There are four resource dispensers currently available with Visual Studio:

- **ODBC resource dispenser** Pools ODBC connections for components
- **Shared property manager** Allows properties to be shared among various components
- **MSMQ dispenser** Enlists MSMQ queues in MTS transactions
- **COM Transaction Integrator** For MTS interaction with mainframe resources for SNA connections for IBM CICS and IMS

Application Executable Utility

You can set up a component's client application to execute components on a remote MTS server without installing MTS to manage the interaction. This can be done by using the Application Executable utility, which creates an executable that can be run on the client machine to create the necessary DCOM references for the component to run remotely.

To activate the utility to create the client executable, open the MTS item in the MMC. Right-click on the My Computer item and open the Properties dialog. On the Options tab in the Replication section, set the Remote server name so the client will be able to reach MTS. Now when you export the package to create the client executable, it will contain the configuration to access the remote server.

Although only an ActiveX-based client solution would require this type of remote execution, it does allow for easy Web installation of a remote component. A reference to the object can be placed on a Web page (using the `<OBJECT>` tag) where the executable is located. When the client browser executes the tag, if there is a newer version of the object on the server, it will be automatically downloaded and installed.

Security Considerations

The security capabilities included in MTS can help to lock down an entire package instead of individual objects. There are six levels of security available for communication between the MTS server and a client. Aside from the No Security setting, the available levels include:

- **Connect** Only the initial connection is checked for authentication.
- **Call** Each call to a component within a package is checked for authentication.
- **Packet** The sender's identity is encrypted.

- **Packet Integrity** The sender's identity and a checksum signature are encrypted to ensure that the received packet is exactly the one sent.
- **Packet Privacy** All of the data of the packet, as well as the sender's identity and a checksum signature, are encrypted.

These security settings mirror those available in DCOM.

Executing a Remote Component

To execute remote components, MTS must be executing on both the calling machine and the machine that executes the component (unless you used the Application Executable described earlier). You must package the components in an MTS executable for installation on the remote machine. Once encapsulated within an executable, the primary server can *push* or *pull* components to or from remote machines.

Pushing the components means installing them on remote machines available and then allowing the primary server to call them for execution. Once the components are installed, a reference in the Remote Computers folder can be made to allow the components to be pulled.

You must have a shared folder that all the machines within this structure can access, where copies of the components will be located. The Remote Component folder of MTS contains the components that are registered on the MTS computer but that will actually execute on a remote computer.

NOTE: Because of security considerations, MTS cannot execute a remote component on a Windows 95/98 machine, although DCOM can. All components that are to be remotely executed by MTS must exist on a Windows NT machine.

Stately Versus Stateless Components

In the ways that you have used COM so far, either an object is completely loaded or it is flushed from memory. As a result, resource execution for Web pages is not as efficient as possible. Ideally, there would be a way to pool components, much like ODBC connections are pooled. With ODBC, connections are re-initialized once they are needed, but they remain in memory to decrease the initialization time.

MTS has stateless components. A stateless component maintains the key resources that are needed for the object (such as the VB runtime) to minimize instantiation. However, the memory taken by an instance (to hold state information and property settings) is released. This prevents the initialization foundation from having to be loaded each time, yet maximizes resources on the server for processes that are active.

DEFINITION: **Stateless components** A component written specifically for use with MTS that signals the MTS context that execution is complete until the component is referenced again.

Traditional components—those that aren't written specifically for MTS—are known as stately components. MTS operates best when stateless components use the methods `SetComplete` and `SetAbort` to explicitly indicate their current status.

Note that components written to be stateless cannot preserve variables unless the information is written into some nonvolatile medium, such as a database. Therefore, stateless components are best for quick and self-contained functions, such as utilities that don't need to access consistent information across method calls.

MTS Spy

To monitor the MTS system and the components that are executing on it, you can use a utility called MTS Spy. The MTS Spy utility displays information on packages, objects, threads, method calls, transactions, resources, and security. To use MTS Spy, you must set your component to generate the same debugging information that is needed to use Visual Debugger.

Debugging a component in MTS requires the use of the Visual Studio Debugger. It is therefore advisable to accomplish most of the debugging of your application before it is deployed to MTS, since the native debugging facilities of your development environment should provide a more robust feature set. For more information on using Visual Studio Debugger with your component, see the debugging section of the Visual C++ manual included in the MSDN Library document that came with Visual Studio.

MTS Spy is available in the Platform SDK in the MTS SDK section. If you don't have this SDK, you can download it from the Microsoft site at http://msdn.microsoft.com/developer/sdk.

Package Properties

You can set a number of properties for each package. They are divided into tabs in the Properties window. The properties will determine the treatment of all of the components held within the package. The tabs include:

- **General** Contains the name of the package and a description of the computer on which it executes.
- **Security** Settings for the roles and authorization checking of the current package.
- **Advanced** Contains settings for the execution of the package within a server process.
- **Identity** Allows you to set the user type that can address this package.
- **Activation** Allows you to set where the execution of the component will take place. A library package executes in-process of the calling application and a server package executes in a server process.

NOTE: For the Activation selections, when a package is selected as a Library Package (where components will be activated in the creator's process), MTS cannot support role checking, process isolation, or component tracking because the components will be running in a process over which MTS has no control. As a Server Package (where they run in the server process), all of these capabilities can be enabled.

Q&A

Q: What type of threading model is used by MTS?

A: Components created for MTS should use the apartment model for threading. Although a component can use the single threading setting, MTS cannot effectively manage resources when the component is configured in this fashion.

Q: Can MTS be used with components built in Visual FoxPro?

A: Yes. Visual FoxPro (VFP), which is reputed to have almost 500,000 developers worldwide, can create complete COM components that are compatible with MTS. Check the Microsoft site for a complete technical note on how components can be created and tested from within VFP.

SUMMARY

Microsoft Transaction Server (MTS) can be used to manage components for security, resource configuration, and transactions. VB components can be easily configured for use in MTS and can access the context of the MTS instance from within the component. In this chapter, you've learned about:

- **MTS** Microsoft Transaction Server allows components to be coordinated for resource sharing and transaction encapsulation on a server.
- **Packages** One or more components are placed within a package on MTS. Settings for a package determine the security, execution location, identity, and resource allocation for all of the components that the package contains.
- **Components** Only ActiveX DLLs designed for MTS can execute on MTS. Visual Basic components comply with all of the MTS specifications, so any DLL built in VB can be used.
- **Role** A role is the declarative security model used by MTS for defining the interfaces that are available for use, and the users who can access them.

CHAPTER 18

Visual Modeler

Creating multitier applications has made enterprise development significantly more complicated than earlier client/server applications. To remedy some of the complexity generated by these new applications, the Enterprise Edition of Visual Studio includes a powerful new tool known as Visual Modeler (VM). Many developers are unaware of the potential benefits that can be achieved by using a modeling program such as VM for prototyping and ongoing development. Visual Modeler can diagram relationships between components in a system, as well as generate object prototypes for new components.

In the past, the design process of most small to mid-level systems used a written proposal or report as the basis for constructing a solution. Often these designs contained a few simple diagrams that generally showed how the data sources, components, and business objects linked together. However, the complexity of even simple programmed systems has been increasing swiftly. For a reasonably well-developed distributed system, these manually created diagrams aren't very useful as the project commences. Changes are made frequently along the way, and in the rush to complete a project, the time and energy required to update a diagram is simply not allocated.

Visual Modeler is the first step toward a change in the way mid-sized systems can be designed. Included with every copy of Visual Studio Enterprise Edition, VM will likely become the almost ubiquitous design and modeling tool for distributed systems. Further, it is integrated with Visual Basic, Visual C++, and Visual FoxPro, to allow these already familiar design platforms to be the launching point for the modeling project. Visual Modeler greatly simplifies the creation of distributed database systems.

VISUAL MODELER FOR COMPONENT SYSTEM MODELING

The Visual Modeler tool is perhaps one of the most important tools included in Visual Studio for coordinating enterprise development. A model created in Visual Modeler provides a bird's eye view of a system and the interaction of the components of that system. VM can even publish models to the Microsoft Repository to make them available throughout your organization. It can be used to unify the modeling, design, and implementation of a development project.

In addition to its deployment features, Visual Modeler can be your gateway into the comprehensive study of system modeling. Since these tools have historically been very high-end, anyone who studies how to use Visual Modeler can enhance their career skills for the more powerful modeling systems.

A modeling system has several purposes:

- To improve the quality of the software being designed
- To provide automatic documentation of the system
- To increase code-generation productivity
- To allow communication among programmers with a standard diagram
- To unite the design and implementation of a distributed application

To aid in both the initial creation and the further maintenance of a distributed system, Visual Modeler can provide new methods for managing a project. New projects can be created or existing projects can be imported into Visual Modeler for examination and modification. Visual Modeler helps automate the construction of complex software systems.

In the past, the paperwork costs alone had relegated modeling to large businesses who could afford it. The low-cost automation introduced by Visual Modeler makes it possible to use modeling wherever it makes sense. There is no reason to use multitier modeling for a single-component project—the sample project in this chapter is a simplified example that would traditionally not warrant implementation in a modeling system. Modeling makes the most sense when the project includes more than four components and multiple tiers.

Power of Visual Modeler

Although the capabilities of Visual Modeler are extensive, it cannot handle all of the modeling tasks that may be desired for a complete system. Before you begin considering implementing a project with VM, it is important to understand how the tool should be used.

In very simple terms, Visual Modeler can do the following:

- Diagram an existing multitier project
- Model and create a new component-based project
- Provide visual connections between components
- Generate stub source code for new classes, methods, and properties

Visual Modeler cannot do the following:

- Verify connection integrity between components
- Code application logic
- Create or access database schema

That means that while a component-based database system can be augmented or added to a project that has an existing data source, it cannot be created completely from scratch in the modeler. VM has no direct method for accessing a database schema. Therefore, the required databases and tables must be created completely outside of the modeler.

Visual Modeler supports code generation for Visual Basic, Visual C++, and Visual FoxPro (when VM is launched from within VFP). No DHTML generation is possible from VM, so front-end Web-project modeling is currently very limited.

NOTE: Visual InterDev is not integrated with Visual Modeler. You cannot include projects from Visual InterDev for reverse-engineering or code generation, as you can from the other tools in Visual Studio. Visual Modeler also does not support advanced Web-based types, such as scriplet components. Therefore, Visual Modeler can only model Web applications in the abstract, without direct access to the various projects. This requires updating your Visual InterDev project by hand for any changes in the Visual Modeler project diagram, and vice versa.

Visual rendering of an object model makes a great deal of sense because of the complexity involved in creating most modern object frameworks. Within the diagram for the object model, spatial relations between objects rarely provides any information beyond grouping of objects within others. If spatial relationships were critical, flexibility would be lost when trying to magnify or reduce the view of the current project. Most of the spatial relations between objects are indicated by connection lines that can be reformatted by the visual modeling tool.

VM is an extremely accessible modeling tool for smaller projects, as well as being an excellent stepping stone to a full-scale modeling tool. However, although Visual Modeler is robust, it does not provide all of the features of a complete modeling tool, such as concurrent team development. For this capability, the software package called Rational Rose (www.rational.com) is available. Visual Modeler is a "lite" implementation of the Rational Rose modeler created for Microsoft by Rational Software. Rational Rose allows a model to use eight different diagram types for designing a system (compared with VM's support for three types). Diagrams created in Visual Modeler can be directly loaded into the Rational Rose system.

TIP: To aid in Visual Modeler development, Rational Software has set up a Web site dedicated to information that relates to the Visual Modeler software (www.rational.com/msvmuser). The site contains information and white papers on using the VM program.

Visual Modeler can be used effectively by a team of three to five component developers. If the team grows bigger, that usually indicates that the project has grown and the management challenge as well. Such changes would suggest that the extra diagrams, the concurrent diagram modification, and the other features of the full Rational Rose package might be more effective for managing the project.

CAUTION: At the time of this writing, Visual Modeler has difficulty coexisting on the same machine as Rational Rose. If you are thinking about downloading the trial version of Rational Rose from the Web site for testing, be aware that it could require a reinstallation of Visual Modeler to resolve problems.

Visual Modeler Overview

Visual Modeler provides a graphical diagramming interface for constructing and designing object-based distributed systems. It is included with the Enterprise Edition of Visual Studio and is contained in the default Visual Studio installation. The Visual Modeler application can be executed through either the Enterprise Tools submenu of the Visual Studio menu or the Add-Ins menus of the various development systems.

Visual Modeler can create a model of a distributed system from scratch, or it can be derived from an existing project. There are three different diagram types that can be used to display various aspects of the system. Each diagram type allows you to model a specific aspect (component distribution, deployment, or data organization) of the complete application.

Diagrams created in Visual Modeler do not have to display all of the information contained in a system. A diagram can provide a filtered view of how the system actually appears. For example, a component might have 100 methods. In the diagram of the system that you're constructing, however, perhaps only 10 of these methods are relevant. The diagram can be made to display only those 10 important methods to prevent cluttering the image. Therefore, a model is much like a map of a territory in that it is *not* the territory itself, but merely a representation of it.

A model of a system within Visual Modeler is made up of a number of diagrams. Each model provides a number of different perspectives from which the system will be viewed. These diagrams, although usually connected, do not have to be related. For example, a class diagram may be a representation of the methods and properties of some of the objects in a component diagram and not others. Each diagram may show a completely different part of the system and need not be generated from the same base data.

In Visual Modeler, each diagram is known as a *view* of the system. There are three view types available:

- **Class or Logical view** Shows the classes of a project separated into three general categories
- **Component view** Displays the components of the system and their interconnections
- **Deployment view** Indicates the physical resources that will be used

In the VM application, the Browse menu allows you to instantly move among these views. Each view displays different objects that represent pieces of the finished system. The objects in one view may be connected with the objects in another, so most item-property dialog boxes provide drill-down support to access the connected model view easily.

Class or Logical View

The Class view (also known as the Logical view) will probably be the most useful view for live design, since the project is displayed as a series of classes. The view displays a diagram of the properties and methods available for each class. In the diagram, the classes are in three categories for display: user, business, and data.

- **User Services** These are the components that will be used on the client side of the system. Usually this will refer to either client-side ActiveX DLLs in a traditional client application or an ActiveX control running within a browser.
- **Business Services** These are components that contain business logic and business rules.
- **Data Services** These are wrapper components that provide database access functionality.

These categories are primarily useful for organizing the project. They do not actually affect the creation of the classes displayed in the view. By organizing components among these three tiers, it is much easier to lay out a project. Figure 18-1 provides an example of a

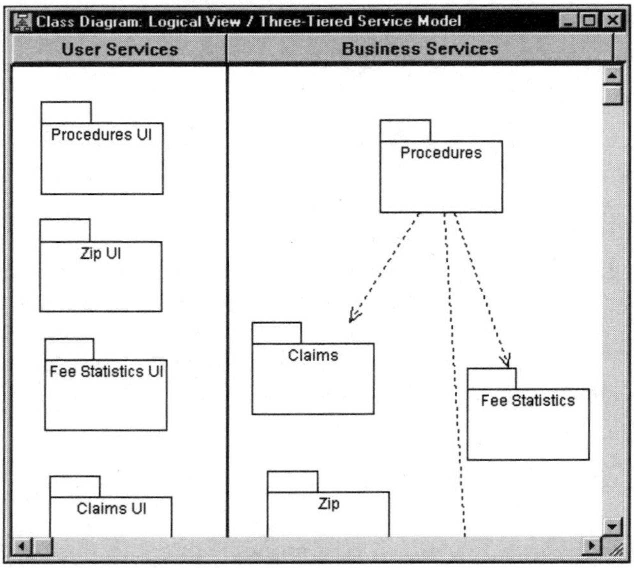

Figure 18-1. A class diagram displays all of the methods available in the class

class diagram that shows a number of classes and their connections. In this class diagram, none of the methods or properties are included for a simplified overview.

From the Browse menu, selecting the Class Diagram option will display the Logical or Class Diagram view of the project. The diagrams can also be accessed from the left window pane containing a tree of all of the diagram types and the current diagrams contained in the project.

> ***TIP:*** It is recommended that you examine an existing model before you start your own from scratch. Although no sample models are included with Visual Modeler, Rational Rose provides a number of examples for download. Check out the Models and Scripts page (www.rational.com/cgi-bin/www/upshow.cgi) for a number of models, including a model of Insurance Network Fees by InterAccess Corp., and a Java 2 class model by Novell, Inc.

Component View

The Component view shows an overview of the components used in the system. Rather than show specifics (such as methods or properties) of each component as the Class view does, the diagram of the Component view was made to easily configure and examine all of the interdependencies of the pieces of a system. A component may actually contain more than one class, but the classes are not articulated in the Component view.

While the class diagram is very specific, the component diagram more generally shows how components within the system are interrelated. A component does not even necessarily have to be an ActiveX component, but may be an application with exposed interfaces, a random-access binary file, or even a legacy system in a component wrapper. The component diagram helps document a system by presenting it as understandable subsystems. Each "component" on the diagram may refer to another diagram that explicitly documents the subsystem with a precise architecture, such as a class diagram.

In Figure 18-2, you can see an example component diagram that shows the component version of the class diagram you viewed previously.

The component diagram shows the objects and dependencies of all of the components in the system. In a component diagram, libraries, tables, EXEs, files, and documents may also be added to appear as components so a complete system diagram can be created. The items in this view support drill-down to the class diagram of the components.

Deployment View

A Deployment view shows a system design as a series of nodes and connections. This form of diagram is not directly connected to the reverse-engineering or code-generating capabilities of Visual Modeler. In Figure 18-3 you can see a simple deployment diagram of a database-access component system.

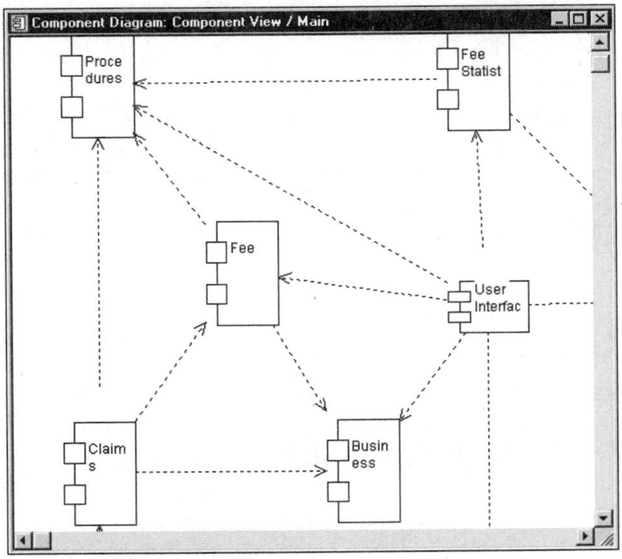

Figure 18-2. The components and attachment of components are displayed in the component diagram

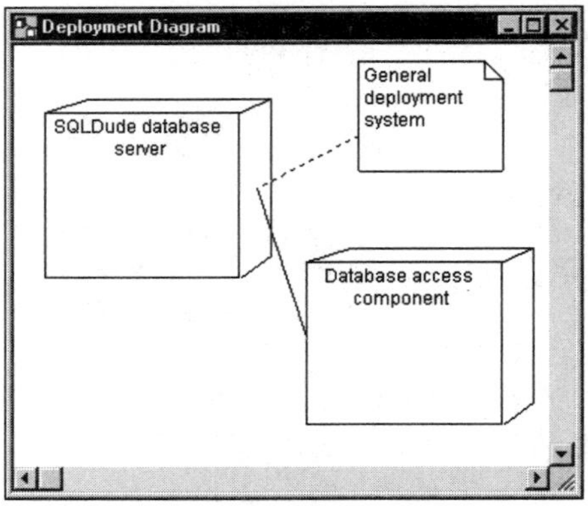

Figure 18-3. Sample deployment view of a programmed system

You can use the Deployment view to map out details of the servers and connectivity that will be used. The Deployment view will be used typically for documentation purposes and not for live project development. For this reason, it is likely to be the least-used diagram type available in Visual Modeler.

Deployment diagrams show the actual hardware and software that will be used to make the system possible. This diagram is of primary use when designing distributed systems to show the location of various pieces of the system. Load-balancing factors can even be placed in the deployment diagram to specify potential transactions and network traffic.

MODELING DESIGN

When a diagram becomes too complicated, you can break it into two or more diagrams. Within a class diagram, each class can be connected with a description of the relationship between the components that the classes define. The *cardinality* of a relation specifies what components are involved in that relation. The *optionality* of an object in a relationship determines whether the object is required or optional.

DEFINITION: **Cardinality** Specifies what classes are involved in the relationship between components.

Think of Visual Modeler as a drawing program with background connections to real world programming constructs. Most of the work you will do in VM, such as drawing interface connections or changing the spatial placement of components on the VM diagram canvas will have no direct effect on the functioning of the system. Diagramming using this tool will help you to visualize and organize a system that is being designed and aid you in understanding not only how the pieces of the system will fit together, but also what pieces are needed.

The various diagrams available within Visual Modeler are not intricately connected. Think of the various diagram types (class, component, and deployment) as hyperlinks that allow you to examine the model from different perspectives. As described earlier, modifications to the placement or connections within these diagrams rarely translates to a change in the final solution. Within the diagram, a number of explanatory symbols can also be added that will not affect the actual functioning of the application.

A tool like Visual Modeler can be used before the user interface prototyping. In fact, many of the pitfalls of generating a quick prototype with Visual Basic can be avoided with this method. Many projects are begun by defining the interface first, with the back-end programming following, only to find that the core deployment structure has been limited by this front to back approach. Visual Modeler can help you design the underlying technology before the interface has been declared.

NOTE: Since the model of the system is visual, consider taking a screen shot of the model and storing it with the system documentation. This diagram can allow others participating in the system construction to see the overall layout without having to understand how Visual Modeler is used. This image can even be placed on a Web page for intranet access. Be sure to date the image clearly so viewers will know when the shot was last updated.

Once the model has been created, maintaining and updating it is simple for Visual Studio projects. Since Visual Modeler can revise the project based on updates to the model, your Visual C++, Visual Basic, Visual FoxPro, or Visual J++ applications can reflect the most current diagram.

Round-Trip Engineering

Round-trip engineering involves taking an existing system, making modifications to the model, and recreating the solution with the new changes. This process creates a cycle where the model is routinely updated to reflect the current state of the project and new class additions are made in the model to be returned to the project. Typically this is accomplished with the Reverse-Engineering Wizard for Visual Basic projects.

Reverse-Engineering Wizard

The Reverse-Engineering Wizard takes an existing project and imports all of the key pieces into a VM model. This wizard is included in Visual Modeler to accept Visual Basic, Visual C++, and Visual J++ projects. After the model is imported, it can be modified within the diagram and later exported into the existing project.

Code Generation Wizard

The Code Generation Wizard is a key part of using Visual Modeler to work with projects. It will take the definitions of new classes and generate the necessary code stubs for these classes in the target development environment (Visual Basic, Visual C++, etc.). All methods and properties for the class that is modeled in VM will be automatically prototyped and placed in the program. By prototyping the overview of the solution in VM, a project can be generated for further development in the destination language.

The Code Generation Wizard also places custom code markers in the new project so that it can be easily re-imported into VM at a later time. These code markers provide a critical piece necessary for round-trip engineering since they allow the modeler to understand what changes have occurred to the project since the last import.

Unified Modeling Language

Visual Modeler is not the only enterprise development tool available. In fact, it was initially designed by Rational Software for Microsoft as a basic enterprise tool. The big brother of Visual Modeler, a program called Rational Rose, provides even more functionality. To allow an exchange of information between enterprise modeling tools, a modeling language called Universal Modeling Language (UML) was created. UML is an open standard and is currently supported by a number of different vendors, including IBM, HP, Microsoft, Rational Software, Object Management Group (OMG), and others.

DEFINITION: **UML** Universal Modeling Language (UML) is a cross-platform standard created by OMG to facilitate a common format for defining classes, relations between classes, and general system modeling.

UML is a general modeling standard that is used to describe the layout and interaction between objects. It is effective in diagramming almost any type of computer system (from client/server to embedded systems) created with almost any language (VB, C++, Java, FoxPro, and so on).

UML originated at Rational Software as a common method of storing modeling files for exchange. Since then, OMG has adopted the standard and now maintains it through their collaborative agreement with numerous companies. Companies that contributed to the UML standard include IBM, Microsoft, Oracle, Rational Software, TI, Unisys, HP, DEC, and more. UML is non-proprietary and combines the semantics and notation of earlier modeling languages, including Booch, OOSE, and OMT.

NOTE: The UML specification is available through the OMG (www.omg.org) or Rational Software's Web site (www.rational.com/uml). For revisions to the UML standard, the http://uml.shl.com Web site contains all of the information on updates. The specification, cryptic and verbose at best, is not written for the average reader. If you want to learn more about UML, it is useful to get a well-written book about UML, such as *The Unified Modeling Language User Guide* by Grady Booch, James Rumbaugh, and Ivar Jacobson (Addison-Wesley, 1998). It describes, in depth, all of the various aspects of UML construction and use.

When you actually begin designing multitier systems, you will need to understand the basics of what UML can do in a general sense of the current features and limitations. Because Visual Studio includes both Microsoft Repository and Microsoft Visual Modeler, you will almost certainly never have to code UML by hand.

The UML specification describes several diagram types and the meaning of those diagrams. More UML models are supported in the professional Rational Rose software than in VM.

The UML standard currently supports the following nine types of diagrams:

- Use case diagrams
- *Class diagrams*
- Sequence diagrams
- *Component diagrams*
- *Deployment diagrams*
- Statechart diagrams
- Collaboration diagrams
- Activity diagrams
- Object diagrams

In this list, you can see that three of the diagram types are in *italics,* and these are the types that are supported by VM. Rational Rose supports five other models not available in VM: object, use case, sequence, collaboration, and statechart diagrams.

NOTE: The usefulness of modeling and of the UML language extends beyond a round-trip engineering application, such as Visual Modeler. The drawing program Visio (www.visio.com) also provides support for UML diagramming. The Professional and Enterprise versions of the Visio application can be used to create UML diagrams that are static, check the semantics of a UML diagram, and export the structure diagrams into the Microsoft Repository. The diagrams also integrate with Visual Modeler. Drawings made in Visio are used as static models.

The usefulness of UML is that it provides a standard for metamodels. A metamodel is a standardized method of describing a model that describes another system. This may seem confusing at first, but it simply describes another level of abstraction. To return to the parallel of maps, a model is used to describe the territory, but is not itself the territory. The metamodel (in this case UML) standardizes the way the map is described.

DEFINITION: **Metamodel** The definition of a standard that unifies the underlying semantics (meaning and rules) of how the model is described.

For example, on a geographic map, latitude and longitude lines provide a metamodel that allow all maps to be examined in a standard way. The computer-based UML standard allows programs to understand how the model is created, particularly for import and export. The UML specification also describes how the models should appear when displayed (types of connecting lines, component icons, etc.) called *common notation.* This standardization allows people unfamiliar with a particular application model to examine and understand it.

DEFINITION: **Common notation** Common notation provides a standard for human rendering of the metamodel. It describes how a model will appear when it is displayed.

The UML standard defines a semantic model but does not provide explicit implementation details. This means that there is no specific interface, file storage, or run-time model that is standardized for UML implementations. As the specification matures, a definition will likely appear. Visual Modeler uses the UML framework to define how the model is constructed.

The UML language was also created to be extensible so that a new standard didn't need to be created when additions were required. Primarily, UML provides the capability of stereotyping. A stereotype allows new model elements to be created that have the same interface of older elements. In many ways, stereotyping works like subclassing and overloading techniques provided in object-oriented languages.

DEFINITION: **Stereotype** A stereotype provides a mechanism through which the UML modeling language can be extended. Stereotyping works much like subclassing for UML model elements.

There are nine core models defined in the UML standard. The Visual Modeler program supports three of these models, whereas Rational Rose supports eight of the nine.

For the implementation of the nine UML diagrams, different levels of compatibility may be supported by a given modeling program. Support of the complexity of models created with UML falls into three rough categories:

- **Static structural modeling** Simple diagramming using a drawing-type program such as Visio allows models to be created that do not actually interact with the programming environment. These models are used primarily for documentation and project coordination.

- **Dynamic behavior modeling** Visual Modeler provides dynamic modeling by allowing round-trip engineering. Changes to the model can be incorporated into the development project and vice versa.
- **Complete model management** Supplied by programs like Rational Rose, complete model management supports team and concurrent development, unified modeling of multiple systems, and other enterprise-wide functionality.

Only the parts of UML that apply to the needs of your development project need be used. In fact, most modelers can only accommodate a subset of the total features of the language.

UML Common Notation

In the UML standard, common notation specifies how the diagram will appear to the user. This includes how the items in the diagram appear, the connectivity of items, and the semantics of the diagram itself. Since Visual Modeler fully complies with common notation, learning how to read a diagram in VM will allow you to understand diagrams in most other UML standard modeling programs.

The primary method of displaying connections between objects is by using lines. In a UML diagram, a line connection can indicate a variety of things, depending on the diagram type. In a class diagram, a line would show the visible connection between two classes. In a deployment diagram, a line can indicate that the item is actually a Within connection, indicating that the resource is contained within the primary resource.

Sample Petal File

There is no standard file format defined in the UML specification. Rational Software has created the petal file format (.ptl and .mdl files) to provide a cross-platform modeling format. A file with the .mdl extension is actually a "monolithic" petal file that contains an entire description of a model, while individual petal files (.ptl) are most commonly used to break up pieces of the model for team development.

Although you will probably never have to create a UML file by hand, it is useful to examine the file format because it is becoming the standard for exchanging modeling data. The ability to load this file format will become an increasingly critical feature of all levels of modeling programs.

A very simple (and trimmed) petal file is shown in the following listing. The text file format does not resemble the HTML file format you are accustomed to. If you load a Visual Basic Form (.frm) or Module (.bas) file into a text editor, however, you will see that many of the characteristics are similar. The designations and properties are divided into areas determined by objects.

```
(object Petal
   version       42
   _written      "Microsoft Visual Modeler 2.0.8139"
   charSet       0)
```

```
(object Design "Logical View"
    is_unit         TRUE
    is_loaded       TRUE
    quid            "3773D6C200CB"
    defaults        (object defaults
    rightMargin      0.250000
    leftMargin       0.250000
    defaultFont      (object Font
       size               9
       face               "Tahoma"
       bold               FALSE
       default_color      TRUE)
    showMessageNum         3
    showClassOfObject      TRUE
    notation               "Unified")
    root_usecase_package      (object Class_Category "Use Case View"
    quid                      "3773D6C200CD"
    exportControl             "Public"
    global                    TRUE
    logical_models            (list unit_reference_list)
   logical_presentations      (list unit_reference_list
      (object UseCaseDiagram "Main"
      quid              "3773D6C9013A"
      title             "Main"
      zoom              100
      items             (list diagram_item_list))))
   root_category        (object Class_Category "Logical View"
   quid                "3773D6C200CC"
   exportControl       "Public"
   global              TRUE
   subsystem           "Component View"
   quidu               "3773D6C200CE"
   logical_models   (list unit_reference_list
       (object Class_Category "User Services"
       attributes   (list Attribute_Set
          (object Attribute
          tool            "VisualBasic"
          name            "TierPackage"
          value           "User Services"))
      quid                "3773D6C901B1"
      documentation       "User services provide the visual interface for
presenting information and gathering data in an application. The user
services connect the user with the application and request the business
and/or data services needed by the user to execute business tasks."
```

```
visible_categories    (list visibility_relationship_list
    (object Visibility_Relationship
    attributes    (list Attribute_Set
       (object Attribute
       tool          "VisualBasic"
       name          "TierPackage"
       value         "Business Services"))
   quid          "3773D6C901D9"
   supplier      "Logical View::Business Services"
   quidu         "3773D6C901B3")
exportControl     "Public"
logical_models    (list unit_reference_list
    (object Class "Browser"
    quid          "3773D6D5006E"))
logical_presentations    (list unit_reference_list
    (object ClassDiagram "Package Overview"
    quid          "3773D6C901B2"
    title         "Package Overview"
    zoom          100
    origin_x      0
    origin_y      0)))
```

The file shown here has been edited greatly to make it easier to study. The unedited file containing a single class covers more than six pages. Examining this excerpt will allow you to see the general format of the text-based file.

NOTE: An attempt to standardize modeling in a common language format is coming in the form of Universal Object Language (UOL). Whether this standard will be adopted remains to be seen. Check the UOL Web site (www.recercai.com) for more information.

Process Patterns

Through process patterns, programmers seek to describe effective methods of object-oriented development. Although a complete description of process patterns is beyond the scope of this book, an introduction to process patterns will help you in understanding how to put Visual Modeler to work. Process patterns have become increasingly popular because the design capabilities of modeling systems allow development to be examined from an overview perspective.

DEFINITION: **Process pattern** A series of coding techniques, tasks, and operations that act as a template for effectively developing object-oriented solutions.

You can choose the pattern that most closely matches the project you need to complete, and then follow the pattern through to completion of your project. These patterns are often proven solutions used to implement other real-world applications.

Although finding an effective method of developing software for complex systems has always been a priority, the increased use of development teams and of component creation has called for a more methodical approach. Studying existing process patterns should help provide this methodology and the benefits that come with it.

MODELING THE FORUM APPLICATION

When you create a project with Visual Modeler, it can be exported to several of the development environments available in the Visual Studio suite. For this project, you will use Visual Basic as the core IDE to model the system that accesses the Forum application. In Chapter 17, you wrapped the key database functionality of the Forum application in an ActiveX component. With Visual Modeler you will extend this system and you will learn how to use round-trip engineering to work with an existing project.

Before you begin using Visual Modeler in conjunction with Visual Basic, you need to properly configure VB so the modeler can access and manipulate the project to add and modify the classes.

Configuring Visual Basic for Modeling

For Visual Basic, the components for using Visual Modeler from the integrated environment are add-ins. You need to add the Visual Modeler extensions to the VB environment before they can be used. Once they are installed, Visual Modeler can reach into VB and manipulate any aspect of the current project. To configure Visual Basic properly, follow these steps:

1. Start Visual Basic.
2. Select the Add-In Manager option under the Add-Ins menu.
3. In the Add-Ins listbox, select the Visual Modeler Add-In and check the Load/Unloaded and the Load on Startup options as shown in the following illustration. The Visual Modeler Add-In allows VM to control Visual Basic.

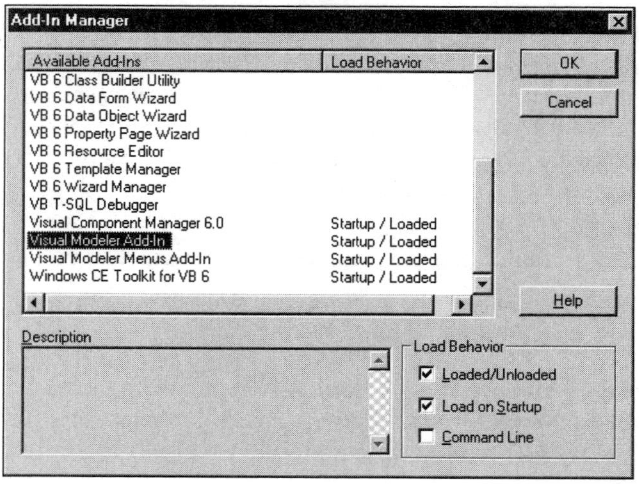

4. Select the Visual Modeler Menus Add-In and again check the Load/Unloaded and the Load on Startup options. This allows VB to activate models in VM.
5. Click the OK button to accept the new add-ins. Under the Add-Ins menu, you should now have a complete Visual Modeler submenu that has Reverse Engineering and Class Diagram Browsing options.

You can either exit Visual Basic now or select the Loaded option (in the Add-Ins window) for the two Add-Ins. With VB open, Visual Modeler can actually reach into the currently loaded project and reverse-engineer it, but it needs the Add-Ins available. By setting the Add-Ins to Load/Startup, they will automatically load when VB is executed.

Reverse-Engineering an Existing Component

To load the model of a class into Visual Modeler, the project must be reverse-engineered. VM is automated well enough that the process is simplified through a Reverse-Engineering Wizard. This wizard lets you select your class and then generates the appropriate UML code to be used by VM. Follow these steps:

1. Start the Visual Modeler application. You will be presented with a blank project. This project will place one component into the Business Services area and another into the Data Services area of the three-tier model.
2. Return to Visual Basic and load the clsForum project that you created in Chapter 17.
3. Select the clsForum class in the Project as shown next.

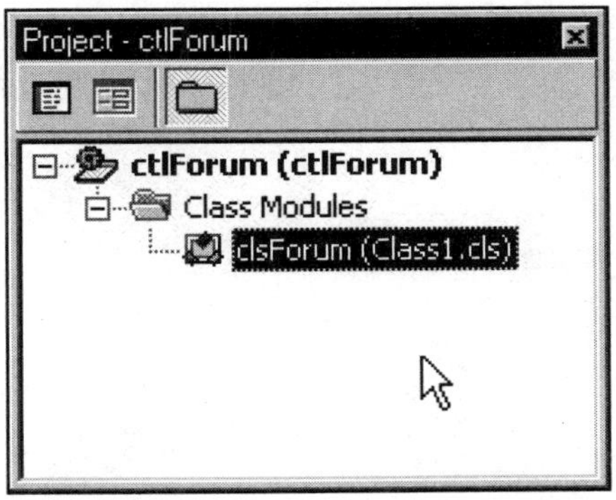

4. Select the Reverse Engineering Wizard option from the Visual Basic submenu of the Add-Ins menu. You will be presented with a window that allows you to select the model that will accept the reverse-engineered project. Since you just launched Visual Modeler, there should be a single item listed as (Untitled).
5. Click OK, and Visual Modeler will run the Reverse Engineering Wizard. A welcome screen will appear and describe the basics of the reverse-engineering process.

6. Click the Next button to proceed to the first page. The first step allows you to select all of the classes or ActiveX controls to be modeled shown in the next illustration.

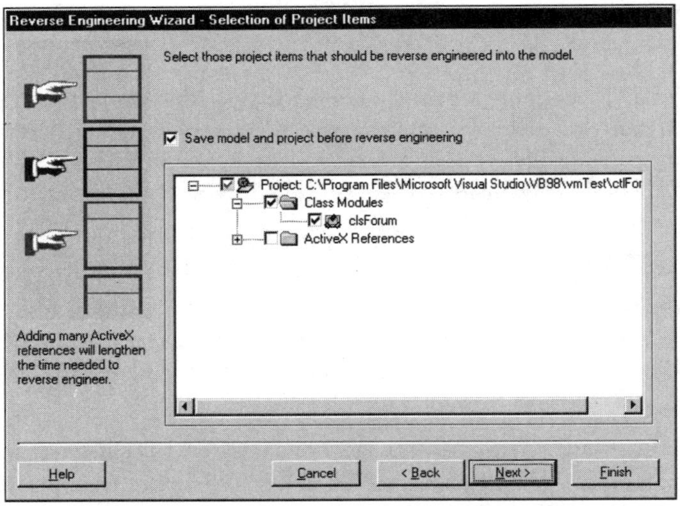

7. Click the Business Services item in the Logical Packages list (see the following illustration). This selection will determine where in the three-tier model the imported items will be placed. After you have selected the folder, any items dragged into the Assigned Project Items pane will be placed in the Business Services tier.

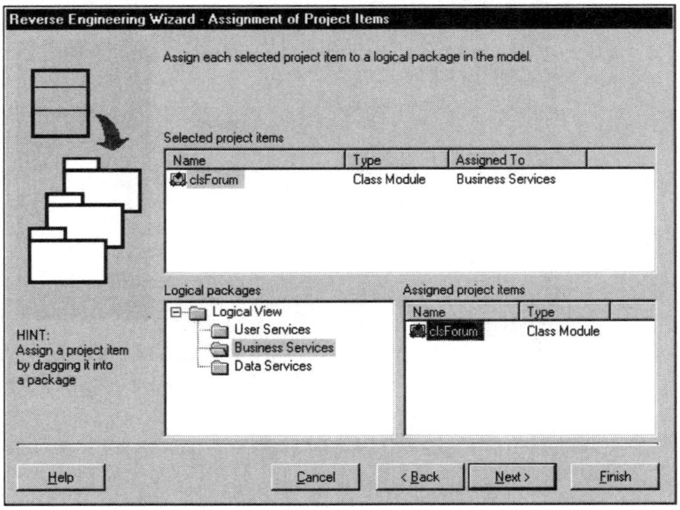

8. Drag the clsForum item into the Business Services folder.
9. Click the Next button to continue to the final page. The wizard will summarize all of the members to be reverse-engineered and estimates the time to complete the process.
10. Click the Finish button to begin reverse-engineering the class.
11. Click the Log tab to examine the steps of the process completed by the wizard (shown next). You will see the warning that explains that the model hasn't been saved, so it may not yet be linked to the Visual Basic project. If you had imported into the existing saved model, this warning would not have appeared.

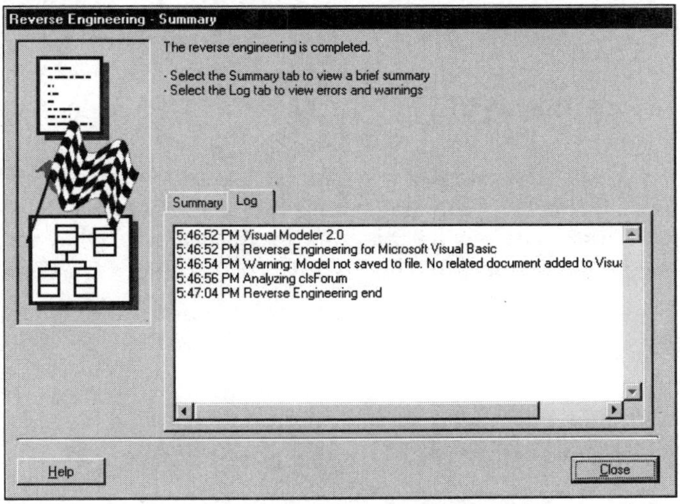

12. Click the Close button to dismiss the wizard.
13. The class will now appear in the Business Services section of the three-tier model.

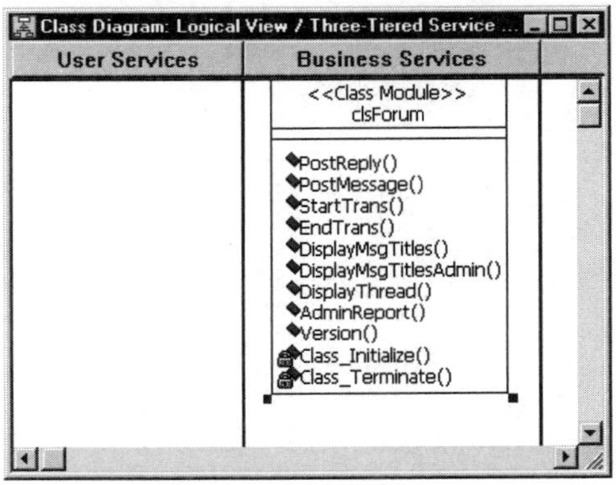

You now have the basis of a diagram for modeling an entire system. Properties and methods can be added to the model that can later be imported into Visual Basic to redefine the class.

Adding a Method

Once you have the component in Visual Modeler, you can manipulate it, make any necessary changes, and then make VM generate the new VB code to change the class. In this section, you'll add a simple method that will return the current version of the component. You should try to always include a version method so that when you are debugging a solution, you can quickly verify that the components that are installed on the machine you're testing are the expected versions.

Activate Visual Modeler and follow these steps:

1. Right-click the class module and select the New Method option. A new method entry will appear highlighted at the bottom of the class definition.
2. Enter `Version` as the name of the method. After you've changed the name, click on a blank space of the diagram. If you then press the ENTER key, the new method will automatically be created. (If you accidentally create a method, you will need to open the Specification dialog box for the entire class to delete it.)
3. In order to create a return parameter for the method, open the Specification dialog box by right-clicking the class and selecting the Open Specification option.
4. Click the Methods tab.
5. Select the Version method shown in the next illustration.

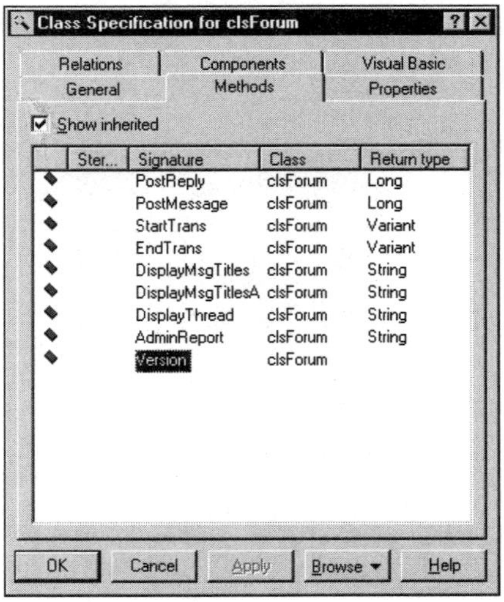

6. Right-click the Version method and select the Specification option from the context menu. You will be presented with all of the information related to the method. Below the Name text box, the Return class item allows you to select the type of data that will be returned from the method.
7. Select the Integer type from the Return class combo box.
8. Click OK to dismiss the Method Specification dialog box.
9. Click OK to dismiss the Class Specification dialog box.
10. Select the clsForum class item in the diagram.
11. Under the Tools menu, select the Generate Code option.
12. Click the Next button four times to accept all of the default options. Because you just imported the class, the wizard will know all of the proper settings.
13. Click the Finish button.
14. Enter ctlForum.mdl as the filename for the model, and click Save.

When the process is complete, the model will be updated to include an initialization and termination method (shown next), necessary for VM compatibility.

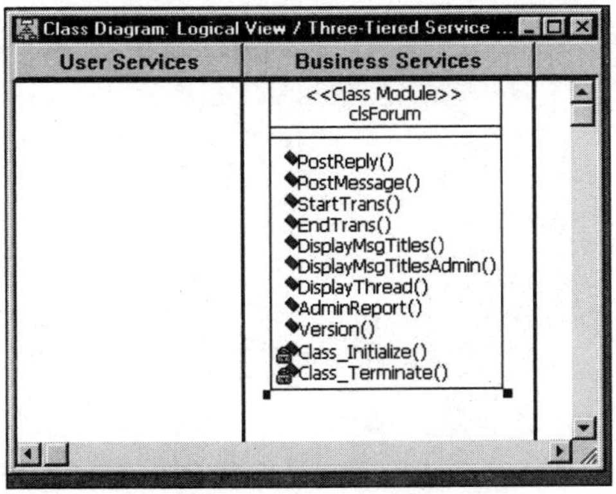

If you view the class in Visual Basic, you will see the new method, as well as two new modules and some new code. These modules and the code additions allow Visual Modeler to coordinate the project with the class diagrams as updates are made.

Opening the Version method will reveal code like this:

```
'##ModelId=37EC1D13029F
Public Function Version() As Integer
    On Error GoTo VersionErr

    'your code goes here...
```

```
    Exit Function
VersionErr:
    Call RaiseError(MyUnhandledError, "clsForum:Version Method")
End Function
```

Adding the following line of code under the "your code goes here" comment will provide the version of the component. Place this line of code in the proper place:

```
    Version = 100
```

The Reverse Engineering Wizard, when used on this project again, will update the model to reflect any methods and properties added to the project and display the changes in the model diagram.

Defining a New Class

You've been augmenting an existing class, but you can also create a new class from scratch in VM that can generate the equivalent code stubs in your final solution. This is one of the fundamental procedures when modeling a new system. Using VM, you can create prototypes for all of the components that you believe you will need for the project, and even create the interfaces.

This example will demonstrate how a data class for the Forum application might be prototyped within Visual Modeler. The Class Wizard in VM will perform all of the necessary operations to diagram the class that will be generated in VB. This example will not create a final class, because the details would be determined by the specifications of the final deployment. Instead it shows how a prototype might be constructed within Visual Modeler.

Properly Setting Default Values

Since Visual Modeler is made to facilitate development in many different languages, it allows settings that may not be permissible in the destination language. An excellent example of this problem in VB is setting default values to method arguments. When the code is generated for the method definition, it will look like this:

```
Function myMethod (myValue = 10 As Integer) As Integer
```

In some languages, property settings can be made in the method definition. Visual Basic does not allow it and will cause an error when you try to execute this program. To make the program work properly, you would either need to make sure the parameter has no default value, or cut the value setting code and place it in the body of the method. Therefore, when using a new feature in VM, try to test it in your destination environment as soon as possible. This will allow you to make certain that the feature is supported.

To create this prototype class, follow these steps:

1. Activate the Visual Modeler application.
2. Select the Class Wizard option under the Tools menu. You will see the opening screen that allows you to enter the name of the class.
3. Enter clsForumData as the class name and click the Next button.

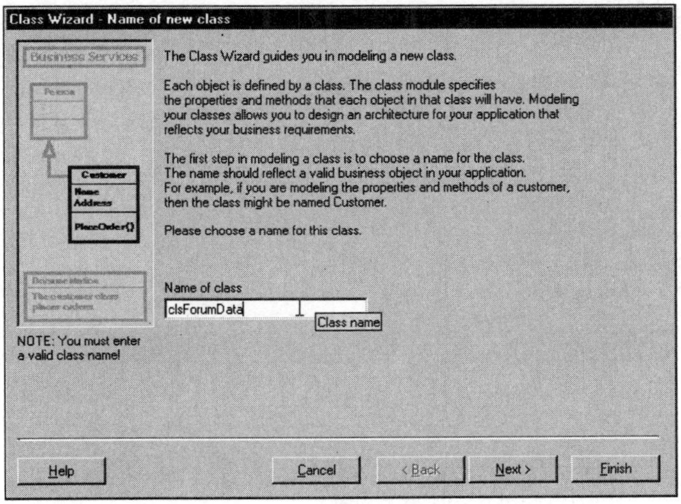

4. Select the Generate Code option and click the Next button. This will create a new project containing the class created in the diagram.
5. Enter a description of the class to be created (shown in the next illustration) and click the Next button. A description is always useful for documenting the functionality provided by the class.

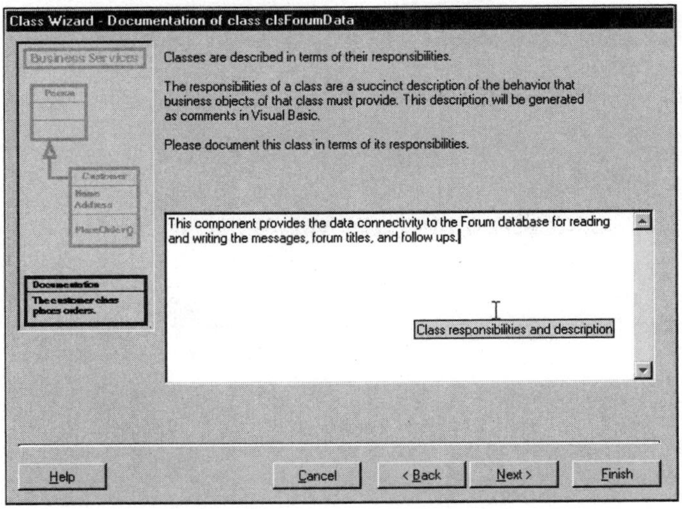

6. Select the Data Services option. This will place the new class in the Data Services tier of the model.

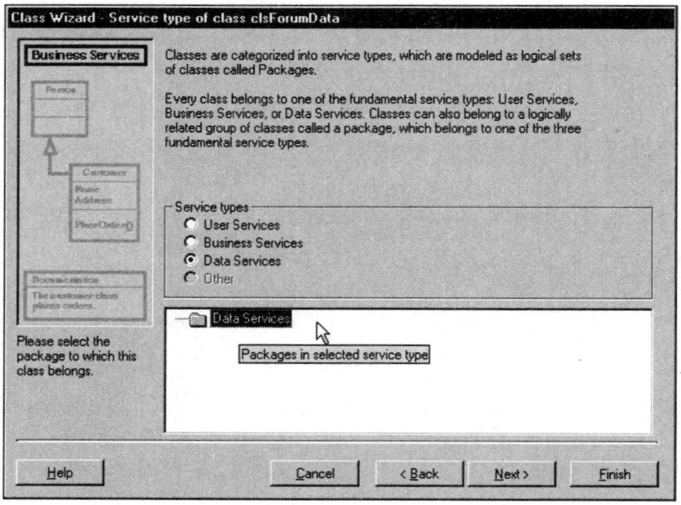

7. Leave the inheritance selections to their defaults and click the Next button. Since Visual Basic does not support inheritance directly, you won't need the wizard option that allows for inheritance in VB projects, so click No so that you won't inherit from another class.

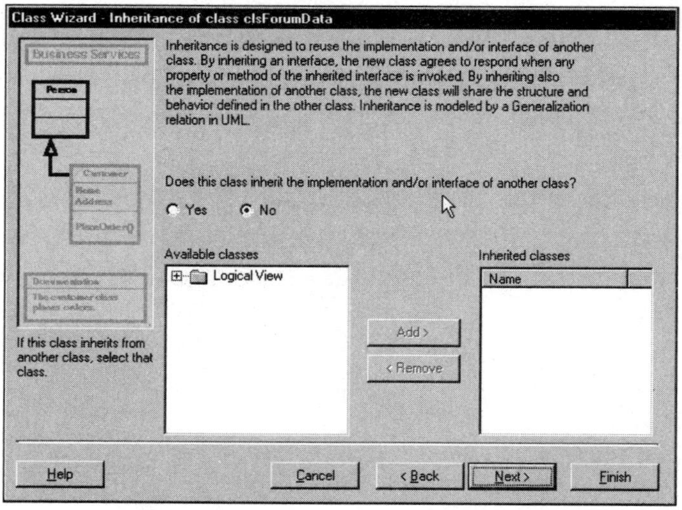

8. For this class, you will need to create a new method. Right-click in the Methods box and select the Insert option shown here. Inserting a method will open the Method Specification dialog box.

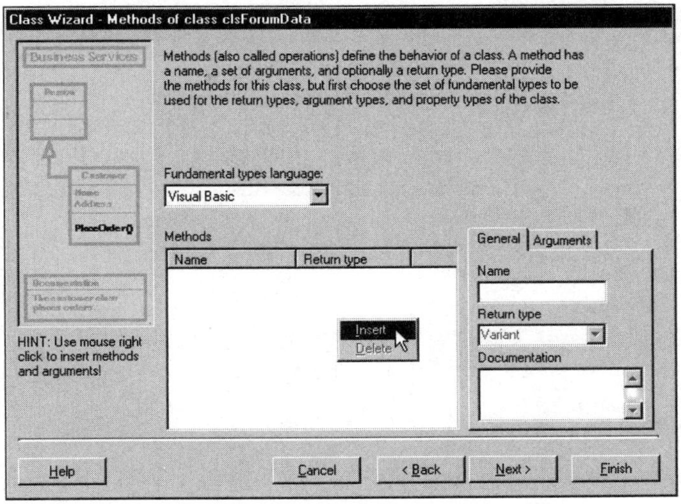

9. In the Name text box, enter GetMessageBody as the method name.
10. Set the return type to String. For each message retrieved, a string containing the contents of the message will be returned.
11. You will also need to pass a message ID to specify which message is to be accessed. Select the Arguments tab.
12. Right-click in the listbox, and select the Insert option.
13. Set the name of the argument to messageID.
14. Set the type of the argument to Long, and click the Next button to accept the method definitions.
15. The next screen allows you to enter the properties that may be needed by the class. In this prototype, no properties are needed. If you want to add some properties, the insert option is available by right-clicking in the Properties listbox.

16. Click the Next button to reach the final configuration box shown here. Finish building the class and add it to the solution diagram.

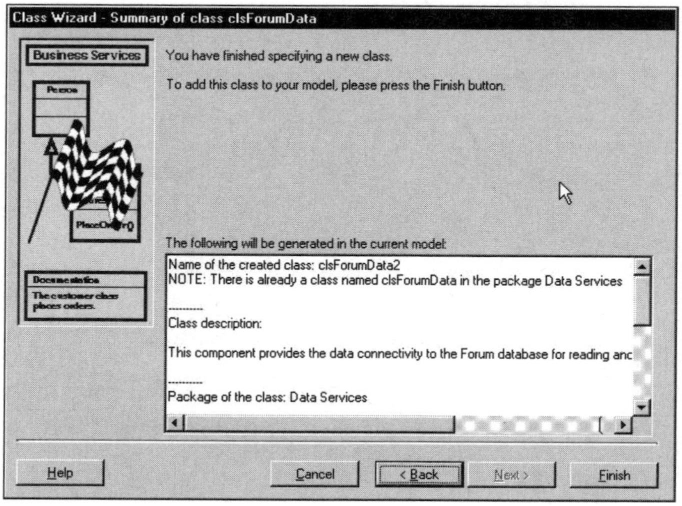

With both classes properly configured, you are ready to make the transition from the model to the coding world. You can use the Generate Code option to take the clsForumData class and store it in a Visual Basic project.

NOTE: Although generating a complete data-access component for the Forum application is beyond the scope of this chapter, there is an excellent piece of software called COM-Gen 2000 by Q&D Software Development (www.q-d.com). It will take an existing data source and create an entire class for database access. It can be very effectively used with Visual Modeler to create component database systems. I cannot recommend this tool highly enough for the professional developer.

Q&A

Q: Can the modeler be used to create or examine database models?

A: Unfortunately, no. Visual Modeler only models the capabilities of components. It has no access to database schema. However, there is an excellent program called COM-Gen 2000 by Q&D Software Development (www.q-d.com). This program will create Visual Basic classes from a database schema for complete database access. The database classes that are generated as part of a Visual Basic program can then be imported into Visual Modeler for prototyping.

Q: Will a Rational Rose model import into Visual Modeler?

A: They both use the same file format, called a petal file (.mdl or .ptl), so no importation is necessary. However, if the model uses one of the five diagram types that is supported in Rational Rose but not available in Visual Modeler, opening the file will generate an error.

SUMMARY

Visual Modeler is a distributed-system graphical modeling program that is included with the Enterprise Edition of Visual Studio. VM provides an entry-level modeling system that can be used to prototype and define components and the relations between them. Through the process of round-trip engineering, an application can be interactively built at the same time as the model. In this chapter, you covered:

- **Visual Modeler** A diagramming and modeling tool for programming systems that allows existing projects to be reverse-engineered for loading into the model. It can be used to generate code for Visual Basic, Visual C++, and Visual J++.
- **Unified Modeling Language** UML is a core standard that is used to describe the appearance and storage format of a model. The standard, which originated with the team at Rational Software, is embraced by Visual Modeler. Visual Modeler supports three of the most common diagram types described in the UML specification.
- **Class diagram** Also called the Logical view, it displays classes in an object-model diagram divided into three categories: user services, business services, and data services.
- **Component diagram** This is an overview diagram that displays unified components and connections between the components.
- **Deployment diagram** This diagram is designed to describe primarily the physical resources and individual items that will be included in your deployment scenario. This diagram is not used to generate code or to directly affect the development of a project.
- **Round-trip engineering** This is the process of reverse-engineering an existing project, making changes to the model or classes involved, and generating code from the changes to modify the project. This cyclical process allows you to evolve the model while the application is being built.

CHAPTER 19

DHTML Intranet Development

Most of the solutions that you've developed so far have been browser independent. Browser-independent applications make it possible for a large number of people to be able to use the solution. Targeting the lowest common denominator of Web application user is not always the best development choice.

For many network administrators, it is possible to specify a browser type for all of an organization's members. Since a baseline level of technology can be assumed when creating an application, it is possible to include many of the user-interface niceties of a stand-alone application without the install and update cycles.

Intranet applications can have robust client-side features through the Internet Explorer browser and its implementation of Dynamic HTML (DHTML). DHTML provides almost complete control over the screen and presentation of the user interface. Unlike the advanced user-interface abilities of older Web standards (such as frames), DHTML can be used to build client-side interactivity into the user interface. DHTML applications can appear as polished and elegant as the compiled applications created with tools such as Visual Basic.

DHTML greatly enhances the power of HTML by allowing complete control over the browser environment. DHTML combines HTML, scripting, display object modeling, and style sheets. DHTML makes the following possible:

- **Dynamic modification of page content** From text replacement to altering the image displayed, any page element can be changed on the client page.
- **Drag-and-drop capabilities** Events can be used in conjunction with page modification to create a drag-and-drop interface.
- **Live formatting of input** The event model, combined with HTML components (such as text boxes, check boxes, and the like), allows live access to user entry for dynamic formatting.
- **Showing and hiding elements** Page elements can be hidden or displayed dynamically so that solutions that need to can offer this display option (for example, expanding or collapsing outline content).
- **Free-form object positioning** Objects or elements can be positioned by specific coordinates instead of having to occur within the HTML display stream.
- **Advanced screen display** Using positioning and events, a variety of client-side additions can be implemented, such as ToolTips (the small yellow boxes that contain information or descriptions of an item that the cursor pauses over) and image animation or transition effects (fading, expanding, or hover effects).
- **Integration with XML** DHTML scripts can access the data stored in the XML by the names given in their tag definitions.
- **Automatic content refreshing** Event- and time-based operations can be used to make dynamically updating page elements, such as stock tickers, current news displays, and so on.

- **Data binding** When DHTML is used with Visual InterDev and RDS, it can provide client-side data binding of HTML components.
- **Scriptlets** DHTML can use HTML pages as client-side components called scriptlets. This allows HTML code to be re-used and exist across multiple page executions like a client-side session object.

DHTML Web page updates occur in the client browser without any additional Web server requests. Although the general implementation of a scripting language (such as JavaScript) alone can access many of the items on a page and even present simple dialog boxes, it cannot reformat the page without complex page reloading. DHTML makes it easier for a script to alter individual items (such as frame formatting or selected image display) without any page reloading. DHTML reduces the load on the Web server and improves the user experience by avoiding round-trip journeys to the server for new content.

NOTE: Since DHTML solutions require client-side processing power, be sure to test them on typical target machines (using the target machine's processor speed, memory, and hard disk resources). Testing on a fast development machine may not make it apparent to a developer that the application will appear slow to the end user.

These DHTML features are not contained in a single Web standard. In fact, there is no specific standard known as DHTML. What is commonly referred to as DHTML is actually the union of several technologies for providing dynamic client-side content, including the following:

- **HTML** DHTML uses standard HTML tags for page description.
- **Document Object Model (DOM)** The DOM is a standardized method by which scripts access the elements of a Web page. It defines the object hierarchy of page items.
- **JavaScript or VBScript** Code that executes to provide the dynamic behavior of the page.
- **Cascading Style Sheets (CSS)** Style sheets provide the ability to define attributes such as font, font size, style, color, border, and so on, for displaying areas of the document.

This set of technologies is used to create dynamic content and to provide the reference platform that supports DHTML.

NOTE: All of the public specifications for the Web technology, including HTML, DOM, CSS, and XML, are available from the World Wide Web Consortium (W3C) on their Web site (www.w3.org).

Microsoft and Netscape have supported different versions of the technologies that make up a DHTML implementation. The two major browsers differ, particularly in the areas of element positioning and the DOM, making a powerful cross-browser application difficult to design. For intranets, however, where the use of a particular browser can be assumed, the features of DHTML make it a compelling choice for advanced application deployment.

Microsoft initially supported DHTML in Internet Explorer 4. All of the primary features of DHTML (including a robust DOM and full-featured scripting) were included in this version. With Internet Explorer 5, Microsoft increased the number of supported features to complete compliance with the proposed W3C standards and made the object model easier to program from the scripting language.

There are two primary methods for a Visual Studio developer to create a DHTML application: through Visual InterDev or Visual Basic. In Visual InterDev, all of the DHTML (except that provided by Design-Time controls) must be coded manually, because the DHTML access capabilities occur within the client-side scripting. For a VB DHTML application, DHTML is integrated with ActiveX controls that execute in the client browser to control the presentation.

NOTE: The IIS Application project type in Visual Basic (where VB builds the ActiveX DLLs and handles the ASP code generation) does not directly support DHTML. If you're going to provide client-side execution of DHTML in an IIS application, you will have to create it manually. The VB DHTML and IIS Application project type are not integrated in the VB environment.

SIMPLE DHTML

To help you grasp how DHTML manipulates a document, let's create the simplest DHTML page available. You can do this coding on any page within Visual InterDev. Since DHTML uses client-side execution, the application can even be written using a simple text editor and loaded directly into the browser—there's no need to place it on a server.

The primary DHTML feature that lets you dynamically address HTML page elements in script code is the ID attribute. An ID attribute is placed within one of the HTML tags to allow the items encapsulated within the tags to be addressed and modified. To add an identifying attribute to a paragraph, for example, you could use code like this:

```
<P ID="textHW">Hello World</P>
```

An ID for a link can look like this:

```
<A HREF="mypage.htm" ID="link1">My Link</A>
```

Once the ID attribute has been set to a unique string, it can then be referenced from the scripting code within your browser. The text within the tags can be read or modified as can the other attributes of the object. Project attributes are accessed using the dot (.) notation, just like properties in Visual Basic code.

Enter the following code into a Visual InterDev application or a text editor. Since all of the execution occurs on the client side, this file does not have to be an ASP file.

```
<HTML>
<BODY>
<P ID="textHW">Hello DHTML World</P>

<SCRIPT language="Javascript">
   // Set the size of the textHW font to 24
   textHW.style.fontSize = 24;
</SCRIPT>

</BODY>
</HTML>
```

You can see that the code changes the size of the font to 24 points when it executes. Without the script code, the paragraph would be displayed in the default size.

By using DHTML, everything on the Web page, from text to links, can be modified through the object model. Properties are used to reflect HTML attributes. Therefore, an image might have an HTML definition like this:

```
<IMG SRC="myPict.gif" WIDTH=200 HEIGHT=100 ID="mypict">
```

The SRC attribute could be changed with JavaScript code such as this:

```
document.mypict.src = "mySecondPict.gif";
```

In this sample, the Document object is specified, whereas in the earlier code (which set the size of textHW) it was not present. When the Document object is not explicitly stated in the scripting code, the scripting engine makes an implicit assumption that the specified element occurs under the selected instantiation of the Document object.

Form items are contained within the Form object. Individual elements that occur on the form must be referenced using the name of the form and then the element name. Code like the following could be used to set the value displayed in a text box inside the myform object:

```
document.myform.txtName.value = "Hello World!"
```

CASCADING STYLE SHEETS

You are probably already familiar with using style sheets in your word processing documents. Style sheets allow you to create a style definition that contains a font, font size, typeface style, paragraph formatting, and so on. Text within a document can then be marked with a particular style type. Any changes to the primary style definition will be immediately reflected in all of the text that is set to that style type. For example, if the style called myBody had a font size setting of 10, changing myBody to 12-point size would reformat all of the text set to that style in the document to the new size.

The W3C has defined a style-sheet standard for the Web called cascading style sheets (CSS). These style sheets can make it much easier to create a generalized common look for your Web pages. The styles available through CSS have many attributes that are customized for Web deployment.

The CSS in HTML allows you to do the following:

- Create font styles including font type, size, style, and leading (line spacing)
- Provide environmental positioning of HTML objects
- Set the current background and foreground colors
- Specify text and graphic spacing
- Provide absolute or relative positioning for page elements
- Add margins and borders
- Set the mouse cursor to a specific type of pointer (for example, an arrow or hand) when the user passes the cursor over a specific area
- Provide filters for transition effects between pages

The CSS standard, which is fully supported in Internet Explorer 4, extends HTML to include 70 style attributes that can be added to HTML tags. Style sheets can be either linked from an external document or embedded directly into the HTML code.

As with DHTML, the implementation of CSS object definitions are different for the Netscape and Microsoft browsers. Netscape has not fully adopted the W3C standard; it selectively implements CSS features, and has added its own definitions for some parts of the style sheet functionality. Therefore, to create a solution that supports style sheets for both browsers, you will need to code for each type of style-sheet definition.

NOTE: Netscape Navigator supports style sheets through JavaScript Accessible Style Sheets (JASS) and dynamic fonts through TrueDoc. These technologies are not defined by the W3C and are therefore unsupported in Internet Explorer.

Adding a Style Sheet to a Document

Adding a style sheet to a Web application is fairly simple, but there is a slight difference in syntax from typical HTML tags or scripting code. Style sheets can be added to an HTML document in four ways:

- **Setting inline style sheets** Styles are selected for individual HTML elements.
- **Embedding the style sheets in the document** The style definitions are created in the document, and can then be used to format elements throughout the body.
- **Linking to a style sheet** An external file can define all of the styles for the document.
- **Importing a style sheet** Styles can be imported from an external file into the current style list.

While these four methods add the style sheet definitions to a document, you also need a way of specifying the parts of the document that will use each style. For most style sheet applications, you will need to group a series of words or paragraphs for a style setting. The HTML tags `<DIV>` and `<SPAN>` allow you to categorize and name a set of elements.

- **`<DIV>`** Used to group a number of HTML elements together. Note that the terminating tag `</DIV>` causes a paragraph break in the HTML display.
- **`<SPAN>`** Used to group smaller elements, such as the text within a sentence instead of separate paragraphs (which would use `<DIV>`). This tag cannot contain paragraph formatting.

The tags are hierarchical and therefore allow styles in encapsulated sections to inherit the styles defined by earlier tags. The characteristics of the text supplied in these definitions are reflected in subsequent displays of those tags.

Inline Styles

The style setting for inline styles is added to a tag by using the `STYLE` attribute. When specified through the inline attribute, the style only affects the text contained within the opening and closing tags. It does not redefine the style for the entire document. To set the color on a section of bold text, you could use code like this:

```
<B STYLE="color:yellow;">This should be bold yellow text.</B>
```

Inline settings can be added to any HTML tag, including `<A>` references. Adding an inline style is primarily useful for layout definitions when you need more exact style settings than are available with HTML tags such as `<H1>` or `<STRONG>`.

Embedded Styles

Embedded styles use the <STYLE> tag to create a series of style-sheet definitions that can be referenced by other HTML elements. Embedded styles are the most popular way of using CSS, because it allows a style to be formatted for the entire document. The style sheets should be defined in the <HEAD> portion of the document so they are available for easy display.

For example, you could define "big" and "little" styles for the text of your documents like this:

```
<HTML>
<HEAD>
<STYLE>

.styBig     {
        font-size: 24;
        text-decoration: underline;
        color: blue;
        }

.stySmall    {
        font-size: 8;
        text-decoration: none;
        color: black;
        }
</STYLE>
```

A style sheet can also omit any one of these attributes and the unspecified attributes will use whatever current setting exists.

Styles can be created as completely new styles (as shown in the preceding code) or they can redefine an existing style. To redefine the settings for the H3 heading style, you could use code like this:

```
<STYLE>
<!-- ' Make style transparent if CSS is not supported
.H3 { font-color:blue; font-style:bold; }
-->
</STYLE>
<H3>Hello Stylized World!</H3>
```

You can see from this code sample that the syntax of the style sheet is different from that of other HTML tags. The name of the style is first specified (in this case, H3) followed by the style settings in the curly brackets {}.

The following style is known as a *class*. A class is defined by starting the declaration with a period. You can reference the class definition within an HTML tag. For example:

```
<STYLE>
<!--
.clsBlue { font-color:blue; }
-->
</STYLE>
```

The style creates a class for the color blue. The definition also includes the HTML comment codes (<!– and -->) which will prevent a browser incapable of supporting the <STYLE> tags from displaying the style code in the document itself. To use the `clsBlue` style, you need to add the `CLASS` attribute to your HTML tags:

```
<B CLASS="clsBlue">This should be blue text.</B>
<STRONG CLASS="clsBlue">This should be bold blue text.</STRONG>
```

The period (.) that precedes the class name only applies to the definition of the style and is not actually part of the identifying name. Therefore, when the class is referenced in a tag, the period is omitted. The prefix of `cls` is not necessary for the attribute, but it is a useful convention that makes it easier to identify the classes in your code.

NOTE: For DHTML access, an inline style is exposed to the scripting language, whereas a style sheet is not. Although you can modify the style object whether it is embedded or inline, only inline styles can be read.

Table 19-1 lists some common property categories that are supported by the CSS standard.

Property	Description
background-color	Background color
border	Border of the current span or object
color	Foreground color
font	Font definition, including type, size, style, and so on
margin	Margin inside the sides of the current window
padding	Distance between the element and its border
text-decoration	Formatting for text, including text blink, strikethrough, underline, overline, and so on

Table 19-1. Properties Supported by the Cascading Style Sheets Specification

The settings for these properties are listed in the CSS specification. There are a variety of settings available within a style, as shown in these examples:

```
text-transform:uppercase;
border:silver thick solid;
background-color:turquoise;
padding:10px;
text-align:center;
text-decoration: none;
```

There are a large number of style and property settings available for style sheets. You can get the entire CSS standard from the W3C Web site (www.w3.org) or get the quick reference from the Stephen Pemberton Web site (www.cwi.nl/~steven/www/css1-qr.html).

Notice that the `padding` property is set to a number followed by a suffix. The suffix defines the units of measure for the setting. The value `10px` specifies 10 pixels should be used for padding. Standard settings include `em`, `pt` (point), and `px` (pixel). The `em` is a relative setting that gets its name from a typesetting standard originally based on the width of a capital letter *M*. Setting values to `em` will allow them to automatically scale if the user increases the size of the font used by the browser.

NOTE: For better accessibility and scaling, try to use the em positioning units because items specified with this scale type will change size with the default font size. If the user changes the default font size in their browser, styles using this gradation will scale properly. On the default settings for Internet Explorer, 1 em equals roughly 10 pixels. To display 18 point type under the default settings, use a 1.5em type size.

Linked Styles

Linked style sheets are contained in a separate file with the `.css` extension. The styles in the CSS file should follow the same syntax as the embedded styles except they should not be contained within `<STYLE>` tags or comment brackets `<!– –>`. Once the styles are linked, they can be used just as if they were defined within the file.

You can place a link in an HTML file with a reference like this:

```
<LINK REL="stylesheet" TYPE="text/css" HREF="mystyles.css">
```

Imported Styles

Linked styles set the specified files as the exclusive definition location for the styles of that document. However, you might need to define other styles for the page, as well. By importing the styles from one of the files, you can augment those settings with additional style definitions of your own. To import styles, place an import flag at the beginning of the definition of a CSS set, like this:

```
<STYLE>
<!--
@import: url(mystyles.css);
H3 { font-color:blue; font-style:bold; background-color:turquoise; }
-->
</STYLE>
<H3>Hello Stylized World!</H3>
```

This import command will load styles from the imported sheet and add them to the set that is being defined. This is especially useful if you have a file that contains master styles, and you also want additional style settings for each page.

Positioning Page Elements

Positioning in an HTML document has always been a problem for designers who want precise control over the location of page elements. Programs such as NetObjects' Fusion could simulate precise control using a table for placement with varying degrees of success. With DHTML, absolute positioning of elements on the display page is now possible.

Any HTML object, such as a paragraph or an image, can be positioned on the page and moved on the fly. Position settings are defined as attributes within the `<STYLE>` definitions.

- **`POSITION`** Specifies either absolute coordinates (coordinates that are determined in relation to the page) or relative coordinates (coordinates that are determined in relation to the parent object)
- **`TOP`** Defines the Y position of the element on the screen
- **`LEFT`** Defines the X position of the element on the screen
- **`Z-INDEX`** Defines where the element appears in the back-to-front display order. The `z-index` actually refers to the `z-order` of the screen object and designates its relative position on the `z-axis`.

An example of using the positioning capabilities is helpful because it is often difficult to visualize. Like other DHTML additions, positioning changes a sequential static HTML page into a dynamic interactive page that is more like a traditional client application. Enter this code into an HTML editor and save the file as `Animate.htm`:

```
<HTML>
<HEAD>
<SCRIPT LANGUAGE="JavaScript">
```

```
function animate() {
   // Setup image in proper place
   document.all.moveImage.style.pixelLeft = document.body.offsetWidth
   // Make image visible
   document.all.moveImage.style.visibility = "visible"
   // Set up interval to call routine
   myTimer = window.setInterval("move()",100)
}

function move() {
   // If there is room available, move
   if (document.all.moveImage.style.pixelLeft > 10) {
      document.all.moveImage.style.pixelLeft -= 10
   }
}
</SCRIPT>
</HEAD>
<BODY>
<H1>DHTML Positioning</H1>
<IMG ID="moveImage"
STYLE="visibility:hidden;position:absolute;top:0;left:0;z-index:-1"
SRC="tile.gif">
<P onclick="animate()">Click here to animate</P>
</BODY>
</HTML>
```

This example takes an image named tile.gif and makes it invisible by changing the style settings. The `animate()` method executes when the text is clicked on. This sets the object's position to the far right of the window, makes it visible, and creates a timed event loop to advance the object across the screen (see Figure 19-1). You might notice that the image actually moves behind the displayed text. This is caused by setting the style's `z-index` (z-order) to `-1`.

NOTE: The Netscape and Microsoft style sheets differ primarily in their positioning capabilities. Netscape Navigator uses the proprietary `<LAYER>` tag to support positioning; Microsoft has adopted the open standard initiated by the W3C.

As part of Microsoft's battle to win the browser wars, it designed Visual InterDev to support Microsoft's implementation of DHTML. For most core DHTML features, you can create code that will execute under either the Microsoft or Netscape browser.

For the Netscape object model, the `document.layers` object path is used to address the various page elements. For Internet Explorer, `document.all` performs the same

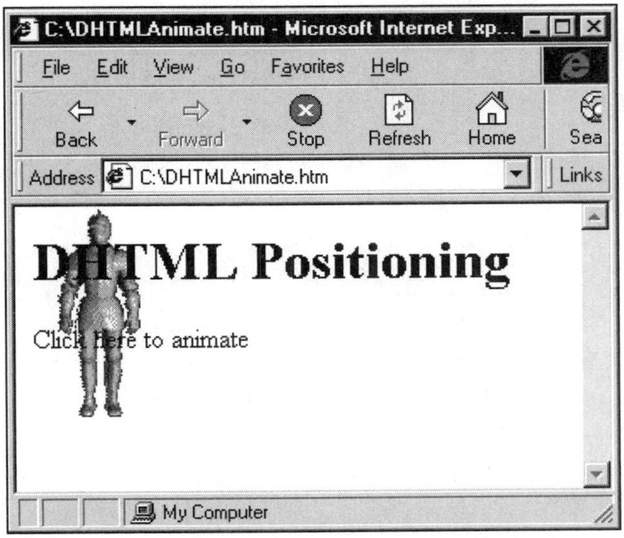

Figure 19-1. The image will advance across the screen until it reaches the left edge

function. To create positioning code that will execute on either browser, you can create a variable that would hold a reference to the document layers. This variable would be filled with the proper object reference depending on the browser type detected and then all subsequent script code (in that HTML document) could use the variable reference to access a specific layer instead of explicitly naming the layer.

The following sample code automatically detects the type of browser available, allows for either DHTML implementation, and fills the docReference variable with the needed pointer:

```
if (document.layers) docReference = document.layers["layerName"];
if (document.all) docReference = document.all["layerName"].style;
```

Once the `docReference` variable has been set, most of the document objects can be addressed for either browser. The image setup code from the Animate.htm example will appear with this reference:

```
docReference.moveImage.style.pixelLeft = document.body.offsetWidth
```

Using Filters

Filters provide multimedia effects in Internet Explorer (these effects are not available in Netscape Navigator). The filter is designed as part of a style sheet. To make an element fade out, you could define a style like this:

```
<IMG ID="image1" SRC="tile.gif" STYLE="filter:revealTrans(Duration=3.0,
Transition=1)">
```

Filtered elements cannot run in their own window, such as in a frames window. Transitions must be applied and then played in order to take effect.

The available filters include:

- **`Alpha`** Sets a transparency level
- **`BlendTrans`** Creates a blending transition
- **`Blur`** Blurs an element
- **`Chroma`** Sets a transparency color
- **`DropShadow`** Adds a drop shadow to an image
- **`FlipV`** Flips an element vertically
- **`FlipH`** Flips an element horizontally
- **`Glow`** Adds a glow to the outside edges of an element
- **`Gray`** Makes an element appear in grayscale
- **`Invert`** Inverts an element
- **`Light`** Makes light appear to be directed at an element
- **`Mask`** Makes a transparency mask from an element
- **`Redirect`** Converts an object to an object that can be used by DirectAnimation
- **`RevealTrans`** Creates a transition
- **`Shadow`** Creates a silhouette of an element
- **`Wave`** Uses a wave distortion to display the image
- **`XRay`** Displays the edges of an object

DOCUMENT OBJECT MODEL (DOM)

The core of DHTML-application creation lies in the ability to access and modify elements on the Web page. The Document Object Model (DOM) defines the objects available within an HTML document, as well as their hierarchy. In Figure 19-2, you can see the objects available to scripting code.

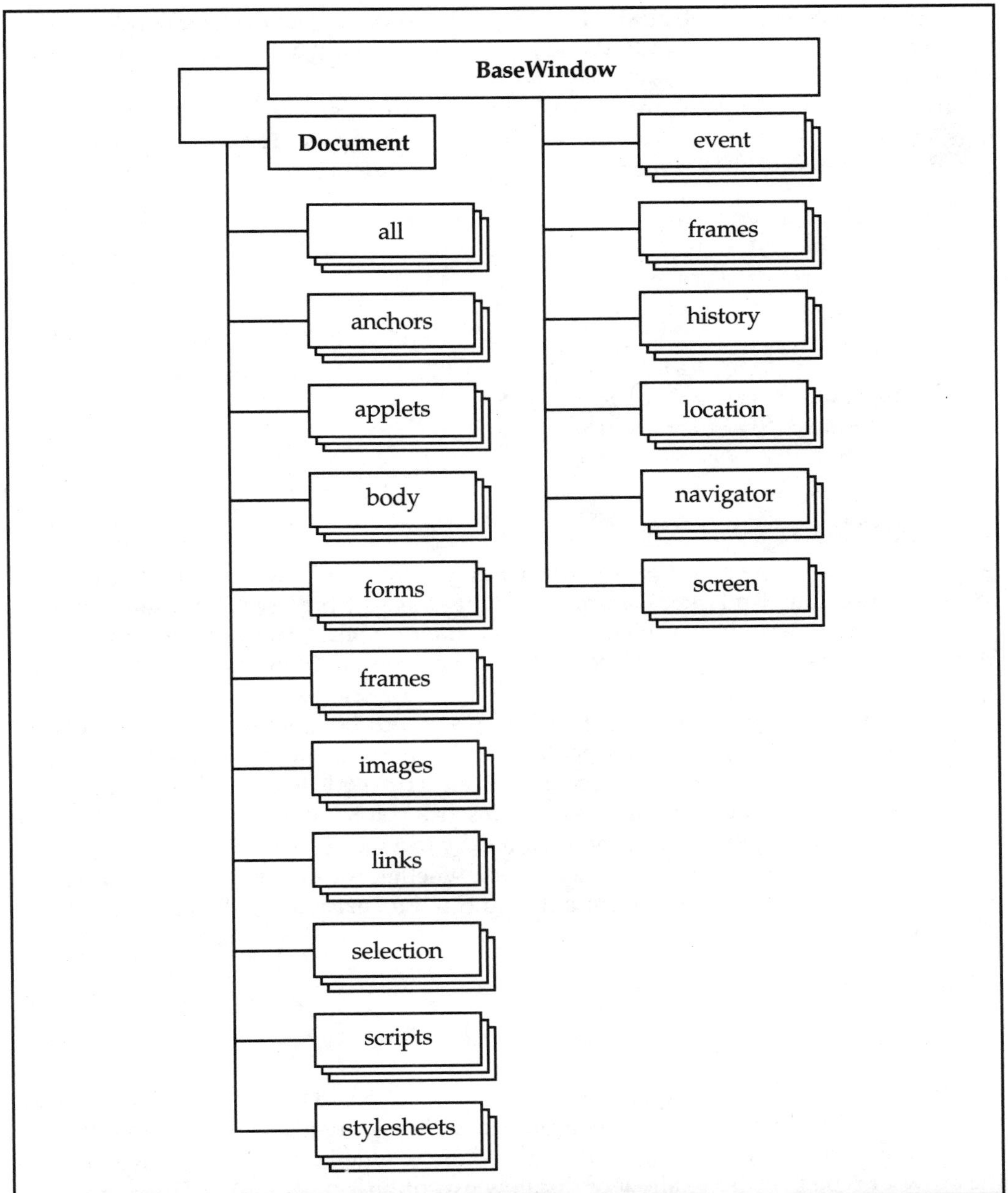

Figure 19-2. The objects of the Document Object Model

Within the object model, most window objects descend from the BaseWindow object, which defines the browser window, and the Document object, which displays the current HTML document.

In DHTML terminology, the objects on a DHTML page are called elements. Headings, images, and styles are all examples of elements on a page. These elements are referenced in code in much the same way that objects are referenced in VB:

```
Private function cmdSearch_onclick() As Boolean
   'Create variables to contain the search criteria.
   Dim lastName as String
   Dim firstName as String

   ' Get from text fields
   lastName=Me.lastName.Value
   firstName=Me.FirstName.Value
End Function
```

Object Detection

Although you can detect the type of browser that is running, browsers might be updated to include previously missing features. With the Netscape browser distributed by AOL, you may see increasing compliance with the international standards bodies, such as W3C. In the near future, Navigator could become compatible with the W3C DHTML specification.

Therefore, for layering and other capabilities, it can be more effective to determine whether the browser supports a particular feature than to make an assumption based on browser type. The `If` statement can be used from script code to detect if an object exists. By including code that tests for an object's presence before attempting to use it, you can make client-side code that can adapt dynamically to a new browser.

In this sample code, the script checks to see whether the document.images are available in the executing browser. If present, you can then execute DHTML code that uses this object:

```
if (document.images) {  // Check if the object exists
   // Execute DHTML code
}
```

Unfortunately, this technique only works for whole objects. It cannot detect the presence of individual methods within an object. If you are going to include methods that are unavailable to all browsers (such as the CreateElement method), you will have to detect the browser type in order to allow or disallow execution.

Using the CreateElement Method

In DHTML, Microsoft has created the `createElement()` method, which can be used to add items to the HTML page on the client side. The most common use of this method is to allow items to be dynamically added to a list or combo box, based on the user's selections of other controls on the page.

NOTE: The `createElement()` method is not supported in Netscape Navigator. If you want this solution to avoid causing an error on Netscape browsers, you will need to add browser type checking code.

To create a button that will add an additional element to an options box named List1, you can use code like this:

```
Function Button1_onclick() As Boolean
   Dim myElement as HTMLOptionElement
   // Create a new option element
   Set myElement = Document.createElement("OPTION")
   // Set the appropriate properties of the element
   myElement.Text=TextField1.Value
   myElement.Value="ListItemValue"
   // Add element to current option box
   List1.Options.Add myElement
End Function
```

This method is particularly useful when you are creating a drag-and-drop interface to allow dynamic element additions. The `createElement()` method can only be used for list, select, and image elements.

VISUAL BASIC DHTML APPLICATIONS

Visual Basic 6 added the ability to create a DHTML application. It can generate a project that mimics many of the capabilities of a standard client application. The VB DHTML application is a hybrid between HTML code and ActiveX controls. VB allows you to use the full capabilities of the VB language for compilation into an ActiveX control. The appropriate DHTML code is generated automatically.

NOTE: Visual Basic has difficulty working with frame-based documents. If you are going to need a frame-set solution, using a VB DHTML application may not be the best choice.

A DHTML application created in Visual Basic allows you to store information between pages, much like the server Session object. It can respond to events on the client-side through the code that has been created in the VB application.

The core object in the DHTML application is the DHTMLPage object. DHTMLPage is the runtime object that has events such as Load, Unload, Initialize, and Terminate. Like a traditional VB application, events execute in this order: Initialize > Load > Unload > Terminate.

Like all ActiveX controls, the code is compiled and is therefore unavailable for examination without the source code. This ability can have special meaning when the code is being stored on the client for execution. The compilation will prevent visitors from stealing or modifying your client code, which is a hazard with traditional client-side script.

For referencing objects in the DHTML object model, you learned that a page element can include an ID attribute so that it can be addressed in the script. The same applies to VB DHTML applications, although all ID attributes used in interfaces in Visual Basic must be unique. This does not apply to standard DHTML, which allows ID overloading. If there are duplicate IDs in the page, VB will automatically append a number to the ID, thereby changing its name.

NOTE: For elements to be used within the VB DHTML environment, don't assign an ID attribute of more than 117 characters. Exceeding this limit will cause an error at run time.

The DHTML application is made up of a number of DHTML pages. You can either save these as designer pages (a VB format) or reference an external HTML page. A designer page is easier to maintain if you are building the application with a team of Visual Basic designers. If a Web designer team needs modification privileges from external editors (such as Microsoft FrontPage), however, you will want to create a reference to an HTML file.

For a DHTML application, Visual Basic uses an internal executing program called a *designer* (like the Data Environment designer used for the DE) to allow management of DHTML files. The `SourceFile` property of the designer file designates the format that the page will be saved in. The property will be empty if the file is saved in the VB project, and it will contain the HTML filename if saved externally.

NOTE: The Visual Basic designer does not allow you to view or edit HTML code directly. Therefore, if you like hands-on access to the HTML, using an external file may be the best choice.

When you open a page in a VB project, the designer window for that page will be displayed. This designer window allows you to setup the DHTML application as well as position elements, design layering, and other DHTML functions. The window provided by the designer is called the *document editor*.

Opening a designer page will provide you with a window specific to DHTML development. On the toolbar in the designer window is an icon that allows you to specify the type of positioning that will be used when you place a new element on the page. Two types of positioning are available:

- **Relative positioning** This is the type of positioning that you are familiar with on an HTML page. Elements are placed within the document, and their positions are determined by the text, `<P>` and `<BR>` tags, and other elements.
- **Absolute positioning** Absolute positioning takes advantage of the DHTML functionality to place an object anywhere in the browser window.

The icon used for positioning, labeled Absolute Position Mode in the ToolTip, defaults to being off. This makes relative positioning the default mode. Clicking the icon will set the mode that specifies how new elements will be placed on the page, as well as changing the positioning mode of the currently selected element.

You can set the z-order of page elements by using the layering options of the toolbar menu (see the following illustration).

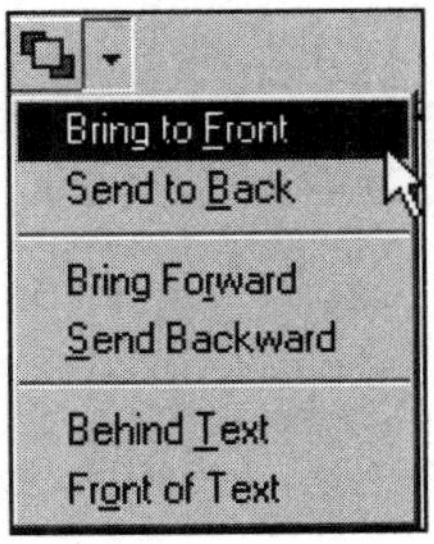

NOTE: The layering attributes of objects only apply when the elements are selected for absolute positioning.

The toolbar also contains icons that can wrap a selected group of elements in a `<DIV>` or `<SPAN>` tag. Simply select the desired objects in the right pane of the window, and click the appropriate icon: Wrap Selection in <DIV>...</DIV> or Wrap Selection in <SPAN>...</SPAN>. The Make Selection into Link icon on the toolbar will change the selected elements into a hyperlink.

The document editor can also create tables. The Table menu (shown in the next illustration) allows you to create a table, insert and delete cells, columns, and rows, as well as split and merge cells.

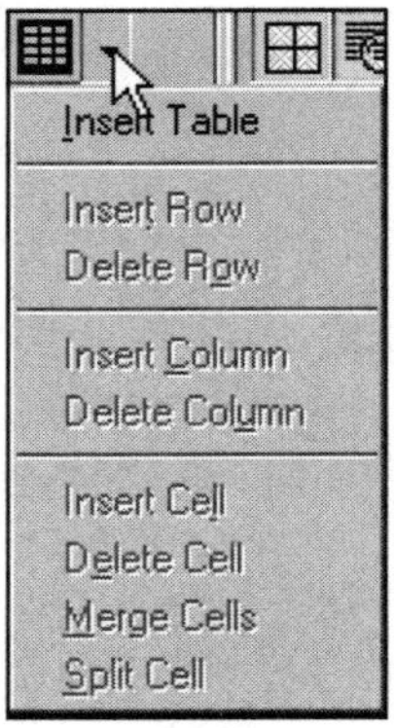

In the document editor, the detail panel in the right pane of the window shows the contents of the HTML page. When you select an element in the left pane, it will also be selected in the details pane.

DHTML events often are prefixed with the letters `on` (for example, `onkeydown`, `onkeypress`, `onkeyup`). Aside from this difference, they largely mirror the events available in Visual Basic. The focus events are different, however, as can be seen in this comparison:

VB	DHTML
`gotfocus`	`onfocus`
`lostfocus`	`onblur`
`selchange`	`onselectstart`, `onselect`
`dragdrop`, `dragover`	`dragstart`

Additionally, several events exist in the DHTML environment for which there are no equivalents in Visual Basic:

- **`onabort`** Activated when the Stop button is clicked to halt the retrieval of a page element
- **`onreset`** Activated when the Reset button is clicked
- **`onsubmit`** Activated when the Submit button is clicked

The event code that is placed in your VB DHTML application receives the activation before the Web browser. Therefore, your code can specify whether to allow the browser to process it or not. In this sample code, an `onclick` event will change the colors of two buttons:

```
Private Function Hyperlink1_onclick() as Boolean
   ' Insert event code
   Button1.style.backgroundColor = "red"
   Button2.style.backgroundColor = "#FF00FF"   '

  ' True = do default, False = don't execute default
   Hyperlink1_onclick = True
End Function
```

Notice that this code uses both a proper style sheet–variable name and a more common RGB color setting for the backgrounds of the two buttons. After the event code executes, it still allows the link to be activated (the default operation for a link click). If the function was set to False, only this code would execute.

NOTE: The Internet Explorer 5 version of DHTML adds an additional method of handling events called *behaviors*. The implementation of behaviors allows you to link a script file external to the normal HTML file that defines how controls will react. This includes the functioning of standard HTML controls, such as the text box. It can also be used to define the behavior of ActiveX controls and Java applets. Check the Internet Explorer 5 document on the MSDN Web site (msdn.microsoft.com) for more information.

Changing DHTML Document Text

DHTML provides a mechanism for changing the text that occurs between an opening and closing tag. In order to make this modification, DHTML includes a special set of methods that specify how the text will be replaced.

- **`innerText`** Holds and can replace the content between the tags with specified text.
- **`innerHTML`** Holds and can replace the HTML between the tags.
- **`outerText`** Holds and can replace the object, including the tags, with specified text. Note that if this is set, the ID reference to the element will be eliminated, so it cannot be accessed again.
- **`outerHTML`** Contains and allows the entire element to be set, including tags and text.

These properties are all read and write capable, so you can use them to retrieve the content stored within the tags as well as to set it. There are also two methods included in DHTML that allow you to add other elements before or after the referenced element:

- **`InsertAdjacentText`** Allows text to be added before or after the referenced element. Use the `beforeBegin`, `afterBegin`, `beforeEnd`, and `afterEnd` parameters to specify where to locate the new text.
- **`InsertAdjacentHTML`** Allows HTML to be added before or after the referenced element. Use the same location settings as `InsertAdjacentText`.

Drag-and-Drop Capabilities

Until recently, drag-and-drop functionality only was available for taking content from the browser window to the destination window of another application. DHTML allows objects to be dragged and dropped within the browser window for rearrangement and event activation. Objects can even be moved between frames.

The dataTransfer object provides most of this capability. The dataTransfer object works much like an internal clipboard that allows objects to be cut, copied, and pasted to and from it. To send data to and retrieve data from the object, you can use the `setData` and `getData` methods, respectively. To place an object with an `ID` setting of `myTable` in the dataTransfer object, you could use code like this:

```
window.event.dataTransfer.setData "myTable"
```

You can even specify the data type that will be used for the transfer of the data. Setting the data type will allow the receiving application to properly process the data included in the dataTransfer object. For example, to specify that an object will be contained in the transfer, you'd use code like this:

```
window.event.dataTransfer.setData "myTable", myObject
```

If data is dropped onto a text box, you can use the `getData` method to place the data into the `Value` property with code like this:

```
window.event.dataTransfer.getData "myTable", myObject
```

You can also use the `innerHTML` and `insertAdjacentHTML` methods to allow an object that is dropped on another designated object to be added to the current contents.

Creating a DHTML Application

Applications developed in Visual InterDev can be effectively customized for use on any browser that supports the proper DHTML browser object. A VB DHTML application, in contrast, can only run on Internet Explorer because it requires the use of ActiveX controls which aren't supported by other browser types. Since natively compiled ActiveX controls are used, processor-intensive functions, such as mathematical or graphics applications, are more feasible in a VB DHTML application than in a scripting environment.

The following example demonstrates how a DHTML application can be created using Visual Basic to change some of the displayed page elements. It will use the `onclick` and mouse movement events to make changes to the document based on user interaction. All of the code will be executing on the client-side like a Visual InterDev DHTML application.

Follow these steps to create the Visual Basic-based DHTML application:

1. *Execute Visual Basic.*
2. *Start a New Project.*
3. *Select the DHTML Application (see Figure 19-3).*

The DHTML palette will display the familiar HTML controls (such as a hyperlink, option list, text box, and so on) as well as the Input Image component that is specific to a VB DHTML application. The project will contain two files: a module and a DHTML designer

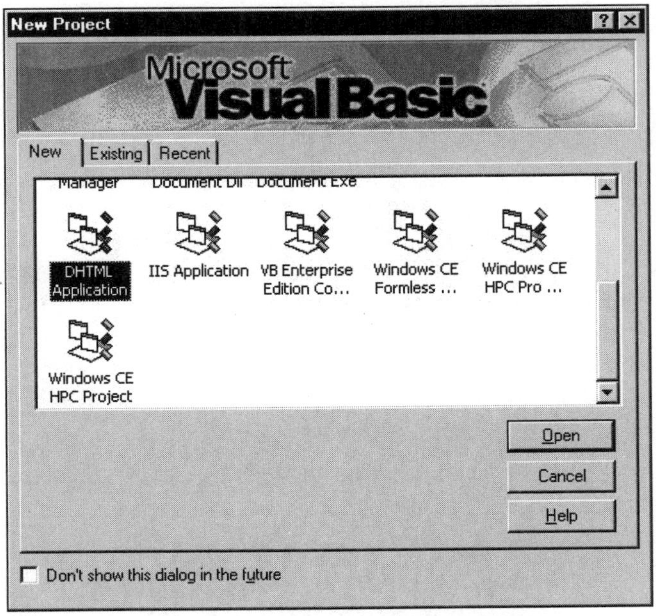

Figure 19-3. The DHTML application is one of the application types for VB 6 generation

file (shown in the next illustration). The module file can be used to hold code or global procedures that will be available to all of the executing pages.

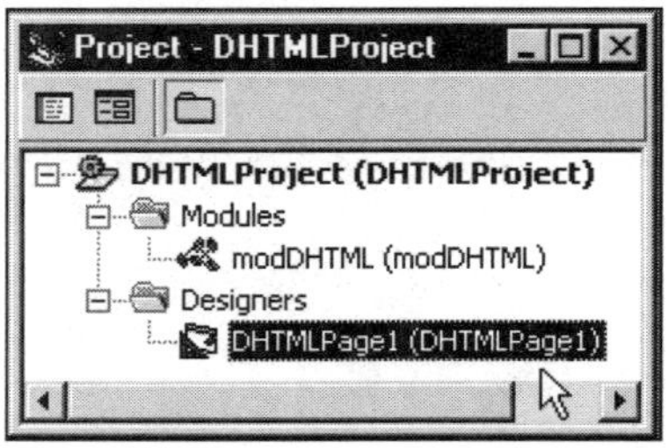

4. *Double-click the DHTMLPage1 file.* This will open the document in a split-pane window view and display a new toolbar. This window is the designer used for DHTML pages. The left pane of the window contains a hierarchical tree of all of the objects contained in the document. The right pane, the detail pane, shows the current content of the document. The toolbar provides a number of formatting icons for alignment properties, z-order manipulation of page elements, table creation, font style properties, and hyperlink creation.

NOTE: The VB DHTML application does not directly support cascading style sheets. Any CSS implementation used must be created by modifying the HTML code outside of Visual Basic.

5. *Click in the detail pane and enter some text.*
6. *Select the paragraph item in the left pane that reads "VB DHTML Application".*
7. *Use the style combo box on the toolbar to set the type to Heading 1.* You will see that the type of item (designated by its icon) changes in the left pane, while the right pane visually reflects the new style (see the following illustration). These elements will be static on the page. To demonstrate the capabilities of the VB DHTML application, you need an element that will be used to attach events. For this element, you can create a standard hyperlink onto which event code will be attached.

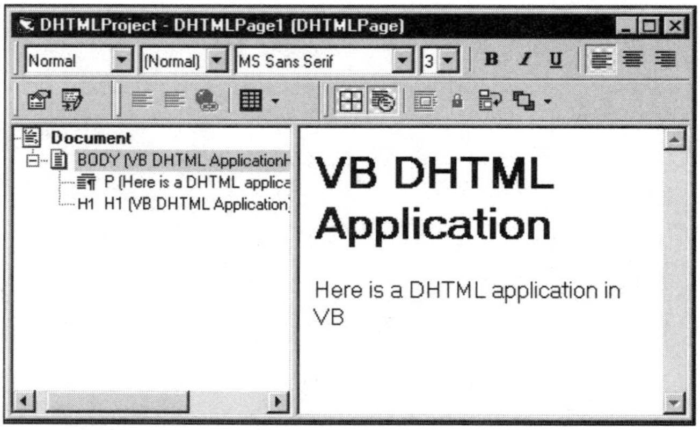

8. *Enter another paragraph at the end of the document with the text* ***Move mouse over and click on this text***. This text label will be used to demonstrate event execution.
9. *Select the new paragraph item in the left pane.*
10. *Display the Properties window by pressing the* F4 *key.* You'll see a number of attributes available for the item. If an ID attribute is set, the element will be accessible for code, events, and other DHTML interaction.
11. *Set the (Id) field to* ***lblText*** *(see Figure 19-4).* When you change the ID, you will notice that the name of the element appears with the element in the left pane of the window. It is now available for access or linking code.
12. *Double-click the lblText item.* This will display the code window with all of the available events. The default `onClick` event will be selected.
13. *Add the following code so that your event will add to the displayed text.* This code might at first seem odd, because the `With...End With` construct is used for only a single line. This coding was done to make you very aware that you are

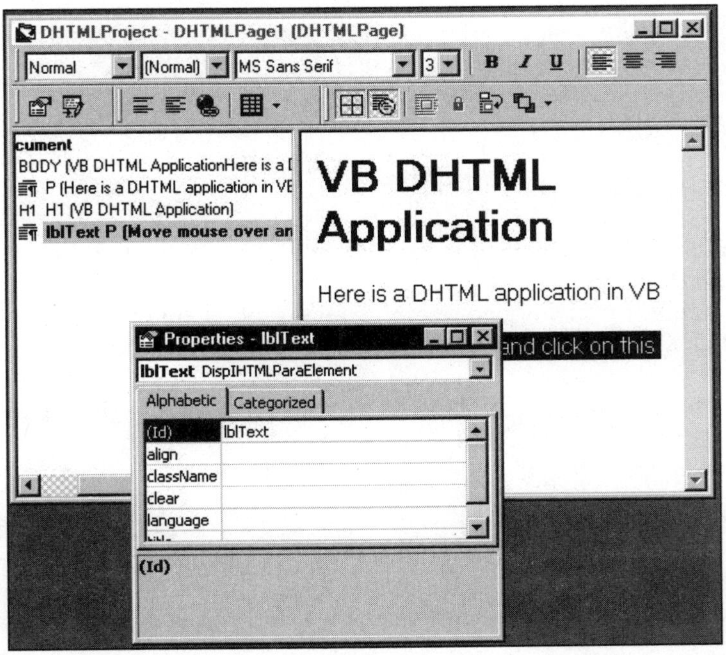

Figure 19-4. Set the ID attribute so that code can reference the element

working in Visual Basic and not VBScript (which doesn't support `With...End With`). Although the code resembles what you've done earlier with VBScript, this application is actually a compiled VB component.

```
Private Function lblText_onclick() As Boolean
   With lblText
       .innerText = .innerText + "...and again"
   End With
End Function
```

14. *Add the following code to the* `onmousemove()` *and* `onmouseout()` *events.* These events will cause the text size and color to be changed when the mouse cursor moves across the paragraph. When the cursor leaves the paragraph, the text will appear as another color.

```
Private Sub lblText_onmousemove()
   With lblText.Style
       .Color = "blue"
       .FontSize = 24
   End With
End Sub
Private Sub lblText_onmouseout()
   With lblText.Style
       .Color = "green"
       .FontSize = 14
   End With
End Sub
```

15. *Execute the application by pressing* F5.

Unlike standard VB 6 projects that would execute the application as a standalone executable, your DHTML application is loaded into the Internet Explorer browser for execution. When the cursor is positioned over the paragraph element, the text will change its size. If you click on the paragraph (see Figure 19-5), text will be added to the existing paragraph.

When you move the cursor off the text, the text will shrink to small green characters. This code could have been accomplished using VBScript, but in addition to providing faster execution speed, using this object protects your client-side source code.

16. *Select the View Source option from the browser View menu.* You will see only code that looks like the code that follows. VB compiles and generates the object to be used by the client-side solution. It is activated by the `<OBJECT>` tag reference, and your actual client-side code never appears for examination or modification.

```
<!--METADATA TYPE="MsHtmlPageDesigner" startspan-->
<object id="DHTMLPage1"
classid="clsid:DD87BB0E-59B3-11D3-AA6D-0080C8833F6C"
```

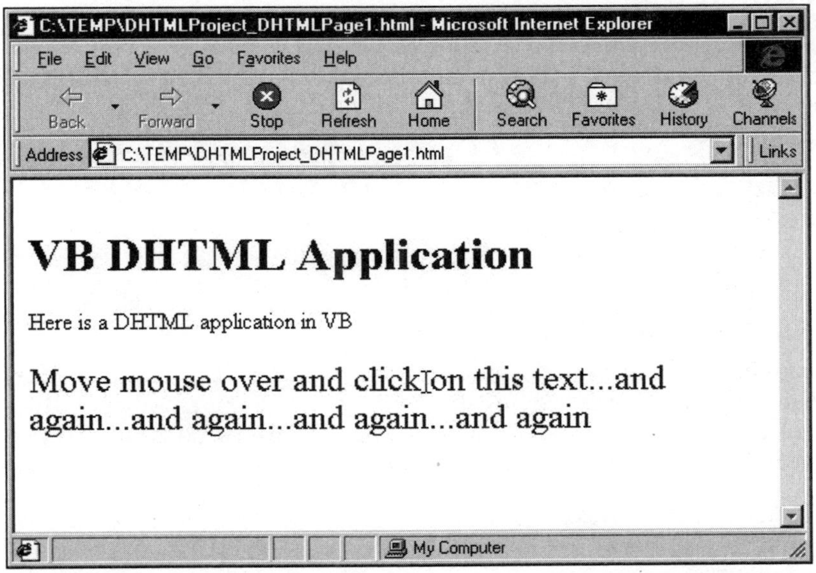

Figure 19-5. The application executes in the Internet Explorer browser and reacts to events

```
width=0 height=0>
</object>
<!--METADATA TYPE="MsHtmlPageDesigner" endspan-->
<BODY>
<H1>VB DHTML Application</H1>
<P>Here is a DHTML application in VB</P>
<P id=lblText>Move mouse over and click on this
text</P>
</BODY>
</HTML>
```

NOTE: If you click the Refresh button while the VB application is paused, all of your breakpoints will be eliminated when you restart it.

This application should aptly demonstrate how VB code can be activated when DHTML events occur. Although the application primarily consists of compiled VB functionality, it can actively modify HTML elements on the Web page.

Navigating with Code

Using the object model, you can even control movement through a Web site. Script code can move the browser from one page to another by using the BaseWindow object's `navigate` method. To move to the second page of your project, you could attach code like this to a button:

```
Private Function Button1_onclick() As Boolean
   BaseWindow.navigate "Project1_DHTMLPage2.htm"
End Function
```

Storing Session Information

You can store information that will stay with the document by using the `PutProperty` method. The data can be retrieved by calling the `GetProperty` method. Values stored in the property are actually recorded to client cookies. Here is some sample source code that places the value stored in a last-name box, and retrieves it to display a message:

```
Private Function PutButton1_onclick() As Boolean
   PutProperty BaseWindow.Document, "lastName", txtLastName.Value
End Function

Private Function GetButton1_onclick() As Boolean
   MyValue.innerText = "LastName: " & _
      GetProperty(BaseWindow.Document, "lastName")
End Function
```

NOTE: If you use the `MsgBox` method in your ActiveX control, it will display the message in the VB environment while it is executing under VB. Click the VB icon on the task bar to view it.

Q&A

Q: Is there a way to make my DHTML code work in both Navigator and Internet Explorer?

A: Yes. Although the DHTML implementation available in Netscape Navigator is more limited than the Internet Explorer version, much of the basic framework is identical. Therefore, you can make compatible style sheets (using the W3C standard, which both browsers support) and use a simple `If...Then` statement to determine which browser's layer settings to apply.

The object model in Netscape, at the time of this writing, was moving toward adoption of the full DOM framework. Check the version of Netscape that is in use for individual objects to make sure they are available.

Q: Does DHTML support client-side data capabilities?

A: Not exactly. Despite the indications of some of the Microsoft documentation, client-side data-source access is provided by client-side ActiveX components used in conjunction with DHTML. DHTML merely provides the object model, which allows access to such items as the table elements, which in turn allow the client-side components to reformat and display the database information.

SUMMARY

Intranet applications have several deployment advantages over Internet applications: the network administrator can often specify a type and version of browser, and larger, more reliable bandwidth is usually available. Both of these considerations make DHTML a promising technology for advanced intranet deployment. The availability of DHTML in a large percentage of browsers allows client-side scripting to dynamically manipulate page content for a more user-friendly application. In this chapter, you covered the following:

- **Dynamic HTML (DHTML)** DHTML provides an object model for accessing and altering any of the objects on an HTML page without reloading the page or making a request to the server. Scripting code in VBScript or JavaScript on the client browser is used to manipulate the DHTML objects.
- **Standard DHTML applications** DHTML objects can be controlled by events and behaviors that are coded in a client-side scripting language. Typically this is a client-side application consisting of HTML code and augmented by script code to provide dynamic changes to the currently viewed Web page.
- **VB DHTML applications** These applications combine the DHTML object model with ActiveX controls that execute in the client browser. DHTML applications created in Visual Basic will automatically generate the necessary scripting code to activate the ActiveX controls.
- **Cascading Style Sheets (CSS)** CSS makes it possible to define a style sheet for a page or multiple documents to standardize the appearance of page elements. For example, an H1 heading can be assigned a particular font, style, size, and color that will be used to present any text appearing within the <H1> tags.
- **Layers or z-order** Layers provide the ability to place one object on top of another in an HTML page. Before style-sheet positioning, there was no method of allowing shapes to appear on top of or behind other text or image items. Using the `z-index` property, the order can be set for tags.
- **Positioning** Positioning gives you the ability to explicitly specify the X and Y coordinates of an object on an HTML page. Exact positioning and movement of objects is critical in order to allow Web pages to provide multimedia or a professionally formatted presentation.

CHAPTER 20

Windows 2000 and Active Directory

The release of Windows 2000 (previously known as Windows NT 5.0) brings Active Directory to the Windows NT operating system. Active Directory will provide global directory services and allow a single login for a variety of network resources including objects, file volumes, networks, printer shares, and databases. Previously, a single login would only allow access to the resources controlled by a single domain controller. With Active Directory, resources across domains can automatically verify authentication so multiple logins and security profiles become unnecessary.

In a large organization, security can literally span hundreds or thousands of machines. Resource management can be a nearly overwhelming task. Active Directory consolidates and extends the login process by allowing permissions to custom resources (such as backup systems) to be maintained for each user. Several years after Novell pioneered centralized directory management with an enterprise management system called Novell Directory Services (NDS), Microsoft has created a robust global directory that benefits from Novell's earlier experience.

With Active Directory, Microsoft has also sought to collapse the worlds of LAN, WAN, and the Internet. Web resources, including file stores, bandwidth settings, and permissions, are now all encapsulated within the Windows 2000 operating system. Microsoft has made TCP/IP, the key protocol of the Web, the native protocol of Windows 2000.

NOTE: With Windows 2000 and Active Directory, Microsoft is making TCP/IP the default and preferred protocol of Windows. Previously the NetBEUI/NetBIOS standard dominated the network. With the release of Windows 2000, resource lookup will occur predominantly through DNS-based directory systems.

Understanding Active Directory is important to managing Web sites, FrontPage extension logins, bandwidth adjustments, and integrated logins for databases and file folders. The traditional Windows NT Challenge/Response system now addresses Active Directory to determine access permissions. Examining Active Directory and some of the new IIS 5 features included with Windows 2000 will prepare you for the new topology of a Windows 2000 network.

ACTIVE DIRECTORY STRUCTURE

Active Directory is a significant improvement on previous NT resource structures in its basic storage and organization. While the domain management available in earlier versions of Windows NT has a flat organization, Windows 2000 features a hierarchical structure. Active Directory is essentially a large centralized database that holds all of the information for all of the resources on the network. Because it is a database, it can take advantage of all the features commonly associated with a database including searchability, replication, and central backup.

One of the immediate benefits of the Active Directory data organization is the ability to have different resources retain the same name as long as they are located in different areas of the hierarchy. For example, with Windows NT 4, it would be impossible to accommodate two users (one in Marketing and one in R&D) who each wanted the username *jsmith* on the same domain. With a hierarchical organization of users, each jsmith can be placed in his or her hierarchical department, thereby avoiding the username conflict. For large organizations where name and resource conflicts are common, this new structure is a significant improvement.

Microsoft has based Active Directory upon the Exchange Server directory capabilities that were initially used to provide e-mail security. Active Directory implements and augments the LDAP protocol for network resource access. Lightweight Directory Access Protocol (LDAP) is an open standard for storing and querying directory information. LDAP is also used by Microsoft Exchange Server for its directory functions.

As Microsoft evolved the directory services already available in Exchange Server, they became the basis for Active Directory. Even the properties stored for each user have been broadened to reflect the extended role that a user record will now play. Many of the characteristics of an Exchange Server user account can be seen in the individual user dialog boxes used by Active Directory (see Figure 20-1).

At the heart of Active Directory lies the replicated data store called a *directory*. This directory is not the same as the file folder directory on a hard drive. It is a specific file type that holds all of the access information that defines the resources within a domain. A directory file exists on each Active Directory domain controller.

DEFINITION: **Directory** In Active Directory services, a directory is the data store or file that contains all of the resource information. It is the directory that is replicated among Windows 2000 machines.

The use of the directory has made NT more flexible since it allows the Active Directory system to provide a unified directory of all resources available through the network. Active Directory eliminates the concept of Primary Domain controllers and Backup Domain controllers, as all domain controllers are treated equally. In the past, servers had to be configured as one or the other during the installation process and could not be changed without a complete re-install. The new Active Directory configuration allows you to easily specify which controller will act in the role of primary controller and which are reserved for backup at any time. This promotes replication and fail-over capabilities in a server network.

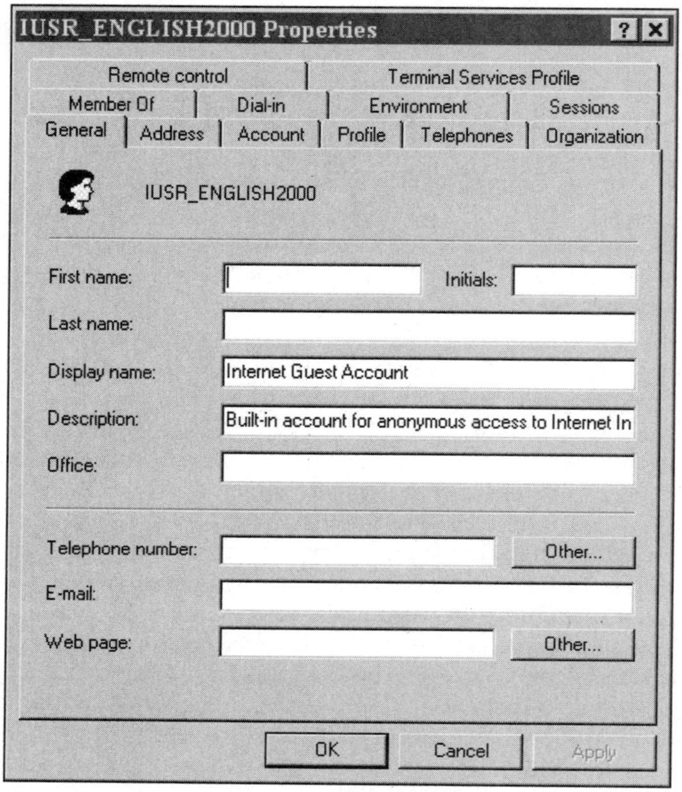

Figure 20-1. User account Properties dialog box

In fact, each domain controller within the domain will have a replicated version of the primary directory file. The directory data is stored within a file named `ntds.dit` on each domain controller.

One of the most attractive aspects of the Active Directory system is the potential of centralizing administration of all of the resources in the enterprise. Previous modifications for common business practices, such as a division reorganization, could create substantial additional work and downtime to reconfigure a Windows NT domain-based system.

Permissions had to be transferred individually to the new server when relocation was required. With Active Directory, that same reorganization would essentially be as simple as deciding what groups and users need to be reassigned. Since all of the resources are held in the directory file, reassignment is instantaneous.

The directory file serves a greater purpose than simply providing security logon services. It also allows you to examine a directory of all the resources on the network that are available to you. All of the listings of the computing resources are stored in a hierarchical database.

Within the directory, Active Directory stores the object information related to users, groups, printers, file shares, computers, domains, organizational units, and security policies. These item types are the ones that ship with Windows 2000, but one of the most important advances in this Active Directory structure is that you can extend it to include new object types linked to user and group security.

Access Control Lists

If you are familiar with NT security, you know that Access Control Lists (ACLs) determine the operations that a user can perform on each object (file share, printer share, etc.). For example, the write or delete permissions for a directory are held in an ACL that is consulted by the NT system when a request is made for that resource.

ACLs are still used by Active Directory. Active Directory uses static ACL inheritance like NT, so when a resource is moved from one place to another, it does not automatically add the permissions of the new parent. You can define security for a folder in the Properties dialog window and click the *Allow Inheritable Permissions from a Parent to Propagate to the Object* setting to make the children that exist under the parent accept the security settings.

This method of configuration can be used for the hierarchical basis of Active Directory. Since the new organization is hierarchical, groups can be contained within other groups, each inheriting the necessary privileges. New resources created under the parent group will then automatically receive existing parental permissions. A user inherits the permissions for all the groups in the direct lineage.

Security for an Active Directory integrates the ACLs to provide user and group authentication for any resource within the list. Through Active Directory, properties within an ACL can be controlled to apply to read/write access, creating and deleting child objects, abandoning replication, checking stale phantoms, performing garbage collection, recalculating hierarchies, and recalculating security inheritance.

Like Windows NT 4, Windows 2000 features a number of built-in users and groups (see Figure 20-2). These will vary depending on the services that you have installed. IIS, DNS, RAS, and other services all install a primary user account for use when the servers are executing. Default groups such as Account and Backup Operators are new to Windows 2000 to support the new Active Directory services.

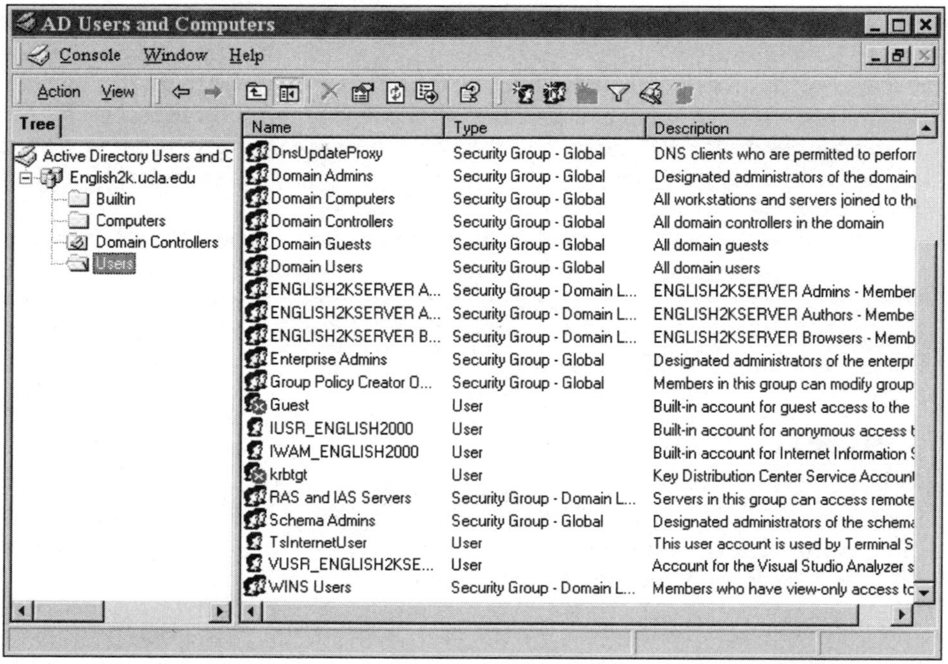

Figure 20-2. Built-in users and groups

Active Directory Name Resolution

Active Directory extends beyond the security to redefine how named resources are accessed. Integration of NT with the Web extends to the way resources are addressed. In the past, Windows NT has relied on the WINS naming structure. A traditional WINS path statement for addressing a computer would look like this:

```
\\mycompany\mycomputer
```

The new Active Directory uses DNS resolution for the primary naming scheme, which is far more familiar to Web developers. The same resource under the DNS directory access might look like this:

```
mycomputer.mycompany.com
```

The WINS protocol in the past has been much easier to manage because the list of resources queried through WINS was built dynamically, while DNS entries had to be specified manually. Active Directory features automatic DNS maintenance and creation by integrating the WINS capabilities. These new dynamic DNS services help unify resources for the new default protocol of Windows NT—TCP/IP.

Change from a domain-based system to an enterprise-wide directory standard will require some reorganization. Domain division typically occurs based on geography. A global directory allows structuring to occur through a logical organization so resource access and privileges can be configured either traditionally (according to geography) or through a more logical structure (dividing resource by organization units).

Users who log in to many domains can also be saved a lot of work. The ability to log into the enterprise and transparently access all of the resources for which you have permission without having to enter the deluge of passwords, logins, and domains, is a significant advance in user friendliness.

KERBEROS SECURITY

The Windows 2000 security provides a new core security protocol called Kerberos. In Windows NT, the NT LAN Manager (NTLM) protocol was a holdover from the original integration between Windows and OS/2. Although NTLM is still supported in Windows 2000, Kerberos is the new standard protocol. Kerberos is used as the primary encryption protocol for the COM and DCOM services.

DEFINITION: **Kerberos** Industry standard security protocol used for distributed security. The Kerberos name comes from a mythological three-headed dog that guards the gates of Hades.

Trusted security between domains is handled by implicit/transitive Kerberos trusts. This means that trusted capabilities are hierarchical. For example, suppose three domains exist: A, B, and C. In Windows NT 4, all trusts between the machines had to be manually configured on each machine. With hierarchical trusts, if A trusts B, and B trusts C, then a user on domain C will have automatic access to domain A through the hierarchical relationship.

DELEGATING AUTHORITY

Under Active Directory, administrative tasks can now be delegated to other user types without granting full administrative control. For example, in the past, a user could not be granted administrative control over a single printer. To allow the user to modify the properties of a printer, the user would have to be given control over all of the printers on the system.

With Windows 2000, administrative control can be granted for individual resources. This includes the ability to give a group manager administrative control of security for all of the users in the group. Being able to manage resources independently is critical in the new paradigm of Web development, where groups of programmers, graphic artists, and others work on different pieces of the same project.

To aid in setting these resources, Active Directory includes a Delegation of Control Wizard (see Figure 20-3) to simplify the configuration of the responsibilities.

Because Active Directory can encompass so many aspects of a system, the granting of rights is based not on resources, but on tasks. These tasks that can be delegated include a number of predefined standard tasks, as well as custom ones that can be added (see Figure 20-4).

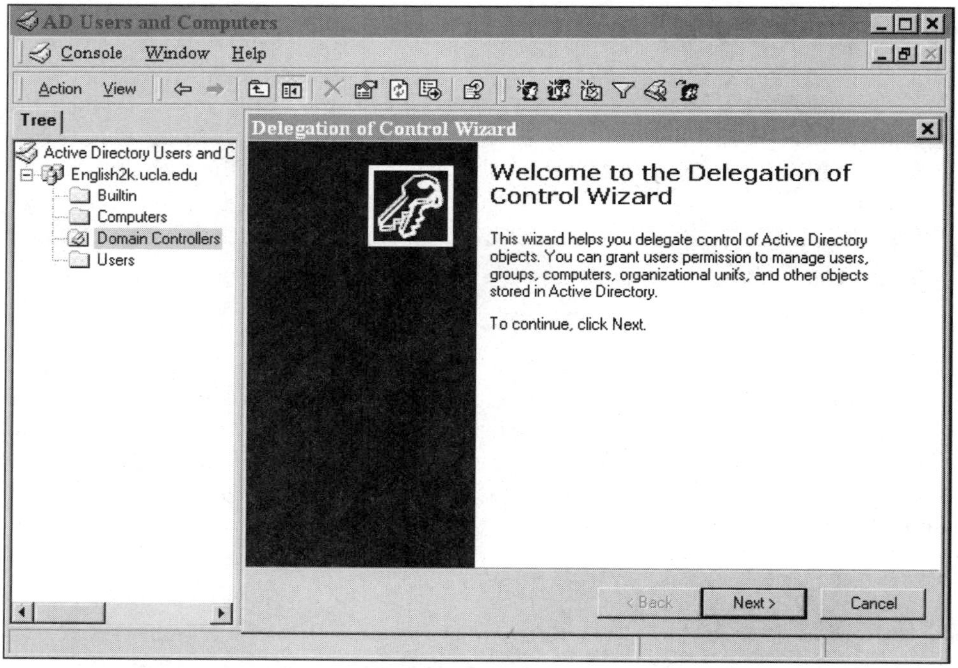

Figure 20-3. The Delegation of Control Wizard allows you to delegate authority

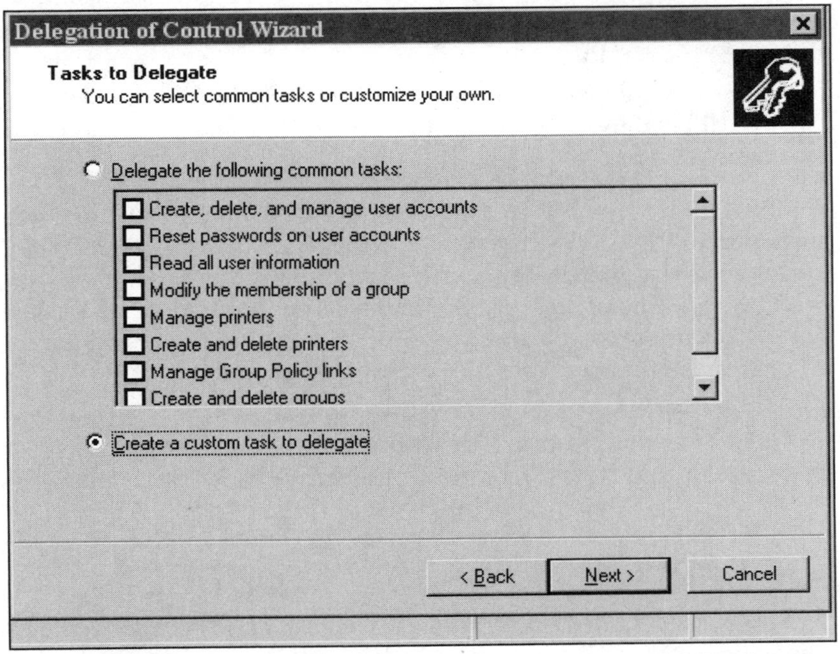

Figure 20-4. Standard and custom tasks are available for delegation

INTERNET AUTHENTICATION SERVICE

Under Windows 2000, an Internet Authentication Service (IAS) allows dial-in users to be remotely authenticated. IAS allows you to manage the authentication, authorization, and accounting of users. The primary function of IAS is the access control for virtual private network (VPN) implementation on an NT-based network. IAS supports a variety of protocols for connection, including the following:

- **Point-to-Point Protocol (PPP)** For traditional dial-in access, PPP is the most popular protocol available for routing TCP/IP packets.
- **Extensible Authentication Protocol (EAP)** For smart cards, certificates, one-time passwords, and token cards, the EAP can integrate with the rest of Active Directory services primarily for hardware authentication of users.

- **AppleTalk Remote Access Protocol (ARAP)** For allowing Macintosh computers to access the Windows NT network, the ARAP is a long awaited addition to NT services.
- **Automatic Number Identification Service (ANI)** Commonly known as Caller ID, this protocol can be used to authenticate and record access requests from remote users.

IAS provides a bridge for authenticating remote users to Active Directory. For a virtual private network (VPN), an authenticated user would then be granted all of the permissions that are allowed through a standard LAN connection.

While IAS provides the protocol access for the various remote services, configuration of the remote access resources (such as modems, bridges, and so on) and the actual VPN occurs through the Routing and Remote Access MMC snap-in.

NOTE: IAS was previously available in the Windows NT Option pack. The Windows 2000 version is greatly expanded to allow access to permission capabilities available through Active Directory.

QUALITY OF SERVICE ADMISSION CONTROL

For Web and other network access, Windows 2000 provides much greater control over when and how the resources of a network may be used. The Quality of Service (QoS) Admission control allows the administrator to control the amount of bandwidth at the subnet level for compatible services on the Active Directory network. The administrator can configure QoS in the MMC to prevent excessive bandwidth usage and to regulate network resources more effectively.

QoS can be used to configure amounts of reserved bandwidth, how the traffic is sent to the requesting computer, and who can reserve priority bandwidth. QoS allows users to reserve network resources and set priorities for resources. Resources allocation can then be partitioned between low priority and high priority traffic. The traffic management also allows end-to-end delivery systems with low-delay guarantees for multimedia or voice transmissions over the network. The system can support multicast transmission of bandwidth-reservation messages.

Bandwidth reservation requests must be sent explicitly to the Windows 2000 server assigned to manage the Quality of Server. To make these requests, the client needs to be running Windows 2000, Windows 98, or an available Subnet Bandwidth Management (SBM) client software. Rarely does the user get involved in the actual requesting process. Primarily a program that would perform optimally with certain bandwidth allocation (such as Real Audio Player) will make the request to the QoS server.

NOTE: Subnet Bandwidth Management (SBM) is a standard adopted by the Internet Engineering Task Force (IETF). Therefore, clients will likely be available in the future for a variety of platforms.

The bandwidth settings that are configured in the QoS can be assigned directly to groups and individual users stored in Active Directory. For Web access, the Quality of Service Admission control also allows settings to be made for unauthenticated users (see Figure 20-5). These settings will allow you to manage a broad range of potential users.

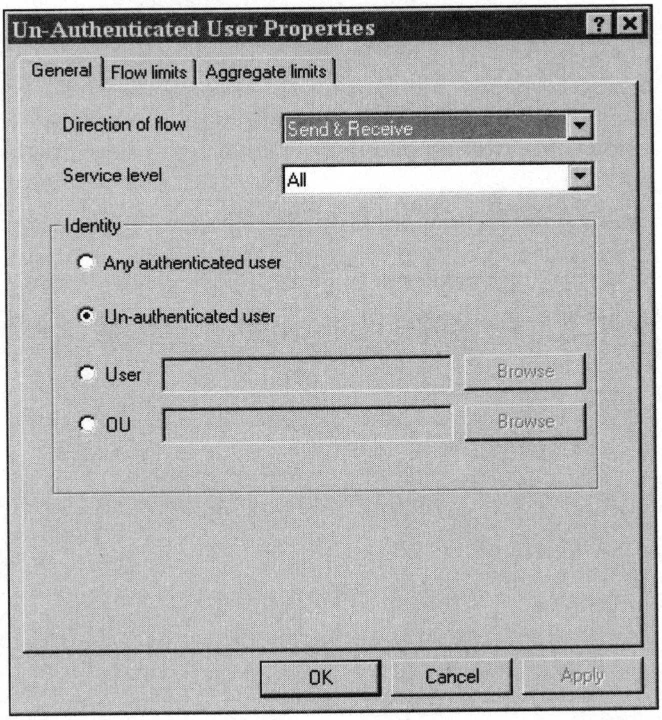

Figure 20-5. Quality of service allows you to set restrictions such as bandwidth flow limits

REPLICATION

Active Directory features multimaster replication. This means that any domain with available writeable directory databases can accept updates from other replicated domains. This provides fault tolerance, because if any of the servers fail, they have an updated backup on the system to take over. Update sequence numbers (USNs) are used to coordinate the replication. The USN acts like a time stamp to indicate when the update needs to occur.

In the Active Directory replication structure, the entire domain must be replicated—an organizational unit cannot be set for exclusive replication. By requiring complete directory replication, any backup domain controller may become the primary controller with a simple configuration setting. To set up the replication options and paths, the Sites and Services MMC snap-in is used. This service is installed on all Windows 2000 domain controllers.

In the Active Directory settings for Sites and Services (see Figure 20-6), the method, route, and authorized servers can be specified. Settings also include configuration of the necessary digital certificates to ensure that the replication is only to authenticated and validated servers. Replication requires the trust relationships ensured by these certificates.

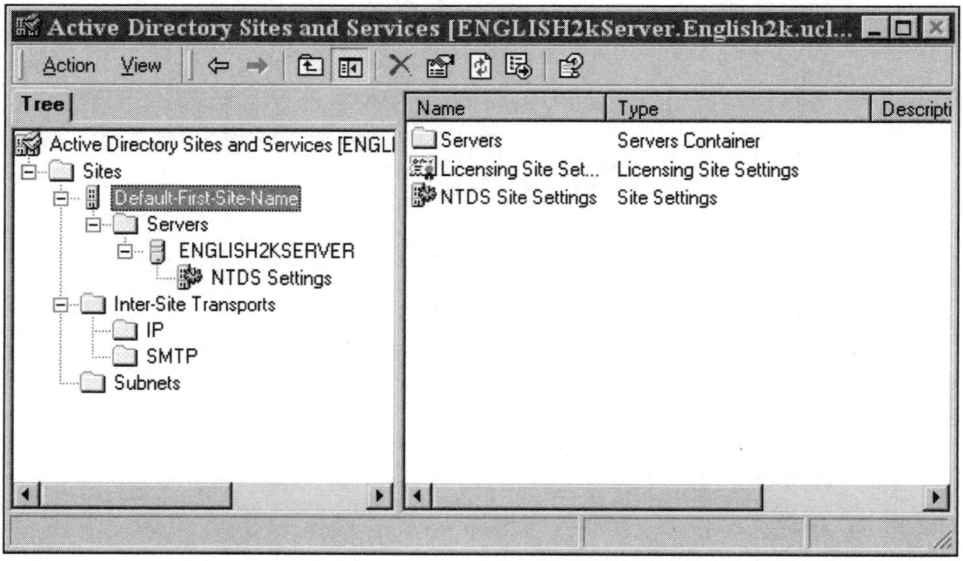

Figure 20-6. Active Directory Sites and Services allows configuration for replication

Trust relationships are the way in which the Windows NT domain system allows multiple domains to share security information. Settings can be made by object type for the entire organizational unit. Trust relationships in Active Directory are automatic and dynamic in contrast to the manual configuration required by older versions of NT. The complex web of trust links that was previously difficult to maintain is now handled seamlessly by Active Directory.

Moving objects from one domain to another used to require that the objects be destroyed on the source domain and recreated on the destination domain. Active Directory allows resources to be quickly and easily moved among logical groups.

Within each domain, a primary domain controller (PDC) and backup domain controller (BDC) would manage all of the users and groups. Active Directory eliminates the concept of the PDC and BDC. Any domain controller can be a primary controller if designated as such. This provides for failover support.

The data for Active Directory is stored in a variation of the Jet engine called the Exchange Jet engine. Windows NT previously used a secure portion of the registry for security settings. It retains the APIs to the registry entries to allow for backward compatibility.

Extending Active Directory

One of the important aspects of Active Directory is its programmability. Through the Active Directory Service Interfaces (ADSI), new applications can be created to use the services provided by the global directory. Directory data visualization, integration with other directory structures such as X.500 and Novell-based systems, server location abstraction, and network bandwidth administration and allocation are just a few of the potential applications now possible with the ADSI technology.

The primary method of adding to the capabilities of Active Directory is augmenting the data types that it can handle. The database included in Active Directory is extensible, which allows developers to add their own resource types for unified management within the directory server.

The standard resources for a server such as file shares, printers, etc. are the default object types stored in the directory schema. The schema holds the metadata (information that describes the data types) of the resource data stored in the directory. The schema can be extended with new object types by developers and administrators, and additional properties can also be added to existing objects.

TIP: If you want to investigate extending the schema of Active Directory, the Active Directory Programmer's Guide is available on the Microsoft Web site (http://msdn.microsoft.com/developer/windows2000/adsi).

Realize that you must be very careful when making modifications to existing schema types. Extending the schema can possibly debilitate your entire Windows 2000 security system. Therefore, instead of modifying existing schema, favor creating a subclass of an existing schema so you don't have to start from scratch. This subclass will have all of the attributes of the superclass, and then you can add the custom attributes you desire.

CAUTION: If possible, avoid modifying existing attributes of a schema. There are likely to be objects that already rely on the schema as it is defined. Modifications can corrupt the foundation of the class type.

IIS 5

IIS under Windows 2000 has a few new options. One of the important options for a Web application developer is the ability to set a level of application protection. Rather than just allow the application to execute in-process with the Web server or in its own isolated process, IIS 5 offers a third option of pooled processes. This option doesn't require all of the processes to be isolated, but simply isolates them from the main Web server. Therefore, a catastrophic failure might take down other applications, but never the Web server itself.

Q&A

Q: Can Active Directory coexist with older systems?
A: Yes, but many of the benefits are lost if your domain controllers remain non–Windows 2000 servers. While client machines will notice almost no difference between the older system and the newer Active Directory resource management, having domain servers on the network forces Windows 2000 to act as a traditional domain controller with all of the limitations that implies. However, since Windows 2000 eliminates the concept of primary and backup domain controllers, Windows 2000 can be gradually adopted in an organization with little negative effect and without needing to purchase numerous new machines.

Q: Is authority to control Web resources stored in Active Directory?
A: Most of the Web settings are not explicitly located in Active Directory. They are controlled by the IIS services located on the individual machines. However, authorization for access to Web directories, such as through the FrontPage extensions, is handled by the Active Directory users and groups authentication.

SUMMARY

Windows 2000, in addition to being a significant upgrade to Windows NT, provides many features, such as Active Directory, that are critical for the OS to be used as a scalable network OS. Active Directory allows all of the domain controllers that were previously isolated from each other to be centralized for both the users and the administrators. In this chapter, you covered:

- **Active Directory** The new Active Directory structure recreates the security service for Windows NT around a global, extensible, and hierarchical directory service featured in Windows 2000. Active Directory can coexist with existing Windows NT installations and Novell's NDS global directory service.
- **Single login** With the domain-wide capabilities of Active Directory, a single login can provide access to all of the resources (files, directories, printer shares, and so on) for which the user has permission.
- **Centralized administration** The users and groups for the entire network can be managed on a single domain controller. This administration cuts the management costs of information systems dramatically.
- **Replication** Linked domains will replicate the changes made to the central one. Replication is at the heart of Active Directory's ability to provide fail-over services if one of the domain controllers faults.

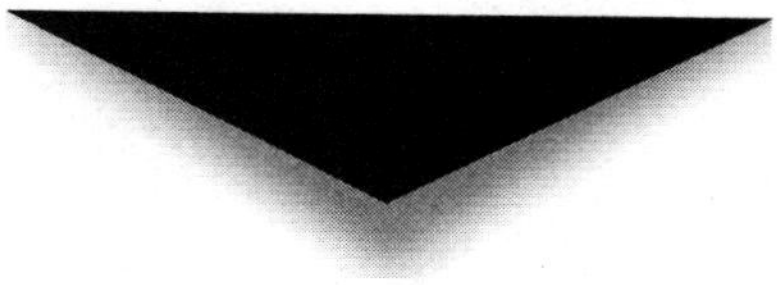

CHAPTER 21

Generating a Formatted Report from Database Information

In Chapter 6, you created a simple report that allowed some basic drill-down capabilities. Web-based reporting is extremely effective for basic examination of data, but often a spreadsheet, such as Microsoft Excel, is needed for comprehensive manipulation and chart creation, especially if the report needs to be included in a submitted document.

A Web application can be an excellent facilitator of such reports, as well as the more traditional HTML display reports. In fact, you can use a Web-based application to generate a report as a formatted data file, and then e-mail the file as an attachment to a designated address. In this chapter, you'll build a solution that creates a formatted report on the fly, using the FileSystemObjects to write it to the server drive.

The generated report file can be downloaded by a Web user and opened in Microsoft Excel. In fact, if you have Excel 97 (or higher) installed, the Excel component will load into the Internet Explorer (Version 3 or above) browser and the formatted report will be displayed within the browser window.

There are often a number of changes that must be made in the presentation of a formatted report before it can be shown to other people. The second part of the solution will use the Microsoft Posting Acceptor to allow you to use IIS to upload a file to a directory. This allows a user to post a formatted report to the Web server for downloading by other users.

THE SYLK FILE FORMAT

The Report application you will create uses the Symbolic Link (SYLK) file format to generate a formatted spreadsheet report. The SYLK format, although poorly documented by Microsoft, is one of the easiest ways to create a spreadsheet with formatting such as fonts, styles, column widths, and so on. Most spreadsheets (Excel, Quatro Pro, and others) can read this file format. Files formatted with this standard use the file extension `.slk`, which Excel will recognize when the file is double-clicked.

An extremely simple SYLK file looks like this:

```
ID;PWXL;N;E
P;P@
F;P0;DG0G8;M255
B;Y2;X2;D0 0 1 1
O;L;D;V0;K47;G100 0.001
C;Y1;X1;K"a1"
C;X2;K"b1"
C;Y2;X1;K"a2"
C;X2;K"b2"
E
```

Although this may seem slightly cryptic, it is really fairly simple. This SYLK file contains a spreadsheet of two columns and two rows. The first row and column contains the text value "a1". The second column has the value "b1" (to match the cell reference values where they are placed). The next row has two matching column values "a2" and "b2". These create a simple table that looks like this:

a1	b1
a2	b2

The first line of the file identifies the creator (`XLW`) using the ID flag (`ID;P`). This line is followed by a series of global formatting commands. The first line of real interest is the one containing the text `C;Y1;X1;K"a1"`. It specifies that there is column data on this line (C), followed by the cell location of the data (Y1;X1, which means row 1, column 1). The next flag (K) specifies that the value contained in quotes will be placed in that cell.

The next line of text nearly matches the previous line except it doesn't contain a Y value. Within a SYLK file, once a row or column is set, it retains this value until it is changed. Therefore, the second value will be placed in the same row as the one above it. In the following line you can see that the row is changed to advance to the second row.

With a general grasp of the file format, you could write a basic SYLK file. Before you begin creating the solution, however, all of the security for the Web server should be in place to allow these files to be created. To simplify the security settings, you can configure the entire solution at once (including the settings for the upload functionality).

SETTING UP SECURITY

For a Report application that will generate a file on the server as well as accept uploaded documents, you will need to create three folders: SReport, Created, and Upload. The SReport folder (Special Report) will contain the executing script code for the creation of reports and for uploading applications. The Created folder will accept the reports that are created by the ASP program in the SYLK file format. The Upload folder will hold the files that are to be uploaded to the Web server.

Begin by creating the SReport folder at the root of the wwwroot directory. It should have the path:

```
C:\InetPub\wwwroot\SReport
```

Once you've created that folder, create two folders within it: one named Created and the other named Upload. You will need to set the proper permissions for the folders to permit the files to be uploaded and allow the reports to be created.

NOTE: Because of the complexity of the security settings, the instructions for this example show how to construct the application by hand rather than by using Visual InterDev for deployment. To create the application in Visual InterDev, simply make sure that the proper permissions have been set on both the staging and deployment server. The deployment presented here will help you understand exactly what settings are needed.

Folder Security

A Web application will use the security of folder settings that are made at the NT operating system level. You will need to make these settings enabled for the report file creation and allow the uploads from users to take place. To set up the file security, follow these steps:

1. In Windows Explorer, right-click the SReport folder and select the Properties option.
2. Select the Security tab in the Properties dialog box.
3. Click the Permissions button. The Directory Permissions dialog box will appear.
4. Click Add to add users and groups.
5. Click the Show all Users button.
6. Select the IUSR_*xxx* entry where *xxx* is the name of your server machine. This user is the default account created by IIS to use for resource access. Giving this user permission to the folder will allow IIS to place files in the folder.
7. Click Add.
8. Select the Change option from the Type of Access box.
9. Click OK.
10. Repeat steps 4–9 to add an Administrators group with Full control, and then limit access for the Everyone group to Read. When you've completed this configuration, the permissions list should look like the one shown in the following illustration.

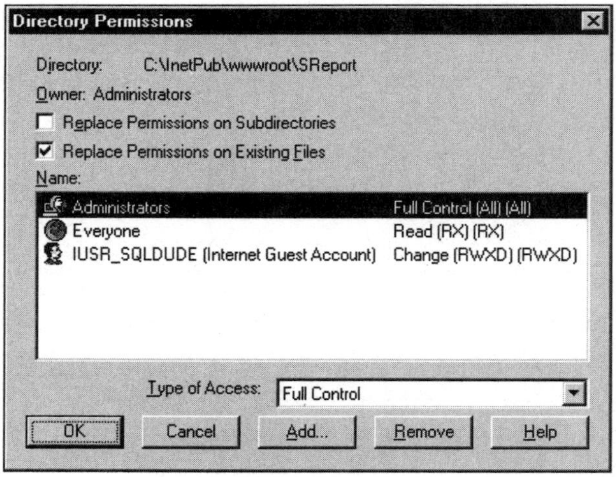

11. Click OK to save these properties.

The other two folders should inherit the permissions that you've set, so the basic folder security should now be in place. To complete the security settings, you must configure the security for Web access.

Internet Security

For this configuration, you will need to load the IIS Service Manager into the MMC. All of the configuring is performed from the Property dialog boxes for the various folders. The SReport directory will have different settings for permissions than the other two folders. The Upload folder, for example, must have Write permission set in its folder attributes to accept the file being sent by the user.

To configure the Web folder access, follow these steps:

1. Start the IIS Service Manager.
2. Open the Default Web Site folder.
3. Right-click the SReport folder, and select the Properties option.
4. In the Application Settings frame, click the Create button to make the SReport folder an application.
5. Set the Permissions to Script to enable scripting capabilities.
6. Click OK to accept these settings.
7. Right-click the Upload folder, and select the Properties option.
8. Check the Write option for Access Permissions. This will allow files that are uploaded to be placed in this folder.
9. Set the Permissions to None to disable all execution capabilities.

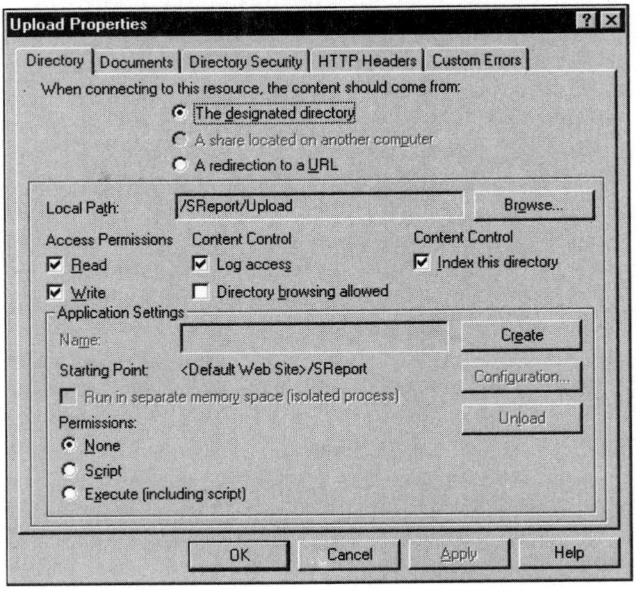

10. Click OK to accept these settings.
11. Repeat steps 7–10 to make the same adjustments to the Created folder.

The security on your application should now be properly configured. Your ASP application will now be allowed to write files into the Created folder, accept uploaded files into the SReport folder, and execute the necessary application scripts.

WARNING: Do not set a folder that will be used for uploads to permit Write and Execute privileges. A malicious user could upload a potentially damaging executable to the directory and then have IIS run the application. When you attempt to set both Write and Execute privileges on a folder, IIS will warn you that this poses a security threat. Think carefully before you accept this dangerous setting.

CREATING THE SOLUTION

This report generator will rely on the Northwind database for report information. The solution has been generalized so that any recordset source could be used in its place. Once the data has been returned from the query, it must be placed within a file that can be easily read by a spreadsheet such as Excel.

Since the FileSystemObjects allow a stream to be output to a file, it is easy to send the data to a text file that can be downloaded as the formatted report. The SYLK file format is a text-based file that will work perfectly when output using the stream objects. Once the file has been created, Excel will be able to load it with the proper column formatting, adjustments, and so on.

To begin creating the application, you will need to enter the ASP script code that will generate the report file. Load a Web page editor (such as Notepad, FrontPage, or Visual InterDev) and enter the code in the following listing. Save the file in the SReport folder with the name `ReportCreate.asp`.

```
<HTML>
<HEAD>
<TITLE>Formatted Report Creator</TITLE>
<META NAME="GENERATOR" Content="Microsoft Visual Studio 6.0">
</HEAD>
<BODY>
<H1>Formatted Report Creator</H1>

<%
   On Error Resume Next
```

```
Dim myConn, myRS
' Set buffer to false so progress has an opportunity
' to be displayed
Response.Buffer = False

Set myConn = Server.CreateObject("ADODB.Connection")
myConn.Open "driver={Microsoft Access Driver (*.mdb)};" & _
   dbq=c:\Program Files\Microsoft Visual Studio\VB98\nwind.mdb"
' Check if the opening was successful: adStateOpen(1)
If myConn.State = 1 Then
   Set myRS = Server.CreateObject("ADODB.Recordset")

   Set myRS.ActiveConnection = myConn
   myRS.CursorType = 2 ' adOpenDynamic
   myRS.CursorLocation = 2 ' adUseServer
   myRS.Open "select * from customers"
   If myRS.State = 1 Then
     tempFName = "Report_" & Now & ".SLK"
     ' Replace slashes in date with underscores
     tempFName = Replace(tempFName,"/","_")
     ' Replace spaces with underscores
     tempFName = Replace(tempFName," ","_")
     ' Replace colons in time with dashes
     tempFName = Replace(tempFName,":","-")

    Set FileObject = Server.CreateObject("Scripting.FileSystemObject")
    outFName =(Server.MapPath ("/SReport") & "/Created/" & tempFName)

' Arguments: True = Overwrite existing file, False = No Unicode
Set outStream= FileObject.CreateTextFile (outFName, True, False)

 ' Identify file creator as Excel
 outStream.WriteLine ("ID;PWXL;N;E")
 outStream.WriteLine ("P;P@")

 ' Create a bold style
 outStream.WriteLine ("P;FArial;M200")
 outStream.WriteLine ("P;EArial;M200;SB")
```

```
' Start global formatting
outStream.WriteLine ("F;P0;DG0G8;M255")
outStream.WriteLine ("B;Y30;X30;D0 0 1 1")
outStream.WriteLine ("O;L;D;V0;K47;G100 0.001")
' Set width of column 1 to 44 characters
outStream.WriteLine ("F;W1 1 44")
' Set width of column 2 to 3 characters
outStream.WriteLine ("F;W2 2 3")
' Set row one to style 1 (bold)
outStream.WriteLine ("F;SDM1;R1")
' write the column header
For i = 1 To myRS.Fields.Count - 1
   ' If first column, must write column (Y) number
    If i = 1 Then
        outStream.WriteLine ("C;Y1;X1;K" & Chr(34) & _
           myRS.Fields(i).Name & Chr(34))
    Else
        outStream.WriteLine ("C;X" & i & ";K" & Chr(34) & _
           myRS.Fields(i).Name & Chr(34))
    End If
Next
rownum = 2
Do Until myRS.EOF
   Response.Write(".")
    For i = 1 To myRS.Fields.Count - 1
        fldValue = "" & myRS.Fields(i).Value
        ' Check for carriage returns and eliminate
        If Instr(fldValue, Chr(13)) then
            ' Replace carriage return
            fldValue = Replace(fldValue, Chr(13), " ")
            ' Replace line feed character
            fldValue = Replace(fldValue, Chr(10), "")
        End If
        ' Check for single quotes and change to double
        If Instr(fldValue, Chr(34)) then
            ' Replace with double quotes
            fldValue = Replace(fldValue, Chr(34), Chr(34) & _
               Chr(34))
        End If
        ' Write field value to SYLK file
```

```
            If i = 1 Then
                outStream.WriteLine("C;Y" & rownum & ";X1;K" & _
                   Chr(34) & fldValue & Chr(34))
            Else
                outStream.WriteLine("C;X" & i & ";K" & Chr(34) & _
                   fldValue & Chr(34))
            End If
        Next
        myRS.MoveNext
        rownum = rownum + 1
    Loop
    outStream.WriteLine ("E")
    Set outStream = Nothing
      Else
         Response.Write("Error. Could not create recordset.<P>")
      End If
     ' Close the connection
     myConn.Close
   Else
      Response.Write("Error. Connection could not be opened.<P>")
   End If
   ' Eliminate the connection
   Set myConn = Nothing
%>
<P>Report created successfully.<P>
<A HREF="./Created/<%=tempFName %>">Download Report</A><P>
</BODY>
</HTML>
```

When the code is entered, try executing the page by accessing the local URL like this:

```
http://localHost/SReport/ReportCreate.asp
```

The page will open a recordset to the Northwind database. If successful, it will open a file for outputting the SYLK information. The first portion of the file output will write the appropriate header information and list the field names of all the columns in the recordset. In the final report, this will become a bold header line. The bold and column width settings occur in this header. All of this formatting occurs before the `Do Until` loop that is used to cycle through all of the records available from the recordset.

Once the header has been output, each record in the recordset is processed and sent to the file. A single period (.) for each record is also sent to the browser through the

Response object as a status indicator. This will prevent the browser from timing out if there are a great number of records to be output.

When the output is completed, the user will be presented with a link to download the report file (see Figure 21-1). The filename is based on the current time and date that the report was generated. Currently, the solution presumes that there will not be two reports generated in the exact same second. If this is a problem, you will need to modify the code to add some type of random extension to prevent file collision.

If the user has Excel 97 or above installed, clicking on the link will open the file in the Excel component in the Internet Explorer browser (see Figure 21-2). You can see that the report has the two primary formatting adjustments that were made: a bold first row and a first column that is 44 characters in width. With additional tags, the report could contain most of the visual cues normally associated with a spreadsheet presentation.

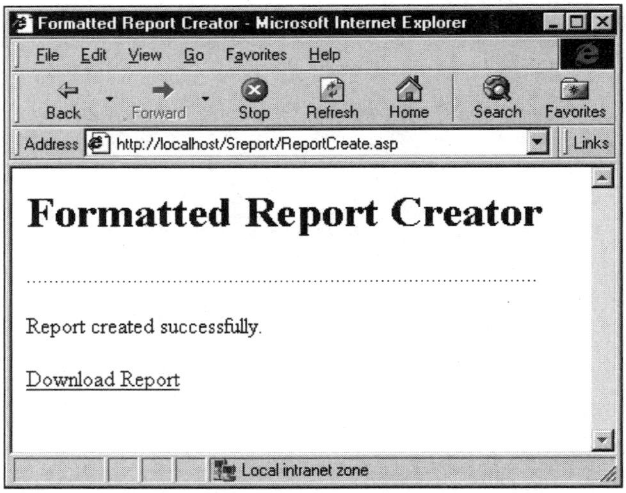

Figure 21-1. The user will be presented with a link to download the report

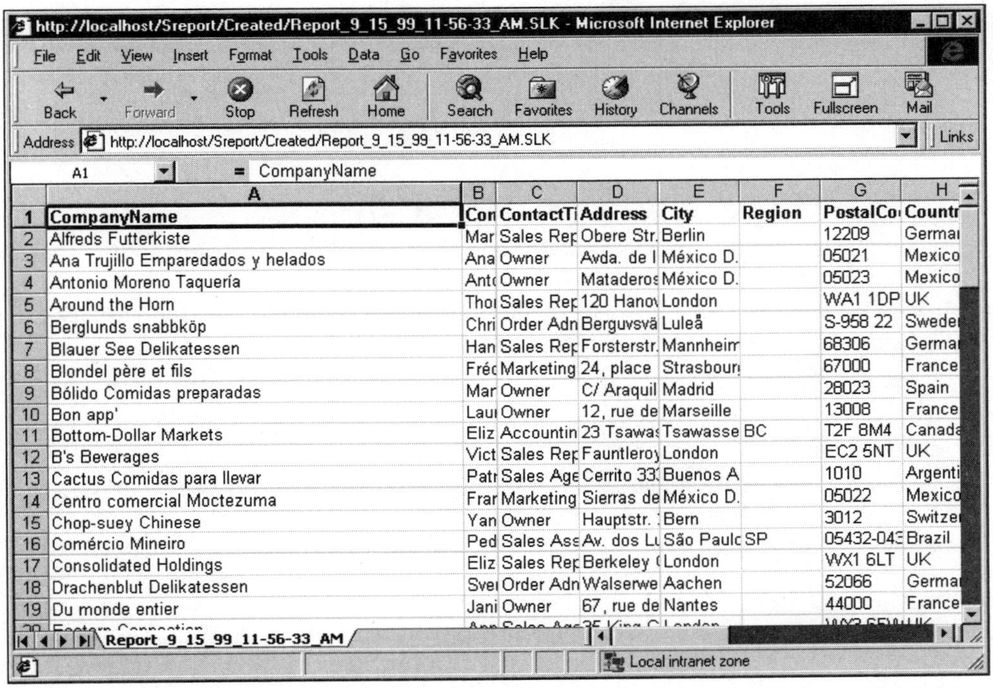

Figure 21-2. The formatted report appears in Excel within the browser

ACCEPTING A FILE UPLOAD

The report that has been generated is stored in a primitive state. After the user has imported it into a spreadsheet, it is likely that additional, more advanced formatting will take place. Perhaps the user will even add charts to clarify the meaning of the data. To share the formatted reports with others, this document could be placed on an Exchange server in a public folder for group access. Another option is to allow the file to be uploaded directly to the Web site, where it could then be viewed by others.

NOTE: Any version of Netscape Navigator greater than 2.02 supports the ability to upload files. For Microsoft Internet Explorer, any version older than 4.0 requires a special ActiveX component to be installed (check msdn.microsoft.com for further details). If your visitors are still using Internet Explorer 3, you should get the posting component from the Microsoft site and place it on your Web page for easy access.

On IIS, the component that can accept file uploads is known as the Microsoft Posting Acceptor. The Posting Acceptor (cpshost.dll) is an ISAPI driver that intercepts a file that is being sent from the browser and writes it into the desired directory rather than sending it to the Web server or ASP engine for processing. This component will receive files that have been sent from the browser using the HTTP `PUT` command. If a file already exists with the same name as the one being sent, it will be overwritten.

NOTE: The *`PUT`* command was added to the 1.1 version of HTTP, and an exact specification can be accessed on the W3C Web site (www.w3c.org) under the name RFC 2068.

On the page sent to the browser, the user will need to have a button that allows the file to be uploaded to be located on the client hard drive. This "browse" button will present a standard open file dialog window and then fill a text field on the Web page with the path selected. With the upload form technology included in the Web browser, the browse button is automatically supplied and activated.

To begin creating this application, you should first examine your Web server system to see if you have the Posting Acceptor installed. Check the scripts directory for the cpshost.dll file:

```
C:\InetPub\scripts\cpshost.dll
```

If it's not installed, get out the Visual Studio CD #2. In the Deploy folder on this CD, there is a Posting Acceptor installer (`pasetup.exe`) that will install the DLL on your Web server. Execute it to place the files on your server.

You need to have the permissions properly set for the Upload folder to accept files. If you didn't set permissions in the "Folder Security" section, go back and do it now. If the permissions are not set properly, you will receive the error message "HTTP 500, you do not have write access to the destination" when an upload is attempted.

To allow for file uploads, you need to create a form that contains a text box to accept the filename of the incoming file and a Submit button to start the upload. To prepare the form for the upload, the `METHOD` attribute of the FORM tag must be set to `post` and the `ENCTYPE` attribute must be set to `multipart/form-data`.

To create this solution, you will need two script files: Upload.asp and UploadFinish.asp. The Upload page will accept the filename and will allow you to submit it. The UploadFinish page will be displayed by the Posting Acceptor after the upload is complete.

Load a Web page editor (Notepad or Visual InterDev) and enter the code in the following listing. Save the file as Upload.asp in the SReport folder.

```
<HTML>
<HEAD>
<TITLE>Upload formatted report</TITLE>
<META NAME="GENERATOR" Content="Microsoft Visual Studio 6.0">
<%
   Dim serverURL, uploadURL, destinationURL
   Dim postAcceptorURL

   ' Get URL reference to local server
   serverURL = "http://" + Request.ServerVariables("SERVER_NAME")

  ' Folder where the file will be uploaded
  uploadURL = serverURL & "/SReport/Upload"
  ' Redirection URL for final page display
  destinationURL = serverURL & "/SReport/UploadFinish.asp"
  ' Location of Posting Acceptor
  postAcceptorURL =  serverURL & "/Scripts/cpshost.dll"
%>
</HEAD>
<BODY>
<H1>Report Upload</H1>
<form enctype="multipart/form-data" action=
<%=postAcceptorURL + "?PUBLISH?" + destinationURL %>
 method="POST">
   <input type="hidden" name="TargetURL" value="<% = uploadURL %>">
        Enter the path of the file to be uploaded:
        <input name="uploadreport" type="file" size="50"><P>
     <input type="submit" value="Upload Report">
    </form>

</BODY>
</HTML>
```

This form uses two types of items: the `file` type and the `submit` type. The `file` type provides the ability to browse on the client machine in order to select the file path to be uploaded. The `submit` button posts the file as multipart form data. You can see that the target for redirection after the upload occurs is placed in the `?PUBLISH?` piece of the query string.

For the redirection destination file, enter the code in the following listing. Save the file as UploadFinish.asp in the SReport folder.

```
<HTML>
<HEAD>
<TITLE>Upload formatted report</TITLE>
<META NAME="GENERATOR" Content="Microsoft Visual Studio 6.0">
</HEAD>
<BODY>
<H2>Upload formatted report</H2>
<%
Dim fName, fPath

' Display info on multi-part upload
For i = 1 To Request.Form("FileName").Count
       fName = Request.Form("FileName")(i) & _
          Request.Form("FileExtention")(i)
       fPath = Request.Form("FilePath")(i)
Next
Response.Write("Uploaded report ")
Response.Write("<B>" & fPath & fName & "</B>")
Response.Write( " was received successfully")
%>
</BODY>
</HTML>
```

The upload portion of the application is now ready for execution. Try executing the code by accessing the local URL, like this:

```
http://localHost/SReport/Upload.asp
```

Select a file for upload by clicking the Browse button (see Figure 21-3). Click the Upload Report button to begin the transmission.

The Posting Acceptor will receive the file and place it in the Upload folder on the server. Once complete, the UploadFinish.asp page will be displayed (see Figure 21-4). The UploadFinish page will display the path of the file that was sent. In a real solution, you would probably only want to display the filename and not the path—otherwise users might become concerned that your server knows more about their local drive than they would like.

The best method for listing all of the uploaded files would be to create a database entry with each upload that stores the path to the uploaded file. All of the available uploads could then be displayed in an easily accessed table. If you need simplicity, you could simply allow browsing access to the Upload folder through directory configuration in IIS.

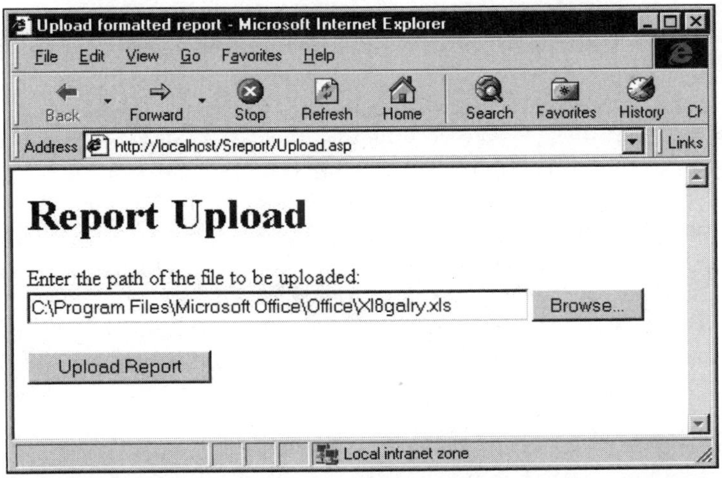

Figure 21-3. Use the Browse button to select a file to upload

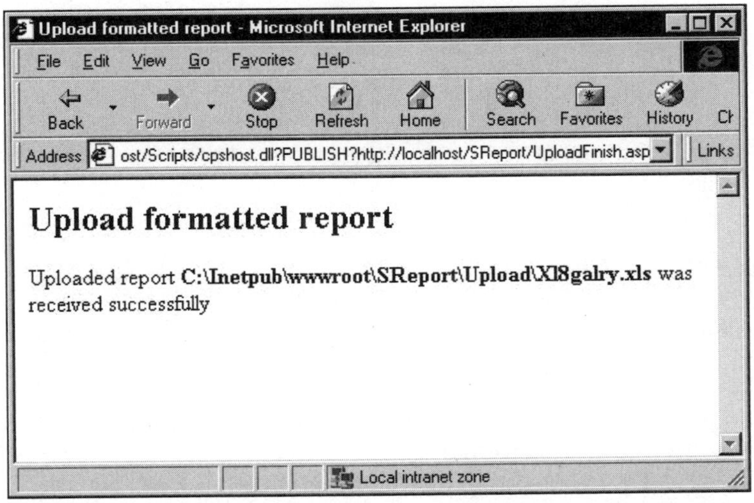

Figure 21-4. The UploadFinish page will confirm that the file was received

Storing Session Variables

One drawback to using the file upload technique is the possibility that all of the Session object variables will be eliminated after the upload. You may have noticed that when you executed the upload, the URL changed dramatically. The file upload actually sends the browser access to the Posting Acceptor which accepts the upload and subsequently redirects the browser to the destination page provided by the script code.

Sometimes the IIS server interprets the redirect to the upload ISAPI driver as a new client. When control returns to the destination page, the Web server will interpret this as another new client, and a new session will be started. This redirection process will cause all of the values stored in the Session object to be cleared.

There are several ways to work around this problem. The most straightforward solution involves embedding existing session values in invisible attributes of the uploading form. For example, you could use ASP code like this:

```
For i = 1 To Session.Count - 1
   Response.Write("<INPUT TYPE=hidden NAME=")
   Response.Write(Session(i))
   Response.Write(" VALUE=" & Session("myVar") & ">")
Next
```

In the HTML, if you had two session variables, the client HTML might look like this:

```
<INPUT TYPE=hidden NAME=mySessionVal1 VALUE=131>
<INPUT TYPE=hidden NAME=mySessionVal2 VALUE=151>
```

To read the data back into the proper session values, the process could be reversed by reading the form values. You could use code like this:

```
For i = 1 To Form.Count - 1
   Session(Form(i).Name) = Form(i).Value
Next
```

All of the variables will be reconstructed as session variables by the receiving page. This method is probably the most straightforward, and it's the one recommended by Microsoft. However, it has several disadvantages:

- *Any non-session values in the form will be turned into session variables.* The destination page code has no way of knowing which form values are not session variables and automatically places them in the Session object.
- *Object references cannot be passed through the form variables.* Any objects you have created within the session will be eliminated. Therefore, recordsets and/or other ActiveX objects will be flushed by the system when the session is terminated.

- *Session information is passed to the client.* Any secure information stored in the Session variables will be exposed to the client in the client-side source code. This creates a potential security risk if private information is placed in any of the session variables.

An alternative to this technique would be to add a random prefix to the session variable names and then transfer them to the Application object. Then the random prefix could be passed in the invisible form variables. When the destination page receives the form data, the prefix will be available.

Since the Application object is not flushed with the creation of the new object, the session variables could be retrieved by checking all of the application variables with the designated prefix. These values could be returned to the session and values in the Application object eliminated. All of this can be accomplished with only slight modifications to the code provided earlier.

Make sure you eliminate the values in the Application object once they have been placed back in the Session object. If the reference to a Recordset object stored in the Application object is not eliminated, the Application object will keep the Recordset object open even after the Session is done with it. This means that the resources used by the Recordset object will remain in limbo until the Application object is flushed from the system. If the application is a popular one, it could mean that the object will remain in memory for days.

Checking a User Login

In Chapter 7, a method was described to allow a user to log in from any browser. Since the Windows NT Challenge/Response security is only available on Internet Explorer browsers, many applications will need this type of browser-independent security access. However, with file uploads, you might need stronger security that restricts access to the upload page to those within the organization. Further, you may be able to specify that only Internet Explorer can be used.

In this case, you could use the Windows NT security to ensure that only the assigned users have access to the upload portions of the Web application. By using the following simple code, you can be assured that the proper Windows NT login procedure has been followed. The server variable LOGON_USER will only contain a value if the login for Windows NT Challenge/Response security has been successfully validated.

```
If Request.ServerVariables("LOGON_USER")="" Then
   Response.Status = "You are not logged onto the site as a valid NT user."
   Response.End
End If
```

Dangers of Uploads

Allowing uploads of data files creates a potential security risk for the Web server. Most of the danger comes from the potential for anonymous placement of files that others can download. Uploaded files might include files that violate copyright (MP3s, porn images, movies, and the like) or files that contain viruses.

To minimize this potential danger, an upload application can use two simple precautions: limiting file uploads to 500K, and only allowing Excel files to be uploaded. The file size and file type can be checked after the upload occurs and the file deleted if it does not meet these criteria.

Even with these safety guards in place, an Excel file might contain a macro virus. However, this danger will not be unique to Web uploads but may occur in any public file repository. To avoid the spread of macro viruses, make sure your users are running some form of antivirus protection, such as McAffee (www.mcaffee.com) or Norton AntiVirus (www.norton.com).

If a file containing a virus is uploaded to the system, you can check the Web log for the time and the date that the file was placed on the site. This will provide at least the IP number of the person who uploaded the file. You can then contact them to alert them that their system is infected.

Q&A

Q: Is there a way to create an actual Excel file on the server for download?

A: Yes, but Microsoft does not recommend it. Since the Excel application can be instantiated like an ActiveX DLL, it can actually be controlled on the server to generate a worksheet or chart that can be saved to a server directory. To make this possible, a switch in the IIS registry must be changed (see IIS documentation) to allow an ASP page to instantiate external objects.

However, Excel is a very large application to be used like a DLL or component. Each loaded instance would take up several megabytes of memory. If a dozen simultaneous users requested an Excel report at the same time, it could very easily overwhelm the average Web server. Therefore, if you are considering such an implementation, consider whether such formatting is really needed (why won't a CSV file do?).

To create such a solution, ensure that either the necessary resources are available on the server or that there will be an extremely low numbers of users accessing this report.

Q: Can the File System Objects be used to write over system files?

A: No, not if the system is configured properly. IIS automatically creates a user called IUSER_xxx (where xxx is the system name) that it uses for all Web access. As long as the write capabilities of that user are limited to specific folders, there is no possibility that even a vicious upload would be able to access critical server files.

Q: Is there an easier way to send Excel data to a client?

A: You can send data directly to the browser and have Excel load and interpret it by changing the MIME type of the returned data from "text/html" to "application/x-msexcel". This method is not as flexible as SYLK files (for example, you cannot specify formatting), but it is much easier. Use tabs to separate the columns, and line feeds to indicate a new row.

SUMMARY

Report generation is one of the most commonly deployed intranet applications. Providing various deployment options for a report can significantly increase its usefulness. In this chapter you covered:

- **File System Objects** These are objects that can be used to create a file on the server from data retrieved from an ADO data source. This allows you to dynamically create a formatted file that can be downloaded by the user.
- **File Uploads** A Web page can accept file uploads to provide Web access to reports related to a Web application. Use caution to avoid either becoming a repository for illegal content or a distribution center for viruses.
- **Microsoft Posting Acceptor** This DLL can be used from IIS to allow uploads from within a browser. Through the HTTP `PUT` command, a binary file can be sent from the client machine to the Web server.

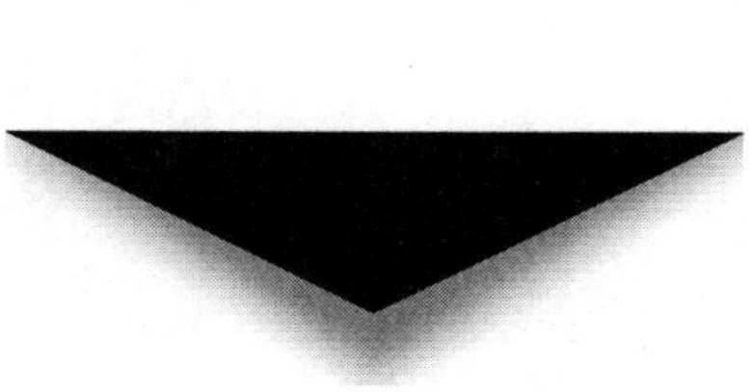

CHAPTER 22

ADO and Advanced Data Types

The capabilities of ADO are much broader than have been demonstrated so far in this book. Because of the added complexity of all of the ADO functions, the primary functionality of ADO is all that is needed in the majority of Web database applications. However, ADO has extra power for more challenging tasks. These are some of the more advanced features that you will learn about in this chapter:

- **Programming and using stored procedures** Stored procedures—compiled code that resides on the data source rather than on the client—can mean faster query execution, better encapsulation, increased security, and substantial update control.
- **Storing large amounts of data in a data source** Large amounts of text, bitmaps, and other binary large objects (BLOBs) can be placed into a field in an ADO data source.
- **Querying using the asynchronous capabilities** An asynchronous query is a query that doesn't require program execution to halt until a result is returned. This provides the ability to submit a query without monopolizing the execution thread until a result is returned.
- **Accessing non-SQL data sources** Rather than using a traditional SQL query, ADO can be used to retrieve various nonstandard data types (such as spatial data) or provide record-level access (such as AS/400 access).

Of these options, you are most likely to use stored procedures in designing a solution. In many professional applications, a majority of all queries occur as stored procedures in order to gain the maximum optimization of query execution.

STORED PROCEDURES

In Chapter 4, you briefly examined the Command object, which was used to access a stored procedure in SQL Server. However, executing existing stored procedures is just the tip of the iceberg when using a full database server. Creating your own code on a database server can offer the following advantages:

- **Faster query execution** A stored procedure that is created on the database server is compiled to optimized code. This allows the server to analyze the execution of the stored procedure and make the most efficient execution choices given the available indexes and other resources. When the stored procedure is activated, it can use the compiled execution plan without having to generate it on the fly.
- **Better encapsulation** Like an object, a stored procedure can hold both data and code. That makes the stored procedure an excellent place for self-contained

business logic. All of the elements relating to the logic can reside in the same location as the data it's affecting.

- **Increased security** The location of the stored-procedure code on the server makes the security of the code easier to administer than if the logic remained in a cleartext ASP page.
- **Substantial update control** A single update to a stored procedure can alter the behavior of all of the clients accessing the system. Like a shared component, stored procedures provide a method for centralizing logic to minimize the expense of updates usually associated with client modifications.
- **Ability to control execution flow** In a stored procedure, control-of-flow structures such as `If...Then` statements can be used to alter the control-of-flow path of a query.

These advantages provide substantial reasons to implement stored procedures in many of your professional database projects. Through ADO, using a stored procedure is no more difficult than directly executing a query.

Execution Steps for a Query and a Stored Procedure

The performance gains of using stored procedures are easy to understand if you examine the process that a submitted query must go through before the query actually begins. After a query is submitted to the database server, seven steps are required to execute it:

1. Parse the query text.
2. Determine the names of the objects named in the query text.
3. Validate the objects named in the query text.
4. Check the security and permissions of the addressed objects.
5. Optimize the query against available indexes.
6. Compile the execution plan for the database engine.
7. Execute the query.

Using a stored procedure cuts the number of steps down to four:

1. Locate the name of the stored procedure in the text.
2. Check security and permissions.
3. Substitute any passed parameters or arguments.
4. Execute the query.

All of the other steps are handled when the stored procedure is initially created on the server. Making a procedure also allows you to determine, before submission, what the process of query execution will be. Whenever a stored procedure is created, the database creates an execution plan to determine how the query will execute. It's common practice to optimize this plan in a stored procedure for best execution.

DEFINITION: **Execution plan** The step-by-step procedure that a database server will follow to return the results requested by a SQL query. Optimizing the execution plan of a procedure is critical to effective query creation.

Stored procedures are unavailable for simple data sources, such as the JET engine in Microsoft Access. However, Access programmers now have the ability to use this technology because of additions made to Office 2000. The Microsoft Data Environment (MSDE), a complete database server, is included with Access 2000. MSDE is feature-compatible with SQL Server and offers Office developers the ability to begin working with stored procedures.

NOTE: The limitations of MSDE include a 2GB database size (the same limit as for Access) and a recommended limitation of five simultaneous users. If you need greater capability, you will want to upgrade to a full SQL Server installation.

For SQL Server and MSDE, stored procedures are written in Transact-SQL—a proprietary Microsoft extension to the SQL language. Transact-SQL provides a database-specific language that can be programmed in a similar way to a traditional procedural language, such as VBScript.

NOTE: All of the code in this section uses Transact-SQL against a SQL Server or MSDE data source. Since SQL extensions are vendor-specific, these code samples will not execute without modification on other database servers (Oracle or Informix, for example). See the documentation of your database server for the specifics of the stored-procedure implementation. Sybase servers will likely be able to execute these simple procedures, because Microsoft SQL Server and the Sybase servers originated from the same code base.

Creating a Stored Procedure

When you first begin creating stored procedures, they will look very much like your traditional queries. To define a stored procedure, you need to provide it with a name. You use the `create proc` command to begin defining a procedure:

```
create proc mySP as select * from authors
```

This example creates a stored procedure named mySP that does a simple `SELECT`. When executed, this procedure will execute the query just as if the `SELECT` statement had been directly entered.

NOTE: This example uses the SQL Server 6.5 Developer's Edition that was included on the Visual Studio CD. If you are using MSDE or SQL Server 7 or above, the interface will look slightly different, although all of the code and commands will be the same. Under SQL Server 7, the SQL Query Tool is named as the SQL Server Query Analyzer on the Tools menu. Although the interface may appear slightly different than the figures and illustrations, it functions identically.

Let's go ahead and create this procedure on the SQL server and execute it by following these steps:

1. Start the SQL Enterprise Manager.
2. Open the SQL Query Tool window (Tools | SQL Query Tool).
3. Change the DB combo box setting to Pubs. This stored procedure will be created in the Pubs database to query the Authors table.
4. Enter the stored-procedure code (the `create proc` command for `mySP`) in the query window (see the following illustration).

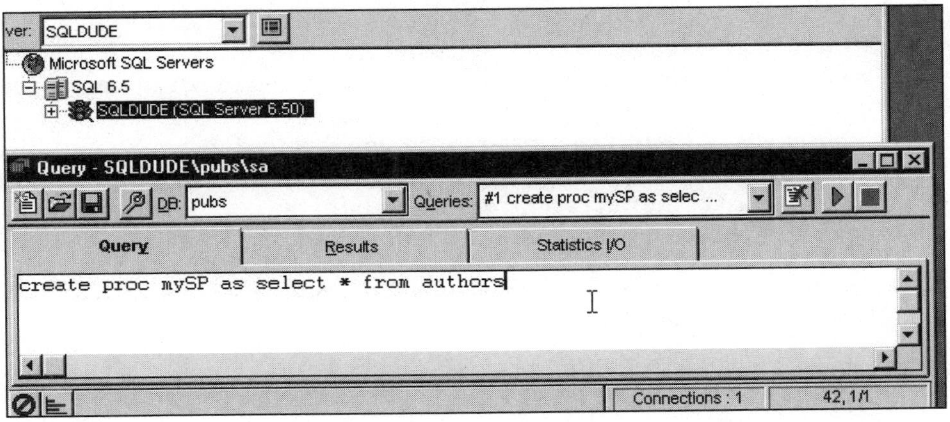

5. Click the green right-facing arrow button (found on the right side of the window) to execute the code and create the stored procedure. The Results tab will tell you that the command did not return any data or rows. The stored procedure has been created and is ready for execution.
6. Click the New Query button on the toolbar (the icon on the far left of the toolbar). This will create a new query so that you can leave the text of the

stored-procedure-creation query intact. You can go back and make modifications to the stored procedure code later.

7. In the new query, under the Query tab, enter the following code:

```
mySP
```

8. Click the green right-facing arrow button to run the stored procedure.

Executing the `mySP` stored procedure will display the results of the query, just as if the query had been entered by hand. The code for the stored procedure is stored within the database so it can be executed by any client accessing the data source.

> ***TIP:*** To see exactly the operations that the database server is performing to execute the query, you can view the query plan for the execution. If you click the Query Options icon on the toolbar, a dialog box will display all of the available preferences. Checking the Show Query Plan option will display the process of the query execution before and after the results of the query. Running the stored procedure again will allow you to observe the execution process.

Adding Parameters to the Procedure

One of the key features that this implementation of a stored procedure doesn't demonstrate is the ability to accept parameters. Without parameter passing, the execution of a procedure would be very limited. By allowing parameters to specify criteria in the query (such as a specific zip code in a mailing list search), a generalized stored procedure can often be used in place of a custom query.

To add the ability to accept a parameter to the stored procedure you've already created, the procedure must first be deleted. Once created, stored procedures cannot simply be redefined; they must be destroyed and recreated. The `drop proc` command is used to eliminate an existing stored procedure.

1. From the Queries combo box at the top of the window, select the stored-procedure definition (item #1).
2. Click the Query tab to return to the Transact-SQL code.
3. Change the code to match the following:

```
/* Check if mySP already exists in the sysobjects */
if exists (select * from sysobjects where
   id = object_id('dbo.mySP') and sysstat & 0xf = 4)
/* if it exists, drop it */
   drop procedure dbo.mySP
/* Execute this part of the query */
GO
```

```
/* Define mySP to accept one argument named @lastName */
create proc mySP @lastName varchar(30)
as
select * from authors
/* Use the argument to match the au_lname field */
where au_lname like @lastName

GO
```

4. Execute the stored procedure. The beginning of the code has a comment that explains the procedure. Unlike VB and VBScript which use the apostrophe (') for a comment, SQL uses the C convention of open and closing brackets (`/*` `*/`). The first statement checks whether or not a stored procedure with that name exists (so that an error isn't generated if it doesn't) and then drops the existing procedure. The `GO` command forces execution of the code entry up to that point.

   The definition of the new procedure follows. This time, the code defines `mySP` to accept a single argument of `@lastName` of varchar type. The argument is subsequently used to match the last-name column in the table.
5. Use the combo box in the query window to return to the mySP execution code (item #2). It will have to be modified now that the query expects to be passed a parameter.
6. Alter the code to read:

   ```
   mySP 'S%'
   ```
7. Execute the code by clicking the green right-arrow button. This time, only three rows should be returned. Unlike Microsoft Access, which uses the asterisk (*) as a wildcard character, SQL Server uses the percent symbol (%). This query, therefore, requests all of the rows where the last-name column begins with the letter *S*.

Now that you have a little experience creating a stored procedure, you will see how to use the procedure from Visual InterDev.

Using a Command Object with the Stored Procedure

The stored procedure you created returns a dataset to match the query that it executes. That means that it can be used as a data source for some of the design-time components. You have used Visual InterDev extensively by now, so create a standard project called StoredProcedure. In this project, you're going to add a Connection object so that it can be referenced by the design-time components.

For the project, create the following:

- **ODBC data source named Pubs** This data source should provide a connection to the MSDE or SQL Server data source that you are using. Make sure that the data source has the default database set to Pubs. When initially created, a SQL Server source defaults to Master.
- **Connection object in the project named conPubs** In your project, add a Connection object that references the Pubs ODBC data source you've created.
- **Command object (under the conPubs connection) named comMySP** In the Properties dialog box, set the Data Object type to Stored Procedure and select the mySP object in the combo box.

When you've created these three items, you should be able to expand the comMySP item in the Project window (shown here) to see the structure of the information returned by the stored procedure.

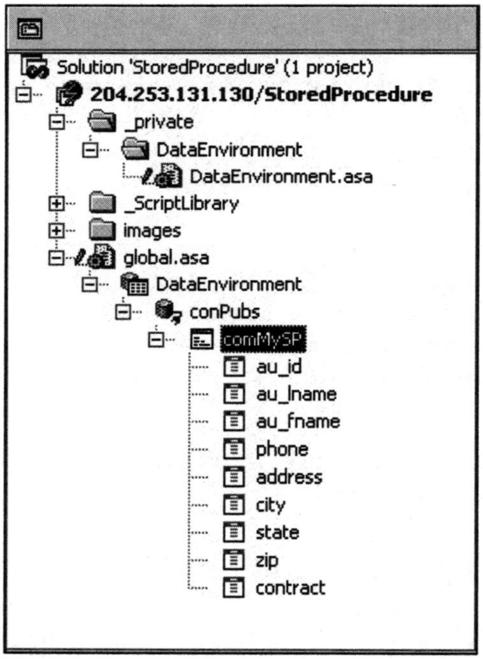

The Data View window (shown next) can also allow you to examine the data source itself. Activate the Data View window and expand the Stored Procedures item in the Pubs tree. You can see that the mySP item contains all of the columns that will be returned by the stored procedure, as well as the argument that must be passed in to allow the procedure to execute.

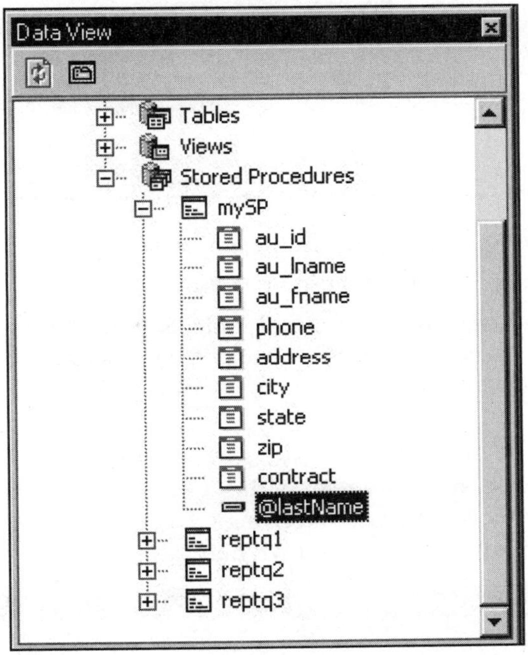

With the project properly configured, you're ready to add a page to display the information returned by the procedure. Follow these steps:

1. Select Page | Add New Page.
2. Set the name of the new page to SPExecute.asp.
3. Select the Design-Time controls tab on the toolbar.
4. Drag a Recordset object onto the page in the Body section (see the following illustration).

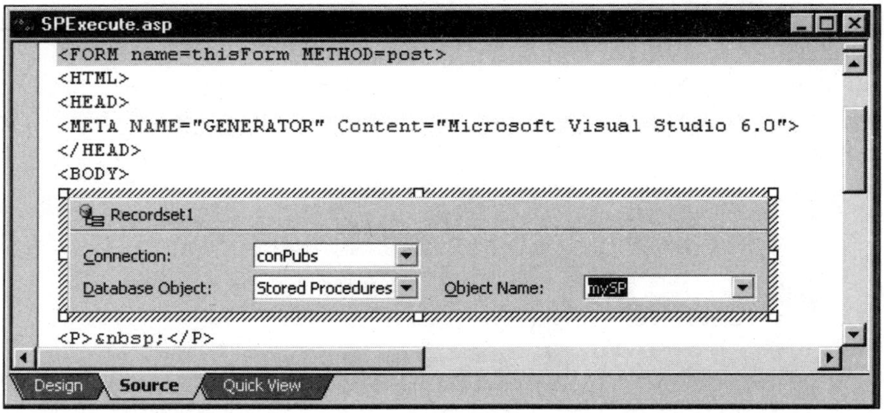

5. Select the conPubs connection on the Recordset component.
6. Set the Database Object to Stored Procedures.
7. Set the Object Name to mySP. Simply selecting the stored procedure will not work in this case because mySP expects to be passed a string parameter. You'll need to set the properties of the component to pass the parameter that you want to use.
8. Right-click the Recordset object and select the Properties option. The Properties window will be displayed for all of the current settings for the Recordset. All of the settings you just made on the Design-Time interface appear on the General tab in the Properties window, shown here:

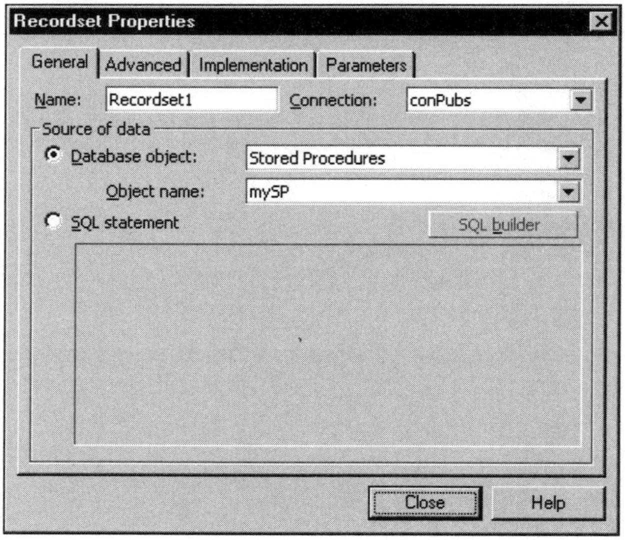

9. Select the Advanced tab and set the Cursor Location to 2 - Use Server-Side Cursors, as shown in the following illustration.

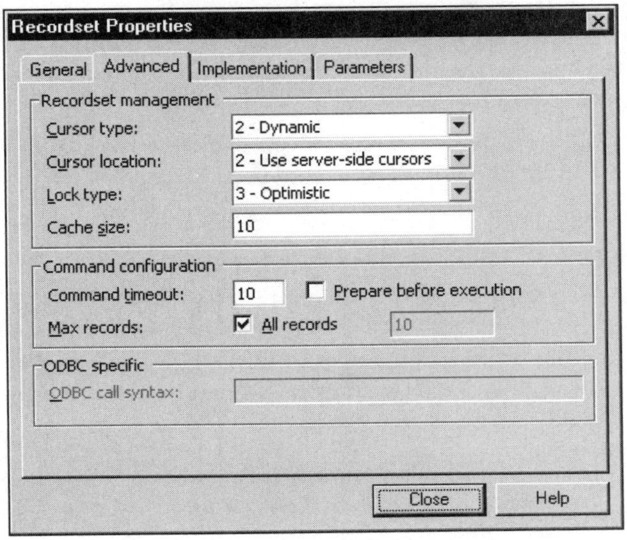

10. Select the Parameters tab and set the `@lastName` parameter to `'s%'`. The default value for this parameter is `nothing`. Entering this query value (as shown in the following illustration) will return the same records as the execution in the SQL Query Tool.

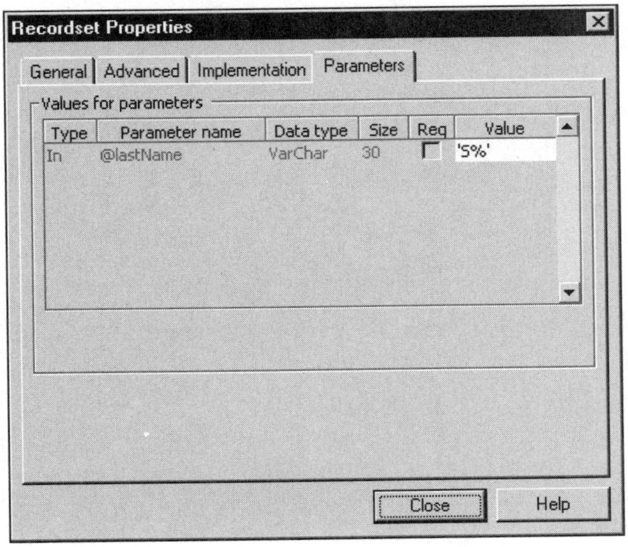

11. Click the Close button to accept these changes. The recordset is now properly configured to execute the stored procedure.
12. There is still nothing in the page for displaying the data returned by the procedure, however. You can use the Grid Design-Time control to easily display the values in the recordset. Drag a Grid object from the toolbox palette into the body of the document below the recordset.
13. Right-click on the Grid object and select the Properties option to configure the recordset to fill the displayed rows and columns.
14. Select the Data tab in the Properties window.
15. Select Recordset1 in the Recordset combo box.
16. Click to check all of the fields displayed in the Available Fields list box (see the following illustration). Each field that is checked will be placed in the Grid Columns list that determines the order in which they'll be displayed in the grid. The up and down arrows to the right can be used to change the order of any of the fields.

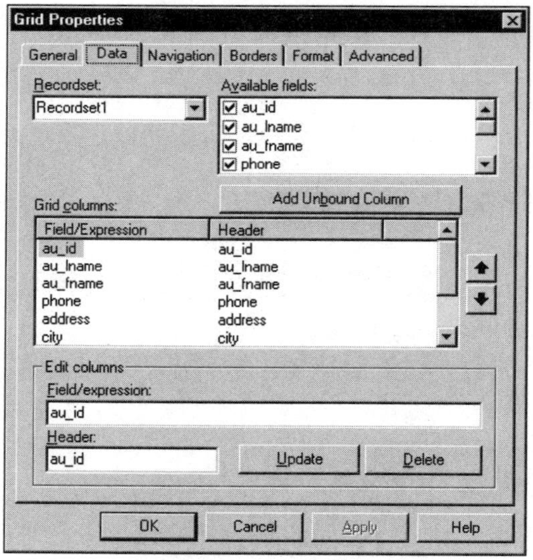

17. Click the OK button to accept the property changes. The solution is now complete; it just needs to be executed.
18. Select View | View in Browser to execute the solution.

When the grid is displayed in the browser, you'll see the three author records that have last names that start with the letter S (shown next). This example provides an effective demonstration of the use of a stored procedure in a Visual InterDev ASP solution.

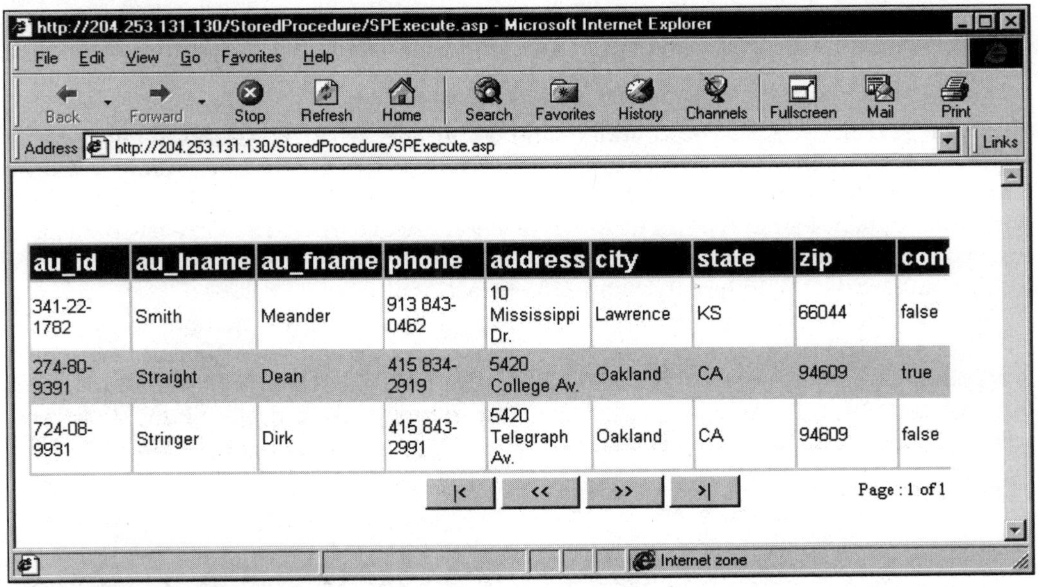

Instead of using the Data Environment in Visual InterDev, ADO could have been used directly in the ASP code. By creating a Command object and adding a Parameter object in the hierarchy to provide the `@lastName` parameter, you could execute it to return the recordset.

PLACING LARGE AMOUNTS OF DATA ON AN ADO DATA SOURCE

In Chapter 21, you used the Microsoft Posting Acceptor to allow a report, once formatted in Excel, to be uploaded into a directory on the Web server. This same code could be used to accept any type of data file, including images. However, having the data reside as a file may be cumbersome if you are trying to associate an image with a database record (such as a personnel photo). You can use ADO to store this information directly to a field of a database.

NOTE: Using a database field to store file data, such an image, is not always the best choice. If the database stores all of the images, the database size can grow dramatically. Also, multiple records cannot store references to the same image. Instead, it must be stored uniquely in each record, taking up more space. You may instead create a common images folder on the Web server and place all of the uploaded images there. Then you need only create a file reference field to allow each record to point to the proper image.

The first concept you should understand before placing this type of data into a data source is that it will be treated as a binary large object (BLOB). A BLOB is simply a large chunk of data that cannot be searched, indexed, or queried in the ways that are possible with other database field types. The most common use of a BLOB field in early databases was to provide a field type that could accept text for a memo that would be too long for a traditional text data field (greater than 255 characters).

In ADO, manipulating binary data is accomplished with two methods on the Field object: `AppendChunk()` and `GetChunk()`. Placing information in a general BLOB field is accomplished by using the `AppendChunk()` method. To retrieve the stored information, the `GetChunk()` method is used. To read an image file and place it in a field, you could use code like this in Visual Basic:

```
Dim fileData() As Byte

Open "c:\myImage.jpg" For Binary Access Read As #1
   ' Expand to entire file size
   Redim fileData(LOF(1))
   ' Grab from file
   Get #1, , fileData()
   ' Append to the recordset
   myRS.Edit
   myRS.Fields("myBLOB").AppendChunk fileData()
   myRS.Update
Close #1
```

This example code expects several database constructs to be in place before it executes. First, it expects to find a recordset that is already opened and stored in the myRS variable. The recordset must be pointing to a data source that contains a field named myBLOB. It also requires a file at the `C:\` root named `myImage.jpg` that will be appended to the current field. Adapting this code to VBScript and ASP would only require the use of the FileSystemObjects for the file access and more exact reading and writing control, because you cannot set the type of the array to Byte.

Using an Image File in a Database

The GetChunk() and AppendChunk() methods can be used to retrieve and place images in database files. For a Web solution, this can cause some difficulties. To retrieve the image, the application would need to read the data from the data source and send it to the browser. The data could instead be written to a file, and then the path to the image could be inserted into the HTML code for transmission to the browser. However, this solution would require constant reads and writes to the server's hard drive which, as described in the last chapter, can have some disadvantages for resource usage and can require extra configuration and authorization.

Broadcasting the image directly to the browser requires a slightly different method of transmission from ASP than you've used before. For the bitmap to be accepted as an image by the browser, the MIME type that tells the browser the type of data that is incoming must send an image notification instead of an HTML notification. To accomplish this, you can use the BinaryWrite() method of the Response object.

For a complete example of how this can be accomplished by creating an ActiveX DLL to retrieve the image and broadcast it directly to the browser, see the tech note Q175261 on the Microsoft Web site (msdn.microsoft.com). This note provides an example of VB, Visual InterDev, and ASP to display the employee images stored in the Northwind database.

To retrieve the image from the field and write it back to a file, you could use the GetChunk() method and code that works in the opposite manner (to write a file instead of read it). Using the GetChunk() method for a file save could be done like this:

```
Dim fileData() As Byte

Open "c:\myImage.jpg" For Binary As #1
   ' Expand to entire field size
   Redim fileData(myRS.Fields("myBLOB").FieldSize)
   ' Retrieve from the recordset
   fileData() = myRS.Fields("myBLOB").GetChunk
   ' Save in file
   Put #1, , fileData()
Close #1
```

Almost every type of database has a field type for large amounts of data. In Microsoft Access, the field type is General, while SQL Server calls it Text, and Oracle calls it Long Raw. Whatever name it is given, the GetChunk() and AppendChunk() methods can be used to store large amounts of information in fields of that type.

ASYNCHRONOUS QUERIES

Many Web database applications will be designed to generate reports, and it is entirely possible that these reports will take more time to produce than the user will want to remain waiting on a single page. Further, the timeout values would have to be extended to the point that they become meaningless. This is particularly true with some data warehouse reports. Using an asynchronous query, the report can be generated while the user continues using the Web application. When the report is ready, it can appear in a Finished Reports page that can be examined by the user.

Using an asynchronous query is possible with the new features added to ADO 2.0. When the query has finished executing and a result set is available, an event is executed to allow processing or display of the recordset. This event can be used to update an HTML page in a Web solution to provide access to the finished query.

DEFINITION: **Asynchronous query** A query that will be processed in the background, returning control to the calling application. Once the query is complete, event code is activated within the query object for recordset processing.

Asynchronous queries are most useful in traditional client applications that use multiple forms such as Visual Basic's Multiple Document Interface (MDI). However, with a Web application, the process can still augment the user experience by providing options such as the ability to manually abort a long query.

NOTE: Using asynchronous queries on a Web site is only effective if the user stays on the Web site for the duration of the query execution. To prevent server resource starvation, the ADO objects are stored in the Session objects, which are eliminated after 20 minutes of disuse. If the user leaves the site for more than this amount of time and the query hasn't been completed, the object will be flushed by the system.

To allow the asynchronous query to execute properly, you will need to set up the ADO object in the Session object. If the ADO object were created on the page, the object would be flushed when the user proceeded to another page.

For a general framework of this type of reporting solution, you could use three ASP pages:

- **StartReport.asp** This page would create the recordset and begin the asynchronous query. Once the query has begun, a variable could be set so the same user cannot begin the query again until it is complete.
- **CheckReport.asp** This page would provide the status of the current query. When the query is complete, this page would contain a link to the final page, DisplayReport.asp.
- **DisplayReport.asp** This page would take the completed recordset and display it in a table format.

This type of asynchronous application is very useful for generating log reports. Log files examination requires individual processing of thousands of individual transactions that may require a large amount of summarization before they can be displayed. Be aware that a great amount of data would have to be processed to justify this advanced technology.

NON-SQL DATA SOURCES

The database industry is simultaneously struggling with old and new technology. The older technology, such as non-SQL databases, still exists in many critical areas of business and government. At the same time, object technology and new data types (such as spatial data) are increasingly being incorporated into the information system framework of organizations.

As described in Chapter 4, Microsoft has launched a program called Universal Data Access (UDA) to provide a way for all data sources, old and new, to be available to current enterprise technology. The ADO object model goes a long way toward fulfilling this promise.

Older Data Sources

In the past, older non-SQL databases either required complex middleware (such as a screen scraper) to make data available to client applications, or an entire SQL engine wrapper had to be created around the data source (this technique is used by some ODBC drivers). These methods can be used effectively for limited applications, but the setup itself requires a substantial amount of time and effort. Additionally, non-native access techniques such as these tend to be fairly slow and make real-time or OLAP systems difficult to implement.

Since SQL processing is not required, ADO has created a new method. By allowing the data provider (the equivalent of a driver in other systems) to access a data source in a non-SQL manner, most existing data sources can be tapped for ADO access. If the proper ADO drivers exist or can be created, direct access to the data source can be used without the problems associated with earlier techniques. Addressing an AS/400 through the VSAM interface is one such data source that is now available for convenient access through an ADO data provider.

Newer Data Sources

In the same way that the flexibility of the ADO framework opens up older data sources, new data source types that don't necessarily fit into the SQL-based query methods benefit from ADO provider implementation. Already the company Object Design, Inc. has an OLE DB provider to access ObjectStore data. Vendors such as Merant (formerly Intersolv) supply a number of OLE DB drivers to access various data sources from MAPI-compliant mail servers, to CISAM, to DB2.

While most of the database industry has been struggling with the decision of whether to include object technology (the ability to store and access object data) in the heart of their database server products, Microsoft has taken advantage of its operating-system dominance to provide a universal middleware solution for servers. Rather than placing all of the object stores into the central database, ADO allows you to access many different servers through the same object model, transparently.

Therefore, an organization could easily run, for example, a database server, an object server, and a Geographic Information System (GIS) server. All of the client code for accessing these servers could use ADO, simply directing the connection to use different data providers. As long as the providers support transaction capabilities, a single transaction could even span all of these servers with abort or commit capabilities.

In fact, the growth of many organizations' reliance on spatial data for demographic decision-making is creating a lucrative market for GIS implementation. Querying by abstract geographical concepts does not lend itself to a traditional SQL statement. For example, imagine a construction company that needed to notify all of the neighbors within a two-mile radius that the noise from jackhammers will only last between 8 A.M. and 10 A.M. Using a traditional database, this becomes a complex problem of coordinating streets with distance and with residential addresses.

On the other hand, for a properly configured spatial database, this query is the essence of simplicity. With street-map coverage, you can literally request the map server to provide all of the addresses within a two-mile radius. Through technologies such as ODBC, building an interface for such a system would be extremely expensive and cumbersome. ADO, however, is ideal for creating just such a provider. In the future, an interface standard could evolve so that a spatial query could be directed against the GIS servers of several different vendors (such as ARC/Info or MapInfo) without any reprogramming.

Another example of non-traditional data access available from ADO is the ability to manipulate an e-mail store. There is no ODBC driver for Microsoft Exchange Server because of the complications it would involve. An Exchange data store is not SQL-based. However, Exchange Server data is available through the ADO interface. You can use the Exchange data provider to retrieve e-mail information through the standard ADO objects.

ADO can even access file information. Data residing in the Windows NT file system is available through the OLE DB provider, which is part of Microsoft Index Server. This data provider allows you to treat files as just another type of data source and provides an excellent example of the flexibility available through ADO for future access needs.

NOTE: For more examples, you can log on to the Web site dedicated to this book in the books section of Client/Server Central (www.coherentdata.com/cscentral). The password for this book is `dwelling`.

Q&A

Q: Where can I get ADO drivers not made by Microsoft?

A: There are a variety of vendors that are making ADO provider software. These include Merant (www.merant.com), MetaWise (www.metawise.com), Object Design (www.odi. com), and Sagent Technology (www.sagenttech.com). However, data providers are most commonly needed for a specific solution, such as access to an AS/400 data store. In that case, you should check with the vendor of the product for the availability of an ADO driver.

If there are no data providers available for the data source you wish to address, and you have competent Visual C++ programmers on your team, you might consider creating your own. On the Microsoft site, there is information on developing your own data providers (www.microsoft.com/data).

Q: Can I use an asynchronous query with MSMQ?

A: While technically possible, there are very few advantages to creating such a system since MSMQ provides asynchronous operation calls. However, I have seen an application that used the asynchronous queries to allow for Web-based data-warehousing activities. In that solution, a query was sent through an object stored in the Application object. When MSMQ returned the results of the query, an event was generated for the object, and it modified the appropriate page. The Web interface was used essentially as an instigator for a long-term process.

SUMMARY

ADO provides much more flexibility than the older technologies of JET or ODBC. Rather than limiting a developer to a sequential SQL environment, ADO provides a multiple data type, multiple provider, non-sequential, middleware option. In this chapter you covered:

- **Stored procedures** Stored procedures are code (including queries) that can be placed on the database server and compiled for faster execution. Through the Command object, ADO has the functionality to create, modify, and access stored procedures.
- **Command objects** In ADO, a Command object can be created to represent a stored procedure. By adding Parameter objects to a Command object that is representing the procedure, arguments can be passed to it.
- **Asynchronous queries** Asynchronous queries are processed in the background, returning control to the calling application. Once the query is complete, event code is activated within the query object for recordset processing.
- **Binary large object (BLOB) storage** Placing BLOBs into an ADO data source is possible because of the `AppendChunk()` method. A program can place binary data into a field and later retrieve it using the `GetChunk()` method.
- **Non-SQL data sources** Whether the data source is an older record-based database or a new object data store, ADO allows providers to be created that can retrieve and modify any type of data. This furthers Microsoft's Universal Data Access (UDA) program which seeks to make any online data accessible through Microsoft enterprise software.

CHAPTER 23

Java Charts

Java has been the most publicized new computer language to come along in many years. Initially, Java promised to be a language that would allow people to write a single program that could be executed on any platform (Windows, Macintosh, UNIX, and others). Four years after its release, however, this promise still remains elusive, but for basic program capabilities, Java excels in cross-platform deployment. One of the functions for which Java is particularly suited is the creation of browser-based interactive graphics, such as generating a bar chart in real-time.

This chapter will introduce you to the capabilities of Java, as well as to its use within a Web-based application. If you are not familiar with the language, this chapter will serve as an excellent introduction for using Visual J++ for Java coding and compiling. You will work step-by-step through the creation of a Java applet that displays a bar chart (see Figure 23-1). Visual Studio includes a copy of Visual J++ that allows you to compile and use a variety of existing Java source code. Although a complete exploration of the Java language could fill a book, this chapter will help you get started with Java.

The example applet in this chapter provides an excellent foundation applet from which you can build a custom bar chart for your enterprise needs. You will see how this applet can be created and deployed in a Web solution.

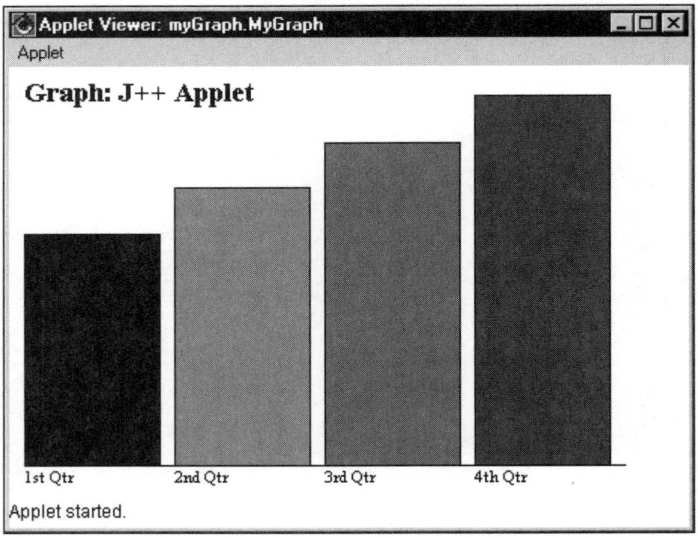

Figure 23-1. The MyGraph applet displays a bar chart based on data received from the HTML page

JAVA LANGUAGE FROM A VB PERSPECTIVE

For a Visual Basic or VBScript programmer, using Java presents some special challenges. Java is a language much more like C++ than VB, which makes Java slightly more powerful but much more complex than Visual Basic. Although the differences from the familiar VB style might seem intimidating at first, learning a second computer language requires far less effort than learning the first one does. Once you get the hang of the general style of Java, you will be able to use it to handle simple functions and rudimentary modifications to existing programs.

Hello World Applet

A simple Hello World program is usually an excellent place to start with a programming language, but since you need a program that will execute in a browser, this task becomes more difficult in Java. To execute in a browser, all of the implementation details for creating an applet must be followed and an applet is an advanced place to start.

Instead, let's take a look at a simple Hello World application that could be compiled and run on a machine outside a browser. All programming in Java requires the creation of a class like the one shown in this listing:

```
public class helloWorld {
   public static void main(String[] args)
   {
      System.out.println("Hello World");
   }
}
```

This program creates a class called helloWorld. The `main()` function is defined as a method of this class. To have a similar program execute in VB, you would need a form or module file to instantiate the class and then execute the `main()` method. In Java, since you are executing the program as if it were an executable file, it will automatically create the instance and run the function named `main()`, passing it any arguments that follow on the command line.

To give you an idea of how such a program would appear in Visual Basic, you would need to create a class in Visual Basic and name it helloWorld. Then, you would enter code such as the following:

```
Public Function main(args As String)
   Debug.Print "Hello World"
End Function
```

The Java version of the Hello World application cannot be practically executed in a browser since an applet must be created as a subclass of the Applet class. Within the Applet class, a graphic canvas much like a window is provided that can be drawn upon. Since this example uses the system `println` function, the output wouldn't be displayed in the browser window.

> ***NOTE:*** This Hello World application can be executed within a browser with the proper security settings, but the displayed message will only appear in a window known as the "Java Console". Both Netscape Navigator and Microsoft Internet Explorer (select the Java Console option under the View menu) include a console output so that programs can display error and debugging information. However, the console is not useful for interacting with users.

When you create an applet, the design and programming will appear strikingly like the work you do to create an ActiveX DLL or control in VB. An applet, like an ActiveX component, needs to be instantiated and have its methods called from outside the component. In the case of an applet, the method calls usually come from the client browser.

Inheritance

Unlike VB, Java was designed from the bottom up as an inherited language. Although VB can achieve somewhat similar functionality through the `Implements` keyword, the starting point is far different. Inheritance allows you to create a child or subclass of a base class so that you can add additional methods or properties. At the same time, the new subclass can maintain the functionality of the parent class.

A key part of inheritance is the `extends` keyword in Java. It is used in a class definition to indicate which parent class the new class will be based upon. To create a Java applet, you will need to *subclass* (create a subclass from) the Applet class. The definition statement for your applet will look like this:

```
class MyGraph extends Applet
```

The new MyGraph class then inherits all of the functions of the Applet class, and you can additionally define new methods and properties.

Directory or Path Structures

For all inheritance, Java uses a method of accessing an object that is very similar to the directory hierarchy on your hard disk. For example, to execute a program that is several directories deep, you could use a fully explicit path call at the command prompt, like this:

```
c:\windows\winipcfg.exe
```

This would execute the winipcfg program that is located down one directory layer in the drive hierarchy. Likewise, in Java you might create a new object that has several layers of inheritance by using the dot (.) command, like this:

```
company.myOrganization.division1.pkgMyClass.myclass.class
```

This class, if the root folder is set to \myOrganization, would have the following directory structure:

```
company\division1\pkgMyClass\myclass.class
```

JAVA PLATFORM

In Chapter 19, you used the DHTML object model to manipulate the client-side user experience. DHTML, when combined with ActiveX controls, can be used to provide a user experience almost as comprehensive as a fully compiled client application. Unfortunately, this type of implementation requires the user to be running Microsoft Internet Explorer. Internet Explorer is the only browser to feature ActiveX and DHTML support.

Outside of the enterprise, it is likely that users will be running a variety of browsers including Netscape Navigator, Mosaic, Hot Java, and others. Although most of these browsers lack a compatible version of DHTML and are unable to support ActiveX controls, almost every available browser can execute basic Java programs.

This cross-platform and cross-browser Java support is provided through the Java virtual machine (VM). The Java VM is essentially a software version of a microprocessor. When source code files (files with the `.java` extension) are compiled to JVM executables (files with the `.class` extension), they can be run on any microprocessor that has a compatible VM. The executable compilation converts the source code into something called Java bytecode.

This process does not come without its drawbacks. Since the bytecode must execute on the virtual microprocessor of the VM, it is much slower than system-specific compiled code. To make execution faster, companies have created technologies such as the Java Just-in-Time (JIT) compilers. These compile the bytecode to native code on-the-fly in the background. To the user there appears to be no difference, but the native code executes much more quickly.

To compile the source code into bytecode files, Visual J++ offers one of the most effective Java compilers on the market. It can also extend the functionality of a Java program to take advantage of native system resources, such as the Windows API (which is useful if your application will be executing on only one machine type).

NOTE: Since you have a complete development environment in Visual J++, you may have no desire to acquire other systems. However, it is usually a good idea to install the free Java Development Kit (JDK) that Sun Microsystems (the inventor of Java) provides as the reference standard for the Java language. You can download the JDK from the Sun/Java Web site (www.javasoft.com).

You can also get IBM's excellent Java IDE, called Visual Age for Java, which supports Enterprise JavaBeans and the 100% Pure Java initiative. An entry-level version (limited to the creation of 500 classes in a project) can be downloaded from the Visual Age Web site (www.software.ibm.com/ad/vajava) for free.

Java is both a platform and a language. It is a platform because it has its own execution environment and has a large number of classes to handle disk access, graphics, windowing, network access, and more. In the early promotion of Java, Sun intended Java to supplant all current operating systems since a program written for the Java platform could be executed on any machine running the Java VM. Not surprisingly, Microsoft did not like this idea—hence, the legal battle that continues to be waged between Microsoft and Sun.

Despite the war over the Java platform implementation, Microsoft has embraced the Java language. The language can be seen as a successor to C++. While the Java language is too large to cover in a single chapter, we can review some of the basic operations needed to understand the source code included for the bar chart application.

NOTE: Unlike Visual Basic, Java is case-sensitive. Therefore, if you enter a variable name as *myVar*, it will not be the same as a variable named *myvar*. Be sure to closely follow the source code you're typing, because capitalization mistakes can prevent proper compiling.

The functions shown in Table 23-1 give a few of the most common keywords and commands available in Java and their VB equivalents.

Java also handles individual lines differently from VB. In Java, each command continues, regardless of line breaks, until it is ended with a semicolon (;) character. This is exactly the opposite of VB, which ends a command at a line break unless you use the underscore (_) to extend the command. Since the command line in Java doesn't end until the semicolon is reached, a single statement can run across many lines like this:

```
myStr = "Hello" +
    " World " +
    " from Java ";
```

Until the semicolon is reached, all of the text regardless of line feeds, is considered a single operation. For the `If...Then` construct, a true or a false value executes a single operation following the `If` statement:

```
if (i == 10) a = 1;
else a = 2;
```

Visual Basic	Java
`If...Then...Endif`	if (...) { ...}
= (variable setting)	=
= (comparison)	==
`' (remark)`	//

Table 23-1. Visual Basic and Java Common Commands

To make multiple operations appear to Java as a single command, the curly brackets {} can be used. For example, the `if` command can be used like this:

```
if (i == 10) {
   a = 1;
   myStr = "Bye.";
}
else {
   a = 2;
   myStr = "Hello.";
}
```

Declaring variables in Java is similar to doing so in VB, except the type is entered first, and one or many variable names may follow. For example:

```
int x,y,z;
```

This code defines three variables (x, y, and z) of the integer data type. The primary variable types for VB compared with Java are shown in Table 23-2.

Java also allows a variable type to be defined on the same line on which it is assigned a value. For example, a new string could be set like this:

```
String myStr = "Hello"
```

This method of declaration works somewhat like the naming characters such as string ($) in Visual Basic:

```
myStr$ = "Hello"
```

With this basic introduction, you should be able to make some sense of the simple source code used for the bar chart applet.

Visual Basic	Java
Integer	int
Long	long
Float	float
Double	double
String	String

Table 23-2. Visual Basic and Java Variable Types

USING VISUAL J++ TO GENERATE THE CUSTOM CHART APPLET

With a basic understanding of Java under your belt, you will be able to use Visual J++ to create a simple applet. To make things even easier, J++ supplies a number of wizards that automate most of the process of creating a Java program. You'll be using a wizard to supply the code for the framework of the graphing applet.

Java Bar Chart Code

Visual J++ shares the Visual InterDev development environment. Since you've already done extensive VI creation, many of the features will be familiar. You will create the bar chart applet that can be used in a Java-capable browser. The code will use the Applet class to define a subclass called MyGraph that will be used to display bar chart information supplied by the HTML page that instantiates it.

To create the bar chart applet, follow these steps:

1. *Start up the Visual J++ development environment.* Visual J++ will automatically open with a dialog box that allows you to select an existing project or create a new one. The J++ environment provides a wizard to automatically generate primitive applet code, so you will have a starting point.
2. *Select the Web Pages folder in the Visual J++ Projects folder.* This Web Pages folder will display the available page types supported in J++.
3. *Select the Applet on HTML item.* (See the following illustration of the New Project dialog box.)

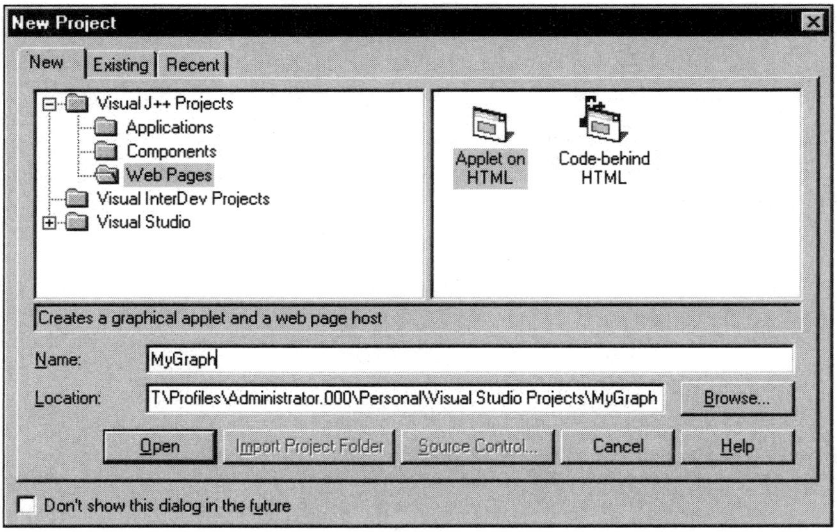

4. *Name the project MyGraph in the Name text box, and click the Open button.* The New Page Wizard will automatically generate a basic applet and an HTML file that will call the applet. Your project window should display these two items now (see the next illustration showing the applet and its page support). The applet will, by default, have the name Applet1.java. For this solution, you will be creating an applet to display a bar chart, so the class should be renamed appropriately.

5. *Right-click the applet item and rename it **MyGraph.java**.* When the name of the applet is changed, there are a number of code references that must be changed as well, since they do not adjust automatically. This first reference is in the applet code itself.
6. *Double-click the MyGraph.java item to open it in the source editor.* The source code for the applet will be displayed in the code window. You will notice that the text Applet1 is underlined in red. This indicates an error—the name of the applet definition must match the name of the file in which it occurs.
7. *Change the "Applet1" text to "MyGraph."* The wizard automatically has placed a large amount of sample code in the applet. This code provides the basic pathway that retrieves parameters passed from the browser, sets the background color, and displays a string. For the moment, you can leave the code so that a test of the applet can be made.

   In order to execute the applet on the Web page constructed by the New Page Wizard, the reference to the applet name must be changed.
8. *Double-click the Page1.htm item in the Project Explorer.* The page will be opened in the Design view, which doesn't provide access to the properties that you need to set. You'll have to change the viewing mode to show the page source.

9. *Select the Source tab to change to the source view mode.* Selecting the applet itself will allow you to change the properties that will be used to generate the HTML page.
10. *Click the applet box that appears under the "Insert HTML here" text.* As shown below, once the applet is selected, the Properties window displays the settings for the applet in the design environment.

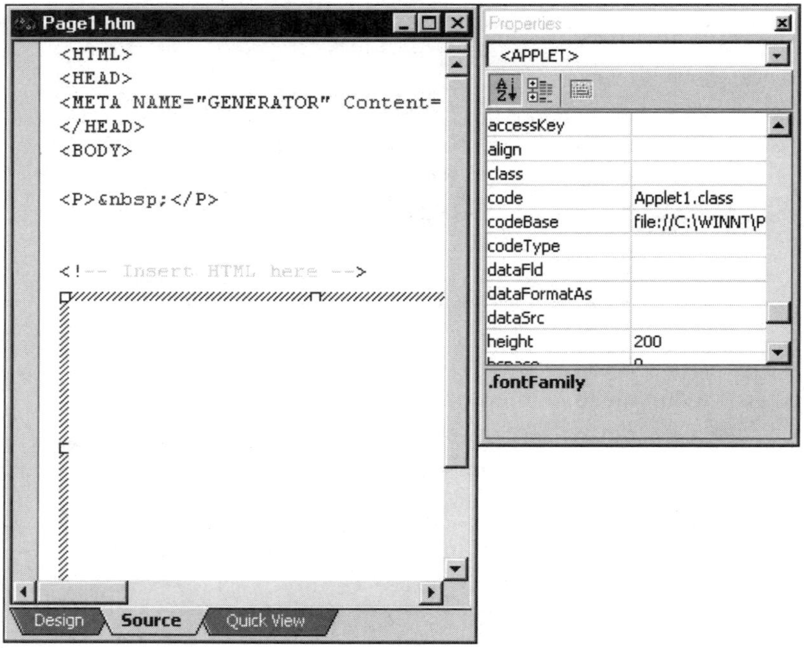

If you examine the `Code` property, you'll see that it is still set to access the Applet1.class file. Since you've changed the name of the class to MyGraph, you will have to alter this property to allow the HTML to properly access it.

11. *Set the text in the `Code` property to MyGraph.class.* You can now test the applet. It will not be run in the Web browser for testing, but instead will run in the Microsoft Applet Viewer. The Applet Viewer is a small program that allows applets to execute effectively in a testing environment which is far more convenient for the loading and reloading cycle common during development.
12. *Select the Start option under the Debug menu or press F5.* The applet will run in the Microsoft Applet Viewer and appear in a small window (as shown in the following illustration). Since this applet is primitive and no parameters were passed to it, it will only display the simple default string. If a reference to the compiled applet was placed in the HTML code of the Page1.htm page and loaded in a browser, it would execute with the passed string as an argument. However, this applet is just a shell for the bar chart applet that needs to be created.

13. *Close the Applet Viewer.* You need to modify the source code of the MyGraph.java file to display a bar chart.

14. *Activate the MyGraph.java source window.* You will need to replace most of the code in this window. The MyGraph applet only consists of four methods: `getAppletInfo()`, `getParameterInfo()`, `init()`, and `paint()`. The `getAppletInfo()` method is a standard method for returning information about the applet to the calling environment (such as Applet Viewer or a browser). The `getParameterInfo()` method returns the description of the various parameters that can be passed to the applet for use.

    The real meat of the applet occurs in the `init()` and `paint()` methods. The `init()` method initializes the primary variables used by the applet and reads the parameters passed from the calling environment, storing them in global variables available to all methods of the class.

    The `paint()` method actually draws the bar chart, based on the parameters specified by the host environment. The size of the bars automatically adjust in height and width to reflect the size of the applet.

    In the MyGraph.java code window, replace the existing wizard-generated code with the following code:

```
import java.awt.*;
import java.applet.*;

/**
 * This class displays a bar graph
 */
public class MyGraph extends Applet
{
   // Setup variables that can be accessed
   // throughout the applet
   private int numberBars = 1;
   private int barVals[] = new int[20];
   private String labelVals[] = new String[20];
   private int xOff = 10,yOff = 20;
   private int maxVal = 0;
   private String title = "";
   private int drawHt = 0;
   private int xPos = 5;

   // Define the font for the title string
   Font titleFont = new Font("TimesRoman", Font.BOLD, 18);
   Font labelFont = new Font("TimesRoman", Font.PLAIN, 10);
```

```
    /**
     * Information about this applet.
     */
    public String getAppletInfo() {
       return "MyGraph\n" +
          "\n" +
          "This applet will display a bar chart of passed information.\n"
          ;
    }

    /**
     * Parameter info for this applet
     */
    public String[][] getParameterInfo() {
       String[][] info = {
          {"title", "String", ""}
       };
       return info;
    }

public void init()
    {
    super.init();

    int tempVal;

    // Get the number of bars passed to the applet
    String barsParam = this.getParameter("num");

    if (barsParam != null)
        numberBars = Integer.parseInt(barsParam);

    if (numberBars > 0) {
       // Read the individual data for the chart
       for(int i=0;i<numberBars;i++) {
          String tempValStr = this.getParameter("d"+ (i+1));
          String tempLabelStr = this.getParameter("l"+ (i+1));
          if (tempValStr != null) {
             barVals[i] = Integer.parseInt(tempValStr);
             // Find the maximum value
             maxVal = Math.max(maxVal,barVals[i]);
          }
          else
             barVals[i] = 0;

          if (tempLabelStr != null)
             labelVals[i] = tempLabelStr;
          else
             labelVals[i] = "";
       }
    }

    String xOffStr = this.getParameter("xOff");
    if (xOffStr != null)
        xOff = Integer.parseInt(xOffStr);
    String yOffStr = this.getParameter("yOff");
    if (yOffStr != null)
        yOff = Integer.parseInt(yOffStr);
    String titleStr = this.getParameter("title");
```

```
    if (titleStr != null)
        title = titleStr;
    }

public void paint(Graphics g) {
    int i,tempWidth,tempOffset,tempVal;
    int tx,ty;
    Double myDouble;
    double tempDouble;
    Rectangle appletRect;
    int drawWidth;

    // Define an array of eight colors for the bars
    Color colorLookup[] = {Color.blue,Color.cyan,Color.green,
          Color.magenta,Color.orange,Color.pink,Color.red,Color.yellow};

    // Calculate the maximum height for the bars
    appletRect = g.getClipRect();
    drawHt = appletRect.height - (yOff*2);
    drawWidth = (appletRect.width  - (xOff*2)) / numberBars;

    // Draw the title of the graph
    g.setFont(titleFont);
    g.setColor(Color.black);
    g.drawString("Graph: " + title, xOff, 24);
    // Set font for labels in the loop
    g.setFont(labelFont);

    // Cycle through all of the bars
    for (i=0;i< numberBars;i++) {
       // Read the bar value from the array
       tempVal = barVals[i];
       // Set the color from the array
       g.setColor(colorLookup[i % 8]);

       // Create a double value that fits the new
       // bar within the height of the applet
       myDouble = new Double(tempVal);
       tempDouble = myDouble.doubleValue();
       tempDouble = (tempDouble/maxVal)*drawHt;
       myDouble = new Double(tempDouble);
       // Get the integer of that value
       tempVal = myDouble.intValue();

       // fill rectangle with a width of 10
       // and a height of tempVal
       g.fillRect(i*drawWidth+xOff,drawHt-tempVal+yOff,drawWidth-10,tempVal);
       // Draw a border on the bar
       g.setColor(Color.black);
       g.drawRect(i*drawWidth+xOff,drawHt-tempVal+yOff,drawWidth-10,tempVal);
       if (labelVals[i] != null)
          g.drawString(labelVals[i], (i*drawWidth)+xOff, drawHt+yOff+12);
    }
    // Draw a baseline to frame the bars
    g.setColor(Color.black);
    g.drawLine(drawWidth,drawHt+yOff,10+(numberBars*drawWidth),drawHt+yOff);
  }
  }
```

When all of the code has been entered, the applet is ready to accept bar values and execute. You might want to save the project at this point. To look at the applet, you will need to run it in the Applet Viewer again.

15. *Run the applet by pressing the F5 key.* Your first question might be "Where are the colored bars that make up the chart?" The answer is that the Applet Viewer that you used to execute the applet hasn't passed any data to display. As a result, the only item displayed in the window is the "Graph:" (shown in the next illustration) text that would be followed by the title of the chart if it had been given one. Although there is no displayed data, the applet does have a feature you can access from the Applet Viewer. The `getAppletInfo()` method can be executed by the viewer itself.

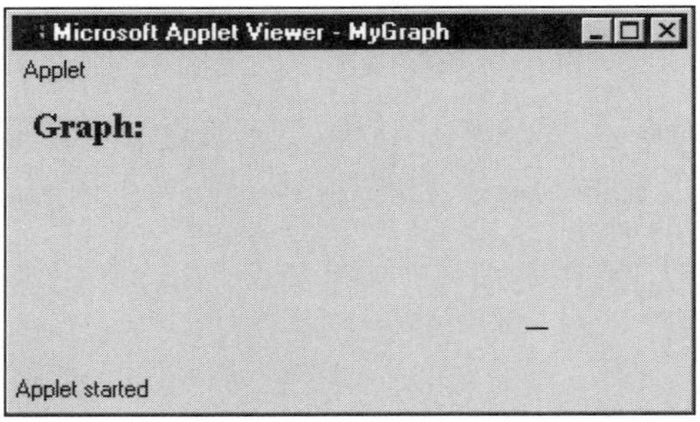

16. *Under the Applet menu, select the Applet Info option.* You will see a dialog window (shown next) that displays the information returned by this routine. To have the applet display actual bar-chart images, you will need to pass in argument information. As in a final application, this information will be provided in the HTML source code that initializes the applet. You now need to create a Web page to pass some sample parameters. Close the applet viewer and return to the HTML page of the project.

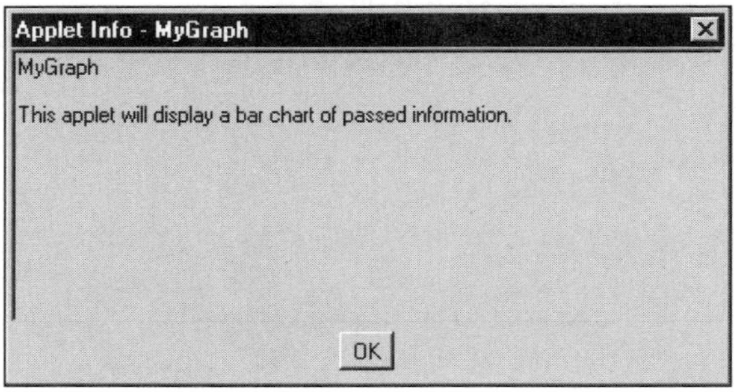

17. *Select the Page1.htm file.*
18. *Under the View menu, select the View Controls as Text option.* By viewing the control (applet) as text, you can see the code that initializes the applet. Since

your chart applet does not need the parameters of the wizard-created applet (such as the background color), but does need bar-chart values, the code will have to be modified.

Modify the code between the <APPLET> tags to match this:

```
<APPLET code=MyGraph.class codeBase=
   "file://C:\WINNT\Profiles\Administrator\Personal\
   Visual Studio Projects\MyGraph\"
   height=200 name=Applet1 style="LEFT: 0px; TOP: 0px"
width=320>
<PARAM name=d1 value=50>
<PARAM name=d2 value=60>
<PARAM name=d3 value=70>
<PARAM name=d4 value=80>
<PARAM name=num value=4>
<PARAM name=l1 value="1st Qtr">
<PARAM name=l2 value="2nd Qtr">
<PARAM name=l3 value="3rd Qtr">
<PARAM name=l4 value="4th Qtr">
<PARAM name=title value="J++ Applet">
</APPLET>
```

These added parameters give the graph a title ("J++ Applet"), set the number of bars (to 4), and provide values and labels for each of the four bars.

19. *Select the Build option from the Build menu.* This will create the class files for the project in the project directory.
20. *For this run, you will need to copy the class file and the HTML page into your Web server directory.* Look in the project folder. You should see a number of files created by Visual J++ (see the following illustration containing the .class and .Java files of the applet).

21. *Copy the MyGraph.class and Page1.htm files into the Web server directory.* At this point the applet is ready to execute.
22. *Start up your browser (either Navigator/Communicator or Internet Explorer), and enter the URL to the Page1.htm on your Web server.* You should now see the applet execute and display four properly labeled bars in the chart (see Figure 23-2). If you modify the width and height parameters of the applet in the source code, the display of the applet will alter to fit the new size.

Now that you've completed this basic applet, you should begin to understand how applets can be developed for a cross-platform, cross-browser solution. Almost more powerful, however, is the ability to use existing applets with dynamically generated values through an ASP solution.

Creating an ASP Page for Java Applet Information

The example HTML page was effective in showing a primitive use of a Java applet, but the functionality becomes really powerful when it is merged with ASP. Since the applet can accept the parameters in the HTML code, an ASP file can execute and retrieve data-

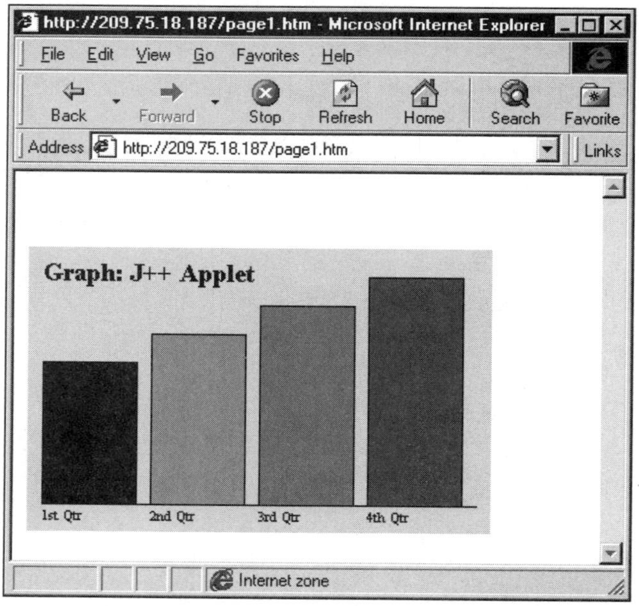

Figure 23-2. The applet executing in the browser

base information for display. These parameters can be supplied to either an applet that you've developed or one of the hundreds that are available for free download.

NOTE: The type of dynamic ASP page presented in this section can easily be modified to become even more elaborate. For example, if separate applets were available for bar, line, pie, and point charts, the ASP page could designate which applet should be sent, based on a user selection.

The code for the ASP page can use the Page1.htm file generated by the project for its foundation. The page will simply randomize some data to be passed in the HTML and sent to the browser. Instead of random data, this code could just as easily retrieve the necessary information from a data source.

Create an ASP file containing the following code:

```
<HTML>
<HEAD>
<META NAME="GENERATOR" Content="Microsoft Visual Studio 6.0">
</HEAD>
<BODY>

<P> </P>


   <APPLET code=MyGraph.class" height=400 name=Applet1 width=320>
   <PARAM name=title value="ASP J++ Applet">
   <PARAM name=num value=10>
<%
   for i = 1 to 10
%>
   <PARAM name=d<%=i%> value=<%=CInt(Rnd*100) %> >
   <PARAM name=l<%=i%> value="Bar #<%=i%>"   <% Next %>
   </APPLET>

</BODY>
</HTML>
```

This ASP code takes the basic applet HTML code and adds a `For...Next` loop to enter values between 0 and 100 into the bar chart. When this ASP page is addressed by a Web server, it will display bars containing ten random values (see Figure 23-3).

This applet did not require sophisticated Java coding to display a graphic solution. With a little more experience, you could modify the applet to reflect your charting needs. For more information, I suggest the excellent *Java Handbook* by Patrick Naughton (Osborne, ISBN: 0-07-882199-1).

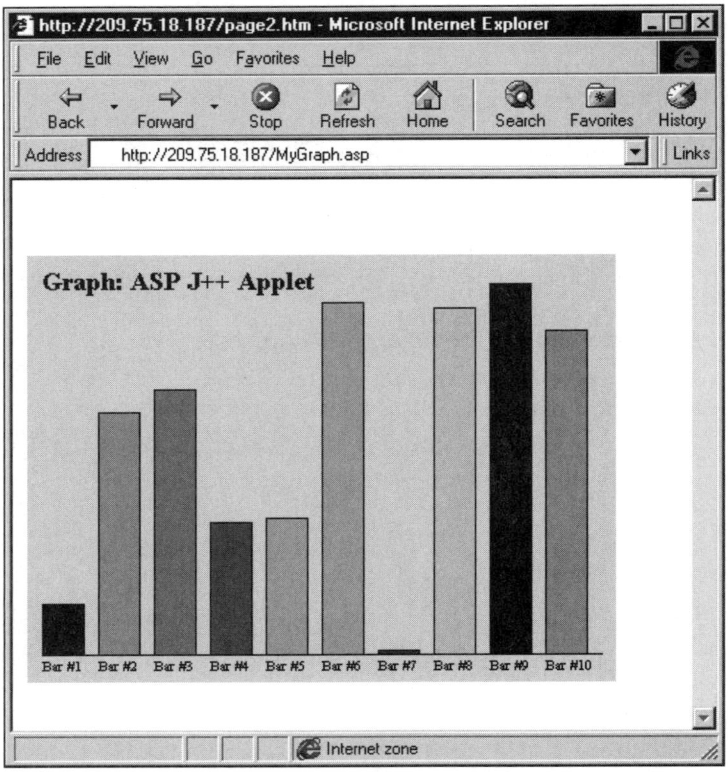

Figure 23-3. The applet displayed with the ASP-generated data

Q&A

Q: Why would someone want to use a natively compiled Java application, since it becomes platform dependent?

A: A natively compiled Java application has one large advantage over bytecode compilation—speed. In most cases of development, speed takes precedence over cross-platform compatibility. After the initial surge of Java development, many IT professionals recognized that often 80 percent or more of their machines were running Windows on an Intel processor. The substantial speed penalties for using Java were difficult to mitigate with the small cross-platform advantage.

However, the Java language provides the perfect evolutionary step from C++. The overall design of Java, as well as its lack of pointers, makes object-oriented programs written in Java far easier to develop and debug than similar programs in C++. In some ways, Java seems to be evolving into the equivalent of C++ 2.0.

Q: How can a Java applet access the local hard drive?

A: Unfortunately, that is a difficult problem to solve. Microsoft and Netscape both support separate standards for digitally signing an applet to provide this type of access. With Microsoft, the secured applet must be contained in a digitally signed CAB file. For Netscape, the signing occurs within a JAR file (a form of Zip compression). Although Internet Explorer can handle JAR files, secure JAR files are not supported. You will need two separately stored versions of the applet to provide for each browser type.

SUMMARY

Within some Web solutions, a client-side Java application can solve problems that are difficult to overcome by other means. By introducing yourself to the Java development environment, you dramatically expand the directions you can take in future application generation. In this chapter you covered:

- **Java** There are two different concepts of Java: the language and the platform. The language is very similar to C++ and provides classes, inheritance, instancing, multithreading, and more. The platform incorporates a set of standard classes for window display, networking, disk access, applet creation, and so on.
- **Virtual machine** The Java VM acts much like a software-based microprocessor. An individual Java VM exists on every Java-compatible platform that can execute Java bytecode.
- **Applet class** Applets are small Java programs that run on the Java VM within a Web browser. For security reasons, they are typically limited in their ability to access desktop resources, such as the hard disk or client networking features.
- **ASP data generation** An ASP page can be constructed to easily feed information to an applet for client display. Since the data are inserted directly into the HTML code (unlike the live-capabilities of the Microsoft Remote Data Services), the applet can be used from any Java-compatible browser.

CHAPTER 24

Primary Challenges to Implementing Distributed Computing

Using the tools that are included in Visual Studio, you have created a distributed system. The Forums application used logic that spread across four tiers (browser, Web server, MTS, and SQL Server) to provide one of the most advanced types of application. This application, however, was already planned and implemented for you. When you need to start from scratch and design a distributed system, there are many factors that need to be taken into account.

This chapter describes some of the planning methodology that can help you achieve an effective implementation. Some "soft tools," such as checklists, charts, and diagrams can aid you in planning and considering your distributed system. When you are working on enterprise development, managing relationships among the people involved is an important part of effectively creating a new system. Graphic aids such as charts can help you work with your development people to guide the project to completion.

The architecture that needs to be defined before a distributed system is deployed includes not only the components and servers that will be used, but also the communication and security pieces of a system. Microsoft has created a model called Distributed InterNetwork Application Architecture (DNA) that attempts to provide a conceptual model for reducing the obstacles in creating a distributed system.

The push for DNA comes in part from the increasingly complex applications (such as e-Commerce deployment) that need to be created for Web database solutions. Often one of the technologies in the DNA framework can overcome shortcomings found in another. For example, ASP scripting can easily become the execution bottleneck in a simultaneous user environment. Deploying the compiled logic of ActiveX components, another DNA technology, largely alleviates the execution speed problem. The effective integration of DNA technology will help to ease deployment of component-based Web projects.

MICROSOFT DISTRIBUTED INTERNETWORK APPLICATION ARCHITECTURE (DNA)

Microsoft Distributed InterNetwork Application Architecture (DNA) is the umbrella under which all of the current Microsoft distributed technology is united. DNA refers to the creation and deployment of distributed applications. All of the DNA technologies are integrated through the COM interface.

According to Microsoft, DNA includes these technologies:

- Internet Information Server (IIS) and Active Server Pages (ASP)
- Component Object Model (COM) and ActiveX components
- Microsoft Transaction Server (MTS)
- Dynamic HTML (DHTML)
- Extensible Markup Language (XML)
- Microsoft Message Queuing Server (MSMQ)

- Active Directory services
- Windows NT security services
- Data Access components (including ADO)
- Java

Windows DNA is essentially just a concept that brings together all of the component and distributed architecture tools available from Microsoft for the Windows platform. However, it is Microsoft's stated object to closely integrate these technologies to define a single interoperable system that can be shaped to fit a desired Internet solution.

Although most of these tools are available for the Windows platform, Microsoft seeks to extend the reach of DNA beyond Windows-based desktops. With COM ported to several Unix operating systems and the DHTML-capable Internet Explorer browser available on Mac OS and Unix, total DNA integration may be possible, depending on the needs of your solution.

Additionally, most of the new Internet technology within DNA relies on open Web standards including DHTML, HTML, TCP/IP, Java, ODBC, X.500, and XML. DNA continues Microsoft's stated objective to "embrace and extend" the open Web standards that have been created by the community.

TIP: The Windows DNA site is available for access at www.microsoft.com/dna. It includes white papers and extensive overview literature on the pieces of technology integrated in the DNA framework. For a multimedia overview of DNA, check out the www.microsoft.com/seminar site. The twenty-minute streamed audio/slide-show presentation provides a clear indication of Microsoft's intentions as to the future of DNA.

Two Phases of DNA Deployment

Microsoft has set two stages for the complete integration and deployment of the DNA framework. The first phase includes the tools that are widely deployed today, including Windows NT 4.0, COM, DCOM, IIS 4, ASP, MTS, MSMQ, and Visual Studio. Most of today's distributed development uses the technology from phase one.

The second phase is defined by the release of Windows 2000 and the widespread use of COM+. As the services and capabilities of these tools are integrated into development tools and general enterprise solutions, they will bring the full creation of the DNA architecture to fruition.

DNA Three-Tier Architecture

DNA is fundamentally structured around the three-tier model that you used in Chapter 18 when designing with Visual Modeler. This separation of logic into three distinct layers provides an effective design approach to the difficult problem of separating a large project into manageable pieces.

To use a simple example, let's imagine that an order entry system needs to be constructed. Normally, the application might be created, top to bottom, with all code integrated into a single application. Now, imagine that the application needed to be modified for use by a portable remote user.

Under the standard application design process, the program would probably need to be rewritten and redesigned almost from scratch. However, if the application had initially been designed using the three-tier DNA approach, it is likely that only the data-storage layer would require modification.

Likewise, moving an application from a single-machine Web database implementation to a multimachine distributed deployment would be much easier if the various pieces were centralized within the specified layers.

The three tiers of a DNA application include the following:

- **User Interface or Presentation** ActiveX controls, DHTML, and Internet Explorer in the DNA framework are included in this tier.
- **Business logic** COM components, programs, ASP, IIS, MTS, and MSMQ are included in this tier.
- **Data storage** ADO, OLE DB, ODBC, Remote Data Services (RDS), and Microsoft Data Access Components (MDAC) all provide integrated data storage capabilities. All of the Universal Data Access (UDA) architecture is included in this tier.

When code logic is placed in one of these three tiers (see Figure 24-1), steps can be taken to deploy the components independently or to provide modification for further generalization.

NOTE: Note that the Remote Data Services actually bridge the User Interface and the Data storage tiers to provide database access from the ADO backend to the control bound in the client browser. RDS may be used from within C++ or VB and is listed in the references library as ADO Recordset library.

The business logic tier is where most of the meat of an application resides. The code in this layer handles the process logic, filtering, calculations, and math for manipulating the information between the data storage and presentation layers.

The presentation layer is often the most difficult to design and implement properly, because it must, in the end, reflect both the data store against which it operates and the final presentation environment. When designing your three-tiered solution, it is often best to examine the presentation and data storage layers first. This will help you decide on the final form of the application.

COM+ and DNA

With the release of Windows 2000, Microsoft is augmenting the functionality of COM to make COM+ one of the cornerstones of DNA. One of the key new services included in the

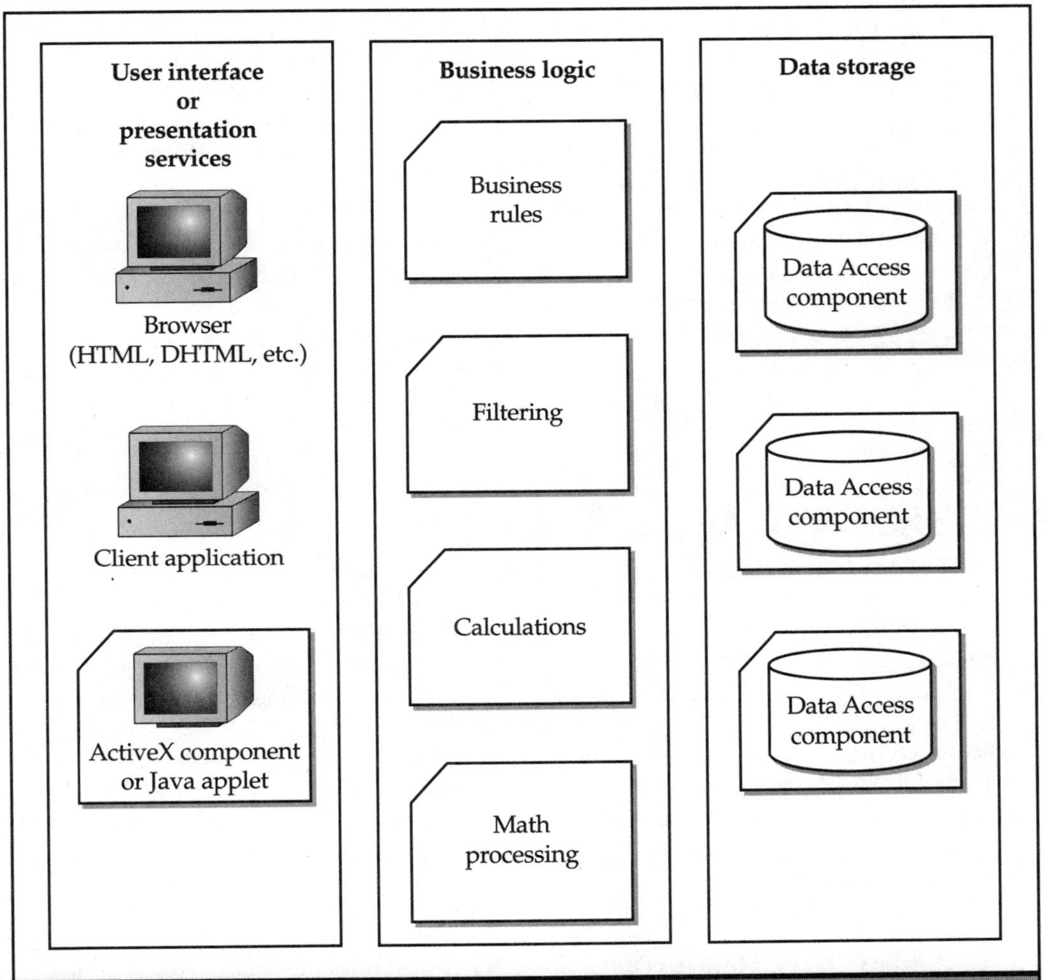

Figure 24-1. Three tiers can be used to define the construction of a distributed application

COM+ implementation is a mechanism called interception. Interception allows functions of a component to be redirected to various services at runtime, allowing for late binding for instance creation, instance deletion, errors, calls, and returns. Interceptors can respond to events allowing for transactions, data access services, and system monitoring.

Interceptors can be easily created at design time simply by setting or defining particular properties that are detailed in the COM+ specification. COM+ will interpret these properties for a component that activates interceptor capabilities and enables the appropriate services.

Many of the capabilities of COM+ are available to Visual Basic 6.0 programmers (such as the `Implements` keyword) since the release of Visual Studio 6. COM+ extends this functionality to be available to any COM+ development system including C++, J++, Delphi, and Powerbuilder. Since the property interception provides one of the central methods of COM+ project implementation, it can be used in any development system that supports the COM+ framework.

COM+ also features complete object replication capabilities. MTS, can provide most of the necessary protection for a fail-over backup system that automatically seizes operations when the primary system fails. The fail-over approach eliminates any downtime for the system. A server can be created to hold backup installations of all of the objects for a distributed system. MTS can then resolve domain names into IP addresses much like an Internet DNS server, and can provide a reference to a remote object. If the server containing the remote object were to fail, the directing entry could be altered to point to the backup server.

UNIVERSAL DATA ACCESS (UDA)

Universal Data Access (UDA) is a strategy that dovetails with the intentions of the DNA architecture. UDA is constructed to include access to both nonrelational data sources (spatial, Paradox, and dBASE, etc.) and relational data sources (for example, SQL Server and Oracle). UDA also attempts to bridge platform considerations so that data can be accessed in a common way, regardless of the location or storage format.

Although this strategy sounds almost utopian, ODBC alone provides a historical example by having made great strides over the last decade toward achieving these integration ends. ODBC has become a unifying cross-platform standard for accessing almost any SQL data source on any platform that supports the standard. As Microsoft gears up its middleware technology through ADO/OLE DB, the long-term potential of UDA becomes increasingly real.

The UDA framework is made up of four database services:

- **ActiveX Data Objects (ADO) and OLE DB** Heterogeneous access methods that establish an object model for database access.
- **Microsoft Data Access Components (MDAC)** Components used for client-side, remote, or connectionless data access. Data binding services are available from within the Web browser to allow for data-bound Web pages.
- **Remote Data Services (RDS)** Remote recordsets and database capabilities, including asynchronous data sets, supported within ADO. RDS was previously known as the Active Data Connector (ADC).
- **ODBC** The venerable middleware for which there are drivers available for connecting to almost every popular relational data source and most query-based nonrelational formats, as well.

Each of these technologies can be used in a DNA solution to support data source access for most data types in most environments (client, server, browser, and so on). All of the UDA pieces are also made to scale for increasing numbers of concurrent users, which is in line with Web-based expectations.

NOTE: At the time of this writing, although the ADO access to a data source is robust and essential for most Web database applications, there is a performance penalty for using ADO. ODBC can be significantly faster for a great number of transactions, especially when accessed at a lower interface level, such as by using Visual Basic RDO or ODBC Direct technologies. If data-access speed is an issue in your Web application, consider using a component that can address the ODBC interfaces more directly.

The SQL language is the primary means of accessing information through these UDA pieces. The ADO query engine itself relies on the ANSI SQL 92 standard to define query construction. The possibilities of the ADO/OLE DB components of UDA will become more prominent as organizations adopt database servers that include object storage capabilities, such as the Informix Dynamic Server 2000 and Oracle 8.

NOTE: Object servers are likely to supercede database servers once the performance issues can be overcome. An object server can store and query data as individual objects. This means that instead of placing individual data elements into field types, such as numbers (Integer, Double, and so on) or characters (Char, Varchar, and the like), a field can be defined as a specific object type. This would allow forms, media, and other data to be accessed and queried as information within the database.

If you are doing database development on multiple platforms (Windows and Unix, for example) you may want to stick with a single vendor to supply the necessary ODBC database drivers. Often, small implementation differences among vendors will make access through one ODBC driver different from access through another. Since ODBC can be accessed through the ADO/OLE DB interface, you can use ODBC drivers for the entire solution even if the programming model requires ADO implementation. Microsoft has developed a thin data provider for ADO that acts as a converter or gateway directly to the ODBC driver. This allows older ODBC drivers to be accessed via the new object interface provided by ADO. You can therefore stay with the single vendor, yet use the advanced ADO features on the Windows platform.

DISTRIBUTED SYSTEM MANAGEMENT

Most deployments of information systems require cooperation between the information systems specialists and the nontechnical management. Communication between these two groups is critical to having the system used properly and avoiding deployment problems and design mistakes.

Likewise, in the management of a distributed system, extra work procedures must be put into places that are uncommon in a normal networked system. For example, if the customer service department is responsible for the customer information component, and their server goes down, will all of the systems within the constellation of distributed objects be crippled? The very nature of the distribution of processing power leads to more potential points of failure, as well as security concerns.

These problems can best be handled if planned for ahead of time. Using a deployment diagram constructed in Visual Modeler is one method of clarifying not only the placement of individual resources, but backup capabilities as well. To properly evaluate a distributed system in light of backup and deployment issues, answer the following questions for each component:

- *Is there a clear, visible sponsorship/responsibility (where management has assigned specific maintenance responsibility to a single person or group) for the component and the system on which it is running?* The goal should be to provide clear and unambiguous roles and responsibilities for each piece of the system.
- *What dependencies are generated by the use of this component? What are the alternatives if it fails?* These dependencies and alternatives should be documented and kept in your development center. Providing a central location for this documentation can allow a developer to check dependent systems before a modified component is introduced to the system.
- *Is there a central person responsible for keeping a centralized repository for the source code (a code librarian) for the component in case changes or upgrades to the component negatively affect other systems?* If there is an assigned code librarian, upgrades are easy to accomplish since the location of all the code is known and properly filed.
- *Can some systems be redirected to an alternate implementation?* Planning for fail-over is a useful activity even if the system is non-mission critical. At the very least, there should be an installer for all of the create objects readily available in case the central system faults.
- *Has the entire distributed system been tested when each individual server is shut down? Is a recovery plan in place?* Doing basic failure testing can help you understand what to expect when a fault does occur.

These questions should provide you with some framework for evaluating the components at the beginning and end of the development cycle. Particularly toward the end of development, relationships that seemed clear and apparent can become hazy. Review these questions for the components of your system when you've completed 80 percent of the milestones of your project.

Object Location Management

For a distributed system, locating the objects on the proper server is a struggle between efficiency and proper organizational placement. Whenever objects are distributed across a network, potential performance and reliability problems become real concerns. In the past, the fail-over capabilities of a distributed system deployed on the Windows platform was not very effective. COM+ promises to change that through its built-in load balancing functionality.

The most appropriate location for any object can be determined by these four factors:

- **Responsibility** The team that will be responsible for the object should be capable of maintaining it.
- **Visible sponsorship** When the component has a problem, who do you call? Everyone involved in the distributed system should know exactly how to contact the appropriate person for problems, bugs, or failure of a component.
- **Reliability** A distributed component should never be placed on an already taxed resource, such as a file server or a personal workstation. The location should be reliable in order to ensure the proper functioning of the entire system.
- **Need for decentralization** What is the compelling reason for locating the object at this location or on this server? Without a clear reason, decentralization simply complicates the system without a clear benefit.

Once these four factors are evaluated, you will be able to locate the component at a location with a reasonable amount of assurance that the distributed system will not fault from a planning oversight.

Eliciting Business Rules

Most discussion about creating business logic overlooks the step of eliciting the business rules from which the logic is built. Since business rules are established primarily by management, which may not be nearly as technologically savvy as the designers of automated systems, it is important to understand the basic guidelines that can be used to determine these rules.

The first step is defining that which in modeling is called the *term* of the rule. This describes the type of information to be modeled, such as a customer, claim, invoice, or case. Terms can be groups, such as invoice items within an invoice. By comparing terms defined in the system, a rule can be created using standard logic. For example, in the invoice example, the following rule might apply:

An *invoice* cannot be completed if an *invoice item* has zero quantity in stock

The italicized words are terms of the business rule. If your business rule stated that an invoice could not be completed if the customer is not within the 48 continental states of the US, you would be introducing another term, the *customer*, which was not defined by the terms of the first rule.

Explicitly defining the terms of a rule will allow you to begin the conversion of a business rule that humans can interpret into the logic needed for implementation within a computer system.

The other primary reason for identifying terms is that you can then examine how rules relate to or interfere with each other. Imagine that the ordering system had these two rules:

1) **An *invoice* cannot be completed if an *invoice item* has zero quantity in stock.**
2) **If an *invoice item* has zero quantity in stock, but the *shipper* can provide stock within 24 hours, presale may be made.**

You can see that these two rules can be combined into a single rule. If they are not, whichever rule is accessed first will prevail in the system. By addressing all of the rules that apply to each term, unified business logic can be created.

Stating business rules individually in a concise manner can also help prevent the confusion that often accompanies the massive flowcharting of a complicated business process. Rules can be examined thoroughly while decisions are being made as to their precedence and compatibility. The inflexibility of most charting systems makes this process difficult in a graphical format.

The examples so far have been of *rule-constraint* logic, which are the easiest to model within a component. The more complex type is *rule-based* logic. This logic usually indicates some type of calculation, such as the amount of income tax due (based on income levels) or figuring the depreciation of an asset. These types of rules are more difficult to model because they cannot generally be diagrammed with a Boolean structure.

Most often, rule-based systems must be implemented to confirm that the understanding of the business rule is accurate. This can often be accomplished in an easy-to-change scripting environment before it is incorporated into a component. It may also be diagrammed in UML, using a complete package such as Rational Rose. This can be useful, because such a diagram will use natural language text.

When the business rules have been documented, decisions must be made to determine the placement of business rules inside routines. Once again, the terms that you defined when documenting the rules will assist you in this task. Rules dominated by particular terms can often be grouped within the same component, if not the same method.

Component Creation Management

The methodology for distributing a system among components has been described extensively throughout this book. Most of the recommendations describe how to break the logic into component pieces based on a functional overview of the system. In many software development circles, code reuse through components has become an accepted concept. Developers often strive to make components general enough to allow for as much component reuse as possible.

It has been my experience that this is generally a waste of time. Nearly always, a project that needs a similar component also needs a few modifications for it to work properly. When creating the components for a project, the designers cannot possibly know how to generalize the interface enough for it to be useful in other projects, because they are too close to the implementation details. Valuable project time ends up being wasted attempting to generalize interfaces that will seldom be comprehensive enough to warrant reuse.

Here's a better method:

- *Write components explicitly, and only for the current project.* Only pay attention to the maintenance aspects of the component for the current project without providing expansion interface (non-working what-if methods and properties).
- *Create a general component-evaluation team.* If a component is to be reused in other projects, it should be apparent to the people who would be considering the reuse. This way, a team made up of different project managers can usually examine and forecast whether they could use that type of functionality.
- *Assign the component to be built as a separate project.* For the components that warrant creation, begin a team specifically to generalize the components as in-house projects.

By divorcing the concern for creating reusable components from the project, the interface can more easily be created without attempting to foresee some general component that might be needed in the future. When the project is complete, the strengths and weaknesses of the component can be accurately judged, including the possible constraints on developing a generalizing component from the existing one.

You may believe that this process will ensure that no components will be built, because your organization will not allocate the necessary resources for independent component development. If your organization does not embrace code reuse, the chances of effectively creating a component within a project process that will be shared, documented, and maintained are slim. Proper code reuse can provide substantial long term savings to an organization, but only if embraced by the organization and if the proper resources are allocated to it. Otherwise, it simply becomes a hindrance to completing the project. Facing the fact that the code will not be adapted to other projects in the future will allow you to more realistically complete the project now. If you cannot implement code reuse effectively, it is probably best not attempted at all.

Security Options in a Distributed System

Planning security at the same time you are designing your project is critical to creating an effective system. Planning security may seem an overwhelming task because of the number of places for security to be implemented. For example, a common solution will require security settings for the following:

- **Active Directory** On Windows 2000–based systems, there is the option to create a single login security profile. Configuration for all primary pieces of a DNA system can be made here.
- **DCOM** DCOM object security is available to Windows NT machines and must be configured for individual registered components. To access Windows NT components from a Windows 95/98 machine, security authentication settings must be disabled.

- **File directories** These permissions are important for Web servers, as well as for execution directories.
- **Web site login** To allow login security, a Web site can either use Windows NT Trusted Security (by setting up directory permissions) or ClearText transmission in a custom ASP login page. This area must be examined most carefully, as it usually has more exposure outside the organization than other aspects of the system. If the login system is breached, access to other areas of the system is possible.
- **MTS roles and component execution** Setting security for roles and packages is one of the most useful aspects of MTS for controlling DCOM remote execution.
- **Data source login and table settings** Whether the data source pointer is stored in source code or in a ODBC DSN (whether it is a user, admin, or file DSN), database security is critical. If the access pointer is stored in the source code, be sure login information for an application is stored in a Global.asa file rather than individual ASP files that are more susceptible to compromise. If stored in a file DSN, make sure the location of the file is secure.
- **IIS component and script execution** Ensure that no directories have unnecessary application and script execution privileges. If a trespasser can find a way to place scripting files in an unmonitored directory (especially one with FTP access), the entire network could be compromised because all components in the distributed system would be available from that machine.
- **Web server certificates** Use of digital certificates in Windows 2000 can provide some of the most effective distributed security.

All of these areas of security can be easily examined by using a Deployment diagram for the distributed system that you're designing. This diagram can be made to represent all of the pieces of the system. It can provide the sort of overview for security that Visual Modeler does for enterprise objects. The entries on this type of diagram will vary dramatically from project to project, but the general category breakdown should help you determine how to divide the functions of a project.

Planning Multitier Deployment with Visual Modeler

The powerful capabilities of Visual Modeler were demonstrated in Chapter 18 when it was used to oversee development of the Forums application. Visual Modeler serves as both a planning and an implementation tool.

Because the Component diagram does not contain the ability to add database functionality, it will be limited to diagramming and designing an entire system. However, the Deployment diagram (see Figure 24-2) can be used to draw an overview of the system more effectively than if it were drawn by hand. The Deployment diagram can also be used to easily communicate the structure of the system to those already familiar with the conventions of UML diagram formats.

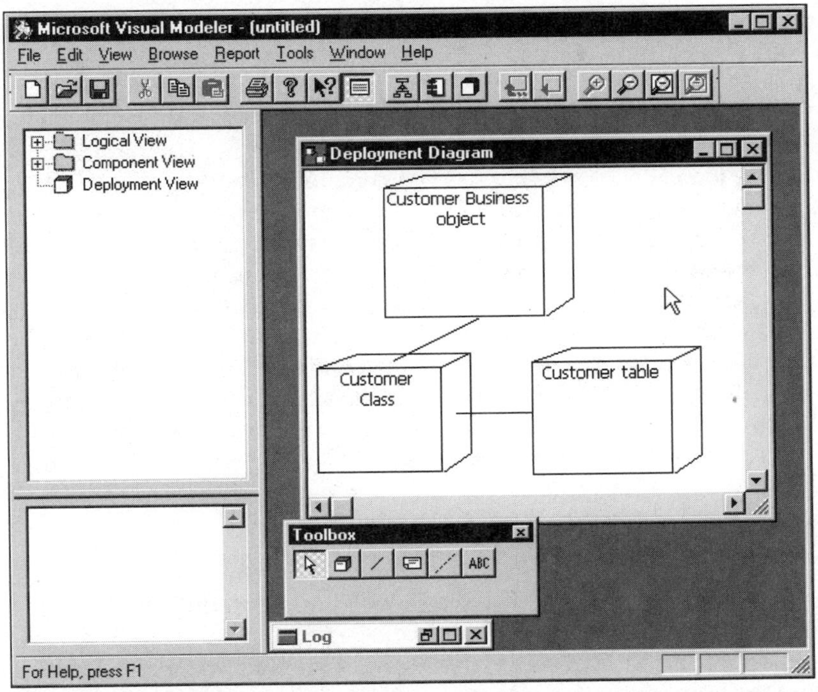

Figure 24-2. A simple Deployment diagram can be constructed to organize the pieces of a component system

Within a Visual Modeler project, you can add as many Deployment diagrams as you want. These diagrams do not affect execution or round-trip engineering of the project at all. It will be easy to demonstrate the usefulness of this diagram type by constructing one for the VM model that you created in Chapter 18 for the Forum application.

While Component and Class diagrams show design-time construction layout, a Deployment diagram shows the run-time entities involved with the system execution. Previously known as Process diagrams under the Booch methodology, a Deployment diagram shows the organization of systems, software, and hardware.

Object Communication over a WAN

As distributed systems grow and information is coordinated with remote machines (either with remote offices or "road warriors"), the possibility of creating a secure distributed solution requires additional consideration. Since most objects in the Microsoft COM/DCOM/COM+ architecture communicate through the TCP/IP protocol, the

Internet can provide a readily available backbone for object communication over a wide area network (WAN). Alternatively, a virtual private network (VPN) can make all of the distant objects appear to be located on the same physical network.

A VPN can allow a virtual network to be created with remote machines appearing to be physically connected to the network. A VPN is explicitly configured to include specific machines. Those machines are then exposed only to the network traffic and resources available on the logical network that has been created.

VPNs are increasingly being adopted by the corporate world because of the flexibility they allow for defining a logical network rather than a physical one. Remote networks can be connected to shared resources including file servers, printers, and objects.

The advantage of a VPN over simple remote communications is the added level of security that is available to the system. Since the objects can be configured to be available only to the local network, a potential trespasser would first have to violate the security of the VPN itself, before access to the object was possible. Although the security available for DCOM objects is robust, it has not been tested to the degree and level of scrutiny that has been used to assure that VPNs are secure.

Employee Involvement Diagram

The employee involvement diagram has, in the past, been extremely useful for the basic documentation of a system. Now this diagram can take on additional significance if applied to the creation of a distributed system.

One of the most difficult parts of creating a distributed system is not the technology involved but the number of people that must be consulted and the division of individual responsibilities for each area. Table 24-1 shows a simple example of such information. You can see that while it is fairly easy to create, it also documents and communicates a great amount of necessary information about the system.

Questions related to security can be answered quickly and easily by consulting this diagram. If an employee needs to be able to add an inventory item, but should not be provided access to examine the existing inventory account balance, such information would be provided here. The employee involvement diagram will likely remain mostly static during the lifetime of the distributed system. Therefore, try to include the diagram in the formal system documentation.

Q&A

Q: Is there a way to automate deployment of a distributed system?

A: Right now, automated deployment is still very primitive. If your entire organization is running with the Windows 2000 operating system from servers to workstations, centralized deployment becomes a possibility. Without a complete Windows 2000 system, distribution becomes more problematic.

	Jim McLiv, Program Analyst	Jill Smith, Human Resources	John Doe, Cost Accounting	Jane Doe, Accounts Payable	Bill Klepsy, Shop Floor Control
Finance database	Maintenance Read Write Logic	Logic Read	Logic Read Write	Read Write	Read
CostControl component	Maintenance Read Write Logic		Logic Read Write	Read	
Inventory component	Maintenance Read Write Logic		Write	Read Write	Logic Read Write

Table 24-1. The Employee Involvement Diagram Shows the Levels that Each Employee Accesses with the System

Because of the object registration and DCOM proxy configuration required, creating an automated solution can be more prohibitive in time and resources than simply doing the initial install by hand. However, once the general setup has been done, traditional update systems, including Microsoft Systems Management Server (SMS) and Web deployment methods, can be used for modification.

Q: Is it really necessary to use the distributed technology in a Web database solution?

A: No. With the complexities involved in any Web database solution, distributed technology is often used when no clear need is evident. With Microsoft's strong promotion of DNA, organizations will increasingly use distributed systems without clearly examining whether the benefits make up for the costs. Try to evaluate whether your system will benefit from the distributed architecture in terms of the extra maintenance, deployment, development, and security costs that will be incurred.

Keep in mind that a multicomponent project can be moved to a distributed structure much more easily than a distributed structure can be returned to single-machine execution. Data security and permissions settings are the primary impediments when moving either way.

SUMMARY

Designing a distributed system will increasingly become a part of creating Web database solutions. With the Microsoft DNA program, the integration of the components will make distribution technology less difficult to use, and the planning of the system will be even more important. In this chapter you've covered the following:

- **DNA** Microsoft has unified all of the distributed technology available to the Windows environment under the name Distributed InterNetwork Application Architecture (DNA). The central pieces of the DNA model include COM+, the Windows NT servers, HTML, DHTML, and other Internet standards.
- **Object location** Choosing the proper location for each component is critical to appropriate deployment. The following four factors should be addressed for all objects used: responsibility, visible sponsorship, reliability, and the need for decentralization.
- **Component creation management** It is often counterproductive to attempt to construct all components for a project so that they can be reused. Instead, initially create the components specifically for the project, and later allow an independent team to evaluate whether they should be adapted for widespread general use.
- **Virtual Private Networks (VPN)** The VPNs provide a new way to define networks around a logical organization rather than the physical structure. For remote systems or geographically dispersed organization units, a VPN can provide the key to the implementation of a component-based distributed system.

APPENDIX A

SQL Primer

When designing almost any type of database solution, you will be using the Structured Query Language (SQL) whether you realize it or not. Even Microsoft Access, with its user-friendly query construction, actually generates SQL code in the background to execute the requested queries. A good understanding of SQL is therefore critical to any Web database solutions that you create.

This SQL primer will describe the basic techniques and syntax for SQL. Although you will need a complete book on the exacting details of SQL query creation if your work will be extensive, this appendix will provide an effective foundation for your beginning SQL needs. If you need more in-depth help, try SQL Server 7: A Beginner's Guide (Petković, 1999).

SQL OVERVIEW

Structured Query Language (SQL) was invented by IBM in the early 1970s. It has since become a nonproprietary language and the de facto standard used to query both small and large databases. The power of the SQL language is substantial because its functionality is both simple and complex; writing a general query takes only the most basic training, but precise retrieval of data with numerous requirements is possible, as well.

Most languages that are used for general programming, such as C++, VB, or Java, are known as procedural languages. These languages use a procedure of step-by-step execution, and all actions are explicitly described by the code. SQL, on the other hand, is a language designed to generate results (see Figure A-1). With SQL, you indicate the results you want, and the database server finds the most effective way of fulfilling your request.

The language itself consists of only four primary keywords used for queries and data handling:

- `Select` Queries a database and returns records
- `Update` Changes the values of certain records
- `Insert Into` Inserts new records into the database
- `Delete` Removes records from the database

All of the other primary keywords (such as `Create Database`, `Alter Database`, and so on) are used to create and manipulate structures within the environment. Although some of these will be briefly covered in this appendix, most of the information will focus on using SQL for data manipulation.

LANGUAGE STRUCTURE

SQL is an industry standard that can be found on every platform and in all large database servers (Oracle, Sybase, Informix, Microsoft SQL Server, and so on). SQL is used in every Microsoft database technology, including Microsoft Access, Visual FoxPro, Visual Basic,

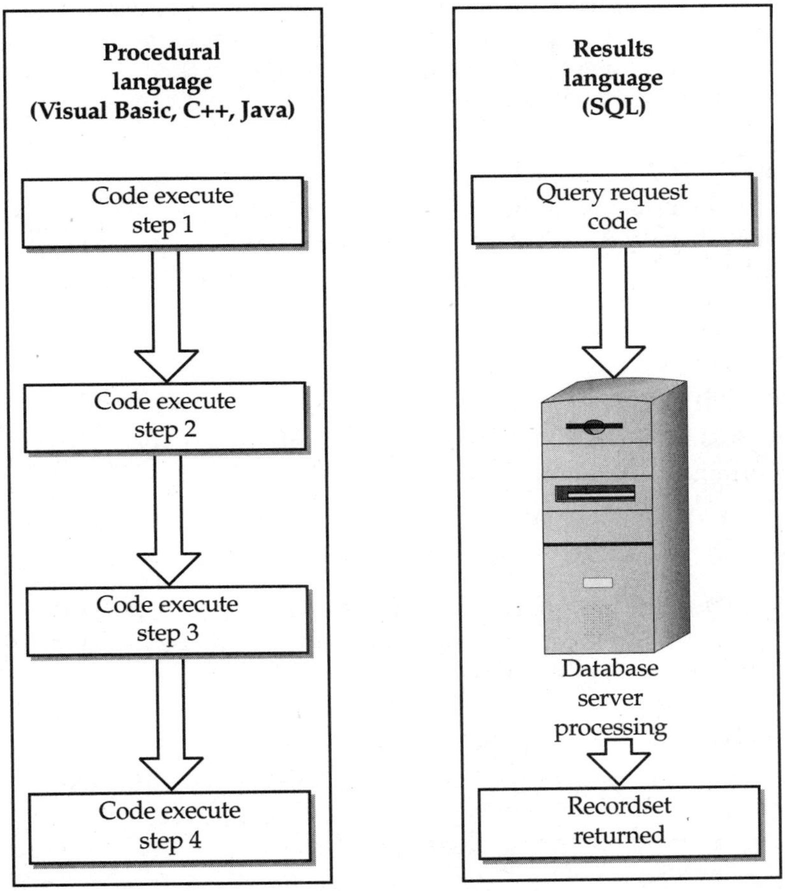

Figure A-1. SQL generates results based on code requests rather than step-by-step code execution

ODBC, OLE DB, ADO, RDO, and DAO. Although not all of these SQL implementations are 100 percent compatible with each other (a query from one will not necessarily execute properly in another), they are close enough that conversion is not a difficult or lengthy process.

In this book there are extensive examples of using SQL with ADO to query both Microsoft Access and SQL Server data sources. Most of these commands can be used with other SQL implementations with little or no change.

NOTE: Most implementations of SQL allow the commands to be entered in a case-insensitive manner. All Microsoft products accept the keywords no matter how they are capitalized. However, if you are using a different SQL system and the commands are not properly recognized, check the database server manual to see if that is the problem.

What Does a Query Do?

What a query actually accomplishes might seem like it should be obvious, but a query can fill so many roles that it is important to define exactly what it can do. All of these roles can be accomplished within a single SQL query statement. The capabilities of a query include:

- Selecting records
- Sorting records
- Grouping records
- Choosing fields to be returned
- Performing calculations
- Making changes to data
- Inserting data that meets query parameters into another table

SQL is ideally suited to accomplishing all of these functions, even within a single line of code. Learning to use the SQL language entails understanding the basic SQL terminology, as well as how SQL commands are used.

Rows and Columns

SQL always refers to records as rows, and to fields as columns. These terms come from the basic structure of a table. The following sample table contains three rows of information (the headings are not considered a row) and four columns. The LastName column of row 2 contains the value *Stark*.

UniqueID	LastName	FirstName	MiddleName
1	Spone	Joe	I
2	Stark	Erik	K
3	Jones	Bill	M

This row and column terminology is used in most of the available SQL documentation. All of the syntax definitions provided for SQL will use these terms to describe what must be passed and what will be returned.

SELECT Command

The most commonly used command, `Select`, allows a number of parameters to be specified that will determine which records will be returned from a data source. The most rudimentary syntax of the `Select` command is:

```
SELECT * FROM myTable
```

The asterisk (`*`) wildcard in this statement indicates that all of the fields (columns) from the table should be returned in the result set.

There are a number of clauses that can be added to the `Select` statement to return exactly the information that is desired. A generalized syntax representation of the `Select` statement would look like this:

```
SELECT columns FROM tables WHERE conditions
   GROUP BY groups ORDER BY orders
```

This `Select` code specifies the fields that should be returned by name, rather than using the asterisk (`*`).

To specify only two fields to be returned (named `myField1` and `myField2`), you might use a command like this:

```
SELECT myField1, myField2 FROM myTable
```

Seldom will you want to return all of the records that exist in a table. The `Where` clause is used to filter the desired records. To select only the records for customers with the last name of Smith, you could use code like this:

```
SELECT * FROM myTable WHERE LastName = 'Smith'
```

In this query, the equal operator (=) is used to make the search case-sensitive. Therefore, this query won't return the record of a customer whose last name is entered as "SMITH".

To make the search ignore case, you can use the `Like` modifier:

```
SELECT * FROM myTable WHERE LastName LIKE 'Smith'
```

While this command provides all of the records that have values matching the criteria, the `Select` statement and Boolean operators can also be used to exclude records. Using the `Not` operator, the `Select` statement will return all of the records that don't match the criteria:

```
SELECT * FROM myTable WHERE LastName NOT LIKE 'Smith'
```

Boolean operators can also be used to specify multiple matches. For example, to return rows that have column values of either Smith or Jones, you could use a statement such as this:

```
SELECT * FROM myTable WHERE LastName LIKE 'Smith'
   OR LastName LIKE 'Jones'
```

To make the search more inclusive for a given criteria, you can use a wildcard search. The wildcard was used previously to select which of the columns should be returned. Inside a search string, however, a wildcard can be used to select column *values*. For example, it could return all of the records for last names that begin with the letters "Sm". To perform this type of search, you can use the SQL wildcard character (%) like this:

```
SELECT * FROM myTable WHERE LastName LIKE 'Sm%'
```

NOTE: Not all SQL implementations use the percent sign (%) for their wildcard character in string searches. In fact, Microsoft Access didn't support this standard until its most recent version. Many SQL implementations, such as those from Oracle and Informix, use the more common asterisk (*) for a wildcard character within string values. If your query issues an error against a data source that you have little experience using, check for the wildcard values.

Wildcards are even more powerful than the preceding example demonstrates. They can also be used to locate any occurrence of a string within a field. Simply encapsulate the search text within two wildcard characters, like this:

```
SELECT * FROM myTable WHERE LastName like '%S%'
```

Don't use a query such as this unless it is necessary to find a particular value. This type of query is very processor intensive and cannot take advantage of any of the indexes created for the table. Wildcards are best used if they can be set for very precise variability.

Another type of wildcard can be used to substitute for a specific number of characters. The underscore character (_) is used for these placeholder wildcard queries. For example, if you know that the last name you are looking for begins with the letter *S* followed by three unknown characters and ending with the letter *H*, you could use code like this:

```
SELECT * FROM myTable WHERE LastName LIKE 'S___h'
```

Using the placeholder wildcard is particularly useful for queries on predefined code numbers (such as license plates) where some characters are known, as is the overall format of the data in the field.

Queries are not limited to searching one table at a time. Related tables can be brought together within a SQL query using an explicit join to connect the foreign key of one table to the primary key of another table. To create a join between two tables, you could use code like this:

```
SELECT * FROM myTable, myTable2 WHERE myTable.userID = myTable2.userID
```

With both tables being included in the From clause, SQL also provides a method of specifying the source table even if the column names in both tables are identical. Referencing columns that are included in the join, you can use the table name with the dot command (.), like this:

```
SELECT myTable.myField1, myTable2.myField1 FROM myTable, myTable2
   WHERE myTable.userID = myTable2.userID
```

The dot command (.) can be used anywhere within the query to designate tables included in the From clause.

Returned Field Aliases

The column names that are returned do not have to match the actual column names. There are many cases for which you will need to specify the column names, sometimes for a basic such as shortening the length of long field references. Results from aggregate functions are also assigned general names by the database server, and it is usually a better idea to explicitly assign an appropriate column name for the returned information.

For example, a normal query that returns all of the last names in the Customers table would look like this:

```
SELECT LastName FROM customers
```

To access this field from ADO, you would use the command:

```
a = myRS.Fields("LastName")
```

If you instead wanted to give the column an alias, you would need to use the As keyword. Your query would look like this:

```
SELECT LastName AS LN FROM customers
```

Now, the ADO access would look like this:

```
a = myRS.Fields("LN")
```

This feature is used most commonly with aggregate functions (see the "Aggregate Functions" section later in this appendix). For example:

```
SELECT SUM(total) AS myTotal FROM invoice
```

The aggregate results for myTotal can be accessed like any other column.

Calculations

Within a query, basic calculations can be made. For example, if you need to multiply two column values for each record to be returned in a field, you could use a SQL statement such as this:

```
SELECT (quantity * cost) AS ItemTotal FROM invoice
```

SQL supports the four standard operators (`*`, `/`, `+`, `-`) as well as `^` and `%`. Additionally, many SQL implementations add more complete mathematical functions. On Microsoft SQL Server, the following trigonometric and other functions are available:

- `COS(`*num*`)` and `ACOS(`*num*`)`
- `SIN(`*num*`)` and `ASIN(`*num*`)`
- `TAN(`*num*`)` and `ATAN(`*num*`)`
- `CEILING(`*num*`)` and `FLOOR(`*num*`)`
- `LOG(`*num*`)` and `LOG10(`*num*`)`
- `ABS(`*num*`)`
- `ROUND(`*expr, numDecPlaces*`)`
- `SIGN(`*num*`)`
- `POWER(`*num, n*`)`
- `SQRT(`*num*`)`
- `RADIANS(`*num*`)` and `DEGREES(`*num*`)`

These operators are used just like the parallel functions available in VBScript and other procedural languages. For the numbers returned by the expressions, each function uses whatever floating point mathematical type is native to the database server.

NOTE: Placing calculations within the query slows down the processing of the query and the return of the result set. Be careful that you don't use too many calculations on an already complicated query, because they may make the return time prohibitively long.

Using Comparison and Boolean Operators

There are three Boolean operators that you can use in a SQL query: `AND`, `OR`, and `NOT`. These operators function just as their procedural language equivalents do in ASP code. You can use parentheses to specify unification and precedence of multiple Boolean comparisons. The comparison operators are shown in the following table.

Comparison Operator	Meaning
>	Greater than
<	Less than
=	Equivalent or equal to
>=	Greater than or equal to
<=	Less than or equal to
!=	Not equal to
!>	Not greater than
!<	Not less than
LIKE	Case-insensitive equal

You might notice that the NOT operators (!=, !>, and !<) are different from what you are accustomed to in VBScript. Since the SQL language grew from a cross-platform standard, these operators match those found in more general languages, such as C.

ORDER BY

The `Order By` clause allows you to specify the order in which the result set should be sorted when it is returned. To return a set of customers sorted by their last names, you could use a statement such as this:

```
SELECT * FROM customers ORDER BY lastname
```

To make the query sort by last name and then first name, you could use a query like this:

```
SELECT * FROM customers ORDER BY lastname, firstname
```

You can also choose whether the sort is ascending (*a* to *z*) or descending (*z* to *a*). If you do not specify a sort order, ascending is the default. To make the sort type explicit, you need to add the keyword after the `Order By statement:`

```
SELECT * FROM customers ORDER BY lastname, firstname ASC
```

The `DESC` command is used to specify that the sort order should be descending.

> ***NOTE:*** In different variations of the SQL language, the statements for ascending and descending may vary. Some require the entire words `ASCENDING` and `DESCENDING` to be spelled out. Microsoft Access and SQL Server can accept either version.

Aggregate Functions

Aggregate functions are used within a SQL query to summarize or encapsulate the information from many records into a condensed record of information. These functions allow a great deal of processing to be done on the database server where optimization is possible rather than requiring post-processing of the query results to be done on the client.

For example, the `Count` aggregate operator can be used to return the actual count of the records returned by a query. To determine the number of people in your customers table with the last name of Smith, you could use a query like this:

```
SELECT COUNT(lastname) AS numRecords FROM customers WHERE lastname LIKE 'Smith'
```

The `Count` function requires a column to be specified, but any column within the table will return the same value, because it is counting records rather than summing values. The returned dataset will contain a single record whose value, from ADO, could be accessed like this:

```
recs = myRS.Fields("numRecords").Value
```

The available aggregate functions include: Count, Sum, Avg, Min, and Max. These commands are used to return summary information for a given column. Note that only the Count command can be used on nonnumeric fields, because the other commands are made to provide mathematical functions.

To compile categories for return by the aggregate functions, you can use the Group By command. The Group By statement groups a number of similar entries into a single record under a unifying field. As an example of the use of this statement, imagine you wanted to determine the total amount of money spent by a customer located in Ohio.

You can use the Having clause to only return information that complies with a specified threshold. For example, if you wanted invoice totals for invoices that have a sum greater than $20, you could use a query like this:

```
SELECT invoiceID, SUM(cost) AS invoiceCost, SUM(quantity) AS
invoiceQuantity
   FROM orders
   GROUP BY invoiceID
   HAVING SUM(cost) > 20
```

Union Clause

Two result sets can be combined by using the Union clause. The most common application of this operator is to unify the result sets of two different queries on the same table. Creating a Union is as easy as specifying a single query with two Select statements with the Union keyword between them.

To return a recordset with two distinct queries on the same table, you could use a query like this:

```
SELECT * FROM customers WHERE state='CA' AND zip='92117'
   UNION SELECT * FROM customers WHERE state='CO'
```

The column titles are taken from the first select statement. If there are some columns missing from either query, all of the rows from that query will contain a blank or null value for the columns that don't match.

INSERT INTO Command

The Insert statement allows you to insert new records into a table. Insert can be used to create completely new records, and to insert existing records from a different table.

```
INSERT INTO customers (lastname, firstname) VALUES ('Smith', 'John')
```

The Into keyword is optional and is included for compatibility with the SQL standard.

If you know the order of the fields in the structure of the table, you can exclude the field list. For example, if the table consisted of three fields (ID, lastname, and firstname), you could use an Insert statement like this:

```
INSERT customers VALUES (10,'Smith', 'John')
```

To insert values from one table into another table, you can use a Select statement in conjunction with the Insert Into command, like this:

```
INSERT INTO stores
   SELECT * FROM newstores
```

You can even specify exactly which fields should be inserted if the two tables are not identical. To select the destination columns, you can use a command like this:

```
INSERT INTO stores (storeID, city, state, zip)
   SELECT * FROM newCustomers
```

The Insert Into command is a powerful tool for transferring data from one table to another. It is particularly useful when you are normalizing an existing database. You can easily transfer the information stored in a single table into the two new related tables.

NOTE: The Insert command has certain limitations imposed by the SQL processor. When using this command to insert a value into a table, a single field argument can typically only accept values with lengths up to 255 characters. Addressing the fields directly through the ADO Fields collection allows you to circumvent this limitation.

UPDATE Command

The Update statement uses a different syntax from the Insert command. Rather than allowing two list (one of field names and one of values), Update uses the equal operator (=) to set fields to new values.

```
UPDATE customers SET LastName = 'Smith'
```

This will set the value of every LastName column to *Smith*. You can use this in conjunction with the Where clause:

```
UPDATE customers SET LastName = 'Smith' WHERE lastname='SMITH'
```

To update multiple fields with a Where clause, you could use SQL code like this:

```
UPDATE customers SET areacode = '760', region=2 WHERE areacode='619'
```

You can even do calculations. For example, to increase the cost on all inventoried goods by 10 percent, you could use code like this:

```
UPDATE products SET cost = cost * 1.10
```

All of the values of the Cost column in the Products table will be increment by 10 percent. You can even encapsulate these changes in a transaction, so the changes can be rolled back if any problems arise.

TIP: The batch updating abilities available using the `Update` statement can be much more efficient than using a loop in ASP code to modify the records through ADO. If you have general batch changes that you need to do frequently in your program, you might consider creating a Command object that uses the `Update` statement to modify the database.

DELETE FROM Command

The `Delete` statement is used to remove records that match certain criteria from a table. This command should be used with care, because a large number of records can be removed from the database with a single command.

To delete every record in the current table, you can use code like this:

```
DELETE FROM customers
```

The `From` keyword, like the `Into` keyword on the `Insert` statement, is optional.

The `Delete` command also features a `Where` clause for specifying what records should be deleted.

```
DELETE customers WHERE state = 'CA'
```

You can also delete with a join.

```
DELETE FROM sales, titles
   WHERE sales.titleID = titles.titleID AND titles.type = 'business'
```

Like the `Update` command, `Delete` can be used effectively to enact a batch process optimized on the database server.

Subqueries

It is possible to embed a `Select` statement within another `Select` statement. You can also nest a `Select` statement within an `Insert`, `Update`, or `Delete` statement.

To query all of the books by authors with the last name of "Jones", for example, you could create a subquery between the two related tables, like this:

```
SELECT title, price FROM titles WHERE titleid IN
   (SELECT titleid
   FROM titleauthor WHERE lastName = 'Jones')
```

To make the match exact, you can use the equivalent operator:

```
SELECT title, price FROM titles WHERE titleid =
   (SELECT titleid
   FROM titleauthor WHERE lastName = 'Jones')
```

To select only the records that exist in the subqueried table, you can use the `EXISTS` command. A query such as the following could be used:

```
SELECT title, price FROM titles WHERE titleid EXISTS
   (SELECT titleid
   FROM titleauthor WHERE lastName = 'Jones')
```

Referential Integrity

Joins were described previously as largely a constructed function of the entered query. In the past, a join didn't really exist outside each individual query. Now, though, most databases actually store these relationships between tables within the database. Although queries must continue to explicitly specify each join, the implicit join structure stored in the database can ensure that the two related tables maintain consistency between themselves.

Connecting the tables within the database server provides for a relationship known as *referential integrity*. Referential integrity ensures that when a record exists in one table, its foreign-key references to other tables are valid. This prevents, for example, an invoice item in an invoice detail table from referencing an invoice in a master table that has been deleted.

DEFINITION: **Referential integrity** Structural technology that ensures that records from related tables are synchronized. This prevents record references from being left "dangling" or invalid when one of the tables is modified.

To implement referential integrity, database servers have added the capability of cascading update and delete. Cascading delete ensures that if a record is deleted in one table, all of the related records in the connected table will be deleted at the same time.

DEFINITION: **Cascading insert and delete** When tables are joined explicitly in the database, a cascading feature makes changes in one table automatically affect the other table. For cascading insert, the proper default records in the connected tables will be automatically created. For cascading delete, a record deleted in one table will delete records hierarchically attached below that table.

All of the referential integrity technology occurs outside of the actual SQL code that is sent to a database server. However, when such integrity is placed on a system, any SQL commands, such as `Insert` and `Delete`, will activate these structures, so their consequences should be recognized.

Inner and Outer Joins

Earlier in this Appendix you linked two tables together with a simple join using the equivalent (=) operator. This creates an implicit join called an `INNER JOIN`. An `INNER JOIN` returns only the records that have matching values in both tables. You can create an explicit `INNER JOIN` using code like this:

```
SELECT categories.CategoryID, Products.ProductID
   FROM categories INNER JOIN products
   ON categories.categoryID = Products.CategoryID;
```

You might need the result set to return all of the records from one table, regardless of whether a matching record was found in the secondary table. This is known as an `OUTER JOIN`. There are actually two types of outer joins: a `LEFT JOIN` and a `RIGHT JOIN`. These indicate which table in the join will include all records, whether matched or not. You can create a `LEFT JOIN` that includes all of the categories using code like this:

```
SELECT categories.CategoryID, Products.ProductID
   FROM categories LEFT JOIN products
   ON categories.categoryID = Products.CategoryID;
```

To include all of the products, a `RIGHT JOIN` can be used code like this:

```
SELECT categories.CategoryID, Products.ProductID
   FROM categories RIGHT JOIN products
   ON categories.categoryID = Products.CategoryID;
```

DISTINCT Keyword

The `Distinct` keyword allows you to prevent duplicate records from appearing in a result set. For example, if the same person was entered twice in a table, using the `Distinct` keyword on the proper column would display only the first record with unique identification.

The `Distinct` feature is most often used with tables that have lists of items, or in conjunction with aggregate functions. For example, a table that contains individual invoice items could be queried to return records with a distinct InvoiceID foreign-key field. If the connected tables have referential integrity, the result set should never have more distinct records than the connected Invoice Summary table.

The `Distinct` or the `DistinctRow` keywords are used in exactly the same manner. Place the keyword after the `Select` command like this:

```
SELECT DISTINCTROW Employees.LastName FROM Employees, Orders
   WHERE employees.EmployeeID = Orders.EmployeeID;
```

Stored Procedures and Triggers

The most recent SQL standard, SQL-92, agreed to in 1992, only provides a bare-bones implementation of the language. Vendors requiring more powerful capabilities have extended the SQL language in a variety of ways. The most common way of providing extensions is adding the ability to handle stored procedures and triggers. There are usually built-in stored procedures in any SQL implementation. These procedures provide such functions as:

- Setting security, passwords, and groups
- Creating and modifying databases
- Compiling queries with specified variables
- Creating rules
- Setting up and maintaining indexes
- Performing transactions
- Maintaining transaction logs
- Sending e-mail
- Setting global parameters
- Shutting down database servers

Writing stored procedures is much more like traditional programming; in that they both can handle conditional statements (`If...Then`), alter program flow, use variables, and so on. New procedures are created using the `CREATE PROC` command. Check the individual implementation of the SQL version you are using for the available stored procedures.

> ***NOTE:*** Once you begin programming for stored procedures and triggers, your SQL code becomes difficult to port because it will be optimized for the specific target platform. If you use a stored procedure, especially in your ASP code, try to include a source code comment to document its function the first time you use it. This will allow either you or a later developer to clearly understand the intended function of the procedure.

SUMMARY

The SQL language has become the standard method of querying and modifying database information. The more effectively you can create a query to return the information you need, the less procedural programming will be required in your ASP application to manipulate the data that has been returned. In this appendix, you covered:

- **SQL standard** Structured Query Language (SQL) is an industry and cross-platform standard query language for almost all database technologies. Invented by IBM, it has been adopted by most software vendors. Microsoft uses SQL to generate results for Access, ODBC, ADO, RDO, and DAO.
- **Select statement** The `Select` statement is used to query a database and return a result set that matches the parameters specified in the statement.

- **Update statement** Making modifications to the records in a database is done using the `Update` statement. For batch changes, using `Update` can be much more efficient than processing individual records through ADO.
- **Insert statement** Inserts one or more new records with values that can be passed to the statement or from the information provided by another table.
- **Stored procedures and triggers** These are vendor-specific code in the database server that provide features not specified in the SQL-92 standard. New stored procedures and triggers can be created within the database. Database servers also include a number of preset stored procedures for system manipulation.

APPENDIX B

Team Development

The complexity of most computer development projects requires a broad range of programming specialties. In most organizations, the intricacy of a modern application nearly guarantees that one person will not possess the skills or have the time to independently create the entire project. Team development has become the standard method of developing all but the smallest solutions.

Despite the increases in team development on Web systems, most Web enterprise applications are managed like traditional projects. A programming project, however, can benefit greatly by using technology such as Visual SourceSafe and Microsoft Exchange to aid in management, coordination, and documentation.

This Appendix reviews some of the ways that team development can be streamlined and incorporated into everyday use through network information-sharing. By updating the practices of development to use this technology, you should also be able to increase the effectiveness of future projects and project updates.

USING MICROSOFT EXCHANGE FOR SHARING

Documenting a solution that is being developed consists of much more than a user's manual. The intricacy of most applications requires that developer documentation must also consist of the information related to: the program's structures, deployment decisions, component layout, and other documents necessary to understand the custom application later. In fact, proper storage and recording of the steps taken to create a project can save a great deal of time and money in the long term by making it easier to maintain and reuse code. For this reason, a central repository for a project is critical to keeping everything together. More important still, the storage should be electronic and convenient to access; otherwise things are simply put in an archive and never used.

A groupware solution, such as Microsoft Exchange, provides a perfect answer to the dilemma of project storage. Not only can all of the project be stored in one easy-to-access, network-accessible place, but it can also be accompanied by notes, pertinent e-mail, and any other attached information that is appropriate.

For a Web database solution, the most common project items stored in a groupware location will include:

- **Source code** Typically posted as a zipped or compressed file of the current version, the stored source code may also contain past revisions. Although the final version deployment set of source code files can be most easily coordinated with Visual SourceSafe, a copy should be kept with the rest of the documentation.
- **Installation image** Storing a version of the current install disks with the project is critical to enabling the recreation of a deployment. When circumstances later demand that the version be reinstalled (and they usually do for reasons ranging from lost files to compatibility issues), the full version installation will be available.

- **Documentation** This is usually in the form of a Microsoft Word, FrameMaker, or other published files. All of the diagrams and screen shots should also be included with the documentation.
- **Modeling files** The models created in Visual Modeler and Web solution diagrams created by programs like Microsoft FrontPage or NetObjects Fusion should be included.
- **Database schema** The structure of the columns and the relationships between tables in the database can be stored either through the Database Designer references in a project or the SQL code that defines the database schema. Most database servers (including SQL Server) can export the SQL code to recreate the tables.
- **Sample database** Often, the database that is used in the application is too large to include with the project. However, it is useful to add a trimmed down version of the data to allow for general examination. Usually this compacted database file will consist of a few records in each table.
- **Bug and additions database** When a project ships, it will almost surely have known bugs and limitations that were either too minor to delay shipment or were not addressed because the deadline forced the ship date. These bugs, along with any additions planned for the next version, should be documented with the project so that fixes and upgrades can be easily addressed.

The preceding list can be used as a checklist to make sure that when the project is compiled for posting, all of the necessary information and files are included. Better yet, make your own checklist as a form in Outlook for posting on the Exchange Server. When a new archive version is created, add the document to the public folder. As additional parts are posted, they can be checked off on the form.

TIP: SQL Server features a Generate SQL Scripts option under the Object menu when a database has been selected in SQL Enterprise Manager. This option will output the SQL code needed to recreate the tables. You can easily generate these SQL scripts for posting to your Exchange server.

Public Folders

The most appropriate method of setting up the source code is to place it in public folders on the Exchange server for remote access. Each person on the project team will be responsible for placing the portion of the system that they worked on into the folder.

Public folders also allow a VBScript form application to be created that can be accessed from any Outlook client. By adding your file attachments and explanatory messages to the folder, the backup and calendaring capabilities of Exchange can also be used.

Posting Source Code

Posting source code can create some security dangers that you must consider. Corporate espionage does exist, and simple sabotage by a disgruntled employee is also a possibility. Having source code for a core program freely available is rarely a good idea. For this reason, it may be best to split an archive into several separate folders with independent security settings.

Often, this arrangement can be broken down into three tiers, much like the model used in Visual Modeler. You might use the following breakdown:

- **User services** Store all of the front-end code, DHTML, compiled ActiveX components, and documentation in this folder.
- **Business services** In this folder, store more private information, such as business logic, components providing business rules, and so on. The core of the project will probably be located in this tier.
- **Data services** The database access resources, particularly if passwords are stored in the access files (such as Global.asa) can be placed in this folder. With the older versions of the database structure archived in this folder, it may also prevent outdated documentation of the database structure from being used. Only the team members for the system can access these important documents.

Security should be considered by everyone working on a project, but primarily by the project manager. Never before have the benefits and dangers of information access been so intertwined. A user can access a public data store at any time from any location with little likelihood that the access will be individually noticed since Web access logs contain such a large volume of information for every user visit.

USING VISUAL SOURCESAFE

Source code control is slowly becoming one aspect of project management that is being embraced by organizations large and small. The proper use of Visual SourceSafe (VSS) is crucial to effective team development since it minimizes code loss, maximizes debugging possibilities on a group build, and provides a historical snapshot of the progress of application construction.

VSS allows you to keep a revision history of every file within a project. Previous versions of the file can be accessed with a few mouse clicks and can be restored or compared with the current version. This is especially helpful in a team building environment where a build of an application may fault on a single developer's code. By examining the changes made to the old file, the problem can be located or the previous clean compiled code can be substituted to allow a complete build until the developer can create corrected files.

Source code control is used to:

- Maintain a record of changes to source code files
- Manage a team project
- Manage parallel project development when multiple projects are being simultaneously developed that share a number of files or components
- Support comparisons of historical source code versions

SourceSafe is built on the analogy that the pieces of a project are like books in a library. Any files within the project can be withdrawn ("checked out") for modification. After changes are made, the file is returned ("checked in") so that the changes are stored in the project library. To minimize disk usage, only the changes between an old and new version are stored with a process known as "storing deltas" of the files. The process of withdrawing the file will copy the current version of the file from the SourceSafe library to a local directory, usually on the hard drive of the developer.

DEFINITION: **Deltas** Rather than storing a complete copy of a source code file every time it's checked in, a delta stores the changes from one version of a file to another. Deltas require far less disk space to keep a source code version history.

One of the most useful recent additions to the Visual Studio application is the integration of SourceSafe capabilities directly within the development system IDE. Like most of the Visual Studio environment, Visual Basic provides a SourceSafe menu (shown in the following illustration) directly on the Tools menu. From this menu, projects and files can be added to an existing project, or a new project can be created.

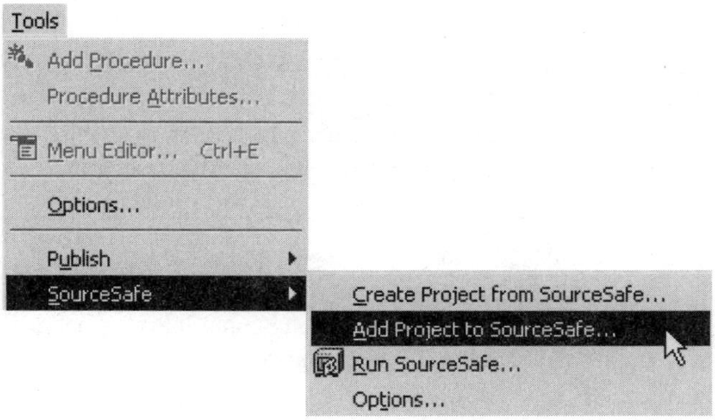

When you begin a Visual SourceSafe project, you declare a set of baseline files. The project baseline forms the starting files for comparison as the history of the project increases.

Every time you release a new version of an application, a snapshot should be taken of the source code. This enables you to examine various project and code files to determine their condition in the released version. In VSS, this means giving the project a label (shown in the following illustration). Labeling a project allows all of the files from a release to be stored consistently.

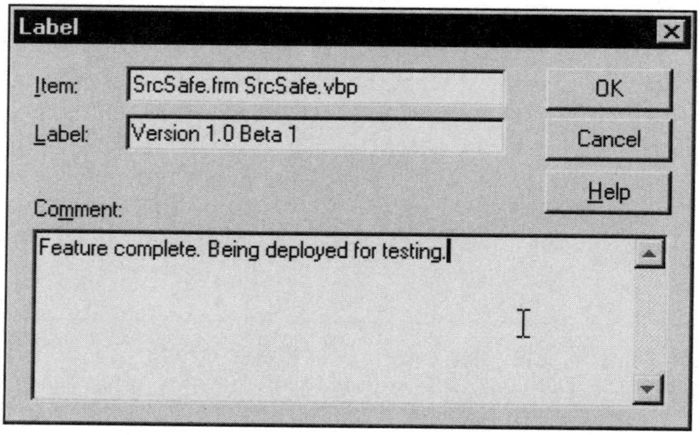

Shared Files

Sharing files among projects can present some special difficulties. Sharing is common, particularly with global files or includes. Extra precautions can be taken with shared files so that a modification to a multiproject file does not cause problems for the other projects in which it is used. Under these circumstances, the share can be broken to allow the other projects to maintain the existing version.

VSS supports project branching that requires the capability of using shared files. Branching consists of a single project being broken down into two or more project branches that can be maintained separately and which may have different security privileges. A branched project may still share files with another project.

NOTE: For the latest information, code, sample files, and utilities, check out the Visual SourceSafe home page (http://msdn.microsoft.com/ssafe) on the Microsoft site. In the samples and downloads section, there are even some files to aid you in adding SourceSafe commands to Office 97 and Word 95. There is also an excellent utility in the Tools section that can be used to produce more readable history reports.

Using SourceSafe within Microsoft Access

Source code control in VSS is not limited to files. VSS provides the option of being used in conjunction with Microsoft Access to provide significant database documentation abilities. In Access, VSS can be used to archive and label parts of the database schema (such as tables and queries). This functionality allows individual queries or database structure to be archived for versioning and historical comparison. Since Microsoft doesn't include a similar tool that can be used with the SQL Server database server, an Access-based database application can actually support more advanced versioning.

To use SourceSafe with Access, you must have the SourceSafe client installed on the development machine. The Microsoft Office Development edition install should include the VSS Add-Ins that will modify the registry to display the SourceSafe submenu in the database application.

NOTE: The Add-In to get SourceSafe functionality for Access is only available in the Development edition of Microsoft Office. When installed in Access, it adds a SourceSafe submenu to the Tools menu, providing Check In and Check Out options, and so on. If you have the Development edition but this menu doesn't appear, rerun the Setup program for Office and make sure the ODE option is checked.

In addition to all of the objects within a database that can be added to source-code control, you can add files external to the Access database file (*.MDB), as well. For SourceSafe control of tables external to the MDB, you can also use the Attached Table options to integrate the current project.

CAUTION: An Access database with security settings enabled cannot be added as a SourceSafe project. If added, all of the settings will be eliminated and you will have to add them again when SourceSafe access is removed from the database.

SourceSafe Administrator

The SourceSafe Administrator application is one of two applications included with the Visual SourceSafe package for source control management. The Administrator primarily serves the purpose of helping you set up security functions. In the Administrator, you can create users and groups. The groups and users should be configured for permission, following the methodology you've established with your file server for development access.

The SourceSafe Administrator also allows you to repair or recover damaged archives, as well as bundle entire archives for backup. The projects and deltas that they contain are stored in an immense number of folders that are inconvenient to back up and restore. The Administrator helps distill the files into a more manageable backup format.

SourceSafe User

The other application used for Visual SourceSafe is the client application that is listed simply as Visual SourceSafe in the Start menu. To access all of the projects stored in SourceSafe outside of an IDE, you will use this application. It is the primary control center for all of the projects that you are managing in SourceSafe (see Figure B-1). In the application, right-clicking provides a context menu for most of the options available for projects and for the items displayed in the application.

All of the project management that occurs within SourceSafe is done by users included in the administrator group. Often it is practical to leave this application running when doing development so that you can access functions that are not provided in the IDE.

From the SourceSafe user application, you can:

- Check files in and out
- Add new projects
- Delete projects or files
- Label a version of a project (for versioning)
- Compare two files for differences
- Examine the history of a file or project

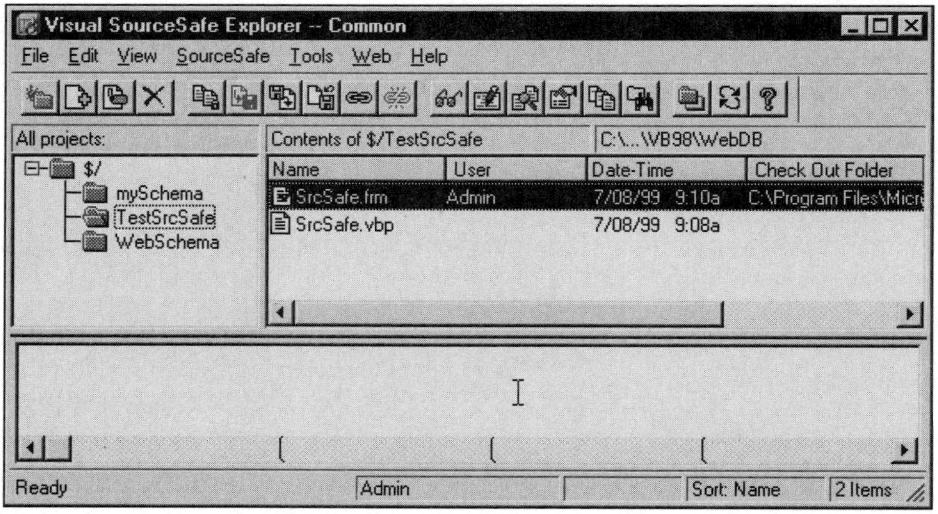

Figure B-1. The Visual SourceSafe application allows you to manage all of the projects added to VSS for source code control

The interface for the application is similar to Windows Explorer. Projects are contained in folders shown in the left pane of the window. The Detail pane, to the right, shows all of the files contained within the selected project.

NOTE: The default administrator name for the server is *Admin* with no password. However, when the SourceSafe application loads and requests a login, the user name is set by default to *Administrator*. You'll need to type *Admin* into the user name text box in order to log in.

SourceSafe within the IDE

SourceSafe can be effectively used through the Administrator or User interfaces, as well as from within the programming environments themselves. Visual Basic, Visual C++, Visual J++, and Visual Modeler all feature the ability to access, add, and check files in or out from within a project. Since all of the interfaces mirror the functionality provided by the SourceSafe User application, there is little need to cover them here.

For information about individual installation of the SourceSafe menu options (if not already present in the IDE), check the documentation for the environment. In most of the Visual Studio applications, the VSS additions can be installed through the Add-In manager.

VSS Automation

In version 6, Visual SourceSafe exposes an OLE Automation interface for scripting. This interface supports both events that activate code as well as objects and methods to completely control the SourceSafe environment.

There are a number of objects used to control the model, including:

- **VSSApp** The primary application object for Visual SourceSafe.
- **VSSCheckOut** Holds references to objects that are currently checked out to the logged on user.
- **VSSDatabase** Contains the information for all projects currently under VSS source code control.
- **VSSUser** Determines whether the logged on user is accessing the current SourceSafe object and information regarding that user.
- **VSSItem** Holds the reference information about VSS items in the VSSCheckOut and VSSDatabase collections.
- **VSSFileStatus** Contains the current status of a file that is under source code control.
- **VSSFlags** Flags stored for individual VSSItems.
- **VSSVersion** Returns the version of a file or project.

Using these objects can allow you to create a custom management application for source code control. The potential for custom solutions is significant since any environment capable of automation access can control the VSS engine. It would be possible, for example, to use ASP to create a Web-based check in/check out utility for intranet access.

The following listing shows code that uses the automation capabilities of Visual SourceSafe from Visual Basic. Add this source code to a project that includes the VSS object model in the References dialog box. When executing the application, the code will create a new project, add a file, check it out, and check it in.

```
Private Sub modProject()
    Dim mySSDatabase As New VSSDatabase
    Dim mySSRoot As VSSItem
    Dim myProject As VSSItem
    Dim myFile As VSSItem
    Dim uName As String, pwd As String
    Dim SrcSafeIni As String
    Dim AddFlags As Long
    Dim CheckOutFolder As String
    Dim objCheckOut As VSSCheckOut

    On Error Resume Next

    uName = "Guest"
    pwd = ""
    SrcSafeIni = "C:\VSS\SRCSAFE.INI"

    mySSDatabase.Open SrcSafeIni, uName, pwd

       Select Case Err

       Case 0
            MsgBox ("Database opened!")
            ' Create reference to the root
            Set objVSSRoot = objVSSDatabase.VSSItem("$/", False)
        Case Else
            MsgBox ("Error logging into SourceSafe!" + vbCrLf + _
            Err.Description)
            Exit Sub
       End Select

    mySSRoot.NewSubproject Name:="MyNewProject", Comment:="My Create Comment"

    Set myProject = objVSSDatabase.VSSItem("$/MyNewProject", False)

    ' Add the file, removing the local copy
    AddFlags = VSSFLAG_DELYES
    objNewProject.Add Local:="C:\Test.txt", Comment:="My Add Comment", _
        iFlags:=AddFlags

    Set objVSSFile = objVSSDatabase.VSSItem(objNewProject.Spec + _
        "/Test.txt", False)

    ' Working directory
```

```
    objNewProject.LocalSpec = "C:\"

    objVSSFile.CheckOut Comment:="My CheckOut Comment", _
        Local:=objNewProject.LocalSpec + objVSSFile.Name, iFlags:=0

    For Each objCheckOut In objVSSFile.CheckOuts
        ' In this sample we will assume that multiple CheckOuts
        ' are disabled in Admin so the first CheckOut we encounter
        ' that is checked out by the current user will be the one
        ' we are looking for
        If objCheckOut.UserName = objVSSDatabase.UserName Then
            CheckOutFolder = objCheckOut.LocalSpec
            Exit For
        End If

    Next
    ' Check in the file
    objVSSFile.CheckIn Comment:="My CheckIn Comment", _
        Local:=CheckOutFolder + objVSSFile.Name, iFlags:=0
End Sub
```

It is also possible to use the object model to create an application that can respond to VSS events. Setting up event execution for SourceSafe requires the creation of an ActiveX DLL that uses the `Implements` keyword to activate the control when the appropriate event occurs. Explaining the creation of a SourceSafe event application is beyond the scope of this book. Visit the SourceSafe portion of the MSDN Web site for more information (http://msdn.microsoft.com/ssafe).

Q&A

Q: Are there other available source-code control utilities?

A: There are numerous source code applications, including the popular PVCS (www.pvcs) and MKS (www.mks) products. While SourceSafe is excellent for the development of Windows-based applications, other products are stronger on the multiplatform front. They also provide features available to all development systems, including non-Microsoft vendors, such as Inprise (Delphi) and Visual Age for Java (IBM).

Other source-code control products integrate some of the aspects of project planning directly into the application. However, none of these offer the level of integration available from SourceSafe that is provided for Visual Studio applications.

SUMMARY

Properly managing team development is critical in a Web-based project environment for which two or more different development systems must commonly be used. Effective coordination of the developers on the project can substantially reduce the project creation time and the time spent debugging. Using groupware systems and source code control can aid in the management of these team efforts. In this Appendix, you covered:

- **Source-code control** These are systems that can archive different versions of source code and other files for historical retrieval. Using the check in/check out methodology enforced by Microsoft Visual SourceSafe prevents multiple developers that are working on the same project from editing the same file at the same time.
- **Visual SourceSafe (VSS)** This source-code application serves four central purposes: archiving past file versions, coordinating multiple developers, managing parallel project development, and supporting historical comparison. VSS is integrated directly into most of the Visual Studio applications, including Visual Interdev, Visual Basic, and Visual C++.
- **Groupware** This is an advanced form of electronic bulletin board that provides a central place to communicate, organize, and archive the source code, documentation, and support files for a project. With many organizations already using Microsoft Exchange Server for public folders and e-mail communication, it is the ideal choice for centralizing project documentation, files, and communication.
- **Versioning** This is the demarcation of time-stamped groups of files. By storing an entire project by version, a new build can be constructed from any archived version. Past files can also be used to recover code that may have been deleted in intervening versions.

APPENDIX C

Multi-Tool Development Strategy

One of the most substantial challenges facing organizations today is coordinating the variety of programming environments and languages. In this book alone, you've used five languages: Visual Basic, VBScript, DHTML, UML, and Java. At the same time, you've used four different development systems: Visual Basic, Visual InterDev, Visual J++, and Visual Modeler. On a typical Web database solution, a single programmer might use two or three of these environments. To successfully create applications using these different tools, you need to master development techniques, application analysis and profiling, and some of the application-wide tools provided with Visual Studio.

DEVELOPMENT TECHNIQUES

Application development initially focuses on learning the tools, because their possibilities and limitations will determine what can be done to create a solution. Once the tools are understood, the process of developing the application becomes the primary concern. Multi-environment development is still a brave new world that designers are grappling with, and examining some of the development techniques available in the Visual Studio family of products can help you develop a new methodology.

To complete a project successfully, you will have to use the tools at your disposal to direct the implementation and guide you in properly managing people and resources. Some of these tools (such as Visual SourceSafe and Visual Modeler) can be used together very easily. Other program utilities included in the Visual Studio suite, such as those for examining or modeling execution processes for final deployment, are designed to be used with any type of project. Reviewing how some of these Visual Studio tools are used will save you time and may prevent frustration as you assemble your application.

Using Visual SourceSafe and Visual Modeler Together

In multi-tool development, both Visual SourceSafe and Visual Modeler take center stage to help you effectively coordinate a team of developers. Visual SourceSafe allows you to synchronize the pieces of the project and produce a coordinated build of the final application. Visual Modeler provides a framework for component design and development on a team project.

Visual Modeler stores the diagrams in the Petal file format. Since the Petal format is a text-based file, the models can be preserved and updated with the source code attached to the rest of the project through source code control procedures. This can provide numerous advantages.

- **Consistent model implementation** Storing the model with the project promotes round-trip engineering.
- **Self documentation** The model will assist a team of programmers in creating the individual pieces in coordination with the whole. It also allows real-time comparisons between initial design plans and the actual implementation.
- **Model comparison** With the text-based model files, the Visual SourceSafe comparison features can be used to examine changes between two models (such as the current model and an older version).

Since both Visual SourceSafe and Visual Modeler operate independently of the development environment, they can be used together with any component-based Web project. When used together, they can also provide an archival history of the design and implementation of the project studied later.

Component Development

Although code reuse has been heavily promoted in the development press, most of the real power in creating components today comes from the ability to use a component in many different environments. The components you've created in this book could be used in Visual Basic, Visual C++, Active Server Pages, Visual InterDev, and so on. The ActiveX architecture was created to allow language independence for component access. Component technology has become a cornerstone of the development process, which requires multiple development environments.

The effective creation and deployment of ActiveX controls and ActiveX DLLs is useful in team development. Every Visual Studio tool, such as Visual Basic, Visual C++, Visual J++, Visual InterDev, and Visual FoxPro can address a component built in the ActiveX framework. Every development system, except Visual InterDev, can create them as well.

NOTE: JavaBeans, the Java component architecture that competes with ActiveX, is not supported by Visual Studio products and is barely supported in Internet Explorer. If you want to use JavaBeans in one of your Visual Studio projects, Sun has an ActiveX control that acts as a JavaBeans container that exposes a JavaBean to the ActiveX environment. This control is available on the Sun Web site (www.javasoft.com) for free download.

When beginning a multi-tool project, consider which functions may need to be shared among team members. The process of encapsulating functionality within a component—particularly the initial component stubbing that takes place early in the design process—can prove to be one of the most effective means of cross-language development.

Visual Basic IIS Applications

If you are developing a project across a number of Visual Studio environments, building an IIS application through Visual Basic would be a poor choice. Since an IIS Application project is compiled in Visual Basic, other members of the Web development team (except the graphic arts department) won't have ready access to modify the solution.

Although an IIS application generates ActiveX DLLs, these are specially designed to work in conjunction within the IIS Application framework. Therefore, they cannot be accessed by any other applications in the way common ActiveX components can be used. An application created using the IIS Application framework is primarily limited to VB development and rudimentary template modification in an HTML editor.

Unifying Through XML

The XML language is powerful enough to become the primary data-type middleware for allowing easy communication among many different types of applications. XML is known as a metadata definition language because it is used to define how the data is structured. XML can provide an effective way to pass data between applications, controls, or even development system add-ins and tools.

The language of XML relies on defining custom tags. For example, you could define a mail list by setting up the data in a series of XML-defined fields, like this:

```
<firstname>John</firstname>
<lastname>Smith</lastname>
<address>1992 LakeView Dr.</address>
```

The XML format also allows hierarchical definition of data. For example, to allow multiple addresses in a mail list, you might use an XML definition like this:

```
<firstname>John</firstname>
<lastname>Smith</lastname>
<addresses>
   <address>1992 LakeView Dr.</address>
   <address>323 Main Rd.</address>
</addresses>
```

The reason that XML is perfect for inter-tool data exchange is the availability of the Microsoft XML control. This control is included with the Visual Studio tools and is also installed by default with each copy of Internet Explorer 5, Windows 98, and Windows 2000. If you examine the controls available on your development machine, the Microsoft XML control is likely to be one of them.

This control makes it possible to load an XML file and automatically parse the file into hierarchical data nodes for easy access. This method dramatically simplifies the following procedures:

- **Creating a data exchange format** Since the format is defined by tags, a tag system can be created to serve almost any data-exchange need.
- **Reading a data file** There is perhaps no easier method of accessing disk-based hierarchical data than that available through the XML control. Information can be accessed in random order, making the access capabilities extremely flexible. Since each piece of data is contained within type-specifying tags, a program accessing the data file can ignore data types that it cannot use or understand.
- **Adding to an existing data file** XML is far superior to using a sequential data file, because data can be added to the XML tree rather than having to perform operation-intensive sequential inserts. XML makes hierarchical file organization easy.
- **Modifying the data format** To modify the format, you simply need to add new tags. Because parsing the XML file involves ignoring tags that are not understood by the interpreting program, multiple levels of compatibility can be maintained.

The potential for creating XML data interchangeability among different types of applications increased with the widespread use of the XML ActiveX component. Designing your applications to use XML as an interchange format can make communication and future maintenance far less difficult.

APPLICATION PERFORMANCE EXPLORER

The Application Performance Explorer (APE) is a low-level tool that allows you to run basic what-if performance scenarios. It does not allow you to actually execute your application and check the performance. Instead, you can create a model of the transaction and interface details in the APE model. The model can then be executed in real time against your current system to perform speed, processing, and functionality tests.

For example, you might be designing an application that has a program (such as an ASP page) that calls an ActiveX DLL. Each call to the DLL takes place across the COM interface. Furthermore, each call passes three values and expects one value in return. The APE model can be configured to simulate these calls on the machine on which it is running. If 1,000 users make the same request at the same time, this would be equivalent to 1,000 requests. APE can be set to test 1,000 calls to a component, and it will return information such as the average time for each query, server resource usage, and response times.

The APE is particularly useful when you need to test various aspects of a distributed system. The APE will allow you to stress-test details of the system to tune for best deployment. Calls through COM, DCOM, MTS, RAS, and SQL Server can all be modeled and analyzed in APE.

The APE is most useful for testing the component pieces of a distributed application. The APE application was designed especially for a component-based application created with a combination of the Visual Studio tools. By examining the execution of an application's performance, features such as connection pooling can be maximized to use the available resources to best advantage.

NOTE: A variety of distributed test examples are included with the Visual Studio installation. Check the source folder in the Visual Studio hierarchy. The standard path to this folder is: `C:\Program Files\Microsoft Visual Studio\Common\Tools\Ape\Source`

The performance monitoring is divided into three different tiers:

- **Clients** The requesting application; the client can be a client program, an ASP page, or even a component that references other components
- **Servers** The services that react to requests from the clients; most often these will be objects, object servers, or other server pieces of the distributed technology
- **Databases** A database engine or server, such as the Jet engine or SQL Server

Each of these tiers appears as a button in the APE window (see Figure C-1). Clicking on the button will display a configuration in which the particular tier may be set to mirror the system you want to model.

NOTE: These tiers do not parallel the three tiers used in Visual Modeler. The Visual Modeler tiers are categorized for segregating component types; the APE tiers define deployment locations.

APE System Overview

For database modeling, APE supports the four primary methods of database access: ADO, DAO, RDO, and ODBC. All of the feedback, along with information from these data access objects is logged as the connectivity that uses the pool manager. The Job Manager defines jobs to be done by the operations and threads that will be used to complete a particular task. The logged cycles are retrieved from client events, MTS events, Pool Manager messages, Job Manager messages, database events, and job-summary information.

To use APE on MTS, you need to install the APE package to MTS to allow it to track performance. The APE package is called Aemtssvc.pak and is located in the `C:\Program Files\Microsoft Visual Studio\Common\Tools\Ape\` folder. Use the

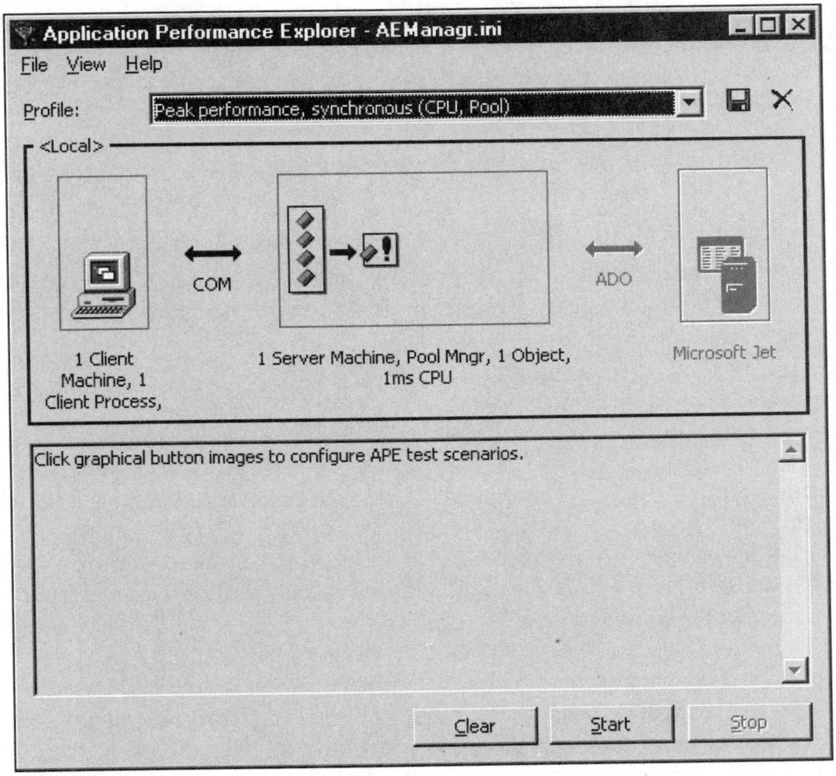

Figure C-1. The APE can help to model performance

Package Wizard to install this prebuilt package. For SQL Server, the standard installation makes the database server available to APE.

Creating a performance evaluation allows you to fine tune and refine the pieces of the system to be deployed. Preconceived estimates about bottleneck locations are often inaccurate. Slow performance that is assumed to be caused by queries to a database, for example, may instead turn out to be the result of a large number of COM requests. The APE allows these stress tests to be run on the actual hardware on which the solution will be deployed.

DCOM Configuration

Because of the distributed nature of a DCOM solution, it requires special configuration to allow APE to communicate with it properly. The access permissions must be set properly to allow the APE to execute the necessary test calls to provide an accurate model. Four different APE services must be configured:

- **Service Manager** Installed on the machine that will host the pooling and queuing resources
- **Client Manager** Installed on the machine where the APE will be executed
- **Remote Client** Installed on a machine that doesn't have the Client Manager; in a two-machine system, it would be installed on the same machine as the Service Manager
- **Remote Worker** Installed on a machine that doesn't have the Service Manager; in a two-machine system, it would be installed on the same machine as the Client Manager

To configure the DCOM system for APE access, make sure the machine is running DCOM properly. Execute the Dcomcnfg.exe utility that is located in the `\Windows\System` directory and ensure that the DCOM services are enabled in the default properties for the machine. With DCOM active, set the Default Authentication Level to None and the Default Impersonation Level to Identity.

CAUTION: While your DCOM system is set up for APE testing, it will be vulnerable to hackers because of the lack of authentication requirements. Make sure you change the settings back to their original values after you finish your testing, to re-enable security.

In the DCOM configuration utility, select one of these applications and open the properties dialog box. On the Identity tab, set the user type to Interactive User. Do the same for the remaining applications.

The system will now be ready to send event information back to the APE from DCOM events. In a distributed system, this information may prove to be crucial for tuning. The Performance Explorer allows you to save the model that you've constructed. By creating various different deployment scenarios, you can effectively estimate performance differences for changes in the system design.

VISUAL STUDIO ANALYZER (VSA)

After a distributed application appears to be executing properly, problems may still need to be resolved before it is placed in a deployment environment. Problems with object allocation commonly have to be resolved. The Visual Studio Analyzer (VSA) can measure application performance, show trouble spots, and show the structure of distributed applications, allowing you to examine the application from the outside (as it appears to the operating system). It can also plot a diagram of the communications and components of your application while it is executing.

Visual Analyzer uses event messages from within an application and statistical information from the Performance Monitor, to generate a picture of application execution. It also allows an execution to be recorded and played back for detailed analysis of a process. In this way, the application can be examined in real time or precisely analyzed once the application has executed.

The Analyzer is used to do the following:

- Analyze the performance of a distributed application
- Examine execution parameters in detail
- Understand the structure of the application
- Isolate problems, bottlenecks, and errors

The analyzer does not act as a live debugger; no breakpoints can be set with it, and individual source code cannot be examined through it. However, breakpoints set in the native development environment (such as VB, Visual C++, and so on) can halt execution and allow you to switch to the Analyzer for execution tracking. The Analyzer allows you to display time usage as a line chart, Gantt chart, or timeline view.

To use the Analyzer, you need to create the following:

- **Analyzer project** The project holds all of the event logs, filters, and resources used to provide analysis for a system.
- **Event log** Events are returned from the following sources: ADO, SQL Server, COMTI, VSA Debug, COM, ODBC, JScript, MTS, VBScript, the Web server, and Performance Monitor.

- **Filters** The filters determine which events are displayed for an analysis. The project can receive a large variety of events and the filters allow you to examine only those that are needed for a particular detail set.

Visual Studio Analyzer is not executable as a separate application but only as part of a development environment. From the IDE shared by Visual InterDev and Visual J++, you can create a new Visual Studio Analyzer project. The Visual Analyzer is primarily used for C++ and J++ projects.

To setup a VSA project, use the following steps:

1. Start Visual InterDev, and when the New Project dialog box appears, expand the Visual Studio folder (see the following illustration).

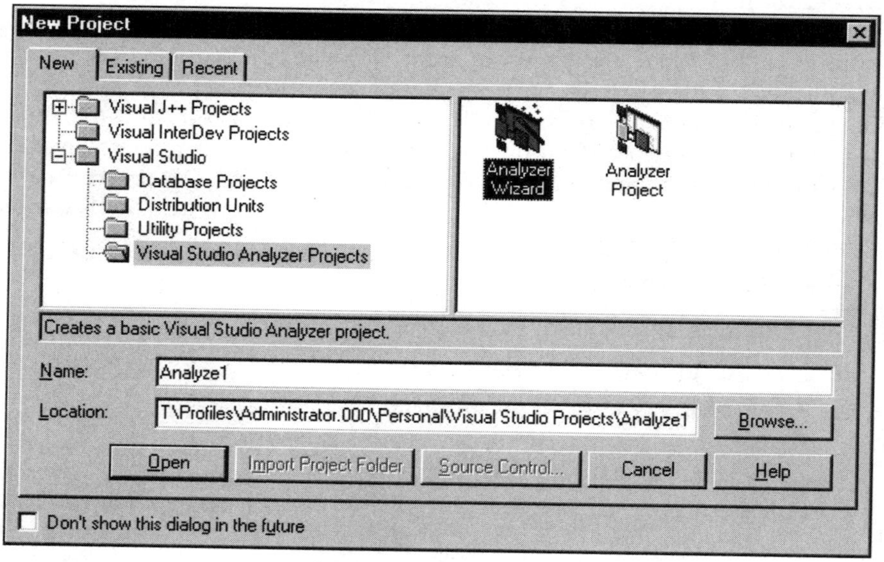

2. Make sure the Analyzer Wizard option is selected, and click the Open button. This will begin the Analyzer Wizard that will lead you step-by-step through the process of defining a VSA project.
3. Leave the default option to automatically scan for machines, and click Next.
4. Make sure the current machine is selected. If you don't want machines that the wizard has identified to be available for event examination, uncheck them here.

You can also add additional machines if the wizard didn't locate one used in your project (such as IP-based machines). Click Next.

5. Leave all default event sources checked, and click Next.
6. The default filter values are fine, so click Next.
7. Click Finish to create the new project.

Most of the development tools require that the Symbolic Debugger logic be activated. In Visual Basic, this option setting is located in the Project Properties window. With the event log activated, occurrences within the program are sent to the Visual Studio Analyzer.

All of the components that are executing within the project system can be seen in the component diagram (see Figure C-2).

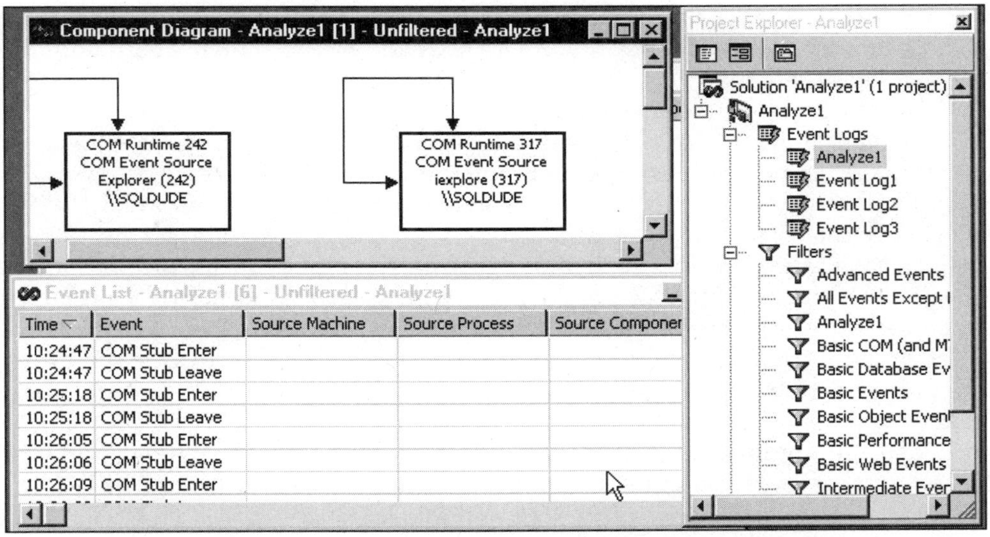

Figure C-2. All of the components are displayed in the Component Diagram window

From here, you can begin recording all of the events for a solution (using the Record button on the toolbar). Executing your application will generate the events to be caught for analysis. All of these events will appear in the event log and any other event logs that you define. Event logs can be filtered to display only the details you require.

VISUAL STUDIO TOOLS

Visual Studio includes a variety of development tools that unfortunately are not well documented, causing them to remain largely unused by many developers. All of these tools were initially created for C++ development, but they operate at the system level, allowing them to be used in conjunction with any application. The OLE client and server tools that allow components to be conveniently tested are particularly useful to the Web database developer.

ActiveX Testing Utilities

There are a number of utilities included with Visual Studio that can aid you in testing and streamlining your ActiveX controls and DLLs, COM objects, and clipboard and drag-and-drop data. These tools allow you to examine aspects of the program constructs both on disk and in an execution environment.

For ActiveX controls, a complete testing environment is included in the ActiveX Test Container (see Figure C-3). This application will instantiate a control, allow you to examine property values, and even execute methods on the control. In the figure, you can see that the TreeView control (the box with the Sample Node items) has been created inside the test container. By selecting the Invoke Methods options, all of the available methods are displayed in the Method Name combo box. In this case, the `SelectedItem PropPut` method is selected. The current value is displayed, and you can also enter a custom value.

This test container allows you to view the changes that take place as a result of changes to the control. The application can also reload the control if it is updated, as would be required when debugging the component.

There is no user interface that can be used to draw and display ActiveX DLLs on a canvas. For these components, the OLE Client Test and OLE Server Test can be used. The OLE Server Test can provide an execution environment for an ActiveX DLL. The test environment provides some sample components for test instantiation.

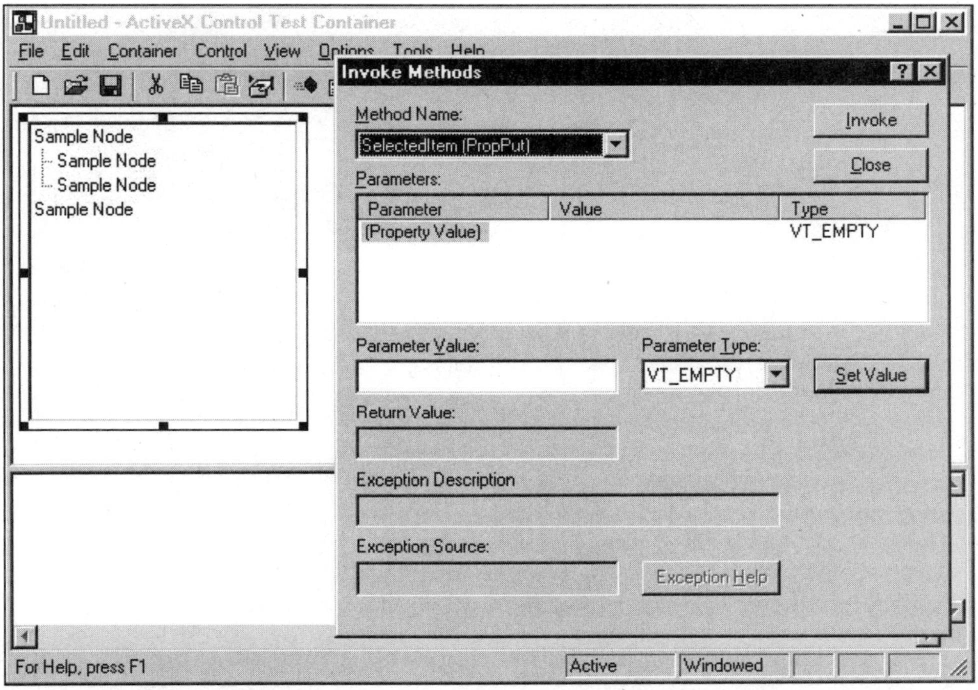

Figure C-3. The ActiveX Test Container for testing your ActiveX controls

The OLE/COM Object Viewer (see Figure C-4) allows you to examine COM objects registered on a system and make alterations to some of their parameters. In the figure, you can see all of the properties of the WebDB component that you created in Chapter 14. Information such as the ClassID is readily available, as well as the proper configuration settings to allow a COM entry to reference a remote instantiation machine through DCOM.

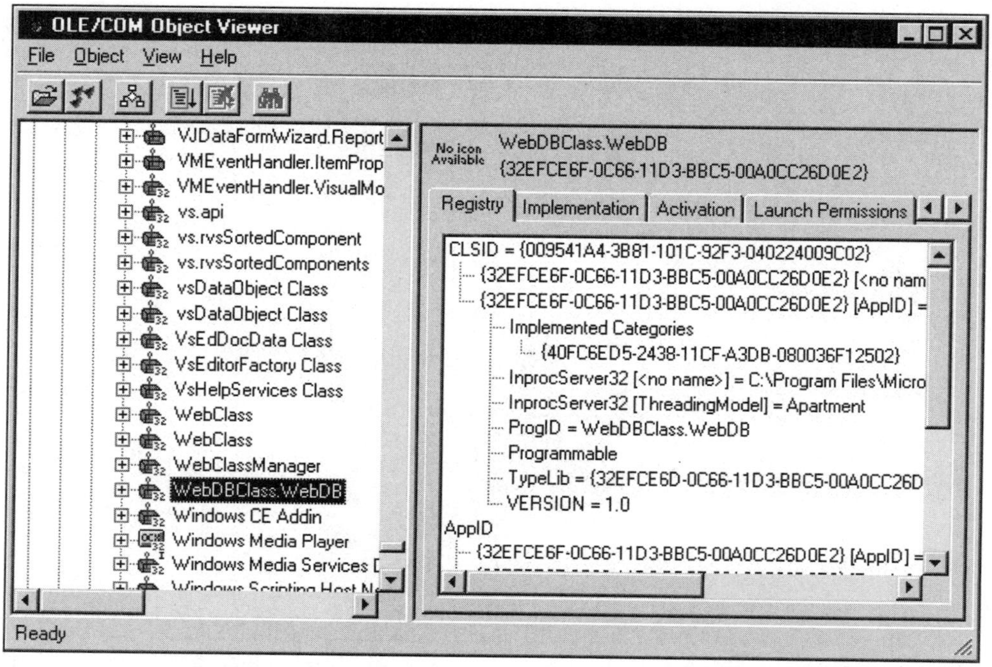

Figure C-4. The OLE/COM Object Viewer

For the drag-and-drop and clipboard aspects of an ActiveX solution, the DataObject Viewer (see the following illustration) will display all of the information that the OLE system has available for inter-application data transport. The DataObject Viewer breaks down all of the data held in the clipboard and drag-and-drop object store by their various data types.

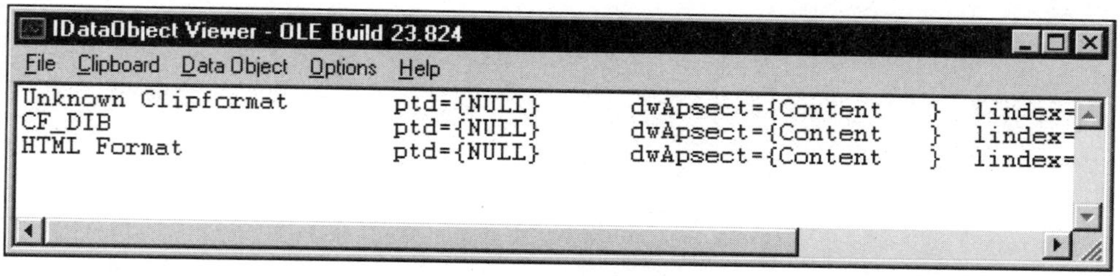

NOTE: Visual Studio also includes a DDE Spy test application. With the OLE/ActiveX framework providing the preferred and dominant method of inter-application communication, this tool is primarily included for testing legacy applications.

When you were reviewing the ActiveX framework in Chapter 14, the OLE Storage capability was briefly described. OLE Storage, also known as OLE Structured Storage, essentially makes a file operate as a hierarchical data structure rather than one stream of sequential characters (a traditional data file). In the OLE Storage file format, data can be stored within hierarchical categories, much like files are placed within folders on a standard hard drive.

If you are using Visual C++ or Visual J++, you can take advantage of this OLE Storage file format—all of the Microsoft Office products use this file format to store their documents. To examine the contents of a structured file, the DocFile Viewer (shown in the following illustration) has been included with Visual Studio. Unfortunately, Visual Basic does not directly support structured storage. To use structured storage with VB, you will have to go through Windows API calls.

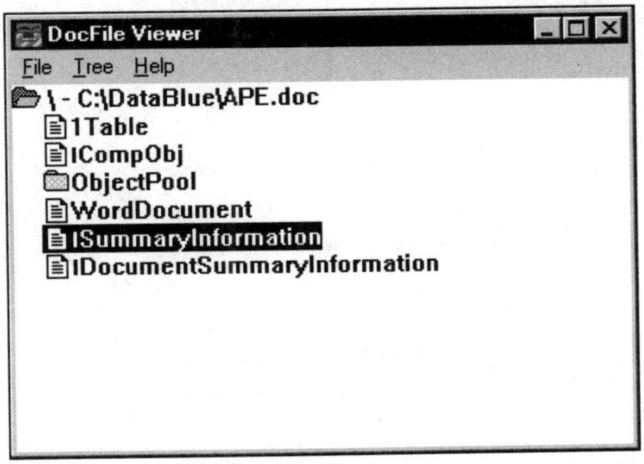

The DocFile Viewer allows you to examine a file in the structured storage format and drill down into the various data categories that it contains. In the preceding illustration, you can see the various structures defined in a common Microsoft Word document. If macros and forms existed in the VBA portion of this document, they would be displayed as additional folders.

API Text Viewer

Even though the object model for Windows available in Visual Basic and VBScript is very robust, it does not provide complete access to all of the functions available in Windows. Additionally, other parts of the system, such as the Winsock interface, are only partially exposed to higher-level applications. From Visual C++, however, every function of the system can be accessed.

To provide accessibility from Visual Basic, the Windows API can be addressed directly through Win32 API calls. These are created using the `Declare` keyword in VB. The declarations for the routines of the Windows API system are not automatically declared in Visual Basic; they must be placed in the appropriate code module.

NOTE: `Declare` statements must be located in a module file unless the statement is preceded by the `Private` keyword. Only in a module file can the declaration be publicly available. Other VB structures (such as forms and classes) must have the declarations set to only be available to the routines within those structures.

The API Viewer (see Figure C-5) can load a file that contains all of the declarations for each constant, function call, and structure needed to access the Win32 API.

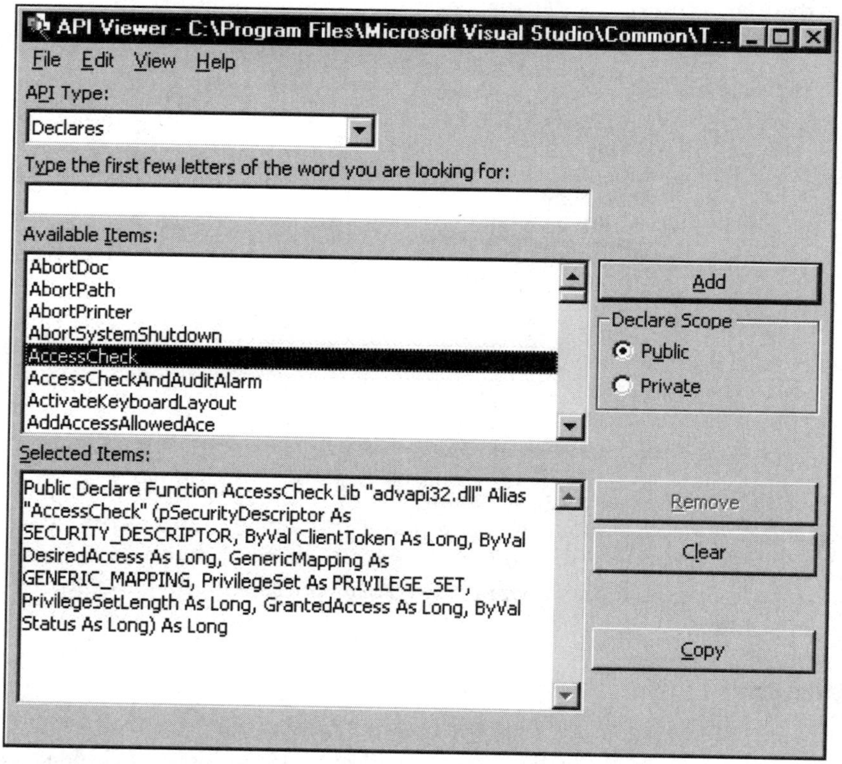

Figure C-5. The API Viewer can copy all of the desired `Declare` statements to the clipboard

A desired function call can be selected from the list and added to the text box below. The Copy button will transfer items from the Selected Items text box to the clipboard for pasting into your VB solution.

NOTE: The `Declare` statement is not available through VBScript, and, therefore, no API calls can be made directly through ASP. However, any functions you need can easily be wrapped in a Visual Basic ActiveX DLL that can, in turn, be called by VB Script code.

Help Workshop

The traditional Windows Help files (.hlp) are fantastic for a traditional application, but in a Web solution they are rather unnecessary. A Web application can include all of the help for the system in the form of additional HTML pages, which makes a single, specific help file unnecessary.

Microsoft is converting its Help system to use HTML technology rather than continuing to evolve the existing Help system. Although this strategy has turned out poorly so far, creating sluggish performance, large memory requirements, expanding file sizes, deficient searchability, and meager interactivity of the Visual Studio documentation, Microsoft promises to improve the HTML Help system in the future.

To define a Windows Help file, Microsoft provides the Help Workshop (see Figure C-6). This tool is fairly primitive, and I would recommend purchasing a commercial Help-writing package, such as RoboHelp (www.bluesky.com) for all but the simplest Help files. Commercial systems can even create a variety of formats, such as Word, HLP, and HTML, so only one coordinated set of documentation needs to exist.

Package and Deployment Wizard

The Package and Deployment Wizard allows you to package items that are not directly associated with a particular development system. It is available from within any of the Visual Studio development environments (look under the Add-Ins menu), and it can also be executed on its own. Since the wizard supplies compression, the splitting of files across multiple floppies, and checksum security, it can be useful for distributing more than applications.

The SQL Server data files are an excellent example of a set of files that often needs to be distributed apart from a specific application or component. Since the wizard provides compression and network-installation options, it is ideal for large data files that need to be placed at a specific location on a client machine.

General Tools

There are also a number of general tools included in Visual Studio that are primarily used to examine the interaction of the application with the system. These tools are less likely to be used when developing a Web application unless you're creating a low-level ISAPI driver or designing a component in Visual C++. However, they may provide another useful way of examining your application.

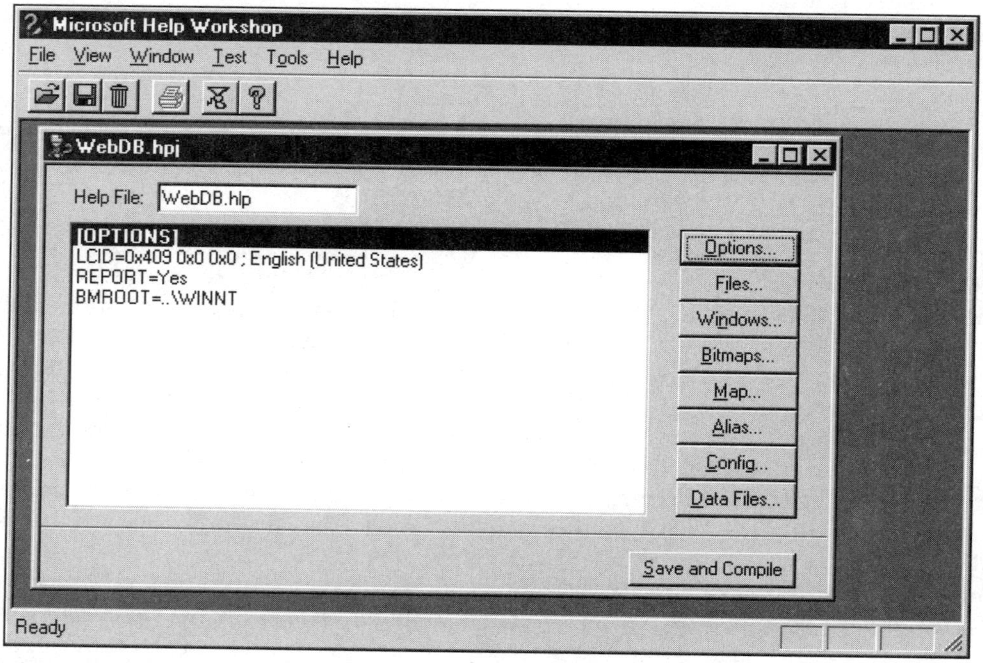

Figure C-6. Microsoft Help Workshop

Error Lookup

The Error Lookup application provides a global list of error codes and their meanings. It allows you to type in an error number, and a description of the error is displayed. You can load extra modules that define other errors by using the Module button.

The Err object is available for all applications, including those created in ASP. Error numbers are valuable in properly handling an error event during execution. However, when an error is generated on a system, it is inconvenient for the programmer to quickly examine the error object to find the description of the fault. This application provides a unified reference for error codes that can be quickly checked.

With the breadth of different systems addressed by the typical Web database application (ADO, Windows, VBScript, ASP, and so on), this application helps combine the error listings into a single area so that during development you can examine the codes you intend to provide to handling events.

Process Viewer

The Process Viewer (see Figure C-7) allows you to watch, update, and even kill processes of executing applications within the viewer. Since MTS provides the option of executing an application within its own memory space, a specific Web application can be directly examined by the Process Viewer. This is extremely powerful when attempting to debug components executing on MTS. You can also set the system processing priorities for various executing threads.

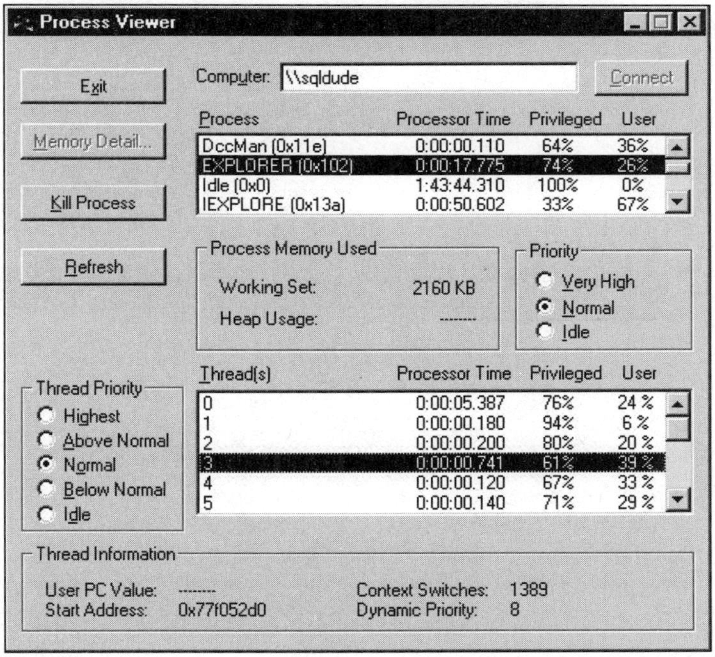

Figure C-7. The Process Viewer can view any memory objects

To examine other libraries and code that are dependent on a running process, you can use the Dependency Walker (see Figure C-8). This application will allow you to step through all of the DLLs used by a program and all of their individual properties. The dependencies in this program can be traced all the way down into the system DLLs that manage the most primitive level of functions.

To closely examine process structures, you can use the Spy++ tool (see Figure C-9). It shows all of the details of the objects and memory allocation used by an application, component, or DLL. It also allows you to examine the Windows messages communicated with that object. The Windows messaging system does not provide messages in the form of e-mail. Instead, it is the foundation of the Windows operating system's event response structure.

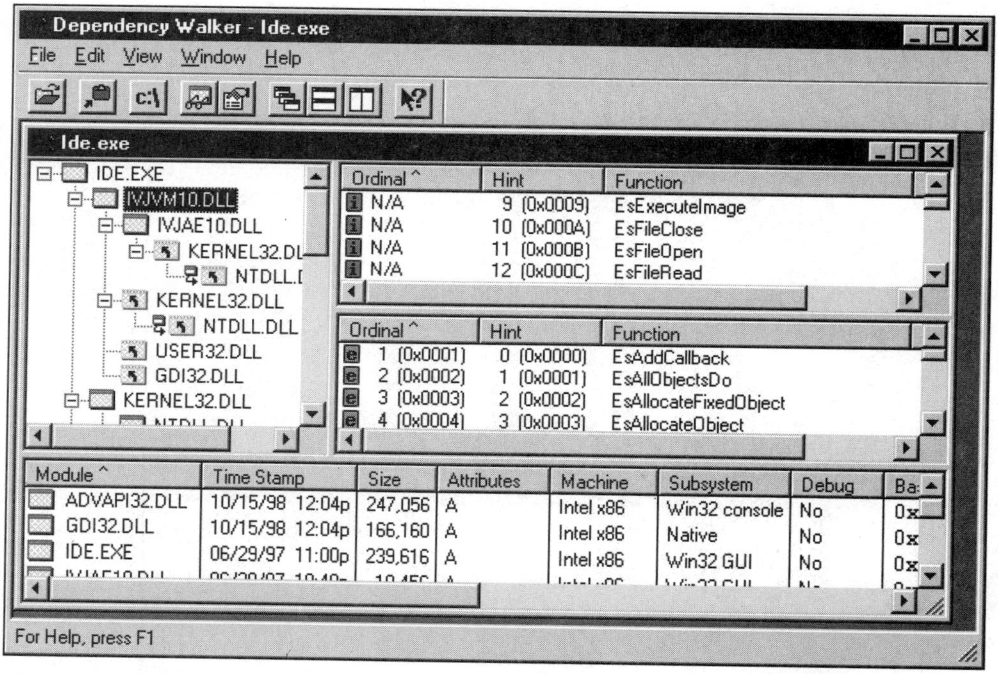

Figure C-8. The Dependency Walker can view information on executing DLLs

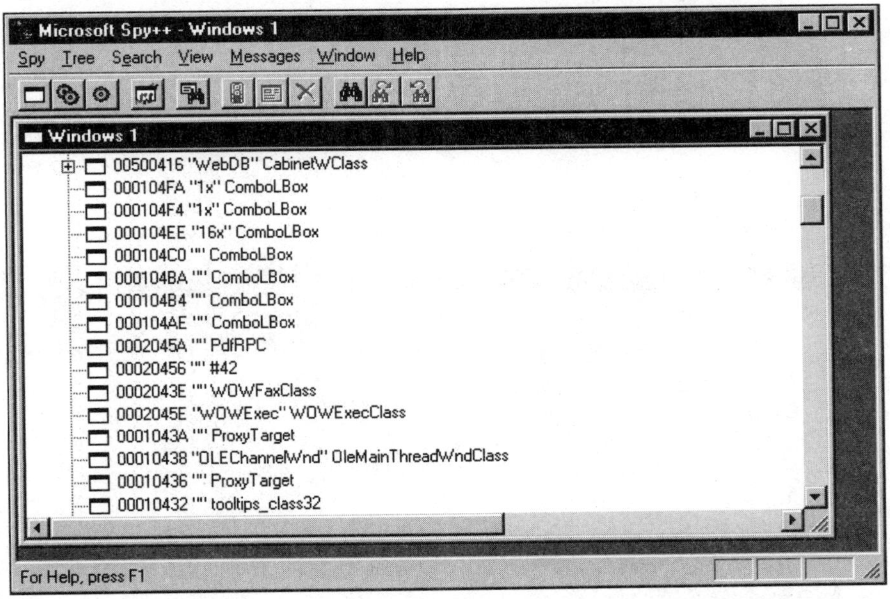

Figure C-9. Use Spy++ to examine Windows system messages

For applications and DLLs directly based on the Microsoft Foundation Classes (MFC), such as those written in Visual C++, the MFC Trace application (shown in the following illustration) can be used to activate various aspects of the MFC system. The traces can occur in user-selectable parts of the MFC framework.

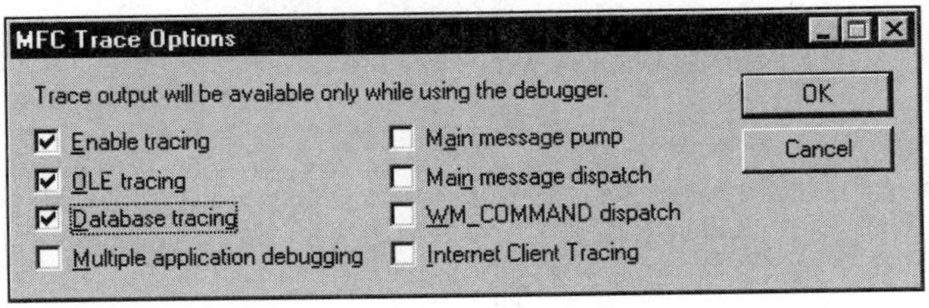

While Visual SourceSafe allows you to examine differences among past versions of a particular file, the WinDiff application (see Figure C-10) can be used to display the differences between two different files. This is a particularly useful function for HTML and scripted files, such as the one shown in the figure, in which HTML changes can be easily examined in a collapsible structure.

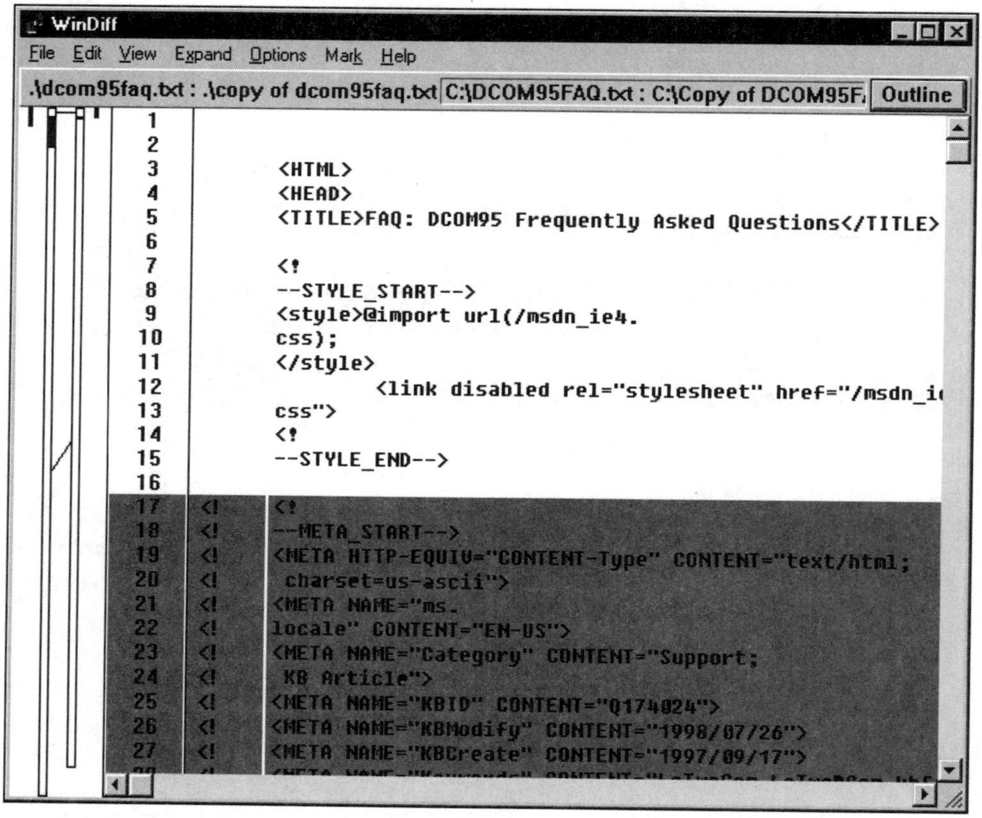

Figure C-10. WinDiff can display the differences between two files

Windows NT Resource Kit

Some of the most powerful tools for system management and examination are included with a subscription to the Microsoft Developer Network (MSDN) in a package called the Resource Kit. The Resource Kit contains close to fifty tools covering categories of management such as configuration, desktop tools, diagnostics (including a domain monitor and network traffic monitor), disk tools, file tools, Internet tools (including a mail service), and management tools.

The Resource Kit is also available for free download at www.microsoft.com/ntserver in the Downloads section. These utilities primarily govern aspects of the operating system, and therefore are more oriented toward a system administrator. However, the file-management and packet-examination tools are very useful for a Web developer. Be sure to check out the kit for tools you might need.

Q&A

Q: Can XML files be loaded by programs other than my own?

A: The XML file format is a metadata format, meaning that it provides data that describes data. Therefore, if a program can understand the tags in your data file that describe what the data it contains actually means, then yes. Even if a program supports XML import, it may not use tags understandable to another application.

As XML becomes increasingly popular, expect to see a number of data-format standards for XML-based files in particular industries. In fact, if you are doing a great deal of development in a particular industry, you might consider creating and publishing a format standard if one isn't currently available. Providing exchange among various applications and promoting compatibility can be a fantastic benefit.

Q: Is it more expensive to develop with multiple languages?

A: Yes. It is always more expensive in time and energy to develop in multiple languages if other factors (such as feature availability) are equal. Unfortunately, in the modern development world, there is little choice but to develop using a variety of tools. However, the more you minimize the number of development environments you use, the more savings you'll achieve. That is one of the reasons the languages for Visual Basic and VBScript are so similar—it minimizes development obstacles.

Each solution must be examined separately to determine which languages should be chosen. For example, although it might be optimal to develop both client and server scripts in VBScript, Netscape cannot execute VBScript code, so most applications use JavaScript for client-side deployment. However, using JavaScript as the standard, and writing the server-side code in this language makes it difficult to use VBScript tools, such as Visual InterDev. Therefore, most applications require the client and server to use different languages. Every application must be examined individually.

SUMMARY

Multi-environment development can present special challenges to a development team. Microsoft has provided a number of tools that can be of use to all applications within the Visual Studio suite. In this chapter you covered:

- **Visual SourceSafe with Visual Modeler** By placing your models within SourceSafe with the project source files, a multi-tool project can be coordinated more easily. The comparison functionality in SourceSafe also allows historical versions of models to be compared with each other.
- **Application Performance Explorer (APE)** APE allows you to model a distributed application to stress-test and examine the performance of a distributed system. APE supports and times calls on COM, DCOM, SQL Server, and RAS.
- **Visual Analyzer** This is a tool for analyzing the performance of a distributed system. The Analyzer can record events from ADO, COM, IIS, Performance Monitor, and more. All of the recorded events can be analyzed through an event log, graphs, filters, and other included capabilities.
- **ActiveX/OLE tools** Tools for examining ActiveX files, registry structures, memory allocation, dependencies, and execution are included with Visual Studio. These tools can aid in the development of components for use with your Web database system.

Index

A

B

C

D

E

F

G

H

I

J

K

L

M

N

O

P

Q

R

S

T

U

V

W

X